MOON HANDBOOKS®

WESTERN CANADA

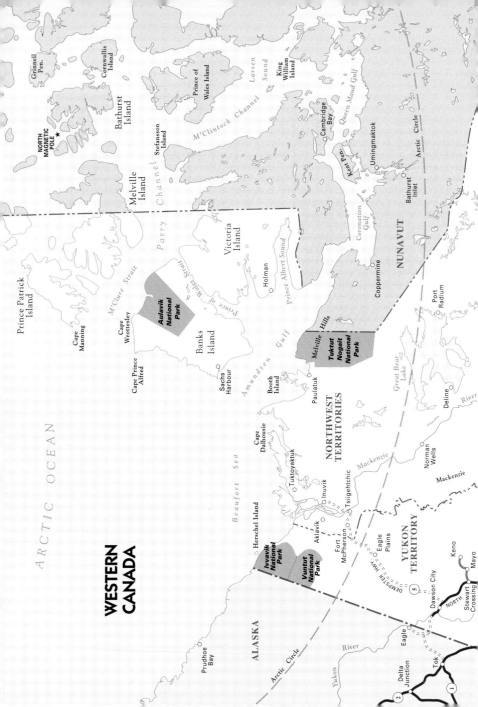

WESTERN CANADA

ARCTIC OCEAN

Grinnell Pen.

Cornwallis Island

Bathurst Island

Prince of Wales Island

Larsen Sound

King William Island

Arctic Circle

NORTH MAGNETIC POLE ★

Stefansson Island

M'Clintock Channel

Cambridge Bay

Queen Maud Gulf

Umingmaktok

Kent Pen.

Bathurst Inlet

Melville Island

Parry Channel

Victoria Island

Prince Albert Sound

Coronation Gulf

NUNAVUT

Prince Patrick Island

M'Clure Strait

Cape Manning

Holman

Coppermine

Cape Wrottesley

Aulavik National Park

Prince of Wales Strait

Cape Prince Alfred

Banks Island

Amundsen Gulf

Melville Hills

Tuktut Nogait National Park

Great Bear Lake

Port Radium

Sachs Harbour

Booth Island

Paulatuk

Deline

River

Beaufort Sea

Cape Dalhousie

NORTHWEST TERRITORIES

Mackenzie

Norman Wells

Mackenzie

Tuktoyaktuk

Inuvik

Tsiigehtchic

Aklavik

Fort McPherson

Eagle Plains

YUKON TERRITORY

Herschel Island

Ivvavik National Park

Vuntut National Park

DEMPSTER HWY.

Keno

Mayo

⑤

Dawson City

NORTH

Stewart Crossing

ALASKA

Arctic Circle

Eagle

River

Yukon

Prudhoe Bay

Eagle

Delta Junction

Tok

②

①

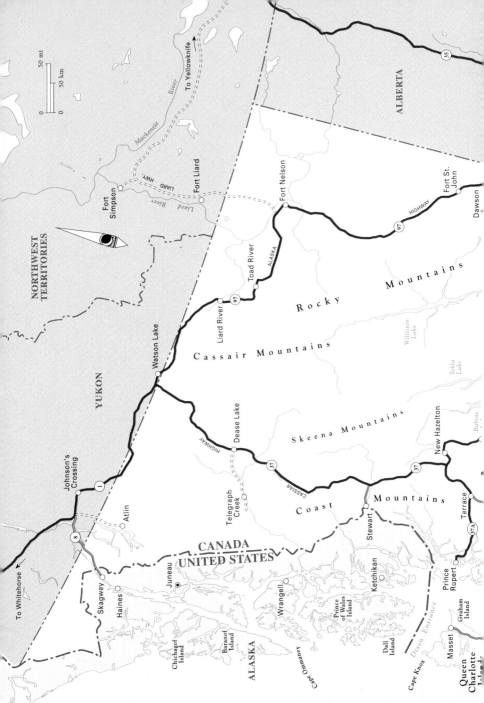

BRITISH COLUMBIA

© AVALON TRAVEL PUBLISHING, INC.

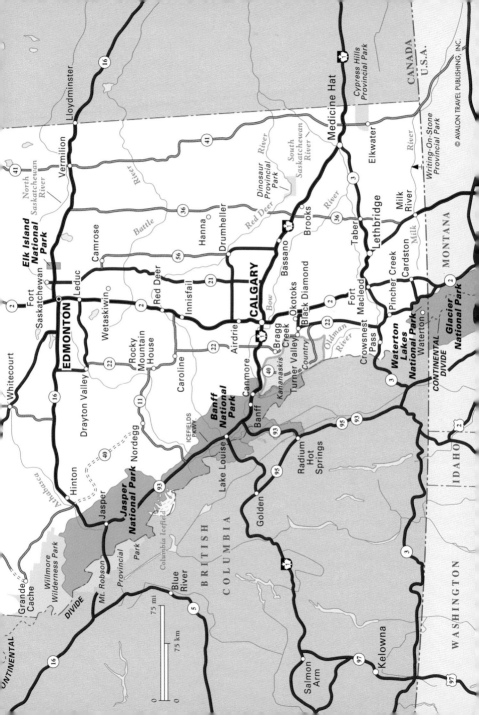

MOON HANDBOOKS®

WESTERN CANADA

FIRST EDITION

ANDREW HEMPSTEAD

AVALON
TRAVEL

MAPS

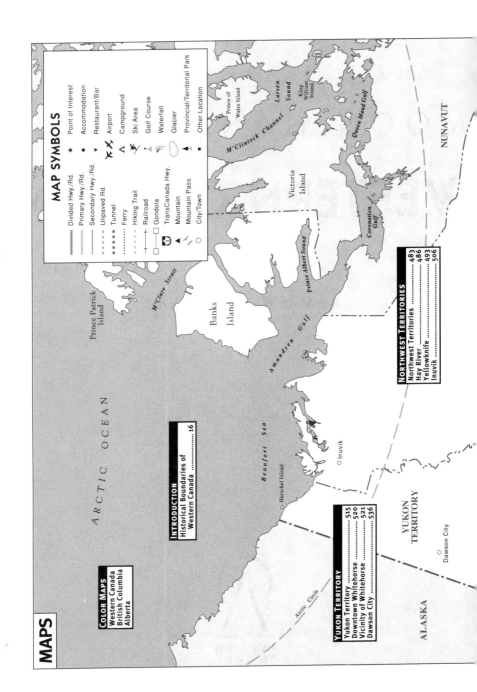

MAP SYMBOLS

Symbol	
Divided Hwy./Rd.	★ Point of Interest
Primary Hwy./Rd.	• Accommodation
Secondary Hwy./Rd.	◆ Restaurant/Bar
Unpaved Rd.	✈ Airport
Tunnel	Λ Campground
Ferry	Ski Area
Hiking Trail	Golf Course
Railroad	Waterfall
Gondola	Glacier
TransCanada Hwy.	▲ Mountain
◄ Mountain Pass	■ Provincial/Territorial Park
○ City/Town	Other Location

COLOR MAPS
Western Canada
British Columbia
Alberta

ARCTIC OCEAN

Prince Patrick Island

M'Clure Strait

Banks Island

Beaufort Sea

Herschel Island

○ Inuvik

M'Clintock Channel

Prince of Wales Island

Larsen Sound

King William Island

Queen Maud Gulf

Victoria Island

Prince Albert Sound

Coronation Gulf

Amundsen Gulf

NUNAVUT

Arctic Circle

ALASKA

YUKON TERRITORY

○ Dawson City

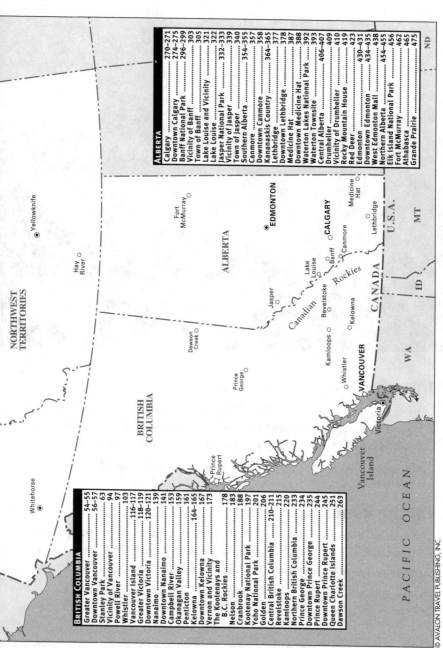

PACIFIC OCEAN

NORTHWEST TERRITORIES

Whitehorse

Yellowknife

Hay River

Fort McMurray

BRITISH COLUMBIA

ALBERTA

Dawson Creek

Prince George

Jasper

EDMONTON

Kamloops

Revelstoke

Kelowna

Lake Louise

Banff

Canmore

Medicine Hat

CALGARY

Lethbridge

Whistler

VANCOUVER

Victoria

Vancouver Island

Canadian

Rockies

CANADA

U.S.A.

WA

ID

MT

ND

Prince Rupert

© AVALON TRAVEL PUBLISHING, INC.

Contents

BRITISH COLUMBIA

Vancouver

Perfectly perched between the sparkling water of the Pacific and the snowcapped peaks of the Coast Mountains, Vancouver takes full advantage of its location with activities that range from scuba diving to downhill skiing. Cultural diversions include fine museums, upscale restaurants, and a thriving theater community.

Downtown; False Creek; West End; Stanley Park; South of Downtown; Richmond; North Shore; East from Downtown

Vicinity of Vancouver

Your route from Vancouver depends on the type of adventure you're seeking. Board a ferry for the sun and sand of the Sunshine Coast; head north to Whistler, one of the world's most acclaimed four-season resort towns; or drive west through the Fraser River Valley amid hot springs, canyons, and rock slides.

Vancouver Island

A short ferry ride from Vancouver, this island is lapped by protected water in the east and battered by the wild Pacific to the west. Hike the West Coast Trail, try your hand at surfing, or go whale-watching, then enjoy the English charms of Victoria, the capital city at the island's southern tip.

Okanagan Valley 158

Find respite from the summer heat by taking to the water in the Okanagan's string of large lakes. In winter, the towns of Penticton, Kelowna, and Vernon become hubs for skiers and snowboarders seeking adventure in the surrounding mountains.

The Kootenays and B.C. Rockies 177

The wonders of mountainous southeastern British Columbia extend from funky towns like Nelson and Rossland to the snowcapped peaks of Kokanee Glacier Provincial Park. Along the provincial border, you'll find the stunning Kootenay and Yoho National Parks.

Central British Columbia 209

*Glacier and Mount Revelstoke National Parks protect a
spectacular swath of mountainous terrain—worthy of as
much time as your schedule allows. Further east, in the
Cariboo region, saddle up for horseback riding, or slip a
canoe into any one of hundreds of lakes.*

Northern British Columbia 232

*The northern part of the province is ruggedly handsome, and
graced with small surprises: fish-filled lakes, friendly towns,
and plentiful wildlife, with an ancient lava flow and
accessible glaciers thrown in for good measure. Adventurous
travelers should jump aboard a ferry bound for the remote
Queen Charlotte Islands—"the Canadian Galapagos."*

ALBERTA

*With its bucking broncos and tight-fitting Wranglers,
the annual Calgary Stampede proves that Cowtown
hasn't forgotten its roots: The fastest-growing city in
Canada is still a small town at heart. But don't let that
fool you—Calgary's filled with cutting-edge galleries,
innovative restaurants, and great live performances.*

Downtown; Chinatown; Canada Olympic Park; Calgary Stampede

*Here you'll find some of the world's most magnificent scenery:
glacial lakes, fast-moving rivers, and unending forests against
a backdrop of snowcapped peaks. The postcard-perfect town
of Banff seems made for idle strolling and shopping,
luxurious lodging, and world-class dining—yet the
wilderness is just minutes away.*

Jasper National Park 331

Drive the stunning Icefields Parkway from Banff to reach neighboring Jasper National Park and the Columbia Icefield, one of the world's largest nonpolar icefields. The park itself is home to soothing hot springs, abundant wildlife, and the most extensive backcountry trail system in Canada.

Southern Alberta 352

This region's diverse landscape ranges from ranching country through arid badlands to the mountain wilderness of Kananaskis Country and Waterton Lakes National Park. You'll also find sights of historical interest, from the petroglyphs and petrographs at Writing-on-Stone Provincial Park to piles of 5,000-year-old buffalo bones at Head-Smashed-In Buffalo Jump.

Central Alberta **405**

Highway 2 may provide the quickest route between Calgary and Edmonton, but tempting detours beckon east and west: the dinosaur-rich Red Deer River badlands, abandoned fur-trading posts at Rocky Mountain House, the remote wilderness abutting Banff National Park, and the summer resort town of Pigeon Lake.

Edmonton **428**

Alberta's capital is a vibrant cultural center, with 14 theater companies and live music from opera to honky-tonk. But the biggest draw is the West Edmonton Mall, the world's largest shopping and amusement complex.

Northern Alberta **452**

Travelers venturing north of Highway 16 will find themselves surrounded by unspoiled wilderness perfect for fishing, bird-watching, or canoeing. Highlights include Elk Island National Park, with high concentrations of bison, moose, and beavers, and the remote oil-sands boomtown of Fort McMurray.

NORTHWEST TERRITORIES

The Accessible North 484

Take advantage of the reliable road system to explore the southern section of the Northwest Territories. Choose between heading east to Wood Buffalo National Park (the world's second largest), or west then north around Great Slave Lake to the modern territorial capital of Yellowknife.

Mackenzie River and Western Arctic 498

Further adventures await in this wild and mostly uninhabited region: Join a rafting trip down the South Nahanni River, cross the Arctic Circle by road, or take a flightseeing trip to remote Tuktoyaktuk.

YUKON TERRITORY

The Alaska Highway snakes its way through the southern Yukon, passing by the famous signpost forest at Watson Lake and the historic capital of Whitehorse before continuing its westward march to Alaska alongside mountainous Kluane National Park.

Trace the path of the biggest gold rush the world has ever known by following the Yukon River north to the Klondike goldfields and the enchanting outpost of Dawson City, where you can relive the glory days by panning for gold; taking a riverboat to Eagle, Alaska; or playing poker at Diamond-Tooth Gerties.

ABOUT THE AUTHOR
Andrew Hempstead

© DIANNE MELTON

Hiking in the Canadian Rockies, golfing the fairways of Whistler, surfing off Long Beach, fishing for steelhead in Northern British Columbia, rafting the South Nahanni River, and skiing the slopes of Red Mountain (for a full season)—Andrew Hempstead has done all of these and more. Not because it's part of compiling a guidebook, but because he loves the great outdoors. On the other hand, it probably wasn't necessary for Andrew to get "Hyderized" in Hyder or gobble down a corndog at the Calgary Stampede to write about it, but he did anyway. These diverse experiences, coupled with a deep respect for native culture and his interest in more modern history, created *Moon Handbooks Western Canada*.

Andrew has been writing since the late 1980s, when, after leaving a career in advertising, he took off for Alaska, linking up with veteran travel writer Deke Castleman to help research and update the fourth edition of *Moon Handbooks Alaska-Yukon*. In the ensuing years he focused on writing about Western Canada, authoring guidebooks to Alberta, British Columbia, the Canadian Rockies, and Vancouver. He is also co-author of *Moon Handbooks Atlantic Canada,* and has been a contributor to *Moon Handbooks San Juan Islands* and *Road Trip USA*. His writing and photographs have also appeared in a wide variety of other media, including *National Geographic Traveler, Travesias, Interval World,* on the Alaska Airlines website, and Microsoft's *Automap*.

Further afield, Andrew is co-author of *Moon Handbooks Australia* and *Moon Handbooks New Zealand*. He has also traveled purely for pleasure through most of the United States, Europe, the South Pacific, and India.

Andrew lives with his wife, Dianne, and their two dogs in Banff, Alberta. When not working on his books, Andrew spends as much time as possible enjoying the wonderful surroundings in which he lives, hiking, fishing, golfing, camping, and skiing.

The website www.westerncanadatravel.com showcases Andrew's work while also providing invaluable planning tips for travelers heading to Canada.

Introduction

It is difficult to capture the true majesty of western Canada with simple words and pictures. They can't re-create the fragrant smells of a flower-filled alpine meadow, the feel of a fresh sea breeze along a coastal trail, the sense of awe as you watch a grazing grizzly bear, and the adrenaline rush of a bucking bull at the Calgary Stampede. They can't express the thrill of hooking a trophy-sized salmon, the solitude of an early-morning mountain hike, and the excitement of white-water rafting. Then you'd want to communicate the tranquility of a rustic lakeside cabin and the flavor of a tender cut of Alberta beef. Of course, the written word and even the most appealing images can't convey any of these things. You have only one option—and that is to discover the wonders of western Canada firsthand.

The Land

Western Canada can be described in one word—vast. The two provinces and two territories have a total land area of 3,440,000 square kilometers (1,327,000 sq. mi.), approximately half the size of the continental United States. The Northwest Territories alone is double the size of Texas, yet has a population of just 64,000. British Columbia is Canada's third-largest province (behind only Ontario and Quebec). Covering 948,596 square kilometers (366,300 sq. mi.), it's four times larger than Great Britain, 2.5 times the size of Japan, larger than all U.S. states except Alaska, and larger than California, Oregon, and Washington combined.

Western Canada is a mostly arbitrary designation for Canada's western regions. This book covers the two western provinces—**British Columbia** and **Alberta**—and two territories—the **Northwest Territories** and the **Yukon.**

Mountains

Mountainous terrain dominates western Canada, a continuation of the same geology that runs along the entire western margin of the United States. The mountain ranges run in a north–south direction, and are separated by a series of parallel valleys. In northern regions, the ranges are lower, wider, and less well defined; they rise to vast plateaus, then give way to endless rolling hills, and eventually to endless arctic tundra and the Canadian Shield.

The steep **Coast Mountains,** an unbroken chain extending for 1,500 kilometers (930 mi.), rise abruptly from the Pacific Ocean and form a stunning backdrop to the seaside city of Vancouver and a winter playground for skiers and snowboarders at Whistler/Blackcomb alpine resort. Their high point, and the highest peak entirely within British Columbia, is 4,016-meter (13,200-foot) **Mount Waddington.** A northern extension of the Coast Mountains is the **St. Elias Range,** which pass through the southwestern corner of the Yukon. These remote mountains include 6,050-meter (19,800-foot) **Mount Logan,** Canada's highest peak. East of the Coast Mountains are the **Columbia Mountains,** the collective name for the **Cariboo, Monashee, Selkirk,** and **Purcell Ranges.** These ranges rise to their high-

Mount Kidd, a classic example of folding and faulting in the Canadian Rockies est points in the south, where they're separated by deep valleys and long lakes. To the east of these ranges are the **Canadian Rockies,** reaching a high point at the summit of 3,954-meter (13,000-foot) **Mount Robson.** Creating a natural border between the provinces of British Columbia and Alberta, the Rockies north of the 49th parallel don't rise to the heights they do in the United States, but the national parks of Banff, Jasper, Kootenay, and Yoho combine to create one of the most magnificent and famous travel destinations on the face of this planet.

Waterways

Western Canada has around 50,000 named lakes, rivers, and streams that lie in dozens of drainage basins separated from each other by **divides,** simply high points of land. The most important of these is the **Continental Divide,** atop the Rocky Mountains and the dividing line between British Columbia and Alberta. From this point all rivers flow either west to the Pacific Ocean or east to the Atlantic and north to the Arctic Oceans.

British Columbia's largest watershed is drained by the **Fraser River.** With its headwaters at the Continental Divide in Mount Robson Provincial Park, this mighty river drains almost 25 percent of the province on its 1,368-kilometer (850-mi.) journey to the Pacific Ocean at Vancouver. The Fraser is not the province's longest river, though. That title belongs to the **Columbia River,** which follows a convoluted course through southeastern British Columbia before crossing the U.S. border and draining into the Pacific Ocean in Oregon, 2,000 kilometers (1,240 mi.) from its source.

Central and most of southern Alberta are drained by the **Saskatchewan River System,** which eventually flows into Hudson Bay and the Atlantic Ocean. Its two notable tributaries are the **North Saskatchewan River,** originating from the Columbia Icefield, and the **Red Deer River,** which flows through "Dinosaur Valley."

The **Peace River,** the only river system to cut across the Canadian Rockies, flows in a northeasterly direction from British Columbia and through northern Alberta to the Mackenzie River System (10th longest in the world), whose waters flow through the Northwest Territories to the Arctic Ocean. Also in the north is the famous **Yukon River.** Although its headwaters are high in the Coast Mountains, it heads north then west on a convoluted course to the Bering Sea.

CLIMATE

The sheer size of western Canada makes for different climates and radically varying temperatures, which rise or fall with changes in elevation, latitude, slope aspect, and distance from the ocean. The coastline of British Columbia boasts

AURORA BOREALIS

The aurora borealis, or northern lights, is an emotional experience for some, spiritual for others, and without exception is unforgettable— an exhibition of color that dances across the sky like a kaleidoscope.

Auroral light is created through a complex process—a spontaneous phenomenon with no pattern and no "season"—that starts with the sun and finishes within the Earth's atmosphere. Essentially a huge atomic-fusion reactor, the sun emits the heat and light that keep us alive, and also emits ions that are thrust through space at high speeds. When these electrically charged particles reach the Earth's rarefied upper atmosphere—about 180 km above the surface—they are captured by the Earth's magnetic field and accelerated toward the poles. Along the way they collide with the atoms and molecules of the gases in the atmosphere, which in turn become temporarily charged, or ionized. This absorbed energy is then released by the ionized gases, often in the form of light. The color of the light varies depending on the gas: Nitrogen atoms produce a violet and sometimes red color, oxygen produces green or, at higher altitudes, orange.

Because the magnetic field is more intense near the north and south magnetic poles, the lights are best seen at high latitudes. In northern latitudes the light show takes place up to 160 nights annually, with displays best north of the 60th parallel. They generally start as a faint glow on the northeastern horizon after the sun has set, improving as the sky becomes darker.

the mildest climate of all Canada, but this comes with one drawback—it rains a lot. The two main cities, Vancouver and Victoria, lie within this zone. As prevailing moisture-laden westerlies blow across British Columbia, the cold heights of interior mountain ranges wring them dry, producing drier, hotter summer temperatures and sunnier skies the farther east you travel. The same is true in winter, except the temperature range is reversed—winter temperatures in Calgary are lower than in the interior of British Columbia and significantly lower than in Vancouver. In winter, the dry winds blasting down the eastern slopes of the Canadian Rockies can raise temperatures on the prairies by up to 40°C (72°F) in 24 hours. Called **chinooks,** these desiccating air currents are a phenomenon unique to Alberta.

Northern Latitudes
In general, the human species lives in the middle latitudes and is accustomed to the particular set of natural phenomena common to those latitudes—

the sun rises in the east each morning and sets in the west each evening; night follows day; vegetation is lush; and water most often occurs as a liquid. But in the far north, these comfortable patterns don't exist. In winter, the sun doesn't rise for days (or, in the high arctic, even months), whereas in summer, it circles endlessly around the horizon. And for more than half the year, lakes, rivers, and the ocean aren't free-flowing water but solid ice. The region's climate is harsh, but the image of the Canadian North being a land of eternal ice and snow is a misconception. During the summer months, from late May to September, the weather can be quite pleasant.

Much of the north is covered by **permafrost**—ground with an average annual temperature below freezing. In much of the mainland, the topsoil melts each summer. This is known as an *active layer* of permafrost. But farther north and in the Arctic Archipelago, the ground remains continuously frozen in a layer 2–500 meters (6–1,640 ft.) deep, which is called *continuous permafrost.*

Flora

Western Canada can be divided into four major geographical areas: the Pacific coast, the mountainous interior, the plains of Alberta, and the arctic. Within each of these four main areas are distinct vegetation zones, the boundaries of which are determined by factors such as precipitation, latitude, and altitude.

COASTAL
Temperate Rainforest
Coastal regions that receive over 1,000 millimeters (40 inches) of rain annually are dominated by temperate rainforest—predominantly evergreens. Just 0.02 percent of the world's land area is temperate rainforest and a full 25 percent of this amount is located in British Columbia. Coastal forest is mostly **hemlock, western red cedar, Sitka spruce,** and, in drier coastal areas, **Douglas fir.** The Queen Charlottes' rainforest is thickly covered in spongy, pale green moss, which grows alongside coastal

Douglas fir. In the region's subalpine areas you'll find **mountain hemlock.**

INTERIOR MOUNTAINS
With vast elevation changes, naturally the flora is diverse, ranging from the cactuses of Canada's only desert in the Okanagan Valley to the equally hardy flowering plants that cling to glaciated peaks, coming alive with color for a few short weeks of summer.

Montane
The montane forest holds the greatest diversity of life of any vegetation zone and is prime winter habitat for larger mammals. But this is also where most development occurs and therefore the habitat is often much changed from its natural state.

In the southern portion of interior British Columbia, valleys are cloaked in montane forest to an elevation of about 1,500 meters (4,900 feet). Drier and south-facing areas support a mixture of

Douglas fir and **ponderosa pine** in the south-central region. Farther east in the Canadian Rockies, **aspen, balsam poplar,** and **white spruce** thrive. **Englemann spruce** take hold at higher elevations and to the north. **Lodgepole pine** is common throughout. The first species to appear after fire, its seed cones are sealed by a resin that is melted only at high temperatures. When fire races through the forest, the resin melts and the cones release their seeds. Large tracts of **fescue** grassland are common in the very driest areas.

Subalpine

Subalpine forests occur where temperatures are lower and precipitation higher than in the montane. In the Canadian Rockies, this is generally from 1,500 to 2,200 meters (4,900 to 7,200 feet) above sea level. In the southern interior of British Columbia, it begins (and ends) at higher elevations. The upper limit of the subalpine zone is the treeline. The climax species are Engelmann spruce and **subalpine fir,** although as in the montane, extensive forests of lodgepole pine occur in areas that have been scorched by fire in the last 100 years. At higher elevations, stands of **larch** are seen. Larches are deciduous conifers. Unlike other evergreens, their needles turn a burnt-orange color each fall, producing a magnificent display for photographers.

Alpine

The alpine zone extends from the treeline to mountain summits. The upper limit of tree growth south of the 60th parallel varies between 1,800 and 2,400 meters (5,900 and 7,900 feet) above sea level, dropping progressively to the north until it meets the treeless tundra of the Northwest Territories. Vegetation at these high altitudes occurs only where soil has been deposited. Large areas of alpine meadows burst with color for a short period each summer as **lupines, mountain avens, alpine forget-me-nots, avalanche lily, moss campion,** and a variety of **heathers** bloom.

THE PLAINS

East of the Canadian Rockies, the mountains dramatically give way to seemingly endless plains.

Although the average elevation is 1,000 meters (3,300 feet) above sea level, the land is incredibly flat; in the southeast corner of Alberta, the Cypress Hills rise 500 meters (1,600 feet) above the surrounding land, yet are the highest point between the Canadian Rockies and Labrador, 5,000 kilometers (3,100 mi.) distant. While it certainly isn't obvious at first, the plains are made up of the following three vegetation zones.

Prairie

Southern Alberta is dominated by prairie, the warmest and driest of Canada's ecological zones. The land is flat open grassland, with trees supported only where water flows. Along most waterways, **cottonwood,** aspen, and poplar provide welcome shade for larger mammals (including *Homo sapiens*) while **willows** clog riverbanks. Water from these rivers is pumped up from the valley floors and diverted by canals across the prairies, making widespread agriculture possible. Native grasses such as rough fescue and **grama** surviving without a helping hand. Amid the seemingly desolate landscape, colorful flowers such as the **wild rose** can be found.

Aspen Parkland

Unique to Canada, this area is a transition zone between the prairie grassland to the south and the boreal forest to the north. As the name suggests, trembling aspen (named for light, flattened leaves that "tremble" in even the slightest wind) is the climax species, but much of this zone has been given over to agriculture. Best known for it mammal populations, Elk Island National Park is one of the few remaining areas of this unique habitat.

Boreal Forest

Technically, the boreal forest, cutting a wide swath across western Canada, is part of the "plains." Encompassing almost half of Alberta and continuing into northern British Columbia and the two territories, the landscape is certainly flat. But it's also heavily treed. Only a few species of trees are able to adapt at these northern latitudes. In the southern part of the boreal forest, aspen and balsam poplar dominate. Farther north, conifers such as white spruce, lodgepole pine, and **balsam fir** are more common, with **jack pine** growing on dry ridges and **tamarack** also present. The entire forest is interspersed with lakes, bogs, and sloughs, where black spruce and larch are the dominant species. In drier, upland areas the lush undergrowth is home to **raspberries, saskatoons,** and **buffalo berries.** To the north, where drainage is generally poor, the ground cover is made up of dense mats of peat.

THE TREELINE AND BEYOND

The treeline is a convoluted line that designates the northernmost extent of tree growth. It occurs below the 60th parallel in Eastern Canada, crossing the Arctic Circle some 500 kilometers (300 mi.) north of Yellowknife before running along the top of the continent and into Alaska. It varies in latitude due to elevation—as a generalization it begins farther north as latitude descends. The treeline is not a line of trees as the name might suggest, but a transition in vegetation types (sometimes called *taiga*) that may be up to 100 kilometers (62 mi.) wide. Where trees do grow in this transition, they are predominantly evergreens of the boreal forest, and because of little precipitation and a short growing season (70–80 frost-free days annually) almost always stunted. Black spruce, white spruce, jack pine (the most northerly of the pines), and aspen are the most common trees

found here. **White birch** is the only deciduous tree able to withstand the region's climate.

Tundra

Above the treeline, in an area of continuous permafrost, is the arctic biome—the tundra. Here a unique selection of vegetation has successfully adapted to the region's extreme seasonal changes of temperature and sunlight, as well as to its lack of precipitation (less than the Sahara Desert). Where water and wind have deposited soil, usually in depressions or along the banks of rivers, the vegetation is more varied. Almost all plants are perennials, able to spring to life quickly after a winter of hibernation. Brightly colored flowers such as **yellow arctic poppies, purple saxifrage, pink rhododendrons,** and **white heather** carpet entire landscapes during the short summer. **Willows** are one of the few woody plants to survive on the otherwise treeless tundra; they're found across the Arctic mainland along with **ground birch** and **Labrador tea.** Other areas are almost completely devoid of soil, supporting little more than arctic ferns, lichens, and mosses. Low temperatures here restrict bacterial action, and as a result, the soil is lacking in the nitrogen necessary for plant growth. Occasional oases of lush vegetation mark spots where the soil received a nitrogen boost—as from a rotting animal carcass or the detritus of an ancient Inuit campsite.

Fauna

Western Canada is one of the best places in the world for wildlife-watching. Thanks to a diverse topography that provides a wide variety of habitat, large mammals are abundant, including elk, moose, bighorn sheep, and bears, all of which are widespread and easily viewed throughout the region. Species diversity in the Northwest Territories and northern Yukon is relatively low compared to other parts of the world. Species concentrations here, however, are enormous, including some of the world's largest populations of caribou, musk oxen, polar bears, whales, and seabirds.

BEARS

Three species of bears are present in western Canada, but only two—black bears and grizzlies—are widespread and abundant. The two can be differentiated by size and shape. Grizzlies are larger than black bears and have a flatter, dish-shaped face and a distinctive hump of muscle behind the neck. *Color is not a reliable way to tell them apart:* Black bears are not always black. They can be brown or cinnamon, causing them to be confused with the brown grizzly.

THE ELUSIVE KERMODE

Little-known outside British Columbia is the Kermode (kerr-MO-dee), an elusive sub-species of black bear inhabiting only the vast tract of wilderness north of Terrace, British Columbia, and uninhabited Princess Royal Island, off the nearby coast.

First studied by Francis Kermode, director of the provincial museum at the turn of the 20th century, the bear was originally thought to be a distinct species. It's slightly larger than other black bears, has a different jaw structure, and, although its color varies, some individuals are pure white. These white bears are not albinos, merely the lightest-colored members of the species.

The Tsimshian called the Kermode "spirit bear" and often rendered it in human form in their artwork. Once close to extinction, the Kermode is now fully protected.

Black Bears

If you spot a bear feeding beside the road, chances are it's a black bear. These mammals are wide-spread throughout all forested areas of western Canada, with an estimated population of 150,000 throughout the region. Their weight varies considerably, but males average 150 kg (330 lbs.) and females 100 kg (220 lbs.). Their diet is omnivorous, consisting primarily of grasses and berries but supplemented by small mammals. They are not true hibernators, but in winter they can sleep for up to a month at a time before changing position. During this time, their heartbeat drops to 10 beats per minute, body temperature drops, and they lose up to 30 percent of their body weight. Females reach reproductive maturity after five years; cubs, usually two, are born in late winter, while the mother is still asleep.

Grizzly Bears

Grizzlies (called brown bears along the B.C. coast), second largest of eight recognized species of bears (only polar bears are larger), have disappeared from most of North America but are widespread throughout Western Canada, numbering around 12,000. Grizzlies are only occasionally seen by casual observers; most sightings occur in alpine and subalpine zones, although sightings at lower elevations are not unusual, especially when snow falls early or late. During fall along the British Columbia coast, salmon runs draw bears to local river systems, almost guaranteeing sightings at a few accessible spots. The bears' color ranges from light brown to almost black, with dark tan being the most common. On average, males weigh 200–350 kg (440–770 lbs.), with those along the coast often weighing a lot more. Apart from the salmon-feasting brown bears, grizzlies eat small and medium-size mammals and berries in fall. Like black bears, they sleep through most of the winter. When they emerge in early spring, the bears scavenge carcasses of animals that succumbed to the winter, until the new spring vegetation becomes sufficiently plentiful. Females first give birth at four years old, and then every three years, the cubs remaining with their mother for up to 3 years.

Polar Bears

Evolved from the grizzly bear 250,000–400,000 years ago, polar bears weigh up to 600 kg (1,300 lbs.) and measure 3.5 meters (11.5 feet) from head to tail. Their most distinctive feature is a pure white coat, but they also have long bodies with large necks. The bears' scientific name, *Ursus maritimus* (maritime bear), aptly refers to their habitat, which is the permanent pack ice of the Arctic Ocean east to Hudson Bay. Polar bears are at home in the sea and have been known to swim hundreds of kilometers. Their most common hunting strategy is to wait, for days at a time, at a hole in the ice for a seal that needs to take a breath.

THE DEER FAMILY

Mule Deer and White-Tailed Deer

These deer are similar in size and appearance. Their color varies with the season but is generally light brown in summer, turning dirty-gray in winter. Though both species are considerably smaller than elk, the mule deer is a little stockier than the white-tailed deer. The mule deer has a white rump, a white tail with a dark tip, and large mulelike ears. It inhabits open forests along valley floors. The white-tailed deer's tail is dark on top, but when the animal runs, it holds its tail erect, revealing an all-white underside. White-tails frequent thickets along rivers, lakes, and highways. They are especially prevalent on Vancouver Island. **Sitka deer,** a subspecies, inhabit the Queen Charlotte Islands.

Moose

The giant of the deer family is the moose, an awkward-looking mammal that appears to have been designed by a cartoonist. It has the largest antlers of any animal in the world, stands up to 1.8 meters (6 feet) at the shoulder, and weighs up to 500 kg (1,100 lbs.). Its body is dark brown, and it has a prominent nose, long spindly legs, small eyes, big ears, and an odd flap of skin called a bell dangling beneath its chin. Apart from all that, it's good-looking. Each spring the bull begins to grow palm-shaped antlers that by August will be fully grown. Moose are solitary animals preferring marshy areas and weedy lakes, but they are known to wander to higher elevations searching out open spaces in summer. They forage in and around ponds on willows, aspen, birch, grasses, and all aquatic vegetation. They are most common in northern British Columbia, often seen by travelers along the Alaska Highway. Although they may appear docile, moose will attack humans if they feel threatened.

Elk

The elk (also known as wapiti) has a tan body with a dark-brown neck, dark-brown legs, and a white rump. This second-largest member of the deer family weighs 250–450 kg (550–1,000 lbs.) and stands 1.5 meters (5 feet) at the shoulder. Beginning each spring, stags grow an impressive set of antlers, covered in what is known as velvet. The velvet contains nutrients that stimulate antler growth. By fall, the antlers have reached their full size and the velvet is shed. Rutting season takes place between August and October; listen for the shrill bugles of the stags serenading the females. During the rut, randy males will challenge anything and can be dangerous. The stags shed their antlers each spring, but don't relax too much because fe-

males protecting their young in spring can be equally dangerous. Elk are common in the Canadian Rockies, where large herds make a home in and around the towns of Banff and Jasper, often nonchalantly wandering along streets and feeding on tasty plants in residential gardens.

Caribou

Native people named the animal *caribou* (hoof scraper) for the way it feeds in winter, scraping away snow with its hooves. The species seems ungainly, but has adapted superbly to life in the harsh northern climates. Standing approximately 1.5 meters (5 feet) tall at the shoulder, Caribou are smaller than elk and have a dark-brown coat with creamy patches on the neck and rump. Both sexes grow antlers, but those of the females are shorter and have fewer points. On average males weigh 180 kg (400 lbs.), females 115 kg (250 lbs.). Like the elk, they breed in fall, with the males gathering a harem. Above the treeline, they congregate each fall for a migration west to the boreal forest. As many as 400,000 of the animals may band together into a single herd. Each spring the process is reversed as they head east to summer calving grounds, high above the Arctic Circle. Small populations of **woodland caribou** inhabit the Yukon, northern British Columbia, and remote corners of the Canadian Rockies.

OTHER LARGE MAMMALS
Bighorn Sheep

Bighorn sheep (also called Dall's Sheep or Rocky Mountain Sheep) are easy to recognize—if you spy an animal with spiraled horns that curve up 360 degrees, it's a bighorn. They spend summers grazing on open slopes or along roadsides, often attracted by natural salt deposits, such as along the Alaska Highway and in Jasper National Park east of the town.

Mountain Goats

The remarkable rock-climbing ability of these nimble-footed creatures allows them to live on rocky ledges or near-vertical slopes, safe from predators. They also frequent the alpine meadows and open forests of the Canadian Rockies, where they congregate around natural licks of salt. The goats stand one meter at the shoulder and weigh 40–530 kg (140–290 lbs.). Both sexes possess a peculiar beard, or rather, goatee. Both sexes have horns. It is possible to determine the sex by the shape of the horns; those of the female grow straight up before curling slightly backward, whereas those of the male curl back in a single arch. The goats shed their thick coats each summer, making them look ragged, but by fall they've regrown a fine, new white woolen coat.

Pronghorn

Found roaming the prairie grasslands of southeastern Alberta, the pronghorn, often called pronghorn antelope, is one of the fastest animals in the New World, capable of sustained speeds up to 80 kilometers (50 mi.) per hour. Other remarkable attributes also ensure its survival, including incredible hearing and eyesight, and the ability to go without water for long periods.

Musk Oxen

These shaggy beasts, hunted to near extinction by the turn of the 20th century, are now restricted to the high arctic. Banks Island is home to around 60,000 musk oxen, the world's highest concentration. The image of them in a defensive circle, protecting the young from predators or the cold, is an endearing symbol of the north. Known to the Inuit as *oomingmak,* meaning "bearded one," they are covered with an underlayer of short, fine wool and a topcoat of shaggy hair up to 60 centimeters (24 inches) long. This gives the animals their characteristic prehistoric appearance and helps protect them from frequent blizzards and winter temperatures that in some areas average -30°C (-22°F).

WILD DOGS AND CATS

Wolves

Now inhabiting only the mountains and boreal forests, the wolf was once the target of a relentless extermination campaign. They weigh up to 60 kg (132 lbs.), stand up to one meter (3.2 feet) high at the shoulder, and resemble large huskies or German shepherds. Their color ranges from snow

white to brown or black. Unlike other predators, they are complex and intriguing animals that adhere to a hierarchical social order and are capable of expressing happiness, humor, and loneliness. British Columbia's vast wilderness is home to an estimated 8,000 wolves. Ironically, the one region that has a declining population is the national parks of the Canadian Rockies.

Coyotes

The coyote is often mistaken for a wolf though in fact it is much smaller, weighing up to only 15 kg (33 lbs.). It has a pointed nose and long bushy tail. Its coloring is a mottled mix of brown and gray, with lighter-colored legs and belly. The coyote is a skillful and crafty hunter, preying mainly on rodents. Coyotes have the remarkable ability to hear the movement of small mammals under the snow, allowing them to hunt these animals without actually seeing them. Their eerie concerts of yips and howls can be heard across much of western Canada and they are often seen patrolling the edges of highways and crossing open meadows in low-lying valleys.

Foxes

The smallest of the North American wild canids is the **swift fox,** which had been eradicated from the Canadian prairies by 1928 but was reintroduced to the southeastern corner of Alberta in 1983. Today, a small population continues to thrive in this dry and desolate landscape, but the species is still considered endangered. It has a gray body with a long, black-tipped bushy tail, large ears, and smoky gray facial spots. The **red fox** is slightly larger than the swift fox and is common throughout Alberta and southern latitudes of the Northwest Territories and the Yukon.

Cougars

Rarely encountered by casual hikers, cougars (known in other parts of North America as mountain lions, pumas, or catamounts) measure up to 1.5 meters (5 feet) long. The average male weighs 75 kg (165 lbs.) and the female 55 kg (120 lbs.). The fur generally ranges in color from light brown to a reddish-tinged gray, but occasionally black cougars are reported. Cougars are versatile hunters whose acute vision takes in a peripheral span in excess of 200 degrees. They typically kill a large mammal such as an elk or deer every 12–14 days, eating part of it and caching the rest. Their diet also includes chipmunks, ground squirrels, snowshoe hares, and occasionally porcupines. The cougar is a solitary animal with distinct territorial boundaries. Although this limits its population density, there are more cougars than ever as the animal expands its traditional range. The cougar population of Vancouver Island is the densest of anywhere in North America, and the species is present as far east as the eastern slopes of the Canadian Rockies (and occasionally sighted within Calgary city limits).

Lynx

The elusive lynx is identifiable by its pointy black ear tufts and an oversized tabby-cat appearance. The animal has broad, padded paws that distribute its weight, allowing it to float on the surface of snow. It weighs up to 10 kg (22 lbs.), but appears much larger because of its coat of long, thick fur. The lynx, uncommon but widespread throughout the region, is a solitary creature that prefers the cover of subalpine forests, feeding mostly at night on snowshoe hares and other small mammals.

SMALL MAMMALS

Beavers

One of the animal kingdom's most industrious mammals is the beaver. Growing to a length of 50 cm (20 inches) and tipping the scales at around 20 kg (44 lbs.), it has a flat, rudderlike tail and webbed back feet that enable it to swim at speeds up to 10 kph (6 mph). The exploration of western Canada can be directly attributed to the beaver, whose pelt was in high demand in fashion-conscious Europe in the early 1800s. The beaver was never entirely wiped out, and today the animals can be found in almost any forested valley with flowing water. Beavers build their dam walls and lodges of twigs, branches, sticks of felled trees, and mud. They eat the bark and smaller twigs of deciduous plants and store branches underwater near the lodge, as a winter food supply.

Squirrels

Several species of squirrel are common in western Canada. The **golden-mantled ground squirrel,** found in rocky outcrops of subalpine and alpine regions, has black stripes along its sides and looks like an oversized chipmunk. Most common is the **Columbian ground squirrel,** which lives in burrows, often in open grassland. It is recognizable by its reddish legs, face, and underside, and a flecked, grayish back. The bushy-tailed **red squirrel,** the bold chatterbox of the forest, leaves telltale shelled cones at the base of conifers. The lightly colored **Richardson's ground squirrel,** which chirps and flicks its thin tail when it senses danger, is found across much of western Canada; on the prairie, it is often misidentified as a gopher. Another species, the nocturnal **northern flying fox,** glides through the montane forests of mountain valleys but is rarely seen.

Hoary Marmots

High in the mountains, above the treeline, hoary marmots are often seen sunning themselves on boulders in rocky areas or meadows. They are stocky creatures, weighing around four kg (9 lbs.). When danger approaches, these large rodents emit a shrill whistle to warn their colony. Marmots are only active for a few months each summer, spending up to nine months a year in hibernation.

Porcupines

This small, squat animal is easily recognized by its thick coat of quills. It eats roots and leaves but is also known as being destructive around wooden buildings and vehicle tires. Porcupines are common and widespread throughout all forested areas, but they're hard to spy because they feed most often at night.

Other Rodents

Widespread throughout western Canada, **muskrats** make their home in the waterways and wetlands of all low-lying valleys. They are agile swimmers, able to stay submerged for up to 12 minutes. They grow to a length of 35 cm (18 inches), but the best form of identification is the tail, which is black, flat, and scaly. Closely related to muskrats are **voles,** which are often mistaken for mice. They inhabit grassed areas of most valley floors.

Shrews

A member of the insectivore family, the **furry shrew** has a sharp-pointed snout and is closely related to the mole. It must eat almost constantly because it's susceptible to starvation within only a few hours of its last meal. Another variety present throughout the region, the **pygmy shrew,** is the world's smallest mammal; it weighs just four grams (0.1 ounces).

Hares and Pikas

Hares and pikas are technically lagomorphs, distinguished from rodents by a double set of incisors in the upper jaw. **Varying hares** are commonly referred to as snowshoe hares because their thickly furred, wide-set hind feet mimic snowshoes. Unlike rabbits, which maintain a brown coat year-round, snowshoe hares turn white in winter, providing camouflage in the snowy climes they inhabit. One of their cousins, the **white-tailed prairie hare,** has been clocked at speeds of 60 kilometers (37 mi.) per hour. Finally, the small, gray-colored **pika,** or rock rabbit, lives among the rubble and boulders of scree slopes above the tree-line, a neighbor of the larger marmot.

Weasels

The weasel family, comprising 70 species worldwide, is large and diverse, but in general, all members have long, slim bodies and short legs, and all are carnivorous and voracious eaters, consuming up to one-third of their body weight each day. Many species can be found in the western regions of Canada, including the **wolverine,** largest of the weasels worldwide, weighing up to 20 kg (44 lbs.). Known to natives as *carcajou* (evil one), the wolverine is extremely powerful, cunning, and cautious. This solitary creature inhabits forests of the subalpine and lower alpine regions, feeding on any available meat, from small rodents to the carcasses of larger mammals. Rarely sighted by humans, the wolverine is a true symbol of the wilderness.

The **fisher** has the same habitat as the wolverine, but is much smaller, reaching just five kg (11 lbs.) in weight and growing up to 60 cm (24 inches) in length. This nocturnal hunter preys on small birds and rodents, but reports of fishers bringing down small deer have been made. Smaller still is the **marten,** which lives most of its life in the trees of the subalpine forest, preying on birds, squirrels, mice, and voles. Three subspecies of the **American badger** inhabit western Canada. A larger member of the weasel family, this creature is uncommon, naturally secretive, and also nocturnal, so sightings are extremely rare. It is endowed with large claws and strong forelegs, making it an impressive digger. Dividing its time between land and water, the badger is found in valley bottoms and on the prairies. A small population was relocated to the Columbia River Valley from Montana in 2003.

River otters have round heads; short, thick necks; webbed feet; long facial whiskers; and grow longer than one meter. These playful characters are active both day and night and prey on both beaver and muskrat. They are widespread but not common throughout the northern half of Alberta. **Mink,** at home in or out of water, are smaller than otters and feed on muskrats, mice, voles, and fish. Mink are especially sought after for their pelts; they are raised in captivity for this purpose at mink farms throughout the province.

As well as being home to the largest member of weasel family, Canada holds the smallest—the **least weasel** (the world's smallest carnivore), which grows to a length of just 20 cm (8 inches) and weighs a maximum of 60 grams (2 ounces). Chiefly nocturnal, it feeds mostly on mice, and lives throughout open wooded areas, but is not particularly common.

REPTILES AND AMPHIBIANS

Reptiles don't like cold climates, and therefore they don't like Canada. Western Canada is home to just 17 of the world's 10,000-odd reptile species. All inhabit dry, hot valleys of grassland, such as the desert areas of the Okanagan Valley and badlands of the Red Deer Valley. The breakdown includes nine species of snakes, five turtles, two lizards, and one species of skink. The only poisonous snake is the extremely rare western rattlesnake. Like other rattlers, it waits for prey rather than actively hunting and won't bite unless provoked.

SEA MAMMMALS

Whales

Once nearly extinct, today an estimated 20,000 **gray whales** swim the length of the British Columbia coast twice annually between Baja Mexico and the Bering Sea. The spring migration (Mar.–Apr.) is close to the shore, with whales stopping to rest and feed in places such as Clayoquot Sound and the Queen Charlotte Islands.

Orcas (also known as "killer whales") are actually the largest member of the dolphin family. Adult males can reach 10 meters (33 feet) in length and up to 10 tons in weight, but their most distinctive feature is a dorsal fin that protrudes more than 1.5 meters (5 feet) from the back.

Belugas—also called "white whales" for their coloring—are common off the Arctic coast. They winter in the Bering Sea and off the west coast of Greenland and migrate to estuarine areas such as the Mackenzie Delta in the western Arctic for summer calving season.

Seals

Five types of seals inhabit western Canadian waters. The most abundant, smallest, and most important to the Inuit are the **ringed seals,** whose name refers to the cream-colored circular markings on their backs. The largest are the **bearded seals,** which weigh up to 250 kg (550 lbs.), and have facial whiskers resembling a beard.

FISH

Salmon

Five species of salmon are native to the tidal waters of British Columbia. Largest is the **chinook,** which grows to 30 kg (66 lbs.) in local waters. Known as "king salmon" in the United States, chinooks are a prized sportfish most recognizable by their size but also by black gums and silver-spotted tails. Averaging 2–3 kg (4.4–6.6 lbs.), **sockeye (red salmon)** are the most streamlined of the Pacific salmon. They are distinguished from other species by a silvery-blue skin and prominent eyes. While other species swim into the ocean after hatching, the sockeye remain inland in freshwater lakes and rivers for at least a year before migrating into the

Pacific. When ready to spawn, the body of the sockeye turns bright red and the head a dark green. **Chum (dog) salmon** are very similar in appearance to sockeye, and the bodies also change dramatically when spawning; a white tip on the anal fin is the best form of identification. Bright, silver-colored **coho (silver) salmon** average 1.5–3 kg (3.3–6.6 lbs.). This species can be recognized by white gums and spots on the upper portion of the tail. Smallest are **pink salmon,** which rarely weigh over four kg (nine lbs.). Their most dominant feature is a tail covered in large oval spots.

Kokanee are a freshwater salmon native to major lakes and rivers of the southern interior. They are directly related to sockeye salmon, spawning in the same freshwater range, and look similar in all aspects but size—kokanee rarely grow to over 30 cm (12 inches) in length.

IT'S A SALMON'S LIFE

The five species of Pacific salmon are *anadromous,* meaning they live in both freshwater and saltwater at different stages. The life cycle of these creatures is truly amazing. Hatching from small eggs in freshwater often hundreds of miles upriver from the ocean, the fry find their way to the ocean, undergoing massive internal changes along the way that allow them to survive in saltwater. Depending on the species, they then spend between two and six years in the open water. After reaching maturity, they begin the epic journey back to their birthplace, to the patch of gravel on the same river from which they emerged. Their navigation system has evolved over a million years, using, it is believed, a sensory system that combines measurements of sunlight, the earth's magnetic field, and atmospheric pressure to find their home river. Once the salmon are in range of their home river, scent takes over, returning them to the exact spot where they were born. Once the salmon reach freshwater they stop eating. Unlike other species of fish (including Atlantic salmon), Pacific salmon die immediately after spawning; hence the importance of returning to their birthplace, a spot the salmon instinctively know gives them the best opportunity for their one chance to reproduce successfully.

Trout

Trout are part of the same fish family as salmon, but, with one or two exceptions, they live in freshwater their entire lives. Interestingly, the trout of western Canada are more closely related to Atlantic salmon than to any of the species of Pacific salmon detailed above. The predominant species is the **rainbow trout,** common in lakes and rivers throughout the region. It has an olive-green back and a red strip running along the center of its body. Many subspecies exist, such as the **steelhead,** an ocean-going rainbow that inhabits rivers flowing into the Pacific Ocean.

Other trout species present include the **bull trout,** which struggles to survive through high levels of fishing and a low reproductive cycle. Throughout the mid-1900s, this truly native Canadian trout was perceived as a predator of more favored introduced species, and was mostly removed. The species is now confined to the headwaters of the Canadian Rockies' river systems, and is classed as a threatened species. Bull trout grow to 70 cm (27 inches) in length and weigh up to 10 kg (22 lbs.). **Cutthroat trout,** found in high-elevation lakes, are named for a bright red dash of color that runs from below the mouth almost to the gills. Colorful **brook trout** can be identified by their dark green backs with pale splotches and purple-sheened sides. It is native to eastern Canada, but was introduced to the Canadian Rockies as early as 1903 and is now widespread throughout lakes and streams on the Alberta side of the Continental Divide. **Brown trout** are the only trout with both black and red spots. This species was introduced from Europe in 1924 and is now found in the Bow and Red Deer watersheds of Alberta. The **lake trout,** which grows to 20 kg (44 lbs.), is native to large, deep lakes of the western provinces. Identified by a silvery-gray body and irregular white splotches along its back, this species grows slowly, taking up to eight years to reach maturity and living up to 25 years. It is technically a member of the char family.

Other Freshwater Species

The **whitefish,** a light gray fish, is native to lower-elevation lakes and rivers across British Columbia and Alberta. Inhabiting northern waters are **arctic grayling** and **Dolly Varden** (named for a colorful character in a Charles Dickens story). **Walleye** (also called "pickerel") grow to 4.5 kg (10 lbs.) and are common in sandy-bottomed areas of lakes in northeastern British Columbia and northern Alberta. The monster freshwater fish of western Canada is the **sturgeon,** growing to over 100 kg (220 lbs.) in size and living for upwards of 100 years. The biggest of this species inhabit the Fraser River.

BIRDS

Bird-watching is popular throughout western Canada, thanks to the approximately 500 resident bird species and the millions of migratory birds that follow the Central and Pacific Flyways each year. All it takes is a pair of binoculars, a good book detailing species, and patience.

Raptors

A wide variety of raptors are present in western Canada—some call the region home year-round, while others pass through during annual spring and fall migrations. British Columbia is home to a quarter of the world's bald eagles. Mature birds can be distinguished by their white heads and tails (immature birds resemble the dark brown–colored golden eagle). **Golden eagles** migrate across the regions, heading north in spring to Alaska and crossing back over in fall en route to Midwest wintering grounds. **Ospreys** spend summers across western Canada, nesting high up in large dead trees, on telephone poles, or on rocky outcrops, but always overlooking water. They feed on fish, hovering up to 50 meters (160 feet) above water, watching for movement, then diving into the water, thrusting their legs forward and collecting prey in their talons.

Falcons have adapted to the prairies and northern treeless landscapes. They are easily distinguished among raptors for their long, pointed wings and narrow tails, allowing them to reach great speeds when in pursuit of prey. Most widespread of is the **prairie falcon,** whose territory extends from the prairies to the foothills. Other falcons present include the **American kestrel,** which is commonly seen perched on fence posts and power poles throughout the prairies; the **merlin,** which tends to nest close to populated areas; and the rare **peregrine falcon,** which has been clocked at speeds of up to 290 kilometers (180 mi.) per hour when diving for prey.

Hawks have adapted to hunting in wooded areas by developing short, rounded wings and long tails. The rust-colored **ferruginous hawk,** the largest hawk in North America, inhabits the treed areas of the prairies. The **marsh hawk** is widespread through the prairies and parkland, and as the name suggests, lives around areas of wetland. Farther north, the **red-tailed hawk** resides in the aspen parkland and southern extent of boreal forest.

Distinct from all previously listed species are a group of raptors that hunt at night. Best known as **owls,** these birds are rarely seen because of their nocturnal habits but are widespread throughout forested areas of the mountains. Most common is the **great horned owl,** identified by its prominent "horns," which are actually tufts of feathers.

Also present is the **snowy owl,** and in the north of the region, the largest of the owls, the **great gray owl,** which grows to a height of 70 cm (2.4 feet).

Shorebirds, Seabirds, and Waterfowl

Nationalistic in name, the **Canada goose** is one of the most common and distinctive birds of western Canada. In the same family, **trumpeter swans, whistling swans,** and the endangered **whooping crane** are also present. In the duck family, **mallards** are present everywhere and **pintails** can often be seen feeding on grain in farmers' fields. The **wood duck** is much less common; identified by a distinctive crest, it can be spied around wetlands. Other widespread waterfowl species include **loons, grebes,** and three species of **teal.** Shorebirds present along the Pacific coast include **plovers, sandpipers, dowitchers, turnstones, gulls, terns,** and **herons.** Many shorebirds migrate vast distances through western Canada to nesting grounds in the Northwest Territories and Alaska, including the **arctic tern,** which makes an annual journey from Antarctica.

THE CANADA GOOSE

Each spring and fall the skies of western Canada come alive with the honking of the Canada goose, a remarkable bird whose migratory path takes it clear across the North American continent. Each spring, family units migrate north to the same nesting site, year after year. These are spread throughout Canada, from remote wetlands of northern Alberta to desolate islands in the Arctic Ocean.

Groups of families migrate together in flocks, the size of the flock varying according to the region, subspecies, and season. Preparation for long flights includes hours of preening and wing-flexing. Once in the air they navigate by the sun, moon, and stars, often becoming disoriented in fog or heavy cloud cover. They are intensely aware of air pressure and humidity. In spring Canada geese hitch a ride north on the strong winds produced by low-pressure systems rolling up from the southwest. In fall they take advantage of Arctic fronts that roar south. If weather conditions aren't right, the geese will rest for a while, usually in farmers' fields (taking advantage of freshly sown crops). The V formation for which the geese are famous

© ANDREW HEMPSTEAD

serves a very specific purpose: Each bird positions itself behind and slightly to the side of the bird immediately ahead. In this way every goose in the flock has a clear view, and all but the leader benefit from the slipstream of the birds ahead.

History

THE EARLIEST INHABITANTS

Approximately 15,000 years ago, at the end of the last Ice Age, human beings began migrating from northeast Asia across the Bering Strait, which was then dry land. At this time, the northern latitudes of North America were covered by an ice cap, forcing these people to travel south down the west coast before fanning out across the ice-free southern latitudes. As the ice cap receded northward, the people drifted north also, perhaps only a few kilometers in an entire generation, and began crossing the 49th parallel about 12,000 years ago. By the time the ice cap had receded from all but the far north and the highest mountain peaks, a number of distinct cultures had formed.

The Northwest Coast

Around 12,000 years ago, Canada's west coast had become ice-free, and humans settled along its entire length. Over time they had broken into distinct linguistic groups, including the Coast Salish, Kwagiulth, Tsimshian, Gitksan, Nisga'a, Haida, and Tlingit, but all these peoples relied on two things: cedar and salmon. Their lifestyle was very different from that of the stereotypical "Indian"—they had no bison to depend on, they didn't ride horses, nor did they live in tepees—but they developed a unique and intriguing culture that remains in place in small pockets along the west coast. These coastal bands lived comfortably off the land and the sea, hunting deer, beaver, bear, and sea otters; fishing for salmon, cod, and halibut; and harvesting edible kelp.

West coast native society emphasized the material wealth of each chief and his tribe, displayed to others during special events called "potlatches." The potlatch ceremonies marked important moments in tribal society, such as marriages, puberty celebrations, deaths, or totem-pole raisings. The wealth of a tribe became obvious when the chief gave away enormous quantities of gifts to his guests—the nobler the guest, the better the gift. The potlatch exchange was accompanied by much feasting, speech-making, dancing, and entertainment, all of which could last many days. Stories performed by hosts garbed in elaborate costumes and masks educated, entertained, and affirmed each clan's historical continuity.

The Interior Salish

Moving north with the receding ice cap around 10,000 years ago, the Salish spread out across most of southwestern and interior British Columbia. After spending summers in the mountains hunting and gathering, they would move to lower elevations to harvest their most precious natural resource—salmon. At narrow canyons along the Fraser River and its tributaries, the Salish put their fishing skills to the test, netting, trapping, and spearing salmon as the fish traveled upstream to spawn. Much of the catch was preserved by drying or roasting, then pounded into a powder known as "pemmican" for later use or to be traded. The Salish wintered in earth-covered log structures known as "pit houses." Depressions left by these ancient structures can still be seen in places such as Keatley Creek, alongside the Fraser River.

Those who settled along the upper reaches of the Columbia River became known as the Shuswap. They spent summers in the mountains hunting caribou and sheep, put their fishing skills to the test each fall, then wintered in pit houses along the Columbia River Valley; they were the only Salish who crossed the Rockies to hunt buffalo on the plains. Within the Salish Nation, three other distinct tribes have been identified: the Lillooet, the Thompson (Nlaka'-pamux), and the Okanagan.

The Kootenay

The Kootenay (other common spellings include Kootenai, Kootenae, and Kutenai) were once hunters of buffalo on the great American plains, but were pushed westward by fierce enemies. Like the Salish did farther west, they then moved north with the receding ice cap. They crossed the 49th parallel around 10,000

HISTORICAL BOUNDARIES OF WESTERN CANADA

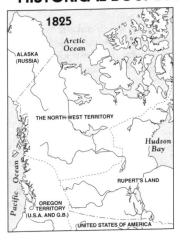

years ago, settling in the Columbia River Valley, along the western edge of the Canadian Rockies. Also like the Salish, they were hunters and gatherers and came to rely on salmon. The Kootenay were generally friendly, mixing freely with the Salish and treating the earliest explorers (including David Thompson) with respect. They regularly traveled east over the Rockies to hunt—to the wildlife-rich Kootenay Plains or farther south to the Great Plains in search of bison.

Blackfoot

The Blackfoot Confederacy was a group of traditional prairie dwellers and was the most warlike and feared of all native groups in Canada. Linguistically linked to the Algonkians, they were the stereotypical Indian depicted in story and film, bedecked in costumes and headdresses and mounted on horses. (This perception is somewhat skewed, however, because the horse was only introduced to North America by the Spanish in the mid-1600s and appeared north of the 49th parallel in the mid-1700s.) Before the arrival of Europeans, the Blackfoot Confederacy ruled the southern half of Alberta and comprised three allied bands, which hunted and camped together, intermarried, shared customs, and spoke dialects of the Algonkian language. They were the **Blackfoot** (best known today as **Siksika**), who lived along the North Saskatchewan River; the **Blood,** along the Red Deer River; and the **Peigan,** along the Bow River.

The **Sarcee** are also considered part of the Blackfoot nation but are of Athabascan linguistic stock. This small tribe divided from the subarctic Beaver in the mid-1800s and integrated themselves with the Blackfoot in customs, lifestyle, and marriage but retained their original tongue.

Assiniboine

Around 1650, the mighty Sioux nation began splintering, with many thousands moving north into present-day Canada. Though these immigrants called themselves Nakoda meaning "people," other tribes called them Assiniboine, meaning the "people who cook with stones."

Totem poles can be viewed in many places along the British Columbia coast, including in Vancouver's Stanley Park (pictured).

© ANDREW HEMPSTEAD

Europeans translated Assiniboine as Stone People, or Stoney for short. Slowly, generation after generation, smaller groups pushed westward along the Saskatchewan River system, allying themselves with the Cree but keeping their own identity, and pushing through the Blackfoot territory of the plains to reach the foothills approximately 200 years ago. They split into bands, moving north and south along the foothills and penetrating the wide valleys where hunting was productive. The evolved a very different lifestyle from that of the plains Indians. Moving with the seasons, they lived in small familylike groups, diversifying their skills, becoming excellent hunters of mountain animals and gathering berries in fall, and becoming less dependent on buffalo. They were a steadfast yet friendly people.

Cree

Before the arrival of Europeans, the Cree had inhabited most of eastern Canada for thousands of years. As the European fur traders pushed westward from Hudson Bay, the Cree followed, displacing enemies and adapting to new environments. By 1800, the Cree had moved as far west as the Peace River and to the northern slopes of the Rocky Mountains. They lived mostly in the forests fringing the prairies, acting as a middleman between Europeans and local natives, searching out furs and trading buffalo hides obtained from plains natives for European goods. Although not related, the Cree and Assiniboine freely mixed together, camping, hunting, and fighting as a group.

The Athabascans

Athabascan (often spelled Athapaskan) is the most widely spread of all North American linguistic groups, extending from the Rio Grande to Alaska. It is believed that Athabascan-speaking people followed the receding ice cap and settled in forested areas throughout the subarctic approximately 7,000 years ago. Athabascans led a simple, nomadic life and were generally friendly toward each other and neighboring tribes. Although culturally diverse, the nature of this tribe's lifestyle left few archaeological remains; therefore, they are the least known of the natives who once lived in western Canada. The largest division of the Athabascans was the Carrier group. They lived throughout the northern reaches of the Fraser River basin and along the Skeena River watershed. The Carrier, along with Athabascan tribes that lived farther north (including the Chilcotin, Tahltan, and Inland Tlingit), adopted many traits of their coastal neighbors, such as potlatch ceremonies and raising totem poles. One Athabascan group inhabiting northern Alberta was the Beaver, who were forced westward, up the Peace River watershed, by the warlike Cree (the name Peace River originated after the two groups eventually made peace). Across the subcontinental divide to the north, the Mackenzie River watershed was the traditional home of another distinct Athabascan band, known today as the Dene (DEN-ay). Like the Beaver, they were nomadic hunters and gatherers but also relied heavily on fishing.

Inuit

A second group of people crossed the Bering land bridge much later than the first—approximately 10,000 years ago—and settled in Alaska. Eventually, people from this group would migrate across the Arctic coast in two major waves. The first wave occurred approximately 4,000 years ago when the people known as the **Dorset culture** began to move east. They lived in skin tents in summer and snow houses—previously unknown in Alaska—in winter. The second eastward migration, that of the **Thule culture,** occurred approximately 1,000 years ago and picked up elements of the Dorset culture, such as snow houses and intricate carvings, as it progressed. The Thule lived in semipermanent villages and specialized in hunting sea mammals. The Thule are ancestors of the Inuit.

Métis

The exact definition of Métis varies across Canada, but the term originated in the 1700s to describe those born of a mixed racial heritage as the result of relationships between French traders and native Cree women. The Métis played an invaluable role in the fur trade because they were able to perform traditional tasks and were bilingual. By the early 1800s, a distinct Métis culture developed, mostly along major trading routes. As the fur trade ended and the great buffalo herds disappeared, many Métis found themselves drawn toward the familiarity of their own people and settled along Central Canada's Red River. Government threats to take their land along the Red River led to the 1869 Riel Rebellion and the 1885 North West Rebellion, after which the displaced Métis drifted back westward to the boreal forests, eking out food by hunting, trapping, and fishing. They were a people stuck between two cultures; they were excluded from treaties signed by full-blooded natives but were not a part of mainstream Canadian society.

EUROPEAN EXPLORATION AND COLONIZATION

By Sea

It was only a little more than 200 years ago that the first European explorers began to chart the northwest corner of North America. In

1774, the ship of Mexican Juan Perez was the first vessel to explore the coastline and trade with the natives. He was quickly followed by Spaniard Don Juan Francisco de la Bodega y Quadra, who took possession of the coast of Alaska for Spain. England's Captain James Cook arrived in 1778 to spend some time at Nootka, becoming the first nonnative to actually come ashore. Cook received a number of luxuriantly soft sea otter furs, which he later sold at a huge profit in China. This news spawned a fur-trading rush that began in 1785 and continued for 25 years. In 1789, Bodega y Quadra established a settlement at Nootka, but after ongoing problems with the British (who also claimed the area), he gave it up. In 1792, Captain George Vancouver, who had been the navigator on Cook's 1778 expedition, returned to the area and sailed into Burrard Inlet, claiming the land for Great Britain.

By Land

Some 100 years before Europeans began exploring the west coast, the British government granted the Hudson's Bay Company the right to govern Rupert's Land, a vast area of western Canada that included all of present-day Manitoba, Saskatchewan, Alberta, and the Northwest Territories. The land was rich in fur-bearing mammals, which both the British and the French sought to exploit for profit. The Hudson's Bay Company first built forts around Hudson Bay and encouraged natives to bring furs to the posts. Soon, however, French fur traders working for the Montreal-based North West Company began traveling west to secure furs, forcing their British rivals to do the same.

Both companies began establishing trading posts, often beside each other, which created a rivalry that continued unabated until they merged in 1821. Most posts were made of solid log construction and were located beside rivers, the main routes for transportation. The first European to reach the coast overland was Alexander Mackenzie, who traveled via the Peace and Fraser Rivers—you can still see the rock in the Dean Channel (off Bella Coola) where he inscribed "Alexander Mackenzie from Canada by land 22nd July 1793." Not far behind came other explorers, including Simon Fraser, who followed the Fraser River to the sea in 1808, and David Thompson, who followed the Columbia River to its mouth in 1811.

The Native Response

The fur trade brought prosperity to the indigenous society, which was organized around wealth, possessions, and potlatches. The traders had no interest in interfering with the natives and, in general, treated them fairly. This early contact with Europeans resulted in expanded trade patterns

DAVID THOMPSON

David Thompson, one of Canada's greatest explorers, was a quiet, courageous, and energetic man who drafted the first comprehensive and accurate map of western Canada. He arrived in Canada from England as a 14-year-old apprentice clerk for the Hudson's Bay Company. With an inquisitive nature and a talent for wilderness navigation, he quickly acquired the skills of surveying and mapmaking. Natives called him Koo-koo-sint, which translates as The Man Who Looks at Stars.

Between 1786 and 1808 Thompson led four major expeditions into what is now Alberta—the first for the Hudson's Bay Company and the last three for its rival, the North West Company. The most important one was the fourth, from 1806 to 1808, during which he discovered the Athabasca Pass through the Continental Divide. For many years, this was the main route across the Canadian Rockies to the Pacific Ocean.

In 1813 Thompson began work on a master map covering the entire territory controlled by the North West Company. The map was four meters (13 feet) long and two meters (6 feet) wide, detailing more than 1.5 million square miles. On completion it was hung out of public view in the council hall of a company fort in the east. It was years later, after his death in 1857, that the map was "discovered" and Thompson became recognized as one of the world's greatest land geographers.

and increased commerce between tribes. But with the Europeans came guns, alcohol, and diseases. And native lifestyle and the boundaries of the various tribes changed dramatically as commerce between the Europeans and locals caused tribes to abandon their traditional home sites and instead to cluster around the forts for trading and protection. While natives of the plains had always slaughtered many buffalo, the population had remained relatively constant. As beaver populations dwindled, however, traders turned to buffalo hides. Within 10 years, the once-prolific herds were practically eradicated. Without their traditional food source, the indigenous plains people were weakened and left more susceptible to diseases such as smallpox and scarlet fever.

Keen to confirm British sovereignty, the British government began colonizing Vancouver Island. Leaving the island in the hands of the Hudson's Bay Company, chief factor James Douglas began "purchasing" land from the natives. He made treaties with the tribes in which the land became the "entire property of the white people forever." Out on the prairies, the now-famous North West Mounted Police had established posts to try to curb the whiskey trade and restore peace. Facing no other choice, the chief of all plains chiefs, Crowfoot, of the powerful Blackfoot Confederacy, signed the first major treaty in 1877, with others following. Relegated to reserves, which consisted of land set aside by the government for specific native bands, the native lifestyle was changed dramatically, and forever. Their self-sufficiency taken away, the tribes were forced to accept what they were given.

BOOMING TIMES

The discovery of gold along the Fraser River in 1858 led to western Canada's first population explosion. At the time only Vancouver Island was part of the British Empire. Realizing that enormous wealth could be buried on the mainland, and with U.S. miners arriving in Victoria by the shipload, the British government quickly responded by creating a mainland colony. At first it was named New Caledonia, but because there was a French territory of the same name, Queen Victoria was asked to change the name, which she did, using "Columbia," which appeared on local maps, and adding "British," just to make sure the United States knew who owned the territory.

The Dominion of Canada

By 1867, some of the eastern provinces were tiring of British rule, and a movement was abuzz to push for Canadian independence. The British government, wary of losing Canada as it had lost the United States, passed legislation establishing the Dominion of Canada, which British Columbia was invited to join in 1871. It joined, with one important condition: that it be connected to the rest of the country by railway. At that time, the North-West Territories—comprising all of western Canada except British Columbia—was a foreign land to those in eastern Canada: Life was primitive and lawless, and no post had more than a couple dozen residents. But in an effort to solidify the Dominion, the government bought the North-West Territories back from the Hudson's Bay Company in 1869.

This region had been divided into districts. One of these, the Yukon, was separated in 1898, the same year the greatest gold rush the world had ever seen was playing out near Dawson City. Thus it was only sensible to declare that boomtown the capital of the Yukon (it was changed to Whitehorse in 1953). Two other districts, Alberta and Saskatchewan, were admitted as provinces of the Canadian Confederation in 1905.

The Coming of the Railway

Scorned in the east as being unnecessary and uneconomical, the rail line reached Winnipeg in 1879, and Calgary then Banff in 1883, before the final spike was driven on November 7, 1885. The completion of a transcontinental railway did more than fulfill a government promise, it changed the face of the west. A northern route through Edmonton to Prince Rupert was completed by the Grand Trunk

Railway in 1914, roads were built, industries—including logging, mining, farming, fishing, and tourism—started to develop, and settlers began pouring in to surveyed land offered at $10 per quarter section (160 acres). Vancouver, at the terminus of the railway, also got a huge boost as overnight it became a transportation hub for the entire Pacific Rim.

Alberta's Black Gold

Fifty years after the Klondike gold rush, Alberta had a gold rush of its own, except it wasn't shiny nuggets that created the excitement, it was black gold—oil. When Leduc Oil Well No. 1, south of Edmonton, began belching black rings of smoke in February 1947, Alberta had hit the jackpot and a new economy for all of Canada had begun. Capitalists poured billions of dollars into Alberta as every valley, hill, and flat was surveyed, and soon farmers' fields throughout the province were littered with beam pumps bobbing up and down. By 1954, eight major fields had been proven to contain eight billion barrels of recoverable crude oil. Calgary became the financial and administrative headquarters of the industry, while Edmonton—at the center of many of the fields—became the technological, service, and

supply center. In less than a decade, the province's population doubled to more than one million.

THE NEW MILLENNIUM

Vancouver, Calgary, and Edmonton have embraced the information-technology boom, diversifying the resource-based economy of both provinces. Nonrenewable resources are still the backbone of western Canada's economy, however.

Since Martin Frobisher took 1,000 tons of fool's gold from the Canadian Arctic back to England in 1576, natural resources have always played a vital role in the exploration and economy of Canada. It looks like this will continue well into the future—the oil sands of Northern Alberta hold the world's second-largest deposit of oil, in the last decade the Northwest Territories has become the one of the world's largest diamond producers, and the potential of vast reserves of natural gas off the British Columbia coast are just being realized.

With a growing, relatively young, and well-educated population, a strong economy, and staggering resources still available in the ground, the future remains bright for Canada's western provinces.

NUNAVUT

On April 1, 1999, the map of Canada was redrawn when the Northwest Territories was divided up and Canada's third territory, Nunavut, was born. Nunavut, meaning Our Land, encompasses the Keewatin, Arctic coast, and Baffin regions—over two million square kilometers—and is home to 29,000 people, of whom 25,000 are Inuit. While native groups around the world dragged issues of land claims through courts, held demonstrations, and, in parts of Canada, took up arms, the Inuit led a low-profile 15-year campaign that on July 9, 1993, culminated in the passage in Canadian Parliament of the historic bill creating Nunavut.

But Nunavut was a lot more than the world's largest land claim. It was an enormous step for the Inuit. Now they assume responsibility for a chunk

of land four times the size of Texas. Although Nunavut was a victory for the Inuit, it hasn't automatically solved the many social problems experienced in the region—unemployment is three times the national average, and the cost of living is twice the national average. Only 21 km of government-maintained roads cross the region, and only 5 percent of its population has completed high school. Nevertheless, after 100 years, the Inuit once again have control of their land.

The capital of the territory is **Iqaluit.** The working language of the government (www.gov.nu.ca) is **Inuktitut.** Tourism is a thriving business in Nunavut. If you're contemplating a trip, start by contacting **Nunavut Tourism** (867/979-6551 or 866/686-2888, www.nunavuttourism.com).

Economy and Government

ECONOMY

The economy of western Canada has always been closely tied to the land—based first on the fur trade, followed by fishing and forestry in British Columbia and agriculture and oil in Alberta. The two western provinces account for one third of Canada's economic output. As a result of its vast natural resources, Alberta leads the way with a GDP of $151 billion.

Energy

Alberta lies above an immense basin of porous rock containing abundant deposits of oil, natural gas, and coal. The **oil** in Alberta occurs in three forms: crude oil, heavy oil, and oil sands. Most is refined for use as gasoline for cars, diesel for trucks, and heating fuel for homes. As technology improves and prices prove extraction to be economically viable, the oil sands of northern Alberta are playing an increasingly important role in meeting world energy demands. The Athabasca Oil Sands, near Fort McMurray, are the world's largest such deposit, with an estimated 315 billion barrels of recoverable oil.

Natural gas was first discovered in southeast Alberta in 1883, but it wasn't seen as a viable source of energy until 1900. Canada has always had more gas than it can use (currently, proven reserves stand at two trillion cubic feet), and 70 percent is exported via pipelines to other provinces and the United States. Gas is mostly used for home heating but is also a source material for the petrochemical industry.

Western Canada's first **coal** mine began operations on Vancouver Island in the 1850s, followed by numerous others across British Columbia and Alberta. Coal was first used to heat homes and provide fuel for steam locomotives, but oil took over those duties in the early 1950s. The industry was revived in the 1960s with the advent of coal-fired electric power plants. This market has since broadened, and today coal is British Columbia's most important mineral export, worth $1 billion annually. Alberta mines more coal, but the value is less.

Minerals

British Columbia is a mineral-rich province, and historically mining has been an important part of the economy. Today, the province is home to 26 major mines and three mineral processing plants that produce $3.6 billion worth of exports. In the Northwest Territories, mining has always been a mainstay of the economy. Currently, eight mines produce $1 billion worth of minerals annually, principally zinc and gold, with yields totaling 25 percent and 10 percent, respectively, of all Canadian production. In the last decade, more than 15,000 diamond claims have been staked in the Canadian Arctic. Currently only two mines are in operation, with the BHP Minerals operation at roadless Lac de Gras producing $500 million of diamonds annually (equivalent to the extraction of 9,000 carats—about five cupfuls—daily).

Forestry

Almost two thirds of British Columbia—some 60 million hectares (148 million acres)—is forested, primarily in coniferous softwood (fir, hemlock, spruce, and pine). These forests provide about half Canada's marketable wood and about 25 percent of the North American inventory. Along the coast the hemlock species is dominant; in the interior are forests of spruce and lodgepole pine. Douglas fir, balsam, and western red cedar are the other most valuable commercial trees. The provincial government owns 94 percent of the forestland, private companies own 5 percent, and the national government owns the remaining 1 percent. Private companies log much of the provincially owned forest under license from the government. Around 75 million cubic meters of lumber are harvested annually, generating $10 billion in exports (more than all other industries combined). Although over half of Alberta is forested, the industry constitutes a tiny percentage of the total economic output, mainly because of the slow regrowth rate of northern forests.

Agriculture

Although oil and gas form the backbone of Alberta's economy, farms and ranches still dominate the landscape. More than 20 million hectares (49.2 million acres) are used for agriculture, half of which is cultivated—a back-breaking job that was started when the first homesteaders moved west. Alberta produces about 20 percent of Canada's total agricultural output, directly employing 50,000 people in the process. The largest portion of the province's $4 billion annual farm income comes from cattle ($1.2 billion). Alberta has four million head of beef cattle—just under half of Canada's total—as well as 140,000 dairy cows. The largest crop is wheat, used mainly for bread and pasta. Barley, used for feeding livestock and making beer, accounts for more than $500 million in annual revenues.

The agricultural facts and figures from British Columbia are very different for a single reason—only 4 percent of this mountainous province is arable, and of this just 25 percent of this land regarded as prime for agriculture. Nevertheless, agriculture is an important part of the provincial economy: 19,000 farms growing 200 different crops contribute $1.4 billion annually to the economic pie. The most valuable sector of the industry is dairy farming, which is worth $260 million. The best land for dairy cattle is found in the lower Fraser Valley. Almost all of British Columbia's fruit crops are grown in the Okanagan Valley; apples are the best known produce, but a burgeoning viticulture industry produces grapes in over 50 vineyards. The province holds around 600,000 beef cattle, including 20,000 run on Canada's largest ranch, the 200,000-hectare (494,000-acre) Douglas Lake Ranch.

Fishing

Commercial fishing, one of British Columbia's principal industries, is worth $1 billion annually and comes almost entirely from species that inhabit tidal waters. The province has 6,000 registered fishing boats and 600 fish farms. The industry concentrates on salmon (60 percent of total fishing revenues come from six species of salmon): Boats harvest the five species indigenous to the Pacific Ocean, and the aquaculture industry revolves around Atlantic salmon, which is more suited to farming. Other species harvested include herring, halibut, cod, sole, and a variety of shellfish, such as crabs. Canned and fresh fish are exported to markets all over the world—the province is considered the most productive fishing region in Canada. Japan is the largest export market, followed by Europe and the United States.

Tourism

Tourism is the second most important industry to the economies of each jurisdiction in western Canada. But it is the largest employer, employing over 200,000 people in British Columbia and Alberta combined. This segment continues to grow, as more and more people become aware of western Canada's outstanding scenery, its numerous national, provincial, historic, and regional parks, and the bountiful outdoor recreation activities available year-round. British Columbia reports 26 million annual "visitor nights" (the number of visitors multiplied by the number of nights they stayed within British Columbia), while Alberta comes up with a figure of 20 million (a figure that counts every visitor only once, but includes intraprovincial travel). The largest number of visitors come from other provinces. Both provinces report over 1,000,000 visitors from the United States, while the United Kingdom, Japan, Germany, and Australia also contribute significant numbers. Tourism British Columbia promotes Canada's westernmost province to the world, while Travel Alberta, a branch of the government's Department of Economic Development, markets that province. North of the 60th parallel, NWT Arctic Tourism and Tour Yukon are the government departments responsible for marketing the two territories.

GOVERNMENT

Canada is part of the British Commonwealth, but the monarchy and the elected government of Great Britain have no control over Canada's political affairs. The British monarchy is represented in Canada by a governor general. The country's constitution is based on five important acts of British Parliament, the most recent being the Canada Act of 1982. That act gave Canada the power to amend its constitution, provided for recognition of the nation's multicultural heritage, and strengthened provincial ownership of natural resources, the latter especially important for Alberta.

The Canadian government operates through three main agencies: the Parliament (made up of the Senate and the House of Commons), which makes the laws; the Executive (Cabinet), which applies the laws; and the Judiciary, which interprets the laws. The leader of the political party voted into power by Canadian citizens becomes the head of government, known as the prime minister. The prime minister then chooses a cabinet of ministers from members of his or her party. Each minister is responsible for the administration of a department. Although elected for a five-year term, the prime minister may call an election at any time.

At a provincial level, the monarchy is represented by a lieutenant governor. Like the governor general, the position is mainly ceremonial.

British Columbia

Under the lieutenant governor are members of the Legislative Assembly (MLAs). Assembly members are elected for a period of up to five years, though an election for a new assembly can be called at any time by the lieutenant governor or on the advice of the premier. In the Legislative Assembly are the premier, the cabinet ministers and backbenchers, the leader of the official opposition, other parties, and independent members. The laws of British Columbia are administered by the cabinet, premier, and lieutenant governor; they are interpreted by a judiciary made up of the Supreme Court of British Columbia, Court of Appeal, and County or Provincial Courts.

The current ruling party is Gordon Campbell's Liberal Party, which swept to power in April 2001. Provincial politics in British Columbia have traditionally been a two-party struggle. In the most recent election, the Liberals defeated the

New Democrats (NDP), who came to be reviled by the business community for tax burdens that stalled the local economy. For information on the provincial government, its ministries, and current issues, visit the website www.gov.bc.ca.

Alberta

The members of the Alberta Legislature are elected on a party system in the same way as those in British Columbia. The leader of the party in power, known as the premier, oversees the running of 18 departments. With so much control over the province's natural resources and, in turn, Alberta's future, many premiers have enjoyed a particularly high profile. One such premier, Peter Lougheed, initiated the Heritage Savings Trust Fund, which collects billions of dollars in oil royalties for the people of Alberta. Initiated in 1976, the fund changed direction in the mid-1990s, steering toward long-term financial returns as opposed to specific projects. Now, the General Reserve Fund holds monies for programs and services, but most of the fund's $12 billion is invested. The Progressive Conservative Party, led by Ralph Klein, is currently in power. Other parties include the New Democratic Party, the Liberal Party, and Alberta Alliance. The website of the Alberta government is www.gov.ab.ca.

Northwest Territories and the Yukon Territory

North of the 60th parallel are three territories (the third is Nunavut). Simply put, these three northern jurisdictions lack the population to qualify as provinces, and therefore fall under the constitutional control of the federal government. Fully elected assemblies give the territories a degree of independence, but there are no political parties. Instead, a single member of each electoral district is voted to the legislative assembly. Members of the assembly then elect a premier and cabinet ministers. At the top of the territorial ladder is a commissioner, who performs a role similar to the lieutenant governor's. For information on the Northwest Territories government go to www.gov.nt.ca; the website of the Yukon government is www.gov.yk.ca.

The People

For thousands of years before the arrival of Europeans to western Canada, several distinct indigenous peoples had lived off the land's abundant natural resources. With the coming of the white man, however, the native groups were overrun and reduced in numbers.

NATIVES

As natives signed treaties, giving up traditional lands and settling on reserves (known as "reservations" in the United States), their lifestyles changed forever. They were no longer free, they no longer hunted or fought, their medicine men could do nothing to stop the spread of the white man's diseases, and they slowly lost their pride. The first Indian Act, drafted in 1876, attempted to prepare natives for "European" society, but it only ended up isolating them from the rest of society.

Natives who are registered as members of a band are known as "status" Indians; that is, they have the right to use designated reserve lands and have access to federal funding. Originally, the Indian Act sought to assimilate natives by removing their "status" when they were considered ready to assimilate, such as when they earned a university degree, or in the case of native women, when they married a nonnative man. The Indian Act has been rewritten many times, including as recently as 1985, when many antiquated sections were repealed. The most important recent change was that natives didn't have to surrender their status to become a Canadian citizen and, therefore, vote and own property. As a direct result of these changes, many natives who had lost their status, or in fact never had it, have been reclaiming it over the last 30 years. Therefore, the population of status Indians has grown considerably in recent years. Today, 130,000 status Indians live in British Columbia and 85,000 in Alberta.

In the Northwest Territories, roughly half the population is of native descent. The Dene

The Indian Village at the Calgary Stampede is a good place to immerse yourself in native culture.

and Métis peoples are along the Mackenzie River Basin and the Inuit live above the treeline and along the Arctic coast. Although the Inuit's physical adaptation has been phenomenal, their Asian origins can be seen in the epicanthic eye fold.

NONNATIVES

When British Columbia joined the confederation to become a Canadian province in 1871, its population was only 36,000, and 27,000 of the residents were natives. A decade later, a Dominion census in 1881 recorded only 18,072 nonnatives in what would later become the province of Alberta. Calgary's nonnative population was recorded at just 75. With the completion of the Canadian Pacific Railway in 1885, Europeans came in droves—drawn first by game and arable land, then by mining, and later by the oil-and-gas boom of Alberta. People of many diverse cultures moved west, forming a melting pot of traditions. As early as 1921, 30 different languages were noted in Alberta alone, in addition to the many distinct languages of the natives.

Today 3.7 million people live in British Columbia and three million in Alberta. The two territories barely register a blip on the population meter, with 64,000 residents in the Northwest Territories and 31,000 in the Yukon. British Columbia holds 12 percent of Canada's total population, while Alberta has a little over 10 percent. Alberta is Canada's fastest-growing province, with an annual population growth of 2 percent, double the national average. British Columbia is Canada's second fastest growing province. Around 60 percent of total population growth is attributed to westward migration across the country. Retirees make up a large percentage of these new arrivals, as to a lesser extent do young professionals.

In British Columbia, the population is concentrated in the southwest, namely in Vancouver, on the south end of Vancouver Island, and in the Okanagan Valley. These three areas make up less than 1 percent of the province, but contain 80 percent of the population. Alberta's population is also concentrated in the cities; Calgary and Edmonton hold well over half the province's total population.

Around 40 percent of western Canadians are of British origin, followed by 30 percent of other European lineage, mostly French and German. To really get the British feeling, just spend some time in Victoria—a city that has retained its original English customs and traditions from days gone by. While the native peoples of western Canada have adopted the technology and the ways of the European, they still remain a distinct group, contributing to and enriching the culture of the province. Asians have made up a significant percentage of the population since the mid-1800s, when they arrived to work on the railway and then in search of gold.

On the Road

The great outdoors: western Canada certainly has plenty of it. With spectacular scenery around every bend, millions of hectares of parkland, and an abundance of wildlife, the region is an outdoorsperson's fantasy come true. Hiking, fishing, golfing, canoeing, kayaking, white-water rafting, scuba diving, downhill and cross-country skiing—it's all here.

Outdoor Recreation

HIKING

Just about everywhere you go in western Canada you'll find good hiking opportunities, from short walks in urban parks to backcountry treks through untamed wilderness. Best of all, it's free.

In British Columbia the regional parks surrounding Vancouver have a wide variety of trails, while over on Vancouver Island the challenging **West Coast Trail** is renowned for its coastal scenery. Many provincial parks scattered through the province—Garibaldi, Manning, Kokanee Glacier, and more—hold a range of hikes, but always with mountain scenery as a backdrop. The national parks of the Canadian Rockies hold the greatest concentration of hiking trails. Here you

can find anything from short interpretive trails with little elevation gain to strenuous slogs up high alpine passes. Some trails are accessible from downtown Banff, while others require some advance planning, like those around Lake O'Hara (Yoho National Park) which are on a quota system.

Heli-hiking is an out-of-the-ordinary way to experience the high alpine without making the elevation gain on foot. The day starts with a helicopter ride into the mountains, where short, guided hikes are offered and a picnic lunch is served. Whistler, Valemount, and Canmore are bases for heli-hiking operations.

CYCLING AND MOUNTAIN BIKING

Cycling is a great way to explore western Canada. The casual pace allows riders time to stop and appreciate the scenery, wildlife, and flowers that can easily be overlooked at high speeds. Some of the most popular areas for road cycling trips are the **Southern Gulf Islands** (quiet, laid-back, loads of sunshine, rural scenery, and lots of artists), **Vancouver Island** (following the Strait of Georgia past lazy beaches and bustling resort towns), and the **Canadian Rockies** (endless mountain scenery). One of the most challenging and scenic on-road routes is the **Icefields Parkway** between Lake Louise and Jasper, which has several well-placed hostels along its length.

Bike rentals are available in all cities and resort towns. Expect to pay $5–10 per hour and $25–30 per day for a regular town bike and from $15 per hour and $45 per day for a full-suspension mountain bike.

Cycle Tours

Backroads (510/527-1555 or 800/462-2848, www.backroads.com) offers cycling tours around the Southern Gulf Islands (Vancouver Island) and through the Canadian Rockies. These excursions are designed to suit all levels of fitness and all budgets. An average of six hours is spent cycling each day, but the less ambitious always have the option of riding in the support van. There's also the option of camping each night (US$1,100 for six days) or staying in grand mountain lodges (US$2,000 for six days). **VBT** (800/245-3868, www.vbt.com) offers a seven-day ride through the Canadian Rockies with mid-range lodging and all meals included in the price of US$1,400. A local company with a long-standing track record is **Backroads Whistler** (604/923-3111, www.whistlermountainbiking.com), with tours through the Whistler Valley and beyond.

HORSEBACK RIDING

Horses are a traditional means of transportation in the Canadian West; many of the roads began as horse trails. Through the foothills of Alberta, ranches still dominate the landscape, and at places like **Griffin Valley Ranch** (Southern Alberta) unguided riding is permitted. Within the national parks of the Canadian Rockies, horse travel is restricted to certain areas, but trail riding is a popular way to enjoy the scenery. Another option in these mountains are overnight pack-trips. On these, expect to ride for up to six hours per day, with nights spent at a remote mountain lodge or a tent camp, usually in a scenic location where you can hike, fish, or ride farther. Rates range $150–200 per person

---

WILDLIFE AND YOU

The abundance of wildlife in western Canada is one of the region's biggest attractions. To help preserve this unique resource, use common sense.

- **Do not feed the animals.** Many animals may seem tame, but feeding them endangers yourself, the animal, and other visitors, as animals become aggressive when looking for handouts.
- **Store food safely.** When camping keep food in your vehicle or out of reach of animals. Just leaving it in a cooler isn't good enough.
- **Keep your distance.** Although it's tempting to get close to animals for a better look or photograph, it disturbs the animal and, in many cases, can be dangerous.
- **Drive carefully.** The most common cause of premature death for larger mammals is being hit by vehicles.

per day, which includes the riding, accommodations, and food.

Guest ranches, where accommodations and meals are included in nightly packages, include ultra-luxurious **Echo Valley Ranch & Spa** (250/459-2386 or 800/253-8831, www.evranch.com) in the Cariboo (Central British Columbia), **Brewster's Kananaskis Guest Ranch,** east of Canmore (403/673-3737 or 800/691-5085, www.brewster adventures.com), and **Black Cat Guest Ranch,** near Hinton in Northern Alberta (780/865-3084 or 800/859-6840, www.blackcatguestranch.ca). Expect to pay from $120 per person per day for accommodations, meals, and trail riding.

FISHING

Freshwater

Fishing is productive in literally thousands of rivers and lakes across western Canada. Hundreds of lakes are stocked at least once annually. Rainbow trout are to western Canada what bass are to the eastern United States—a great fighting fish. They are found in lakes and rivers throughout the west and are the most common of the stocked fish because they're easy to raise and can adapt to various conditions. You can catch them on artificial flies, small spinners, or spoons.

One particular type of rainbow trout, the large anadromous steelhead, is renowned as a fighting fish. They are caught along the Pacific Coast in northern rivers such as the Skeena. The largest species of trout is the lake trout. The largest

"lakies" generally come from northern lakes, including Cold Lake (Northern Alberta). A more central spot is Lake Minnewanka (Banff National Park). Both these lakes have boat rentals and guides. Fishing for cutthroat, which inhabit the highest mountain lakes, requires using the lightest of tackle because the water is generally very clear. Brook trout are found in rivers and lakes throughout the Canadian Rockies. Brown trout are widespread: Most often caught on dry flies, they are difficult to hook onto.

Kokanee rarely grow over one kilogram (2.2 lbs.), but this freshwater salmon is an excellent sport fish inhabiting lakes of interior British Columbia. Feeding near the surface and caught on wet or dry artificial flies, they taste great, especially when smoked. Walleye (also called pickerel) grow to 4.5 kg (10 lbs.) and are common in sandy-bottomed areas of lakes throughout the prairies and northern British Columbia. They are a popular catch with anglers, mostly because they taste so good. The largest northern pike (up to 17 kg/38 lbs.) inhabit northern lakes and rivers. Jigging with a large lure around the weedy extremes of large lakes gives the angler the best chance of hooking one of these monsters. Perch, at the other end of the size scale from pike but inhabiting the same shallow waters, are a fun, easy-to-catch fish—if you see kids fishing off a pier, chances are they're after perch. Arctic grayling, easily identified by a large dorsal fin, are common in cool clear lakes and streams throughout the far north of Alberta. These delicious-tasting fish are most often taken on dry flies, but their soft

ON THE ROAD

NATIONAL PARK PASSES

Passes are required for entry into all national parks. The cost of a **National Parks Day Pass** varies between parks in the range of adult $5–7, senior $4.25–6, and child $2.50–3.50. There is a maximum per-vehicle entry fee of double the adult (or senior) rate. Passes are interchangeable between parks and are valid until 4 P.M. the day following purchase. An annual **National Parks of Canada Pass,** good for entry into all Canadian national parks for one year from the date of purchase, is adult $45, senior $38 to a maximum of $89 per vehicle ($76 for two or more seniors). The **Discovery Package** includes entry into Parks Canada–managed National Historic Sites for adult $59, senior $49 to a maximum of $118 ($98 for two or more seniors).

Passes can be purchased at park gates, at all park information centers, and at campground fee stations. For more information, check the Parks Canada website (www.pc.gc.ca).

mouths make keeping them hooked somewhat of a challenge.

The Northwest Territories is a legendary destination for serious anglers. Inland lakes and rivers are the domain of trophy-size lake trout, arctic grayling, walleye, and northern pike (jackfish). Great Bear Lake holds world records in *every* class of lake trout and arctic grayling (including a 34.5-kg/76-lb. lake trout). The arctic char, caught in rivers, lakes, and the open ocean of the Arctic coast and Arctic archipelago, is famous both as a fighting fish and as an acclaimed Northern delicacy.

Freshwater Licenses

British Columbia licenses: Prices vary according to your age and place of residence. B.C. residents pay $36 for a freshwater adult license, good for one year. Other Canadians pay $55, and international visitors pay $80. Single-day licenses are $10 for B.C. residents and $20 for everyone else. Eight-day licenses (resident $20, other Canadian $36, non-Canadian $56) are another option. For more information contact the Ministry of Water, Land, and Air Protection (250/387-4573, www.gov.bc.ca/wlap).

Alberta licenses: Alberta has an automated licensing system, with licenses sold in sporting stores, gas stations, and so forth. To use the system, a **Wildlife Identification Number** (WIN) card is needed. These cards are sold by all license vendors and cost $8 (valid for five years). An annual license for Canadian residents age 16 and older is $21; for nonresidents it is $60, or $40 for a five-day license. For information, contact Wildlife Division, Sustainable Resource Development (780/944-0313, www3.gov.ab.ca/srd/info).

Northwest Territories licenses: In the NWT, a three-day license costs $15 for Canadians, $30 for nonresidents. A season license is $20 or $40, respectively. To download a *Northwest Territories Sport Fishing Guide* go to the website of the government's Wildlife and Economic Development Ministry (www.rwed.gov.nt.ca).

Yukon licenses: The Department of Environment website (http://environmentyukon .gov.yk.ca) is the best source of Yukon license information. Canadians pay $5 for one day, $15 for six days, or $25 to fish for the entire season. Nonresidents of Canada pay $5, $20, and $35 respectively.

National park licenses: Fishing in national parks requires a separate license, which is available from park offices and some sport shops; $7 for a seven-day license, $20 for an annual license.

Tidal

The tidal waters of British Columbia hold some of the world's best fishing—Port Alberni, Tofino, Campbell River, and Port Hardy, all on Vancouver Island, are popular bases. The five species of Pacific salmon are most highly prized by anglers. The chinook (king) salmon in particular is the trophy fish of choice. They commonly weigh over 10 kg (22 lbs.) and are occasionally caught at over 20 kg (44 lbs). Other salmon present are coho (silver), pink (humpback), sockeye (red), and chum (dog). Other species sought by recreational anglers include halibut, ling cod, rockfish, cod, perch, and snapper.

A resident tidal-water sportfishing license, good for one year from 31 March, costs $21.47 ($11.34 for those 65 and over); for nonresidents of British Columbia, the same license costs $108.07, or pay $7.49 for a single-day license, $20.33 for three days, or $34.17 for five days. A salmon conservation stamp is an additional $6.42. Licenses are available from sporting stores, gas stations, marinas, and charter operators. For further information contact **Fisheries and Oceans Canada** (604/666-0561, www.pac .dfo-mpo.gc.ca).

The **Sport Fishing Institute of British Columbia** (604/689-3438, www.sportfishing.bc.ca) produces a free annual magazine, *Sport Fishing,* that lists charter operators and fishing lodges and details license requirements.

OTHER WATER-BASED RECREATION

Canoeing and Kayaking

Canoes are a traditional form of transportation throughout western Canada. You can rent one at many of the more popular lakes, but if you bring your own you can slip into any body of water whenever you please, taking advantage of an unparalleled opportunity for admiring scenery

ALPINE CLUB OF CANADA

The Alpine Club of Canada (ACC), like similar clubs in the United States and Great Britain, is a nonprofit mountaineering organization whose objectives include the encouragement of mountaineering through educational programs, the exploration and study of alpine and glacial regions, and the preservation of mountain flora and fauna.

The club was formed in 1906, mainly through the tireless campaign of its first president, Arthur Wheeler. A list of early members will be familiar to all Canadian mountaineers—Bill Peyto, Tom Wilson, Byron Harmon, Mary Schäffer. Today the club membership includes 3,000 alpinists from throughout Canada.

The club's ongoing projects include operating the Canadian Alpine Centre (Lake Louise Hostel), maintaining a system of 20 huts throughout the backcountry of the Canadian Rockies, and publishing the annual *Canadian Alpine Journal*—the country's only record of mountaineering accomplishments. A reference library of the club's history is kept at the Whyte Museum of the Canadian Rockies in Banff.

For further information and membership details, contact club headquarters in Canmore, Alberta (403/678-3200, www.alpineclubof canada.ca).

The British Columbia coastline is great for sea kayaking, and rentals are available in most coastal communities. The Southern Gulf Islands (Vancouver Island) are ideal for kayakers of all experience levels, while destinations such as Desolation Sound (Vicinity of Vancouver), the Broken Group Islands (Vancouver Island), and the Queen Charlotte Islands (Northern British Columbia) are the domain of experienced paddlers.

Most outfits offering kayak rentals also provide lessons and often tours. One such Vancouver operation is the **Ecomarine Ocean Kayak Centre** (604/689-7575). Tofino, on Vancouver Island's west coast, is a popular base for sea kayakers. Here, **Tofino Sea Kayaking Company** (250/725-4222 or 800/863-4664, www.tofino-kayaking .com) rents kayaks and leads tours through local waterways.

White-Water Rafting

The best and easiest way to experience a white-water rafting trip is on a half- or full-day trip with a qualified guide. In the vicinity of Vancouver, the Green, Fraser, Nahatlatch, and Thompson Rivers are run commercially. In the Canadian Rockies, the Kicking Horse River, Sunwapta, and Kananaskis Rivers provide the thrills. Expect to pay $90–100 for a full day's excitement, transfers, and lunch.

For those with some experience in both river *and* wilderness travel, there are some excellent opportunities for extended river trips. Close to Vancouver, the classic of these runs the Chilko, Chilcotin, then Fraser Rivers and lasts up to two weeks. In the far north of the province, the Tatshenshini and Alsek Rivers are a popular destination, while in the Northwest Territories the legendary South Nahanni River is at the top of many people's to-do list.

Boating

British Columbia's 25,000 km (15,535 mi.) of coastline, in particular the sheltered, island-dotted Strait of Georgia between Vancouver Island and the mainland, is a boater's paradise. Along it are sheltered coves, sandy beaches, beautiful marine parks, and facilities specifically designed

and viewing wildlife from water level. One of the most popular backcountry canoe routes is in Bowron Lake Provincial Park (Central British Columbia), where a 117-kilometer (73-mi.) circuit leads through a chain of lakes in the Cariboo Mountains. The **Canadian Recreational Canoe Association** (613/269-2910 or 888/252-6292, www.crca.ca) represents qualified guides and can recommend canoe routes. Another handy website is www.paddlingcanada.com.

Anywhere suitable for canoeing is also prime kayaking territory, although most keen kayakers look for white-water excitement. The best wilderness kayaking experiences are in the interior of British Columbia and the Canadian Rockies.

ON THE ROAD

for boaters—many accessible only by water. One of the most beautiful marine parks is Desolation Sound, north of Powell River (Vicinity of Vancouver).

Scuba Diving

Some of the world's most varied and spectacular cold-water diving lies off the coast of British Columbia. Diving is best in winter, when you can expect up to 40 meters (130 ft.) of visibility. The diverse marine life includes sponges, anemones, soft corals, rockfish (china, vermilion, and canary), rock scallops, and cukes. Plenty of shipwrecks also dot the underwater terrain. *Diver* magazine is a good source of local information; its scuba directory lists retail stores, resorts, charter boats, and other services. The most popular dive sites are off the Gulf Islands, Nanaimo, Campbell River, and Powell River (the scuba diving capital of Canada). Many of the coastal communities along Vancouver Island and the Sunshine Coast have dive shops with gear rentals and air tanks, and many can put you in touch with charter dive boats and guides. Being landlocked, Alberta is not renowned for scuba diving. A few interesting opportunities do exist, however, including the flooded townsite of Minnewanka Landing in Banff National Park.

GOLF

With beautiful scenery, long sunny days, and more than 500 courses, western Canada is an ideal spot for golfers. Some of the world's best-known golf courses are in western Canada, along with hundreds you've probably never heard of, including a few in the Northwest Territories and the Yukon with artificial grass greens. Municipal courses offer the lowest greens fees, generally $10–25, but the semi-private, private, and resort courses usually boast the most spectacular locations. At these courses, greens fees can be over $200. At all but the smallest municipal courses, club rentals, power carts, and lessons are available, and at all but the most exclusive city courses, nonmembers are welcomed with open arms.

SKIING AND SNOWBOARDING

Most of the developed winter recreation areas are in the southern third of British Columbia and in the Canadian Rockies. Whether you're a total beginner or an advanced daredevil, you'll find slopes to suit. The price of lift tickets is generally reasonable, and at the smaller, lesser-known resorts, you don't have to spend half your day lining up for the lifts. Generally resorts are open December–April. The best known of the British Columbian resorts is **Whistler/Blackcomb** (Vicinity of Vancouver), but others scattered through the southern interior provide world-class skiing and snowboarding on just-as-challenging slopes. The best of these include **Big White Ski Resort** and **Silver Star Mountain Resort** (Okanagan Valley); **Red Mountain, Whitewater, Fernie Alpine Resort,** and **Panorama Resort** (Kootenays); and **Sun Peaks Resort** (Central B.C.). Banff National Park is home to Canada's second-largest resort, **Lake Louise,** as well as **Sunshine Village** and **Ski Banff @ Norquay. Nakiska** (Southern Alberta) was developed for the 1988

Banff Springs Golf Course

Olympic Winter Games, while Whistler is preparing to host the downhill events at the 2010 games.

Heli- and Sno-Cat Skiing and Snowboarding

Alternatives to resorts are also available. If you're an intermediate or advanced skier or snowboarder, you can go heli-skiing and heli-boarding in the mind-boggling scenery and deep, untracked powder of the Coast and Chilcotin Ranges, the central Cariboo Mountains, and the Bugaboos. The world's largest heli-ski operation is **CMH Heli-skiing** (403/762-7100 or 800/661-0252, www.cmhski.com), which includes almost limitless terrain over five mountain ranges accessed from 11 lodges. **Mike Wiegele Helicopter Skiing** (250/673-8381 or 800/661-9170, www.wiegele.com) offers heli-skiing and heli-boarding in the Monashee and Cariboo Mountains from a luxurious lodge at Blue River (Central British Columbia).

Another, less-expensive alternative is to hook up with one of the many Sno-Cat operations in the province. Sno-Cats are tracked, all-terrain vehicles (similar to snow groomers but capable of carrying passengers) that can transport skiers and snowboarders up through the snow to virgin slopes in high-country wilderness. British Columbia has been a world leader in this type of skiing, and many operators are scattered through the province. Revelstoke is the Sno-Cat capital of the province. In this central B.C. town, **CAT Powder Skiing** (250/837-5151 or 877/422-8754, www.catpowder.com) offers day trips or overnight packages from its Revelstoke base. Thanks to its location amid some of the continent's most consistent powder snow, **Island Lake Lodge** (near Fernie, 250/423-3700 or 888/422-8754, www.islandlakelodge.com) has gained a reputation for both its Sno-Cat skiing and its luxurious lodgings.

Arts and Entertainment

MUSEUMS

The best way to gain insight into western Canada's unique and colorful history is to visit its many museums. Almost every town has a small museum showcasing the surrounding area, but the larger facilities attract the most attention. In Victoria, don't miss the **Royal British Columbia Museum,** a magnificent facility that catalogs the province's entire natural and human history. In Vancouver, the **Museum of Anthropology** boasts a fantastic collection of totem poles and other native artifacts. Outside of the major cities, museums generally reflect local heritage; the pick of the bunch are the **Historic O'Keefe Ranch** outside Vernon, the **Museum of Northern British Columbia** in Prince Rupert, and the **Haida Gwaii Museum** out on the Queen Charlotte Islands. In Alberta, the **Royal Tyrrell Museum,** located in the dinosaur-rich badlands of the Red Deer River Valley (Central Alberta), is the largest paleontological museum in the world. Inside you'll find more than 50 full-size dinosaurs on display. If you visit only one museum in Alberta,

make it this one. Other major Alberta museums include the **Provincial Museum of Alberta** in Edmonton; **Glenbow Museum** in Calgary; **Remington-Alberta Carriage Centre** at Cardston (Southern Alberta), which houses more than 200 carriages, buggies, and wagons; and the **Reynolds-Alberta Museum** on the outskirts of Wetaskiwin (Central Alberta), which catalogs the history of machinery in western Canada. The **Prince of Wales Northern Heritage Centre** in Yellowknife is the largest museum in the NWT, while across the border in the Yukon, plan on visiting Whitehorse's **MacBride Museum** of local history and the **Yukon Beringia Interpretive Centre** to learn more about mammals that roamed the earth during the last ice age.

PERFORMING ARTS

British Columbia's largest city boasts a lively performing-arts community: More than 30 theater groups call Vancouver home, and the city also supports an opera, an orchestra, and Ballet British Columbia. Vancouver's magnificent Ford

Centre hosts world-class productions. Victoria, Kamloops, and Prince George also have noteworthy performing-arts communities. Alberta, a province that prides itself on a Western heritage, has a surprising number of cultural diversions. Edmonton alone has a dozen professional theater companies, equal to any North American city of comparable size. Both Edmonton and Calgary have ballet troupes, an orchestra, and an opera company.

NIGHTLIFE

The bar scene in western Canada is really no different than anywhere else in North America. Most cities have a plethora of bars and nightclubs playing everything from disco to hip hop. Western heritage lives on at country-music bars. **Ranchman's** in Calgary, **Cook County Saloon** in Edmonton, and dozens of small-town bars across the region keep the Western image alive.

FESTIVALS AND EVENTS

You'll find at least one festival or event going on somewhere in either of the two provinces or territories every weekend through spring, summer, and fall. Many towns hold winter events featuring zany happenings such as snow golf, bed races on ice, and anything they can come up with that's good for a laugh. The following section lists some highlights; see the Festivals and Events sections of the particular town listings in this book for more or check tourism websites listed in the Internet Resources.

Spring

Raise a glass to the beginning of a packed festival season at the **Vancouver Playhouse International Wine Festival,** in early April. The year's first major event for cowboys is the **Rodeo Royal** held at Calgary's Saddledome in late March, followed the next weekend by the **Spring Outdoor Rodeo** in Medicine Hat (Southern Alberta) and in April by the **Makin' 8 Silver Buckle Rodeo** in Red Deer (Central Alberta). For a full rodeo schedule, contact the Canadian Professional Rodeo Association (403/250-7440, www.rodeocanada.com).

Kids of all ages with love Calgary's **International Children's Festival** in late May, or a month later, the **Vancouver International Children's Festival** at Vanier Park, in late June.

Winter resorts throughout western Canada usually have snow on the ground until late spring, and many hold events near season's end, such as the **World Ski & Snowboard Festival** at Whistler (Vicinity of Vancouver) at the end of April and the **Slush Cup** at Sunshine Village (Banff National Park) in May.

Spring musical gatherings in Victoria (Vancouver Island) include the **TerrifVic Jazz Party** the third weekend of April, **FolkFest** in late June, and **Rootsfest** one month later.

Many of the Okanagan's biggest festivals relate to the planting or harvesting of crops. The first of these is the **Spring Wine Festival** throughout the valley's wineries in late April. Following closely is the **Apple Blossom Festival** in Kelowna every May.

The Gathering comes to Pincher Creek (Southern Alberta) in mid June . . . hear cowpokes read poems by the light of the, uh, stars? Stars of another type come to perform at the **Jazz Festival Calgary,** through the last week of June—the festival draws famous jazz musicians from around the world.

The longest day of the year, June 21 is widely celebrated through northern latitudes, including in Yellowknife (**Raven Mad Daze** and a **midnight sun golf tournament**) and Inuvik (**Midnight Madness**).

Summer

Summer is the biggest event season in western Canada. Edmonton boasts a major festival almost every weekend. Highlights are the early-July **International Street Performers Festival**, with more than 1,000 free performances; **Klondike Days Festival,** a late-July celebration centered around the city's connection to the Yukon goldfields; the **Edmonton Folk Music Festival** that picks and strums its way into town in early August; and **The Fringe,** held mid-August, that is North America's largest alternative theater festival.

Canada Day, July 1, is a national holiday celebrated in many towns with various events—look for pancake breakfasts, parades, and fireworks. Steveston (Vancouver) celebrates with a **salmon barbecue.** The **Williams Lake Stampede** (Northern British Columbia) is the biggest Canada Day weekend rodeo, while across the border, the **Ponoka Rodeo** (Central Alberta) is also a major draw. Vegreville (Northern Alberta) celebrates its multicultural past on this weekend with the **Ukrainian Pysanka Festival.**

The best known of western Canada's events is the **Calgary Stampede,** with 10 days of action and a final-day, winner-take-all format. This Western extravaganza is a not-to-be-missed event that takes place over 10 days from the second Friday in July. Equestrian events of a very different kind take place throughout summer just outside the Calgary city limits at **Spruce Meadows,** one of the world's finest international riding centers. The first event on the calendar, in early June, is the **National,** a show-jumping competition attracting thousands of enthusiasts.

In the Kootenays, Kimberley's **International Old Time Accordion Championship** attracts a mass of accordion players to the Bavarian city in mid-July. In late July, crowds gather along the Nanaimo (Vancouver Island) foreshore for the annual **World Championship Bathtub Race,** with competitors racing around local waters in motorized bathtubs. The mood is a little less zany that same weekend in Inuvik (Mackenzie River), which hosts the **Great Northern Arts Festival.** July ends on a high note with the **Red Deer International Air Show** (Central Alberta) on the last weekend, featuring performances by some of the world's best stunt pilots.

Aside from the Edmonton Folk Music Festival, two other southern Albertan events stand out on the August long weekend (first full weekend in August): **Whoop-Up Days** in Lethbridge and Canmore's **Folk Music Festival.** Also in early August, held over four nights, is one of Vancouver's best-attended events: the **Festival of Light,** a magnificent musical fireworks display over the harbor.

Enjoy the traditions of show jumping at Spruce Meadows.

Fall

The biggest of the Okanagan's many wine gatherings is the **Fall Wine Festival,** which showcases local wines to the world through early October. Some harvest celebrations are on a smaller scale, such as the October **Pumpkin Festival** at Davison Orchards, on the outskirts of Vernon.

Just when all of the summer festivals are winding down, the action at Spruce Meadows equestrian center (Calgary) is heating up. Held the first weekend of September, **Spruce Meadows Masters** is the world's richest show-jumping event and the finale to a packed season. Jointly hosted by Calgary and Banff, the mid-October **Wordfest** is a popular literary gathering. The first weekend of November is **Banff Mountain Festivals** (Banff National Park), a gathering of the world's greatest makers of adventure films.

Winter

For the month of December, an evening visit to Vancouver's VanDusen Botanical Garden is made memorable by a dynamic light show and seasonal displays called the **Festival of Lights.** Also in Vancouver through December, the **Carol Ships Parade of Lights** brings the festive season alive as boats filled with carolers motor around city waterways. One of western Canada's many mid-winter festivals is the **Winter Carnival** in Canmore (Southern Alberta), with ice-sculpting and dogsled races. The early-February **Yukon Quest,** between Whitehorse (Southern Yukon) and Fairbanks, Alaska, is another mushing race, this one regarded as the world's toughest.

SHOPPING

Shops are generally open Monday–Friday 9 A.M.–5 P.M., Saturday 9 A.M.–noon, and are closed on Sunday. Major shopping centers and those in resort towns like Whistler and Banff are often open until 9 P.M. and all weekend. Banks are open Monday–Friday 9:30 A.M.–3:30 P.M. and until 4:30 or 5 P.M. on Friday.

Arts and Crafts

The arts and crafts of Canada's indigenous people are available throughout western Canada. It tends to fall into one of two categories: "arts" such as woodcarving and painting, argillite carving, jade- and silverwork, and totem restoration (all generally attended to by the men); and "handicrafts" such as basketry, weaving, beadwork, skinwork, sewing, and knitting (generally created by women). Today, all of these arts and crafts contribute significant income to First Nations communities.

Painting and woodcarving are probably the most recognized art forms of Pacific Northwest natives. Along the Pacific Coast—in museums and people's homes, outdoors, and of course in all the shops—you can see brightly colored carved totems, canoes, paddles, fantastic masks, and ceremonial rattles, feast dishes, bowls, and spoons. Fabulous designs, many featuring animals or legends, are also painstakingly painted in bright primary colors on paper.

Basketry comes in a variety of styles and materials. Watch for decorative cedar-root (fairly rare) and cedar-bark baskets, still made on the west coast of Vancouver Island; spruce-root baskets from the Queen Charlotte Islands; and beautiful, functional, birch-bark baskets from Fort Liard (NWT). In Alberta, jewelry, beaded moccasins, baskets, and leatherwork such as headdresses are favorite souvenirs. And all outdoorspersons should consider forking out for a heavy, water-resistant, raw sheep's-wool sweater; they're generally white or gray with a black design, and much in demand because they're warm, good in the rain, rugged, and last a lifetime. One of the best places to get your hands on one is the Cowichan Valley (Vancouver Island).

Carved argillite (black slate) miniature totem poles, brooches, ashtrays, and other small items, highly decorated with geometric and animal designs, are created exclusively by the Haida on the Queen Charlotte Islands (Northern British Columbia).

Accommodations

The good news is that western Canada has a wide range of accommodations to suit all budgets. The very best options are detailed through the following chapters, while this section broadly describes various accommodation types, as well as some hints on saving money along the way.

Tourism offices in Alberta (**Travel Alberta,** 780/427-4321 or 800/252-3782, www.travelalberta.com) and British Columbia (**Tourism British Columbia,** 250/387-1642 or 800/435-5622, www.hellobc.com) produce annual accommodation guides that include hotels, motels, lodges, and bed-and-breakfasts, with prices included. The same departments in the Northwest Territories (**NWT Arctic Tourism,** 867/873-7200 or 800/661-0788, www.explorenwt.com) and the Yukon (**Tourism Yukon,** 403/667-5340, www.touryukon.com) include lodgings in their general travel guides. Each of the above departments will send out these guides for free, or you can download them from their websites.

All rates quoted in this handbook are for the cheapest category of rooms during the most expensive time period (summer). Accommodation prices in Whistler and the national parks of the Canadian Rockies are slashed by as much as 70 percent in shoulder seasons, while in major cities weekend rates are discounted up to 50 percent. To all rates quoted, you must add the 7 percent Goods and Services Tax (GST) and either an 8 percent provincial room tax (British Columbia) or a 5 percent provincial room tax (Alberta). The GST is refundable to nonresidents of Canada (keep receipts).

HOTELS AND MOTELS

Hotels and motels of some sort exist in just about every town through western Canada. Check your favorite chain—most are represented, as are locals such as upscale **Delta Hotels** (www.deltahotels.com) and **Fairmont Hotels and Resorts** (www.fairmont.com), and the mid-priced **Sandman Hotels** (www.sandmanhotels.com).

Ubiquitous park-at-your-door, single-story road motels are located in all towns and on the outskirts of all major cities. In most cases, rooms are fine, but check before paying, just to make sure. Most motels have a few rooms with kitchenettes, but these fill fast. In the smaller towns, expect to pay $40–70 s, $50–80 d.

Most major towns and all cities have larger hotels, each of which typically has a restaurant, café, lounge, and pool. At these establishments, expect to pay from $60 s, $70 d for a basic room. Downtown hotels in Vancouver, Victoria, Calgary, and Edmonton begin at $100 s or d. A good deal can be suites or executive suites, with kitchenettes and one or two bedrooms for little more than a regular room.

Finding inexpensive lodging in resort areas is difficult in summer. By late afternoon the only rooms left are in the more expensive categories, and by nightfall all of these rooms are booked, too. Hotel rooms in Whistler and Banff begin around $150.

BED-AND-BREAKFASTS

Bed-and-breakfast accommodations are found throughout western Canada. Staying at this type of accommodation is a great way to meet the locals. They're usually private residences, with up to four guest rooms, and as the name suggests breakfast is included. Rates fluctuate enormously. In Vancouver and Banff, for example, they start at $80 s, $90 d and go up and over $200. Guests can expect hearty home cooking, a peaceful atmosphere, personal service, knowledgeable hosts, and conversation with fellow travelers. On the downside, facilities and the amount of privacy afforded can vary greatly. This uncertainty as to what to expect upon arrival can be off-putting for many people, especially sharing a bathroom with other guests—which is a common and accepted practice in European bed-and-breakfasts. If having a bathroom to yourself is important to you, clarify with the bed-and-breakfast operator when reserving. Here is one interpretation of terms:

En suite: Refers to a bathroom that is private,

© ANDREW HEMPSTEAD

The Fairmont Chateau Lake Louise in Banff National Park is one of the world's finest mountain resorts.

inside, and attached to the sleeping unit (literally "in suite").

Private: A bathroom that is for the sole use of a particular sleeping unit but may be outside of the room.

Shared or semiprivate: Bathrooms that are used in common by more than one room. No more than two guest rooms should share a single bathroom.

These descriptions are courtesy of the **Western Canadian Bed and Breakfast Innkeepers Association** (604/255-9199, www.wcbbia .com), which represents more than 140 bed-and-breakfasts. The association produces an informative brochure with simple descriptions and a color photo of each property, but it doesn't take bookings. In the world of the Internet, **Bed and Breakfast Online** (www.bb-canada.com) is an old-timer, having been online since 1995. You can't make bookings through this company, but links are provided and an ingenious search engine helps you find the accommodation that best fits your needs.

HOSTELS

Budget travelers are enjoying more and more options in western Canada, ranging from a treehouse on Salt Spring Island (Vancouver Island) to a luxurious log lodge at Lake Louise (Banff National Park). **Hostelling International** (formerly the Youth Hostel Association) has undergone a radical change in direction and now appeals to all ages, with a limited number of privately run "hostels" providing other options. Either way, staying in what have universally become known as "backpackers" hostels is an enjoyable and inexpensive way to travel. Generally, you need to provide your own sleeping bag or linen, but most hostels supply extra bedding (if needed) at no charge. Accommodations are in bunk beds (2–10 in each room) or double rooms that share bathrooms. Each also offers a communal kitchen, lounge area, and laundry facilities, while most have Internet access, bike rentals, and organized tours.

Hostelling International-Canada (613/237-7884, www.hihostels.ca) operates 18 hostels in British Columbia and 17 in Alberta (none in the NWT or Yukon). For a dorm bed, members of Hostelling International pay $13–28 per night, nonmembers pay $17–32; single and double rooms are more expensive. Whenever you can, make reservations in advance, especially in summer. The easiest way to do this is through Hostelling International's **International Booking Network** (www.hostelbooking.com) or by contacting the individual hostel.

If you plan to travel extensively using hostels, join Hostelling International before you leave home (otherwise it's $4 extra per night). In Canada, an annual membership for Hostelling International-Canada is $35.In the United States, membership for **HI-USA** (301/495-1240, www.hiayh.org) is US$28. Other contacts include **YHA England and Wales** (0870/770-8868, www.yha.org.uk), **YHA Australia** (02/9261-1111, www.yha.com), and **YHA New Zealand** (03/379-9970 or 0800/278-299, www.yha.co.nz). For other countries, click through the links provided at www.iyhf.org.

The privately owned **SameSun Backpacker Network** (877/562-2783, www.samesun.com) comprises 12 hostels spread across the two provinces.

CAMPING AND RV PARKS

Almost every town in western Canada has at least one campground—picnic tables, cook shelters, showers, and powered hookups are standard amenities. Often those campgrounds in smaller towns are a bargain—it's not uncommon to pay less than $10 for a site with hookups and hot showers. In resort towns, camping isn't such a bargain, with most sites in the $25–35 range and a few places charging over $40 per night. If you're planning a summer trip to Vancouver, Vancouver Island, the Sunshine Coast, Whistler, the Okanagan Valley, Calgary (especially during Stampede), or Edmonton, you should try to book in advance.

Camping facilities in national parks are excellent; most parks have at least one campground with hot showers and hookups. National park campgrounds have always operated on a first-come, first-served basis but in 2005 **Parks Canada** (www.pc.gc.ca) will begin taking campsite bookings ($12 per reservation) for a limited number of sites in the most popular campgrounds. Most provincial and territorial parks have a campground; prices are $12–22 depending on facilities available. Some have powered hookups, showers, and boat rentals. In British Columbia, you can reserve a spot at the 60 most popular provincial parks by calling the **Discover Camping** hotline (604/689-9025 or 800/689-9025, www.discovercamping.ca). Reservations are taken between 15 March and 15 September for dates up to three months in advance. The reservation fee is $6.42 per night, to a maximum of $19.26, and is in addition to applicable camping fees. In national and provincial parks, firewood is supplied, but at a cost. In the national parks, a nightly Fire Permit costs $6, but includes as much wood as you need.

Food and Drink

Canada is not world-renowned for its culinary delights, but the western region does have two specialties. **West Coast** cuisine (also called fusion cooking), meaning an abundance of local seafood (halibut, salmon, crab) and fresh produce prepared with an Asian influence, is currently the flavor of the month in British Columbia, while **Alberta beef,** the staple of that province, is delicious and served in most restaurants. **Game meats** such as elk and bison as well as caribou and musk ox farther north are also widely available. Otherwise, Canadian food is similar to American food—in general, bland and not very interesting.

If you're RVing it or camping, eating cheaply in western Canada is easy. The three largest grocery chains—**Safeway, I.G.A.,** and **Overwaitea**—generally have the least expensive groceries, with prices slightly higher than in the United States. In most I.G.A. stores, you'll find an excellent bakery. If you're barbecuing, know that most urban campgrounds discourage open fires, and provincial and national parks charge up to $6 for a small bundle of firewood.

For a three-course meal in a family-style restaurant, including a steak dish, expect to pay $25–30 per person—double that in the better eateries. Vancouver, Victoria, Edmonton, Calgary, and Banff have an astonishing array of ethnic restaurants (Banff, a town of 8,000, has more than 100 restaurants). Inexpensive options are **Husky** restaurants, located in gas stations of the same name along all major routes; **Boston Pizza,** a chain of Canadian family-style restaurants; and **Tim Hortons,** best known for coffee and donuts.

British Columbian wine is highly regarded, having won awards throughout the world. The province is one of the few places in the world capable of producing ice wines, made by a process in which the grapes aren't harvested until after the first frost; the frost splits the skins and the fermentation process begins with the grapes still on the vine. These concentrated juices from classic varietals such as Riesling and Gewürztraminer create a super-sweet wine. Ice wine is generally marketed in a distinctively narrow 375-ml bottle and promoted as a dessert wine. The largest concentration of vineyards is in the Okanagan Valley, with more than 40 wineries ranging from large-scale commercial operations to small plots of grapes grown on hobby farms. Expect to pay $12–30 for a bottle of locally produced wine. For more information on the province's wine industry contact the **B.C. Wine Information Centre** (250/490-2006, www.bcwine.com).

Vancouver, Victoria, Calgary, and Edmonton each have specialty brewers that brew boutique beers for sale in the immediate area. Alberta's largest home-grown brewery is **Big Rock** in Calgary. With one of North America's most modern breweries, Big Rock is unique in that it uses all natural ingredients and doesn't pasteurize the finished product; this shortens the shelf life, but a great deal more of the natural flavor is retained. **Kokanee,** brewed in Creston and widely available

WINES OF BRITISH COLUMBIA

Wines from the Okanagan Valley receive acclaim worldwide, although this success is only recent. In fact, it was doubted that quality grapes could be grown north of the 49th parallel until the late 1980s, when most of the original vines were ripped out and replaced with classic European varietals. The valley's climate—long summer days and cool nights—produces small grapes with higher than usual sugar content, creating intensely flavored and aromatic wines. A wide variety of red and white wine grapes are planted, with the reds thriving in the warmer south end of the valley, where Merlot, Cabernet Franc, and Pinot Noir grapes produce the best local wines. The entire winemaking process in the Okanagan has been one of experimentation, and along the way more unusual varietals such as Ehrenfelser and Auxerrois have been grown with success, which makes tasting local wines all the more interesting.

throughout western Canada, is a fine-tasting beer that should be taken on all camping trips. All the popular Canadian and American beers are available at bars and liquor stores.

The legal drinking age varies throughout

Canada. In Alberta, the Northwest Territories, and the Yukon it's 18. In British Columbia it's 19. From the United States, visitors may bring 1.1 liters of liquor or wine or 24 cans or bottles of beer into Canada free of duty.

Getting There

BY AIR

Vancouver International Airport (YVR) is the gateway to Canada from around the Pacific Rim. Regularly scheduled service to and from Vancouver is offered by major airlines throughout the world. Victoria may be the capital of British Columbia, but it falls a distant second when it comes to international flights; the only destinations served from its international airport are major Canadian cities and Seattle. Calgary and Edmonton have international airports served by major airlines from throughout the world.

Many flights from the south are routed through Vancouver or Calgary before continuing to Edmonton, giving you a choice of final destinations for little or no price difference. Getting to Yellowknife or Whitehorse generally requires a plane change in Vancouver, Calgary, or Edmonton. Flights to these northern destinations, as well as smaller centers throughout the region, are usually made by local airlines that have code-share agreements with Air

Canada, so you should have no trouble booking flights and making connections to even the most out-of-the-way place.

Air Canada

Canada's national carrier is Air Canada (888/247-2262, www.aircanada.ca). It offers direct flights to Vancouver from the following North American cities: Whitehorse, Calgary, Edmonton, Winnipeg, Toronto, Ottawa, Montreal, Halifax, Boston, Chicago, Dallas, Denver, Honolulu, Los Angeles, New York (JFK), Portland, San Francisco, Seattle, Spokane, and Washington, D.C. Air Canada also offers direct flights to Calgary from all major Canadian cities, as well as from Honolulu, Los Angeles, San Francisco, Spokane, Las Vegas, Phoenix, Denver, Houston, and Chicago. Direct flights to Edmonton originate in all major Canadian cities west of Montreal, while flights from the U.S. cities noted above are routed through Vancouver or Calgary. From Europe, Air Canada flies direct from London to Calgary and Vancouver, and from other major cities via Toronto. South Pacific and Asian cities served include Sydney, Melbourne, Brisbane, Auckland, Bangkok, Kuala Lumpur, Hong Kong, Taipei, Nagoya, Beijing, and Tokyo, some by code-sharing agreements with other airlines. Air Canada flights originating in the South American cities of Buenos Aires and São Paulo are routed through Toronto.

Other Canadian Airlines

Canada's second-largest airline is **WestJet** (403/444-2484 or 800/538-5956, www.westjet.com). Based in Calgary, this carrier is one of the success stories of the airline industry, having grown to become one of the world's most profitable airlines while offering extremely competitive fares,

FLIGHT TAXES

The federal government imposes an **Air Transportation Tax** of 7 percent of the ticket price, plus $6 (to a maximum of $55) on all flights departing Canada for the United States and all other international destinations. The **Air Travellers Security Tax** is set at $14 for domestic flights and $24 for international flights. Vancouver, Calgary, and Edmonton International Airports charge an **Airport Improvement Fee** ($12–15) for all departing passengers. These taxes are generally built into the ticket purchase price, but it pays to ask when booking.

CUTTING FLIGHT COSTS

Price structuring for air travel is so complex that sometimes even travel agents have problems coming to grips with it. The first step when planning your trip to Canada is to use airline websites to search out the best available fares for the time of year you wish to travel. Then shop around the travel agencies (take along a printout of the online airline quote for reference). Also, check the Sunday travel section of most newspapers for an idea of current discount prices.

Tickets can be bought in one of numerous "classes," which have no relation to the actual seating arrangement on the plane. Many cheaper classes have tight restrictions regarding changes of flight dates, length of stay, and cancellations. A general rule is the cheaper the ticket, the more restrictions.

Within Canada, **Travel Cuts** (866/246-9762, www.travelcuts.com), with offices in all major cities, consistently offers the lowest airfares available. In London, **Trailfinders** (225 Kensington High St., Kensington, 020/7937-5400, www.trailfinders.com) always has good deals to Canada. Two major online agencies are **Expedia** (www.expedia.com) and **Travelocity** (www.travelocity.com). Enter the flight date and destination at either of these sites and they'll come up with the "best fare available," while also offering options, such as a cheaper flight the following day.

Edward Hasbrouck's *Practical Nomad Guide to the Online Travel Marketplace* (Avalon Travel Publishing) is an excellent resource for working through the web of online travel-planning possibilities.

friendly and efficient service, and expanding to serve all of Canada, all since its inaugural flight in 1996. It serves all major Canadian cities, as well as smaller hubs such as Abbotsford, 72 km (45 mi.) east of downtown Vancouver.

Air Canada operates a number of smaller affiliated airlines. **Tango** (800/315-1390, www.flytango.com) is a no-frills carrier with flights to Vancouver, Calgary, and Edmonton from across Canada. **Air Canada Jazz** (514/369-1386 or 888/247-2262, www.flyjazz.com) links regional centers throughout western Canada.

U.S. Airlines

Air Canada offers to most flights into western Canada from the United States, but Vancouver, Calgary, and/or Edmonton are also served by the following U.S. carriers: **Alaska Airlines** (877/502-5357, www.alaska-air.com), **American Airlines** (800/433-7300, www.aa.com), **Continental Airlines** (800/231-0856, www.continental.com), **Northwest Airlines** (800/225-2525, www.nwa.com), **Skywest** (800/221-1212, www.skywest.com), and **United Airlines** (800/864-8331, www.ual.com).

International Airlines

In addition to Air Canada's daily London–Vancouver flight, **British Airlines** (800/247-9297, www.britishairlines.com) also flies this route daily. **KLM** (604/278-3485, www.klm.nl) flies nonstop to Vancouver from Amsterdam, and **Lufthansa** (800/563-5954, www.lufthansa.de) from Frankfurt.

Qantas (800/227-4500, www.qantas.com.au) flies from Sydney, Melbourne, and Brisbane to Vancouver via Honolulu. **Air New Zealand** (800/663-5494, www.nzair.com) operates in alliance with Air Canada, with a change of airline in Honolulu or Los Angeles. This airline makes stops throughout the South Pacific, including Nandi (Fiji). **Air Pacific** (800/227-4446, www.airpacific.com) flies from points throughout the Pacific to Honolulu and then on to Vancouver.

BY RAIL

This form of transportation, which opened up the West to settlers, began to fade with the advent of efficient air services. Today, however, improved service, a refitting of carriages, a competitive pricing structure, and the luxurious privately operated Rocky Mountaineer have helped trains regain popularity in western Canada. Scheduled services along the original transcontinental line through Calgary and Banff ended in 1991, but continue along a northern route.

VIA Rail

The *Canadian* runs between Toronto and Vancouver via Edmonton and Jasper three days a week in either direction and provides two classes of travel: Economy, which features lots of leg room, reclining seats, reading lights, pillows and blankets, and a Skyline Car complete with bar service; and Silver and Blue, which is more luxurious, featuring a variety of sleeping-room configurations, daytime seating, a domed lounge and dining car reserved exclusively for passengers in this class, shower kits for all passengers, and all meals. At Jasper (Alberta) the westbound transcontinental line divides, with one set of tracks continuing slightly north to Prince Rupert. Along this route, the *Skeena* makes three trips a week. It's a daytime-only service, with passengers transferred to Prince George accommodations for an overnight stay. It also offers first-class travel, in Totem Class.

For all VIA Rail travel, discounts of 25 percent (40 percent if booked seven days in advance) apply to travel October–June (applicable to all classes). Those travelers older than 60 and younger than 25 receive a 10 percent discount, which can be combined with other seasonal fares. Check for advance-purchase restrictions on all discount tickets.

The **Canrailpass** allows unlimited travel anywhere on the VIA Rail system for 12 days within any given 30-day period. During high season (May 15–Sept. 15) the pass is $719, and $448 the rest of the year. Extra days are $61 and $39, respectively. Even if you plan limited train travel, the pass is an excellent deal—but remember, if you travel on a service that, for example, departs at 10 P.M. and arrives at 2 A.M., it counts as two days of travel. VIA Rail has recently cooperated with **Amtrak** (800/872-7245) to offer a **North America Rail Pass,** with all of the same seasonal dates and discounts as the Canrailpass. The cost is $975 for 30 days of unlimited travel anywhere in North America.

Pick up a train schedule at any VIA Rail station or call 416/366-8411 or 800/561-8630. In the United States, call any travel agent. The VIA Rail website (www.viarail.ca) provides route, sched-ule, and fare information as well as links to towns and sights en route.

BY BUS

Greyhound (403/260-0877 or 800/661-8747, www.greyhound.ca) serves areas throughout Canada. From the east, buses depart Toronto daily for Vancouver via two different routes—one through Calgary, the other through Edmonton. From Vancouver, the main routes are north through Prince George to Whitehorse, west along the TransCanada Highway to Banff and Calgary, and a more northern route through to Jasper and Edmonton.

Travel by Greyhound is simple—just roll up at the depot and buy a ticket. No reservations are necessary. Greyhound bus depots in all cities and towns are centrally located and linked to other public transportation (or, at the very least, cabs meet all arrivals). Always check for any promotional fares available at the time of your travel. Regular-fare tickets are valid for one year and allow unlimited stopovers between paid destinations.

Greyhound's **Discovery Pass** comes in many forms, including passes valid in all of North America, only in Canada, and only in the western states and provinces. The Canada Pass is sold in periods of seven days ($275), 10 days ($345), 15 days ($415), 21 days ($455), 30 days ($515), 45 days ($575), and 60 days ($655) and allows unlimited travel west of Montreal. The Domestic West Coast Pass, valid for Greyhound travel through western Canada and the western United States is valid for 10 days (US$285) and 21 days (US$385). You can buy the passes at any bus depot. In the United States, the pass can be bought from most travel agents. From outside North America, passes can be bought online; with advance purchase, a small discount is applied.

BY FERRY

One of the most pleasurable ways to get your first view of Canada is from sea level. Many scheduled ferry services cross from Washington

State to Victoria (Vancouver Island), but no ferries run to Vancouver from south of the border.

From Washington State

The **Victoria Clipper** (206/448-5000 or 800/888-2535, www.victoriaclipper.com) is a fast passenger-only service connecting Seattle's Pier 69 with Victoria. From farther north, at Anacortes, **Washington State Ferries** (250/381-1551, www.wsdot.wa.gov/ferries) runs a once-daily passenger and vehicle service to Sidney, 30 km (18.6 mi.) north of Victoria. If you're traveling up the east coast of Washington State to Vancouver Island and want to bypass the built-up corridor between Tacoma and the international border, consider heading out to Port Angeles on the Olympic Peninsula, where the **MV Coho** (360/457-4491, www.cohoferry.com) departs for a twice daily crossing to Victoria. For details on all of the above options see Getting There under Victoria in the Vancouver Island chapter.

BY CAR OR RV

Most visitors to western Canada travel in their own vehicle, or rent one upon arrival. Driver's licenses from all countries are valid in Canada for up to three months. You should also obtain a one-year **International Driving Permit** before leaving home (U.S. licensed drivers do not require an IDP to drive in Canada). Inexpensive and available from most motoring organizations, they allow you to drive in Canada (in conjunction with your regular license), without taking a test,

for up to three months. You should also carry car registration papers or rental contracts. Proof of insurance must also be carried, and you must wear seat belts. All highway signs in Canada give distances in **kilometers** and speeds in **kilometers per hour** (kph). The speed limit on most major highways is 100 kph (62 mph).

Insurance

If entering Canada from the United States in your own vehicle, check that your insurance covers travel in Canada. U.S. motorists are advised to obtain a Canadian Non-resident Inter-provincial Motor Vehicle Liability Insurance Card, available through U.S. insurance companies, which is accepted as evidence of financial responsibility in Canada.

When renting a vehicle in Canada you have the option of purchasing a Loss Damage Waiver, along with other types of insurance, such as for your personal effects. Before leaving home, find out if you're already covered. Many people are—through gold credit cards, higher levels of motoring association membership, or home insurance (in the case of personal effects)—and the additional coverage may be unnecessary.

Crossing into Canada by Land

Ports of Entry (border crossings) are spread at regular intervals along the entire U.S./Canada border. The main port of entry into British Columbia is **Peace Arch,** south of Vancouver. **Coutts/Sweetgrass,** north of Great Falls, Montana, along Hwy. 14, is the main crossing into Alberta. Both posts are open 24 hours daily.

Getting Around

BY AIR

Air Canada Jazz (514/369-1386 or 888/247-2262, www.flyjazz.com), a connector airline for Air Canada, offers scheduled flights to all cities and many larger towns within British Columbia and Alberta. **Pacific Coastal Airlines** (800/663.2872, www.pacific-coastal.com) flies to towns on Vancouver Island and along the Sunshine Coast from Vancouver and Victoria. **Harbour Air** (604/274-1277 or 800/665-0212, www.harbour-air.com) links Vancouver, Victoria, and Nanaimo with scheduled seaplane service. **Hawk Air** (250/635-4295 or 800/487-1216, www.hawkair.net) flies throughout northern British Columbia and to Grande Prairie (Alberta). **Central Mountain Air** (888/865-8585, www.flycma.com) serves towns throughout both British Columbia and Alberta, but has no flights between the two provinces. **Peace Air** (780/624-3060 or 800/563-3060, www.peaceair.com) links Calgary and Edmonton to the northern town of Peace River. **First Air** (613/688-2635 or 800/267-1247, www.firstair.ca) flies to Edmonton, Inuvik, Whitehorse, and throughout Nunavut from Yellowknife. **Air North** (867/668-2228 or 800/764-0407, www.flyairnorth.com) flies through the Yukon and Mackenzie River Valley.

BY RAIL

The only scheduled rail service in western Canada is along the transcontinental line from Vancouver to Jasper and Edmonton (see the earlier section). The other option is the privately operated Rocky Mountaineer.

Rocky Mountaineer

Rocky Mountaineer Railtours (604/606-2245 or 800/665-7245, www.rockymountaineer.com) operates a summer-only luxurious rail trip through the spectacular interior mountain ranges of British Columbia between Vancouver and Banff or Jasper. Travel is during daylight hours

only, so you don't miss anything. Trains depart in either direction in the morning (every second or third day), overnighting at Kamloops. One-way travel in Signature Service, which includes light meals, nonalcoholic drinks, and Kamloops accommodations, costs $669 per person between Vancouver and either Banff or Jasper, and $729 from Calgary. GoldLeaf Service is the ultimate in luxury. Passengers ride in a two-story, glass-domed car, eat in a separate dining area, and stay in Kamloops' most luxurious accommodations. GoldLeaf costs $1,299 from Vancouver to Banff or Jasper and $1,399 to Calgary. During value season (mid-April–May), fares are reduced by $120–300.

BY BUS

Greyhound (800/661-8747, www.greyhound.ca) bus routes radiate from all major cities including Vancouver, Calgary, and Edmonton. Northern terminuses of Greyhound service are Hay River (Northwest Territories) and Whitehorse (Yukon).

Aside from the territories, the largest chunk of western Canada where Greyhound doesn't operate is Vancouver Island. There, **Island Coach Lines,** operated by Grayline (250/388-0818 or 800/318-0818, www.grayline.ca), runs up the east coast to Port Hardy and to the west coast town of Tofino. Getting to the island itself is easy with **Pacific Coach Lines** (604/662-8074, www.pacificcoach.com), which provides bus service between Victoria and both Vancouver city center and Vancouver International Airport.

BY FERRY

Many interior lakes and rivers are crossed by ferries owned and operated by the government. Of course, no service is available between freeze-up and breakup, but the rest of year, expect daily service from 6 A.M. until at least 10 P.M. Some of the ferries are small, capable of carrying just two vehicles, while others can transport up to 50. Passage is free on all these ferries, including the 45-minute sailing across Kootenay Lake between

Balfour and Kootenay Bay (the Kootenays)—the world's longest free ferry trip.

BC Ferries

Government-owned BC Ferries (250/386-3431 or toll-free in B.C. 888/223-3779, www.bc ferries.com) serves 46 ports with a fleet of 40 vessels. All fares listed for "vehicles" in this book cover vehicles up to 20 feet long and under seven feet high (or under six ft., eight in. high on a few routes). Larger vehicles such as RVs pay more. Also note that prices listed for all types of vehicles are in addition to the passenger price; the vehicle's driver is not included in the vehicle fare.

Vancouver has two major ferry terminals. From Tsawwassen, south of downtown, ferries run regularly across the Strait of Georgia to the Vancouver Island centers of Swartz Bay (north of Victoria) and Nanaimo. From Horseshoe Bay, west of downtown Vancouver, ferries ply the strait to Nanaimo. Also from Horseshoe Bay, ferries run across Howe Sound to Langdale, gateway to the Sunshine Coast. From Powell River, at the north end of the Sunshine Coast, ferries depart for Comox (Vancouver Island), making it possible to visit both Vancouver Island and the Sunshine Coast without returning to Vancouver. BC Ferries also provides regular services from Vancouver Island to populated islands in the Strait of Georgia.

From Port Hardy at the northern tip of Vancouver Island, a ferry runs north up the coast to Prince Rupert. From the end of May–September the ferry goes every other day, October–April once a week, and during May twice a week. The trip takes 15 hours and links up with the Alaska Marine Highway (see Prince Rupert in the Northern British Columbia chapter). Also from Prince Rupert, ferries run out to the Queen Charlotte Islands. These longer sailings require reservations, which should be made as far in advance as possible.

CAR AND RV RENTAL

All major car-rental agencies have outlets at Vancouver, Victoria, Calgary, and Edmonton International Airports as well as at smaller airports like Kelowna, Yellowknife, and Whitehorse. To ensure that a vehicle is available for you when you arrive, book in advance, especially during the busy June–September period.

In summer, expect to pay around $60 per day for an Economy or Compact car, $75 for an Intermediate, $85–100 for a Full Size, and over $100 for an SUV. Between late September and mid-June all vehicles are heavily discounted, with smaller vehicles available from $30 per day and $200 per week. Most major agencies now offer unlimited mileage, but not for rentals originating in Banff or Jasper National Parks. Check to make sure about this policy. In all cases, insurance costs from $20 per day and is compulsory unless covered by a personal policy or on your credit card. Charges apply if you need to drop off the car at an agency other than the rental location. All agencies provide free pickup and drop-off at major city hotels.

Vehicles can be booked through parent companies in the United States or elsewhere using the Web or toll-free numbers. **Discount** (403/299-1202 or 800/263-2355, www.discount car.com) is a Canadian company with 200 rental outlets across the country. Their vehicles are kept in service a little longer than the other majors, but they provide excellent rates—even through summer—especially if booked in advance. Other major rental agencies include **Avis** (800/879-2847, www.avis.com), **Budget** (800/268-8900, www .budgetcanada.com), **Dollar** (800/800-4000, www.dollar.com), **Enterprise** (800/325-8007, www.enterprise.com), **Hertz** (800/263-0600, www.hertz.com), **Lo-Cost** (604/689-9664 or 800/986-1266, www.locost.com), **National** (800/227-7368, www.nationalcar.com), **Rent-A-Wreck** (800/327-0116, www.rentawreck.ca), and **Thrifty** (800/847-4389, www.thrifty.com).

RV Rental

Camper vans, RVs, and travel trailers are a great way to get around western Canada without having to worry about accommodations each night. The downside is cost. The smallest vans, capable of sleeping two people, start at $100 per day with 100 free kilometers (62 mi.) per day. Extra charges include insurance, a preparation fee (usually around $50 per rental), a linen/cutlery charge (around $60 per person per trip), and taxes. Major agencies, with rental outlets in Vancouver and Calgary, include **Cruise Canada** (403/291-4963 or 800/327-7799, in U.S. 800/784-7368, www .cruiseamerica.com), **Go West** (403/240-1814 or 800/240-1814), **Canadream** (604/572-3220 or 800/461-7368, www.canadream.com), and **C.C. Canada Camper** (877/327-3003, www.canada camper.com). In most cases, a drop-off fee of $400 applies to drop-offs made in Vancouver from rentals originating in Calgary, or vice versa.

Information and Services

VISAS AND OFFICIALDOM

Entry for U.S. Citizens
U.S. citizens are required to show proof of citizenship—a passport, birth certificate, baptismal certificate, or voter registration card (which proves citizenship). It must either be a photo ID (passport) or accompanied by some other form of photo ID (like a driver's license). The best practice is to be prepared and at least carry a passport (a driver's license isn't considered proof of citizenship). Check the Citizenship and Immigration Canada website (www.cic.gc.ca) for the latest regulations.

Other Foreign Visitors
Visitors from countries other than the United States require a valid passport and, in some cases, a visa for entry to Canada. Presently, citizens of the British Commonwealth and Western Europe are granted a Temporary Resident Permit upon arrival and do not require a visa, but check with the Canadian embassy in your home country. The standard entry permit is valid for six months; proof of onward tickets and/or sufficient funds are required in order to obtain the permit. Extensions are possible from Citizen and Immigration Canada (www.cic.gc.ca) offices in Vancouver, Victoria, Calgary, and Edmonton ($75 per person).

Employment and Study
Anyone wishing to work or study in Canada must obtain authorization *before* entering Canada. Authorization to work will be granted only if no qualified Canadians are available for the work in question. Applications for work and study are available from all Canadian embassies and must be submitted with a nonrefundable processing fee.

The Canadian government has a reciprocal agreement with Australia for a limited number of **holiday work visas** to be issued each year. Australian citizens under the age of 30 are eligible; contact your nearest Canadian embassy or consulate for more information.

HEALTH AND SAFETY
Compared to other parts of the world, Canada is a relatively safe place to visit. Vaccinations are required only if coming from an endemic area. That said, wherever you are traveling, carry a medical kit that includes bandages, insect repellent, sunscreen, antiseptic, antibiotics, and water-purification tablets. Good first-aid kits are available at most camping shops. Health care in Canada is mostly dealt with at a provincial level.

Taking out a travel-insurance policy is a sensible precaution because hospital and medical charges start at around $1,000 per day. Copies of prescriptions should be brought to Canada for any medicines already prescribed.

Giardia
Giardiasis, also known as beaver fever, is a real concern for those heading into the backcountry. It's caused by an intestinal parasite, *Giardia lamblia*, that lives in lakes, rivers, and streams. Once ingested, its effects, although not instantaneous, can be dramatic; severe diarrhea, cramps, and nausea are the most common symptoms. Preventive measures should always be taken, including boiling all water for at least 10 minutes, treating all water with iodine, or filtering all

water using a filter with a pore size small enough to block the *Giardia* cysts.

Winter Travel

Travel through western Canada during winter months should not be undertaken lightly. Before setting out in a vehicle, check antifreeze levels, and always carry a spare tire and blankets or sleeping bags. **Frostbite** is a potential hazard, especially when cold temperatures are combined with high winds (a combination known as **windchill**). Most often, frostbite leaves a numbing, bruised sensation, and the skin turns white. Exposed areas of skin, especially the nose and ears, are most susceptible.

Hypothermia occurs when the body fails to produce heat as fast as it loses it. It can strike at any time of the year but is more common during cooler months. Cold weather, combined with hunger, fatigue, and dampness, creates a recipe for disaster. Symptoms are not always apparent to the victim. The early signs are numbness, shivering, slurring of words, dizzy spells, and, in extreme cases, violent behavior, unconsciousness, and even death. The best way to dress for the cold is in layers, including a waterproof outer layer. Most important, wear headgear. The best treatment is to get the victim out of the cold, replace wet clothing with dry, slowly give hot liquids and sugary foods, and place the victim in a sleeping bag. Warming too quickly can lead to heart attacks.

MONEY

As in the United States, Canadian currency is based on dollars and cents. Coins come in denominations of one, five, 10, and 25 cents, and one and two dollars. The one-dollar coin is the 11-sided, gold-colored "loonie," named for the bird featured on it. The unique two-dollar coin is silver with a gold-colored insert. Notes come in $5, $10, $20, $50, and $100 denominations.

All prices quoted in this book are in Canadian dollars. American dollars are accepted at many tourist areas, but the exchange rate is more favorable at banks. Currency other than U.S. dollars can be exchanged at most banks, airport

CURRENCY EXCHANGE

The Canadian dollar reached record lows against the greenback in 2002, but rallied back. At press time, exchange rates (into C$) for major currencies were:

US$1	=	$1.30
AUS$1	=	$1
€1	=	$1.60
HK$10	=	$1.80
NZ$1	=	$.85
UK£	=	$2.40
¥100	=	$1.20

On the Internet, check current exchange rates by using the Universal Currency Converter (www.xe.com/ucc).

money-changing facilities, and foreign exchange brokers in Vancouver, Victoria, Whistler, Calgary, Banff, Jasper, and Edmonton. Travelers checks are the safest way to carry money, but a fee is often charged to cash them if they're in a currency other than Canadian dollars. All major credit cards are honored at Canadian banks, gas stations, and most commercial establishments. ATMs can be found in almost every town.

Costs

The cost of living in Canada is comparable to the United States. By planning ahead, having a tent or joining Hostelling International, and being prepared to cook your own meals, it is possible to get by on less than $60 per person per day. Gasoline is sold in liters (3.78 liters equals one U.S. gallon) and currently costs 70–80 cents per liter (at 80 cents, that's around US$2.30 per gallon) for regular unleaded. In the Northwest Territories and the Yukon, the price is higher, up to 90 cents per liter.

Tips are not usually added to a bill, and in general 15 percent of the total amount is given. Tips are most often given to restaurant servers, taxi drivers, doormen, bellhops, and bar staff.

Taxes

Canada imposes a 7 percent **Goods and Ser-**

vices Tax (GST) on most consumer purchases. Nonresident visitors can get a rebate for the GST they pay on short-term accommodations and on most consumer goods bought in the country and taken home. Items not included in the GST rebate program include gifts left in Canada, meals and restaurant charges, campground fees, services such as dry cleaning and shoe repair, alcoholic beverages, tobacco, automotive fuels, groceries, agricultural and fish products, prescription drugs and medical devices, and used goods that tend to increase in value, such as paintings, jewelry, rare books, and coins. The rebate is available on services and retail purchases that total at least $100 and were paid for within 60 days before your exit from the country. Rebates can be claimed any time within one year from the date of purchase. Most visitors apply for the rebate at duty-free shops (also called Visitor Rebate Centres) when exiting the country. The duty-free shops can rebate up to $500 on the spot. For rebates of more than $500, you'll need to mail your completed GST rebate form directly to Revenue Canada. In either case, you need to keep all receipts. If claiming from outside of Canada, you must have receipts validated upon leaving Canada. Rebate checks sent to the United States are issued in U.S. dollars; elsewhere checks are sent in Canadian funds. For more information, call toll-free from anywhere in Canada 800/668-4748; from outside Canada, phone 902/432-5608; or see the website www.rc.gc.ca/visitors.

British Columbia also charges a 7.5 percent **provincial sales tax (PST)** on everything except groceries and books. So when you are looking at the price of anything, remember that the final cost you pay will include an additional 14 percent in taxes. Alberta has no PST, nor do the two territories.

COMMUNICATIONS
Postal Services
All mail posted in Canada must have Canadian postage stamps attached. First-class letters and postcards are 49 cents to destinations within Canada, 80 cents to the United States, and $1.40

POST, TELEPHONE, AND TIME

POSTAL ABBREVIATIONS
British Columbia: BC
Alberta: AB
Northwest Territories: NT
Yukon: YK

TELEPHONE AREA CODES
Lower B.C. mainland including Vancouver: 604
Rest of British Columbia: 250
Southern Alberta including Calgary: 403
Northern Alberta including Edmonton: 780
Northwest Territories: 867
Yukon: 867

TIME
British Columbia: PST
Alberta: MST
Northwest Territories: MST
Yukon: PST

Mountain Standard Time (MST) is two hours behind Eastern Standard Time and one hour ahead of Pacific Standard Time (PST).

ON THE ROAD

to all other destinations. Post offices are open Monday–Friday only. If you would like mail sent to you while traveling, have it addressed to yourself, c/o General Delivery, Main Post Office, in the city or town you request, ending with the province or territory name, and "Canada." The post office will hold all general delivery mail for 15 days before returning it to the sender. The website of **Canada Post** is www.canadapost.ca.

Telephone
Except for local calls, all numbers must be dialed with the area code, including long-distance calls from within the same area code. The country code for Canada is 1, the same as the United States. Public phones accept five-, 10-, and 25-cent coins. Local calls from payphones are usually 35 cents and most long-distance calls cost at least $2.50 for the first minute from public phones. Pre-paid **phone cards,** which are available from gas stations

and drug and grocery stores, provide considerable savings for those using public phones. They come in $5–50 amounts.

Internet

It will probably surprise no one that public Internet access is available across western Canada. The best place to try first is local libraries, where more often than not, you only need to show some identification to use a computer. Internet booths can also be found in airports, cafés, and some shopping malls. Most larger hotels either have in-room Internet access (for a small charge) or a communal business center.

MAPS

Specialty map shops are the best source for accurate, high-quality maps. In Vancouver, try **International Travel Maps and Books** (552 Seymour St., 604/687-3320, www.itmb.com) or **Wanderlust** (1929 W. 4th Ave., Kitsilano, 604/739-2182); in Victoria, check out **Crown Publications** (521 Fort St., 250/386-4636). In Calgary, my recommendation is **Map Town** (400 5th Ave. SW, 403/266-2241). There's also a location in Edmonton (10344 105th St., 780/429-2600). All five stores sell specialty maps designed specifically for hiking (topographical maps), camping (road/access maps), fishing (hydrographic charts of more than 100 lakes), and canoeing (river details such as gradients). **Gem Trek** (403/266-2241

TOURISM OFFICES

NWT Arctic Tourism: 867/873-7200 or 800/661-0788, www.explorenwt.com

Tourism British Columbia: 250/387-1642 or 800/435-5622, www.hellobc.com

Tourism Yukon: 403/667-5340, www.touryukon.com

Travel Alberta: 780/427-4321 or 800/252-3782, www.travelalberta.com

or 877/921-6277, www.gemtrek.com) is an Albertan company that produces some of the best and most useful maps you're ever likely to find. They specialize in the Canadian Rockies and the maps are available throughout that region. **Map Art** (905/436-2525, www.mapart.com) produces a variety of maps for Canada, including atlases to both British Columbia and Alberta.

WEIGHTS AND MEASURES

Like every country in the world except the United States, Liberia, and Myanmar, Canada is on the metric system (see the "Metric System" chart at the back of this book), although many people talk about distance in miles and supermarket prices are advertised by ounces and pounds.

Electricity

Electrical voltage is 120 volts, the same as in the United States.

British Columbia

B ritish Columbia, the westernmost province of Canada, stretches from the Pacific Ocean to the towering heights of the Canadian Rockies. Sandwiched in between is some of this planet's most magnificent scenery—an enormous variety of terrain including spectacular mountain ranges, glaciers, rivers, lakes, rugged coastline, and hundreds of islands within 948,596 square kilometers (366,300 sq. mi.).

The province's overall population is 3.8 million, and its largest city is **Vancouver,** a splendid conglomeration of old and new architectural marvels, parks and gardens, and sheltered beaches set around a sparkling blue harbor. The provincial capital is old-world **Victoria,** perched at the southeastern tip of Vancouver Island, just across the Strait of Georgia from Vancouver. Victoria boasts an intriguing mixture of old English architecture, customs, and traditions, along with modern attractions, cosmopolitan restaurants, and an infectious joie de vivre.

But most of British Columbia lies away from the cities, in the surrounding vastness. The protected coastal waterways, the rugged west coast of **Vancouver Island,** the stark beauty of the **Okanagan Valley,** the famous Canadian Rockies and many other mountain ranges, and the intriguing **Queen Charlotte Islands** provide experiences you'll never forget, along with enough ooh-and-aah scenery to keep even the most jaded jet-setter in awe. In these wild areas, you'll find endless opportunities for hiking or canoeing, viewing the abundant wildlife, fishing in the hundreds of lakes and rivers, skiing or snowboarding at any of the dozens of resorts, or immersing yourself in native culture.

Note: Please see front color map **British Columbia.**

Vancouver

Let your mind fill with images of dramatic, snowcapped mountains rising vertically from a city's backyard. Century-old inner-city buildings and steel-and-glass skyscrapers facing the sheltered shores of a large, wide inlet. Manicured suburbs perching along the edge of the sea, fringed by golden sandy beaches. Lush tree-filled parks and brilliant flower gardens overflowing with color. Overhead, flocks of Canada geese noisily honking to one another as they fly toward the setting sun. These are the magnificent images of Vancouver, Canada's third-largest city (population 1.85 million).

If you view this gleaming mountain- and sea-dominated city for the first time on a beautiful sunny day, you're bound to fall for it in a big way. See it on a dull, dreary day when the clouds are low and Vancouver's backyard mountains are hidden and you may come away with a slightly less enthusiastic picture—you'll have experienced the "permagray," as residents are quick to call it with a laugh. But even gray skies can't dampen the city's vibrant, outdoorsy atmosphere. Rain or shine, night or day, Vancouver is an alluring and unforgettable city.

BRITISH COLUMBIA

GREATER VANCOUVER

Howe Sound

To Squamish and Whistler

Ferry to Langdale

Bower Island

Porteau Beach

Bowen Island

SNUG COVE

Ferry to Nanaimo (Vancouver Island)

SEA TO SKY HIGHWAY

99

North Shore Range

River

Cypress Provincial Park

CYPRESS MOUNTAIN

CRYPESS BOWL RD.

HORSESHOE BAY

WEST VANCOUVER

GLENEAGLES GOLF COURSE

MARINE DR.

Lighthouse Park

Capilano Lake

Lynn Headwaters Regional Park

Lynn Creek

GROUSE MOUNTAIN SKYRIDE

Creek

Capilano River Regional Park

CAPILANO SALMON HATCHERY

CAPILANO SUSPENSION BRIDGE

RD.

CAPILANO DR.

Mosquito Creek

LYNN CANYON ECOLOGY CENTRE

Lynn Canyon Park

Seymour River

MT. SEYMOUR PKWY.

MOUNT SEYMOUR

Mount Seymour Provincial Park

Pinecone Burke Provincial Park

Coquitlam River

PIPELINE RD.

COAST MERIDIAN RD.

PORT COQUITLAM

7

To Golden Ears

7

COQUITLAM VISITOR INFO CENTRE

EAST RD.

LOCO RD.

ST. JOHNS ST.

COMO LAKE AVE.

COQUITLAM

AUSTIN

AVE.

ANMORE

Buntzen Lake

SUNNYSIDE RD.

PORT MOODY

Port Moody

HWY. 7A

CLARK RD.

BARNET

Belcarra Regional Park

Indian Arm

DEEP COVE

SIMON FRASER UNIVERSITY

BARNET ST.

Burnaby Mountain Park

BURNABY

Burnaby Lake

LOUGHEED

7

Deer

ROYAL OAK AVE.

EXHIBITION PARK

HASTINGS

7A

BROADWAY

Queen Elizabeth

VANCOUVER

1ST AVE.

NORTH VANCOUVER

LONSDALE QUAY

Harbour

MARINE DR.

NORTH VANCOUVER VISITOR CENTRE

B.C. RAIL TERMINAL

99

Vancouver

First Narrows

Stanley Park

Ambleside Park

Burrard Inlet

English Bay

HASTINGS

99

Kitsilano Beach

Granville

16TH AVE.

Kitsilano

W. 4TH AVE.

Shaughnessy

Jericho Beach

Locarno Beach

Spanish Banks Beach

Point Grey

W. 10TH AVE.

Grey

BURNABY ST.

UNIVERSITY GOLF CLUB

MUSEUM OF ANTHROPOLOGY

UNIVERSITY OF B.C.

Point Grey

NITOBE MEMORIAL GARDEN

BOTANICAL GARDEN

Wreck Beach

SEE "DOWNTOWN VANCOUVER" MAP

Coquitlam

ST.

1ST ST.

ST.

ST.

99A

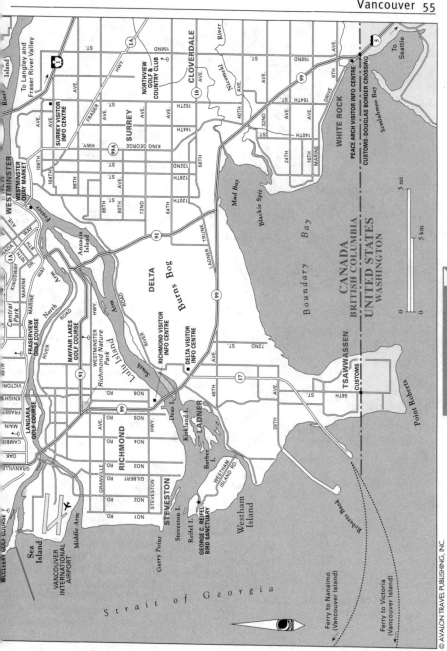

BRITISH COLUMBIA

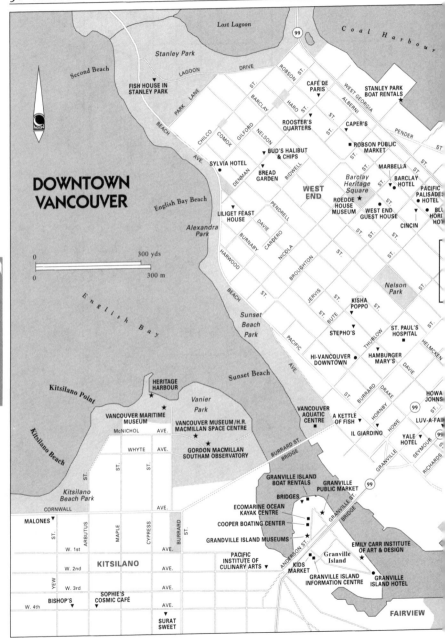

DOWNTOWN VANCOUVER

Lost Lagoon

Coal Harbour

Stanley Park

Second Beach

LAGOON DRIVE

FISH HOUSE IN STANLEY PARK

PARK LANE

BEACH AVE.

English Bay Beach

CHILCO ST.

COMOX ST.

GILFORD ST.

NELSON ST.

DENMAN ST.

BIDWELL ST.

BARCLAY ST.

HARO ST.

ROBSON ST.

WEST GEORGIA

ALBERNI ST.

PENDER ST.

CAFÉ DE PARIS

STANLEY PARK BOAT RENTALS

CAPER'S

ROOSTER'S QUARTERS

ROBSON PUBLIC MARKET

BUD'S HALIBUT & CHIPS

SYLVIA HOTEL

BREAD GARDEN

MARBELLA

Barclay Heritage Square

BARCLAY HOTEL

PACIFIC PALISADES HOTEL

BLU HORI HOT

WEST END

ROEDDE HOUSE MUSEUM

WEST END GUEST HOUSE

CINCIN

LILIGET FEAST HOUSE

PENDRELL ST.

DAVIE

BURNABY

CARDERO

NICOLA

BROUGHTON ST.

Alexandra Park

HARWOOD

BEACH

Sunset Beach Park

English Bay

JERVIS ST.

BUTE ST.

KISHA POPPO

Nelson Park

ST.

STEPHO'S

ST. PAUL'S HOSPITAL

THURLOW

HELMCKEN

PACIFIC

HI-VANCOUVER DOWNTOWN

HAMBURGER MARY'S

DAVIE

0   300 yds
0   300 m

Kitsilano Point

HERITAGE HARBOUR

Vanier Park

VANCOUVER MARITIME MUSEUM

McNICHOL AVE.

VANCOUVER MUSEUM/H.R. MACMILLAN SPACE CENTRE

GORDON MACMILLAN SOUTHAM OBSERVATORY

WHYTE AVE.

Sunset Beach

BURRARD

DRAKE

VANCOUVER AQUATIC CENTRE

A KETTLE OF FISH

IL GIARDINO

HORNBY

HOWE

GRANVILLE

SEYMOUR

RICHARDS

HOWA JOHNS

LUV-A-FAIR

YALE HOTEL

BURRARD ST. BRIDGE

Kitsilano Beach

Kitsilano Beach Park

CORNWALL

MALONES

ARBUTUS ST.

MAPLE ST.

CYPRESS ST.

BURRARD ST.

W. 1st AVE.

KITSILANO

W. 2nd AVE.

YEW ST.

W. 3rd AVE.

SOPHIE'S COSMIC CAFÉ

BISHOP'S

W. 4th

SURAT SWEET

GRANVILLE ISLAND BOAT RENTALS

GRANVILLE PUBLIC MARKET

BRIDGES

ECOMARINE OCEAN KAYAK CENTRE

COOPER BOATING CENTER

GRANDVILLE ISLAND MUSEUMS

PACIFIC INSTITUTE OF CULINARY ARTS

ANDERSON ST.

KIDS MARKET

Granville Island

EMILY CARR INSTITUTE OF ART & DESIGN

GRANVILLE ISLAND INFORMATION CENTRE

GRANVILLE ISLAND HOTEL

GRANVILLE ST. BRIDGE

FAIRVIEW

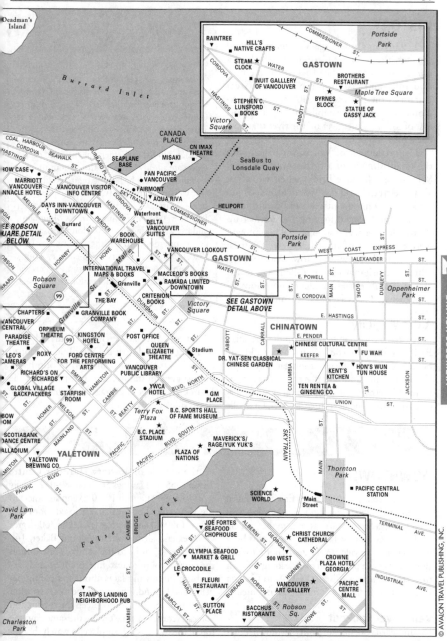

Deadman's Island

Burrard Inlet

GASTOWN (detail)
Portside Park
COMMISSIONER ST.
RAINTREE
HILL'S NATIVE CRAFTS
GASTOWN
CORDOVA
STEAM CLOCK
WATER ST.
BROTHERS RESTAURANT
INUIT GALLLERY OF VANCOUVER
HASTINGS ST.
STEPHEN C. LUNSFORD BOOKS
Maple Tree Square
BYRNES BLOCK
ABBOTT
STATUE OF GASSY JACK
Victory Square

COAL HARBOUR SEAWALK
CORDOVA
HASTINGS
CANADA PLACE
CN IMAX THEATRE
SEABus to Lonsdale Quay
HOW CASE
MARRIOTT VANCOUVER PINNACLE HOTEL
MELVILLE
SEAPLANE BASE
MISAKI
PAN PACIFIC VANCOUVER
FAIRMONT
AQUA RIVA
VANCOUVER VISITOR INFO CENTRE
HELIPORT
DAYS INN-VANCOUVER DOWNTOWN
Burrard
PENDER
Waterfront
DELTA VANCOUVER SUITES
SEE ROBSON SQUARE DETAIL BELOW
BOOK WAREHOUSE
VANCOUVER LOOKOUT
Portside Park
WEST COAST EXPRESS
GASTOWN
ALEXANDER ST.
Robson Square
99
INTERNATIONAL TRAVEL MAPS & BOOKS
MACLEOD'S BOOKS
RAMADA LIMITED DOWNTOWN
WATER ST.
E. POWELL
HORNBY
Granville
CRITERION BOOKS
E. CORDOVA
MAIN
GORE
DUNLEVY
Oppenheimer Park
THE BAY
SEE GASTOWN DETAIL ABOVE
Victory Square
E. HASTINGS ST.
CHAPTERS
GRANVILLE BOOK COMPANY
CHINATOWN
VANCOUVER CENTRAL
ORPHEUM THEATRE
POST OFFICE
E. PENDER
CHINESE CULTURAL CENTRE
PARADISE THEATRE
99
KINGSTON HOTEL
KEEFER
FU WAH
LEO'S CAMERAS
ROXY
FORD CENTRE FOR THE PERFORMING ARTS
QUEEN ELIZABETH THEATRE
Stadium
DR. YAT-SEN CLASSICAL CHINESE GARDEN
KENT'S KITCHEN
HON'S WUN TUN HOUSE
RICHARD'S ON RICHARDS
VANCOUVER PUBLIC LIBRARY
COLUMBIA
TEN RENTEA & GINSENG CO.
JACKSON
GLOBAL VILLAGE BACKPACKERS
STARFISH ROOM
YWCA HOTEL
BLVD. NORTH
GM PLACE
UNION ST.
BOW ROOM
NELSON
CAMBIE
Terry Fox Plaza
B.C. SPORTS HALL OF FAME MUSEUM
SCOTIABANK DANCE CENTRE
HOMER
B.C. PLACE STADIUM
BLVD. SOUTH
MAVERICK'S/ RAGE/YUK YUK'S
SKY TRAIN
PALLADIUM
YALETOWN BREWING CO.
MAINLAND
YALETOWN
PACIFIC
PLAZA OF NATIONS
Thornton Park
PACIFIC BLVD.
David Lam Park
False Creek
CAMBIE ST.
BRIDGE ST.
SCIENCE WORLD
Main Street
PACIFIC CENTRAL STATION
TERMINAL AVE.
STAMP'S LANDING NEIGHBORHOOD PUB
MAIN ST.
INDUSTRIAL AVE.
Charleston Park

ROBSON SQUARE (detail)
JOE FORTES SEAFOOD CHOPHOUSE
ALBERNI ST.
GEORGIA
CHRIST CHURCH CATHEDRAL
OLYMPIA SEAFOOD MARKET & GRILL
THURLOW ST.
900 WEST
CROWNE PLAZA HOTEL GEORGIA
LE CROCODILE
HARO ST.
FLEURI RESTAURANT
BURRARD
ROBSON
HORNBY
VANCOUVER ART GALLERY
PACIFIC CENTRE MALL
SUTTON PLACE
BARCLAY ST.
BACCHUS RISTORANTE
Robson Sq.
HOWE ST.
CAMBIE

BRITISH COLUMBIA

HISTORY

In 1792, Captain George Vancouver cruised through the Strait of Georgia in search of a northwest passage to the Orient, charting Burrard Inlet and claiming the land for Great Britain in the process. In 1808 fur trader/explorer Simon Fraser established a trading post east of today's Vancouver on the river that now bears his name.

The settlement of Vancouver began with the establishment of a brickworks ("Bricks? Why on earth make bricks when we've got all these trees?" said the Woodcutters' Union spokesman) on the south side of Burrard Inlet. Sawmills and related logging and lumber industries followed, and soon several boomtowns were carved out of the wilderness. The first was Granville (now downtown Vancouver), which the original settlers called "Gastown" after one of its earliest residents, notorious saloon owner "Gassy Jack" Deighton.

A Growing City

Selected as the western terminus for the Canadian Pacific Railway in 1887, Vancouver suddenly became Canada's transportation gateway to the Orient and an important player in the development of international commerce around the Pacific Rim. Over the next three decades, Granville Island and the far reaches of Burrard Inlet sprawled with industry, the West End developed as a residential area, the University of British Columbia grew in stature, and the opening of the Lions Gate Bridge encouraged settlement on the north side of Burrard Inlet.

2010 OLYMPIC WINTER GAMES

The date July 2, 2003, is one that Vancouverites will be talking about for many years. It was on this day that the International Olympic Committee awarded the 2010 Olympic Winter Games to a joint Vancouver/Whistler bid. The actual games are a long way off (February 12–28, 2010), and much of the infrastructure is already in place, but the excitement and sense of expectation are already being felt throughout the city.

Vancouver will be hosting figure skating (Pacific Coliseum), hockey (GM Place), speed skating (Pacific Coliseum and Simon Fraser University), snowboarding (Cypress Mountain), and freestyle skiing (Cypress Mountain), as well as the opening and closing ceremonies (BC Place). All alpine events, cross-country skiing, ski jumping, luge, and bobsled competitions will be held at Whistler. For more information, check out the official website of the 2010 games at www.winter2010.com.

Sights

DOWNTOWN

Granville Street was Vancouver's first commercial corridor, and if today you stand at its junction with West Georgia Street, you're as close to the "center" of the city as it's possible to be. From this busy intersection, Granville Street extends north toward Burrard Inlet as a pedestrian mall, leading through the central business district (CBD) to Canada Place and the main tourist information center.

Vancouver Lookout

For immediate orientation from downtown, catch the high-speed, stomach-sinking glass elevator up the outside of 40-story **Harbour Centre Tower** (555 W. Hastings St., 604/689-0421, daily 9:30 A.M.–9 P.M., until 10:30 P.M. in summer) to the Vancouver Lookout, an enclosed room 167 meters (550 ft.) above street level. The 360-degree views extend all the way to Mount Baker, 140 kilometers (87 mi.) to the south. Walk around the circular room to read interpretive panels describing interesting facts about the panorama below and beyond. The trip to the top costs adult $10, senior $9, student $7; keep the receipt and you can return any time during the same day (the top of the tower is a great place to watch the sun setting over the Strait of Georgia).

Canada Place

The stunning architectural curiosity with the billowing 27-meter-high (89-foot-high) Teflon-coated fiberglass "sails" on Burrard Inlet—the one that looks as if it might weigh anchor and cruise off into the sunset at any moment—is Canada Place, a symbol of Vancouver and a city icon. Built for Expo86, this integrated waterfront complex is primarily a convention center and cruise-ship dock, with an upscale hotel (the glass marvel with domed top), restaurants, shops, and an IMAX theater thrown in for good measure. Don't miss walking the exterior promenade—three and a half city blocks long—for neck-straining views of the city close up, splendid views of the harbor, the North Shore, the Coast Mountains, and docked Alaska-bound cruise ships.

Gastown

"Gassy Jack" Deighton, an English boat pilot, offered locals all the whiskey they could drink in return for helping him build a saloon beside Burrard Inlet in 1867. The town that grew around the saloon was officially named Granville in 1869, but it has always been known as Gastown. The district's tree-lined cobblestone streets and old gas lamps front brightly painted restored buildings housing galleries, restaurants, and an abundance of gift and souvenir shops.

Most of the action centers along **Water Street,** which branches east off Cordova Street, an easy five-minute walk from Canada Place. As you first enter Water Street, you're greeted by **The Landing,** a heritage building that has had its exterior restored to its former glory and its interior transformed into an upmarket shopping arcade. Down the hill, at Cambie Street, is a **steam clock,** one of only two in the world. Built by a local clockmaker, it's powered by a steam system originally put in place to heat buildings through an underground pipeline that snakes through downtown. Watch for the burst of steam every 15 minutes, which sets off steam whistles to the tune of Westminster chimes.

Continue east along Water Street to the 1899 **Dominion Hotel** and a string of other buildings built after the Great Fire of 1886. The **Byrnes Block** (2 Water St.) stands on the site of **Deighton House,** Gassy Jack's second and more permanent saloon.

Vancouver Art Gallery

Vancouver's imposing neoclassical-revival courthouse is home to the city's public art gallery (750 Hornby St., 604/662-4700, daily 10 A.M.–5:30 P.M., closed Mon. in winter, adult $12.50, senior $9, youth $8, children under 12

GETTING ORIENTED

Vancouver isn't a particularly easy city to find your way around, although an excellent transit system helps immensely. Downtown lies on a spit of land bordered to the north and east by **Burrard Inlet,** to the west by **English Bay,** and to the south by **False Creek,** which almost cuts the city center off from the rest of the city. Due to the foresight of city founders, almost half of the downtown peninsula has been set aside as parkland.

The **City of Vancouver** officially extends south and west from downtown, between Burrard Inlet and the Fraser River. Here lie the trendy beachside suburb of **Kitsilano** (known as "Kits" to the locals) and **Point Grey,** home of the University of British Columbia. To the east, the residential sprawl continues, through the suburbs of **Burnaby, New Westminster,** and **Coquitlam,** which have a combined population of well over 250,000.

Farther south, the low-lying Fraser River Delta extends all the way south to the border. Between the north and south arms of the river is **Richmond,** home of Vancouver International Airport. South of the south arm is the mostly industrial area of **Delta,** as well as **Tsawwassen,** departure point for ferries to Vancouver Island. Southeast of the Fraser River lie **Surrey** and the Fraser River Valley towns of **Langley, Abbotsford,** and **Chilliwack**—all part of the city sprawl.

Across Burrard Inlet to the north of downtown, **North Vancouver** is a narrow developed strip backed up to the mountains and connected to the rest of the city by the Lions Gate Bridge. To its west are **Horseshoe Bay,** departure point for Sunshine Coast and Vancouver Island ferries, and **West Vancouver,** an upscale suburb.

BRITISH COLUMBIA

free). The highlight of the large collection is the gallery of works by Canada's preeminent female artist, Emily Carr. Combining native influences with techniques acquired during periods of living in London and Paris, her work is unique, and the gallery is well worth visiting for these alone. The Carr collection is on the third floor, along with the works of many other local artists. The gallery also holds other contemporary pieces from both North America and Europe, as well as an impressive collection of historical art.

Christ Church Cathedral and Vicinity

One block northwest from the art gallery, on the corner of West Georgia and Burrard Streets, is the gracious Christ Church Cathedral. When built in 1895, it was in the heart of a residential area. Over the ensuing century, it has been engulfed by modern developments and is today Vancouver's oldest church.

Across West Georgia Street from the cathedral is the Hotel Vancouver. Built in 1887, the original hotel on this site featured 200 rooms, half of which had private bathrooms—unheard of in that day. It burnt to the ground in 1932 and was replaced by the hotel that stands today, which reflects the heritage of CPR-built hotels across the country with its distinctive chateau-style design topped by a copper roof.

Chinatown

With the second-largest Chinese community in North America and one of the largest outside Asia, Vancouver's Chinatown is an exciting place any time of year. But it's especially lively during a Chinese festival or holiday, when thronging masses follow the ferocious dancing dragon, avoid exploding firecrackers, sample tasty tidbits from outdoor stalls, and pound their feet to the beat of the drums.

Chinatown lies several blocks southeast of Gastown, along East Pender Street between Carrall and Gore Streets. Its commercial center is the block bordered by Main, East Pender, Gore, and Keefer Streets. Stroll through the neighborhood to admire the architecture—right down to the pagoda-roofed telephone booths—or to seek out one of the multitude of restaurants.

Designed primarily to host community programs for the local Chinese population, the **Chinese Cultural Centre** also has a museum (555 Columbia St., 604/687-0282, Tues.–Sun. 11 A.M.–5 P.M., adult $5, senior $3) cataloging the history of Chinese-Canadians in Vancouver.

Gardening enthusiasts won't want to miss **Dr. Sun Yat-Sen Classical Chinese Garden** (behind the Cultural Centre at 578 Carrall St., 604/662-3207, daily from 10 A.M., adult $8, senior and child $6), which features limestone rockeries, a waterfall and tranquil pools, and beautiful trees and plants hidden away behind tall walls.

To get to Chinatown from downtown catch bus no. 19 or 22 east along Pender Street. Try to avoid East Hastings Street at all times; it's Vancouver's skid row, inhabited by unsavory characters day and night.

FALSE CREEK

False Creek, the narrow tidal inlet that almost cuts downtown off from the rest of the city, has been transformed from an industrial wasteland to an attractive area of waterfront parks and a bona fide tourist attraction. If you walk from downtown, **B.C. Place** (777 Pacific Blvd., 604/669-2300), the world's largest air-supported domed stadium, is a worthwhile stop.

Science World

This impressive, 17-story-high geodesic silver dome (it's best known locally as "the golf ball") sits over the waters of False Creek on the southeast side of city center (1455 Quebec St., 604/443-7440, open daily 10 A.M.–5 P.M., adult $17.75, senior and child $13.50; includes admission to one Omnimax film). Built for Expo86, this Vancouver landmark is now home to a museum providing exhibitions that "introduce the world of science to the young and the young at heart." The three main galleries explore the basics of physics, natural history, and music through hands-on displays. The audiovisual presentation *Over Canada* is a highlight. An **Omnimax theater** (like IMAX) features science-oriented documentaries.

© ANDREW HEMPSTEAD

Science World

The most enjoyable way to get to Science World is aboard a False Creek Ferry from Granville Island or the Vancouver Aquatic Centre. You could also take the SkyTrain to Main Street Station.

Granville Island

Follow Granville Street southwest through downtown and cross False Creek by bridge or ferry to reach Granville Island, regarded as one of North America's most successful inner-city industrial site redevelopments. The jazzed-up island is the place to go on a bright sunny day—allow at least several hours or an entire afternoon for this hive of activity.

Even though you'll be keen to start browsing, it's worth making your first stop the **Granville Island Information Centre** (1398 Cartwright St., 604/666-5784, daily 9 A.M.–6 P.M., closed Mon. in winter) to view the audiovisual presentation detailing the island's colorful history.

You can spend the better part of a day just walking around the island looking at the many specialty businesses reflecting the island's maritime heritage, fresh food markets, and gift shops. **Granville Island Public Market** (daily 9 A.M.–6 P.M.) is a hub of activity from dawn to dusk and a lot more than a tourist attraction.

The market sells all kinds of things to eat—fresh fruit and vegetables, seafood from local waters, a wide variety of meats, specialty ingredients, and prepared ready-to-go meals. The **Stock Market** has mouthwatering soups (from $4), but it's worth the extra for a huge serving of red-snapper chowder ($6).

Near the island's vehicular access point, **Granville Island Museums** (1502 Duranleau St., 604/683-1939, daily 10 A.M.–5:30 P.M., adult $4.50, senior $4, child $3) combines three museums under one roof. If you're into fishing, the Sport Fishing Museum is worth a visit just for the collection of historic rods, reels, flies, and gaffs, as well as fishing-related artwork and the photographic history of fishing in British Columbia. Of the other two sections, one displays model ships, the other model trains that run on operational tracks. The **Emily Carr Institute of Art and Design** (1399 Johnston St., 604/844-3800) also has two galleries open to the public.

To get to the island by boat, jump aboard one of the small **False Creek Ferries** (604/684-7781) at one of many docks around the bay. Single fare is $2–5, or buy an all-day Adventure Pass for adult $12, senior $10, child $8. Parking on the island is almost impossible, especially on weekends when locals do their fresh-produce shopping. If you do find a spot, it'll have a three-hour maximum time limit.

WEST END

The West End (not to be confused with the West Side, south of downtown, or West Vancouver, on the north side of the harbor) lies west of the central business district between Burrard Street and English Bay Beach, the gateway to Stanley Park. On foot, walk along Robson Street, then south on Denman Street, to reach pretty, park-fringed English Bay Beach. The golden sands, tree-shaded grassy roadsides, and sidewalks at the west end of the West End are popular with walkers, joggers, cyclists, and sun worshippers year-round.

Robson Street

If you like to shop in trendy boutiques, sample European delicacies, and sip cappuccinos at

BRITISH COLUMBIA

sidewalk cafés, saunter along this colorful and exciting street linking downtown to the West End. Once the center of a predominantly German neighborhood, Robson Street is also known as Robsonstrasse. At 1610 Robson (the west end), **Robson Public Market** occupies an impressive atrium-topped building filled with meat, seafood, dairy products, fruits and veggies, nuts, flowers, craft vendors, fresh juice and salad bars, and an international food fair.

Roedde House Museum

Most of the West End's original buildings are long gone, but a precinct of nine homes built between 1890 and 1908 has been saved and is preserved as **Barclay Heritage Square.** The only one open to the public is Roedde House (1415 Barclay St., 604/684-7040). Built in 1893, this Queen Anne Revival–style home is a classic example of Vancouver's early residential architecture. It was restored using historical records to ensure accuracy—right down to the color of the walls and interior furnishings. Tours of the house cost adult $5, senior $4, and are conducted Tuesday–Friday at 11 A.M.

STANLEY PARK

Beautiful Stanley Park, a lush 405-hectare (1,000-acre) tree- and garden-carpeted peninsula jutting out into Burrard Inlet, is a sight for sore eyes in any weather. Unlike other famous parks—New York's Central Park or London's Royal Park, for example—Stanley Park is a permanent preserve of wilderness in the heart of the city, complete with dense coastal forests and abundant wildlife.

Walk or cycle the 10-kilometer (6.2-mi.) **Seawall Promenade** or drive the perimeter via **Stanley Park Drive** to take in beautiful water and city views. Travel along both is one-way counterclockwise (those on foot can go either way, but if you travel clockwise you'll be going against the flow). For vehicle traffic, the main entrance to Stanley Park is the beginning of Stanley Park Drive, which veers right from the end of Georgia Street; on foot, follow Denman Street to its north end to find a pathway leading around Coal Harbour into the park. Either way,

you'll pass a small information booth where park maps are available.

Horse-drawn trams leave regularly from the information booth (604/681-5115, mid-Mar. to Oct. daily 9 A.M.–5:30 P.M., adult $21, senior and child $19) on a one-hour tour in a 20-person carriage. Riding a bike around the Seawall is also popular. Rent a bike (under $20 a day) from one of the many bike shops around the corner of Robson and Denman Streets. The least expensive is **Alley Cat Rentals** (1779 Robson St., 604/684-5117). If you decide to walk, it will take about three hours to complete the loop.

Vancouver Aquarium

In the forest behind the information booth is Canada's largest aquarium (July–Aug. daily 9:30 A.M.–7 P.M., rest of year daily 10 A.M.–5:30 P.M., adult $16, senior and child $12). Guarding the entrance is a five-meter-long killer whale sculpture by preeminent native artist Bill Reid. More than 8,000 aquatic animals and 600 species are on display, representing all corners of the planet, from the oceans of the Arctic to the rainforests of the Amazon. A number of exhibits highlight regional marine life, including the Wild Coast pool and Pacific Canada Pavilion. At the far end of the aquarium, a large pool holds beluga whales—distinctive pure white marine mammals—and sea lions, representing Arctic Canada. They can be viewed from above or below ground.

Seawall Sights

The following sights are listed counterclockwise from the information booth. From this point, Stanley Park Drive and the Seawall Promenade pass the **Royal Vancouver Yacht Club** then **Deadman's Island,** the burial place of the last of the Coast Salish people. At **Brockton Point** is a collection of authentic totem poles from the Kwagiulth people, who lived along the coast north of present-day Vancouver. Before rounding the actual point itself, you'll pass the **Nine O'Clock Gun,** which is fired each evening at, you guessed it, 9 P.M. The **Lions Gate Bridge** marks the halfway point of the seawall and a change in scenery. From this point to Second Beach the

STANLEY PARK

North Vancouver

Burrard Inlet

First Narrows

LIONS GATE BRIDGE

Prospect Point
PROSPECT POINT LOOKOUT
PROSPECT POINT CAFÉ

Promenade Trail

Seawall

First Narrows

Siwash Rock

Third Beach

Ferguson Point

TEAHOUSE RESTAURANT

HOLLOW TREE

PAULINE JOHNSON MEMORIAL

STANLEY PARK

Marrizes

Rawlings

Lovers

Bridle Path

Lees

Walk

Beaver Lake

PIPELINE

STANLEY PARK

CHILDREN'S FARMYARD

ROSE GARDEN

ROAD

Hummingbird Trail

JAPANESE FIGUREHEAD
GIRL IN WETSUIT

DRIVE

AVISON WAY

VANCOUVER AQUARIUM

Brockton Point

TOTEM POLES

NINE O'CLOCK GUN
Hallelujah Point

BROCKTON OVAL

STANLEY PARK

DRIVE

ROYAL VANCOUVER YACHT CLUB

Deadman's Island
(no public access)

Coal Harbour

MALKIN BOWL

INFORMATION BOOTH

VANCOUVER ROWING CLUB

CAUSEWAY

LOST LAGOON DRIVE

Lost Lagoon

NATURE HOUSE

PITCH AND PUTT GOLF

FISH HOUSE IN STANLEY PARK

LAGOON

DRIVE

STANLEY PARK

Promenade

Second Beach

Seawall

English Bay

WEST GEORGIA ST.
WEST END

ALBERNI ST.
ROBSON ST.
HARO ST.
BARCLAY ST.
NELSON
COMOX

DENMAN ST.
BIDWELL ST.

GILFORD
CHILCO

PARK LANE

ALLEY CAR RENTALS
STANLEY PARK RENTALS

BAYSHORE BICYCLES

BRITISH COLUMBIA

Burrard Inlet

300 yds
300 m
0
0

© AVALON TRAVEL PUBLISHING, INC.

views are westward toward the Strait of Georgia. This stretch of pleasant pathway, about two kilometers (1.2 mi.) long, is sandwiched between the water and steep cliffs, with **Siwash Rock** the only distinctive landmark. Continuing south, the seawall and Stanley Park Drive converge at the south end of **Third Beach,** a popular swimming and sunbathing spot (and a great place to watch the setting sun). From Second Beach it's only a short distance to busy Denman Street and English Bay Beach, or you can cut across the park past Lost Lagoon and back to Coal Harbour.

SOUTH OF DOWNTOWN

This largely residential area of the city extending west to Point Grey and the University of British Columbia is home to Vancouver's three largest museums and a number of public gardens. It also encompasses Vancouver's hippest suburb, **Kitsilano,** overlooking the beach and boasting a young, active population. Much of the foreshore is parkland, including **Kitsilano Beach,** Vancouver's most popular beach, which attracts hordes of bronzed (and not so bronzed) bodies for its warm shallow waters, spectacular mountain views, the city's largest outdoor pool, beach volleyball, and surrounding cafés and restaurants.

Vancouver Museum

Regional history from Precambrian times to the present comes to life at Vancouver Museum (1100 Chestnut St., Vanier Park, 604/736-4431, daily 10 A.M.–5 P.M., and Thurs. until 9 P.M., adult $10, senior $8, child $6). The West Coast Archaeology and Culture galleries hold ravishing masks, highly patterned woven blankets, and fine baskets. The Discovery and Settlement Gallery details European exploration of British Columbia, both by land and by sea. After browsing through the forestry and mill-town displays and the metropolis of Vancouver exhibit, you end up in the gallery of changing exhibitions, where you never know what you'll find.

In the same building as the museum is the **H.R. MacMillan Space Centre** (604/738-7827, June–Sept. daily 10 A.M.–5 P.M., closed Mon. the rest of the year, adult $13.50, senior and child

$10.50), which features displays related to planet Earth, the surrounding universe, and space exploration. Many of these exhibits—like the Cosmic Courtyard and Virtual Voyage—are hands-on and enjoyable for all ages, while others—Groundstation Canada and the Star Theatre—combine learning with exciting audiovisual presentations. The adjacent **Gordon MacMillan Southam Observatory** is open for public stargazing Friday–Saturday 7–11 P.M. when the skies are clear.

The most enjoyable way to reach this museum complex is by ferry from Granville Island or the Aquatic Centre at Sunset Beach. There's also plenty of free parking.

Vancouver Maritime Museum

Just a five-minute stroll from Vancouver Museum is Vancouver Maritime Museum (1905 Ogden Ave. at the end of Cypress Ave., Vanier Park, 604/257-8300, June–Sept., daily 10 A.M.–5 P.M., rest of year Tues.–Sat. 10 A.M.–5 P.M. and Sun. noon–5 P.M., adult $8, child $5.50). British Columbia's seafaring legacy is the focus here. Exhibits chronicle everything from the province's first sea explorers and their vessels to today's oceangoing adventurers, modern fishing boats, and fancy ships. Kids will love the Children's Maritime Discovery Centre and its model ships, computer terminals, underwater robot, and telescopes for viewing ships out in the harbor. The historic RCMP vessel *St. Roch,* the first patrol vessel to successfully negotiate the infamous Northwest Passage, is dry-docked within the building.

When you're through with the inside of the museum, you can wander down to the water to view the small fleet of historic vessels docked in the manmade harbor.

Museum of Anthropology

Containing the world's largest collection of arts and crafts of the Pacific Northwest native peoples, this excellent museum at the University of British Columbia (6393 Northwest Marine Dr., 604/822-5087, June–Sept. daily 10 A.M.–5 P.M., Oct.–May Tues.–Sun. 11 A.M.–5 P.M., adult $9, senior and child $7) should not be missed. Perched on a high cliff overlooking the Pacific Ocean and mimicking the post-and-beam struc-

After you've toured the Maritime Museum, wander down to the water to view a small collection of historic vessels, including the *Black Duck*, which was used as a search and rescue boat in the 1950s.

tures favored by the Coast Salish, your first glimpse inside is the entrance ramp, lined with impressive sculptures by renowned modern-day carvers. This leads to the Great Hall, a cavernous room dominated by totem poles collected from along the coast. A museum highlight is the collection of works by Haida artist Bill Reid, which includes *The Raven and the First Men,* a sculpture carved from a four-ton chunk of cedar. Other displays include intricate carvings, baskets, and ceremonial masks, fabulous jewelry, and European ceramics. Many of the research collections are stored in the main museum—in row upon row of glass-enclosed cabinets and in drawers that visitors are encouraged to open. Details of each piece are noted in handy catalogs.

Outside, a deliciously scented woodland path on the left side of the museum leads to a reconstructed Haida village and a number of contemporary totem poles with descriptive plaques.

Other Sights on the University Campus

Immediately south of the Museum of Anthropology is the serene **Nitobe Memorial Garden** (604/822-9666, summer daily 10 A.M.–6 P.M.,

adult $3.50, senior and child $2.25; rest of year Mon.–Fri. only, admission free). This traditional Japanese garden of shrubs and miniatures has two distinct sections: the Stroll Garden, laid out in a form that symbolizes the journey through life, and the Tea Garden, the place to contemplate life from a ceremonial teahouse.

Continue around Marine Drive for two kilometers (1.2 mi.) to reach the **UBC Botanical Garden** (6804 Marine Dr., 604/822-9666, mid-Mar.–mid-Oct. daily 10 A.M.–6 P.M., adult $5, senior $3, child free). Set among coastal forest, the 44-hectare (109-acre) garden features eight separate sections representing specific regions or environments, including a B.C. Native Garden alive with the plants, flowers, and shrubs found along the Pacific Northwest coast.

VanDusen Botanical Garden

In the heart of upscale Shaughnessy, the VanDusen Botanical Garden (5251 Oak St. at 37th Ave., 604/878-9274, adult $7.25, senior and youth $5.50) is home to more than 7,500 species from every continent except Antarctica. It's the place to feast your eyes on more than 1,000 varieties of rhododendrons, as well as roses, all kinds of botanical rarities, winter blossoms, an Elizabethan hedge maze, and a children's topiary garden featuring animal shapes. It's open year-round, daily from 10 A.M., with closing hours varying from 4 P.M. in winter to 8 P.M. in summer. To get there by bus, take no. 17 south along Burrard Street.

Queen Elizabeth Park

Less than two kilometers (1.2 mi.) from the VanDusen Botanical Garden, this 53-hectare (131-acre) park sits atop 152-meter (500-foot) high **Little Mountain,** the city's highest point, with magnificent views of Vancouver and the Coast Mountains. It's a paradise of sweeping lawns, trees, flowering shrubs, masses of rhododendrons (at their brightest in May and June), formal flower gardens, and mature plantings of native trees from across Canada. In the heart of the park is **Bloedel Floral Conservatory** (604/257-8584, summer Mon.–Fri. 9 A.M.–8 P.M. and Sat.–Sun. 10 A.M.–9 P.M., the rest of the year daily 10 A.M.–5 P.M.), a glass-domed structure containing a humid tropical jungle with a profusion of exotic flowering plants and a resident avian population including multihued parrots. Visitors are free to wander around the park, but an admission is charged to the conservatory (adult $4.50, senior and child $3). The main entrance is by the junction of 33rd Avenue West and Cambie Street; to get there from downtown take bus no. 15 south on Burrard Street.

RICHMOND

South of the city, the incorporated city of Richmond is actually on an island at the mouth of the Fraser River. Most visitors to Vancouver cross the island on their way north from the United States on Highway 99, or to or from the airport or Tsawwassen Ferry Terminal.

Steveston

The historic fishing village of Steveston, southwest of Richmond proper (take the Steveston Highway west from Highway 99), is a lively spot worth a visit. In the 1880s it had more than 50 canneries and was the world's largest fishing port (the harbor still holds Canada's largest fleet of commercial fishing boats). On the harborfront sits the **Gulf of Georgia Cannery National Historic Site** (12138 4th Ave., 604/664-9009, June–Aug. daily 10 A.M.–6 P.M., Apr.–May and Sept.–Oct. Thurs.–Mon. 10 A.M.–5 P.M., adult $6.50, senior $5, child $3.25), a cannery that operated between 1894 and 1979. Much of the original cannery has been restored. In addition to canning-line exhibits and demonstrations of the various machinery, an audiovisual presentation is offered in the Boiler House Theatre, and the Discovery area is set aside for children. Another historic site, the **Britannia Heritage Shipyards** (5180 Westwater Dr., 604/718-8050, June–mid-Sept. Tues.–Sat. 10 A.M.–4 P.M., Sun. noon–4 P.M.) is reached by following the signs east along Moncton Street. Steveston's downtown waterfront is lined with fishing-supply outlets, shops selling packaged seafood products, boutiques, and restaurants, and it bustles with activity in summer. Below the landing, fishing boats sell the day's catch, which could be halibut, salmon, crab, or shrimp. To watch all the action, grab a seat on the deck of **Shady Island Seafood** (3800 Bayview Rd., 604/275-6587), where a bowl of creamy clam chowder costs $6.

George C. Reifel Bird Sanctuary

Pass under the south arm of the Fraser River via Highway 99 and the George Massey Tunnel and you'll emerge in Delta. Take Highway 17 (Exit 28) south from Highway 99 and turn right on Ladner Trunk Road then continue along River Road and you'll find yourself in a time-warp of intriguing fishing shacks, maritime-related businesses, and floating houses. Here, an old wooden bridge provides a link to low-lying **Westham Island,** a stopover for thousands of migratory birds in spring and fall. The best time to visit the sanctuary (year-round daily 9 A.M.–4 P.M., adult $5, senior and child $2.50), at the far end of the island, is during the spectacular snow goose migration, which runs from early November to mid-December. Otherwise, you'll see abundant migratory birdlife anytime between October and April. The island also serves as a permanent home for many bird species, including bald eagles, peregrine falcons, herons, swans, and owls, and a parking lot is filled with ducks.

NORTH SHORE

North of downtown lie the incorporated cities of **North Vancouver** and **West Vancouver,** both of which are dramatically sandwiched between the North Shore Range of the Coast Mountains and Burrard Inlet. Road access from downtown is via the **Lions Gate Bridge,** but more enjoyable than getting caught up in bridge traffic is taking the SeaBus from Waterfront Station to **Lonsdale Quay** (adult $3 one way). At the lively quay you'll find a small information center (to the right as you come out of the SeaBus terminal) as well as transit buses that depart regularly for all the sights listed below.

Capilano Suspension Bridge

Tucked into the forested lower slopes of the North Shore Mountains, **Capilano River Canyon** is spanned by a wood-and-wire suspension bridge (3735 Capilano Rd., 604/985-7474, June–Aug. daily 8 A.M.–dusk, Sept.–May daily 9 A.M.–5 P.M.) a fearsome 70 meters (230 feet) above the Capilano River. Allow at least one hour to walk the bridge and the nature trails on the far side, view the totem-pole carvers in the Big House, and browse the requisite gift shop. Admission is a bit steep—adult $17, senior $12.50, child $8.50—but it's one of Vancouver's most popular sights. (If you don't want to spend the money, you can get much the same thrill by crossing the free bridge in Lynn Canyon Park.) To get there by public transportation, jump on the SeaBus and take bus no. 236 from Lonsdale Quay.

Capilano Salmon Hatchery and Regional Park

If you've always wanted to know more about the miraculous life cycle of salmon, or want some facts to back up your fish stories, visit this hatchery (Capilano Park Rd., 604/666-1790, daily 8 A.M.–4 P.M., free admission) on the Capilano River, two kilometers (1.2 mi.) upstream from the suspension bridge. Along with educational displays and nature exhibits you can see what the fish see from an underwater point of view. From July through October, magnificent adult coho and chinook salmon fight their way upriver to the hatchery.

Grouse Mountain

Continuing north, Capilano Road becomes Nancy Greene Way and ends at the base of the **Grouse Mountain Skyride** (604/980-9311, year-round daily 9 A.M.–10 P.M. adult $25, senior $23, child $14), North America's largest aerial tramway. Views from the top are unbeatable—downtown Vancouver, Stanley Park, the Pacific Ocean, and Mount Baker (Washington). The trip to the top is a lot more than a gondola ride. It's easy to spend the better part of a day exploring the surrounding area and taking advantage of the attractions included in the price of the ride up. Theatre in the Sky shows a bird's-eye, wide-screen presentation of the outdoor wonders of British Columbia. In addition, the Peak Chair continues higher up the mountain, and paved paths and nature trails skirt mountain meadows. Other highlights include a logging show (June–mid-Oct. daily 12:30 P.M., 2:30 P.M., and 4:30 P.M.), a refuge for orphaned bear cubs, the Birds in Motion raptor flying demonstration (June–mid-Oct. daily 11:30 A.M., 1:30 P.M., and 3:30 P.M.), and a First Nations longhouse with dancing and storytelling (adult $65, child $29; includes a five-course native feast), and helicopter rides (from $75 pp).

Mountaintop dining facilities include a café and bistro, a picnic area, and the summer-only Rusty Rail outdoor barbeque, and the fancy Observatory Restaurant, which provides free Skyride tickets with dinner reservations (daily 5–10 P.M.).

Lynn Canyon Park

On its way to Burrard Inlet, Lynn Creek flows through a deep canyon straddled by this 240-hectare (600-acre) park. Spanning the canyon is the "other" suspension bridge. The one here, built in 1912, is half as wide as its more famous counterpart over the Capilano River, but it's a bit higher and, best of all, it's free. An ancient forest of Douglas fir surrounds the impressive canyon and harbors a number of hiking trails. Also visit **Lynn Canyon Ecology Centre** (604/981-3103, daily 10 A.M.–5 P.M., free), where displays, models, and free slide shows and films explore plant and animal ecology.

Lynn Canyon Park is seven kilometers (4.3 mi.) east of the Capilano River. To get there by car, take the Lynn Valley Road Exit off Highway 1, east of the Lions Gate Bridge. By public transport, take the SeaBus to Lonsdale Quay, then bus no. 228 or 229.

Mount Seymour Provincial Park and Vicinity

Hikers and skiers flock to this 3,508-hectare (8,670-acre) park 20 kilometers (12 mi.) northeast of downtown. The park lies off Mt. Seymour Parkway, which spurs east off the TransCanada Highway just north of Burrard Inlet. The long and winding access road to the park climbs steadily through an ancient forest of western hemlock, cedar, and Douglas fir to a small facility area at an elevation of 1,000 meters (3,280 feet). From the parking lot, trails lead to the summit of 1,453-meter (4,770-foot) **Mount Seymour;** allow one hour for the two kilometer (1.2-mi.) trek.

If you continue along Mount Seymour Parkway instead of turning north toward the park, you end up in the scenic little village of **Deep Cove** on the west shore of Indian Arm (off the northeast end of Burrard Inlet)—an excellent spot for a picnic.

Cypress Provincial Park

This 3,012-hectare (7,440-acre) park northwest of downtown encompasses a high alpine area in the North Shore Mountains. To get to the park, take the TransCanada Highway 12 kilometers (7.5 mi.) west of Lions Gate Bridge and turn north onto Cypress Bowl Road (Exit 8). Even the park access road up from the TransCanada Highway is worthwhile for the views. At the fourth major switchback, pull into the turnout to see an old-growth yellow cedar tree. Estimated to be over 1,000 years old, this ancient giant stands 40 meters (130 feet) tall and has a base circumference of 10 meters (33 feet). At the 15-kilometer (9.3-mi.) mark, the road dead-ends at a parking lot.

Cypress is best known for its wintertime skiing and snowboarding, but there's plenty of hiking in the vicinity. From the main day lodge, well-marked hiking trails radiate out like spokes, through alpine meadows, to a subalpine lake, and to low peaks with views across Howe Sound. With a vivid imagination, maybe you'll spot Say-

noth-kai, the two-headed sea serpent of native Salish legend, believed to inhabit the sound.

Lighthouse Park

On a headland jutting into Howe Sound, 70-hectare (173-acre) Lighthouse Park lies eight kilometers (five mi.) west of the Lions Gate Bridge. Trails lead through the park to coastal cliffs and a lighthouse that guides shipping into narrow Burrard Inlet. Views from the lighthouse grounds are spectacular, extending west over the Strait of Georgia and east to Stanley Park and the Vancouver skyline. Get there along Marine Drive or aboard bus no. 250 from Georgia Street.

Bowen Island

This small island lies in Howe Sand and is a mix of residential areas and forest. General information (including on island accommodations) is available on the website www.bowenisland.org. It is linked to the mainland by ferry from **Horseshoe Bay** (604/669-1211, daily 6 A.M.–9:45 P.M., adult $6.50, child $4). Ferries depart once an hour and the trip takes around 20 minutes.

The ferry docks at the island's main settlement, aptly named **Snug Cove,** where you'll find all the services of a small town, including bed-and-breakfasts and cafés. There's good swimming at **Mannion Bay,** near Snug Cove, and **Bowen Island Sea Kayaking** (604/947-9266) rents kayaks and offers tours, but the rest of island is also good to explore. A two-kilometer (1.2-mi.) trail leads from Snug Cove to **Killarney Lake,** where birdlife is prolific and roads lead across to the island's west coast.

Harbour Air (604/274-1277 or 800/665-0212, www.harbour-air.com) offers an interesting evening tour to Bowen Island. For $169 you'll be whisked from downtown to the island by floatplane, enjoy dinner at an island restaurant, and return to your hotel by ferry and limousine.

EAST FROM DOWNTOWN

When you leave Vancouver and head due east, you travel through the most built-up and heavily populated area of British Columbia, skirting modern commercial centers, residential suburbs, and zones of heavy industry. Greater Vancouver extends almost 100 kilometers (62 mi.) along the Fraser Valley, through mostly residential areas. The main route east is the TransCanada Highway, which parallels the Fraser River to the south, passing through Burnaby, Langley, and Abbotsford. The original path taken by this highway crosses the Fraser River at New Westminster, the capital of British Columbia for a short period in the 1860s.

Vicinity of Coquitlam

Coquitlam is a residential area at the head of Burrard Inlet. Immediately north is 38,000-hectare (93,900-acre) **Pinecone Burke Provincial Park,** which extends along the west shoreline of Pitt Lake and as far west as the Boise Valley, scene of a short-lived gold rush in the late 1800s. Much of the park was logged over 100 years ago, but a few sections of old-growth forest remain, including a 1,000-year-old stand of cedar in the Cedar Spirit Grove. To get to the park from Highway 7, take Coast Meridian Road north to Harper Road, which leads to Munro and Bennett Lakes.

An even bigger tract of wilderness is protected by **Golden Ears Provincial Park,** which encompasses 55,590 hectares (137,000 acres) of the North Shore Mountains east of Coquitlam. To reach the park, follow Highway 7 east from Coquitlam to Maple Ridge, then follow signs north along 232nd Street and 132nd Avenue. The park access road ends at **Alouette Lake,** with fair fishing and lots of nearby hiking. **Lower Falls Trail** is an easy hike that everyone can enjoy. It begins at the end of the road and leads 2.7 kilometers (1.7 mi.) to a picturesque waterfall; allow one hour each way.

New Westminster

"New West," as it's best known, is a densely populated residential area 15 kilometers (9.3 mi.) southeast of downtown. Its strategic location, where the Fraser River divides, caused it to become a hub of river transportation and a thriving economic center. It was declared the capital of the mainland colony in 1859, then the provincial capital in the years 1866–1868. Only a few historic buildings remain, and the old port area has been totally overtaken by modern developments. Although still a busy inland port, the north side of the river, along Columbia Street, boasts a riverside promenade linking attractive stretches of green space to the Westminster Quay development and other modern shopping areas. The center of the action is **Westminster Quay Market,** which holds markets of fresh produce, takeout food stalls, and specialty shops. In the vicinity, the **Fraser River Discovery Centre** (788 Quayside Dr., 604/521-8401, Tues.–Sat. 10 A.M.–4 P.M., Sun. 1–4 P.M.) holds displays on the human history of the river and the role it has played in the development of New Westminster. Immediately to the south is the *Samson V,* built in 1937 and the last remaining paddlewheeler left on the river when it was retired in 1980. It's now open for public inspection (604/527-4640, June–Sept. daily Wed.–Sun. noon–5 P.M.).

The easiest way to reach New West from downtown is by SkyTrain.

Recreation

BICYCLING

Stanley Park is a mecca for cyclists; among its network of bike paths is the popular Seawall Promenade, which hugs the coast for 10 kilometers (bike travel is one-way counterclockwise). On the south side of English Bay, a cycle path runs from Vanier Park to Point Grey and the university, passing some of the city's best beaches on the way. On the north side of Burrard Inlet, hard-core mountain-bike enthusiasts tackle the rough trails of Cypress Provincial Park and Grouse Mountain.

Near the entrance to Stanley Park, where Robson and Denman Streets meet, is a profusion of bike-rental shops. These include **Alley Cat Rentals** (1779 Robson St., 604/684-5117), **Bayshore Bicycles** (745 Denman St., 604/688-2453), and **Stanley Park Rentals** (1798 W. Georgia St., 604/688-5141). With this many outlets crowded around one block, competition is fierce. Alley Cat Rentals offers the best deals, at $7 per hour or

VANCOUVER'S BEST HIKING

While Vancouver is not a particularly good city to explore on foot, it does have a number of wonderful urban and wilderness parks where taking a walk is a wonderful way to leave the hustle and bustle of the city behind. Here are a few favorites.

Stanley Park
Stanley Park, an urban oasis crisscrossed with hiking trails and encircled by a 10-km (6.2-mile) promenade that hugs the shoreline. The promenade is always busy, especially in late afternoon and on weekends, but you'll find most other trails a lot less used. A good alternative to one long section of the promenade is to ascend the steps immediately north of Lions Gate Bridge to Prospect Point (and maybe stop for a snack at the café), then continue west along the **Merilees Trail,** which follows the top of the cliff band to Third Beach. Along the way, an old lookout point affords excellent views of Siwash Rock and the Strait of Georgia.

Pacific Spirit Regional Park and Vicinity
This 762-hectare (1,880-acre) park out near the university offers 35 km (22 miles) of hiking trails through a forested environment similar to that which greeted the first European settlers over 200 years ago. A good starting point is the Park Centre (604/224-5739), which has a supply of trail maps. The entire park is crisscrossed with trails, so although getting seriously lost is impossible, taking the wrong trail and ending up away from your intended destination is easy. The **Imperial Trail,** starting at the corner of King Edward and 29th Avenues, is a personal favorite. It passes through a forest of red cedar and fir, crosses Salish Creek, then emerges on Southwest Marine Drive, at a monument commemorating the journey of Simon Fraser. From this lofty viewpoint, the view extends across the Strait of Georgia. This trail is 2.8 km (1.7 miles) one way (allow one hour).

North Shore
The provincial parks along the North Shore contain outstanding scenery and wildlife, crystal-clear lakes and rivers, and established hiking trails that are generally well maintained and easy to follow. (These trails are covered under North Shore in the Sights section.)

$20 per day for a basic mountain bike and $12 per hour or $40 per day for a suspension bike.

GOLF

Golf in Vancouver has come a long way since 1892, when a few holes were laid out across the sand dunes of Jericho Beach. Today, the city is blessed with over 50 courses, most of which are open to the public. It is often quoted that in Vancouver it is possible to ski in the morning and golf in the afternoon, and because most courses are open year-round this really is true.

The Courses
Vancouver Parks and Recreation operates three 18-hole courses on the south side of the city: **McCleery Golf Course** (7188 McDonald St., Southlands, 604/257-8191) is a flat, relatively easy layout with wide fairways; **Fraserview Golf Course** (7800 Vivian Dr., Fraserview, 604/257-6923) winds through a well-established forest; and **Langara Golf Course** (6706 Alberta St. off Cambie St., South Cambie, 604/713-1816) is the most challenging of the three. Each course offers carts and club rentals. Greens fees at all three courses are $46 during the week and $49 on weekends. Make bookings up to five days in advance by calling 604/280-1818, or call the courses direct on the day you want to play.

One the best Vancouver courses open to the public is the **University Golf Course** (5185 University Blvd., Point Grey, 604/224-1818). The course has no affiliation with its namesake, but does have a strong teaching program. It features fairways lined with mature trees and plays to 6,584 yards. The clubhouse exudes old-world charm and features an adjacent golf museum. Greens fees are a reasonable $45; reservations can be made up to a week in advance.

Water comes into play on 13 holes of the **Mayfair Lakes & Country Club** (5460 No. 7 Rd.,

If the ocean water is a little cold for your liking, head for the public pool at Kitsilano Beach.

Richmond, 604/276-0505), but its most unusual feature is the salmon that spawn in its waterways. It plays to a par of 71 and 6,641 yards from the back markers. Greens fees Monday–Thursday are $75, $85 Friday and weekends, with discounted twilight and off-season rates.

Formerly a private club, **Gleneagles Golf Course,** on the North Shore (6190 Marine Dr., West Vancouver, 604/921-7353), is a sloping nine-hole layout with ocean views. Operating on a first-come, first-served basis, greens fees for nine holes are just $22.

The **Golf Shuttle** (604/730-1032 or 888/599-6800, www.golf-shuttle.com) transports golfers to a "course of the day" and includes hotel pickups, a booked tee time, greens fees, clubs, a power cart, and even umbrellas and sunscreen. This company also organizes overnight Vancouver and Whistler golf packages.

WATER SPORTS
Swimming and Sunbathing
All of Vancouver's best beaches are along the shoreline of **English Bay;** 10 have lifeguards on duty through the summer months 11:30 A.M.–8:45 P.M. Closest to downtown is **English Bay Beach,** at the end of Denman Street. Flanked by a narrow strip of parkland and a wide array of cafés and restaurants, this is the beach for people-watching. From English Bay Beach, the Seawall Promenade leads north to **Second** and **Third Beaches,** both short, secluded stretches of sand. To the south is **Sunset Beach,** most popular with families.

Swimmers take note: Even at the peak of summer, the water here only warms up to about 17°C (63°F), tops. If that doesn't sound very enticing, continue to the south end of Sunset Beach to **Vancouver Aquatic Centre** (1050 Beach Ave., 604/665-3424).

On the south side of English Bay, **Kitsilano Beach** offers spectacular views back across the bay to downtown and the mountains beyond. Take a dip in the adjacent public pool. The beach and pool are an easy walk from both Vanier Park and a False Creek Ferries dock.

Canoeing and Kayaking
Granville Island is the center of action for paddlers, and the calm waters of adjacent False Creek make the perfect place to practice your skills. For a wide choice of equipment, head to **Eco-marine Ocean Kayak Centre** (1668 Duranleau St., 604/689-7575, www.ecomarine.com), where you can rent sea kayaks for two hours (single $32, double $44), four hours (single $42, double

$54), or 24 hours (single $52, double $74). If you've never kayaked before, join a 2.5-hour paddle around False Creek ($49) or take an inexpensive lesson.

The **Indian Arm** of Burrard Inlet allows for a real wilderness experience, right on the city's back doorstep. Deep Cove is the only settlement on the waterway. Here you'll find **Deep Cove Canoe and Kayak** (2156 Banbury Rd., Deep Cove, 604/929-2268) with rentals and tours. **Lotus Land Tours** (604/684-4922 or 800/528-3531, www.lotuslandtours.com) goes farther afield, with full-day and overnight trips throughout the region.

Boating and Yachting

The calm waters of False Creek and Burrard Inlet are perfect for boating and are always busy with pleasure craft. For puttering around the inner-city waterways, rent a motorboat from **Stanley Park Boat Rentals** (Coal Harbour Marina, 566 Cardero St., 604/682-6257) or **Granville Island Boat Rentals** (1696 Duranleau St., 604/682-6287). Both companies will suggest a trip to suit your boating ability and schedule, while also providing bait and tackle and directing you to the fishing hot spots.

Yachties and yachties-to-be should head for **Cooper Boating Center** (1620 Duranleau St., Granville Island, 604/687-4110, www.cooperboating.com), which boasts Canada's largest sailing school and also holds the country's biggest fleet for charters. For those with experience, Cooper's rents yachts for a day's local sailing (from $180 per day for a Catalina 22), or you can take to the waters of the Strait of Georgia on a bareboat charter (from $1,500 per week for a Catalina 27).

SKIING AND SNOWBOARDING

While Vancouver is the gateway to world-renowned Whistler/Blackcomb (see Whistler in the Vicinity of Vancouver chapter), the city boasts three other alpine resorts on its back doorstep. They don't offer the terrain or facilities of Whistler, and their low elevations can create unreliable conditions, but a day's skiing or riding at any one of the three sure beats being stuck in the hustle and bustle of the city on a cold winter's day.

Grouse Mountain

Towering above North Vancouver, the cut slopes of Grouse Mountain (604/986-0661, www.grousemountain.com, mid-Dec.–Apr.) can be seen from many parts of the city, but as you'd expect, on a clear day views from up there are much more spectacular. Access to the resort is by gondola from the end of Nancy Greene Way. Four chairlifts and a couple of T-bars serve 24 runs and a vertical rise of 365 meters (1,200 feet). Advanced skiers and snowboarders shouldn't get too excited about a day on the slopes here—even the runs with names like Purgatory and Devil's Advocate are pretty tame. Most runs are lighted for night skiing and overlook the city of Vancouver, laid out in all its brilliance far below. Lift tickets are adult $42, youth and senior $30, child $18. Night skiing (after 4 P.M.) costs adult $30, youth and senior $24, and child $18 until closing at 10 P.M.

Cypress Mountain

This small resort (604/926-5612, www.cypressmountain.com) will be on the world stage in 2010 when it hosts the snowboarding and freestyle skiing events of the 2010 Olympic Winter Games. In the meantime, local skiers and snowboarders enjoy about 25 runs on a vertical rise of 534 meters (1,750 feet), most suited to beginners and intermediates. Spectacular views take in Howe Sound and Vancouver Island. Other facilities include a terrain park, rental shop, ski and snowboard school, café, and lounge. Lift tickets are adult $42, youth $53, senior and child $19. Cypress also caters to cross-country skiers; 16 kilometers (10 mi.) of groomed and track-set trails lead from the historic Hollyburn Lodge. To get to the resort, take the TransCanada Highway 12 kilometers (7.5 mi.) west from Lions Gate Bridge and turn north on Cypress Bowl Road.

Mount Seymour

With the highest base elevation of Vancouver's three alpine resorts, Seymour (604/986-2261, www.mountseymour.com) has somewhat reliable snow, but the area's relatively gentle terrain will be of interest only to beginning and intermediate skiers and snowboarders. Four chairlifts serve 20 runs and a vertical rise of 365 meters (1,200 feet). On-hill facilities include a terrain park, toboggan run, and massive day lodge with rental shop. Weekend lift passes are adult $34, senior $24, child $18, while through the week rates are discounted to $28, $17, and $13 respectively. To get there, head north off the Trans-Canada Highway 15 kilometers (9.3 mi.) east of the Lions Gate Bridge, following the Mt. Seymour Parkway to Mt. Seymour Road.

SPECTATOR SPORTS

Vancouverites love their sports—not just being involved themselves, but supporting local teams. With a long season and outside activities curtailed by the winter weather, ice hockey—known in Canada simply as "hockey"—draws the biggest crowds.

Hockey

In 1911 the world's second (and largest) artificial ice rink opened at the north end of Denman Street, complete with seating for 10,000 hockey fans. The local team, then known as the Vancouver Millionaires, played in a small professional league, and in 1915 Vancouver won its first and only Stanley Cup, the holy grail of professional hockey. Today, the **Vancouver Canucks** (604/899-4625 or 604/280-4400, www.canucks.com) struggle to get the best players in a U.S. dollar–oriented market, but came close to capturing the Cup in 1994 before they lost in the finals. The team plays out of General Motors Place (across from B.C. Place Stadium on Griffith Way) from October to April; ticket prices range $35–95.

Football

The **B.C. Lions** (604/589-7627 or 604/280-4400, www.bclions.com) are Vancouver's Canadian Football League franchise. Although Vancouver isn't a hotbed of football fans, the team usually performs well enough to make the playoffs, last winning the Grey Cup in 2000. Home games are played at B.C. Place, on the south side of downtown. The season runs

June–November, with most games played in the evening; tickets range $18–32.

ARTS AND ENTERTAINMENT

There's never a dull moment in Vancouver when it comes to nightlife. The city's unofficial entertainment district extends southwest along Granville Street from Granville St. Mall, and south from this strip to False Creek. Cinemas line Granville St. Mall, while beyond the mall is a smattering of nightclubs. Performing arts and concert venues are scattered through the city, but the three largest—Ford Centre for the Performing Arts, Queen Elizabeth Centre, and B.C. Place Stadium—are south of Granville Street along Georgia Street.

For complete listings of all that's happening around the city, pick up the free weekly *Georgia Straight* or check their website (www.straight .com). Friday and weekend editions of Vancouver's two daily newspapers, the *Province* or the *Vancouver Sun,* offer comprehensive entertainment listings.

As in all other major cities across Canada, Ticketmaster (604/280-3311, www.ticketmaster.ca) has a monopoly on ticket sales to major entertainment events; have your credit card ready.

Theater

Vancouver has theaters all over the city—for professional plays, amateur plays, comedy, and "instant" theater. In total, the city boasts 30 professional theater companies and more than 20 regular venues. One of the great joys of summer in the city is sitting around Malkin Bowl in Stanley Park watching **Theatre under the Stars** (604/687-0174). The show runs Monday–Saturday at 7 P.M.; $20 per person. Another summer production is **Bard on the Beach** (604/739-0559), a celebration of the work of Shakespeare that takes place in huge, open-ended tents in Vanier Park. Tickets are well priced at just $18–30.

The **Ford Centre for the Performing Arts** (777 Homer St., 604/602-0616) hosts the biggest musical hits, with matinees costing from $50 and evening shows ranging $55–90. The **Arts Club** (604/687-1644) always offers excellent theater productions at two Granville Island locations. Productions range from drama to comedy and improv. Tickets run $21–35; book in advance and pick up your tickets at the door 30 minutes prior to showtime.

The **Playhouse Theatre Company** (160 W. 1st St., 604/873-3311) offers seven productions each year ranging from classical to contemporary, with 8 P.M. start times and tickets ranging $34–48.

Classical Music

The **Queen Elizabeth Theatre** (630 Hamilton St.) is the home of **Vancouver Opera** (604/683-0222); tickets begin at $35, rising to $90 for the best seats. The **Orpheum Theatre** (corner of Smithe and Seymour Streets) dates to 1927 and houses its original Wurlitzer organ. Now fully restored, the theater provides excellent acoustics for the resident **Vancouver Symphony** (604/684-9100).

Bars

Take a break from seeing the downtown sights at the **Steamworks Brewing Co.** (375 Water St., 604/689-2739, daily 11:30 A.M.–10 P.M.). The atmosphere is casual yet stylish, and you'll have great views across Burrard Inlet.

Yaletown Brewing Co. (1111 Mainland St., 604/688-0039) is the premier drinking hole for the hip residents of inner-city Yaletown. Up the hill, the old **Yale Hotel** (1300 Granville St., 604/681-9253) is primarily a blues venue, but is a pleasant place for a quiet drink even without the music. Toward the head of False Creek from Yaletown, **Maverick's** (770 Pacific Blvd. S, 604/683-4436) is the quintessential bar for college-age drinkers. Always lively, Maverick's patio (Vancouver's largest) overlooks the water and is generally crowded and noisy. Across False Creek, the **Stamp's Landing Neighbourhood Pub** (610 Stamp's Landing, just east of Granville Island, 604/879-0821) has live music on weekends and great sunset views overlooking the harbor.

Nightclubs

Nightclubs change names and reputations regularly, so check with the free entertainment news-papers or the website www.clubvibes.com for the latest hot spots. Naturally, weekends are busiest, with the most popular clubs having cover charges up to $10 and long lines after 9 P.M. The rest of the week, cover charges are reduced and many places hold promotions with giveaways or discounted drinks.

Downtown, nightclubs are concentrated along and immediately south of Granville Street. Best known as Dick's on Dicks, **Richard's on Richards** (1036 Richards St., 604/687-6794) has been a staple of the Vancouver nightclub scene for over 20 years. It's most popular with the late-20s and over-30s crowd. Best known as "the Fair," **Luv-A-Fair** (1275 Seymour St., 604/685-3288) is a longtime favorite with serious dancers. Expect a line at the **Palladium** (1250 Richards St., 604/688-2648), which is the home of Vancouver's underground music scene and a pretentious Saturday-night crowd.

Away from the main entertainment district, Gastown holds a number of nightclubs, including **Purple Onion** (15 Water St., 604/602-9442), which combines the Lounge, an intimate live music (usually jazz) venue; and the Club, a crowded, hot, and sweaty dance floor.

Live Music

Attracting a huge crowd every night of the week at the classic **Roxy** (932 Granville St., 604/331-7999), two house bands play rock 'n' roll music from all eras to a packed house during the week, with imported bands on weekends. The young hip crowd, good music, and performance bartenders make this the city's most popular live-music venue, so expect a line on weekends. A similar venue is the **Starfish Room** (1055 Homer St., 604/682-4171), although the acts have been more diverse in recent years, ranging from alternative to country.

Check the website of the **Coastal Jazz and Blues Society** (www.jazzvancouver.com) for listings of all the city's jazz and blues events. The **Hot Jazz Society** (2120 Main St., 604/873-4131) regularly presents live jazz; cover charge is $6–9. Serious blues lovers head for the **Yale Hotel** (1300 Granville St., 604/681-9253), which has hosted some of the greatest names in the business.

Sunday is the only night without live performances, although a jam session starts up about 3 P.M. on Saturday and Sunday afternoons.

Cinemas

Cinemas are in all the major shopping malls and elsewhere throughout the city. Combined, **Cineplex Odeon** (604/434-2463) and **Famous Players** (604/272-7280) operate 20 cinemas in Vancouver. Call the respective numbers or check the two daily papers for locations and screenings. The **Paradise Theatre** (919 Granville St., 604/681-1732) features commercial hits for the bargain-basement price of $5. If you're staying at a Robson Street or West End accommodation, head over to **Denman Place Discount Cinema** (corner of Denman and Comox Streets, 604/683-2201) for first- and second-run hits for $2.50–5.

SHOPPING

Vancouver has shopping centers, malls, and specialty stores everywhere. Head to **Gastown** for native arts and crafts, **Robson Street** for boutique clothing, **Granville St. Mall** for department stores, **Granville Island** for everything from ships' chandlery to kids' clothing, **Yaletown** for the trendy clothes of local designers, the **Eastside** for army-surplus stores and pawnbrokers, and **Chinatown** for Eastern foods.

Gastown

Hill's Native Crafts (165 Water St., 604/685-4249) sells $10 T-shirts, towering $12,000 totem poles, and everything in between, including genuine Cowichan sweaters and carved ceremonial masks. Also featuring traditional native art is **Images for a Canadian Heritage** (164 Water St., 604/685-7046). The **Inuit Gallery of Vancouver** (206 Cambie St., 604/688-7323) exhibits the work of Inuit and northwest coast native artists and sculptors. Among the highlights are many soapstone pieces by carvers from Cape Dorset, a remote Inuit village in Nunavut. A couple of blocks from Water Street in the Sinclair Centre is **Dorothy Grant** (757 W. Hastings St., 604/681-0201), a clothing store named for its owner. Dorothy and her husband are renowned for their contemporary Haida-inspired designs.

Granville Island

Arts and crafts galleries on Granville Island include **Wickaninnish Gallery** (1666 Johnston St., 604/681-1057), selling stunning native art, jewelry, carvings, weavings, and original paintings; **Gallery of B.C. Ceramics** (1359 Cartwright St., 604/669-5645), showcasing the work of the province's leading potters and sculptors; and **Forge & Form** (1334 Cartwright St., 604/684-6298), which creates and sells gold and silver jewelry.

Quarterdeck (1660 Duranleau St., 604/683-8232) stocks everything from marine charts to brass shipping bells, while a few doors down, **Ocean Floor** (1522 Duranleau St., 604/681-5014) sells a similar range of treasures, including seashells and model ships.

BRITISH COLUMBIA

Outdoor and Camping Gear

A small stretch of West Broadway, between Main and Cambie Streets, holds Vancouver's largest concentration of outdoor-equipment stores. The largest of these, and the largest in British Columbia, is **Mountain Equipment Co-op** (130 W. Broadway, 604/872-7858, Mon.–Wed. 10 A.M.–7 P.M., Thurs.–Fri. 10 A.M.–9 P.M., Sat. 9 A.M.–6 P.M.), a member-owned co-operative (to make a purchase, you must be a "member"—a once-only charge of $5). The store holds a massive selection of clothing, climbing and mountaineering equipment, tents, backpacks, sleeping bags, books, and other accessories.

FESTIVALS AND EVENTS

Festivals of some kind take place in Vancouver just about every month of the year. Most of the popular festivals are held during summer, the peak visitor season, but the rest of the year is the main season for performances by the city's dance, theater, and music companies, and not-to-be-missed events such as the Christmas Carol Ships Parade.

Spring

The spring event schedule kicks off in a big way with the early April **Vancouver Playhouse International Wine Festival** (604/873-3311, www.winefest.bc.ca), bringing together representatives from more than 150 wineries.

The streets of New Westminster come alive in late May for **Hyack Festival** (604/522-6894, www.hyack.bc.ca), in celebration of spring and the history of British Columbia's one-time capital. Farther east, the country comes to the city for one of British Columbia's biggest rodeos, the **Cloverdale Rodeo and Exhibition** (604/576-9461, www.cloverdalerodeo.com) on the third weekend of May. The last week of May is the **Vancouver International Children's Festival** (604/708-5655, www.vancouverchildrensfestival.com) at Vanier Park; it's a kid's paradise, with face painting, costumes, plays, puppetry, mime, sing-alongs, storytelling, and fancy-hat competitions.

Summer

Two of summer's most popular cultural events take place from mid-June through to late in the season, meaning you can enjoy them at any time through the warmer months. **Bard on the Beach** (604/739-0559, www.bardonthebeach.org) comprises three favorite Shakespeare plays performed in open-ended tents in Vanier Park, allowing a spectacular backdrop of English Bay, the city skyline, and the mountains beyond. Tickets are well priced at just $15–21.50 for 1 P.M. and 4 P.M. matinees and from $25 for 7:30 P.M. evening performances.

The other popular summer event, the **Kitsilano Showboat** (604/734-7332), takes place at nearby Kitsilano Beach. Amateur variety acts have been taking to this stage since 1935. Performances are Monday, Wednesday, and Friday nights over a 10-week summer season.

The last week of June, Vancouver taps its feet to the beat of the annual **Vancouver International Jazz Festival** (604/872-5200, www.jazzvancouver.com), when more than 1,500 musicians from countries around the world gather to perform traditional and contemporary jazz at 40 venues around the city. **Canada Day** is July 1. The main celebrations—music, dancing, and fireworks—are held at Canada Place, but if you head out to the **Steveston Salmon Festival** (604/277-6812) you'll come across a massive salmon barbecue and be granted free admission to the Gulf of Georgia Cannery.

Year after year, Vancouverites await with much anticipation the early August **Celebration of Light** (604/641-1193, www.celebration-of-light.com), the world's largest musical fireworks competition. Each year, three countries compete—each has a night to itself (the last Sat. in July, then the following Wed. and Sat.), putting on a display that lasts up to an hour from 10:15 P.M. Then on the final night (second Wed. in Aug.), the three competing countries come together for a grand finale. The fireworks are let off from a barge moored in English Bay, allowing viewing from Stanley Park, Kitsilano, Jericho Beach, and as far away as West Vancouver. Music that accompanies the displays can be heard around the shoreline.

Summer's busy event schedule winds up at the Pacific National Exhibition Grounds with **The Fair** (Pacific National Exhibition; 604/253-2311, www.pne.bc.ca), which includes an agricultural exposition and the RCMP musical ride, a precision drill performed by Canada's famous Mounties.

Fall

Beginning the second week of September, the **Fringe Festival** (604/257-0350, www.vancouver fringe.com) schedules around 500 performances by 100 artists from around the world at indoor and outdoor stages throughout Granville Island.

Winter

Through the month of December, VanDusen Botanical Garden is transformed each evening by over 80,000 lights and seasonal displays such as a nativity scene during the **Festival of Lights** (604/878-9274). Another popular pre-Christmas event is the **Carol Ships Parade of Lights** (604/878-9988, www.carolships.org). For three weeks leading up to Christmas Eve, the waterways of Vancouver come alive with the sounds of the festive season as each night a flotilla of up to 80 boats, each decorated with colorful lights, sails around local waterways while onboard carolers sing the songs of Christmas through sound systems that can clearly be heard from along the shoreline.

While most normal folk spend New Year's Day recovering from the previous night's celebrations, up to 2,000 brave souls head down to English Bay Beach and go swimming. The information hotline for the **Polar Bear Swim** is 604/732-2304, but all you really need to know is that the water will be very cold.

Accommodations

Whether you're looking for a campsite, hostel, bed-and-breakfast inn, motel, or luxury hotel, Vancouver has accommodations to suit your whim and budget. It is essential to reserve a room ahead of time in summer, but if you haven't, head to the **Vancouver Visitor Info Centre** (200 Burrard St., 604/683-2000), the best place to get all accommodations information and make bookings.

All rates quoted below are for high season (summer). Expect to pay less on weekends, especially for downtown accommodations, and outside of the busy July–August period.

DOWNTOWN

Under $50

The **HI–Vancouver Downtown** (1114 Burnaby St., 604/684-4565 or 888/203-4302, www.hi hostels.ca) offers a large kitchen, library, game room, public Internet access, a travel agency, bike rentals, bag storage, and a laundry. The dormitories hold a maximum of four beds but are small. For these beds, members of Hostelling International pay $24, nonmembers $28; private rooms range $57–66 s or d. **HI–Vancouver Central** (1025 Granville St., 604/685-5335 or 888/203-4302, www.hihostels.ca) has similar facilities, as well as a downstairs bar; members from $24, nonmembers from $28.

Global Village Backpackers (1018 Granville St., 604/682-8226 or 888/844-7875, www .globalbackpackers.com) is excellent in all respects. Each of the smallish rooms has been tastefully decorated, and the communal lounge and kitchen areas serve guests well. Other facilities include a separate TV room, public Internet access, and a rooftop patio. Rates are $23 pp in a dorm or $62–70 d for a private room, with discounted winter rates.

$50–100

The three-story **Kingston Hotel** (757 Richards St., 604/684-9024 or 888/713-3304, www.kingston hotelvancouver.com) dates to the early 1900s but has been extensively renovated. The small "sleeping rooms" (shared bath) are exactly that, but well priced at $50 s, $60 d. Moving up in size, rates range $68–98 s, $78–115 d, the more expensive rooms with a private bathroom. Amenities include a laundry, a TV room where old-time movies are screened each evening, and an adjacent parkade (parking extra). All rates include a light breakfast.

For traveling females, couples, and families on a budget, the **YWCA** (733 Beatty St., 604/895-5830 or 800/663-1424, www.ywcahotel.com, $56–72 s, $69–111 d) is a good choice. Each room offers basic but modern amenities, including a telephone and television (private rooms only). Communal facilities include two kitchens, three lounges, and two laundries.

$100–150

The **Howard Johnson** (1176 Granville St., 604/688-8701 or 888/654-6336, www.hojo vancouver.com) was totally revamped in the late 1990s, creating a good-value, centrally located property. The cheerful rooms are air-conditioned and guests have use of a small fitness room. Rates start at $139 s or d, but the rooms from $149 up are much larger and are discounted well below $100 in winter.

$150–200

Most accommodations in this price range are scattered between the central business district and Granville Island. Least expensive of the CBD hotels is **Days Inn–Vancouver Downtown** (921 W. Pender St., 604/681-4335 or 800/329-7466, www.daysinnvancouver.com, $155–195 s or d). The 85 rooms are small, and surrounding high-rises block any views. But each room is decorated in bright and breezy pastel colors, and high-speed Internet access is provided along with other niceties like coffeemakers and a daily paper.

While guest facilities at **Ramada Limited Vancouver Downtown** (435 W. Pender St., 604/488-1088 or 888/389-5888, www.ramadalimited.org) are limited compared to other properties in this price category, like the Days Inn, the location is very central. As the hotel is old, its 80 rooms are small, but they're well appointed and come with everything from hair dryers to Nintendo. The advertised summer rate is $149 s or d.

$200–250

Granville Island Hotel (1253 Johnston St., 604/683-7373 or 800/663-1840, www.granville islandhotel.com) enjoys a fabulous location on the island of the same name immediately south of downtown. Contemporary and elegant, the rooms are very spacious and furnished with Persian rugs, marble-floored bathrooms, and modern amenities such as high-speed Internet access. Most also have water views. Summer rates range $200–220 s or d, discounted below $150 the rest of the year.

$250–300

Delta Vancouver Suites (550 W. Hastings St., 604/689-8188 or 800/268-1133, www.delta hotels.com) holds 226 spacious units, each with a separate bedroom and comfortable lounge area. In-room business facilities include a work desk stocked with supplies, two phone lines, high-speed Internet access, and personalized voice mail. Other guest facilities include a health club, indoor pool, saunas and a whirlpool, and a street level New York–style restaurant open for breakfast, lunch, and dinner. Rack rates are $279 s or d, but check the website for deals.

The centrally located **Marriott Vancouver Pinnacle Hotel** (1128 W. Hastings St., 604/684-1128 or 800/236-2427, www.marriott.com) is a full-service property with 434 spacious rooms, each with stylish furniture, elegant bathrooms, a writing desk full of office supplies, two telephones (including a cordless) with voice mail and Internet access, a coffeemaker, ironing facilities, and also an umbrella for Vancouver's occasional rainy days. Guests also enjoy complimentary use of the hotel's health club, which features a big indoor pool, a hot tub, a sauna, and a large outdoor patio area. Advertised rates are from $309, discounted to $199 and $219 outside of summer.

$300–400

The Georgian-revival-style **Crowne Plaza Hotel Georgia** (801 Georgia St., 604/682-5566 or 800/663-1111, www.hotelgeorgia.bc.ca) is a relative bargain compared to Vancouver's other upscale hotels. The oak-paneled lobby, brass elevator, and original oak furnishings have been restored and all facilities upgraded, including a fitness center and various eating establishments. Summer rates start at $369 s or d but drop to $169 in winter.

One block from the city end of Robson Street is the super-luxurious, European-style **Sutton Place** (845 Burrard St., 604/682-5511 or 800/961-7555, www.suttonplace.com), which gets a precious five-diamond rating from the American Automobile Association. This hotel, Vancouver's most elegant accommodation, features original European artworks in public areas and reproductions in the 397 rooms. Rooms are furnished with king-size beds, plush bathrobes, and two phone lines, and guests enjoy a twice-daily maid service, complete with fresh flowers; from $385 per night.

Over $400

For all the modern conveniences along with unbeatable city and harbor views, head for the sparkling **Pan Pacific Vancouver** (604/662-8111 or 800/327-8585, www.panpac.com). It's part of the landmark Canada Place, whose Teflon sails fly over busy, bustling sidewalks and a constant flow of cruise ships. Each of the 504 spacious rooms boasts stunning views, contemporary furnishings, a luxurious marble bathroom, and in-room video checkout. Rooms start at $490 s or d, while weekend rates outside of summer are under $300.

ROBSON STREET AND THE WEST END

Under $100

Overlooking English Bay and the closest beach to downtown, the **Sylvia Hotel** (1154 Gilford St., 604/681-9321, www.sylviahotel.com) is a local landmark sporting a brick and terra-cotta exterior covered with Virginia creeper. Built in 1912 as an apartment building, today it provides excellent value, as rates range $95–205 s or d (the less expensive rooms are fairly small), with more expensive rooms featuring fantastic views and full kitchens. The Sylvia also has a restaurant and lounge.

$100–150

One block from Robson Street, the **West End Guest House** (1362 Haro St., 604/681-2889, www.westendguesthouse.com) has been lovingly refurbished in Victorian-era colors and furnished with stylish antiques to retain its original charm. Each of the seven guest rooms has a brass bed complete with cotton linen and a goose-down duvet, an en suite bathroom, a television, and a telephone. Rates range $139–215 s or d, which includes a full breakfast.

The European-style **Barclay Hotel** (1348 Robson St., 604/688-8850, www.barclayhotel .com, $95 s, $115 d) holds 80 medium-size rooms, a small lounge, and an intimate restaurant. The rooms are stylish in an unpretentious way; each holds a comfortable bed, writing desk, couch, and older television. Rates include a light buffet breakfast.

$150–200

At the 214-room **Blue Horizon Hotel** (1225 Robson St., 604/688-1411 or 800/663-1333, www.bluehorizonhotel.com, $159–199 s or d) facilities include an indoor lap pool, a fitness room, a sauna, and a variety of services for business travelers. Rooms are large, brightly lit, and have a private balcony, work desk, and coffeemakers.

$200–250

The **Pacific Palisades Hotel** (1277 Robson St., 604/688-0461 or 800/663-1815, www.pacific palisadeshotel.com) is touted as being a cross between "South Beach (Miami) and Stanley Park," a fairly apt description of this chic Robson Street accommodation. Interior designers have given the entire hotel a "beachy," ultra-contemporary feel—each of the 233 spacious rooms is decorated with sleek furnishings in a dynamic color scheme. Rates are a reasonable $200–225 s or d.

HOTELS AND MOTELS ON THE NORTH SHORE

The best reason to stay on the North Shore is to enjoy the local hospitality of one of the many bed-and-breakfasts, but a number of hotels and motels are also scattered through this part of the city.

$100–150

Charming **Thistledown House** (3910 Capilano Rd., North Vancouver, 604/986-7173 or 888/ 633-7173, www.thistle-down.com, from $135 s or d) has been restored to resemble a country-style inn. My pick of the five guest rooms is Under the Apple Tree, with a king-size bed, split-level sitting room with a fireplace, a sun-drenched patio, and a large bathroom complete with a whirlpool tub.

The Tudor-style **Park Royal Hotel** (540 Clyde Ave., West Vancouver, 604/926-5511 or 877/926-5511, www.parkroyalhotel.com, $149–249 s or d) sits on the banks of the Capilano River—you can fish for salmon and steelhead right on the property—and is surrounded by well-maintained gardens. Inside you'll find an English-style pub with a congenial atmosphere, elegant dining in the Tudor Room, and an inviting lounge area with fireplace. The 30 rooms are small, but each has a brass bed.

Over $150
If you're prepared to book well ahead, **Beachside B&B** (4208 Evergreen Ave., West Vancouver, 604/922-7773 or 800/563-3311, www.beach.bc.ca) is an excellent choice, with views extending across Burrard Inlet to Stanley Park and downtown. The two larger suites have water views, semiprivate patios, and whirlpool tubs; $250 s or d. The smallest of the three rooms, which opens to a private patio, is $175 s or d.

HOTELS AND MOTELS SOUTH OF DOWNTOWN

If you have your own transportation, the lodgings south of downtown are worth consideration. They're generally less expensive than the downtown hotels, and you won't have to worry about parking (or paying for parking).

Under $50
HI–Vancouver Jericho Beach (1515 Discovery St., Point Grey, 604/224-3208, www.hihostels.ca) is in a fantastic location, in scenic parkland and linked to downtown by extensive biking and walking trails. Expect all the usual facilities of hostel living, as well as a café, public Internet access, and a shuttle to downtown. Members pay $18 per night, nonmem-

bers $22 for a dorm bed, or $45 and $53 respectively for a double room.

$50–100
Behind City Hall between Cambie and Yukon Streets, **Cambie Lodge** (446 W. 13th Ave., Mt. Pleasant, 604/872-3060 or 888/872-3060, www.cambielodge.com) has the reputation of being a friendly, clean, and comfortable place to stay for international travelers. Each room has a TV and heritage-style furnishings, while communal facilities include a TV lounge and a small garden. Rates for the six rooms range $95–105 s or d, which includes a cooked breakfast.

$100–150
On the southern edge of Shaughnessy, **Beautiful B&B** (off Cambie at 428 W. 40th Ave., 604/327-1102, www.beautifulbandb.bc.ca) is a Colonial-style two-story home on a high point of land where views extend across the city to the North Shore Range. Both Queen Elizabeth Park and VanDusen Botanical Garden are within walking distance. The house is decorated with antiques and fresh flowers from the surrounding garden. Two rooms share a bathroom ($125–160 s or d) while a third comes with a fireplace, panoramic views, and a huge en suite bathroom complete with soaking tub ($235 s or d).

VANCOUVER INTERNATIONAL AIRPORT AND VICINITY

The following Richmond accommodations are good choices for those visitors who arrive late at or have an early departure from the international airport. Also, if you arrive in Vancouver and want to head straight over to Vancouver Island, staying in this vicinity saves an unnecessary trip into downtown. All accommodations detailed in this section offer complimentary airport shuttles.

$100–150
The kid-friendly **Delta Pacific Resort & Conference Centre** (10251 St. Edwards Dr., 604/278-9611 or 800/268-1133, www.deltahotels.com, $139 s or d) offers a wide range of facilities, including a fitness center, large

water slide, one indoor and two outdoor pools, tennis and squash courts, a business center, and bike rentals.

Farther from the airport, the **Coast Vancouver Airport Hotel** (1041 Southwest Marine Dr., 604/263-1555 or 800/663-1144, www.coast hotels.com) has 134 modern rooms, a fitness center, sports bar, and family restaurant. Instead of paying the rack rate ($139 s or d), inquire about the Coast's many packages suited to arriving and departing air passengers.

Halfway between the airport and ferry terminal, the **Delta Town and Country Inn** (6005 Hwy. 17, 604/946-4404 or 888/777-1266, www.deltainn.com, $105 s or d) enjoys a parklike setting and well-priced rooms.

$150–200

Right at the international airport, the **Fairmont Vancouver Airport** (604/207-5200 or 800/866-5577, www.fairmont.com, $199 s or d) is a technological wonder. Rooms are equipped with remote-controlled everything, right down to the drapes, fog-free bathroom mirrors, and floor-to-ceiling soundproofed windows. As a Fairmont guest, you can check into the hotel at the arrivals level of the international terminal.

CAMPGROUNDS

You won't find any campgrounds in the city-center area, but a limited number dot the suburbs along the major approach routes. Before trekking out to any of them, ring ahead to check for vacancies.

North

The closest campground to downtown is **Capilano RV Park** (295 Tomahawk Ave., North Vancouver, 604/987-4722, www.capilanorv park.com). To get there from downtown, cross Lions Gate Bridge, turn right on Marine Drive, right on Capilano Road, and right again on Welch Street. It's about an hour's walk to downtown from the campground, over Lions Gate Bridge and through Stanley Park. Amenities include a swimming pool and hot tub, a TV and games room, Internet access, and a laun-

dry. Limited tent camping is $25, while hookups range $35–45. Reservations recommended for summer.

South

Large **Richmond RV Park** (6200 River Rd., 604/270-7878 or 800/755-4905, www.richmond rvpark.com, Apr.–Oct.) is 16 kilometers (10 mi.) south of downtown. Aside from noise from the nearby airport, the riverside location is excellent. Facilities include free showers, a coin-op laundry, and a game room. Tent sites are $20, while serviced sites range $29–35. To get there, take Exit 36 from Highway 99, head west along Westminster Highway, then take No. 2 Road north to River Road and turn right.

Parkcanada (52nd St. exit north from Highway 17, then the first left, 604/943-5811, www.park canada.com) is very convenient to the BC Ferries terminal at Tsawwassen, a 30-minute drive south of city center. The campground has a small outdoor pool (next door is a much larger waterpark—perfect for the kids), convenience store, launderette, lounge, and free showers. Unserviced sites, suitable for tents, are $18; serviced sites range $24–37 depending on the size of the RV or trailer and the amp required.

East

Adjacent to Burnaby Lake Regional Park, **Burnaby Cariboo RV Park** (8765 Cariboo Place, Burnaby, 604/420-1722, www.bcrvpark.com) offers lots of facilities, including a large indoor heated pool, fitness room, hot tub, sundeck, playground, lounge, barbecue area, grocery store, and laundry facility. Most sites come with full hookups (power, water, sewer, cable TV, Internet access) for $37–42 per night. Sites in the private, walk-in tent area cost $25 per night. The park is 17 kilometers (10.6 mi.) east of downtown. To get there, take Exit 37 (Gaglardi) from the TransCanada Highway, turn right at the first traffic light, then take the first left, then the first right into Cariboo Place.

Anmore Camp & RV Park is tucked away on Buntzen Lake north of Coquitlam (3230 Sunnyside Rd., Anmore, 604/469-2311). To get there, head north along Highway 7 from Exit 44 of the TransCanada Highway; take Highway 7A west, back toward the city, then Ioco Road north, and follow the signs. It's the forested setting that makes this campground worth the drive, but other amenities include a small heated pool, canoe and bike rentals, a barbecue area, a laundry, and a small general store. Tent sites are $25 per night, hookups $30–34.

Food

With an estimated 2,000 restaurants and hundreds of cafés and coffeehouses, Vancouver is a gastronomical delight. The city is home to more than 60 different cultures, so don't be surprised to find a smorgasbord of ethnic restaurants. The local specialty is West Coast or "fusion" cuisine, which combines fresh Canadian produce, such as local seafood and seasonal game, with Asian flavors and ingredients, usually in a healthy, low-fat way. Vancouver has no tourist-oriented, San Francisco–style Fisherman's Wharf, but however and wherever it's prepared, seafood will always dominate local menus. Pacific salmon, halibut, snapper, shrimp, oysters, clams, crab, and squid are all harvested locally.

DOWNTOWN
Dining Classics
While the best known of Vancouver's restaurants are judged by their food, the service, the decor, and the crowd they attract, none of that matters to the following places. At these places, you can expect hearty portions, inexpensive prices, and, at all except the infamous Elbow Room, friendly service.

Breakfast is the meal of choice at the **Elbow Room** (560 Davie St., 604/685-3628, Mon.–Fri. 7:30 A.M.–3:30 P.M., Sat.–Sun. 8:30 A.M.–4 P.M.), a Vancouver institution where portions are huge and the prices reasonable ($9 for the Lumberjack breakfast). But it's the service, or lack of it, that you'll remember long after the meal. The waiters take no nonsense, and the constant banter from the open kitchen is unique. It's all in good fun, though, and if you get abused you'll join a long list of celebrities whose photos adorn the walls. If you don't finish your meal, you must make a donation to a local charity; if it's a pancake you can't finish, you're advised to "just rub it on your thighs, because that's where it's going anyway!" (Sunday morning is when the kitchen and wait staff are at their wittiest.)

In the vicinity of the Elbow Room are another couple of greasy spoons: **Grade A Café** (1175

GETTING A CAFFEINE FIX

One thing that will soon become apparent to first-time visitors is the amount of coffee consumed by the locals. Specialty coffeehouses are everywhere, but nowhere are they as concentrated as along Robson Street.

Starbucks alone has more than 85 Vancouver outlets, including two sitting kitty-corner from each other on Robson Street, along with two others on that same street. **Blenz** is equally well represented throughout the city, with three cafés on Robson Street.

Rather than diving straight into Starbucks, I recommend trying one of the local places. It is only a cup of coffee after all. My pick for coffee and a light snack is the **Bread Garden,** with 20-odd cafés scattered throughout the metropolitan area. One central location is half a block off busy Robson Street at 812 Bute Street (604/688-3213). It's open 24 hours a day and is always busy—so much so that patrons often need to take a number and wait for service. The coffee is great, as are the freshly baked muffins and pastries. Salads and healthy sandwiches are also available.

Gastown's best coffee is ground and brewed at **La Luna Café** (131 Water St., 604/687-5862). The café's striking yellow and black interior, daily papers, great coffee, and inexpensive light snacks make this a pleasant escape from touristy Water Street.

HOTEL DINING

Generally, hotels have a reputation for ordinary and overpriced restaurants—in existence only for the convenience of guests—but Vancouver is the exception to that rule. Since the first Canadian Pacific Railway passengers arrived at the end of the line to be spoiled by European chefs at the Hotel Vancouver, locals and visitors alike have headed to the city's best hotels to enjoy fine dining in all its glory.

The Wedgewood Hotel's signature dining room, the **Bacchus Ristorante** (845 Hornby St., 604/608-5319), has the feeling of a romantic European bistro with its dark cherrywood paneling, stone fireplace, and elegant table settings over white linen. The emphasis is on Italian cuisine, but the menu relies heavily on local produce, changing with the seasons—such as salmon, roasted in a red wine jus and served on a bed of crab ravioli, when I last splurged here—and ranging $28–35. Afternoon tea ($21) is served daily 2–4 P.M.

Also open for afternoon tea—scones and cream, finger foods like cucumber sandwiches, and more—is **Fleuri** (Sutton Place Hotel, 845 Burrard St., 604/642-2900) in what is generally regarded as one of the world's best hotels. The dinner menu ($25–34 for an entrée) gets more serious, with local produce given classic European treatment.

At **900 West** (Fairmont Hotel Vancouver, 900 W. Georgia St., 604/669-9378, daily 6–10 P.M.), enjoy the atmosphere of a luxurious cruise-ship dining room. The contemporary North American menu is varied, with classic preparations of B.C. seafood and Alberta beef starting at $26.

Typifying the new wave in Vancouver's hotel dining scene is **Show Case**, at street level of the Marriott Vancouver Pinnacle (1128 W. Hastings St., 604/639-4040). Floor-to-ceiling windows and contemporary styling create an environment very different from the elegant old-world feel of Vancouver's other top-end hotel restaurants. Exotic dishes prepared using local seafood and game are simply and stylishly presented; the tasting menu gives diners the opportunity to experience a variety of dishes, accompanied by matching wines. Entrées range $22–35.

Granville St., 604/669-7495) keeps the locals happy with a classic Canadian and Chinese menu, while **The Templeton** (1087 Granville St., 604/685-4612) comes with twist-vinyl booths, jukeboxes, and adventurous dishes such as veggie burgers and jambalaya. **Hamburger Mary's** (1202 Davie St., 604/687-1293) is a classic diner, where delicious hamburgers attract the crowds. Starting at $6, they aren't particularly cheap, but they come with fries, and extras such as salad are just $1. Breakfast ($5 for eggs, bacon, hash browns, and toast) begins daily at 7 A.M., and the last burgers are flipped in the early hours of the morning. Wash down your meal with one of Mary's famous milkshakes.

West Coast and Seafood

With its prime waterfront location between Canada Place and Gastown, **Aqua Riva** (200 Granville St., 604/683-5599) features stunning views across Burrard Inlet. The least expensive way to enjoy the dramatic view is with a pizza baked in a wood-fired oven ($13–16). Other entrées—mostly seafood, including a delicious alderwood-grilled salmon—are all under $30 (pastas average $20).

One of Vancouver's finest seafood restaurants is **A Kettle of Fish** (near the Burrard Street Bridge at 900 Pacific St., 604/682-6853). The casual decor features café-style seating and abundant greenery, while the menu swims with schools of piscatory pleasures. New England clam chowder ($7.50) is one of over 20 appetizers, while traditionally prepared entrées such as grilled snapper ($22) or a seafood platter for two ($45.50) make up the main menu.

Raintree (375 Water St., 604/688-5570, daily 11:30 A.M.–2:30 P.M. and 5:30–10 P.M.), in one of Gastown's many historic buildings, is an elegant room with fantastic water views. Exposed beams, red-brick walls, and a slate floor all give class to what was originally a warehouse. The least-expensive lunch items are the pastas, which cost under $15, while seafood dishes are only a couple of dollars more. Dinner entrées, ranging $20–30, take advantage of local produce, such as salmon, which is served with goat cream cheese from the Southern Gulf Islands.

On Granville Island's northern tip is the bright yellow **Bridges** (1696 Duranleau St., 604/687-4400), with stunning water views. Diners have the choice of four dining areas, but the most popular spot is the Dock, an outside, absolute-waterfront eating area that entails waiting for a table whenever the sun is shining. The menu features typical wide-ranging bistro-style fare of hamburgers, salads, and pastas, as well as basic seafood dishes such as a platter to share for $34.

Fish House in Stanley Park (8901 Stanley Park Dr., 604/681-7275, daily for lunch and dinner) lies in parklike surroundings on a rise in the southwest corner of the famous park, away from the crowded promenade. Seating is in one of three rooms or out on a deck, the service is efficient, and the food is well prepared. All the usual seafood dishes are offered, as well as a few unique dishes, such as a personal favorite, Alaskan scallops grilled in a sweet chili glaze. Dinner entrées range $18–30.

European

Of Vancouver's many Italian restaurants, one of the most popular is **Il Giardino** (1382 Hornby St., 604/669-2422, Mon.–Fri. noon–2:30 P.M. and daily 5:30–11 P.M.), in a distinctive yellow Italian-style villa with light, bright furnishings and an enclosed terrace. Expect to pay $12–16 for lunch entrées, $16–33 for featured Tuscan cuisine in the evening.

In Gastown, the unique decor at **Brothers Restaurant** (1 Water St., 604/683-9124) features monastery-like surroundings of wood, brick, stained glass, chandeliers, and monkish murals. Enjoy delicious soups, salads, sandwiches, and a variety of entrées ($9.50–17), all served by waiters appropriately dressed as monks and accompanied by congregational sing-alongs and laser light shows. The daily lunch specials are a good value, as are the early dinner deals available Monday–Thursday before 6 P.M.

For Vancouver's finest French cuisine, go to the small, intimate **Le Crocodile** (909 Burrard

St., 604/669-4298, lunch Mon.–Fri., dinner Mon.–Sat.), which has won innumerable awards over its two decades as one of Vancouver's premier restaurants. The smallish menu relies heavily on traditional French techniques and style and is complemented by an extensive wine list. It's not as expensive as you might think: Entrées range $15.50–24.

Expect to wait for a table at **Stepho's** (1124 Davie St., 604/683-2555, daily noon–11:30 P.M.), one of Vancouver's best-value restaurants. Locals and savvy travelers line up here to enjoy the atmosphere of a typical Greek taverna—complete with a terracotta floor, white stucco walls, arched doorways, blue and white tablecloths, travel posters, and lots of colorful flowering plants. All the favorite Greek dishes are offered, such as souvlakis or a steak and Greek salad combination for under $10, and portions are generous. Save room for the delicious baklava, which costs just $3.50.

Asian

Dining in **Chinatown,** a few blocks east of downtown, offers two distinct options—traditional eateries where you'll find the locals and the larger Westernized restaurants that attract non-Chinese and a younger Chinese crowd. A perfect combination of the two is **Kent's Kitchen** (232 Keefer St., 604/669-2237), a modern café-style restaurant where the service is fast and efficient, the food freshly prepared, and the prices incredibly low. Two specialty dishes, rice, and a can of pop make a meal that costs just $6. Next door to Kent's, **Hon's Wun Tun House** (230 Keefer St., 604/688-0871) is a large, bright, and modern restaurant that attracts a younger Chinese crowd for mostly Westernized Chinese under $10 per entrée. Around the corner from Keefer Street, Gore Street is less Westernized; here you'll find **Fu Wah** (555 Gore St., 604/688-8722), which has a ridiculously inexpensive lunchtime dim sum menu.

Misaki (Canada Place, 604/891-2893) offers the peace and tranquility of an upmarket Tokyo restaurant and combines traditional Japanese and contemporary fusion cooking. It's not particularly cheap (expect to pay $100 for two, sans alcohol), but dining here costs half of what you would pay in Tokyo.

At the other end of the price spectrum, **Kisha Poppo** (1143 Davie St., 604/681-0488) serves up Westernized Japanese food in a sterile diner-style atmosphere. But the price is right: All-you-can-eat soup, starters, sushi, hot entrées such as teriyaki, and dessert is $9.50 at lunch and $14.50 at dinner.

Pacific Institute of Culinary Arts

Students from around the world are attracted to this Vancouver-based private cooking school (1505 W. 2nd Ave., 604/734-4488) for its state-of-the-art facilities and world-class teachers, led by Chef Walter Messiah. Cuisine prepared by these budding chefs is served up to the public in the institute's 50-seat dining room. The quality of the food is impossible to fault, and its presentation is also impeccable. Lunch is offered weekdays 11:30 A.M.–2 P.M. and dinner Monday–Saturday 6–9 P.M. The three-course set menus are a bargain at $22 and $34 respectively.

ROBSON STREET AND THE WEST END

Linking downtown to the West End, Robson Street holds the city's largest concentration of eateries, including dozens of cafés sprinkling the sidewalks with outdoor tables—perfect for people-watching.

Seafood

Joe Fortes Seafood and Chophouse (777 Thurlow St., 604/669-1940, daily 11:30 A.M.–10:30 P.M.) is a city institution. The comfortable interior offers elegant furnishings, bleached-linen tablecloths, a rooftop patio, and an oyster bar where you can relax while waiting for your table. At lunch, the grilled fish goes for $14–18. The dinner menu is slightly more expensive. While the oysters at Joe's are hard to beat, those at the **Olympia Seafood Market and Grill** (820 Thurlow, 604/685-0716, daily 11 A.M.–8 P.M.) come pretty close. Eat in or take out.

Bud's Halibut and Chips (1007 Denman St., 604/683-0661, daily 11 A.M.–10 P.M.) has been serving up battered fish and crispy fries for over 20 years. The portions are generous, and all fish comes with a massive dollop of creamy tartar sauce. One piece of halibut and chips is just $5. If you want to eat down on the beach, the staff will happily wrap your meal in paper for you.

West Coast

Head for the West End for fine First Nations cuisine at the native-owned and -operated **Liliget Feast House** (1724 Davie St., 604/681-7044, daily 5–10 P.M.). The dining room is styled on a traditional longhouse. Peeled cedar columns rise from the hardwood floor, native artwork adorns the walls, and traditional music plays softly in the background. Menu items include *oolichan* in lemon butter, bannock bread, a traditional salmon soup, seafood or caribou barbecued over an alderwood fire, and steamed fern shoots. Dining here isn't particularly cheap, but it's an experience you won't forget in a hurry. Most people opt for the Liliget Feast Platter (salmon and game such as venison and buffalo), which lets you sample a variety of delicacies ($56 for two).

Chicken

For chicken cooked to perfection, head to **Rooster's Quarters** (836 Denman St., 604/689-8023), a casual eatery chock-full of chicken

picnicking at Stanley Park's Third Beach

memorabilia. A full chicken with accompanying vegetables and fries (for two) is a reasonable $19.

European

Diners at **Marbella** (1368 Robson St., 604/681-1175, lunch Tues.–Sat., dinner Tues.–Sun.) eat from stylish tiled tables, listen to traditional music, and generally immerse themselves in the culture of Spain. The 20 tapas range $2.50–5 each, while the rest of the menu features entrées from $14.50. Try the Spanish-style soup at lunch.

CinCin (1154 Robson St., 604/688-7338) is a Mediterranean-style restaurant with a loyal local following. The specialty is pizza cooked in a wood-fired oven (from $14), but the oven is also used to cook dishes such as halibut roasted in a lightly flavored mint broth and accompanied by fresh mussels ($35). This restaurant has been honored by dozens of awards, including for its wine list, featuring over 300 well-priced choices. It's open for lunch Monday–Saturday and daily for dinner.

Café de Paris (745 Denman St., 604/687-1418, lunch Mon.–Fri., dinner daily) is an intimate yet casual city-style French bistro. Classic French main courses (don't dare call them entrées at this very French restaurant) range $19–30, but the daily three-course table d'hôte is the best value at around $29. Wines offered are almost exclusively French.

KITSILANO

Biceps and butts are the order of the day along trendy Kitsilano Beach, and when the beautiful people have finished sunning themselves they head across the road to **Malone's Bar and Grill** (2202 Cornwall Ave., 604/737-7777) for cold drinks and pub fare.

Cool and Casual

Away from the beach, cafés line West 4th Avenue between Burrard and Vine Streets. This part of the city was the heart of hippiedom 30 years ago, and while most restaurants from that era are long gone, a few remain, and other, newer additions to the local dining scene reflect that period of the city's history. **Sophie's Cosmic Café** (2095 W. 4th Ave. at Arbutus St., 604/732-

6810, daily 8 A.M.–9:30 P.M.) typifies the scene, with a definite "cosmic" look, but also providing good value (daily specials under $10). Expect a wait for Sunday breakfast.

Vegetarian

A throwback to the hippie era of the 1960s is **Naam** (2724 W. 4th Ave. at Stephens St., 604/738-7151), a particularly good natural-food restaurant in a renovated two-story private residence. Boasting large servings, excellent service, and an easy-going atmosphere that has become legendary, it's open 24 hours a day, every day of the week. Veggie burgers start at $5, while full meals range $8–13.

Surat Sweet (1938 W. 4th Ave. between Cypress and Maple Streets, 604/733-7363, Tues.–Sat. lunch and dinner) needs a coat of paint, but the decor plays second fiddle to the food, which is remarkably inexpensive. The menu is entirely vegetarian and vegan—even eggs aren't used. Apart from the curries, most diners will be unfamiliar with many of the dishes, such as *bhajia*, a deep-fried potato dish covered in a coconut chutney ($6.50).

European

The much-lauded **Bishop's** (2183 W. 4th Ave., 604/738-2025, daily 5:30–10 P.M.) is very French in all aspects. Owner and longtime Vancouver restaurateur John Bishop makes all diners feel special, personally greeting them at the door, escorting them to their table, and then describing the menu and wine list as required. Elegant surroundings, starched white linen, and soft jazz background music complete the picture. The menu features French classics, but changes as seasonal foods such as salmon and halibut become available. Expect to pay around $100 for three courses for two. Reservations required.

NORTH SHORE

If you've crossed Burrard Inlet on the SeaBus, visit **Lonsdale Market** for local produce, including a couple of market stalls selling seafood fresh from the trawlers. Lonsdale Avenue, which climbs from the waterfront to the residential heart of North Vancouver, holds many eateries on its lower end.

Seafood

On the north side of Burrard Inlet, **Salmon House on the Hill** (2229 Folkstone Way, West Vancouver, 604/926-3212, Mon.–Sat. 11:30 A.M.–2:30 P.M., daily from 5 P.M., and Sun. brunch 11 A.M.–2:30 P.M.) offers a relaxed atmosphere while providing panoramic views to Stanley Park and the city center from its elevated mountainside location. The intriguing interior is full of northwest coast native arts and crafts—including a dugout canoe suspended over the main dining area. Out front, a rhododendron garden blooms in stark contrast to the surrounding forest of Douglas fir. For an appetizer, the seafood chowder ($7.25) is my recommendation—it's thick, creamy, and delicious. The house specialty of salmon barbecued over an open-flame, alderwood-fired grill is hard to go past as an entrée ($24–27). Sunday brunch is a popular affair. Choose an omelet and your own fillings or try the smoked-salmon eggs Benedict; both are $14.

Information and Services

Many organizations make planning a trip to Vancouver easy. Tourism Vancouver (604/682-2222, www.tourismvancouver.com) promotes the city throughout the world. Their website is an excellent source of information for pretrip planning—what there is to do and see, an online booking form for accommodations, a currency converter, weekly event updates, and more.

Downtown

The city's main information center is **Vancouver Visitor Info Centre** (one block from Canada Place at 200 Burrard St., 604/683-2000, May–Sept. daily 8 A.M.–6 P.M., rest of year Mon.–Sat. 8:30 A.M.–5:30 P.M.). Brochures line the lower level, while on the upper level specially trained staff members provide free maps, brochures, and public transportation schedules; book sightseeing tours; and make accommodations reservations. In summer, information booths also operate in Stanley Park and downtown on the corner of Granville and Georgia Streets.

Other Information Centers and Contacts

Information centers are dotted throughout Vancouver. Run by local chambers of commerce, they are usually open daily in summer and weekdays only the rest of the year. They are all well signposted along major thoroughfares.

If you approach Vancouver from the south on Highway 5 (Highway 99 in Canada), the first official information center you'll come to is the **Peace Arch Visitor Info Centre** (July–Aug. daily 8 A.M.–8 P.M., rest of year daily 9 A.M.–5 P.M.). Also on the south side of the city is the **Delta Visitor Info Centre** (6201 60th Ave., 604/946-4232, www.deltachamber.com) and another operated by **Tourism Richmond** (604/271-8280 or 877/247-0777, www.tourismrichmond.com).

On the North Shore, look for a small information booth at Lonsdale Quay or stop at the **North Vancouver Visitor Info Centre,** along Marine Drive between the Lions Gate Bridge and Lonsdale Quay (131 E. 2nd St., 604/987-4488, www.nvchamber.bc.ca).

East

If you're approaching the city from the east along Highway 1, **Chilliwack Visitor Info Centre** (44150 Luckakuck Way, 604/858-8121 or 800/567-9535, www.tourismchilliwack.com) is a good place to stop, stretch your legs, and gather some brochures. Continuing toward the city you'll find **Abbotsford Visitor Info Centre** (take Exit 92 to 2462 McCallum Rd., 604/859-1721, www.abbotsfordchamber.com), **Langley Visitor Info Centre** (take Exit 66 south to 5761 Glover Rd., 604/530-6656, www.langleychamber.com), and the **New Westminster Visitor Info Centre** (810 Quayside Dr., 604/526-1905, www.tourism newwestminster.org).

BOOKS, MAGAZINES, AND NEWSPAPERS

Vancouver Public Library

The magnificent nine-story Vancouver Public Library (350 W. Georgia St., 604/331-3603, Mon.–Thurs. 10 A.M.–8 P.M., Fri.–Sat. 10 A.M.–5 P.M., and also Sun. 1–5 P.M. Oct.–Apr.) features an elliptical facade containing a glass-walled promenade rising six stories above a row of stylish indoor shops and cafés. Once inside, you'll soon discover that the city not only had enough money to build one of the world's great modern libraries, but also had enough left over to stock the shelves—the library holds over one million books. To help you find that one book you're searching for, use the self-guided tour brochure available at the information desk.

More than 20 other affiliated libraries are spread across the city. Call 604/331-3600 or go to www.vpl.vancouver.bc.ca for addresses and opening hours. One branch library of particular interest is the **Carnegie Reading Room** (corner of East Hastings and Main Streets). It is named for its benefactor, U.S. philanthropist Andrew Carnegie, whose $50,000 donation went a long way toward its 1902 completion as Vancouver's first permanent library.

General Bookstores

Per capita, residents of Vancouver buy more books than the residents of any other North American city. And they buy them from a huge number of bookstores scattered throughout the city. The Canadian bookstore giant **Indigo/Chapters** has multiple Vancouver stores, each stocking over 100,000 titles. Public-accessible computers help search out particular subjects, authors, and titles. The stores maintain a large collection of local and Canadian fiction and nonfiction, an extensive newsstand, discounted books, and an in-store Starbucks coffeehouse. Downtown, Chapters is at 788 Robson St. (at Howe St., 604/682-4066) and south of False Creek at 2505 Granville St. (at Broadway, 604/731-7822).

Two of the best independent bookstores are **Duthie Books** (2239 W. 4th Ave., Kitsilano, 604/732-5344, www.duthiebooks.com, Mon.–Fri. 9 A.M.–9 P.M., Sat. 9 A.M.–6 P.M., Sun. 10 A.M.–6 P.M.) and, on Granville Island, **Blackberry Books** (1663 Duranleau St., 604/685-6188, www.bbooks.ca, daily 9 A.M.–6 P.M.). To save a few bucks on current titles or pick up new books at bargain prices, search out the **Book Warehouse** in the heart of the central business district at 550 Granville Street (604/683-5711), southwest of downtown at 1181 Davie Street (604/685-5711), or farther out at 632 W. Broadway (604/872-5711) and 2388 West 4th Avenue (604/734-5711).

Travel Bookstores

International Travel Maps & Books (downtown at 539 West Pender St., 604/687-3320, www.itmb.com, Mon.–Fri. 10 A.M.–6 P.M., Sat. 10 A.M.–5 P.M.) is the city's most central specialty travel bookstore. Another, smaller branch of International Travel Maps & Books is at 530 W. Broadway (604/879-3621). With over 10,000 titles, Canada's largest travel bookstore is **Wanderlust** (just west of Cypress St. at 1929 W. 4th Ave., Kitsilano, 604/739-2182 or 866/739-2182, www.wanderlustore.com, Mon.–Fri. 10 A.M.–7 P.M., Sat. 10 A.M.–5 P.M., Sun. noon–5 P.M.). As well as general travel guides, Wanderlust stocks maps, atlases, and a range of travel accessories. Also in Kits is **Travel Bug** (3065 W. Broadway, 604/737-1122, www.travelbugbooks.ca).

Secondhand and Antiquarian Bookstores

Vancouver has some fantastic secondhand bookstores, including a few specializing entirely in nonfiction. The largest concentration lies along West Pender Street between Richards and Hamilton Streets. They include **Macleod's Books** (455 W. Pender St., 604/681-7654), which stocks a wide range of antiquarian titles, among them many of the earliest works on western Canada; **Criterion Books** (434 W. Pender St., 604/685-2224), stocking newer titles, but the western Canada section is just as good; and **Stephen C. Lunsford Books** (corner of W. Hastings and Hamilton Streets, 604/681-6830), with plenty of old Canadian nonfiction titles.

Newspapers and Periodicals

Vancouver's two newspapers are the *Province* and the *Vancouver Sun,* and you'll find links to online versions of both at www.canada.com/vancouver. *Georgia Straight* is a free weekly featuring articles on local issues, as well as a full entertainment rundown for the city.

SERVICES

Emergency Services

For emergencies call 911. For medical emergencies contact **St. Paul's Hospital** (1081 Burrard St., 604/682-2344), which has an emergency ward open 24 hours a day, seven days a week. Other major hospitals are **Vancouver General Hospital** (899 W. 12th Ave., 604/875-4111), **Lions Gate Hospital** (231 E. 15th St., 604/988-3131), and **Seymour Medical Clinic** (1530 W. 7th Ave., 604/738-2151). For the **RCMP** call 911 or 604/264-3111.

Visitors with Disabilities

For information on travel considerations for visitors with disabilities, contact the British Columbia chapter of the **Canadian Paraplegic Association** (604/324-3611, www.canparaplegic .org). In general, visitors with disabilities are well cared for, with most major hotels taking disabilities into consideration. Vancouver's public transit system, Translink, has HandyDART buses that provide door-to-door wheelchair-accessible service for about the same price you'd pay on regular buses (call 604/453-4634 for bookings), and the SkyTrain and SeaBus are wheelchair accessible. **Vancouver Taxi** (604/871-1111) has wheelchair-accommodating cabs.

Post Offices

Vancouver's main post office is at 349 W. Georgia Street (604/662-5722). It's open Monday–Saturday. Postal Station A (757 W. Hastings St.) and the branch at Bentall Centre (595 Burrard St.) are also open on Saturdays.

Money Exchange

Custom House (200 Granville St., 604/608-1763, Mon.–Fri. 9 A.M.–5 P.M., Sat.–Sun. 10 A.M.–5 P.M.) is a centrally located currency exchange. They have another bureau in Canada Place that's closed weekends.

Telephone and Internet

Local calls from public phones cost 35 cents; long-distance calls are much more expensive. The area code for Vancouver and the southwest mainland is 604, while the rest of the province, including Vancouver Island, is 250.

Downtown Internet cafés include **Internet Coffee** (1104 Davie St., 604/682-6668) and **Webster's Internet Café** (opposite the library at 340 Robson St., 604/915-9327).

Transportation

GETTING THERE
By Air

Vancouver International Airport (www.yvr.ca) is on Sea Island, 15 kilometers (9.3 mi.) south of Vancouver city center. Over 16 million passengers pass through the terminal annually. The newish (1996) three-story International Terminal and adjacent Domestic Terminal hold coffee shops and restaurants, car-rental agencies, a post office, currency exchanges, newsstands, gift shops, and duty-free shops. Numerous information boards provide a quick airport orientation, and an information booth on Level 3 of the International Terminal offers tourist brochures, bus schedules, and taxi information.

The **Vancouver Airporter** (604/946-8866 or 800/668-3141, www.yvrairporter.com) leaves the Arrivals level of both terminals every 15–30 minutes between 6:30 A.M. and midnight daily, shuttling passengers along three routes between the airport and more than 40 downtown accommodations and Pacific Central Station. The one-way fare is adult $12, senior $9, child $5, with a slight discount offered for a round-trip purchase. Buy tickets from the driver or from the ticket offices on the Arrivals levels of both terminals. To get to downtown by public transport, jump aboard bus no. 100 (Midway Connector) on Level 3 (basic fare $2.25) and get off at 70th Street and Granville, then take bus no. 20 (Vancouver) to downtown. A cab from the airport to downtown takes 25 minutes or more and runs around $30. Cabs line up curbside on the Arrivals level of both the international and domestic terminals 24 hours daily.

Canada's national airline, **Air Canada** (604/688-5515 or 888/247-2262, www.aircanada.ca), has the most flights to Vancouver from international destinations. Another Canadian airline serving Vancouver International Airport, **WestJet** (604/606-5525 or 800/538-5696, www.westjet.com), is based at Abbotsford, 72 kilometers (45 mi.) east of downtown, but flies to and from both destinations. Air Canada offers the most flights into Vancouver from the United States, but the city is also served by the U.S. carriers listed in the On the Road chapter.

By Rail and Bus

The **VIA Rail** (888/842-7245, www.viarail.ca) terminus is **Pacific Central Station** (1150 Station St.), two kilometers (1.2 mi.) southeast of downtown. This is also the main **Greyhound** (604/482-8747 or 800/661-8747, www.greyhound.ca) bus depot, with daily service to points throughout western Canada and beyond. Also from here, **Pacific Coach Lines** (604/662-8074 or 800/661-1725, www.pacificcoach.com) runs bus service to Victoria.

Pacific Central Station is a $7 cab ride or just a few minutes on the SkyTrain from downtown. Inside you'll find a currency exchange, cash machines, lockers, a newsstand, information boards, and a McDonald's.

GETTING AROUND
Translink

Translink (604/953-3333, www.translink.bc.ca) operates an extensive network of buses, trains, and ferries that can get you just about anywhere you want to go within Vancouver. The free brochure *Discover Vancouver on Transit* is available from all city information centers and is an invaluable source of information. The brochure includes details of many attractions and how to reach them by public transportation.

Buses run to all corners of the city between 5 A.M. and 2 A.M. every day of the year. **SkyTrain** is a computer-operated (no drivers) light-rail transit system that runs along two lines—the Expo Line from downtown through New Westminster and over the Fraser River to Surrey and the Millennium Line to Westminster then back

FERRYING OUT OF TOWN

Vancouver has two ferry terminals, with services heading out of the city to **Vancouver Island** and the **Sunshine Coast.** All ferries are operated by **BC Ferries** (250/386-3431 or 888/223-3779, www.bcferries.com) and reservations (select routes only) can be made online or by phone. In high season (June–Sept.), the ferries run about once an hour, 7 A.M.–10 P.M. The rest of the year they run a little less frequently. Expect a wait in summer, particularly if you have an oversized vehicle (each ferry can accommodate far fewer large vehicles than standard-size cars and trucks).

Tsawwassen Ferry Terminal
Located 30 km (18.8 miles) south of downtown Vancouver, ferries run from Tsawwassen to the **Southern Gulf Islands; Swartz Bay,** 32 km (20 km) north of Victoria, Vancouver Island; and to **Nanaimo,** also on Vancouver Island. To get to the terminal from downtown, follow Highway 17 south—in summer this road gets crazy with traffic. Buses also link the ferry terminal with downtown; catch no. 601 from downtown.

Horseshoe Bay Terminal
The other ferry route linking the mainland to Vancouver Island runs between Horseshoe Bay and **Nanaimo.** Horseshoe Bay is on the north side of Burrard Inlet, a 20-minute drive northwest of downtown. You don't save any money on this route—the fares are the same—and the wait is often longer. This is also the departure point for ferries to the **Sunshine Coast.**

to downtown via Coquitlam—from four underground city-center stations. The double-ended, 400-passenger **SeaBus** links downtown Vancouver to North Vancouver in just 12 minutes. The downtown terminus is **Waterfront Station**, beside Canada Place and a five-minute walk from the Vancouver Visitor Info Centre.

On weekdays between 5:30 A.M. and 6:30 P.M. the city is divided into three zones (Zone 1 encompasses downtown and Greater Vancouver; Zone 2 covers all the North Shore, Burnaby, New Westminster, and Richmond; and Zone 3 extends to the limits of the Translink system), and fares vary for each sector: adult $3–5, senior $1.50–3. After 6:30 P.M., all weekend travel anywhere in the city costs $2. Pay the driver (exact change only) for bus travel or purchase tickets from machines at any SkyTrain station or SeaBus terminal. A DayPass costs adult $8, senior $6 and allows unlimited travel for one day anywhere on the Translink system. They are available at all SeaBus and SkyTrain stations and FareDealers (convenience stores such as 7-Eleven and Mac's) throughout the city.

Vancouver Trolley Company

From the main pick-up point, a trolley-shaped booth at the top end of Water Street, this company (604/801-5515 or 888/451-5581, www .vancouvertrolley.com) operates an old-fashioned trolley through the streets of downtown Vancouver. The two-hour City Attractions Loop Tour stops at 23 tourist attractions, from Stanley Park in the north to Science World in the south. Trolleys run April–October daily 9 A.M.–4 P.M., coming by each stop every half hour. Tickets are adult $26, child $13. Reservations aren't necessary.

Boat

Apart from the SeaBus (see *Translink*), the only other scheduled ferry services within the city are on False Creek. Two private companies, **Granville Island Ferries** (604/684-7781) and **Aquabus** (604/689-5858), operate on this narrow waterway. From the main hub of Granville Island, ferries run every 15 minutes to the foot of Hornby Street, and under the Burrard Street Bridge to the Aquatic Center (at the south end of Thurlow Street) and Vanier Park (Vancouver Museum). Every 30–60 minutes both companies also run down the head of False Creek to Stamps Landing, the Plaza of Nations, and Science World. Fares range $3–5 each way, with discounts for seniors and kids; schedules are posted at all docking points.

Taxi

Cabs are easiest to catch outside major hotels or transportation hubs. Fares in Vancouver are a uniform $2.30 flag charge plus $1.25 per kilometer (plus 30 cents per minute when stopped). Trips within downtown usually run under $10. The trip between the airport and downtown is $30. A 10–15 percent tip to the driver is expected. Major companies include **Black Top** (800/494-1111), **Vancouver Taxi** (888/871-8294), and **Yellow Cab** (604/681-1111 or 800/898-8294). A number of wheelchair-accommodating taxicabs are available from Vancouver Taxi, with fares the same as regular taxis.

Car Rental

Vancouver is full of car-rental agencies offering a wide range of vehicles, prices, and deals. Some throw in extras such as coupon books giving you discounts at attractions and certain restaurants. All major companies have outlets at the airport and downtown. Rental agencies and their local numbers include **Avis** (604/606-2869), **Budget** (604/668-7000), **Discount** (604/310-2277), **Dollar** (604/689-5303), **Enterprise** (604/688-5500), **Hertz** (604/606-3700), **Locost** (604/689-9664), **National** (604/609-7150), **Rent-A-Wreck** (604/688-0001), and **Thrifty** (604/647-4599). See Internet Resources at the back of this book for websites.

Bicycle

Downtown Vancouver is not particularly bicycle friendly, but nearby areas such as Stanley Park and the coastline west of Kitsilano are perfect places for pedal power. The main concentration of rental shops surrounds the corner of Robson and Denman Streets, two blocks from Stanley Park. Expect to pay from $7 per hour or $20 per day for the most basic mountain bike and $12 per hour or $40 per day for a front-suspension mountain bike. Most of the shops also rent in-line skates and tandem bikes. Companies are **Alley Cat Rentals** (1779 Robson St., 604/684-5117), **Bayshore Bicycles** (745 Denman St., 604/688-2453), and **Stanley Park Rentals** (1798 W. Georgia St., 604/688-5141).

TOURS

If you don't have a lot of time to explore Vancouver on your own, or just want an introduction to the city, consider one of the many tours available—they'll maximize your time and get you to the highlights with minimum stress.

Bus Tours

Gray Line (604/879-3363 or 800/667-0882, www.grayline.ca) offers a large variety of tours. The 3.5-hour Deluxe Grand City Tour (adult $45, child $31) includes Stanley Park, Grouse Mountain, Chinatown, Gastown, Robson Street, and English Bay. Another option with Gray Line is a downtown loop tour aboard an old English double-decker bus. You can get on and off as you please at 22 stops made on the two-hour loop (adult $27, child $15), and tickets are valid for two consecutive days. Farther afield, Gray Line has daily tours from Vancouver to Whistler ($79) and a 12-hour tour to Vancouver Island ($117). All ticket prices include pick-ups at major downtown hotels.

Harbor Cruises

From June to September, **Harbour Cruises** (604/688-7246 or 800/663-1500, www.boatcruises.com) offers a 70-minute tour of bustling Burrard Inlet on the paddlewheeler MV *Constitution*. Tours depart from the north foot of Denman Street, Coal Harbour, three times daily (adult $20, child $16). In the evening (7 P.M. departure), the paddlewheeler heads out onto the harbor for a three-hour Sunset Dinner Cruise. The cruise costs $69, which includes dinner and, if booked through Gray Line (604/879-3363), hotel transfers.

Flightseeing

Flightseeing tours of the city are offered in floatplanes by **Harbour Air** (west side of Canada Place, 604/274-1277). A 20-minute flight is $89 pp, or include the Sunshine Coast one-hour flight for $215.

Vicinity of Vancouver

Once you've reluctantly decided to drag yourself away from Vancouver, you'll be confronted by a variety of things to see and do within a day's drive of the city.

North of Vancouver and only accessible by ferry, the Sunshine Coast is perfect for swimming, sunbathing on sandy beaches, canoeing and kayaking, beachcombing, scuba diving, boating, and fishing. Spectacular Highway 99, the aptly named Sea to Sky Highway, leads you northeast out of Vancouver to the resort town of Whistler. This year-round outdoor-sports destination offers outstanding opportunities for hiking, biking, golfing, fishing, and other warm-weather pursuits. But it's best known for its alpine resort: Whistler/Blackcomb.

From Vancouver two routes head east through the fertile and obviously agricultural

BRITISH COLUMBIA

VICINITY OF VANCOUVER

To Kamloops
Quilchena
Coalmont
Princeton
Merritt
Cache Creek
Manning Provincial Park
COQUIHALLA HWY.
Thompson River
Ashcroft
Lytton
Fraser River
HELL'S GATE ★
Yale
Hope
Chilliwack
CANADA
UNITED STATES
Lillooet
Harrison Lake
Sasquatch Provincial Park
D'Arcy
Harrison Hot Springs
Mission
Abbotsford
Gold Bridge
Mount Currie
Nairn Falls Provincial Park
Stave Lake
Golden Ears Provincial Park
Pemberton
Garibaldi Provincial Park
Alice Lake Provincial Park
Pitt Lake
FORT LANGLEY N.H.S. ★
Whistler
THE CHIEF
Brandywine Falls Provincial Park
Britannia Beach
Porteau Cove Provincial Park
Horseshoe Bay
Brackendale
Squamish
Howe Sound
VANCOUVER
Georgia
Egmont
Skookumchuck Narrows P.P.
Gibsons
Sechelt
Saltery Bay
Powell River
Texada Island
Malaspina Strait
Strait
Nanaimo
To Victoria
Lund
Desolation Sound
Vancouver Island

15 mi
15 km

© AVALON TRAVEL PUBLISHING, INC.

Fraser River Valley, converging at Hope. After exploring Hope's spectacular canyon formations, you have another choice of routes: north along the Fraser River Canyon, northeast to Kamloops along the Coquihalla Highway, or east along Highway 3 to the picturesque lakes and alpine meadows of Manning Provincial Park.

The Sunshine Coast

The 150-kilometer (93-mi.) Sunshine Coast lies along the northeast shore of the Strait of Georgia between Howe Sound in the south and Desolation Sound in the north. This rare bit of sun-drenched Canadian coastline is bordered by countless bays and inlets, broad sandy beaches, quiet lagoons, rugged headlands, provincial parks, and lush fir forests backed by the snowcapped Coast Mountains. Boasting Canada's mildest climate, the Sunshine Coast enjoys moderately warm summers and mild winters. Boaters and kayakers can cruise into a number of beautiful marine parks providing sheltered anchorage and campsites amid some of the most magnificent scenery along the west coast, or anchor at sheltered fishing villages with marinas and all the modern conveniences.

Gibsons

A delightful hillside community of 4,000 a two-minute drive from the ferry dock at Langdale, Gibsons has two sections: the original 100-year-old fishing village around the harbor and a commercial corridor along the highway. Around the harbor, Gower Point Road is a charming strip of seafaring businesses, antique dealers, arty shops, and cafés. Down on the harbor itself is a marina and the pleasant Gibsons Seawalk, a scenic 10-minute meander (lighted at night).

Elphinstone Pioneer Museum (716 Winn Rd., 604/886-8232, summer daily 9 A.M.–5 P.M.) features Coast Salish displays and holds what must be one of the largest seashell collections on the planet (some 25,000).

Gibsons has a surprisingly good selection of eateries, most in the original part of town on a hill above the marina. For homestyle cooking at reasonable prices, try the **Waterfront Restaurant** (442 Marine Dr., 604/886-2831) overlooking the marina. **Gibsons Visitor Info Centre** is at the east entrance to town (604/886-2325, daily 9 A.M.–5 P.M.).

Sechelt and Vicinity

The native cultural center and regional service center of Sechelt (pop. 7,800) perches on the isthmus of the Sechelt Peninsula between the head of Sechelt Inlet and the Strait of Georgia. At nearby **Porpoise Bay Provincial Park,** four kilometers (2.5 mi.) north of town, you'll find a broad, sheltered sandy beach along the eastern shore of Sechelt Inlet. Hiking trails connect the

> ## FERRYING ALONG THE SUNSHINE COAST
>
> Although the Sunshine Coast is part of the mainland, there is no road access. To reach Powell River, at the end of the road, entails travel with **BC Ferries** (250/386-3431 or 888/223-3779). From Horseshoe Bay, at the west end of Vancouver's north shore, ferries regularly cross Howe Sound to **Langdale.** From there Highway 101 runs up the coast 81 kilometers (50 mi.) to **Earls Cove,** where another ferry crosses Jervis Inlet to **Saltery Bay.** These trips take 40 and 50 minutes respectively and run approximately every two hours between 6:30 A.M. and 11:30 P.M. The cost is adult $8.25, child $4.25, vehicle $28.75, which includes one-way travel on both ferries or round-trip travel on just one ferry. From Saltery Bay, it's 35 kilometers (22 mi.) to Powell River, and you can return from there along the same route or loop back on Vancouver Island on the Powell River–Comox ferry (adult $7.75, child $4, vehicle $26). The Circlepac fare is designed for those who plan to complete this loop. Savings are around 15 percent and the only catch is that you must travel outside of peak hours.

beach with a day-use area and campground, and a woodland trail meanders along the bank of Angus Creek, where chum and coho salmon spawn in fall. Out of town to the west, **Lord Jim's Resort Hotel** (604/885-7038 or 877/296-4593, www.lordjims.com) is a waterfront complex overlooking Halfmoon Bay. It features a wonderful restaurant (both for the food and the view) and rooms from $115 s, $145 d.

Pender Harbour to Earls Cove
Pender Harbour is orca habitat. These highly intelligent gentle giants, also known as "killer whales," travel in pods of up to 100. Feeding on salmon found year-round in these waters, they grow up to nine meters (29.6 ft.) long, weighing as much as eight tons. Keep your eyes on the water and your camera ready to capture their triangular dorsal fins slicing through the waves.

Just before Earls Cove, take the road north to Egmont, then the 3.5-kilometer (2.1-mi.) hiking trail along Sechelt Inlet to **Skookumchuck Narrows Provincial Park.** Meaning "turbulent water" in Chinook, Skookumchuck is a narrow, rock-strewn waterway where tidal water roars through four times a day. The resulting rapids and eddies boisterously boil and bubble to create fierce-looking whirlpools—fascinating to see when your feet are firmly planted on terra firma. You'll also see abundant marine creatures in tidal pools—it's a fascinating spot. Take a picnic lunch, pull up a rock, and enjoy the view.

Earls Cove marks the end of this section of Highway 101. From here, BC Ferries offers regular service across Jervis Inlet to Saltery Bay. The 16-kilometer (10-mi.) crossing takes 50 minutes.

Saltery Bay and Vicinity
Less than two kilometers (1.2 mi.) from the Saltery Bay ferry terminal is 140-hectare (346-acre) **Saltery Bay Provincial Park,** one of the Sunshine Coast's diving hot spots. Waters off the park are accessible from the shore and are full of marine life, including a bronze mermaid. The park also features good beaches and salmon fishing (from late April). Camping is $14 per night.

From Saltery Bay, it's 31 kilometers (19.2 mi.) of winding road to Powell River. Along the way

you'll cross **Lois River,** the outlet for large Lois Lake, and pass a string of coastal communities clinging to the rocky shoreline of Malaspina Strait.

POWELL RIVER AND VICINITY
Situated between Jervis Inlet and Desolation Sound along the edge of Malaspina Strait, Powell River (pop. 16,500) is almost surrounded by water. It's a thriving center for the region's abundant outdoor recreation opportunities, including salmon fishing (good year-round), trout fishing, scuba diving, sailing, canoeing, kayaking, and hiking. Through downtown (also called Westview) is the original townsite, occupied by an ugly waterfront pulp mill and a number of boarded-up buildings.

Sights and Walks
Visiting the excellent **Powell River Historical Museum** (Marine Ave., 604/485-2222, summer daily 10 A.M.–5 P.M., rest of year Mon.–Fri. only) is like wandering back in time. Peruse the vast collection of photographs (the province's third-largest archives) and other displays to learn about this seashore community and to see what the area was like before the town was established. Also see well-preserved artifacts, native carvings and baskets, and the shanty home of a hermit who once lived along Powell Lake.

While most visitors to Powell River spend their time enjoying water-oriented sports, the hiking around town is also good—and chances are you'll have the trails to yourself. From Powell River's municipal campground, the one-kilometer (0.6-mi.) **Willingdon Beach Trail** spurs north past interpretive boards describing natural features. The trail ends at a viewpoint overlooking the historic townsite and pulp operations. The **Sunshine Coast Trail** extends 180 kilometers (112 mi.) from Saltery Bay to Sarah Point, beyond Powell River and north of Lund. Most hikers complete just sections of the trail. For trail details, visit www.sunshinecoast-trail.com.

Fishing and Diving
Saltwater fishing for chinook salmon is good year-round, but it's particularly good in autumn and midwinter. Coho salmon usually arrive around

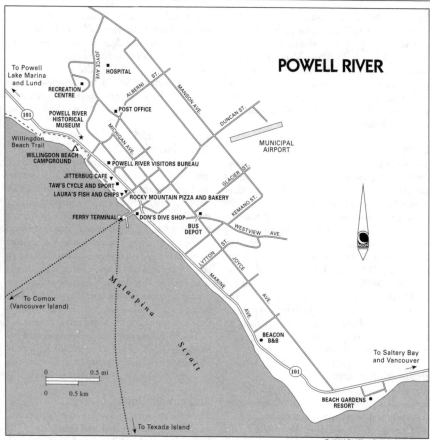

POWELL RIVER

To Powell
Lake Marina
and Lund

JOYCE AVE.

HOSPITAL

RECREATION
CENTRE

ALBERNI ST.

MANSON AVE.

DUNCAN ST.

POWELL RIVER
HISTORICAL
MUSEUM

POST OFFICE

MICHIGAN AVE.

MUNICIPAL
AIRPORT

Willingdon
Beach Trail

WILLINGDON BEACH
CAMPGROUND

POWELL RIVER VISITORS BUREAU

GLACIER ST.

JITTERBUG CAFE

TAW'S CYCLE AND SPORT

LAURA'S FISH AND CHIPS

ROCKY MOUNTAIN PIZZA AND BAKERY

KEMANO ST.

FERRY TERMINAL

DON'S DIVE SHOP

BUS
DEPOT

WESTVIEW AVE.

Malaspina

LYTTON ST.

JOYCE

To Comox
(Vancouver Island)

MARINE

AVE.

Strait

BEACON
B&B

To Saltery Bay
and Vancouver

0   0.5 mi

0   0.5 km

101

BEACH GARDENS
RESORT

To Texada Island

MooN

© AVALON TRAVEL PUBLISHING, INC.

BRITISH COLUMBIA

April or May. Sport anglers also pursue red snapper, perch, flatfish, ling cod, and rockfish. Dangle a line from the wharf, docks, or breakwaters, or hurl it out from the shore. Local tackle stores include **Marine Traders** (6791 Wharf St., 604/485-4624) and **Taw's Cycle and Sport** (4597 Marine Ave., 604/485-2555).

Known as the "Diving Capital of Canada," the Strait of Georgia provides divers with exceptionally clear, relatively warm water and more than 100 exciting dives mapped by local experts. Conditions are particularly excellent in winter, when visibility reaches 30 meters (100 ft.). Expect to see underwater cliffs and abundant marine life, including sponges, giant octopuses, wolf eels, perch, ling cod, tubeworms, sea anemones, nudibranchs (including intriguing hooded nudibranchs), sea stars, crabs, and tunicates. The highlight for wreck divers on the Sunshine Coast is the HMCS *Chaudiere,* through which giant holes have been cut to enable adventurous divers to do some inside exploration.

Diving gear and a list of charter operators are available at **Don's Dive Shop** (4552 Willingdon Ave., 604/483-3456, www.donsdiveshop.com). Beach Gardens Resort is a popular diver's hangout.

Canoeing and Kayaking

The many inland waterways along the Sunshine Coast provide opportunities for canoeing and kayaking. One of the best-known local paddles is the **Powell Forest Canoe Route,** a four- to eight-day backcountry trip that requires a few portages, or just paddle a single section. **Mitchell's Guided Tours** (604/487-1699, www.canoeingbc.com) provides a wide range of services for paddlers, including canoe rentals ($27 per day) and other accessories, shuttles to and from launch sites, and a three-day guided paddle ($299 pp).

Lund

Twenty-eight kilometers (17.4 mi.) north of Powell River, Highway 101 dead-ends on the old wooden wharf of Lund, a tiny fishing village founded in 1889. The drive out is well worth it for the relaxed atmosphere and surrounding beauty—wander around the marina or cruise over to the white sand beaches of **Savary Island** by water taxi (departs 4–5 times daily, $10 round-trip; 604/483-9749). The **Historic Lund Hotel** (604/483-2400, www.lundhotel.com; from $95 s, $105 d) sits right beside the marina and offers small but comfortable rooms above a row of waterfront shops. Even if you don't stay overnight, take advantage of the hotel's magnificent deck by stopping by for lunch.

Desolation Sound

Named by Captain Vancouver in 1792—he was obviously unimpressed—much of this remote waterway is now protected as a marine park. A wilderness-seeker's paradise, the park is totally undeveloped and without road access.

The sheltered waters of **Okeover Arm**—a southern arm of Desolation Sound—are much more accessible, with road access along Malaspina Road, off Highway 101 south of Lund. Forested four-hectare (10-acre) **Okeover Arm Provincial Park** lies on the water; it's a small, rustic park with just a few undeveloped campsites ($12), a pit toilet, and a kayak- and boat-launching ramp, but it's a great spot to camp if you're into canoeing or kayaking.

North of the park **Desolation Resort** (2694 Dawson Rd., 604/483-3592, www.desolation resort.com) offers a wonderful escape at reasonable prices. Accommodation is in freestanding wood chalets set high above the lake edge on stilts. All

feature rich-colored wood furnishings, and even the smallest (the bottom half of one unit) has a king-size bed, large deck, kitchen, separate living and dining areas, and a barbecue. Rates start at just $120 for the unit detailed above. Chalet 7 ($230 in summer, $150 in the off-season) is my favorite. Fishing, canoeing, and kayaking are practically right out your door at the private marina.

Texada Island

A 35-minute ferry trip from the Powell River, Texada is one of the largest of the gulf islands (50 km/31 mi. from north to south), but the permanent population is only 1,400 and services are limited. Originally home to a whaling station, the island has also housed a couple of mining operations and a distillery that supplied illegal liquor to the United States during Prohibition. From the ferry terminal at Blubber Bay, the island's main road winds south for eight kilometers (five mi.) to **Van Anda,** a historic village that once boasted saloons, an opera house, and a hospital. Take a walk along Van Anda's Erickson Beach to appreciate the island's natural beauty.

The 35-minute hop over to the island with **BC Ferries** (604/485-2943) costs adult $5.50, child $3, vehicle $14.50. Ferries depart about every two hours 8 A.M.–11 P.M.; no reservations taken.

Accommodations

The most attractive and welcoming local accommodation is **Beacon Bed and Breakfast** (3750 Marine Dr., two km/1.2 mi. south of the ferry terminal, 604/485-5563 or 800/485-5563, www .beaconbb.com), directly across the road from the water and with views extending to the peaks of Vancouver Island. Within the two-story home are three guest rooms, each with ocean views. Facilities include a lounge area overlooking the water and an outdoor hot tub. Two of the rooms are around the $100 mark while the huge Sunset Suite, complete with a private sitting room, runs $135 s, $145 or d. A memorable breakfast will keep you going for the day.

Five kilometers (3.1 mi.) south of the ferry terminal is **Beach Gardens Resort** (7074 Westminster Ave., 604/485-6267 or 800/663-7070, www.beachgardens.com, $125–180 s or d), which boasts an indoor swimming pool, sauna, tennis courts, a fitness room, and a restaurant/pub. It also has a marina with boat rentals and a dive shop (it's a great base for scuba enthusiasts). The biggish rooms are practically furnished for the setting and most come with a balcony and water views.

Camping
Willingdon Beach Municipal Campground (Marine Ave., 604/485-2242) enjoys a great waterfront location one kilometer (0.6 mi.) north of the ferry terminal. You'll find sheltered and very popular campsites along the beach, as well as a launderette and washrooms with free hot showers. Basic tent sites are $18, hookups $20–24.

Food
Head to **Rocky Mountain Pizza and Bakery Co.** (4471 Marine Ave., 604/485-9111) for great bakery items, coffee as strong (or as weak) as you like it, and daily newspapers. The rest of the day it's pizza, pizza, and more pizza. Right by the ferry terminal is **Laura's Fish and Chips** (4454 Willingdon Ave., 604/485-2252). It's a takeout-only place, but the waterfront and a number of ideal picnic spots are across the road.

Jitterbug Café (4643 Marine Ave., 604/ 485-7797, Tues.–Sun. 11 A.M.–3 P.M., Fri.–Sat. 5–8 P.M.) occupies a restored cottage with an outdoor deck offering views of Malaspina Strait. In the same house is Wind Spirit Gallery, and many local artworks from the gallery are displayed in the

café. The menu offers interesting yet remarkably inexpensive choices, such as a salad of fresh, locally grown greens covered in a strawberry vinaigrette ($5) and a delicious salmon pasta ($11).

Getting to Powell River
Pacific Coastal (604/483-2107) flies between Powell River and its hub at the South Terminal of Vancouver International Airport. The airport is east of town and cabs meet all incoming flights. The bus depot (corner of Joyce Ave. and Glacier St.) is served by **Malaspina Coach Lines** (604/485-5030), which runs buses daily from Vancouver's Pacific Central Station.

To Vancouver Island
The ferry terminal in Powell River is at the foot of Duncan Street, right downtown. **BC Ferries** (604/669-1211) offers regular sailings between Powell River and Comox on Vancouver Island. One-way fares for the 75-minute sailing are adult $7.75, child $4, vehicle $26. You can't make reservations—just roll up and join the queue.

Information
Powell River Visitors Bureau is along the main strip of shops (4690 Marine Ave., 604/485-4701 or 877/817-8669, www.discoverpowellriver.com, June–early Sept. Mon.–Sat. 9 A.M.–9 P.M., Sun. 9 A.M.–5 P.M.; rest of year weekdays only). Coming off the ferry from Vancouver Island, drive up the hill to Marine Avenue and turn left; it's three blocks down on the right.

BRITISH COLUMBIA

Sea to Sky Highway

The spectacular, aptly named Sea to Sky Highway (Highway 99) runs 105 kilometers (65 mi.) between Horseshoe Bay and Whistler. With the almost-vertical tree-covered Coast Mountains to the east and island-dotted Howe Sound to the west, this cliff-hugging highway winds precariously through a dramatic glacier-carved landscape.

In anticipation of the 2010 Winter Olympics, much road work is currently taking place along this stretch of highway. Expect some delays, as well as tight corners, narrow stretches, and

enough traffic to keep your concentration at an optimum.

HORSESHOE BAY TOWARD SQUAMISH
Porteau Cove Provincial Park
On the east shore of Howe Sound, Porteau Cove is best known among the diving fraternity for its artificial reef of four sunken wrecks, but it also offers good swimming and fishing. In addition, the

area's strong winds and lack of waves make for perfect windsurfing conditions. The park holds boat-launching and scuba-diving facilities, an ecology information center, picnic tables, and a waterfront campground for tents and RVs ($22 per night). The day-use fee is $5 per vehicle.

Britannia Beach

Small Britannia Beach is worth a stop to visit the **B.C. Museum of Mining** (800/896-4044, mid-May–mid-Oct. Mon.–Fri. 9 A.M.–4:30 P.M.). In the early 1930s the Britannia Beach Mine was the British Empire's largest producer of copper, producing more than 600 million kilograms. Today it's not a working mine but a working museum. Ever wondered what it's like to slave away underground? Here's your chance to don a hardhat and raincoat, hop on an electric train, and travel under a mountain, without even getting your hands dirty. See fully functional mining equipment, along with demonstrations and displays on the techniques of mining. Then take a step into the past in the museum, where hundreds of photos and artifacts tell the story of the mine. You can even try your hand at gold panning. The tour is adult $13, senior and student $11.

Murrin Provincial Park and Vicinity

Straddling the highway, this small park provides good fishing, swimming, and walking trails, as well as steep cliffs that attract novice and intermediate rock climbers. The park has picnic tables but no campsites.

Farther up the highway, stop at **Shannon Falls Provincial Park** to view the spectacular 335-meter (1,100-ft.) namesake falls from a platform at the base. You can picnic here or hike a few trails. No campsites are available, but just across the road is **Klahanie Campground and RV Park** (604/892-3435), with sites for $19.50-27 and an adjacent restaurant with spectacular views (open daily 6:30 A.M.–9 P.M.).

SQUAMISH

Squamish (pop. 17,000), 67 kilometers (41.7 mi.) north of Vancouver, enjoys a stunning location at the head of Howe Sound, surrounded by snowcapped mountains. The name Squamish is a native Coast Salish word meaning Mother of the Wind—the town gets stiff breezes year-round. Today lumber is still the lifeblood of the area—the town holds four sawmills, and along Mamquam Blind Channel on the east side of town you can see logs being boomed in preparation for towing to other mills—but it's also the center of a growing recreation-based economy.

Sights and Recreation

See around 65 vintage rail cars and engines in a mock working railyard, complete with a station garden, replica workers' home, and a restored station at the **West Coast Railway Heritage Park** (Industrial Way, 604/898-9336, May–Oct. daily 10 A.M.–5 P.M., $7). Along 2nd Avenue, at Victoria Street, a colorful mural covers the exterior of the Ocean Pub, depicting the natural and human elements of life along the west coast.

At first it may be difficult to see past the industrial scars along Squamish's waterways, but on the west side of downtown a large section of the

---

THE "CHIEF"

Towering over Squamish and clearly visible across the highway is the **Stawamus Chief,** one of the world's largest granite monoliths. Rising 762 meters (2,500 ft.) from the forest floor, it formed around 100 million years ago when massive forces deep inside the earth forced molten rock through the crust—as it cooled, it hardened and fractured. This created a perfect environment for today's climbers, who are attracted by a great variety of free and aided climbing on almost 1,000 routes.

If you've never climbed or are inexperienced, consider using the services of **Squamish Rock Guides** (604/815-1750, www.squamishrock-guides.com) for a variety of courses with equipment supplied; expect to pay around $175 for a full day's instruction. **Vertical Reality** (38154 2nd Ave., 604/892-8248) offers a full range of climbing equipment and sells local climbing guidebooks. Camping at the base of the mountain is $9 per night.

delta where the Squamish River flows into Howe Sound has escaped development. It comprises tidal flats, forested areas, marshes, and open meadows—and over 200 species of birds call the area home. Hiking trails lace the area, and there are three main access points: Industrial Road, the end of Winnipeg Street, and the end of Vancouver Street, all of which branch off Cleveland Avenue.

Accommodations

The best place to stay around Squamish is **Dryden Creek Resorts** (six km/3.7 mi. north of town, 604/898-9726 or 877/237-9336, www.dryden creek.com). Set on six hectares (15 acres) of landscaped parkland with Garibaldi Provincial Park as a backdrop, each of six suite-style studios has a vaulted ceiling, large skylights, and a fully equipped kitchen with handcrafted wooden cabinets. Rates of $80 s, $90 d are an excellent value, but check their website for deals—which may include golfing or skiing. The resort's campground offers a choice of forested or creekside sites; unserviced sites $20, hookups $26.

In Squamish itself, **Howe Sound Inn** (37801 Cleveland Ave., 604/892-2603 or 800/919-2537, www.howesound.com, $105 s or d) is light years ahead of the other downtown choices for comfort and style. The rooms hold a distinct mountain feel, with stylish wood furnishings and views across The Chief. The inn also has a restaurant and boasts an in-house brewery.

Information

For detailed information on Squamish, local provincial parks, and Whistler, follow the signs from the highway downtown to **Squamish Visitor Info Centre** (37950 Cleveland Ave., 604/892-9244, www.squamishchamber.bc.ca, June–Aug. daily 9 A.M.–5 P.M., rest of year Mon.–Fri. 9 A.M.–4 P.M.).

NORTH TOWARD WHISTLER

The Eagles of Brackendale

If you're traveling the Sea to Sky Highway in winter, you're probably making a beeline for Whistler, but a stop at Brackendale, just north of Squamish, is well worthwhile. Through the colder months of the year, the riverflats behind this sleepy little town are home to a larger concentration of **bald eagles** than anywhere else on the face of the earth. Over 3,000 of these magnificent creatures descend on a stretch of the Squamish River to feed on spawned-out salmon that litter the banks. The birds begin arriving in late October, but numbers reach their peak around Christmastime, and by early February they're gone. The best viewing spot is from the dike that runs along the back of Brackendale. The best place to learn more about these creatures is the **Brackendale Art Gallery** (604/898-3333, www.brackendaleartgallery.com, Jan. daily noon–5 P.M., weekends only rest of year), "Eagle Count Headquarters," for slide presentations, talks, and other eagle-related activities. To get there, follow the main Brackendale access road over the railway tracks, take the first right and look for the gallery nestled in the trees on the right.

Alice Lake Provincial Park

Alice Lake, surrounded by a 400-hectare (1,000-acre) park of open grassy areas, dense forests, and impressive snowcapped peaks, is particularly good for canoeing, swimming, and fishing for small rainbow and cutthroat trout. A 1.4-kilometer (0.9-mi.) trail encircles the lake, while others lead to three smaller bodies of water. Entry to the day-use area is $5 per vehicle. A campground with showers and picnic tables is open year-round; walk-in sites are $17, while other sites are $22 per night. The park entrance is 13 kilometers (eight mi.) north of Squamish and the lake just under two kilometers (1.2 mi.) from the highway.

Brandywine Falls Provincial Park

Stop at this roadside park 45 kilometers (28 mi.) north of Squamish and take the short trail to the base of these 66-meter (220-ft.) falls. It's the kind of trail that excites all your senses—magnificent frosty peaks high above, dense lush forest on either side, a fast, deep river roaring along on one side, the pungent aroma and cushiness of crushed pine needles beneath your feet. It's most magnificent early in summer. (The falls were named by two railroad surveyors who made a wager on guessing the falls' height, the winner to receive bottles of, you guessed it, brandywine.) Access is $3.

Whistler

Magnificent snowcapped peaks, dense green forests, transparent lakes, sparkling rivers, and an upmarket, cosmopolitan village right in the middle of it all: Welcome to Whistler (pop. 10,000), one of the world's great resort towns, 120 kilometers (75 mi.) north of Vancouver along Highway 99. The Whistler Valley has seen incredible development in recent years and as co-host of the 2010 Olympic Winter Games, construction will be continuing for many years to come. The crowds (1.5 million visitors annually) and the costs might not be for everyone, but there is a great variety of things to do in Whistler, and the village takes full advantage of magnificent natural surroundings, making a trip north from Vancouver well worthwhile at any time of year.

Best-known among skiers and snowboarders, the town is built around the base of one of North America's finest resorts, **Whistler/Blackcomb,** which comprises almost 3,000 hectares (7,400 acres) on two mountains accessed by an ultra-modern lift system. A season stretching from November to May doesn't leave much time for summer recreation, but the "off season" is almost equally busy. Among the abundant summertime recreation opportunities: lift-served hiking and glacier skiing and snowboarding; biking through the valley and mountains; water activities on five lakes; horseback riding; golfing on some of the world's best resort courses; and fishing, rafting, and jet-boating on the rivers. The more sedentary summer visitor can simply stay in bustling Whistler Village and enjoy a plethora of outdoor cafés and restaurants.

SUMMER RECREATION
Whistler/Blackcomb
In the few months they aren't covered in snow, the slopes of the resort come alive with locals and tourists alike enjoying hiking, guided naturalist walks, mountain biking, and horseback

A MODERN BOOMTOWN

Although natives took advantage of the abundant natural resources of the Whistler Valley for thousands of years, the history of Whistler as a resort town doesn't really begin until the 1960s, and is associated almost entirely with the development of the ski area. At that time the only development was a bunch of ramshackle summer holiday houses around Alta Lake (which was also the name of the "town," pop. 300). When the road up from Vancouver was paved in 1964, the first ski lifts were constructed. Early skiers were impressed, and so were investors, who began plans for major base-area facilities. The idea of a European-style ski-in, ski-out village was promoted throughout the 1970s, but it wasn't until 1980 that Whistler Village officially opened. The following year, lift capacity doubled with the opening of an adjacent resort on Blackcomb Mountain. Lift construction continued unabated on both mountains through the 1980s and 1990s and in 1997 the inevitable

happened, and the two mountains came under the control of one company, **Intrawest,** which created the megaresort of **Whistler/Blackcomb.**

Meanwhile, development on the mountains was being overshadowed by construction in the valley below—new base facilities, resort-style golf courses, and upscale accommodations—where the population increased tenfold in 20 years. Through it all, a future cap on development has pushed the cost of living skyward—an empty lot goes for $3.5 million, a family home for $10 million, and a 240-unit development sold out in five hours at an average of $600,000 per condo. And all this *before* Whistler was chosen to co-host the 2010 Olympic Winter Games.

The best place to learn the full story of development in the valley is the magnificent new **Whistler Museum** (4329 Main St., 604/932-2019, July–Aug. daily 10 A.M.–4 P.M., Sept.–June Thurs.–Sun. 10 A.M.–4 P.M.).

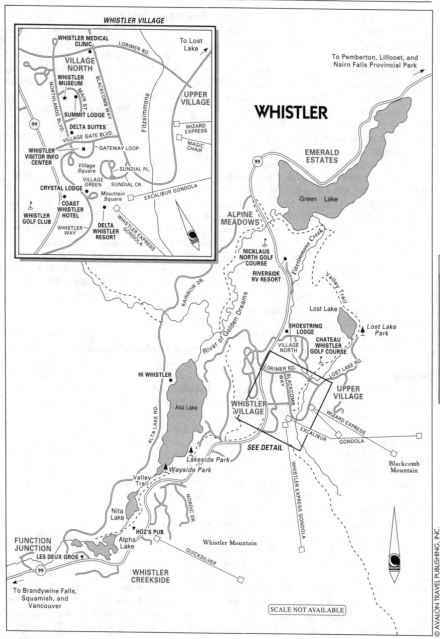

WHISTLER VILLAGE

To Lost Lake

WHISTLER MEDICAL CLINIC

LORIMER RD

VILLAGE NORTH

WHISTLER MUSEUM

UPPER VILLAGE

SUMMIT LODGE

DELTA SUITES

VILLAGE GATE BLVD.

GATEWAY LOOP

WHISTLER VISITOR INFO CENTER

Village Square

SUNDIAL PL.

VILLAGE GREEN

SUNDIAL CR.

CRYSTAL LODGE

Mountain Square

EXCALIBUR GONDOLA

COAST WHISTLER HOTEL

WHISTLER GOLF CLUB

WHISTLER WAY

DELTA WHISTLER RESORT

NORTHLANDS BLVD.

MAIN ST.

BLACKCOMB WAY

Fitzsimmons

WIZARD EXPRESS

MAGIC CHAIR

99

WHISTLER

To Pemberton, Lillooet, and Nairn Falls Provincial Park

EMERALD ESTATES

99

Green Lake

ALPINE MEADOWS

NICKLAUS NORTH GOLF COURSE

RIVERSIDE RV RESORT

Fitzsimmons Creek

Valley Trail

Lost Lake

Lost Lake Park

RAINBOW DR.

River of Golden Dreams

SHOESTRING LODGE

VILLAGE NORTH

CHATEAU WHISTLER GOLF COURSE

LORIMER RD.

LOST LAKE RD.

HI WHISTLER

Alta Lake

WHISTLER VILLAGE

BLACKCOMB WAY

UPPER VILLAGE

WIZARD EXPRESS

ALTA LAKE RD.

Lakeside Park

SEE DETAIL

EXCALIBUR GONDOLA

Blackcomb Mountain

Wayside Park

Valley Trail

NORDIC DR.

WHISTLER EXPRESS GONDOLA

Nita Lake

FUNCTION JUNCTION

LES DEUX GROS

HOZ'S PUB

Alpha Lake

QUICKSILVER

Whistler Mountain

99

To Brandywine Falls, Squamish, and Vancouver

WHISTLER CREEKSIDE

SCALE NOT AVAILABLE

BRITISH COLUMBIA

© AVALON TRAVEL PUBLISHING, INC.

riding, or just marveling at the mountainscape from the comfort of the lifts. Rates for the sightseeing lifts are adult $23, senior $19, children $6. Summer lift hours are late June–early September daily 10 A.M.–5 P.M. Over 50 kilometers (31 mi.) of hiking trails wind around the mountains, including trails through the high alpine to destinations such as beautiful Harmony Lake and the toe of a small glacier. Or for an adrenaline rush, take the gondola up then ride down the mountain, or hone your skills at the Whistler Bike Park, which has a leg-numbing vertical drop of 1,040 meters (3,400 ft.). **Backroads Whistler** (behind Affinity Sports, Whistler Village, 604/932-3111) rents full-suspension bikes ($70 for a half day) and leads a variety of tours. Die-hard skiers will even find mid-summer skiing and snowboarding (June–July; adult $42, child $21) on the Horstman Glacier. Dining facilities are available on both mountains, or grab a picnic-basket lunch from any of the delis down in the village. A good source of information is the **Whistler Activity and Information Centre** (4010 Whistler Way, 604/938-2769) or contact the resort itself (604/932-3434, www.whistlerblackcomb.com).

Hiking

The easiest way to access the area's most spectacular hiking country is to take a sightseeing lift up Whistler or Blackcomb Mountain. But many other options exist. Walking around Whistler Valley you'll notice signposted trails all over the place. **Valley Trail** is a paved walkway/bikeway in summer, a cross-country ski trail in winter. It makes an almost complete tour of the valley, from Whistler Village to Lost and Green Lakes, along the River of Golden Dreams, and past three golf courses to Alta, Nita, and Alpha Lakes, and finally to Highway 99 in the Whistler Creekside area. If you'd rather do a short walk, head for **Lost Lake** via the two-kilometer (1.2-mi.) trail from Parking Lot East at the back of Whistler Village, or take the free Whistler Transit System bus from the middle of the village. Once at the beautiful lake, you can saunter along the shore, picnic, or swim.

Mountain Biking

The Whistler Valley is a perfect place to take a mountain bike—you'd need months to ride all the trails here. Many of the locals have abandoned their cars for bikes (some of which are probably worth more than the vehicles). The **Valley Trail,** a paved walk/bikeway that links the entire valley, is the resident bicyclists' freeway. Another popular place for mountain bikers is beautiful Lost Lake, two kilometers (1.2 mi.) northeast of Whistler Village. If you didn't bring a bike, not to worry—they're for rent. Rental rates range $15–20 per hour, $40–100 per day. Or perhaps a guided bicycle tour of the local area sounds appealing—it's not a bad idea to have a guide at first. **Backroads Whistler** (Whistler Village North, 604/932-3111) offers tours throughout the valley. Other rental outlets include **Can-Ski** (4573 Chateau Blvd., 604/938-7755), **Sportstop** (4112 Golfers Approach, 604/932-5495), **Whistler Bike Co.** (4050 Whistler Way, 604/938-9511), and **Wild Willies** (Nester's Square, 604/938-8036).

Water Sports

Sunbathers head for the public beaches along the shores of **Alta Lake. Wayside Park,** at the south end of the lake, has a beach, an offshore pontoon, and a grassy area with picnic tables. At **Lakeside Park,** also on Alta Lake, **Whistler Outdoor Experience** (604/932-3389) rents canoes (one hour $20, half-day $60) and kayaks (one hour $16, half-day $48). They also have a rental center on quieter **Green Lake,** where you have the option of taking a canoe tour (adult $30, child $15), and they lead white-water rafting adventures down the tame Green River ($69) and the wild and wooly Birkenhead River ($149).

Golf

Whistler boasts four world-class championship golf courses, each with its own character and charm. The entire valley has gained a reputation as a golfing destination, with many accommodations offering package deals that include greens fees (check hotel websites). The golfing season runs mid-May–October, so in late spring you can ski in the morning and golf in the afternoon. The greens fees quoted below are high season—

look for discounted rates outside of the busiest July–August season and daily after 4 P.M. Also budget for cart rental if not included ($40) and club rental (from $40).

Designed by Arnold Palmer, **Whistler Golf Club** (between Whistler Village and Alta Lake, 604/932-4544, $165) offers large greens and narrow wooded fairways over a challenging 6,676-yard, par-72 layout. On the other side of the village is **Chateau Whistler Golf Club** (Blackcomb Way, 604/938-2092, $195). Designed by renowned golf-course architect Robert Trent Jones Jr., this 6,635-yard course takes advantage of the rugged terrain of Blackcomb Mountain's lower slopes through holes that rise and fall with the lay of the land. **Nicklaus North** (just north of Whistler Village, 604/938-9898, $210) holds numerous water hazards, boasts 360-degree mountain vistas, and plays to a challenging 6,900 yards from the back markers.

SKIING AND SNOWBOARDING

No matter what your ability, the skiing at **Whistler/Blackcomb** (general information 604/932-3434, snow reports 604/932-4211, www.whistlerblackcomb.com), consistently rated as North America's No. 1 ski destination, makes for a winter holiday you won't forget in a hurry. The two lift-served mountains, Whistler and Blackcomb, are separated by a steep-sided valley, with lifts converging at Whistler Village. Skiing is over 2,863 hectares (7,071 acres), comprising more than 200 groomed runs, hundreds of unmarked trails through forested areas, three glaciers, and 12 bowls. The lift-served vertical rise of Blackcomb is 1,609 meters (5,280 feet), the highest in North America, but Whistler is only slightly lower at 1,530 meters (5,020 feet). In total, the resort has 35 lifts, including three gondolas. The length of season is also impressive, running November–May. For many skiers, the resort can be overwhelming. Trail maps detail all marked runs, but can't convey the vast size of the area. A great way to get to know the mountain is on an orientation tour; these leave throughout the day from various meeting points (ask when and where when you buy your ticket)

and are free. Lift tickets are adult $78, senior and youth $65, child $42.

ENTERTAINMENT

Throughout the year you can usually find live evening entertainment in Whistler Village. At **Buffalo Bill's** (Timberline Lodge, 4122 Village Green, 604/932-6613) expect anything from reggae to rock. Another longtime hotspot is **Tommy Africa's** (4216 Gateway Dr., 604/932-6090), popular with the younger crowd, pumping out high-volume reggae across the valley's most popular dance floor. The **Boot Pub** (Shoestring Lodge, Nancy Greene Way, 604/932-3338) offers some of the cheapest drinks in the valley and occasional live music. The **Garibaldi Lift Co. Bar & Grill** (2320 London Lane, 604/905-2220) features live entertainment most nights—often blues and jazz—and good food at reasonable prices.

Black's Pub (Mountain Square, 604/932-6945) offers more than 90 international beers and a quiet atmosphere in a small upstairs English-style bar. Finally, for a more refined atmosphere, the **Mallard Bar** (Fairmont Chateau Whistler, 4599 Chateau Blvd., 604/938-8000) offers comfortable lounge chairs and a wide range of wines by the glass.

EVENTS

The winter season is packed with ski and snowboard races, but the biggest is the **World Ski & Snowboard Festival** (604/938-3399, www.wssf .com) in mid-April. This innovative event brings together the very best winter athletes for the World Skiing Invitational and the World Snowboarding Championship. These are only the flagships of this 10-day extravaganza, which also includes demo days, exhibitions, and a film festival. The last weekend of May is the official end of the ski season, with a **Slush Cup** and live music.

Each weekend in May and June and daily through summer, the streets of Whistler come alive with street entertainment such as musicians, jugglers, and comedians. **Canada Day,** July 1, is celebrated with a parade through Whistler Village. On the second weekend of August, the valley

BRITISH COLUMBIA

hosts the **Whistler Classical Music Festival,** which includes a program of events ranging from Brass on a Raft to a concert by the Vancouver Symphony Orchestra high up on the slopes of Whistler Mountain. The **Alpine Wine Festival,** early in September, showcases the province's best wineries with daily wine-tasting at Pika's Restaurant, on Whistler Mountain.

ACCOMMODATIONS AND CAMPING

Whistler's accommodations range from a hostel and inexpensive dorm beds to luxury resorts. It's just a matter of selecting one to suit your budget and location preference. Skiers and snowboarders may want to be right in Whistler Village or by the gondola base in Whistler Creekside so they can walk to the lifts, but you'll be paying for the privilege. (The term "slopeside" describes accommodations within a five-minute walk of the lifts.)

Accommodation pricing in Whistler is very complex, especially in winter. The best advice I can give is to shop around using the phone or Internet. Contact the lodgings themselves, then the booking agencies listed below to get a comparison. Winter is most definitely high season, with the week after Christmas and all of February and March a high season within a high season.

If you plan on skiing or golfing, a package deal is the way to go. These, along with room-only accommodations, can be booked through the **Tourism Whistler** reservation service (604/664-5625 or 800/944-7853, www.mywhistler.com) or other agencies, such as **Whistler Resort Reservations** (604/904-7060 or 888/403-4727, www.whistlerblackcomb.com).

Under $100

HI–Whistler (5678 Alta Lake Rd., 604/932-5492, www.hihostels.ca) is on the western shore of Alta Lake, boasting magnificent views across the lake to the resort. It's relatively small (just 32 beds), with facilities including a communal kitchen, dining area, and big, cozy living area. Bike and canoe rentals are available. It's understandably popular year-round; members $19.50,

nonmembers $23.50. Check-in is 4–10 P.M. To get there from the south, take Alta Lake Road to the left off Highway 99 and watch for the small sign on the lake side of the road.

The **Shoestring Lodge** (7124 Nancy Greene Dr., 604/932-3338 or 877/551-4954, www.shoestringlodge.com) is a popular local pub with dorm beds for $21 per night and private rooms with en suites and a TV for $80 s or d through summer, rising to $31 and $125 in winter.

$100–200

On the edge of the village and adjacent to one of the valley's best golf courses is **Coast Whistler Hotel** (4005 Whistler Way, 604/932-2522 or 800/663-5644, www.coastwhistlerhotel.com). Each of the 194 rooms is simply but stylishly decorated in pastel colors. Facilities include a heated outdoor pool, exercise room, hot tub, restaurant, and bar. Summer rates start at a reasonable $189 (under $100 in spring and fall), with lots of online packages deals. The winter rate of $285 s or d is a little steep considering you're away from the ski lifts.

Crystal Lodge (4154 Village Green, 604/932-2221 or 800/667-3363, www.crystal-lodge.bc.ca) stands out as excellent value in the heart of the action of Whistler Village. The spacious rooms have a homey feel and guests have the use of an outdoor hot tub and heated pool. Rates start at $178 s or d for a regular hotel-style room, rising to $238 for a one-bedroom suite with a balcony.

With the best location of any lodging, right where the gondolas for both Whistler and Blackcomb converge, is **Delta Whistler Resort** (4050 Whistler Way, 604/932-1982 or 800/515-4050, www.deltawhistler.com). This 288-room hotel has a full-service health club with an outdoor pool, two restaurants, and a bar. Rack rates through summer are from $179 s or d. Across the village, **Delta Whistler Village Suites** (4308 Main St., 604/905-3987 or 888/299-3987, www.delta-whistler.ca, from $180 s or d outside winter) combines the conveniences of a full-service hotel with more than 200 kitchen-equipped units—the only such property in Whistler. In both cases, check the website for promotional deals.

Over $200

Summit Lodge (4359 Main St., 604/932-2778 or 888/913-8811, www.summitlodge.com) is a luxurious European Alps–style boutique hotel. Each of the 81 units features comfortable furnishings, a slate floor, a fireplace, a balcony, and a small kitchen. Summer rates start at $260 s or d, rising to $450 in winter.

Campgrounds

Enjoying a pleasant location just over two kilometers (1.2 mi.) north of Whistler Village, **Riverside RV Resort** (604/905-5533 or 877/905-5533, www.whistlercamping.com) is the only campground within town boundaries. It offers a modern bathroom complex, hot tub, laundry, convenience store, and café (open daily at 7 A.M.). Tent camping is $30, RVs pay $45, and luxurious, self-contained log cabins are $175 s or d. Out of town, the closest campgrounds are in **Brandywine Falls Provincial Park,** 11 kilometers (6.8 mi.) south, and **Nairn Falls Provincial Park,** 28 kilometers (17.3 mi.) north. Both are open April–November and charge $14 per night.

FOOD

Cafés

One of the best places in Whistler Village for breakfast is **Chalet Deli** (4437 Sundial Place, 604/932-8345, daily from 7:30 A.M.). Light breakfasts cost from $5 and the service is fast and efficient. The rest of the day the deli is a great choice for hamburgers and healthy sandwiches and salads. Scattered through the village are a number of coffeehouses, including **Moguls Coffee Bean** (4208 Village Square, 604/932-1918).

North American

For steaks, seafood, a salad bar, fresh hot bread, and plenty of food at a reasonable price, the **Keg Restaurant** (Whistler Village Inn, 4429 Sundial Place, 604/932-5151) is a sure thing. Expect to pay from $15 for an entrée. The rustic decor and great Canadian food at **Garibaldi Lift Co. Bar & Grill** (at the base of the Whistler Village gondola, 604/905-2220) is always a hit. For Western-style atmosphere, head to the **Longhorn Saloon and Grill** (4290 Mountain Square, 604/932-5999).

Hy's, in the Delta Whistler Village Suites (4308 Main St., 604/905-5555), undoubtedly offers the best steaks in the valley. The scene is upscale, with elegant tables set within rich-colored wood walls. Appetizers range $10–15, and steaks start at $29.

European

For great Greek food, **Zeuski's Taverna** (4314 Main St., Town Plaza, Village North, 604/932-6009) is open daily for lunch and dinner and is always busy. For something different, sample the souvlaki cooked on the barbecue.

Restaurant entrepreneur Umberto Menghi operates numerous eateries in Vancouver and two restaurants in Whistler Village. Both are reasonably priced with menus influenced by the cuisine of Tuscany. Check out **Il Caminetto di Umberto** (4242 Village Stroll, 604/932-4442) for its warm, welcoming atmosphere and a long

© ANDREW HEMPSTEAD

Delta Whistler Village Suites

BRITISH COLUMBIA

menu of pastas around the $20 mark, or **Trattoria di Umberto** (4417 Sundial Place, 604/932-5858), which is less expensive and attracts a more casual crowd.

Ristorante Araxi (4222 Village Square, Whistler Village, 604/932-4540) consistently wins awards for its traditional Italian menu, which takes advantage of produce from around the Lower Mainland. It also boasts an extensive wine list.

INFORMATION AND SERVICES

Tourism Whistler (www.mywhistler.com) promotes the resort town throughout the world. The local Chamber of Commerce operates the **Whistler Visitor Info Centre** (4230 Gateway Drive, 604/932-5528, daily 9 A.M.–5 P.M.), which is in the middle of the action in Whistler Village. **Whistler Public Library** (4329 Main St., 604/932-5564) is open Monday, Tuesday, and Thursday 10 A.M.–8 P.M., Friday–Sunday 10 A.M.–5 P.M.

In Whistler Village you'll find a post office, banks, a currency exchange, launderette, supermarket, and liquor store. **Whistler Medical Centre** (604/932-3977) is at 4380 Lorimer.

TRANSPORTATION

Getting There

Vancouver International Airport, 130 kilometers (80 mi.) to the south, is the main gateway to Whistler. **Perimeter** (604/266-5386 or 877/317-7788) provides bus service between the two up to five times daily. One way fares are adult $58, child $39. **Greyhound** (604/932-5031) runs six buses daily between Vancouver's Pacific Central Station and Whistler Village ($24 one-way), with airport transfers an extra $10. A schedule is posted online at www.whistlerbus.com.

Getting Around

Once you're in Whistler, getting around is pretty easy—if you're staying in Whistler Village, everything you need is within easy walking distance.

Whistler Transit System (604/932-4020) operates extensive bus routes throughout the valley daily 6 A.M.–midnight.

For a cab call **Sea to Sky Taxi** (604/932-3333) or **Whistler Taxi** (604/938-3333).

THE GOLD NUGGET ROUTE

The route north between Whistler and Lillooet is best traveled in good weather—the scenery is so spectacular you don't want to miss anything. You'll see beautiful lakes, fast-flowing rivers, summer wildflowers, snowcapped mountains, steep ravines, never-ending forests, and vistas in every shade of green imaginable. Campgrounds and picnic areas mark all the best locations.

Pemberton

A small logging town and service center surrounded by mountains, trees, lakes, and rivers, Pemberton sits in the fertile Pemberton Valley 32 kilometers (20 mi.) north of Whistler. Best known for its potatoes, locals affectionately call the area "Spud Valley." It's only a short distance south of the Lillooet River, a main transportation route to the Cariboo during the 1860s' gold-rush days. Today's visitors mostly leave their gold pans at home, coming mainly to fish or to hike in the beautiful valleys around Pemberton.

North to Lillooet

The most direct route between Pemberton and Lillooet is paved Highway 99. Three kilometers (1.9 mi.) out of Mount Currie, the highway begins switchbacking, as it climbs abruptly into the Coast Mountains to **Joffre Lakes Provincial Park,** where a 500-meter (0.3-mi.) trail leads to **Lower Joffre Lake.** Beyond the park, Highway 99 crests a pass, and then loses over 1,000 meters (3,300 ft.) of elevation in its descent to Lillooet. Along the way is narrow **Duffey Lake** (the highway itself is referred to locally as the "Duffey Lake Road"), backed by the steep-sided Cayoosh Range. At the north end of the lake is a provincial park with camping ($14 per night).

East from Vancouver

FRASER VALLEY

When you leave Vancouver and head due east, you travel through the most built-up and heavily populated area of British Columbia, skirting modern cities, residential suburbs, and zones of heavy industry. However, it's not an unattractive area—the main roads follow the mighty Fraser River through a fertile valley of rolling farmland dotted with historic villages, and beautiful mountains line the horizon in just about any direction. You have a choice of two major routes. The Trans-Canada Highway, on the south side of the Fraser River, speeds you out of southeast Vancouver, while Highway 7 meanders along the north side of the Fraser River to Harrison Hot Springs and crosses over the Fraser River to Hope.

Fort Langley National Historic Site

This important site (23433 Mavis St., Fort Langley, 604/513-4777, Mar.–Nov. daily 10 A.M.–5 P.M., adult $6, child $3) re-creates a Hudson's Bay Company settlement that was part of a network of trading posts across western Canada. Through its formative years, the fort played a major role in the development of British Columbia. Out its gates have vamoosed native fur and salmon traders, adventurous explorers who opened up the interior, company traders, and fortune seekers heading for the goldfields of the upper Fraser River. When British Columbia became a crown colony on November 19, 1858, the official proclamation was uttered here in the "big house." Today the restored riverside trading post springs to life as park interpreters in period costumes animate the fort's history. To get there, take Exit 66 from Highway 1 and head north on 232nd Street, for five kilometers (3.1 mi.). The park is within walking distance of Fort Langley village, where many businesses are built in a heritage style and you'll find dozens of antiques shops, boutiques, restaurants, and cafés along its main tree-lined street.

Harrison Hot Springs

A popular resort, self-described as "The Spa of Canada," Harrison Hot Springs (pop. 1,100) lies on the sandy southern shores of southwestern B.C.'s largest body of water, **Harrison Lake,** 125 kilometers (78 mi.) east of Vancouver. Only Harrison Hot Springs Resort has water rights to the hot springs, but the hotel operates **Harrison Public Pool** (604/796-2244, summer daily 8 A.M.–9 P.M., rest of year daily 9 A.M.–9 P.M., adult $8, senior or child $6). The lake itself provides many recreation opportunities, with good swimming, sailing, canoeing, and fishing for trout and coho salmon. Through town to the north is 1,220-hectare (3,020-acre) Sasquatch Provincial Park, named for a tall, hairy, unshaven beast that supposedly inhabits the area. The park extends from a day-use area on the bank of Harrison Lake to two picturesque tree-encircled lakes, each with road access, short hiking trails, and day-use areas ($5 per day). In early September, Harrison Hot Springs hosts the **World Championships of Sand Sculpture** (www.harrisand.org), a gathering of sand sculptors aiming to create a masterpiece that will crown them world champion (and net a share of the $37,000 prize money). The event is unique in that the inland venue has no tides to wash away the sculptures, which stay in place for a month after judging.

The aforementioned lakeside **Harrison Hot Springs Resort** (100 Esplanade, 604/796-2244 or 800/663-2266, www.harrisonresort.com) is the town's most elegant accommodation, offering guests use of a large indoor and outdoor complex of mineral pools, complete with grassed areas, lots of outdoor furniture, and a café. Other facilities include boat and canoe rentals, sailing lessons, and a restaurant and lounge bar. Most of the 300 rooms have a private balcony, many with spectacular views across the lake. Rates range $160–240, but check the Web for discounts. The pick of three campgrounds along the road into town is **Bigfoot Campgrounds** (670 Hot Springs Rd., 604/796-9767; tent sites $16, hookups $18–22), which features large shaded sites, free showers, a laundry, and a game room. Camping at **Sasquatch Provincial Park,** through town to the north, is $14.

Harrison Hot Springs Visitor Info Centre (604/796-3425, summer daily 8 A.M.–6 P.M.) is beside the main road into town.

HOPE AND VICINITY

Locals say "all roads lead to Hope"—and they're right. On a finger of land at the confluence of the Fraser and Coquihalla Rivers, 158 kilometers (98 mi.) east of Vancouver, Hope (pop. 7,000) really is a hub, with four highways converging here. The town itself is nothing special, but the surrounding mountains and rivers are just a short drive away.

Town Sights

To find out more about the history of Hope, visit **Hope Museum** (919 Water Ave., 604/869-2021, May–June daily 9 A.M.–5 P.M., July–Aug. daily 8 A.M.–8 P.M.), in the same building as the **information center.** Outside, climb on the Hope Gold Mill, a restored gold-ore concentrator. Also don't miss the tree-stump art in Memorial Park. The eagle holding a salmon in its claws (in front of the district office) was carved from a tree with root rot, with carvings added since, and it was one of the original tree-stump works of art. As the years go by, more and more carvings (28 at last count) are added by chainsaw artist Pete Ryan. During summer look for him in the park, working on his latest creation.

Finally, since I don't want you to think this book wasn't thoroughly researched, it has to be mentioned—Hope was the setting for the first Rambo movie, *First Blood.* The multimillion-dollar blockbuster starring Sylvester Stallone transformed the quiet streets of Hope into a movie set. Buildings were constructed just to be blown away, local businesses were renamed to suit the film, and the wilderness action scenes were shot almost entirely in Coquihalla Canyon.

Othello–Quintette Tunnels

These five huge tunnels through a steep gorge of Coquihalla Canyon were carved out of solid gran-

ite by the Kettle Valley Railway, completing a route for the company's steam locomotives between Vancouver and Nelson. The tunnels have been abandoned now for almost 50 years; today a short walk takes you from the **Coquihalla Canyon Provincial Park** parking lot to and through the massive, dark tunnels, a popular tourist attraction. To get to there from downtown, take Wallace Street to 6th Avenue and turn right. Turn left on Kawkawa Lake Road, crossing the Coquihalla River Bridge and railway tracks. At the first intersection take the right branch, Othello Road, and continue until you see a sign to the right (over a rise and easy to miss) pointing to the recreation area. The tunnels are closed November–April.

Accommodations and Camping

Hope's newer accommodations are east of the TransCanada Highway on Old Hope-Princeton Way, but a couple of choices are downtown, including the **Park Motel** (832 4th Ave., 604/869-5891 or 888/531-9933, $65 s, $70 d). Four kilometers (2.5 mi.) north of Hope, **Beautiful Lake of the Woods Resort** (604/869-9211 or 888/508-2211, www.lakewoods-resortmotel.com) sits on a lake with views of the surrounding mountainscape. Accommodations are in regular rooms ($65–75 s or d) or small cabins ($85 s or d). Facilities include a restaurant and canoe rentals.

Along the road up to the tunnels, **Coquihalla Campground** (Kawkawa Lake Rd., 604/869-7119 or 888/869-7118, $18–25) sits right beside the river. Trees surround most sites, and facilities include hot showers, a barbecue area, laundry, and game room.

FRASER RIVER CANYON

From Hope, the old TransCanada Highway runs north along the west bank of the fast-flowing Fraser River. Although the new Coquihalla Highway is a much shorter option for those heading for Kamloops and beyond, the old highway offers many interesting stops and is by far the preferred route for those not in a hurry. Head north through downtown Hope, cross the Fraser River, take the first right and you're on your way.

Yale

This small town of 200 has quite a history. In 1858 Yale was a flourishing gold-rush town of 20,000, filled with tents, shacks, bars, gambling joints, and shops. But when the gold ran out so did most of the population. If you want to find out more about Yale's historic past, the gold rush, the Cariboo Wagon Road, and railway construction, visit the **Yale Museum** (Douglas St., 604/863-2324, summer Wed.–Sat. 9:30 A.M.–5:30 P.M.) and the adjacent historic St. John's Church (built 1863).

Hell's Gate

At well-known Hell's Gate, the Fraser River powers its way through a narrow, glacier-carved gorge. When Simon Fraser saw this section of the gorge in 1808 he called it "the Gates of Hell" and the name stuck. In 1914 a massive rockslide rocketed down into the gorge, blocking it even further and resulting in the almost total obliteration of the sockeye salmon population that spawned farther upstream. In 1944 giant concrete fishways were built to slow the waters and allow the spawning salmon to jump upstream—the river soon swarmed with salmon once again. Today you can cross the canyon aboard the 25-passenger **Hell's Gate Airtram** (604/867-9277, summer daily 9 A.M.–6 P.M., adult $12, senior $10, child $7.50). Across the river you can browse through landscaped gardens, learn more about the fishway and salmon, or sink your teeth into a fresh salmon at the Salmon House Restaurant (same telephone number as the Airtram).

COQUIHALLA HIGHWAY

Opened in late spring 1986, the Coquihalla Highway is the most direct link between Hope and the interior of British Columbia. It saves at least 90 minutes by cutting 72 kilometers (44.7 mi.) from the trip between Hope and Kamloops and bypassing the TransCanada Highway's narrow, winding stretch along the Fraser River Canyon. Along the 190-kilometer (118-mi.) route are many worthwhile stops, but only one that's compulsory—a toll plaza at Coquihalla Pass, 115 kilometers (71.5 mi.) from Hope, where $10 is collected from each vehicle.

The highway ascends and descends through magnificent mountain and river scenery to dry, semiarid grasslands. You'll cruise through the valleys of the Lower Coquihalla River and Boston Bar Creek, climb to the 1,240-meter (4,070-ft.) summit of Coquihalla Pass near Coquihalla Lake, descend along the Coldwater River, then climb the Coldwater's eastern valley slope to Merritt.

Merritt

This town of 8,000 in the Nicola Valley provides the only services along the Coquihalla Highway. It's also the exit point for those heading east to the Okanagan on the Okanagan Connector. Make your first stop off the highway at **Merritt Visitor Info Centre** (250/378-2281, daily 9 A.M.–5 P.M.), on a high point east of the highway. Upstairs in this large log building is an intriguing forestry exhibit.

Since the Coquihalla Highway opened, many chain motels have been built around Merritt. But by far the best choice is one of the originals, the **Quilchena Hotel** (23 km/14.3 mi. east of town on Hwy. 5A, 250/378-2611, www.quilchena.com, $75–135 s or d). Built in 1908, this grand old three-story hostelry features a café, restaurant, and antiques-decorated rooms. The hotel sits beside a beautiful lake where you can go swimming or rent a boat and go fishing. Horseback riding and mountain-bike rentals are also offered.

HOPE TO THE OKANAGAN VALLEY

Manning Provincial Park

This spectacular 70,844-hectare (175,060-acre) park in the Cascade Mountains, 64 kilometers (40 mi.) east of Hope along Highway 3, stretches down to the Canada–U.S. border. Highway 3 makes a U through the park, from the northwest to south to northeast corners. But to really appreciate the park, you need to get off the highway—take in the beautiful bodies of water, drive up to a wonderful stretch of high alpine meadows, or hike on the numerous trails. Wildlife is abundant, including populations of black bear, moose, elk, coyote, and beaver.

© ANDREW HEMPSTEAD

BRITISH COLUMBIA

dawn at Cascade Lookout, Manning Provincial Park

A park highlight is the paved road immediately across Highway 3 from Manning Park Resort; it climbs steadily to **Cascade Lookout,** a viewpoint offering a magnificent 180-degree panoramic view. Beyond the lookout, the road turns to gravel and continues climbing for nine kilometers (5.6 mi.), ending at a flower-filled alpine meadow. Take time to soak up the color by taking one of the short trails originating from the parking lot. If it's between late July and mid-August, you won't believe what you'll see—a rich yellow, orange, and white carpet of wildflowers.

Along Highway 3 are some short self-guided nature trails. Just east of the Visitor Information Centre, on the south side of the road, is the 500-meter (0.3-mi.) **Beaver Pond Trail.** If you notice people arriving on foot in this parking lot with worn soles, bent backs, and great big smiles on their faces, give them a pat on the back—they may have just completed one of the world's greatest long-distance hikes, the **Pacific Crest Trail** which runs 3,860 kilometers (2,400 mi.) from the U.S.–Mexico border to this small and undistinguished trailhead.

Along Highway 3, **Manning Park Resort** (250/840-8822 or 800/330-3321, www.manning parkresort.com) is a full-service lodging providing comfortable hotel rooms, cabins, and triplexes, as well as a dining room, self-serve cafeteria, small grocery store, and an open fireside lounge. Other facilities include saunas, an indoor pool, a TV room, a fitness center, and tennis courts, a coin-operated laundry, and a gift shop. Through summer, rooms in the main lodge start at $85 s or d, and chalets with kitchens range $119–249. The most popular of four park campgrounds is **Lightning Lake,** two kilometers (1.2 mi.) west of Manning Park Resort, which has showers; $22.

The park's **Visitor Information Centre** is one kilometer (0.6 mi.) east of Manning Park Resort (250/840-8836, summer daily 8:30 A.M.–4:30 P.M.). Inside you'll find displays on recreation opportunities and on the area's natural and cultural history, as well as maps and detailed information about park facilities.

Princeton and Vicinity

At the confluence of the Similkameen and Tulameen Rivers, surrounded by low, tree-covered hills, lies the small ranching town of Princeton (pop. 3,000). The **Princeton and District Pioneer Museum** (167 Vermilion Ave., 250/295-7588, Mon.–Fri. 1–5 P.M.) features pioneer artifacts from Granite City, Chinese and Interior Salish artifacts, and a good fossil display.

Step back in time by crossing the river at the north end of Princeton's Bridge Street and turning left, continuing on to **Coalmont** (about 18 km/11.2 mi.), an old gold-rush town. You can't help but notice that the town's residents have a sense of humor—the welcoming sign states that Coalmont has no industry, but plenty of activity in the form of sleeping and daydreaming. The attractive old **Coalmont Hotel** (circa 1911) still stands, along with quite a number of homes—some with backyards crammed with eclectic collections of rusting mine machinery.

Through Coalmont is **Granite City,** site of a gold strike in 1885. After the initial discovery, a 13-saloon gold-rush city sprang to life, quickly becoming the third-largest city in the province. Not much remains of Granite City—a few fallen-down cabins among wild lilac bushes and trees—leaving it to your imagination to re-create the good ol' days.

Just a short stroll from downtown Princeton, **Riverside Motel** (307 Thomas Ave., 250/295-6232, $45 s, $50 d) was built in 1934 as a hunting and fishing lodge (ask the owner to show you a photo of the place taken in 1937—the cabins still look exactly the same). Each basic cabin has a toilet, a shower, and a kitchen. **Princeton Castle** (Hwy. 5A three km/1.9 mi. north of town, 250/295-7988 or 888/228-8881, www.castle resort.com, mid-May–mid-Oct.) provides campsites ($20) as well as accommodations in cabins that share bathrooms ($65), larger chalets (from $115), and lodge rooms ($79–89). The forested setting is beautiful, but what makes this place a little more interesting is the history. The "Castle" is actually the concrete and stone ruins of a massive cement plant, slowly being reclaimed by nature. There are lots of activities, including hiking and gold panning.

Cathedral Provincial Park

Wilderness hikers and mountaineers should not miss the turnoff to this spectacular 33,000-hectare (81,540-acre) park. Vehicular access is restricted to guests staying at **Cathedral Lakes Lodge** (250/492-1606 or 888/255-4453, www .cathedral-lakes-lodge.com) or those on a day trip (booked through the lodge; $75 pp). The resort provides various accommodations, including lodge rooms and rustic cabins. Rates starting at $305 pp for two nights include meals, use of canoes and a recreation room, and transportation to and from the base camp. Hiking trails lead from the resort to a variety of striking and enticingly named rock formations, including Stone City, Giant Cleft, Devil's Woodpile, Macabre Tower, Grimface Mountain, Denture Ridge, and Smokey the Bear.

Keremeos

As you approach mountain-surrounded Keremeos from the west, the road is lined with lush, irrigated orchards and fruit stands, one after another, which is probably what inspired the town's claim to fame as the "Fruit Stand Capital of Canada." You'll find cherries, apricots, peaches, pears, apples, plums, and grapes—if they're not in season you can buy them in jams and preserves. The town's main attraction is the **Grist Mill** (250/499-2888, mid-May–mid-Oct., $5), a restored water-powered mill built in 1877. This is where pioneer Similkameen Valley settlers used to grind locally produced wheat into flour. Take a guided tour of the mill, then try your hand at the many informative and entertaining hands-on displays at the Apple House Theatre, or enjoy traditional foods in the Summer Kitchen.

Vancouver Island

Vancouver Island, the largest isle in North America's Pacific, stretches for more than 450 kilometers (280 mi.) off the west coast of mainland British Columbia. Victoria, the provincial capital, lies at the southern tip of the island and is connected to the much larger city of Vancouver by regular ferry services. Its deeply entrenched British traditions make Victoria unique among North American cities. North of the capital, a chain of rugged mountains, sprinkled with lakes and rivers and pierced by deep inlets, effectively divides the island into two distinct sides: dense, rain-drenched forest and remote surf- and wind-battered shores on the west, and well-populated, sheltered, beach-fringed lowlands on the east.

Victoria

Victoria, the elegant capital of British Columbia, boasts a mild climate, friendly people, and a distinct holiday atmosphere somewhat unusual for a capital city. Standing proudly at the southern tip of Vancouver Island, the fashionable city of 360,000 projects an intriguing mixture of images, old and new. Well-preserved century-old buildings line inner-city streets; ancient totem poles sprout from shady parks; restored historic areas house trendy shops, offices, and exotic restaurants; double-decker buses and horse-drawn carriages compete for summer trade; and the residents keep alive the original traditions and atmosphere of Merry Olde England.

Many people view the city for the first time from the Inner Harbour, coming in by boat the way people have for almost 150 years; on rounding Laurel Point, Victoria sparkles into view. Ferries, fishing boats, and seaplanes bob in the harbor, backdropped by manicured lawns and flower gardens, quiet residential suburbs, and striking inner-city architecture. Despite the pressures that go with city life, easygoing Victorians still find time for a stroll along the waterfront, a round of golf, or a typically English high tea.

HISTORY

Needing to establish British presence on the continent's northwest coast, the Hudson's Bay Company built Fort Victoria—named after Queen Victoria—on the southern tip of Vancouver Island in 1843. Three years later, the Oregon Treaty fixed the U.S.–Canada boundary at the 49th parallel, with the proviso that the section of Vancouver Island lying south of that line would be retained by Canada. To forestall any claims that the United States may have had on the area, the British government went about settling the island, opening up the land around Fort Victoria to British settlers.

The Growth of Victoria

In the late 1850s gold strikes on the mainland's Thompson and Fraser Rivers brought thousands of gold miners into Victoria, the region's only port and source of supplies. Overnight, Victoria became a classic boomtown, but with a distinctly British flavor; most of the company men, early settlers, and military personnel firmly maintained their homeland traditions and celebrations. Even after the gold rush ended, Victoria remained an energetic bastion of military, economic, and political activity, and was officially incorporated as a city in 1862. In 1868, two years after the colonies of Vancouver Island and British Columbia were united, Victoria was declared the capital.

INNER HARBOUR SIGHTS

Initially, Victoria's Inner Harbour extended farther inland; prior to the construction of the massive stone causeway that now forms the marina, the area was a mudflat. Overlooking the Inner Harbour, the pompous, ivy-covered 1908 **Empress Hotel** is Victoria's most recognizable landmark. It's worthwhile walking through the hotel lobby to gaze—head back, mouth agape—at the interior razzle-dazzle, and to watch people-watching people partake in traditional afternoon tea (see Food section).

Royal British Columbia Museum

Canada's most-visited museum and easily one of North America's best, the **Royal British Columbia Museum** (675 Belleville St., 250/356-7226, daily 9 A.M.–5 P.M., adult $11, senior and youth $7.70) is a must-see attraction for even the most jaded museum-goer. Its fine Natural History Gallery displays are extraordinarily true to life, complete with appropriate sounds and smells. Come face-to-face with an ice-age woolly mammoth, stroll through a coastal forest full of deer and tweeting birds, meander along a seashore or tidal marsh, then descend into the Open Ocean Exhibit in a submarine—a very real trip not recommended for claustrophobes. The First Peoples Gallery holds a fine collection of artifacts from the island's first human inhabitants, the

continued on page 122

BRITISH COLUMBIA

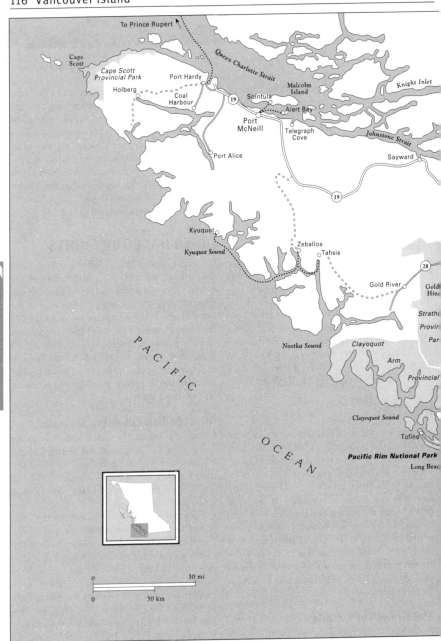

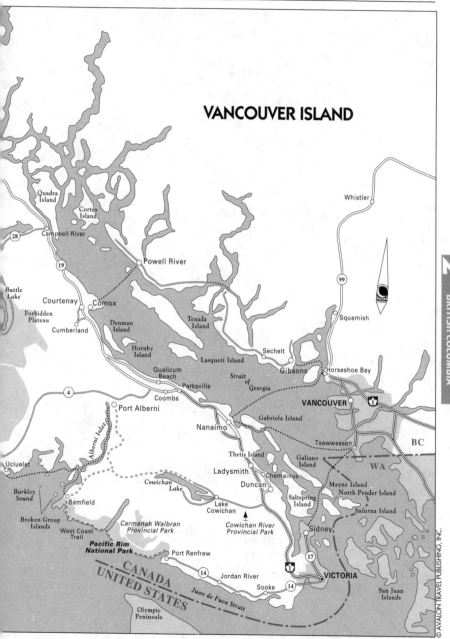

VANCOUVER ISLAND

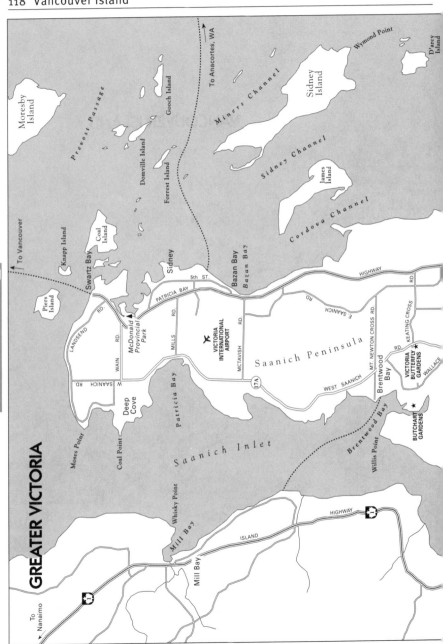

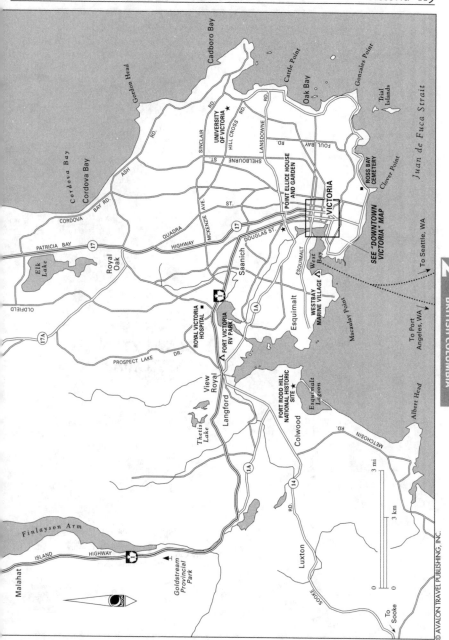

BRITISH COLUMBIA

© AVALON TRAVEL PUBLISHING, INC.

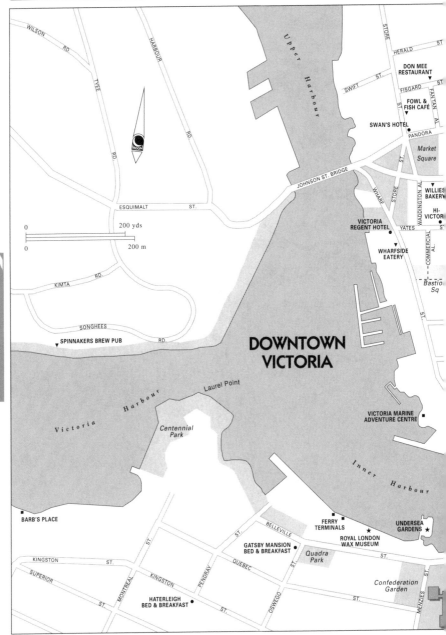

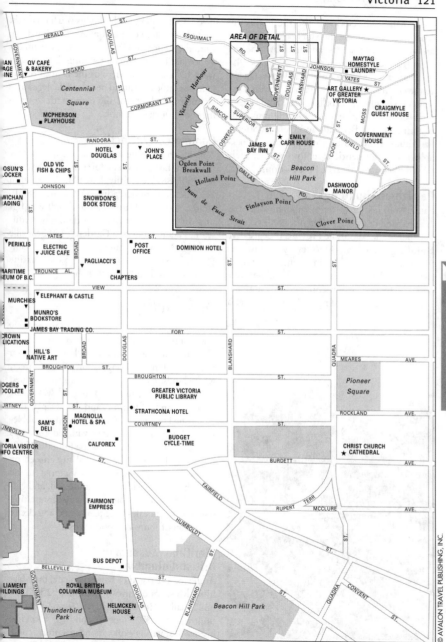

Nuu-chah-nulth (Nootka). Also within the museum is an excellent gift shop for books and natives arts and crafts, a tearoom, and an IMAX theatre.

In front of the museum, the 27-meter (89-ft.) **Netherlands Centennial Carillon** was a gift to the city from British Columbia's Dutch community. The tower's 62 bells toll at 15-minute intervals daily 7 A.M.–10 P.M. On the museum's eastern corner, at Belleville and Douglas Streets, lies **Thunderbird Park,** a small green spot chock-ablock with authentic totem poles intricately carved by northwest coast First Nations.

Parliament Buildings

Satisfy your lust for governmental, historic, and architectural knowledge all in one go by taking a free tour of the harborside **Provincial Legislative Buildings** (250/387-3046, every 20 minutes 9 A.M.–noon and 1–5 P.M. in summer). Dating to the 1890s, these impressive stone buildings were designed by Francis Rattenbury. The exterior is British Columbia Haddington Island stone, and

if you walk around the buildings you'll no doubt spot many a stern or gruesome face staring down from the stonework. Walk through the main entrance and into the memorial rotunda, look skyward for a dramatic view of the central dome, then continue upstairs to peer into the legislative chamber, the home of the democratic government of British Columbia.

Commercial Attractions

A former harborside steamship terminal is now the **Royal London Wax Museum** (470 Belleville St., 250/388-4461, daily 9:30 A.M.–5 P.M., until 7:30 P.M. in summer, adult $10, senior $8.50, child $5), which features around 300 wax figures direct from London. Beside the wax museum, **Pacific Undersea Gardens** (490 Belleville St., 250/382-5717, daily 10 A.M.–7 P.M., adult $9, child $7) boasts more than 5,000 marine specimens in their "natural" habitat.

OLD TOWN

The oldest section of Victoria lies immediately north of the Inner Harbour, between Wharf and Government Streets. Start by walking north from the Inner Harbour along historic Wharf Street, where Hudson's Bay Company furs were loaded onto ships bound for England, gold seekers arrived in search of fortune, and shopkeepers first established businesses. Cross the road to cobble-stoned **Bastion Square,** lined with old gas lamps and decorative architecture dating from the 1860s to 1890s. This was the original site chosen by James Douglas in 1843 for Fort Victoria. At one time the square held a courthouse, jail, and gallows. Today restored buildings house interesting restaurants and cafés, nightclubs, and an eclectic collection of shops and boutiques.

Maritime Museum of British Columbia

At the top (east) end of Bastion Square, the Maritime Museum of British Columbia (250/385-4222, daily 9:30 A.M.–4:30 P.M., until 6 P.M. in summer, adult $7, senior $6, child $3) traces the history of seafaring exploration, adventure, commercial ventures, and passenger travel through

© ANDREW HEMPSTEAD

Parliament buildings

displays of dugout canoes, model ships, Royal Navy charts, figureheads, photographs, naval uniforms, and bells. One room is devoted to exhibits chronicling the circumnavigation of the world, and another holds a theater.

SOUTH OF THE INNER HARBOUR

Emily Carr House

In 1871, artist Emily Carr was born in this typical upper-class 1864 Victorian-era home at 207 Government St. (250/383-5843, mid-May–mid-Oct. daily 10 A.M.–5 P.M., adult $6, senior and child $5). Carr moved to the mainland at an early age, escaping the confines of the capital to draw and write about the British Columbian natives and the wilderness in which she lived. She is best remembered today for her painting, a medium she took up in later years.

Beacon Hill Park and Vicinity

This large, hilly city park—a lush, sea-edged oasis of grass and flowers—extends from the back of the museum, along Douglas Street, and out to cliffs that offer spectacular views of Juan de Fuca Strait and, on a clear day, the distant Olympic Mountains. Add a handful of rocky points to scramble on and many protected pebble-and-sand beaches and you've found yourself a perfect spot to indulge your senses. Catch a sea breeze and gaze at all the strolling, cycling, dog-walking, and pram-pushing Victorians passing by.

If you're driving (or riding a bike), incorporate Beacon Hill Park on a coastal drive that follows the water's edge all the way from the Inner Harbor to the University of Victoria. For the first few kilometers, the Olympic Mountains in Washington State are clearly visible across the Strait of Georgia, and many lookouts allow you to stop and take in the panorama, including **Clover Point.** Just beyond the point, volunteers are on hand at **Ross Bay Cemetery** to point out the final resting place of prominent Victoria residents such as artist Emily Carr and Billy Barker of gold rush fame. Continuing east, Dallas Road leads through upscale residential areas, past small

pebble beaches covered in driftwood, and into the ritzy mansion district east of downtown. Beyond the oceanfront fairways of Victoria Golf Club and the Royal Victoria Yacht Club, the road reaches the university. From here head southwest along Cadboro Bay Road then Yates Street to get back downtown.

ROCKLAND AND OAK BAY

This historic part of downtown lies behind the Inner Harbour, east of Douglas Street, and is easily accessible on foot.

Christ Church Cathedral

Built in 1896, in 13th-century Gothic style, this distinctive cathedral (Quadra and Courtney Streets 250/383-2714, Mon.–Fri. 8:30 A.M.–5 P.M. and Sun. 7:30 A.M.–8:30 P.M.) is one of Canada's largest churches. It's open for self-guided tours and free choral recitals each Saturday at 4 P.M.

Art Gallery of Greater Victoria

From Christ Church Cathedral, walk up Rockland Avenue through the historic Rockland district, passing stately mansions and colorful gardens on tree-lined streets. Turn left on Moss Street and you'll come to the 1889 **Spencer Mansion** and its modern wing, which together make up the Art Gallery of Greater Victoria (1040 Moss St., 250/384-4101, Mon.–Sat. 10 A.M.–5 P.M., Thurs. 10 A.M.–9 P.M., and Sun. 1–5 P.M., adult $6, child $3). The gallery contains Canada's finest collection of Japanese art, a range of contemporary art, Emily Carr pieces, and traveling exhibits, as well as a Japanese garden with a Shinto shrine.

Government House

Continue up Rockland Avenue from the art gallery to reach Government House, the official residence of the lieutenant governor, the queen's representative in British Columbia. The surrounding gardens—including an English-style garden, a rose garden, and a rhododendron garden, along with green velvet lawns and picture-perfect flower beds—are open to the public throughout the year.

WEST OF DOWNTOWN

Point Ellice House and Garden

Built in 1861, this restored mansion sits amid beautiful gardens on Point Ellice, less than two kilometers (1.2 mi.) from the Inner Harbour (Pleasant St., 250/380-6506, mid-May–mid-Sept., daily 10 A.M.–5 P.M., adult $5, senior $4, child $3). Victorian-era artifacts clutter every nook and cranny of the interior, but the real reason to visit is to indulge in a traditional English afternoon tea (daily noon–4 P.M., $18.95 includes admission). Rather than driving, jump aboard a Victoria Harbour Ferry (250/708-0201, $3) to reach the property.

Fort Rodd Hill National Historic Site

Clinging to a headland across the harbor entrance from CFB Esquimalt, this picturesque site (603 Fort Rodd Hill Rd., Colwood, 250/478-5849, daily 10 A.M.–5:30 P.M., adult $4, senior $3, child $2.50) comprises Fort Rodd, built in 1898 to protect the harbor, and Fisgard Lighthouse, which dates from 1873. It's an interesting place to explore: Audio stations bring the sounds of the past alive, workrooms are furnished as they were at the end of the 19th century, and the fully restored lighthouse is open to visitors.

Goldstream Provincial Park

Lying 20 kilometers (12 mi.) from the heart of Victoria, this 390-hectare (960-acre) park straddles Highway 1 northwest of downtown. The park's main natural feature is the **Goldstream River,** which flows north into the Finlayson Arm of Saanich Inlet. Forests of ancient Douglas fir and western red cedar flank the river, orchids flourish in forested glades, and forests of lodgepole pine, western hemlock, and maple thrive at higher elevations. From the picnic area parking lot two kilometers (1.2 mi.) north of the campground turnoff, a trail leads 500 meters (0.3 mi.) to an interpretation center (250/478-9414, daily 9 A.M.–5 P.M.) where the life cycle of salmon that spawn in the river (Nov.–Dec.) is described. Continue beyond the center for five minutes to reach the head of Finlayson Arm (a great bird-watching spot).

SAANICH PENINSULA

The Saanich Peninsula is the finger of land that extends north from downtown. It holds Victoria's most famous attraction, Butchart Gardens, as well as Victoria International Airport and the main arrival point for ferries from Tsawwassen.

Butchart Gardens

These delightful gardens on Tod Inlet are Victoria's best-known attraction. They're approximately 20 kilometers (12 mi.) north of downtown (800 Benvenuto Dr., Brentwood Bay, 250/652-4422). They were developed in the early 1900s to beautify an abandoned quarry, the owners creating what has evolved into one of the world's premier private gardens. The gardens now contain more than 5,000 varieties of flowers, and the extensive nurseries test-grow some 35,000 new bulbs and more than 100 new roses every year. Go there in spring, summer, or early autumn to treat your eyes and nose to a marvelous sensual experience. Summer visitors are in for a special treat on Saturday nights (July and Aug. only), when a spectacular fireworks display lights up the garden.

The gardens are open every day of the year from 9 A.M., closing in summer at 10 P.M. and in winter at 4 P.M. Admission in summer is adult $21, student $10.50, child $2, dropping by 50 percent in mid-winter. To get there from downtown take Highway 17 north to the Brentwood–Butchart Gardens turnoff, turn left on Keating Crossroad, and follow the signs.

Victoria Butterfly Gardens

In the same vicinity as Butchart Gardens, Victoria Butterfly Gardens (corner of Benvenuto Rd. and W. Saanich Rd., 250/652-3822, Mar.–Oct. daily 9 A.M.–4:30 P.M., adult $9, senior $8, child $5) offers you the opportunity to view and photograph some of the world's most spectacular butterflies at close range. Thousands of these beautiful creatures live here, flying freely around the enclosed gardens and feeding on the nectar provided by colorful tropical plants.

Sidney

The small town of Sidney, on the east side of the

Saanich Peninsula, is a pleasant spot in which to spend a sunny afternoon. From the marina, the **Sidney Harbour Cruise** (250/655-5211, $18 pp) runs four tours daily around the harbor and to a couple of the inner Gulf Islands. The only official attraction is **Sidney Museum** (next to the marina at 9801 Seaport Pl., 250/656-2140, summer daily 10 A.M.–5 P.M.), with a whale of a display (including skeletons).

RECREATION

All of Vancouver Island is a recreational paradise, but Victorians find plenty to do around their own city. Walking and biking are especially popular, and from the Inner Harbour, it's possible to travel on foot or by pedal power all the way along the waterfront to Oak Bay.

The **Victoria Marine Adventure Centre,** based on a floating dock just around the corner from the information center along Wharf Street (250/995-2211 or 800/575-6700, www.marine-adventures.com), represents a range of operators and rents bikes and boats. Their specialty is whale-watching trips, which cost around $80.

Water Sports

Ocean River Sports (1824 Store St., 250/381-4233 or 800/909-4233, www.oceanriver.com) leads three-hour guided paddles in the Inner Harbour ($60 pp) as well as full-day trips, and kayaking courses. Rentals are also available.

The best beaches are east of downtown. At **Willows Beach,** Oak Bay, most of the summer crowds spend the day sunbathing, although a few hardy individuals brave a swim. Closer to downtown, at the foot of Douglas Street, the foreshore is mostly rocky, but you can find a couple of short sandy stretches here and there. **Elk Lake,** toward the Saanich Peninsula, and **Thetis Lake,** west of downtown along Highway 1, are also popular swimming and sunbathing spots.

Biking

For those keen on getting around by bike, it doesn't get much better than the bike path following the coastline of the peninsula on which Victoria lies. From downtown, ride down Government Street to Dallas Road, where you'll pick up the separate bike path running east along the coast to the charming seaside suburb of Oak Bay. From there, Oak Bay Road takes you back into the heart of the city for a round-trip of 20 kilometers (12.4 mi.). You can rent bikes at **Sports Rent** (611 Discovery St., 250/385-7368) for $6–8 per hour, $25–35 per day.

ARTS AND ENTERTAINMENT

Victoria has a vibrant performing arts community, with unique events designed especially for the crowds of summer. The city lacks the wild nightlife scene of neighboring Vancouver, but a large influx of summer workers keeps the bars crowded and a few nightclubs jumping during the busy season. The city does have more than its fair share of British-style pubs, and you can usually get a good meal along with your pint of lager. The magazine *Monday* (www.monday.com) offers a comprehensive arts and entertainment section.

Theater and Music

Dating from 1914, the grand old **McPherson Playhouse** at the corner of Pandora Avenue and Government Street hosts a variety of performing arts. For schedule information and tickets for both the "Mac" and the **Royal Theatre** (805 Broughton St.), call the Royal & McPherson Theatre Society (250/386-6121 or 888/717-6121). Performing arts on a smaller scale can be appreciated at the **Belfry Theatre** (1291 Gladstone St., 250/385-6815, Oct.–Apr., from $25 pp).

Pacific Opera Victoria (250/385-0222) performs three productions each year (usually through the winter months) in the McPherson Playhouse. Tickets run $20–65.

Bars

The **Strathcona Hotel** (919 Douglas St., 250/383-7137) is Victoria's largest entertainment venue, featuring four bars, including one on a magnificent rooftop patio and the Sticky Wicket, an English bar complete with mahogany paneling. Closer to the Inner Harbour and converted from an old grain warehouse is **Swans**

Hotel (506 Pandora St., 250/361-3310), which brews its own beer using traditional methods, such as allowing the brew to settle naturally rather filtering it. The beer is available at the hotel's bar, in its restaurants, and in the attached liquor store. A few blocks farther north and right on the water is the **Harbour Canoe Club** (450 Swift St., 250/361-1940), which is popular for its large deck.

Also offering magnificent water views is **Spinnakers Brew Pub** (308 Catherine St., 250/384-6613, daily 11 A.M.–2 P.M.). Opened in 1984 as Canada's first brew pub, Spinnakers continues to produce its own European-style ales, including the popular Spinnakers Ale. A casual atmosphere, large waterfront deck, and great food make this place well worth the diversion. It's across the Inner Harbour from downtown.

SHOPPING

Government Street is the main strip of tourist and gift shops. The bottom end, behind the Empress Hotel, is where you'll pick up those tacky T-shirts and such. Farther up the street are more stylish shops, such as **James Bay Trading Co.** (1102 Government St., 250/388-5477), which specializes in native arts from coastal communities; **Hill's Native Art** (1008 Government St., 250/385-3911), selling a wide range of authentic native souvenirs; and **Cowichan Trading** (1328 Government St., 250/383-0321), featuring Cowichan sweaters. Traditions continue at **Rogers Chocolates** (913 Government St., 250/384-7021), which is set up like a candy store of the early 1900s, when Charles Rogers first began selling his homemade chocolates to the local kids.

In Old Town, the colorful, two-story **Market Square** courtyard complex was once the haunt of sailors, sealers, and whalers who came ashore looking for booze and brothels. It's been jazzed up, and today shops here specialize in everything from kayaks to condoms. Walk out of Market Square on Johnson Street to find camping-supply stores and the interesting **Bosun's Locker** (580 Johnson St., 250/386-1308), filled to the brim with nautical knickknacks.

FESTIVALS AND EVENTS

The second half of May has always been a busy time for festivals in Victoria, and in recent years these events have come to be known collectively as the **Victoria Harbour Festival.** The "festival" incorporates the **Luxton Pro Rodeo** (250/478-4250), the **Swiftsure International Yacht Race,** a writing festival, special events at Fort Rodd Hill National Historic Site, and a parade of bands in front of the parliament buildings.

For eight days from the last Sunday in June, the **FolkFest** (250/388-4728, www.icavictoria .org) features contemporary and traditional jazz along Wharf Street. Hosted by the local symphony orchestra, the **Summer Cathedral Festival** (250/386-6121, www.victoriasymphony .bc.ca) showcases soloist and orchestra performances over 10 evenings in the historic surroundings of Victoria's best-known church. The first Sunday in August brings the unique **Symphony Splash,** when the local symphony orchestra performs from a barge moored in the Inner Harbour to masses crowded around the shore. Running the last week of August, the **Victoria Fringe Festival** (250/383-2663, www .victoriafringe.com) sees over 300 acts performing at venues throughout the city, including the harbor foreshore.

ACCOMMODATIONS

Finding a room in Victoria can be difficult during the summer months, when gaggles of tourists compete for a relative paucity of rooms. If you're after a regular motel room, check the provincial accommodation guide. If you're after something a little more special, you won't go wrong at any of the following places.

Under $50

In the heart Old Town is HI–Victoria (516 Yates St., 250/385-4511 or 888/883-0099, www.hi hostels.ca), enjoying a great location only a stone's throw from the harbor. Separate dorms and bathroom facilities for men and women are complemented by two fully equipped kitchens, a large meeting room, lounge, library, game room, travel services, public Internet terminals, and an informative bulletin board. Members pay $20 per night, nonmembers $24; private rooms range $50–64 s or d. Housed in the upper stories of an old commercial building, **Ocean Island Backpackers Inn** (791 Pandora Ave., 250/385-1788 or 888/888-4180, www.ocean island.com; $22 pp) has all the usual hostel facilities along with an upbeat atmosphere and plenty of space for relaxing.

$50–100
In a quiet residential area immediately east of downtown, **Craigmyle Guest House** (1037 Craigdarroch Rd., Rockland, 250/595-5411 or 888/595-5411, $75 s, $90–100 d) is a rambling old home full of character, comfortable furnishings, and lots of original stained-glass windows. An inviting living room with a TV, a bright sunny dining area, and friendly longtime owners make this a real home-away-from-home.

The centrally located **Hotel Douglas** (1450 Douglas St., 250/383-4157 or 800/332-9981, www.hoteldouglas.com) is one of Victoria's many old hotels, this one with 75 refurbished rooms. Guests have use of a coin laundry, and downstairs is a 24-hour café and quiet bar. Rooms with shared bathroom (but with a wash basin) are $60 s or d, while larger rooms with their own bathroom are $80–90 s or d.

Selkirk Guest House (934 Selkirk Ave., Esquimalt, 250/389-1213 or 800/974-6638, www .selkirkguesthouse.com) is right on the Gorge Waterway three kilometers (1.9 mi.) from the Inner Harbour. The only thing separating the house from the water is the manicured garden, complete with a hot tub that sits under an old willow tree. Three of the guest rooms share bathrooms and a kitchen while the more spacious Rose Room has an en suite bathroom, patio, fireplace, and its own kitchen ($85 s or d). Breakfast is an additional $5 pp.

$100–150
Dating from 1911 and once home to artist Emily Carr, **James Bay Inn** (270 Government St., 250/384-7151 or 800/836-2649, www.james bayinn.bc.ca) is within easy walking distance of all city sights. The place has an old-fashioned look but a bright and breezy decor and new beds in the simply furnished rooms. Rates start at $125–150 s or d; outside of summer, pay for five nights and receive two nights free. All guests enjoy discounted meals at the in-house restaurant and pub.

Away from the water, but still just one block from Douglas Street, is the 1876 **Dominion Hotel** (759 Yates St., 250/384-4136 or 800/663-6101, www.dominion-hotel.com). Millions have been spent restoring the property with stylish wooden beams, brass trim and lamps, ceiling fans, and marble floors re-creating the Victorian era. Yet staying at the Dominion is still reasonable. Advertised rates are $119–139 s, $129–149 d, but off-season deals here are especially attractive, such as one night's accommodation and a three-course dinner for $99 d.

$150–200
Separated from downtown by Beacon Hill Park, **Dashwood Manor** (1 Cook St., 250/385-5517 or 800/667-5517, www.dashwoodmanor.com), a 1912 Tudor-style heritage house on a bluff overlooking Juan de Fuca Strait, enjoys a panoramic view of the entire Olympic mountain range. The 14 rooms are elegantly furnished, and host Derek Dashwood will happily recount the historic details of each room. Rates range from $165 s or d up to $295 for the Oxford Grand, which holds a chandelier, stone fireplace, and antiques.

$200–300
Right on the Inner Harbour, **Gatsby Mansion** (309 Belleville St., 250/388-9191 or 800/563-9656, www.bellevillepark.com) has the most central position of any local bed-and-breakfast. Dating from 1897, this 20-room inn has been elegantly restored, with stained-glass windows, a magnificent fireplace, lots of exposed wood, crystal chandeliers under a gabled roof, and antiques decorating every corner. Afternoon tea is served in a comfortable lounge area off the lobby, and the restaurant has a nice veranda. Through summer, rooms start at $235 s, $245 d; the biggest and best of these, with a king-size bed and harbor view, is $309 s, $319 d. Packages offered make staying at the Gatsby Mansion

more reasonable, or visit in winter for as little as $129 s, $139 d.

The **Magnolia Hotel & Spa** (623 Courtney St., 250/381-0999 or 877/624-6654, www.magnoliahotel.com, $260–300 s or d) is a European-style boutique hotel. The rooms are elegantly furnished and feature floor-to-ceiling windows, heritage-style furniture in a contemporary room layout, down duvets, a work desk with cordless phone, and coffeemakers. Many also feature a gas fireplace. The bathrooms are huge, each with marble trim, a soaking tub, and separate shower stall. The Magnolia is also home to a day spa, two restaurants, and a small in-house brewery.

A few blocks back from the Inner Harbour, but still within pleasant walking distance, **Haterleigh Heritage Inn** (243 Kingston St., 250/384-9995, www.haterleigh.com, $230–375 s or d) has been beautifully restored to its early 1900s glory, complete with period furnishings and stained-glass windows. Each of the six spacious rooms features a luxurious en suite bathroom.

Over $300
Completely restored in 1996, the grand old **Fairmont Empress** (721 Government St., 250/384-8111 or 800/257-7544, www.fairmont.com) is Victoria's best-loved accommodation. Covered in ivy and with only magnificent gardens separating it from the Inner Harbour, it's also in the city's best location. Rooms are offered in 90 different configurations; like other hotels of the era, most are small, but each is filled with Victorian period furnishings and antiques. The least expensive Fairmont Rooms start at $329, but check the website for deals.

CAMPGROUNDS
West
The closest camping to downtown is at **Westbay Marine Village** (across Victoria Harbour at 453 Head St., Esquimalt, 250/385-1831, www.westbay.bc.ca). Facilities at this RV-only campground include full hookups and a launderette. It's part of a new marina complex comprising floating residences and commercial businesses such as restau-

rants and fishing charter operators. Water taxis connect the "village" to downtown. Rates are $36 per night.

Fort Victoria RV Park (340 Island Hwy., 250/479-8112, $30) is six kilometers (3.7 mi.) northwest of the city center on Highway 1A. This campground provides hookups (no official tent sites), free showers, laundry facilities, and opportunities to join charter salmon-fishing trips.

North Along Highway 1
Continuing west from Fort Victoria RV Park, Highway 1 curves north through **Goldstream Provincial Park** (19 km/11.8 mi. from downtown, $22) and begins its up-island journey north. The southern end of the park holds 161 campsites scattered around an old-growth forest—it's one of the most beautiful settings you could imagine close to a capital city. The campground offers free hot showers but no hookups. In Malahat, seven kilometers (4.3 mi.) farther north along Highway 1, is **KOA Victoria West** (250/478-3332 or 800/562-1732, www.koa.com). Facilities include free showers, an outdoor pool, laundry, store, and game room. Unserviced sites are $24, hookups $28–32, and Kamping Kabins from $54.

FOOD
Coffeehouses and Cafés
Murchies (1110 Government St., 250/381-5451) is a large coffeehouse on Victoria's busiest downtown street. It has all the usual choices of coffee concoctions as well as light snacks. Continuing away from the harbor and across the road, is the **Electric Juice Café** (1223 Government St., 250/380-0009). Here you'll find a huge selection of fruit and vegetable juices mixed to your liking and with the option of adding extras such as ginseng and bee pollen.

In Old Town, **Willies Bakery** (537 Johnson St., 250/381-8414) is an old-style café offering cakes, pastries, and sodas, with a quiet cobbled courtyard in which to enjoy them. Across the road, on the second story of Market Square, the **Bavarian Bakery** (560 Johnson St.,

250/388-5506) also sells a wide range of bakery delights.

While tourists flock to the cafés and restaurants of the Inner Harbour, Douglas Street remains the haunt of lunching locals. Reminiscent of days gone by, **John's Place** (just off Douglas St. at 723 Pandora Ave., 250/389-0711) serves up excellent value for those in the know. The food is good, the atmosphere casual, and the waitresses actually seem to enjoy working here. It's breakfast, burgers, salads, and sandwiches through the week, but weekend brunch is busiest, when there's nearly always a line spilling onto the street.

Casual Dining

Right across from the information center, and drawing tourists like a magnet, is **Sam's Deli** (805 Government St., 250/382-8424, daily 7:30 A.M.–10 P.M.). Many places nearby have better food, but Sam's boasts a superb location and cheerful atmosphere. The ploughman's lunch, a staple of English pub dining, costs $8.50, while sandwiches range $5.50–8 and salads are all around $6–9. If you want to know what the weather in Victoria is like, check the restaurant's Sam Cam at www.samsdeli.com.

A few blocks up Government Street from Sam's is the **Elephant and Castle** (at View St., 250/383-5858), an English-style pub featuring exposed beams, oak paneling, and traditional pub decor. A few umbrella-shaded tables line the sidewalk out front. All the favorites, such as steak and kidney pie and fish and chips, range $8–14.50.

The **James Bay Inn** (270 Government St., 250/384-7151) also serves up typical English pub food at reasonable prices. Look for dishes such as kippers and poached eggs for breakfast, ploughman's lunches, and roast beef with Yorkshire pudding or steak and kidney pie in the evening.

Seafood

Fish and chips is a British tradition and is sold as such at **Old Vic Fish & Chips** (1316 Broad St., 250/383-4536, Mon.–Sat. 11 A.M.–7 P.M.). Away from the tourist-clogged streets of the Inner Harbour, right at sea level, is **Barb's Place,** on Fisherman's Wharf (St. Lawrence St., 250/384-6515).

The specialty is fish and chips to go, but the seafood chowder is also good.

Wharfside Eatery (1208 Wharf St., 250/360-1808) is a bustling waterfront complex with a maritime theme and family atmosphere. Behind a small café section and a bar is the main dining room and a two-story deck, where almost every table has a stunning water view. The menu features lots of local seafood—halibut, salmon, snapper—as well pizza from a wood-fired oven. The seafood-oriented tapas menu is a good choice for sharing a variety of dishes between two or more, and includes oysters ($2), a skewer of prawns ($4), and the like.

At street level of Swan's Hotel is the **Fowl & Fish Café** (1605 Store St., 250/361-3150, daily from 5 P.M.). The red-brick and exposed-beam interior reflects its past use as a grain warehouse. The cuisine can best be described as "fusion"—local seafood and game prepared using Asian techniques. Appetizers include a creamy oyster chowder and seafood tapas for $5–8, while most main dishes, including salmon and halibut, are around $20–25.

European

One of the most popular restaurants in town is **Pagliacci's** (1011 Broad St., 250/386-1662, daily 11:30 A.M.–midnight), known for hearty Italian food (entrées $12–18), homemade bread, great desserts, and loads of atmosphere.

A good place to go for traditional Greek food, and live entertainment on weekends, is **Periklis** (531 Yates St., 250/386-3313). Main courses range $12–25, and almost anything can be happening on the floor—from belly dancers to Greek dancing.

The **Garlic Rose Café** (1205 Wharf St., 250/384-1931) offers a Mediterranean-inspired menu (lots of herbs are used), with seating out front, inside, and upstairs. Dinner entrées range $18–22, but the daily specials include an appetizer for around the same price.

Chinese

Victoria's small Chinatown surrounds a short, colorful strip of Fisgard Street between Store and Government Streets. Near the top (east) end of

© ANDREW HEMPSTEAD

Head to Chinatown for an inexpensive meal.

Fisgard is **QV Café and Bakery** (1701 Government St., 250/384-8831), offering inexpensive Western-style breakfasts in the morning and Westernized Chinese the rest of the day. Named for the Chinese province renowned for hot and spicy food, **Hunan Village Cuisine** (546 Fisgard St., 250/382-0661) offers entrées ranging $8–15. It's open Monday–Saturday for lunch and daily for dinner.

Empress Dining

Afternoon tea is served just about everywhere in Victoria—it's a local tradition—but the most popular place to indulge is the Fairmont Empress (721 Government St., 250/389-2727). It's also the most over-commercialized, but try to keep in mind that you're taking part in one of the oldest Victorian rituals. Sample English honey crumpets, homemade scones with cream and jam, finger sandwiches, pastries, and an Empress blend tea, while enjoying the soft music of a pianist for $42 per person ($32 outside summer). It's served in three different areas of the hotel, including the most traditional location, tableside in the Tea Lobby. Sittings take place five times an afternoon from noon, still, it's so pop-

ular that reservations are necessary up to two weeks in advance.

The **Empress Room** is the hotel's most formal restaurant (and the most expensive; entrées start at $30), dishing up West Coast cuisine in an elegant setting accompanied by the soft tones of a harpist. Dress is smart casual, with no jeans allowed.

You needn't spend a fortune to dine at the Empress, although a buffet is a far cry from the two options detailed above. Head to the hotel's **Bengal Lounge** for a curry lunch buffet 11:30 A.M.–3 P.M. or a curry dinner buffet Sunday–Thursday 6–9 P.M. Friday and Saturday evenings an à la carte East Indian menu is offered, with live background jazz. Prices range from $6.50 for soup to a reasonable $14–23 for main courses.

INFORMATION AND SERVICES
Tourist Information

Tourism Victoria (www.tourismvictoria.com) runs the bright, modern **Victoria Visitor Info Centre** (812 Wharf St., 250/953-2033 or 800/663-3883, daily 9 A.M.–5 P.M.) down on the Inner Harbour. Coming off the ferry from Vancouver, stop in at **Saanich Peninsula Visitor Info**

Centre (250/656-0525, daily 9 A.M.–5 P.M.) three kilometers (1.9 mi.) south of the terminal.

Books and Bookstores

Greater Victoria Public Library (735 Broughton St., 250/382-7241) is open Monday–Friday 9 A.M.–6 P.M., Saturday 9 A.M.–1 P.M. **Crown Publications** (521 Fort St., 250/386-4636) is a specialty bookstore with a great selection of western Canadiana and maps. Right downtown, **Munro's Bookstore** (1108 Government St., 250/382-2464) is in a magnificent neoclassical building that originally opened as the Royal Bank in 1909. Munro's may be the grandest bookstore in town, but it's not the largest. That distinction goes to **Chapters** (1212 Douglas St., 250/380-9009). For second-hand and rare west coast and nautical titles, search out **Wells Books** (824 Fort St., 250/360-2929).

Emergency Services

In a medical emergency call 911 or contact **Royal Jubilee Hospital** (1900 Fort St., 250/370-8000). For non-urgent cases, a handy facility is **James Bay Medical Treatment Centre** (230 Menzies St., 250/388-9934).

Other Services

The main post office is on the corner of Yates and Douglas Streets.

To change your money to the colorful Canadian variety, head to any of the major banks or to **Calforex** (Victoria Conference Centre, 724 Douglas St., 250/384-6631). **Lens & Shutter** (615 Fort St., 250/383-7443) offers full photographic services, including one-hour photofinishing, sales, and repairs. **Maytag Homestyle Laundry** (250/386-1799) is at 1309 Cook Street.

GETTING THERE

By Air

Vancouver Island's main airport is on the Saanich Peninsula, 20 kilometers (12 mi.) north of Victoria's city center. The terminal building houses a lounge, café, and various rental car agencies. The **AKAL Airporter** (250/386-2525 or 877/386-2525) operates buses between the airport and major downtown hotels every 30 minutes; $14

per person each way. A taxi costs approximately $45 to downtown.

Scheduled flights link the international airports of Vancouver and Victoria, but it's such a short flight (25 minutes from terminal to terminal) that unless you're on a connecting flight, the alternatives are more practical.

Smaller airlines, including those with floatplanes and helicopter services, provide a direct link between Victoria's Inner Harbour and the downtown Vancouver waterfront. **Harbour Air** (250/384-2215 or 800/665-0212) charges $100 each way, with those over 65 and prepared to go standby paying just $50.

By Bus

The main Victoria bus depot is behind the Empress Hotel at 710 Douglas Street. **Pacific Coach Lines** (604/662-8074 or 250/385-4411, www.pacificcoach.com) operates bus service between Vancouver's Pacific Central Station and downtown Victoria, via the Tsawwassen–Swartz Bay ferry. In summer the coaches run hourly 6 A.M.–9 P.M.; $30 one-way, $56 round-trip, which includes the ferry fare. The trip takes 3.5 hours. This same company also runs three daily buses from Vancouver International Airport directly to Victoria for a few bucks extra.

By Ferry

From Tsawwassen (Vancouver): BC Ferries (250/386-3431, www.bcferries.com) run regularly across the Strait of Georgia from Tsawwassen, 30 kilometers (18.8 mi.) south of Vancouver, to the Swartz Bay Ferry Terminal, 32 kilometers (20 mi.) north of Victoria. Through summer, ferries run hourly 7 A.M.–10 P.M., the rest of the year slightly less frequently. The crossing takes 90 minutes. You can expect a wait in summer; limited vehicle reservations are accepted (604/444-2890 or 888/724-5223; $15 per booking). Peak fares are adult $10, child 5–11 $5, vehicle $34.75.

From Seattle: Clipper Navigation (206/448-5000 or 800/888-2535, www.victoriaclipper.com) has a fleet of foot-passengers-only ferries connecting Seattle's Pier 69 with Victoria's Inner Harbour. Its turbojet catamaran, the *Victoria Clipper IV,* traveling at speeds up to 45 knots, makes the crossing in two hours. One-way fares are adult US$77, senior US$71, child US$38.50, with discounts for round-trip tickets, advance purchase, and off-season travel. The service runs year-round, with up to five sailings daily.

From Anacortes: Washington State Ferries (206/464-6400 or 250/381-1551, www.wsdot.wa.gov/ferries) run between Anacortes and the San Juan Islands, with the 7:50 A.M. sailing continuing to Sidney (32 km/20 mi. north of Victoria). The return sailing departs Sidney at 11.45 A.M. The one-way fare is adult US$13.10, senior US$6.50, vehicle and driver US$33.25. Reservations must be made at least 24 hours in advance.

From Port Angeles: The **MV *Coho*** (360/457-4491, www.cohoferry.com) crosses Juan de Fuca Strait in just over 90 minutes, arriving in Victoria's Inner Harbour. It makes four crossings daily in each direction mid-May–mid-October, two crossings daily the rest of the year. The one-way fare is adult US$8.50, child US$4.40, vehicle and driver US$33.

GETTING AROUND

Bus

Most of the inner-city attractions can be reached on foot. However, the **Victoria Regional Transit System** (250/385-2551, www.transitbc.com) is an excellent bus network, and it's easy to jump on and off and get everywhere you want to go. Pick up an *Explore Victoria* brochure at the information center for details of all the major sights, parks, beaches, and shopping areas, and the buses needed to reach them. Fares are charged per zone: Zone 1 covers most of the city (adult $1.75, senior or child $1.10), while Zone 2 covers outlying areas such as the airport and Swartz Bay ferry terminal (adult $2.50, senior or child $1.75). For extensive bus travel, consider a Day Pass (adult $5.50, senior or child $4).

Water Taxi

Take to the water with **Victoria Harbour Ferry** (250/708-0201). The company's distinctive 12-passenger boats ply two routes departing from the Inner Harbour. One takes in harborside docks,

including Fisherman's Wharf, Ocean Pointe Resort, and Westbay Marine Village, while the other heads up the Gorge Waterway; $3 per sector; or make the round-trip as a tour for $14.

Taxi

Taxis operate on a meter system, charging $2.75 at the initial flag drop plus around $2 per kilometer. Call **Blue Bird Cabs** (250/382-3611 or 800/665-7055), **Empress Taxi** (250/381-2222), or **Victoria Taxi** (250/383-7111).

Car Rental

Victoria is home to all the major car-rental agencies. Demand is high through summer, so book well in advance. Rental agencies and their local numbers include **Avis** (250/386-8468), **Budget** (250/953-5300), **Enterprise** (250/475-6900), **Hertz** (250/656-2312), **Island Auto Rentals** (250/384-4881), **National** (250/386-1213), **Rent-a-Wreck** (250/384-5343), and **Thrifty** (250/383-3659).

TOURING VICTORIA

The classic way to see Victoria is from the comfort of a horse-drawn carriage. Throughout the day and into the evening **Tally-Ho** (250/383-5067) has carriages lined up along Menzies Street at Belleville Street awaiting passengers. A 30-minute tour costs $70, a 45-minute tour costs $90, or take a 60-minute Royal Tour for $130. These prices are per carriage (up to four passengers). Tours run 9 A.M.–midnight and bookings aren't necessary, although there's often a line.

Big red double-decker buses are as much a part of the Victoria tour scene as horse-drawn carriages. These are operated by **Gray Line** (250/388-6539) from beside the Inner Harbour. There are many tours to choose from, but to get yourself oriented while also learning some city history, take the 90-minute Grand City Drive. It departs from the harborfront every half hour 9:30 A.M.–4 P.M.; adult $18, child $9. The most popular of Gray Line's other tours is the one to Butchart Gardens ($42, including admission price).

Vicinity of Victoria

Two highways lead out of Victoria: Highway 14 heads west and Highway 1 heads north. Highway 14 is a spectacular coastal route that ends in Port Renfrew, the southern terminus of the rugged and remote West Coast Trail. Highway 1 leads north from Victoria to Duncan, Chemainus, and Ladysmith, each with its own particular charm. West of Duncan are massive Cowichan Lake, an inland paradise for anglers and boaters, and Carmanah Walbran Provincial Park, protecting a remote watershed full of ancient Sitka spruce that miraculously escaped logging.

SOOKE TO PORT RENFREW

About 34 kilometers (21 mi.) from Victoria, Sooke (pop. 4,500) is best known for a lodge that combines luxurious accommodations with one of Canada's most renowned restaurants. As far as actual local sights go, at **Sooke Regional Museum** (Sooke Rd. and Phillips Rd., 250/642-6351, daily 9 A.M.–6 P.M.) browse the indoor displays, then wander out back to count all 478 growth rings on the cross-section of a giant spruce tree.

Sooke Harbour House

Combining the elegance of an upmarket country-style inn with the atmosphere of an exclusive oceanfront resort, **Sooke Harbour House** (1528 Whiffen Spit Rd., 250/642-3421, www.sooke harbourhouse.com; $375–575 including breakfast) is one of British Columbia's finest accommodations as well as one of its most renowned restaurants. It sits high above the ocean on a bluff that affords panoramic views across the ocean. Each of the 28 well-appointed rooms has views, with the more expensive ones featuring a hot tub and fireplace. The restaurant features simple, country-style decor, not that anything could possibly take away from the food and views. The menu changes daily, but most dishes feature local seafood, prepared to perfection with vegetables and herbs picked straight from the surrounding garden. Many diners disregard the cost and choose the eight-course table d'hôte menu ($99 pp), which represents a wide variety of seafood, including wild sea asparagus harvested from tidal pools below the restaurant.

West from Sooke

The first worthwhile stop west of Sooke is **French Beach Provincial Park,** where a short trail winds through a lush forest of Douglas fir and Sitka spruce to a rocky beach. It's a great place for a picnic or a walk—watch for gray whales. Along this stretch of coast are two great accommodations. The first, three kilometers (1.9 mi.) beyond French Beach, is **Point No Point Resort** (250/646-2020, www.pointno-pointresort.com, $150–240 s or d), whose 26 beautiful log cabins each have views, a full kitchen, and a fireplace. Explore the shore out front, relax on the nearby beach, or scan the horizon for migrating whales, with the Olympic Mountains as a backdrop. Meals are available in the lodge restaurant. Two kilometers (1.2 mi.) farther west, high upon oceanfront cliffs, **Fossil Bay Resort** (250/646-2073, www.fossilbay.com) offers six modern cottages, each with a hot tub, private balcony, fireplace, king-size bed, and full kitchen; $220 s or d, discounted for more than two nights.

Jordan River and Vicinity

When you emerge at the small logging town of Jordan River, take time to enjoy the smells of the ocean and the surrounding windswept landscape. The town comprises only a few houses and a local logging operation; beside the ocean is a small recreation area where surfers often camp overnight, waiting for the swells to rise and the long right-handed waves known as Jordan's to crank up.

Three kilometers (1.9 mi.) west of Jordan River, a 700-meter (0.4-mi.) trail leads through Sitka spruce to pebbly China Beach, which is strewn with driftwood and backed by a couple of protected picnic sites. Camping (back up by the highway) is $14 per night.

WEST COAST TRAIL

The magnificent West Coast Trail meanders 75 kilometers (47 mi.) along Vancouver Island's untamed western shoreline, through **Pacific Rim National Park.** It's one of the world's great hikes—exhilaratingly challenging, incredibly beautiful, and very satisfying. The very quickest hikers can complete the trail in four days, but by allowing six, seven, or eight days you'll have time to fully enjoy the adventure. The trail extends from the mouth of the Gordon River near Port Renfrew to Pachena Bay, near the remote fishing village of Bamfield on Barkley Sound. Along the way you'll wander along beaches, steep clifftops, and slippery banks; cross rivers by rope, suspension bridge, or ferry; climb down sandstone cliffs by ladder; tread slippery boardwalks, muddy slopes, bogs, and deep gullies; and balance on fallen logs. But for all your efforts you're rewarded with panoramic views of sand and sea, dense lush rainforest, waterfalls cascading into deep pools, all kinds of wildlife—gray whales, eagles, sea lions, seals, and seabirds—and the constant roar and hiss of the Pacific surf pummeling the sand.

The trail can be hiked from either direction—Port Renfrew is the preferred start, as the more demanding terrain is covered first, but you have a better chance of scoring a spot in the daily quota at the other end.

Permits, Transport, and Information

The trail is open mid-May–mid-October. For June–September travel, reservations (250/387-1642 or 800/435-5622, $25) are necessary. Ten spots are released each day at 1 P.M. at the registration offices at either end of the trail (expect a 1–2 day wait for your turn to come up). All hikers must obtain a Park Use Permit ($90) and take a quick orientation session before heading out. The only other cost is $28 for two river crossings en route; this is collected at the time of your booking.

West Coast Trail Express (250/477-8700 or 888/999-2288, www.trailbus.com) departs Victoria daily for both ends of the trail ($35–55), and also links the two trailheads ($50), the latter perfect for those who drive to either Port Renfrew or Bamfield. The company also rents camping and hiking gear.

The best source of trail information is the **Parks Canada website** (www.pc.gc.ca), which includes an overview of what to expect, instructions on trail-use fees, a list of equipment you should take, and a list of relevant literature. Seasonal park information/registration centers are in Port Renfrew (250/647-5434) and Pachena Bay (250/728-3234).

Port Renfrew

This small seaside community clings to the rugged shoreline of Port San Juan, 104 kilometers (65 mi.) from Victoria. An eclectic array of houses leads down the hill to the waterfront. Follow the signs to **Botanical Beach,** a fascinating intertidal pool area where low tide exposes all sorts of marine creatures at the foot of scoured-out sandstone cliffs. The road to the beach is rough and can be impassable in winter.

Accommodations are available at the **Trailhead Resort** (250/647-5468, www.trailhead-resort.com). Choose between motel-style rooms ($85 s or d) or spacious wood cabins with kitchens ($105 s or d). Ask about fishing packages. Right on the water, **Arbutus Beach Lodge** (5 Queesto Dr., 250/647-5458, www.arbutusbeachlodge.com, $75–105 s or d, includes light breakfast) offers basic accommodations and a great communal lounge and deck area overlooking the ocean. Beyond town, at the mouth of the San Juan River, **Port Renfrew Marina and RV Park** (250/647-5430; $17–20) offers open tent sites but no showers. Boat charters and fishing gear are available.

DUNCAN AND VICINITY

Duncan, self-proclaimed "City of Totems," lies at the junction of Highways 1 and 18, about 60 kilometers (37 mi.) north of Victoria. Native carvers, many from the local Cowichan band, have created some 80 intricate and colorful totem poles here. Look for them along the main highway near the information center, beside the railway station in the old section of town, and inside local businesses.

Two distinctly different native carvings stand side by side behind City Hall—a Native American carving and a New Zealand Maori carving.

Apart from the famous totem poles, Duncan's main attraction is the excellent **Quw'utsun' Cultural Centre** (200 Cowichan Way, 250/746-8119, daily 9 A.M.–6 P.M., adult $10, senior $8, child $6). Representing the arts, crafts, legends, and traditions of a 3,500-strong Quw'utsun' population spread through the Cowichan Valley, this facility features a longhouse, a carving shed, dance performances, and a café with native cuisine.

Cowichan River

This famous salmon and steelhead fishing river has its source at Lake Cowichan. Much of its length is protected by **Cowichan River Provincial Park,** which extends over 750 hectares (1,850 acres) and 20 kilometers (12 mi.). There are three access points to the park, including Skutz Falls, where salmon spawn each fall. Camping is $14. The paved road inland dead ends 32 kilometers (20 mi.) from Duncan at **Lake Cowichan,** a popular spot for canoeing, swimming, and especially fishing—the lake is stocked with kokanee

and a variety trout. Logging roads encircle the lake (75 km/47 mi. round-trip) and provide hikers access into the adjacent wilderness, including **Carmanah Walbran Provincial Park.**

Practicalities

Give Duncan's chain motels a miss and head west to **Sahtlam Lodge and Cabins** (5720 Riverbottom Rd. W, 250/748-7738, www.sahtlamlodge .com), where you can enjoy the tranquility of a riverside location from your own private cabin. Each is equipped with an old-style fireplace, woodstove, and full kitchen. Rates of $150 s, $180 d include a breakfast basket delivered daily to your cabin. Overlooking the river, the original 1920s lodge now houses an intimate restaurant open Wednesday and Friday–Saturday for dinner.

Always crowded with locals, **Arbutus Café** (Kenneth St. and Jubilee St., 250/746-5443) concocts a great shrimp salad for $8, sandwiches and hamburgers for $5–9, and specialty pies from $5.

Stop at **Duncan Visitor Info Centre** (Overwaitea Plaza, 250/746-4636, www.duncan cc.bc.ca, Mon.–Sat. 9 A.M.–5 P.M.) for the complete rundown on the area.

Southern Gulf Islands

This group of islands lies in the Strait of Georgia, off the southeastern coast of Vancouver Island and just north of Washington's San Juan Islands, which are part of the same archipelago. Five of the islands—Salt Spring, North Pender, Galiano, Mayne, and Saturna—are populated. The largest of the islands, Salt Spring, is home to more than triple the combined population of the other four.

The islands' mild, almost Mediterranean climate, beautiful pastoral scenery, driftwood-strewn beaches, and prolific marinelife (sea lions, bald eagles, harbor seals, killer whales, blue herons, cormorants, and diving ducks, among other species) are a haven from the hectic urban life of nearby Vancouver and Victoria. These appealing qualities have attracted creative people in search of life in the slow lane, as

well as swarms of hikers, campers, cyclists, canoeists, fishermen, beachcombers, island-hoppers, and art lovers.

SALT SPRING ISLAND

Largest of the Southern Gulf Islands, Salt Spring (pop. 9,500) lies close to the coast of Vancouver Island, immediately north of Saanich Inlet. Ferries link the south and north ends of the island to Vancouver Island, and myriad roads converge on the service town of Ganges. The laid-back island is home to a large number of artisans, along with hobby farmers, retirees, and those attracted by island life.

Salt Spring Island Visitor Info Centre (121 Lower Ganges Rd., Ganges, 250/537-5252, www.saltspringisland.bc.ca) is open in summer daily 8 A.M.–6 P.M., the rest of the year Monday–Friday 8:30 A.M.–4:30 P.M.

Sights and Recreation

From the **Fulford Harbour** ferry terminal, take Beaver Point Road east to 486-hectare (1,200-acre) **Ruckle Provincial Park.** The access road ends at the rocky headland of Beaver Point, from where trails lead north along the coastline, providing great views across to North Pender Island. Although the island offers good hiking opportunities, it's better known for water-oriented activities such as kayaking, boating, and fishing. Based at Fulford Harbour, **Saltspring Kayak & Cycle** (250/653-4222) offers guided trips, including a two-hour sunset paddle for $35 pp. **Salt Spring Marine Rentals** (Salt Spring Marina, 250/537-9100) rents boats and offers fishing charters.

Accommodations and Camping

The island's least expensive accommodation is **HI–Salt Spring Island** (640 Cusheon Lake Rd., 250/537-4149, mid-Mar.–mid-Oct.). As well as regular dorms, three tepees and two tree houses are spread through the four-hectare (10-acre) property. One of the tree houses is accessed by a ladder and hatch. The interior features a tree through the middle, a skylight over the bed, and wicker furniture. Rates start at $17 for members.

Maple Ridge Cottages (301 Tripp Rd., 250/537-5977, $110–140 s or d) is a lakefront property with canoes and kayaks available for guest use. Each of the nine cottages has a kitchen, private deck, and fireplace.

The campground in **Ruckle Provincial Park** is in a forest of Douglas fir overlooking Swanson Channel. All sites are a short walk from the parking lot, making this place unsuitable for RVs; $14 per night. On the north side of the island on St. Mary Lake, **Lakeside Gardens Resort** (250/537-5773) offers sites with full hookups for $20–26 and self-contained cottages for $60–100, along with showers and a beach with boat rentals.

Transportation

Closest of the Southern Gulf Islands to Vancouver Island, Salt Spring is served by **BC Ferries** (250/386-3431). Ferries run 10–12 times daily between Swartz Bay and Fulford Harbour, and even more frequently between Vesuvius Bay, at the island's north end, and Crofton. Fares for travel on either route are the same, and as all prices are for the round-trip you can leave the island from either end at no extra charge. Peak round-trip fares are adult $6.50, child $3.50, vehicle $22.50.

NORTH PENDER ISLAND

A short ferry ride from Salt Spring Island's Long Harbour ferry terminal, this smallish island (pop. 2,000) has many great little beaches and provides ocean access at over 20 points. One of the nicest spots is **Hamilton Beach** on Browning Harbour. This is also the main service area, from which roads radiate out to all points of the island. One road leads across a rickety old wooden bridge to South Pender Island, site of **Beaumont Provincial Marine Park.**

Pender Island Visitor Info Centre (250/629-6541, June–mid-Sept. daily 9 A.M.–6 P.M.) is east of the ferry terminal, up the hill.

Accommodations and Camping

The least expensive way to enjoy an overnight stay on North Pender Island is to camp at **Prior Centennial Provincial Park,** six kilometers (3.7 mi.) south of the Otter Bay ferry terminal. Sites are primitive, with no showers or hookups, but the location is excellent; $14 per night. The island's premier accommodation is the **Oceanside Inn** (250/629-6691, www.penderisland.com). The three guest rooms are comfortably furnished and a wide deck takes full advantage of the glorious waterfront location. Off-season rates start at $129 s or d, rising to $209–269 in summer. Breakfast, included in the rates, is a real treat, and dinner is available on request.

Transportation

Up to seven times a day ferries depart the Swartz Bay terminal (250/656-5571) for North Pender Island. Most sailings are direct (40 minutes), although a couple of the early-morning trips go via Galiano and Mayne Islands (over two hours), so check the timetable carefully before boarding. The peak round-trip fare is adult $6.50, child $3.50, vehicle $22.25.

GALIANO ISLAND

Named for a Spanish explorer who sailed through the Strait of Georgia over 200 years ago, this long, narrow island, 27 kilometers (16.7 mi.) from north to south but only three kilometers (1.9 mi.) wide, lies north of Salt Spring Island. Most of the population lives in the south, around the ferry terminal at Sturdies Bay. Right at the terminal is **Galiano Island Visitor Info Centre** (250/539-2233, www.galianoisland.com, July–Aug. daily 9 A.M.–5 P.M.).

Sights and Recreation

One of the best ways to explore local waterways is with **Galiano Island Kayaking** (Montague Harbour, 250/539-2442). Three-hour guided tours, either early in the morning or at sunset, are $40. Another tour takes in the local marinelife on a six-hour paddle for $65. Those with previous experience can rent a kayak at $40 per day for a single or $60 for a double.

Climbing out of Sturdies Bay, Porlier Pass Road crosses through **Montague Harbour Provincial Park,** which protects 89 hectares (220 acres) of coastline. The park offers a variety of short hikes through bird-filled forests of Douglas fir and along the shoreline—or follow a trail of your own along beaches strewn with broken seashells. Manmade piles of shells lie at the park's north end. Known as "middens," they accumulated over centuries of native use.

Accommodations and Camping

Within walking distance of the ferry terminal and set right on the water is **Bellhouse Inn** (29 Farmhouse Rd., 250/539-5667 or 800/970-7464, www.bellhouseinn.com, $135–195 s or d). The more expensive rooms feature a hot tub, private balcony, and fireplace. Rates include a full breakfast and niceties like tea or coffee delivered to your room before breakfast.

As with all provincial park campgrounds through the Southern Gulf Islands, the one at

Montague Harbour Provincial Park, 10 kilometers (6.2 mi.) from the ferry, has a superb setting, but facilities are limited to picnic tables, pit toilets, and drinking water; $14 per night.

Transportation

BC Ferries (250/539-2622) schedules four sailings daily between Swartz Bay and Galiano Island; peak round-trip fare is adult $6.50, child $3.50, vehicle $22.25. From the B.C. mainland, Galiano Island is the first stop for the Gulf Islands ferries, which depart at least twice daily from the Tsawwassen terminal. Peak one-way fare is adult $9, child $4.50, vehicle $35.50. Galiano Island is linked to Mayne Island by four sailings daily, with a couple of those continuing to the other islands. Interisland travel is adult $3, child $1.50, vehicle $7.

MAYNE ISLAND

Separated from Galiano Island by a narrow channel, Mayne Island is laced with country roads leading to all corners of the island. Village Bay has no village; all commercial facilities are at nearby **Miners Bay,** which got its name during the Cariboo gold rush, when miners used the island as a stopping point. Island beaches are limited to those at **Oyster Bay,** but visitors can enjoy interesting shoreline walks or take the road to the low summit of **Mount Park** for panoramic views.

Accommodations

Set on four hectares (10 acres) overlooking a protected waterway, guest rooms at **Oceanwood Country Inn** (630 Dinner Bay Rd., 250/539-5074, www.oceanwood.com) blend pastel color schemes with contemporary styling. My favorite is the Lavender Room—with a fireplace, four-poster bed, soaking tub, and private balcony—but each has its own charm. Within the lodge itself are four communal areas, including a well-stocked library and comfortable lounge. Gracious hosts Jonathan and Marilyn Chilvers cook up a gourmet storm for breakfast, with dinner (four courses for $48) also a memorable affair. Rates start at $179 s or d; rooms with ocean views range $269–344.

Transportation

From Swartz Bay, **BC Ferries** (250/539-2321) schedules four sailings daily to Mayne Island; peak round-trip fare is adult $6.50, child $3.50, vehicle $22.25. Sailings from the Tsawwassen ferry terminal (604/669-1211) depart at least once daily, with a stop at Galiano Island en route; the peak one-way fare is adult $10, child $5, vehicle $36.50.

SATURNA ISLAND

Most remote of the populated Southern Gulf Islands, Saturna protrudes into the heart of Georgia Strait and features a long, rugged northern coastline. From the ferry dock at **Lyall Harbour,** the island's main road follows this stretch of coast for 14 kilometers (8.7 mi.), ending at **East Point.**

Accommodations

Within walking distance of Lyall Harbour is **Sat-** **urna Lodge** (130 Payne Rd., 250/539-2254 or 888/539-8800, www.saturna-island.bc.ca). Right on the water, this modern accommodation offers seven guest rooms, a hot tub, and extensive gardens. Rates range $135–195, including a full breakfast. The lodge's small restaurant has a big reputation for seafood and local game and produce. The owners are involved in various projects around the island, including a successful vineyard and winery.

Transportation

Although Saturna is the most difficult of the main islands to reach by ferry, fares are no higher than on other routes. Direct ferries are available, but you might want to take one of the other ferries and explore one or more of the other islands on the way out to Saturna. Peak one-way fare on any interisland route is adult $3, child $1.50, vehicle $7.

Nanaimo and Vicinity

Nanaimo (na-NYE-mo) sprawls lazily up and down the hilly coastal terrain between sparkling Nanaimo Harbour and Mount Benson, on the east coast of Vancouver Island. With a population of 78,000, it's the island's second-largest city. It's also a vibrant city enjoying a rich history, mild climate, wide range of visitor services, and a direct ferry link to both of Vancouver's ferry terminals.

The Nanaimo Parkway bypasses the city to the west along a 21-kilometer (13-mi.) route that branches off the original highway five kilometers (3.1 mi.) south of downtown, rejoining it 18 kilometers (11.2 mi.) north of downtown.

History

Five native bands lived here (the name Nanaimo is derived from the Salish word Sney-Ny-Mous, or "meeting place"), and it was they who innocently showed dull, black rocks to Hudson's Bay Company employees in 1851. For most of the next century, mines in the area exported huge quantities of coal. Eventually, oil-fueled ships replaced the coal burners, and by 1949 most of the mines had closed. Surprisingly, no visible traces of the mining boom remain in Nanaimo, aside from a museum (built on top of the most productive mine) accurately depicting those times and a sturdy fort (now a museum) built in 1853 in case of a native attack.

SIGHTS

Downtown Nanaimo lies in a wide bowl sloping down to the waterfront, where forward thinking by early town planners has left wide expanses of parkland. Right in front of the Civic Arena is **Swy-A-Lana Lagoon,** a unique manmade tidal lagoon full of interesting marinelife. A promenade leads south from the lagoon to a bustling downtown marina filled with commercial fishing boats and leisure craft. Beside the marina is a distinctive mastlike sculpture that provides foot access to a tiered development with various viewpoints.

The Bastion

Overlooking the harbor at the junction of Bastion

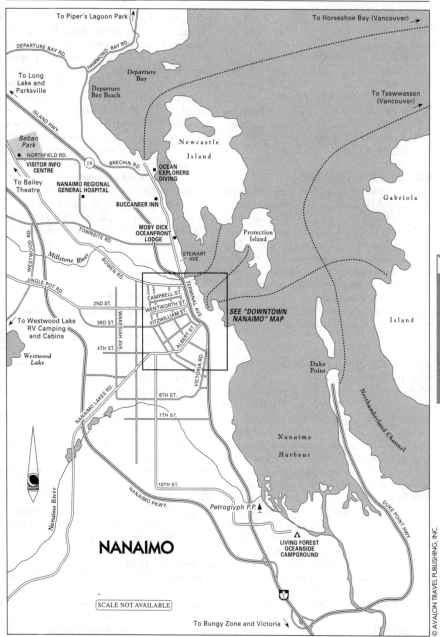

SEE "DOWNTOWN NANAIMO" MAP

NANAIMO

SCALE NOT AVAILABLE

BRITISH COLUMBIA

© AVALON TRAVEL PUBLISHING, INC.

and Front Streets stands the Bastion, a well-protected fort built in 1853 by the Hudson's Bay Company to protect employees and their families against attack by natives. Originally used as a company office, arsenal, and supply house, today the fort houses the **Bastion Museum** (summer daily except Tues. 10 A.M.–4 P.M., $2). For the benefit of tourists, a group of local university students dressed in appropriate gunnery uniforms and led by a piper parades down Bastion Street daily at noon in summer.

Nanaimo District Museum

In Piper Park, just across Front Street from the Bastion and up the stairs, is Nanaimo Museum (100 Cameron St., 250/753-1821, July–Aug. daily 10 A.M.–5 P.M., rest of year Tues.–Sat. 10 A.M.–5 P.M., $2). Walk around the outside to appreciate harbor, city, and mountain views, as well as replica petroglyphs of animals, humans, and spiritual creatures. Then allow at least an hour for wandering through the two floors of displays inside, which focus on life in early Nanaimo and include topics such as local geology, native peoples, and pioneers.

Newcastle Island Provincial Marine Park

Newcastle Island is a magnificent chunk of wilderness separated from downtown Nanaimo by a narrow channel. It's mostly forested, ringed by sandstone cliffs and a few short stretches of pebbly beach. Wildlife inhabitants include deer, raccoons, beavers, and more than 50 species of birds. A 7.5-kilometer (4.7-mi.) trail (allow 2–3 hours) encircles the island, leading to picturesque Kanaka Bay, Mallard Lake, and a lookout offering views east to the snowcapped Coast Mountains.

Meals are available in the **Pavilion Restaurant** (9 A.M.–7:15 P.M.). Ferries depart for the island from **Maffeo-Sutton Park** in summer daily 10 A.M.–7 P.M. on the hour, with extra sailings at 8 P.M. and 9 P.M. on Friday and Saturday. The round-trip fare is adult $5, senior or child $4. For details call **Scenic Ferries** (250/753-5141).

Other Parks

On the road into downtown Nanaimo from the south, two kilometers (1.2 mi.) north of the Nanaimo Parkway intersection, **Petroglyph Provincial Park** features a short trail leading to ancient petroglyphs (rock carvings). Petroglyphs, found throughout the province and common along the coastal waterways, were made with stone tools, and they recorded important ceremonies and events. The designs at this park were carved thousands of years ago and are believed to represent human beings, animals (real and supernatural), bottom fish, and the rarely depicted sea wolf, a mythical creature part wolf and part killer whale.

Along Hammond Bay Road, north of downtown and beyond Departure Bay, is **Piper's Lagoon Park,** encompassing an isthmus and a rocky headland that shelter a shallow lagoon. A trail from the parking lot leads to the headland, with views of the mainland across the Strait of Georgia.

RECREATION
Boating and Diving

The obvious way to appreciate the harbor aspect of Nanaimo is by boat. To arrange a cruise, wander down to the marina below the Bastion and inquire among the fishing and sightseeing charter boats, or stop by the Nanaimo Visitor Info Centre and ask for a list of local guides and charters, plus current prices.

A great variety of dives can be accessed from Nanaimo, including the HMAS *Saskatchewan,* a 120-meter (400-ft.) navy destroyer escort sunk off the city for the pleasure of divers. Marinelife is also varied, and divers mix with harbor seals, anemones, sponges, salmon, and "tame" wolf eels. Near the Departure Bay ferry terminal, **Ocean Explorers Diving** (1956 Zorkin Rd., 250/753-2055 or 800/233-4145, www.oceanexplorersdiving.com) is a well-respected island operation, offering equipment rentals, charters ($50 pp per dive), and courses.

Bungee Jumping

Nanaimo is home to North America's only bridge-based commercial bungee jump, **Bungy Zone** (250/716-7874). The jump site, 13 kilometers (eight mi.) south of downtown, is a bridge 42 meters (140 ft.) above the Nanaimo River. A single jump costs $95.

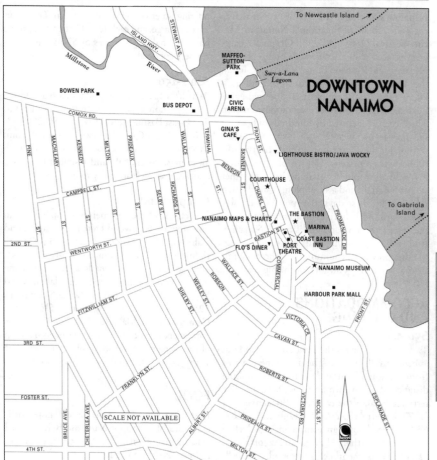

DOWNTOWN NANAIMO

To Newcastle Island

Millstone River

ISLAND HWY.
STEWART AVE.

MAFFEO-SUTTON PARK

Swy-a-Lana Lagoon

BOWEN PARK

BUS DEPOT

CIVIC ARENA

COMOX RD.

GINA'S CAFE

FRONT ST.

LIGHTHOUSE BISTRO/JAVA WOCKY

PINE
MACHLEARY
KENNEDY
MILTON
PRIDEAUX
WALLACE
TERMINAL
SKINNER ST.
BENSON ST.
CHAPEL ST.
BASTION ST.

COURTHOUSE

CAMPBELL ST.
RICHARDS ST.
SELBY ST.

NANAIMO MAPS & CHARTS

THE BASTION

MARINA

COAST BASTION INN

To Gabriola Island

PROMENADE DR.

2ND ST.
WENTWORTH ST.

FLO'S DINER

PORT THEATRE

COMMERCIAL

NANAIMO MUSEUM

FITZWILLIAM ST.
WALLACE ST.
ROBSON
WESLEY ST.
SHELBY ST.

HARBOUR PARK MALL

FRONT ST.

VICTORIA CR.

3RD ST.

CAVAN ST.

ROBERTS ST.

FOSTER ST.
BRUCE AVE.
CHETERLEA AVE.

FRANKLYN ST.

ALBERT ST.
PRIDEAUX ST.

VICTORIA RD.
NICOL ST.
ESPLANADE ST.

SCALE NOT AVAILABLE

4TH ST.

MILTON ST.

© AVALON TRAVEL PUBLISHING, INC.

ARTS AND ENTERTAINMENT

Lovers of the arts will find Nanaimo to be quite the cultural center, with the epicenter of the action at the **Port Theatre** (125 Front St., 250/754-8550). This magnificent 800-seat theater in an architecturally pleasing circular concrete-and-glass building opposite the harbor showcases theater productions, musicals, and music performances by a wide range of artists. The **Nanaimo Theatre Group** (250/758-7246) presents live performances at the Port Theatre as well as in the **Bailey Theatre** (2373 Rosstown Rd.).

The best place in Nanaimo for a quiet drink in a relaxing atmosphere is upstairs in the **Lighthouse Pub** (50 Anchor Way, 250/754-3212), built out over the water in front of downtown. This casual pub gets very busy in summer, with nightly drink specials, a pool table, and a good selection of pub food. For nautical atmosphere, head over to the **Dinghy Dock Marine Pub** (250/753-2373), moored at Protection Island; ferries depart regularly from Nanaimo Boat Basin.

World Championship Bathtub Race

On the fourth Sunday of every July the waters off

Nanaimo come alive for this fun event that is the grand finale of the annual **Nanaimo Marine Festival** (250/753-7223). Originally, competitors raced across the Strait of Georgia between Nanaimo and Kitsilano Beach, Vancouver. Today, they leave from downtown, racing around a 57-kilometer (36-mi.) course in a modified bathtub fitted with a 7.5-horsepower outboard motor. The racers are escorted by hundreds of boats of the more regular variety, loaded with people just waiting for the competitors to sink! Every bathtubber wins a prize—a golden plug for entering, a small trophy for making it to the other side of the strait, and a silver plunger for the first tub to sink! These days, the sport and the festivities around it have grown enormously, attracting tens of thousands of visitors to Nanaimo. And "tubbing," as the locals call it, has spread to other provincial communities, where preliminary races qualify entrants for the big one.

ACCOMMODATIONS AND CAMPING

$50–100

Two motels, both on the same street, stand out as being excellent value. The first of these, across from the waterfront and within easy walking distance of downtown and the Departure Bay ferry terminal, is the two-story **Buccaneer Inn** (1577 Stewart Ave., 250/753-1246 or 877/282-6337, www.thebuccaneerinn.com). Bedecked with a nautical-themed mural and colorful baskets of flowers, the motel is surrounded by well-maintained grounds, a sundeck, picnic tables, and a barbecue facility. The rooms themselves are spacious and brightly decorated, and each holds a desk, coffeemaker, and small fridge. The smallest rooms are $65 s, $70 d, while kitchen suites, some with gas fireplaces, range $100–160 s, $110–170 d. Friendly owner/operators provide a wealth of information on the local area (as does the motel website).

A few blocks toward downtown from the Buccaneer is the **Moby Dick Oceanfront Lodge** (1000 Stewart St., 250/753-7111 or 800/663-2116, www.mobydicklodge.com). This four-story waterfront motel faces Newcastle Island,

offering water views from every room. The rooms are extra large, and each has a kitchen and private balcony, making the rates of $70 s, $80 d extremely good value.

$100–150

As you'd expect, accommodations right downtown are more expensive than those farther out. The **Coast Bastion Inn** (11 Bastion St., 250/753-6601 or 800/663-1144, www.coasthotels.com, $155 s or d) is a full-service 179-room hotel with an exercise room, café and restaurant, lounge, and water views from every room.

Campgrounds

The closest of the commercial campgrounds to downtown is **Westwood Lake RV Camping and Cabins** (380 Westwood Rd., 250/753-3922). It's right on the edge of beautiful Westwood Lake, offering fishing, canoe rentals, a few short hiking trails, a barbecue area, game room, laundry, and hot showers. Unserviced sites are $20, hookups $25, cabins $65. **Living Forest Oceanside Campground** (6 Maki Rd., 250/755-1755, www.campingbc.com, $18–24) is by the braided mouth of the Nanaimo River south of downtown. The setting is delightful and the facilities modern.

FOOD

First things first. This is the place to taste a delicious chocolate-topped **Nanaimo Bar**, a layered delicacy that originated in this city; try **Nanaimo Bakery** (2025 Bowen Rd.).

Cafés and Cheap Eats

Right on the harbor, in the Pioneer Waterfront Plaza, is **Javawocky** (90 Front St., 250/753-1688), a modern coffeehouse with all the usual coffee drinks, great milkshakes, inexpensive cakes and pastries, and light lunchtime snacks. In the heart of downtown, a few greasy spoons make good stops for breakfast. Pick of the bunch is **Flo's Diner** (187 Commercial St., 250/753-2148), complete with a counter, vinyl booths, and kitschy decorations. Breakfast portions are hearty, especially the filled omelets (as big as anywhere on the island), which are around $7–8.

Seafood

Head down to the marina at the foot of Wharf Street for seafood straight from the fishing boats. You can buy salmon, halibut, cod, snapper, shrimp, crabs, mussels, or whatever the day's catch might be at very reasonable prices—perfect if you're camping or have a motel room with a kitchen (many local accommodations also have outdoor barbecue facilities). Also at the marina is **Troller's** (250/741-7994), with tables and chairs set up around a small takeout counter on one of the arms of the floating dock. Expect to pay $6–8 for fish and chips. The nearby **Lighthouse Bistro** (50 Anchor Way, 250/754-3212, 11 A.M.–11 P.M.) is built over the water and has a large, heated outdoor deck. The salmon chowder ($6) is excellent and the halibut and chips ($12) comes exactly as it should—with crisp batter surrounding succulent fish.

Dinghy Dock Marine Pub (250/753-2373, daily 11 A.M.–11 P.M.) is a floating restaurant moored at nearby Protection Island. Well known for great food and plenty of seagoing atmosphere, the pub also hosts live entertainment on Friday and Saturday nights May–September. To get to the restaurant, take a ferry from Nanaimo Boat Basin. Ferries depart hourly 9:10 A.M.–11:10 P.M.

PRACTICALITIES

Information

Nanaimo is promoted to the world by **Tourism Nanaimo** (250/756-0106 or 800/663-7337, www.tourismnanaimo.bc.ca). The main **Nanaimo Visitor Info Centre** is north of downtown and off the main highway in the grounds of Beban Park at 2290 Bowen Road. For maps, nautical charts, and books about Vancouver Island, visit **Nanaimo Maps and Charts** (8 Church St., 250/754-2513).

Services

The post office is on Front Street in the Harbour Park Mall. For medical concerns, contact **Nanaimo Regional General Hospital** (1200 Dufferin Cres., 250/754-2141) or **Pharmasave** (530 5th St., 250/753-8234).

Transportation

BC Ferries (250/386-3431) operates ferries between Vancouver and Nanaimo along two

Down on the dock, Troller's is a great place to enjoy fish and chips.

routes. Fares on both are the same (adult $10, child $5, vehicle $34.75). Limited reservations are taken (604/444-2890 or 888/724-5223; $15 per booking). Ferries leave Vancouver's Tsawwassen terminal up to eight times a day for the two-hour trip to Nanaimo's **Duke Point** terminal, 20 minutes south of downtown. At the north end of Stewart Avenue, is the **Departure Bay,** where ferries from Horseshoe Bay arrive up to 11 times a day. The **Nanaimo Seaporter** (250/753-2118) meets all ferries, transporting passengers to downtown.

GABRIOLA ISLAND

Like the Southern Gulf Islands, Gabriola (pop. 3,400) is partly residential, but also holds large expanses of forest, abundant wildlife, and long stretches of unspoiled coastline. Take Taylor Bay Road north from the ferry terminal to access the island's best beaches, including those within five-hectare (12-acre) **Gabriola Sands Provincial Park.** Walk out to the park's southern headland to view sandstone cliffs eroded into interesting shapes by eons of wave action. The North and South Roads encircle the island, combining for a 30-kilometer (18.6-mi.) loop perfect for a leisurely bike ride. Many scenic spots invite you

to pull off—at petroglyphs, secluded bays, and lookouts.

Practicalities
Marina's Hideaway (943 Canso Dr., 250/247-8854 or 888/208-9850, www.marinashideaway .com, from $135 s or d) is a luxurious bed-and-breakfast overlooking Northumberland Channel. Each of the three guest rooms in this magnificent waterfront home has a king-size bed, gas fireplace, private entrance, and balcony. The least expensive way to overnight on the island is by camping at **Gabriola Campground** (595 Taylor Bay Rd., 250/247-2079, Apr.–Oct., $17). Facilities are limited (no showers or hookups), but it's a great little spot right on the ocean.

Basic services are available at **Folklife Village,** a little over one kilometer (0.6 mi.) from the ferry terminal on North Road. There you'll find a café, grocery store, and **Gabriola Island Visitor Info Centre** (250/247-9332, www.gabriolaisland.org, mid-May–mid-Sept. daily 9 A.M.–6 P.M.).

BC Ferries (250/386-3431) schedules 15 sailings daily between the terminal off Front Street in Nanaimo (downtown, across from Harbour Park Mall) and Gabriola Island. The trip takes 20 minutes each way. The peak round-trip fare is adult $5.50, child $2.75, vehicle $14.

West Coast

From Nanaimo, it's 35 kilometers (21.7 mi.) northwest up Highway 19 to one of Vancouver Island's main highway junctions, where Highway 4 spurs west to Port Alberni and the island's west coast. Follow Highway 4 to its end to reach Pacific Rim National Park, a long, narrow park protecting the wild coastal strip and some magnificent sandy beaches, and Tofino, a picturesque little town that makes the perfect base for sea kayaking, whale-watching, or fishing excursions.

HIGHWAY 4 TOWARD PORT ALBERNI

After turning off Highway 19, make your first stop at **Englishman River Falls Provincial Park,**

where the Englishman River cascades down a series of beautiful waterfalls. Within the park you'll find a picnic area, easy hiking trails to both the upper and lower falls, crystal-clear swimming holes, and plenty of campsites among tall cedars and lush ferns ($17 per night; no showers).

Coombs to Port Alberni
This small community comprises a row of old-fashioned country stores scattered around **Coombs Emporium and Frontier Town.** The shops sell everything from pottery planters, jewelry, and assorted knickknacks to tasty snacks and cool drinks. Check out **Wood and Bone Crafts** for a unique souvenir, and cast your eyes toward the grass-covered roof of Old Country

Market, where several goats can be seen contentedly grazing, seemingly oblivious to the amused, camera-clicking visitors.

Little Qualicum Falls Provincial Park is a 440-hectare (1,100-acre) reserve 10 kilometers (6.2 mi.) west of Coombs. The park's main hiking trail leads alongside the Little Qualicum River to a picturesque waterfall. Take your fishing pole along the riverside trail and catch a trout, stop for an exhilarating dip in one of the icy emerald pools, or stay the night in a sheltered riverside campsite ($17). The source of the Little Qualicum River is **Cameron Lake,** a large, deep-green, trout-filled body of water just outside the western park boundary. Magnificent old-growth forest encircles the lake, and at the west end is **MacMillan Provincial Park,** bisected by Highway 4. Here a short trail leads to majestic Cathedral Grove, a stand of Douglas fir up to 800 years old and 70 meters (230 ft.) high.

PORT ALBERNI AND VICINITY

If you hit Port Alberni on a cloudy day, you won't know what you're missing—until the sky lifts! Then beautiful tree-mantled mountains suddenly appear, and Alberni Inlet and the Somass River turn a stunning deep blue. Situated at the head of the island's longest inlet, Port Alberni is an industrial town of 19,500 centered around the forestry and fishing industries. Port Alberni has much to offer, including a couple of interesting museums, nearby provincial parks, and a modern marina filled with both charter fishing boats and tour boats, including the famous MV *Lady Rose.*

Sights

Follow the signs from Highway 4 to brightly decorated **Alberni Harbour Quay.** On the quay is the **Forestry Visitor Centre,** operated by the logging giant Weyerhaeuser (250/720-2108, July–Aug. daily 9:30 A.M.–5:30 P.M.). Find out more about the origins of the famous West Coast Trail, see a collection of native artifacts, or tinker with a variety of operational motorized machines from the forestry industry at the **Alberni Valley Museum** (10th Ave. and Wallace St., 250/723-2181, Tues.–Sat. 10 A.M.–5 P.M.).

Fishing

The main salmon runs occur in fall, when hundreds of thousands of salmon migrate up Alberni Inlet to their spawning grounds. To get the rundown on fishing charters head down to **Port Alberni Marina** (5104 River Rd., 250/723-8022). The owners, local fishing guides, have put together all kinds of printed information on local fishing. They know all the best spots and know how to catch the lunkers. Expect to pay around $250 for two people for a four-hour guided charter. The marina also rents boats (from $15 per hour or $90 per day, plus gas) and fishing rods ($12 per day).

MV *LADY ROSE*

This vintage Scottish coaster (250/723-8313 or 800/663-7192, www.ladyrosemarine.com) has been serving the remote communities of Alberni Inlet and Barkley Sound since 1949 as a supply and passenger service. But because of the spectacular scenery along the route, the cruise is also one of the island's biggest tourist attractions. Depending on the time of year, orcas and gray whales, seals, sea lions, porpoises, river otters, bald eagles, and all sorts of seabirds join you on your trip through magnificent Barkley Sound.

Year-round, the MV *Lady Rose* departs Alberni Harbour Quay Tuesday, Thursday, and Saturday at 8 A.M., reaching Bamfield at 12:30 P.M. After a one-hour layover, she docks back in Port Alberni at 5:30 P.M. In July and August, sailings are also made to Bamfield on Sunday, with a special stop for kayakers in the Broken Group Islands. If you want to stay longer in Bamfield, accommodations are available. June–mid-September an extra route is added to the schedule, with the vessel departing Monday, Wednesday, and Friday at 8 A.M. for the Broken Group Islands, arriving at Ucluelet at 12:30 P.M. for a 90-minute layover before returning to Port Alberni around 7 P.M. One-way fares from Port Alberni are Kildonan $12, Bamfield $23, Broken Group Islands $20, Ucluelet $25. Children half price.

Accommodations and Camping

Within walking distance of the quay is **Blue-bird Motel** (3755 3rd Ave., 250/723-1153 or 888/591-3888), which charges $65 s, $70 d for a standard motel room. The **Coast Hospitality Inn** (3835 Redford St., 250/723-8111 or 800/663-1144, www.coasthotels.com, $135 s, $145 d), part of an upscale Northwest chain, has large, brightly decorated rooms with super-comfortable beds.

The best camping is out of town at **China Creek Park Marina** (250/723-9812), where you have a choice of open or wooded full-facility sites ($16–28 per site), plus a marina, sailboard rentals, great views of the inlet from a sandy log-strewn beach, and lots of bald eagles for company. To get there take 3rd Avenue south to Ship Creek Road and follow it for 14 kilometers (8.7 mi.).

Food

At any time of day, the best place to find something to eat is down at Alberni Harbour Quay. At the entrance to the quay is **Blue Door Café** (5415 Argyle St., 250/723-8811, daily from 5 A.M.), a small old-style place that's a real locals' hangout. Breakfasts are huge; an omelet with all the trimmings goes for $6–7.50, and bottomless self-serve coffee is an extra buck. On the quay itself, **Turtle Island Fish & Chips** (5440 Argyle St., 250/723-4227) features delicious salmon and chips for $8.50 as well as other seafood delicacies. Eat at the couple of tables supplied, or, better still, down on the grassy waterfront area.

Information

On the rise above town to the east is **Port Alberni Visitor Info Centre** (2533 Redford St., 250/724-6535, late June–Sept. daily 8 A.M.–6 P.M., rest of year Mon.–Fri. 9 A.M.–5 P.M.). The best source of pretrip planning is the **Alberni Valley Chamber of Commerce** (www.avcoc.com).

BAMFIELD

One of the island's most remote communities, this tiny fishing village lies along both sides of a narrow inlet on Barkley Sound. Most people arrive here aboard the MV *Lady Rose* from Port Alberni,

but the town is also linked to Port Alberni by a rough 100-kilometer (62-mi.) logging road. It's well worth the trip out to go fishing, explore the seashore, or just soak up the atmosphere of this picturesque boardwalk village. Bamfield is also the northern terminus of the West Coast Trail (see Vicinity of Victoria, earlier in this chapter).

Practicalities

On the boardwalk, but across the channel from the road side of the village, **Bamfield Lodge** (250/728-3419, www.bamfieldlodge.com) comprises self-contained cabins set among trees and overlooking the water. The cabins are $100 per night, which includes water-taxi transfers. The lodge owners also operate the Boardwalk Bistro and a charter boat for fishing and wilderness trips.

UCLUELET

A small town of 1,800 on the northern edge of Barkley Sound, Ucluelet (yoo-CLOO-let) was first established centuries ago by the Nuu-chal-nulth people as a fishing village. In the native language, the town's name means "people with a safe landing place."

Many visitors are anglers who chase chinook salmon (Feb.–Sept.) and halibut (May–July), keeping a fleet of charter boats busy through summer. Head south through town, passing **He-tin-kis Park,** where a short trail leads through a littoral rainforest to a small stretch of rocky beach, to the end of Peninsula Road, where a lighthouse—one of the most accessible along Canada's west coast—guides shipping along the coast.

Practicalities

At unique **Canadian Princess Resort** (Peninsula Rd., 250/726-7771 or 800/663-7090, www.obmg.com) you can spend the night aboard the 75-meter (250-ft.) steamship *Canadian Princess,* which is permanently anchored in Ucluelet Harbour. The least expensive rooms aboard this historic gem are small and share bathroom facilities, but they're still a good value at $75 s, $85 d. The resort also offers modern, more expensive onshore rooms and has a large fleet of boats for fishing charters. Most people staying here do so on a multinight fishing package. Fisherfolk also congregate at **Island West Fishing Resort** (160 Hemlock St., 250/726-7515, www.islandwestresort.com), which has a marina, charter boats, a waterfront restaurant, and a pub. Kitchen-equipped rooms are a reasonable $95 s or d and RV parking (no tents) costs $28.

Ucluelet Visitor Info Centre (227 Main St., 250/726-7289) is open daily in summer and Monday–Friday only the rest of the year.

PACIFIC RIM NATIONAL PARK

Named for its location on the edge of the Pacific Ocean, this park encompasses a long, narrow strip of coast that has been battered by the sea for eons. The park comprises three "units," each very different in nature and each accessed in different ways. This section of text covers the **Long Beach Unit,** named for an 11-kilometer (6.8-mi.) stretch of beach accessed by Highway 4 to Tofino. (To the south, in Barkley Sound, is the Broken Group Islands Unit, while farther south still is West Coast Trail Unit, named for the famous hiking trail between Port Renfrew and Bamfield covered in Vicinity of Victoria, earlier in this chapter).

You're not charged a fee just to travel straight through to Tofino, but if you stop anywhere en route a strictly enforced charge applies. A one-day permit is $10.

Flora and Fauna

Like the entire west coast of Vancouver Island, Pacific Rim National Park is dominated by littoral (coastal) rainforest. Closest to the ocean, clinging to the rocky shore, a narrow windswept strip of Sitka spruce is covered by salty water year-round. These forests of spruce are compact and low-growing, forming a natural windbreak for the old-growth forests of western hemlock and western red cedar farther inland. The old-growth forests are strewn with fallen trees and lushly carpeted with mosses, shrubs, and ferns.

The park's largest land mammal is the black bear, some of which occasionally wander down to the beach in search of food. Also present are blacktail deer, raccoons, otters, and mink. Bald eagles are year-round residents, but it's the migratory birds that arrive in the largest numbers—in spring and fall, thousands of Canada geese, pintails, mallards, and black brants converge on the vast tidal mudflats of Grice Bay, in the north of the park beyond the Tofino golf course.

Long Beach

Ensconced between rocky headlands is 11 kilometers (6.8 mi.) of hard-packed white sand, covered in twisted driftwood, shells, and the occasional Japanese glass fishing float. Dense rainforest and the high snowcapped peaks of the Mackenzie Range form a beautiful backdrop, while offshore lie craggy surf-battered isles home to myriad marinelife. You can access the beach at many places, but first stop at the **Wickaninnish Centre** (250/726-4212, mid-Mar.–mid-Oct. daily 10:30 A.M.–6 P.M.), which overlooks the beach from a protected southern cove. This is the place to learn about the natural and human history of both the park and the ocean through exhibits and spectacular hand-painted murals.

Through summer Long Beach attracts hordes of visitors. Most just wander along the beach soaking up the smells and sounds of the sea, but some brave the cool waters for swimming or surfing (rent boards and wetsuits in Ucluelet or Tofino). In winter, hikers dress for the harsh elements and walk the surf-pounded beach in search of treasures, or admiring the ocean's fury during the many ferocious storms.

Hiking

The most obvious place for a walk is Long Beach, but other options are worth consideration. From the Wickaninnish Centre, an 800-meter (0.5-mi.) trail (15 minutes each way) leads south around a windswept headland, passing small coves and **Lismer Beach,** then descending a boardwalk to pebbly **South Beach.** Back up the hill, the 2.5-kilometer (1.6-mi.) **Wickaninnish Trail** leads over to Florencia Bay (around 90 minutes for the round-trip). Continuing northwest toward Tofino, the **Rainforest Trail** traverses an old-growth littoral rainforest in two one-kilometer (0.6-mi.) loops (allow 20 minutes for each). Farther north, at the back of the Combers Beach parking lot, is the trailhead for the 1.6-kilometer (one-mi.) **Spruce Fringe Loop.** This trail leads along the beach past piles of driftwood and through a forest of Sitka spruce.

Camping

The park's one official campground fills up very fast every day through summer. But it's in a marvelous location behind Green Point, a beautiful bluff above the beach. Facilities include drive-in sites, washrooms, picnic tables, an evening interpretive program, and plenty of firewood, but no showers or hookups. Mid-March–mid-October, walk-in sites are $15 per night, semiserviced $22; the rest of the year they're $12 and $18 respectively. The closest commercial campgrounds are between the park and Tofino.

Information

The **Park Information Centre** (250/726-4212, mid-Mar.–mid-June daily 10:30 A.M.–6 P.M., mid-June–Aug. 8 A.M.–8 P.M., Sept.–mid-Oct. 10 A.M.–6 P.M.) is on the north side of Highway 4 just inside the park boundary (coming from Port Alberni, turn right toward Tofino at the Ucluelet–Tofino highway junction).

TOFINO

The bustling fishing village of Tofino sits at the very end of a long narrow peninsula, its only road access to the outside world the winding Highway 4. Victoria is 340 kilometers (211 mi.) distant. Originally the site of a native Clayoquot village, Tofino was one of the first points in Canada to be visited by Captain Cook.

Fishing has always been the mainstay of the local economy, but Tofino is also a supply center for the several hundred hermits living along the secluded shores of the sound and for the hordes of visitors that come in summer to visit Pacific Rim National Park, just to the south. An influx of environmentally conscious residents over the last two decades has added flavor to one of the west

coast's most picturesque and relaxing towns. And due to a large number of aware residents who like Tofino exactly the way it is, it's unlikely that high-rise hotels or fast-food chains will ever spoil this peaceful coastal paradise.

Sun, Sand, and Surf

If you fancy a long walk along a fabulous shell-strewn stretch of white sand, like to sit on craggy rocks watching the waves disintegrate into white spray, or just want a piece of sun all your own to lie in and work on your tan, head for **Chesterman Beach,** just south of Tofino. From that beach at low tide you can walk all the way out to **Frank Island** to watch the surf pound the exposed side while the tide creeps in and cuts you off from civilization for a few hours. The turnoff (not marked) to Chesterman Beach is Lynn Road, on the right just past the Dolphin Motel as you leave Tofino. Surfers wanting to hit the water should head south of town to **Live To Surf** (1182 Hwy. 4, 250/725-4464), where boards are $30 per day and wetsuits $25.

Whale-Watching

Each spring around 20,000 gray whales migrate between Baja and Alaska, passing through the waters off Tofino between March and May. Most of them continue north, but some stay in local waters through summer and are accessible by a 20-minute boat trip. On the whale-watching trips, you'll likely spy other marinelife as well—sea lions and puffins sunning themselves on offshore rocks, dolphins and harbor seals frolicking in the bays and inlets, and majestic bald eagles gracefully swooping around in the sky or perching in the treetops. Trips depart mid-February–October and generally last 2–3 hours. Expect to pay about $50–60 per person with one of the follow companies: **Adventures Pacific** (120 4th St., 250/725-2811 or 888/486-3466), **Jamie's Whaling Station** (606 Campbell St., 250/725-3919 or 800/667-9913), **Remote Passages** (71 Wharf St., 250/725-3330 or 800/666-9833), or the **Whale Centre** (411 Campbell St., 250/725-2132 or 888/474-2288). Even with all these operators, business is brisk, so book ahead if possible.

Sea Kayaking

Exploring the waters around Tofino by sea kayak is extremely popular. **Tofino Sea Kayaking Company** (320 Main St., 250/725-4222, www.tofino-kayaking.com) has designed tours to meet the demand and suit all levels of experience. Excursions range from a 2.5-hour harbor paddle ($49 per person) to an overnight trip to a remote lodge on Vargas Island ($390 per person). The company's experienced staff will also help adventurous, independent paddlers plan an itinerary—many camping areas lie within a one-day paddle of Tofino. Kayak rentals start at $45 per day.

Eagle Aerie Gallery

This gallery (350 Campbell St., 250/725-3235, summer daily 9 A.M.–8 P.M., rest of year daily 9:30 A.M.–5:30 P.M.) features the distinctive paintings, prints, and sculptures of Roy Henry Vickers, a well-known and highly respected Tsimshian artist. You can watch a video about the artist, then browse among the artworks—primarily native Canadian designs and outdoor scenes with clean lines and brilliant colors. The gallery itself is built on the theme of a west coast native longhouse, with a carved and painted exterior and interior totem poles.

Accommodations

Tofino boasts plenty of accommodations, but getting a room in summer can be difficult if you just turn up, so book as far ahead as possible. Without exception, all accommodations offer deeply discounted off-season rates.

Tofino's least expensive accommodation is **Whalers on the Point Guesthouse** (81 West St., 250/725-3443, www.tofinohostel.com). Affiliated with Hostelling International, it is a world away from hostels of old, appealing to all travelers. The building is a stylish log structure in a stunning waterfront location of which the communal lounge area takes full advantage. Other facilities include a modern kitchen, laundry, large deck with a barbecue, game room, and bike rentals. Dorm beds are $24 for members, $26 for nonmembers. Private rooms start at $70 s or d.

A good choice for anglers is **Tofino Swell Lodge** (341 Olsen Rd., 250/725-3274), above a busy marina. Shared use of a fully equipped kitchen and living room (complete with stereo, TV, and telescope) are included in the rates of $90 s, $100 d. The stunning views across Tofino Inlet are priceless.

Out of town to the south are a number of oceanfront resorts, including **Middle Beach Lodge** (250/725-2900, www.middlebeach.com). It comprises two distinct complexes: "At the Beach," more intimate, with its own private beach (lodge rooms $110–150 s or d including a big, healthy breakfast), and "At the Headland," with luxurious self-contained chalets ($160–320 s or d) built along the top of a rugged headland. A short trail links the two, and guests are welcome to wander between them.

Cable Cove Inn (201 Main St., 250/725-4236 or 800/663-6449, www.cablecoveinn.com) overlooks a small cove yet is only a short stroll from the center of town. Well-furnished in a casual yet elegant style, each of the six rooms features a private deck and a fireplace. The least expensive room is $160 s or d, but the others, ranging $185–205, each have a hot tub.

Camping

All Tofino's campgrounds are on the beaches south of town, but enjoying the great outdoors comes at a price in this part of the world, with some campsites costing over $50 a night. Best of the bunch is **Bella Pacifica Campground** (250/725-3400, www.bellapacifica.com, $22–38), which is right on MacKenzie Beach and offers protected tent sites, full hookups, coin-operated showers, and a laundry. Along the same stretch of sand, **Crystal Cove Beach Resort** (250/725-4213, www.crystalcove.cc) is one of the province's finest campgrounds. Facilities are modern, with personal touches such as complimentary coffee each morning and a book exchange. Many of the sites are in a private heavily wooded area while others are right along the beach (unserviced $37, hookups $47).

Food

At the **Common Loaf Bake Shop** (180 1st St., 250/725-3915, daily 8 A.M.–6 P.M.), sit outside or upstairs, where you'll have a magnificent view down Tofino's main street and across the sound. Another popular café is the **Coffee Pod** (4th St., 250/725-4246), serving healthy sandwiches, salads, and cakes and pastries.

The best views in town are from the nautical-themed **Sea Shanty** (300 Main St., 250/725-2902), part of the Himwitsa Lodge complex above the marina. Breakfasts are around $7, pastas $13–15, and seafood delicacies—the bulk of the menu—over $18. In the less pretentious Weigh West Marine Resort's **Blue Heron Restaurant** (634 Campbell St., 250/725-3277), kick off a meal with super-creamy clam chowder ($7.50), and then dive into battered halibut and chips ($14) or splurge on a full crab ($24).

Information

Tofino Visitor Info Centre (121 3rd St., 250/725-3414, www.tofinobc.org) is open in summer daily 9 A.M.–9 P.M., the rest of the year Monday–Friday 11 A.M.–4 P.M.

Transportation

Laidlaw (250/725-3101 or 800/318-0818) runs one bus daily between Victoria and Tofino. The bus departs Victoria at 8:05 A.M. and Nanaimo at 11 A.M. before heading west along Highway 4, arriving in Tofino at 3:30 P.M. The return service departs Tofino at 4:10 P.M., arriving back in Nanaimo at 8:05 P.M. and Victoria at 11 P.M. **North Vancouver Air** (604/278-1608 or 800/228-6608) flies from its base near Vancouver's South Terminal to Tofino.

Northern Vancouver Island

Back on the east side of the island, the Inland Island Highway north of the Highway 4 junction bypasses a stretch of coast that has developed as a popular holiday area, with many beaches, resorts, and waterfront campgrounds. Approximately halfway up the island is the Comox Valley, a popular year-round destination where you'll find more great beaches and fishing.

North of the Comox Valley, Vancouver Island is mountainous, heavily treed, dotted with lakes, riddled with rivers and waterfalls, and almost completely unsettled. Just one main highway serves the region, passing through the gateway to the north, Campbell River, on its long journey to Port Hardy, terminus for ferries heading north to Prince Rupert.

PARKSVILLE TOWARD COURTENAY

Parksville

Golden sand fringes the coastline between Parksville (pop. 11,000) and Qualicum Beach. **Parksville Beach** claims "the warmest water in the whole of Canada." When the tide goes out along this stretch of the coast, it leaves a strip of sand up to 1,000 meters (3,300 ft.) wide exposed

to the sun. When the water returns, voila—sand-heated water. **Rathtrevor Beach Provincial Park,** a 347-hectare (860-acre) chunk of coastline just south of Parksville, protects a long sandy beach, a wooded upland area, nature trails, and bird-watching action that's particularly good in early spring, when seabirds swoop in for an annual herring feast. Plenty of campsites are available, but in summer line up early in the morning to stake your claim; walk-in sites $14, pull-throughs $22. Day-use only is $5. Also on Rathtrevor Beach is the sprawling **Gray Crest Seaside Resort** (1115 Island Hwy. E, 250/248-6513 or 800/663-2636, www.graycrest.com, from $125 s or d), with swimming off the beach out front or in the large outdoor pool complex. The rooms are well appointed, if a little motel-like, and each has a deck or patio with water views.

On the southern outskirts of town is the **Parksville Visitor Info Centre** (1275 Island Hwy. E, 250/248-3613, July–Aug. daily 8 A.M.–8 P.M., rest of year Mon.–Fri. 9 A.M.–5 P.M.).

Qualicum Beach

This beach community (pop. 7,000) is generally quieter than Parksville, but it shares the same golden sands of Georgia Strait and attracts the same droves of beach-goers, sun worshippers, anglers, and golfers on summer vacation. The beachfront highway through town is lined with motels, resorts, and RV parks. The attractive downtown area, locally known as "the Village," is off the main highway and up a steep hill to the west. Plan on taking a break from the beach to visit the **Old Schoolhouse Arts Centre** (122 Fern Rd. W, 250/752-6133), where you can watch artists at work daily and listen to live jazz on Sunday (2:30 P.M.; $10).

Of the many local resorts, none is better for families than **Qualicum Bay Resort** (north of town at 5970 West Island Hwy., 250/757-2003 or 800/663-6899, www.resortbc.com). Separated from the water by a road, facilities include a man-made swimming lake, a playground, a games room, an ice cream stand, and a restaurant. Tent sites are $15 and hookups $22–30. The cabins and motel rooms (from $85 s or d) are a little dated, but as you'll be outside most of the time, that's of little consequence.

Horne Lake Caves

To reach these caves (250/248-7829, www.horne lake.com), continue 11 kilometers (6.8 mi.) beyond Qualicum Beach and turn off at the Horne Lake Store, following the road for 16 kilometers (10 mi.) to where the Qualicum River drains into Horne Lake. A 90-minute tour includes a short walk as well as underground exploration and explanation (adult $17, child $15), while the more adventurous have a variety of options, including the three-hour Wet & Wild Adventure (adult $49, child $42). Two caves are open for exploration without a guide, but you are required to wear a helmet and light (rentals available for $5).

Denman Island

Island-hoppers can catch a ferry (daily on the hour, 7 A.M.–11 P.M., adult $5, child $2.50, vehicle $12.25) over to Denman Island from Buckley Bay. Fishing, kayaking, and scuba diving are prime draws here, and you'll also find good beaches, parks, and an artisan community.

Just a short walk from the ferry, the downtown area boasts a number of early-20th-century buildings. Across the island, **Fillongley**

Provincial Park features forested trails, long stretches of beach, and camping ($17). At **Boyle Point Provincial Park** in the south, an 800-meter (0.5-mi.) loop trail (15 minutes round-trip) leads to a lookout with views across to Chrome Island, where a lighthouse stands.

Hornby Island

Every hour, 8 A.M.–6 P.M., a small ferry departs the southern end of Denman Island for Hornby Island (same fare as to Denman Island). The best beaches on this small, seldom-visited island are along **Tribune Bay.** Right in the beach, **Tribune Bay Campsite** (250/335-2359, www.tribune bay.com) is nestled in a quiet forest, yet is within walking distance of shops and a restaurant. Tent sites are $25, powered sites $28. Continue beyond the bay and take St. John's Point Road to **Helliwell Provincial Park,** on a rugged, forested headland where trails lead through an old-growth forest of Douglas fir and western red cedar to high bluffs. Allow 90 minutes for the full five-kilometer (3.1-mi.) loop.

COMOX VALLEY

The communities of Courtenay, Cumberland, and Comox lie in the beautiful Comox Valley, nestled between Georgia Strait and high snow-capped mountains to the west. The valley lies almost halfway up the island, 220 kilometers (138 mi.) from Victoria, but also linked to the Sunshine Coast (see Vicinity of Vancouver chapter) by ferry.

Sights

The valley's largest town, **Courtenay** (pop. 22,000) sprawls around the head of Comox Harbour. It's not particularly scenic but has a few interesting sights and plenty of accommodations. The main attraction is the downtown **Courtenay and District Museum** (207 4th St., 250/334-0686, June–Aug. daily 10 A.M.–5 A.M., rest of year Tues.–Sat. 10 A.M.–5 P.M.). The highlight is a full-size replica of an elasmosaur, found nearby. Also of interest are realistic dioramas and a replica of a longhouse containing many native artifacts and items.

Comox, six kilometers (3.7 mi.) east of Courtenay, is worth visiting for **Filberg Heritage Lodge and Park** (Comox Ave., 250/339-2715). The flower-filled 3.6-hectare (nine-acre) grounds stretch along the waterfront and are open year-round 8 A.M. to dusk. Built by an early logging magnate, the lodge dates from 1929 and is open June–August daily 10 A.M.–5 P.M.; admission $3. On the first weekend of August, the **Filberg Festival** features gourmet food, free entertainment, and unique arts and crafts from the best of B.C.'s artisans. At the base of the mountain is a network of groomed cross-country ski trails and a large self-contained village.

Accommodations and Camping

The valley's least expensive motels are strung out along the highway (Cliffe Ave.) as you enter Courtenay from the south. Rates here are generally lower than on other parts of the island. The least expensive choice is **Courtenay Riverside Hostel** (1380 Cliffe Ave., 250/334-1938), which has private or shared rooms ($17–32 pp), public Internet access, a games room, and a reading room. **Kingfisher Oceanside Resort** (4330 South Island Hwy., 250/338-1323 or 800/663-7929, www.kingfisherspa.com) is set on well-manicured gardens right on the water. The resort also holds a spa facility, a lounge with outdoor seating, and a restaurant renowned for its West Coast cuisine (and a great Sunday brunch buffet). Choose between regular rooms ($125 s, $130 d) or newer beachfront suites, each with a fireplace, hot tub, and kitchen (from $165 s or d).

Just north of the ferry terminal, **King Coho Fishing Resort** (1250 Wally Rd., 250/339-2039, www.kingcohoresort.bc.ca, $23–26) is popular with camping anglers (especially after the Aug. 1 chinook opening). Its facilities include a boat ramp, boat rentals (from $18 per hour), guided charters, a tackle shop, and a weigh station. Continuing north 20 kilometers (12 mi.), **Miracle Beach Provincial Park** has rustic wooded camping ($22) as well as commercialized camping at **Miracle Beach Resort** (250/337-5171, www.miraclebeachresort.com) with oceanfront hookups for $34.

Food

Occupying one of Courtenay's original residences, the **Old House Restaurant** (1760 Riverside Lane, 250/338-5406) sits among landscaped gardens right on the river. Downstairs is a casual restaurant/pub with a large outdoor deck, while upstairs is a more formal eatery with the ambience of an elegant country lodge (entrées mostly under $20). Both are open daily for lunch and dinner, with the Sunday brunch buffet (10 A.M.–2 P.M.; $18) filling the restaurant with hungry patrons.

Transportation

BC Ferries (250/386-3431) offers sailings four times daily between Comox and Powell River, at the top end of the Sunshine Coast. The regular one-way fare for this 75-minute sailing is adult $7.75, child $4, vehicle $26.

Information

Comox Valley Visitor Info Centre (2040 Cliffe Ave., 250/334-3234, www.tourism-comox-valley .bc.ca, July–Aug. daily 8:30 A.M.–6 P.M., Sept.–June Mon.–Fri. 9 A.M.–6 P.M.) is on the main highway leading into Courtenay—look for the totem pole out front.

CAMPBELL RIVER

This scenic resort town of 30,000 stretches along Discovery Passage, 260 kilometers (162 mi.) north of Victoria and 235 kilometers (146 mi.) southeast of Port Hardy. Views from town—of tree-covered Quadra Island and the magnificent white-topped mountains of mainland British Columbia—are superb, but most visitors come for the salmon fishing.

Sights and Recreation

The best place to absorb some of the local atmosphere is the **Saltwater Fishing Pier,** enjoyable for a stroll whether you're fishing or not. Anglers of all ages spin cast for salmon, bottomfish, and the occasional steelhead, hauling them up in nets on long ropes. Inexpensive rod rentals are available at the pier (don't forget you also need a license). Along the pier are built-in rod holders, fish-cleaning stations, and colorful signs

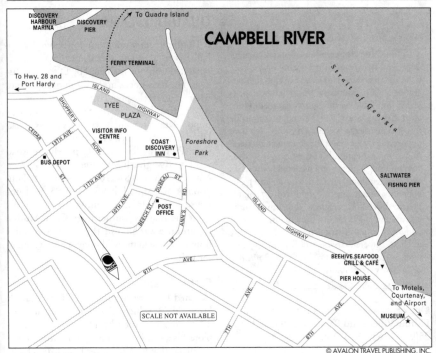

CAMPBELL RIVER

To Quadra Island

DISCOVERY HARBOUR MARINA
DISCOVERY PIER
FERRY TERMINAL

To Hwy. 28 and Port Hardy

ISLAND

TYEE PLAZA

HIGHWAY

VISITOR INFO CENTRE

COAST DISCOVERY INN

Foreshore Park

CEDAR

13TH AVE.

ROW

SHOPPER'S

BUS DEPOT

11TH AVE.

10TH AVE.

BEECH ST.

DUBEAU ST.

POST OFFICE

ST. ANN'S RD.

ISLAND

HIGHWAY

SALTWATER FISHNG PIER

Strait of Georgia

9TH AVE.

BEEHIVE SEAFOOD GRILL & CAFÉ

PIER HOUSE

To Motels, Courtenay, and Airport

7TH AVE.

8TH AVE.

MUSEUM

SCALE NOT AVAILABLE

© AVALON TRAVEL PUBLISHING, INC.

BRITISH COLUMBIA

describing the fish you're likely to catch. To really get in on the action, you'll need to get out on the water. Salmon are pursued year-round in this area, but May–October is peak season. The local information center will help you decide which type of trip is best for your needs and budget.

Within easy walking distance of the pier is the **Museum at Campbell River** (Island Hwy. and 5th Ave., 250/287-3103, May–Aug. daily 9 A.M.–5 P.M., rest of year Tues.–Sun. noon–4 P.M., $3). Native displays—mystical artifacts, a mask collection, carved-wood boxes, button blankets, totem poles, and more—are highlights. Worth watching in the museum's theater is *Devil Beneath the Sea,* cataloging the destruction of nearby Ripple Rock by the world's largest nonnuclear explosion.

Accommodations and Camping
As Campbell River is a resort, every kind of accommodation you could possibly want is here, from campgrounds and RV parks to luxury hotels and exclusive fishing lodges.

Bed-and-breakfast accommodations are provided at **Pier House** (across from the Saltwater Fishing Pier at 670 Island Hwy., 250/287-2943). The old antiques-filled house has a library and three guest rooms with shared or private bathrooms. Rates range $60–80 s, $80–100 d, including a cooked breakfast. Along the highway south of town, only the road separates several motels from the water. Least expensive of these is **Big Rock Motel** (1020 Island Hwy., 250/923-4211 or 877/923-4211), with smallish rooms for $55 s, $64 d, and a few kitchenettes for $70. Best Western and Super 8 are also represented along here, but the contemporary-styled rooms at the downtown **Coast Discovery Inn** (975 Shopper's Row, 250/287-7155 or 800/663-1144, www.coasthotels.com, $145 s, $155 d) are the nicest in town.

Many campgrounds line the highway south of town, but although they're close to the water, the surroundings are generally nothing special.

TYEE CLUB

If you're fishing between July 15 and September 15, you may want to try qualifying for Tyee Club membership. This exclusive club, famous among anglers around the world, has been dedicated to upholding the traditional methods of **sportfishing** since 1924. Several rules must be followed in order to become a member: You have to preregister your intent to fish under club rules; troll around the mouth of the Campbell River without using a motor; and use a rod between six and nine feet long, an artificial lure, and a 20-pound-maximum line (not more than 20 pounds pretested breaking weight). Most importantly, you need to land a trophy-size (30 lbs.) chinook salmon. The information center supplies a list of charter operators who will fish under these rules, or contact the club directly at 250/287-2724, www.tyeeclub.org.

One of the better choices is **Campbell River Fishing Village and RV Park** (260 Island Hwy., 250/287-3630, $20–26).

Food

The **Beehive Seafood Grill & Café** (921 Island Hwy., 250/286-6812) has an outstanding choice of local seafood. Combine this with a waterfront location and sharp service, and you have the best restaurant in town—hands-down. In the café, dishes like traditional halibut and chips and the creative honey-sesame halibut on a bun are all under $15, while in the upstairs restaurant, things get serious with a Surf and Turf Feast ($26) and paella loaded with non-Spanish delicacies like prawns, scallops, and halibut ($37 for two).

Information and Services

Park in the large parking lot of **Tyee Plaza** and you're within easy walking distance of all services, including the post office and **Campbell River Visitor Info Centre** (250/287-4636, www.campbellrivertourism.com, late June–early Sept. daily 8 A.M.–8 P.M., rest of year Mon.–Fri. 9 A.M.–5 P.M.).

QUADRA ISLAND

A 10-minute ferry ride from downtown Campbell River takes you to this beautiful island, separated from the mainland by Discovery Passage. The ferry docks in the south of the island, where most of the population resides. This narrow peninsula widens in the north to a vast unpopulated area where wildlife such as black-tailed deer, raccoons, and squirrels is abundant. From the ferry, take Cape Mudge Road south to **Kwagiulth Museum** (250/285-3733, May–Sept. Mon.–Sat. 10 A.M.–4:30 P.M., Sun. noon–4:30 P.M., adult $5, child $3) and immerse yourself in native culture.

At the island's southern tip, **Cape Mudge Lighthouse** was built in 1898 to prevent ships from wrecking in the wild surging waters around the point.

Cortes Island

Reached by ferry from Quadra Island (adult $6, child $3, vehicle $25), Cortes Island (cor-TEZ—it was named by an early Spanish explorer) is a relatively remote place, closer to the mainland than to Vancouver Island. Two highlights are **Manson's Landing Provincial Park,** a beautiful little spot sandwiched between a large tidal lagoon and the forested shoreline of Hague Lake; and **Smelt Bay Provincial Park,** a great spot for swimming, beachcombing, and camping ($14).

Practicalities

Adjacent to Cape Mudge Lighthouse is **Tsa-Kwa-Luten Lodge** (250/285-2042 or 800/665-7745, www.capemudgeresort.bc.ca, May–Sept., $130–180). Built by the local Kwagiulth people, the centerpiece of this magnificent waterfront lodge is the foyer, built in the style of a longhouse (a traditional meeting place) in locally milled woods. The rooms are decorated in northwest native theme and the restaurant specializes in native foods.

BC Ferries (250/286-1412) offers services from Campbell River to the island, every hour on the hour 6 A.M.–11 P.M.; round-trip fare is adult $5, child $2.50, vehicle $12.50.

HIGHWAY 28

Running west from Campbell River, Highway 28 provides access to Strathcona Provincial Park and the west coast. The first place to stop is 1,087-hectare (2,700-acre) **Elk Falls Provincial Park,** six kilometers (3.7 mi.) west of Campbell River. Here you can follow beautiful forest trails to waterfalls, go swimming and fishing, and stay the night (Apr.–Oct.) in a wooded campsite ($14).

Strathcona Provincial Park

British Columbia's oldest and Vancouver Island's largest park, Strathcona preserves a vast 250,000-hectare (618,000-acre) inland wilderness, including the island's highest peak, 2,220-meter (7,300-ft.) **Golden Hinde.** You'll get a taste of Strathcona's beauty along Highway 28, but to get into the park proper turn south off Highway 28 halfway between Campbell River and Gold River. This access road hugs the eastern shore of **Buttle Lake,** passing many well-marked nature walks and hiking trails. One of the first is the 10-minute walk to **Lupin Falls,** which are more impressive than the small creek across from the parking lot would suggest. Apart from numerous picnic areas along Buttle Lake, the only facilities within the park are two campgrounds ($14) with unserviced sites only.

NORTH TO PORT HARDY

Highway 19, covering the 235 kilometers (146 mi.) between Campbell River and Port Hardy, traverses relatively untouched wilderness of forested mountains (try to ignore the logged hillsides), sparkling rivers, and cascading waterfalls.

Telegraph Cove

Most visitors come to Telegraph Cove to go whale-watching on Johnstone Strait, but the village itself is well worth the eight-kilometer (five-mi.) detour from the highway. Built around a deep sheltered harbor, it's one of the last existing "boardwalk" communities on the island. Many of the buildings stand on stilts and pilings over the water, linked by a boardwalk. Fewer than 20 people live here year-round, but the population swells enormously during late spring and summer when whale-watching, diving, and fishing charters do a roaring trade, and canoeists

an unnamed stream in Strathcona Provincial Park

THE WHALES OF JOHNSTONE STRAIT

Johnstone Strait, offshore from Telegraph Cove, is an unparalleled destination for viewing **orcas** (killer whales) up close and personal. These magnificent, intelligent mammals spend the summer in the waters around Telegraph Cove and are most concentrated in Robson Bight, where they rub on the gravel beaches near the mouth of the Tsitka River.

Stubbs Island Whale Watching (604/928-3185 or 800/665-3066, www.stubbs-island.com) pioneered whale-watching trips in the early 1980s and was involved in the establishment of Robson Bight as an ecological reserve. The company's two boats, *Lukwa* and *Gikumi,* depart Telegraph Cove on 3.5-hour whale-watching cruises daily from late May to early October. The experienced crew takes you out to view the whales in their natural habitat and to hear their mysterious and beautiful sounds through a hydrophone (underwater microphone). Both boats are comfortable, with covered areas and bathrooms. The cost is adult $70, senior or child $60. Make reservations as far ahead as possible. Dress warmly and don't forget your camera for this experience of a lifetime.

and kayakers arrive to paddle along Johnstone Strait. Some of the cabins and houses on the boardwalk can be rented by the night, but they generally need to be reserved well in advance. The cabins are simply furnished, have kitchens, and enjoy an incredible setting ($100–250 s or d). **Telegraph Cove Campground,** a short walk from the village, has wooded sites as well as showers, a launderette, boat launch, and store. Sites are $20–25. For reservations at any of the above options, contact **Telegraph Cove Resorts** (250/928-3131, www.telegraphcoveresort.com).

PORT HARDY

Port Hardy (pop. 5,000) lies along sheltered Hardy Bay, on the edge of Queen Charlotte Strait. It's the largest community north of Campbell River and the terminus for ferries sailing the Inside Passage to and from Prince Rupert. The ferry is the main reason most people drive this far north.

Sights and Recreation

As you enter the Port Hardy area, take the scenic route to town via Hardy Bay Road. You'll pass several original chainsaw woodcarvings and skirt the edge of peaceful Hardy Bay before entering downtown via Market Street.

One of the most enjoyable things to do in town is to stroll along the seawall to **Tsulquate Park,** where you can appreciate native carvings and do some beachcombing if the tide is

out. Many bald eagles reside around the bay, and if you're lucky you'll see them swooping about in the neighborhood. At **Quatse River Hatchery** (Byng Rd., 250/949-9022, Mon.–Fri. 8 A.M.–4:30 P.M.) you can observe incubation and rearing facilities for pink, chum, and coho salmon, as well as steelhead.

Accommodations and Camping

Accommodations in Port Hardy are limited and often fill up, especially on the night prior to ferry departures. Check the accommodation guide for a bunch of choices in the $80–100 range, or stay at one of the two places I recommend, both south of downtown overlooking Port Hardy's busy harbor. The **Quarterdeck Inn** (6555 Hardy Bay Rd., 250/902-0455 or 877/902-0459, www.quarterdeckresort.net) offers harbor views from each of its 40 smallish rooms. Facilities include a fitness room, sauna, and a laundry. At $95 s, $105 d, including a light breakfast, this place is an excellent value. The adjacent **Glen Lyon Inn** (6435 Hardy Bay Rd., 250/949-7115 or 877/949-7115, www.glenlyoninn.com) is similar in standards and price and the in-house Oceanside Restaurant provides the perfect excuse to stay "home" in the evening.

The closest camping to downtown is at **Sunny Sanctuary Campground** (near the ferry terminal turnoff at 8080 Goodspeed Rd., 250/949-8111 or 866/251-4556, $18–24). Facilities include a barbecue shelter, modern bathrooms, firewood and fire rings, and a small store.

Food

Port Hardy doesn't offer a large variety of dining options. Wander around town and you'll soon see what there is. At **Captain Hardy's** (Market St., 250/949-7133) the advertised breakfast specials are small and come on plastic plates, but cost only about $3.50. The rest of the day, this place offers good fish and chips from $6. Dine at the **Oceanside Restaurant,** south of downtown in the Glen Lyon Inn (Hardy Bay Rd., 250/949-3050) for the opportunity to see bald eagles feeding right outside the window.

Transportation

Most people arriving in Port Hardy do so with the intention of continuing north by ferry to Prince Rupert and beyond. The ferry terminal is at Bear Cove, eight kilometers (five mi.) from downtown Port Hardy. The *Queen of the North* departs Port Hardy at 7:30 A.M. every second day, arriving in Prince Rupert the same evening at 10:30 P.M. The service runs year-round, but departures are less frequent outside of summer. Peak one-way fare is adult $102.50, child 5–11 $51.25, vehicle $241.50. Cabins and meal packages are also available. For reservations (as far in advance as possible in summer) contact **BC Ferries** (250/386-3431, www.bcferries.com).

Information

By the waterfront is **Port Hardy Visitor Info Centre** (7250 Market St., 250/949-7622, summer daily 8 A.M.–8 P.M., rest of year Mon.–Fri. 9 A.M.–5 P.M.).

Okanagan Valley

This warm, sunny valley 400 kilometers (250 mi.) east of Vancouver extends 180 kilometers (112 mi.) between the U.S.–Canada border in the south and the TransCanada Highway in the north. Lush orchards and vineyards, fertile irrigated croplands, low rolling hills, and a string of beautiful lakes line the valley floor, where you'll also find 40 golf courses, dozens of commercial attractions, and lots and lots of people—especially in summer.

The Okanagan Valley's three main cities—Penticton, Kelowna, and Vernon—are spread around long, narrow Okanagan Lake and collectively hold the bulk of interior British Columbia's population. Numerous smaller communities also ring the lakeshore, doubling or tripling in size between May and September when hordes of vacationers turn the valley into one big resort. Most of these summer pilgrims are Canadians from cooler climes, who come in search of guaranteed sunshine, lazy days on a beach, and a take-away tan. In winter, the valley draws pilgrims of another sort—skiers and snowboarders on their way to the world-class slopes flanking the valley.

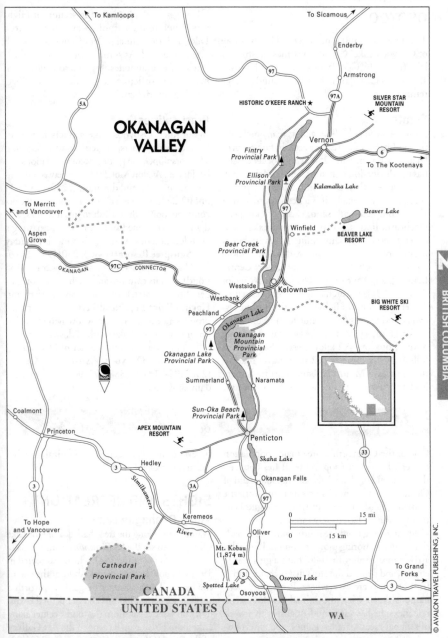

To Kamloops
To Sicamous
Enderby
97
Armstrong
97A
SILVER STAR MOUNTAIN RESORT
HISTORIC O'KEEFE RANCH ★

OKANAGAN VALLEY

5A
Vernon
Fintry Provincial Park
6
To The Kootenays
Ellison Provincial Park
Kalamalka Lake
97
To Merritt and Vancouver
Beaver Lake
Aspen Grove
Winfield
BEAVER LAKE RESORT
Bear Creek Provincial Park
OKANAGAN 97C CONNECTOR
Westside
Kelowna
Westbank
BIG WHITE SKI RESORT
Peachland
Okanagan Lake
97
Okanagan Mountain Provincial Park
Okanagan Lake Provincial Park
Coalmont
Summerland
Naramata
Princeton
Sun-Oka Beach Provincial Park
APEX MOUNTAIN RESORT
Penticton
Hedley
3
Skaha Lake
3
Okanagan Falls
33
3A
97
Simikameen
To Hope and Vancouver
Keremeos
River
0   15 mi
0   15 km
Mt. Kobau (1,874 m) ▲
Oliver
To Grand Forks
3
Spotted Lake
3
Osoyoos Lake
Cathedral Provincial Park
CANADA
Osoyoos
UNITED STATES
WA

BRITISH COLUMBIA

© AVALON TRAVEL PUBLISHING, INC.

OSOYOOS

This town of 4,500 is nestled on the west shore of Osoyoos Lake, Canada's warmest freshwater lake (up to 24°C/75°F in summer). The town also boasts Canada's highest year-round average temperature.

Sights

Away from the valley floor and its many orchards, the landscape is surprisingly arid. In one particular area, a 100-hectare (250-acre) "pocket desert" has the distinction of being Canada's driest spot, receiving less than 300 millimeters (11 in.) of precipitation annually. It is a desert in the truest sense, complete with sand, cacti, prickly pear, sagebrush, lizards, scorpions, rattlesnakes, and other desert dwellers, including 23 invertebrates found nowhere else in the world. Learn more about this unique landscape at the **Desert Centre** (250/495-2470 or 877/899-0897, adult $6, senior $5, child $3), a research and interpretive facility. To get there follow Highway 97 north from Osoyoos, and take 146th Avenue to the west.

For a bird's-eye view of the lake, take Highway 3 west from town 12 kilometers (7.5 mi.), then follow a 20-kilometer (12-mi.) gravel road to the summit of **Mount Kobau.** Short trails there lead to viewpoints of the Similkameen and Okanagan Valleys. Along the section of Highway 3 before the turnoff, watch for **Spotted Lake,** a bizarre natural phenomenon on the south side of the road. As summer progresses and the lake's water evaporates, high concentrations of magnesium, calcium, and sodium crystallize, forming colorful circles.

Practicalities

In summer, Osoyoos Lake attracts hordes of boaters, water-skiers, anglers, windsurfers, and sun worshippers, so getting accommodations can be difficult. **Avalon Motel** (Hwy. 3 between the information center and downtown, 250/495-6334 or 800/264-5999) is a clean and comfortable accommodation with smallish rooms for $65 s, $70 d and self-contained suites for $120. Boasting a great location down on the lakeshore is **Holiday Inn Sunspree Resort** (Hwy. 3, 250/495-7223 or 877/786-7773, www.holidayinosoyoos.com, $135 s or d) with its own private beach, a rooftop garden, fitness center, boat rentals, and a restaurant. **Haynes Point Provincial Park** ($20 per night) protects an extremely narrow low-lying spit that juts into Osoyoos Lake south of downtown.

In a parking lot at the corner of Highways 3 and 97 is the **Osoyoos Visitor Info Centre** (250/495-7142 or 888/676-9667, June–Sept. daily 8:30 A.M.–4:30 P.M.).

Penticton

One of the Okanagan's three major population centers, Penticton (pop. 35,000) lies between the north end of Skaha Lake and the south end of Okanagan Lake. The city gets its name from the nomadic Salish natives, in whose tongue Penticton means "place to stay forever."

Approaching from the south, you'll see a roadside plaque honoring pioneer Thomas Ellis, who arrived in the valley in 1886, built a great cattle empire, and planted the area's first orchard. Today fruit orchards are everywhere. Penticton's nickname is Peach City; the annual Peach Festival celebrates the harvest in mid-August with a week of sailboat races, parades, games, and entertainment. Penticton also participates in another fruitful event, the Okanagan Wine Festival, the first weekend of October.

SIGHTS AND RECREATION
Along Okanagan Lake

Wander west along the tree-shaded shores of Lake Okanagan to see the **SS Sicamous** (summer daily 7 A.M.–7 P.M.; admission $4), which was retired in 1951 and now rests on the lakeshore at the end of the beach. The adjacent rose garden is worth a stroll to see perfect blooms and manicured lawns.

If you wander east from the tourist center along Lakeshore Drive, you'll come to the **Art Gallery of the South Okanagan** (199 Front St., 250/493-

2928, Tues.–Fri. 10 A.M.–5 P.M., Sat.–Sun. 1–5 P.M.). The craft shop is a good place to pick up creative treasures and handmade souvenirs. Continue east from the gallery to the local marina—another enjoyable spot for a lakeside stroll.

Penticton Museum

This museum (787 Main St., 250/490-2451, Mon.–Sat. 10 A.M.–5 P.M.) houses an excellent collection of western Canadiana, covering natural history, local native peoples, the fur-trading days, railways, early Chinese residents, and sternwheelers. It also features an enormous taxidermy section; mining, ranching, and ghost-town artifacts and treasures; and assorted military miscellany. Allow at least an hour or two in here.

Wine and Wineries

The best introduction to the valley's vinous offerings is the **British Columbia Wine Information Centre** (888 Westminster Ave., 250/490-2006, June–Sept. daily 9 A.M.–5:30 P.M.). As much a wine shop as anything else, it offers plenty of information along with wine-tour maps and knowledgeable staff to set you off in the right direction. The closest wineries to Penticton are northeast of the city along Naramata Road, including the renowned **Hillside Estate** (1350 Naramata Rd., 250/493-6294 (open for tours daily 10 A.M.–6 P.M. and for lunch daily from 11 A.M.), where an impressive three-story wooden building holds the main winery. Hillside is known for its pinot noir, but it also produces an unusually dry but fruity riesling. In Naramata itself is **Lang Vineyards**

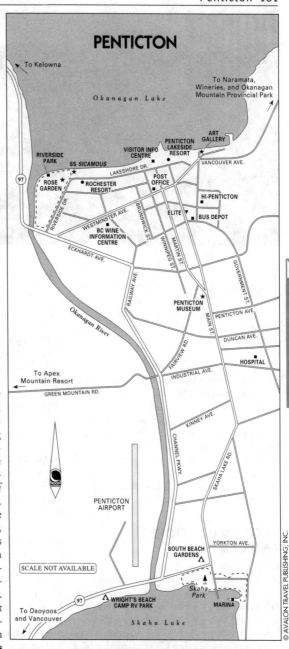

© AVALON TRAVEL PUBLISHING, INC.

BRITISH COLUMBIA

Okanagan Valley vineyard

(Gammon Rd., 250/496-5987, May–Oct. daily 10 A.M.–5 P.M.), one of the Okanagan's premier boutique wineries, for inexpensive whites, pinot noir, and a selection of more expensive ice wines.

Skiing and Snowboarding

Sunniest of the Okanagan ski areas is **Apex Mountain Resort** (250/292-8222 or 877/777-2739, www.apexresort.com) 33 kilometers (20.5 mi.) west of Penticton, which has a vertical rise of 610 meters (2,000 ft.) and 56 runs over 450 hectares (1,100 acres). Most of the expert terrain is off Beaconsfield Mountain, while snowboarders are catered to with a terrain park and half-pipe. Lift tickets are adult $49, senior and child $39.

ACCOMMODATIONS AND CAMPING

Under $50

As you'd expect in a resort town, the only accommodation under $50 is in a dormitory. **HI–Penticton** (464 Ellis St., 250/492-3992 or 866/782-9736, www.hihostels.ca) occupies a historic residence close to the heart of downtown. Facilities include a kitchen, laundry, bike rentals, and an outdoor barbecue area; $17 per night for members of Hostelling International, $21 for nonmembers.

$100–150

The least expensive of several lodgings on Lakeshore Drive, close to both the lake and downtown, is the 36-room **Rochester Resort** (970 Lakeshore Dr., 250/493-1128 or 800/567-4904, $99 s, $109 d). The rooms are probably more expensive than they should be, but the beach is across the road.

$150–200

For a million-dollar lake view, consider the six-story **Penticton Lakeside Resort** (21 Lakeshore Dr. W, 250/493-8221 or 800/663-9400, www.pentictonlakesideresort.com), the only downtown accommodation right on the lake. The full-service hotel has over 200 rooms, an indoor pool overlooking the lake, a whirlpool, saunas, two tennis courts, a bar with a lakeside deck, and a restaurant. In July and August, standard rooms are $180–200, but if you're going to spend this kind of money, you may as well take one of the suites ($30–50 more) with upgraded everything, better views, and jetted tubs.

Campgrounds

All Penticton's commercial campgrounds are south of downtown around the north end of Skaha Lake. They're very popular in summer, so make reservations in advance if possible. The least-crowded seems to be **Wright's Beach Camp RV Park** (Hwy. 97, 250/492-7120, $28–36), which is a little bit surprising as it's right on the lake and many sites are shaded. Across from Sudbury Beach and adjacent to Highway 97 is **South Beach Gardens** (3815 Skaha Lake Rd., 250/492-0628), which charges $21 for an unserviced site and $24–29 for hookups.

FOOD

Many Penticton restaurants feature outdoor eating areas, allowing diners to take advantage of the mild climate. One of the most popular of these is **Magnums on the Lake,** the signature restaurant of the Penticton Lakeside Resort (21 Lakeshore Dr. W, 250/493-8221). The adjacent bar also serves food, and both places have an outdoor deck area overlooking the lake.

On Main Street between Okanagan and Skaha Lakes are several decent eateries. For home cooking at inexpensive prices, try the family-style **Elite Restaurant** (340 Main St., 250/492-3051, daily 7 A.M.–9 P.M.). Good-value daily specials (soup or salad, main course, dessert, and coffee) go for around $7–8.

TRANSPORTATION

From the **Greyhound** (307 Ellis St., 250/493-4101) terminal, buses head south to Osoyoos, linking up with services along Highway 3, and north through the Okanagan Valley to Salmon Arm on the TransCanada Highway.

Getting around town is easy on **Penticton Transit System** (250/492-5602), or use pedal power and rent a bike from the **Bike Barn** (300 Westminster Ave. W, 250/492-4140) from $30 a day.

INFORMATION

You can't miss the **Penticton Visitor Info Centre,** north of downtown right on the shore of Okanagan Lake (250/493-4055 or 800/663-5052, www.penticton.org, June–early Sept. daily 8 A.M.–8 P.M., rest of year Mon.–Fri. 9 A.M.–5 P.M., Sat.–Sun. 10 A.M.–4 P.M.). If it's closed when you're there, you can still orient yourself to local surroundings with the gigantic town map and directory outside the entrance.

NORTH OF PENTICTON

Highway 97 links Penticton and Kelowna, running along the west side of Okanagan Lake for the entire 60 kilometers (37 mi.). The first worthwhile stop is tiny **Sun-Oka Beach Provincial Park,** which offers trees galore, picnic tables, beaches, and good swimming.

Summerland

As you enter picturesque Summerland, nestled between Giants Head Mountain and the lake, turn west (away from the lake) at either of the stoplights and follow the signs to Prairie Valley Station, the departure point for the **Kettle Valley Steam Railway** (250/494-8422 or 877/494-8424). This steam train, dating from the early 1900s, runs along a historic 10-kilometer (6.2-mi.) stretch of track, through orchards and vineyards and over a trestle bridge. Departures are mid-May–mid-October Saturday–Monday at 10:30 A.M. and 1:30 P.M., with additional trips in July and August on Thursday and Friday. The fare is adult $16, senior $15, child $10.

Another sweet stop is **Summerland Sweets** (Canyon View Rd., 250/494-0377), where you can watch syrups, jams, and candy being made from fresh and frozen fruit; from Highway 97 take the Dunn Street or Arkell Road exit west, turn right on Gartrell Road, and follow the signs.

Sumac Ridge Estate (one km/0.6 mi. north of Summerland, 250/494-0451) was British Columbia's first estate winery. Today, this well-recognized name appears on a wide variety of red and white wines, including an award-winning cabernet franc and one of the Okanagan's few sparkling wines. Tours and tastings are offered May–October daily 10 A.M.–4 P.M. on the hour, and a bistro is open daily for lunch.

Kelowna

British Columbia's largest city outside the Lower Mainland and Victoria, Kelowna (pop. 105,000) lies on the shores of Okanagan Lake, halfway between Penticton in the south and Vernon in the north. The city combines a scenic location among semiarid mountains with an unbeatable climate of long, sunny summers and short, mild winters. The low rolling hills around the city hold lush terraced orchards, and the numerous local vineyards produce some excellent wines. Visitors flock here in summer to enjoy the area's sparkling lakes, sandy beaches, numerous provincial parks, and golfing; in winter they come for great skiing and snowboarding at nearby Big White.

History

For thousands of years before the arrival of the first Europeans, the nomadic Salish peoples inhabited the Okanagan Valley, hunting (*kelowna* is a Salish word for grizzly bear), gathering, and fishing. Since Father Pandosy planted the first apple trees at his mission in 1859, Kelowna has thrived as the center of the Okanagan fruit, vegetable, and vineyard industry (the valley is Canada's largest fruit-growing region). In 1960, Kelowna's population stood at 24,000, but as local services improved, the region has become more attractive to older, retired people. Since the opening of the Okanagan Connector in 1986, traveling time between Vancouver and Kelowna has been cut from around six hours to under four hours, and the population has exploded, with the number of wineries doubling since the mid-1980s, luxurious resorts being built along the lake, new golf courses opening every year, and exclusive subdivisions carving away land formerly given over to agriculture.

Over 200 homes were destroyed and 30,000 residents were evacuated in 2003 when wildfires swept down into the city from Okanagan Mountain.

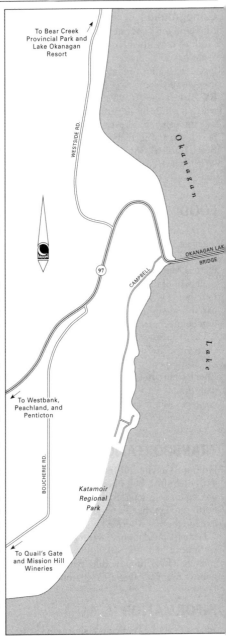

KELOWNA

Knox Mountain Park

KNOX MOUNTAIN DR.

CROWLEY AVE.

TRAIN STATION

Waterfront Park

City Park

HARVEY AVE.

SEE "DOWNTOWN KELOWNA" MAP

BERNARD AVE.

SUTHERLAND AVE.

CADDER AVE.

SPRINGFIELD RD.

HOSPITAL

SPORTS RENT

K.L.O. RD.

SIESTA MOTOR INN

LANFRANCO

Gyro Beach

Rotary Beach

HIAWATHA RV PARK

MANTEO RESORT

HOTEL ELDORADO

To Okanagan Mountain Provincial Park

Pandosy Mission Provincial Historic Site

Mission Creek Regional Park

KELOWNA LAND & ORCHARD COMPANY

THE HARVEST GOLF CLUB

To Kettle Valley Railway and Gallagher's Canyon Golf & Country Club

SCALE NOT AVAILABLE

RICHTER ST.
ETHEL ST.
ELLIS ST.
ABBOTT ST.
PANDOSY ST.
GORDON DR.
HIGH RD.
GLENMORE RD.
GLENMORE DR.
DILWORTH DR.
BENVOULIN RD.
DUNSTER RD.
EAST KELOWNA RD.
MCCULLOCH RD.
WENRICK CRES.
LEATHEED RD.

To Winfield, Airport, and Vernon

DAYS INN
33

To Big White Ski Resort and Grand Forks

BUS DEPOT

97

EAST KELOWNA RD.

Mission Creek

BRITISH COLUMBIA

© AVALON TRAVEL PUBLISHING, INC.

FATHER PANDOSY

The first European to settle in the valley, Father Pandosy, an oblate priest, established a mission on the southern outskirts of present-day downtown Kelowna in 1859. He operated a church, school, and farm here, ministering to natives and whites until his death in 1891. His mission claimed a lot of "firsts"—first white settlement in the Okanagan Valley, first school in the valley, first fruit and vine crops in the valley, and first Roman Catholic mission in the B.C. interior. Now protected as **Pandosy Mission Provincial Heritage Site** (Benvoulin Rd., daily 8 A.M.–dark, $2 donation), the site remains virtually untouched since Fr. Pandosy's day, including a chapel and a barn filled with antique farming equipment.

SIGHTS

Along the Waterfront

Right downtown, beautiful **City Park** is the largest of Kelowna's many parks. Hugging the lakeshore, it holds beds of colorful flowers and large shady trees, expansive lawns, and a long sandy beach. Near the entrance to the park is the large, sparkling-white, attention-grabbing Dow Reid sculpture *Sails,* as well as a replica of the famed lake-dwelling serpent, **Ogopogo,** a friendly Loch Ness–style sea serpent that allegedly lives in Lake Okanagan. Thousands of sightings of the mysterious monster have been made over the years, which, consensus says, is a snakelike creature with small humps, green skin, and a nice big smile, the latter feature confirmed by enterprising locals who print its image on T-shirts, posters, and postcards.

A promenade leads north from the Ogopogo statue past a large marina and a prime waterfront site undergoing redevelopment. Beyond the construction is the Grand Okanagan, the Okanagan's most luxurious accommodation. Even if you can't afford a lakefront suite, the resort holds a bar and restaurant with water views, and full spa services. Beyond the resort, the promenade crosses a small lock, which allows boaters to travel between the higher water level of an artificial lagoon and the lake itself.

Other Downtown Sights

The **Kelowna Museum** (470 Queensway Ave., 250/763-2417, summer Mon.–Sat. 10 A.M.–5 P.M., rest of year Tues.–Sat. 10 A.M.–5 P.M., donation) holds a mishmash of fascinating displays, including horse-drawn carriages; fossils found in the Princeton area; indigenous arts, crafts, clothing, jewelry, beads, and furs; children's books and games; radio equipment; pioneer artifacts; recreations of an 1861 Kelowna trading post and a Chinese store; and a display of the interior of a Salish winter dwelling. **Kelowna Art Gallery** (1315 Water St., 250/762-2226, Tues.–Sat. 10 A.M.–5 P.M., Sun. 1–5 P.M., donation) is a modern facility hosting touring exhibitions and maintaining a permanent collection of contemporary and historical works by artists from throughout the province.

In an old downtown packinghouse, complete with exposed red-brick walls and hand-hewn wooden beams, the **B.C. Orchard Industry Museum** (1304 Ellis St., 250/763-0433, Tues.–Sat. 10 A.M.–5 P.M.) tells the story of the local orchard industry through rare photographs, displays, and a hands-on discovery corner. In the same building, the **Wine Museum** (250/868-0441, Mon.–Sat. 10 A.M.–5 P.M., Sun. noon–5 P.M.) has information on local wineries and tours, and sells the finished product.

Wineries

Most of the local wineries welcome visitors with tours and free tastings year-round (but call ahead outside of summer to check hours). Due to the popularity of visiting the wineries, most charge a small fee for tasting.

One of the province's oldest wineries, in operation since 1932, is **Calona Vineyards** (downtown at 1125 Richter St., 250/762-9144, 9 A.M.–7 P.M.). There's no actual vineyard, just a large winery that uses grapes grown throughout the valley. Calona offers tours throughout the year at 2 P.M. (more frequently in summer), with tastings and sales in a room set up as a cellar.

Across Okanagan Lake from Kelowna is **Mission Hill Family Estate** (1730 Mission Hill Rd., Westbank, 250/768-7611, daily 10 A.M.–7 P.M.), high atop a ridge and surrounded by vineyards

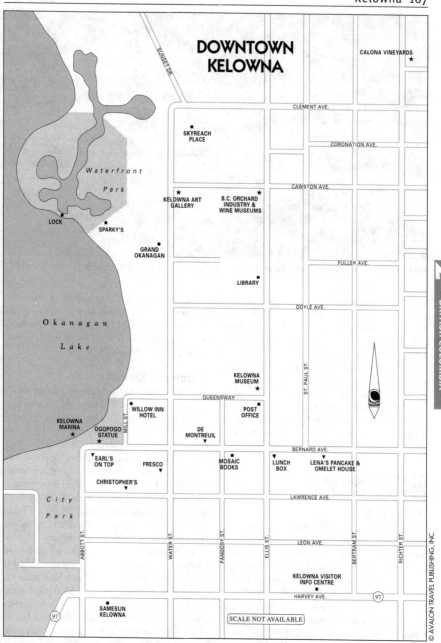

DOWNTOWN
KELOWNA

CALONA VINEYARDS ★

CLEMENT AVE.

SKYREACH
PLACE ■

CORONATION AVE.

*Waterfront
Park*

CAWSTON AVE.

★
KELOWNA ART
GALLERY

B.C. ORCHARD ★
INDUSTRY &
WINE MUSEUMS

LOCK

■ SPARKY'S

● GRAND
OKANAGAN

FULLER AVE.

■ LIBRARY

DOYLE AVE.

*Okanagan
Lake*

ST. PAUL ST.

KELOWNA ■
MUSEUM ★

QUEENSWAY

POST ■
OFFICE

KELOWNA
MARINA ★

● WILLOW INN
HOTEL

OGOPOGO
STATUE ★

DE
MONTREUIL
▼

BERNARD AVE.

▼ EARL'S
ON TOP

FRESCO
▼

MOSAIC ■
BOOKS

▼ LUNCH
BOX

LENA'S PANCAKE &
OMELET HOUSE

CHRISTOPHER'S

LAWRENCE AVE.

*City
Park*

ABBOTT ST.

WATER ST.

PANDOSY ST.

ELLIS ST.

LEON AVE.

BERTRAM ST.

RICHTER ST.

KELOWNA VISITOR
INFO CENTRE

97

● SAMESUN
KELOWNA

HARVEY AVE.

97

SCALE NOT AVAILABLE

BRITISH COLUMBIA

© AVALON TRAVEL PUBLISHING, INC.

golfing Okanagan style—at the Harvest Golf Club, Kelowna, with apple trees lining the fairways

with stunning lake views. Tours depart three times daily, each ending with an informal tasting session. At nearby **Quail's Gate Estate Winery** (3303 Boucherie Rd., 250/769-4451), the reserve pinot noir is a signature wine—enjoy a glass or two alfresco at the winery bistro. Winery tours are conducted four times daily.

Back on the main highway, farther south is **Hainle Vineyards Estate Winery** (5355 Trepanier Bench Rd., Peachland, 250/767-2525, Tues.–Sun. 10 A.M.–5 P.M.), a world leader in the development of commercially viable ice wines.

RECREATION AND ENTERTAINMENT

On the Lake

During the warm and sunny months of summer, Okanagan Lake comes alive with a colorful array of watercraft, fishermen, and swimmers out on the water, and sunbathers dot the surrounding sandy beaches. The busiest spot is the stretch of sand fronting **City Park,** right downtown. Beyond the beach's northern end, you can rent watercraft from **Sparky's** (in front of the Grand Okanagan, 250/862-2469), rent small motor boats at **Kelowna Marina** (250/861-

8001), or go parachuting behind a boat with **Kelowna Parasail Adventures** (250/868-4838).

Gyro Beach and adjacent **Rotary Beach** are beautiful stretches of sand southeast of downtown along Lakeshore Drive.

Hiking and Biking

The abandoned **Kettle Valley Railway,** which winds around the back of Kelowna, may be protected as a national historic site, but unfortunately nothing could protect 14 of 18 trestle bridges from 2003 wildfires. Plans are in place to have them rebuilt, but until then, opportunities for extended trips along the rail bed are somewhat limited. It's still an interesting spot, though, and well worth the effort to reach. To get there take K.L.O. Road east, then McCulloch Road south to Myra Forest Service Road, and follow this unpaved road south for 8.5 kilometers (5.3 mi.). From the parking lot at this point, it's under one kilometer (0.6 mi.) to the first of the burnt trestles.

The cactus-covered top of **Knox Mountain** offers great lake and city views. A hiking trail and a paved road popular with bicyclists both lead to the summit. To get there head north out of town along the lakeshore, passing pretty, lakeside **Sutherland Park,** then take Knox Mountain

Drive up to Knox Mountain Park, stopping at Crown Viewpoint on the way to the top.

Golf

A profusion of resort-style golf courses in and around Kelowna combine with a mild climate and relatively well-priced greens fees to make the Okanagan one of the country's finest golfing destinations. All the courses offer club rentals, power carts (generally around $30), and on-course dining facilities. Quoted greens fees are for peak season. Expect savings of 60 percent outside of summer and for twilight rates.

The **Harvest Golf Club** (250/862-3103 or 800/257-8577, greens fee $95), sitting on terraced land southeast of downtown, features fairways lined with fruit trees, large greens, lots of water hazards, and a magnificent clubhouse. Continue east from the Harvest Golf Club and you'll eventually reach **Gallagher's Canyon Golf & Country Club** (250/861-4240, greens fee $100), one of Canada's finest golf courses. Not particularly long, this immaculately manicured course snakes through a canyon and opens up to fairways lined with mature pine trees.

Skiing and Snowboarding

Big White Ski Resort (250/765-3101 or 800/663-2772, www.bigwhite.com), 57 kilometers (35.4 mi.) east of Kelowna on Highway 33, is the second-largest alpine resort in British Columbia. Much of the expansion has been over the last few years, including a new high-speed quad that almost doubled the lift-served terrain to 850 hectares (2,100 acres). Lift tickets are adult $56, senior $48, child $30, 70 and over and under five free. Adjacent to the main lift-served area is Happy Valley Adventure Centre, a tube park with its own lift. Big White is also home to a terrain park, half-pipe, cross-country trails, and an ice-skating rink. On-mountain facilities in the 9,000-bed base village include rental shops, a ski and snowboard school, accommodations, restaurants and cafés, and a large mall.

Nightlife

Enjoy a drink overlooking Okanagan Lake in the stylish lounge at the **Hotel Eldorado** (500 Cook Rd., 250/763-7500). Right downtown, **Sgt. O'Flaherty's** (Royal Anne Hotel, 348 Bernard Ave., 250/860-6409) is a friendly pub with bands churning out a variety of music styles nightly from 9 P.M.

Don't expect the ritz and glitz of Las Vegas at **Lake City Casino** (Grand Okanagan, 1310 Water St., 250/860-9467)—this is gambling Canadian style, with the action restricted to slot machines, blackjack, roulette, Caribbean stud poker, and mini baccarat, and everyone's ushered out the front door at 2 A.M.

Sunshine Theatre (250/763-4025) puts on three to four plays throughout the summer; pick up a schedule at the information center. For first-run movies, head to the **Uptown Cinema Centre** (1521 Water St., 250/762-0099).

Festivals and Events

The **Spring Wine Festival** (250/861-6654, www.owfs.com) is somewhat less pretentious than the fall equivalent, with many wineries not normally open to the public offering tours and tasting sessions through late April. On the first weekend of May, the **Apple Blossom Festival** coincides with the beginning of the apple-picking season. The event features fun family events out at the Kelowna Land and Orchard Company on Dunster Road.

Through the middle of July, the mobile **Mozart Festival** (250/762-3747) takes place at venues throughout the city, including at local churches and museums. **Parks Alive** is another summertime music event, this one held through July and August at city parks Wednesday–Saturday nights; expect everything from classical to country. On the first weekend of August, the Sunshine Theatre Co. (250/763-4025) presents the **Kelowna Comedy Festival** at various indoor and outdoor venues.

The valley's biggest event is the **Fall Wine Festival** (250/861-6654, www.owfs.com), held annually over 10 days from the last full weekend of September to celebrate the end of the grape harvest. Thousands of visitors participate in food and wine tastings, releases of new wines, cooking classes, and art displays with all sections of the industry participating.

ACCOMMODATIONS AND CAMPING

Under $100

Samesun Kelowna (245 Harvey St., 250/763-5013 or 888/562-2783, www.samesun.com) is a three-story, purpose-built backpacker lodge across the road from the downtown core. Inside the distinctive building are 120 beds, many in private rooms, with communal kitchens, bathrooms, a large lounge area, and public Internet access. Out back is a pleasant grassed barbecue area and a beach volleyball court. Rates are $20 for a dorm bed, with private rooms ranging $59–119 s or d.

Aside from the Samesun Kelowna, the least expensive place to stay right downtown is the old **Willow Inn Hotel** (235 Queensway Ave., 250/762-2122 or 800/268-1055) offering big boxy rooms, each with a writing desk and lounge. Summer rates are $85 s, $95 d, from $55 s, $65 d the rest of the year.

A MOUNTAIN HIDEAWAY

High in the hills northeast of Kelowna, **Beaver Lake Resort** (250/762-2225, www.beaverlakeresort.com, May–Oct.) is very different from the beachy resort complexes down on the valley floor. Set in a forest on the edge of a lake famed for rainbow trout fishing, the resort comprises a restaurant, a horseback riding operation (with afternoon pony rides for kids), and a fishing shop. Boat rentals are well-priced at $45 per 24 hours, including gas. Canoes, kayaks, and belly boats are $30 per day. Cabins range from tiny "camping cabins" that share bathrooms ($35 s or d) to peeled-log chalets with full kitchens ($125). Cabin No. 9 is typical—it's rustic, but enjoys an absolute lakefront setting, a private floating dock, big deck, full kitchen, log fireplace, one bedroom, and a loft—and costs about the same as a room at the Best Western downtown. Make cabin reservations well in advance—locals know a bargain when they see one and book their favorite up to a year in advance. Camping is $18 (no hookups). To get there, head north to Winfield, then 16 kilometers (10 mi.) east on Beaver Lake Road.

$100–150

South of downtown, the **Siesta Motor Inn** (3152 Lakeshore Rd., 250/763-5013 or 800/663-4347, www.siestamotorinn.com) offers a beachside atmosphere one block from the water. Rooms open onto a wide balcony overlooking a courtyard and pool. Rates start at $109 s or d, or pay from $129 for a kitchenette.

Highway 97 (also known as Harvey Ave.) north of downtown holds many motels tucked between shopping malls, gas stations, and fast-food restaurants. Along this strip is **Days Inn Kelowna** (2469 Hwy. 97 N, 250/868-3297 or 800/337-7177, www.daysinn.com), with large, modern rooms decorated in Santa Fe style, as well as an outdoor pool and hot tub; the smallest rooms cost $109 s or d, but it's worth an extra $20 for a much-larger suite.

$150–200

The **Hotel Eldorado** (500 Cook Rd., 250/763-7500, www.eldoradokelowna.com) was built in 1926 and moved to its present lakeside location in the 1980s. This delightful lakeside accommodation offers just 20 rooms, each furnished with antiques and many offering a lake view and private balcony. Hotel facilities include a lakefront café, a restaurant, a lounge, and a marina with boat rentals. Summer rates range $169–219, with only the more expensive rooms having water views. In the off-season, these same rooms are discounted to $69–99 s or d.

The funky looking **Manteo Resort** (3766 Lakeshore Rd., 250/860-1031 or 888/462-6836, www.manteo.com) gets plenty of repeat family business, with lots of kid-friendly activities including a waterslide, pool complex, and small movie theater. The resort takes full advantage of its waterfront location with a private beach and marina. Rates start at $225 s or d ($255 s or d with a water view) for a spacious self-contained unit.

Over $200

The grandest of Kelowna's accommodations is the **Grand Okanagan Resort** (1310 Water St., 250/763-4500 or 800/465-4651, www.grandokanagan.com), a sprawling downtown lakeside development set around a private lagoon/swimming pool and with its own private lock and watercraft rentals. Summer rates start at $259 s or d, but check the website for packages.

On the west side of the lake, **Lake Okanagan Resort** (17 km/10.6 mi. north along Westside Rd., 250/769-3511 or 800/663-3273, www.lake okanagan.com, from $224 s or d) sprawls over 100 hectares (250 acres) of lakeside land with eye-popping views back across the water. You can play tennis, golf a par-3 course, swim in the pools or lake, rent a motor boat, or go trail riding, and then dine at a casual café or upscale restaurant. Some rooms are a little stuffy and dated, but each has a kitchen. Rates drop drastically outside the mid-June–mid-September high season.

Campgrounds

South of downtown and just one block from the lake is **Hiawatha RV Park** (3787 Lakeshore Rd., 250/861-4837 or 888/784-7275, www.hiawatha rvpark.com, tents $34, hookups $42–44), with a separate tenting area, showers, a launderette, game room, and playground.

Most of the other commercial campgrounds are on the west shore of Okanagan Lake at Westbank. Rating them on beach frontage alone, **West Bay Beach Resort** (3745 West Bay Rd., 250/768-3004, www.westbaybeachresort.com) wins hands-down. It offers all amenities, as well as a few extras like nightly beachside bonfires and an alpaca farm. Rates are $31–39, with some rooms right on the beach. On the same side of the lake, but to the north nine kilometers (5.6 mi.) is **Bear Creek Provincial Park** ($20), a world away from the commercial campgrounds.

FOOD

Downtown Kelowna has a great number of dining choices, for everything from a quick coffee to a full meal, but many of the city's finer restaurants are away from the business core, along quiet country roads or at the many golf clubs.

Cafés

The business of breakfast doesn't get going until around 8 A.M. in the downtown area, but one exception is **Lena's Pancake & Omelet House** (553 Bernard St.), which opens its doors at 6:30 A.M.—the perfect place for a meal after an early morning walk along the lakefront; cooked breakfasts start at $4. Back toward the lake is the friendly little **Lunch Box** (509 Bernard St., 250/862-8621, Mon.–Fri. 8 A.M.–8 P.M. and Sat. 9 A.M.–4 P.M.). A full cooked breakfast is just $4, healthy muffins and sandwiches are on the menu for lunch, and in the evening no main meal is over $12.

Family-Style Dining

Opposite City Park, **Earl's on Top** (upstairs at 211 Bernard Ave., 250/763-2777, Sun.–Mon. 11:30 A.M.–11 P.M., Tues.–Sat. 11:30 A.M.) does a booming business, deservedly. The atmosphere features a shiny, black-and-white decor with flashy neon lighting (nothing beats a neon palm tree) and a mass of plants. Grab a table on the rooftop garden patio and absorb the lake view, or just pretend you're outside (not hard to do with all the plants). No surprises on the menu here, just burgers, chicken, seafood, steak, and pasta dishes all under $20.

Other Restaurants

The **de Montreuil** (368 Bernard St., 250/860-5508, Mon.–Fri. for lunch, daily for dinner) is a starkly decorated yet stylish restaurant, with casual yet professional service. The menu offers many mouthwatering choices—think pan-seared snapper with dill hollandaise and Australian rack of lamb basted in fresh rosemary and garlic—with the three table d'hôte menus offering best value (two courses $32, three courses $38, four courses $44). **Christopher's** (242 Lawrence Ave., 250/861-3464) has a light and breezy decor and a menu that concentrates on steak and seafood. **Fresco** (1560 Water St., 250/868-8805) is a chic eatery in the surrounds of a heritage commercial building. The menu is typically West Coast, but more adventurous than you'd expect this far from Vancouver. Mains range $20–26.

PRACTICALITIES

Information

Kelowna Visitor Info Centre (544 Harvey Ave., 250/861-1515, www.kelownachamber.org, late

June–mid-Sept. daily 8 A.M.–7 P.M., rest of year daily 9 A.M.–5 P.M.) is along Highway 97 in the heart of the city.

Mosaic Books (411 Bernard Ave., 250/763-4418 or 800/663-1225, open daily) is an independent bookseller that has been serving the valley for over 30 years. As well as an excellent collection of western Canadian titles, it has a wide selection of magazines and an in-house coffee bar.

Services

The post office is right downtown on Queensway Avenue. **Kelowna General Hospital** (250/862-4000) is on the corner of Strathcona Avenue and Pandosy Street.

Transportation

Kelowna Airport is 15 kilometers (9.3 mi.) north of downtown along Highway 97. It's served by **Air Canada** (250/542-3302) and **WestJet** (800/538-5696), both of which offer daily flights to and from Vancouver, Calgary, and Edmonton. All major car-rental agencies have vehicles at the airport.

Greyhound (2366 Leckie Rd., 250/860-3835) provides bus service throughout the Okanagan and beyond.

Local buses are run by **Kelowna Regional Transit System** (250/860-8121), and the downtown terminal is on Bernard Avenue at Ellis Street. For a taxi, call **Kelowna Cabs** (250/762-4444) or **Checkmate Cabs** (250/861-1111).

Vernon and Vicinity

The city of Vernon (pop. 38,000) lies between Okanagan, Kalamalka, and Swan Lakes, at the north end of the Okanagan Valley 50 kilometers (31 mi.) from Kelowna. The city itself holds little of interest; the surrounding area boasts the main attractions. Among the area highlights: many sandy public beaches; local provincial parks; Silver Star Mountain Resort, a year-round recreation paradise east of the city; and fishing in more than 100 lakes within an hour's drive of the city.

SIGHTS AND RECREATION

In Town

Greater Vernon Museum and Archives (3009 32nd Ave., 250/542-3142, summer Mon.–Sat. 10 A.M.–5 P.M., rest of year Tues.–Sat. 10 A.M.–5 P.M.) holds photos from the early 1900s and a large collection of pioneer and native artifacts. Displays cover natural history, recreation, period clothing, and steamships. In the same vicinity is **Vernon Public Art Gallery** (3228 31st Ave., 250/545-3173, Mon.–Fri. 10 A.M.–5 P.M., Sat. noon–4 P.M.), featuring works by local artists as well as touring exhibitions.

Polson Park (Hwy. 97 at 25th Ave.) has a Chinese teahouse and Japanese garden, but most people go to stare at the spectacular floral clock—nine meters (29.6 ft.) wide, made up of more than 3,500 plants, and the only one of its kind in western Canada.

Historic O'Keefe Ranch

Established in 1867, the O'Keefe Ranch (13 km/eight mi. north of Vernon toward Kamloops on Hwy. 9, 250/542-7868, mid-May–early Oct. daily 9 A.M.–5 P.M., adult $7, senior $5.50, child $5) was one of the Okanagan's first cattle ranches. Today you can tour the opulent, fully furnished O'Keefe Mansion and other noteworthy outbuildings, including a furnished old log house that was the O'Keefe's original home; a working blacksmith's shop; the still-in-use St. Ann's Church, where services have been held since 1889; a fully stocked general store where you can buy postcards and old-fashioned candy; and the Chinese cook's bunkhouse. If you worked up an appetite in your explorations, visit the Homestead Restaurant, open daily for lunch and weekends for dinner.

Davison Orchards

Dozens of farms surround Vernon, but one in particular, **Davison Orchards** (west of downtown off Bella Vista Rd., 250/549-3266, daily 8 A.M.–8 P.M.) is worth a visit. Set on a sloping hill

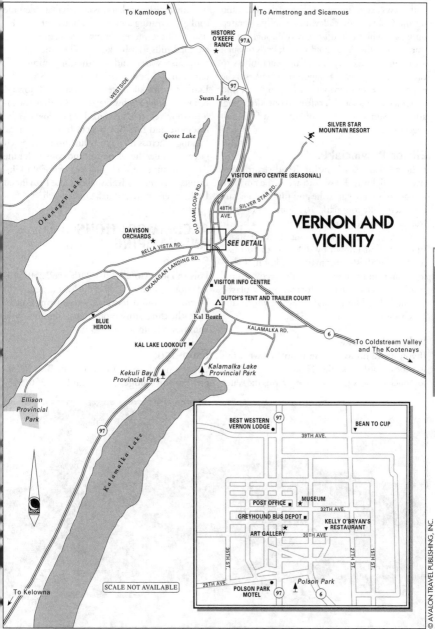

To Kamloops ↑

↑ To Armstrong and Sicamous

HISTORIC O'KEEFE RANCH ★

97A

97

Swan Lake

WESTSIDE

Goose Lake

SILVER STAR MOUNTAIN RESORT

Okanagan Lake

VISITOR INFO CENTRE (SEASONAL) ■

48TH AVE.

SILVER STAR RD.

OLD KAMLOOPS RD.

VERNON AND VICINITY

DAVISON ORCHARDS ★

BELLA VISTA RD.

SEE DETAIL

OKANAGAN LANDING RD.

VISITOR INFO CENTRE ■

DUTCH'S TENT AND TRAILER COURT △

BLUE HERON

Kal Beach

KALAMALKA RD.

6

To Coldstream Valley and The Kootenays

KAL LAKE LOOKOUT ■

Kekuli Bay Provincial Park

Kalamalka Lake Provincial Park

Ellison Provincial Park

97

Kalamalka Lake

MOON

To Kelowna ←

SCALE NOT AVAILABLE

BEST WESTERN VERNON LODGE ●

97

39TH AVE.

BEAN TO CUP ▼

MUSEUM

POST OFFICE ■ ★

32ND AVE.

GREYHOUND BUS DEPOT ■

KELLY O'BRYAN'S RESTAURANT ▼

ART GALLERY ★

30TH AVE.

35TH ST.

27TH ST.

15TH ST.

25TH AVE.

POLSON PARK MOTEL

97

Polson Park ▼

6

BRITISH COLUMBIA

© AVALON TRAVEL PUBLISHING, INC.

with views extending across Kalamalka Lake and up the Coldstream Valley, this family-operated business is a hive of tourist activity throughout the warmer months. A self-guided walk leads through a garden where everything from cucumbers to cantaloupe is grown, a wagon tour traverses the entire 20-hectare property (daily 6 P.M.), and there's a Critter Corral, a café with outside dining, an ice cream stand, and, of course, a fruit and vegetable market.

Ellison Provincial Park

Follow Okanagan Landing Road (from 25th Ave. off Highway 97) west to access the northern reaches of Okanagan Lake and this 200-hectare (500-acre) lakefront park, 16 kilometers (10 mi.) from downtown. Most of the park is on a bench, with trails leading to and along the rocky shore. Ellison is best known by divers as British Columbia's first freshwater marine park. Enjoy shallow-water snorkeling and diving, weed beds full of life, underwater rock formations, a plastic bubble "Dive Dome," a deep-water wreck, and beach showers. Camping is $17.

Kalamalka Lake

If you drove up to Vernon from Kelowna, this was the beautiful lake that Highway 97 paralleled for much of the way. As summer warms the water, the limestone bedrock forms crystals that reflect the sunlight, creating a distinctive aquamarine color that is all the more stunning with surrounding parched hills as a backdrop. The emerald and turquoise water and surrounding mountain panorama is best appreciated from **Kal Lake Lookout,** five kilometers (3.1 mi.) back toward Kelowna along Highway 97. Just south of the information center, a steep road winds down to the lakeshore and fine **Kal Beach,** fringed by trees. Parking is across the railway line from the beach (access is under the rail bridge) and costs $1 for the day. Continue beyond the beach for eight kilometers (five mi.) to **Kalamalka Lake Provincial Park,** where trails lead to a sandy beach.

ACCOMMODATIONS AND CAMPING

$50–100

Polson Park Motel (3201 24th Ave., 250/549-2231 or 800/480-2231) is the least expensive of Vernon's 20-odd motels. Across from Polson Park, the three-story motel has an outdoor pool and rooms from $55 s, $65 d.

$100–150

On the north side of downtown, **Best Western Vernon Lodge** (3914 32nd St., 250/545-

Kal Beach, a popular escape on a hot summer day

3385 or 800/663-4422, www.rpbhotels.com, $109 s, $119 d) has spacious, stylishly decorated rooms overlooking an enclosed three-story tropical atrium. Other facilities include an indoor pool with a whirlpool, a café, a restaurant, and a pub.

Campgrounds

Dutch's Tent and Trailer Court (three km/1.9 mi. south of downtown on Kalamalka Rd., 250/545-1023) is a two-minute walk from Kal Beach and Kalamalka Lake. The park has hot showers, a launderette, and a snack bar. Tent sites are $21, hookups $23–27.

Two provincial parks within a 15-minute drive of downtown provide campsites. **Ellison Provincial Park** ($17 per night) lies 16 kilometers (9.9 mi.) southwest of town on Okanagan Landing Road on the east shore of Okanagan Lake, while south along Highway 97 toward Kelowna, **Kekuli Bay Provincial Park** ($22) sits right on Kalamalka Lake, but it's open to the elements.

FOOD

The dining choices in Vernon have improved vastly in recent years, as has the coffee scene. The best coffee joint is **Bean to Cup** (3903 27th St., 250/503-2222, daily 6 A.M.–midnight), in a converted 1914 residence with a heated patio. Coffee is roasted in-house, tea-lovers are catered to with over 20 varieties, and the food is excellent (panini, healthy sandwiches, chili or clam chowder in a bread bowl, and more). Rounding out its appeal is inexpensive public Internet access.

At **Kelly O'Bryan's Restaurant** (2933 30th Ave., 250/549-2112, daily 11 A.M.–midnight) tuck into burgers, steak, seafood, salads, and pasta, all well under $20. The **Blue Heron** (7673 Okanagan Landing Rd., 250/542-5550) is a few kilometers west of downtown, but well worth the drive. It sits right on Okanagan Lake, and a large deck right on the water is the most popular of the pub's three dining areas. The menu is fairly standard, with lots of dishes to share, but as it's off the tourist path, prices are reasonable.

INFORMATION

Vernon Visitor Info Centre (250/542-1415 or 800/665-0795, www.vernontourism.com, daily 8:30 A.M.–6 P.M.) is in a spruced-up heritage house on Highway 97 at the south end of town. If you're driving into town from the north, make a stop at the seasonal visitors center (6326 Hwy. 97 N).

SILVER STAR MOUNTAIN RESORT

For summer or winter recreation, head up to Silver Star Mountain Resort (250/542-0224 or 800/663-4431, www.silverstarmtn.com), 22 kilometers (13.6 mi.) northeast of Vernon (take 48th Ave. off Highway 97), a colorful gold-rush-era style, fully self-contained village.

Summer Activities

Starting at the end of June, a chairlift ($10 per ride, or $28 all day) runs from the village to the top of Silver Star Mountain for terrific views of Vernon and surrounding lakes. Much of the alpine area around the summit is protected by a provincial park laced with hiking trails, but a guided hike is the best way to fully appreciate the natural history. If you want to spend the day riding the mountain trails on a bike, pay $42 for an all-day lift pass and the use of a bike. Also in summer you can go horseback riding ($27 per hour) on beautiful trails adjacent to the village.

Skiing and Snowboarding

From November through April, skiers and snowboarders mob Silver Star, coming for great terrain and the facilities of an outstanding on-hill village. The two main faces—Vance Creek, good for beginners, and Putnam Creek, for intermediates and experts—are served by five chairlifts and a couple of T-bars. The resort's 80 runs cover 1,100 hectares (2,720 acres) with a vertical rise of 760 meters (2,500 feet). Lift tickets are adult $56, senior and child $48; those over 70 and under six ski free. Through winter a shuttle bus operates between Kelowna Airport and the mountain.

Accommodations

The base village contains numerous types of accommodations; book year-round through central reservations (800/663-4431) or contact each accommodation directly. The rates quoted below are for summer, which is low season. Through winter, expect to pay double (except at the Samesun property).

Least expensive is **Samesun Backpacker Lodge** (877/562-2783, www.samesun.com), Canada's only ski-in, ski-out backpacker lodge. Facilities include a modern communal kitchen, plenty of table space for dining and 140 beds in dorms and private rooms. Dorm beds are $20, private rooms $49.50. The **Kickwillie Inn** (250/542-4548 or 800/551-7466, www.pinnacles.com) is part of the adjacent and much larger Pinnacles Suite Hotel, but has the better value rooms; from $80 s or d with a kitchen. The most luxurious on-mountain lodging is **Silver Star Club Resort** (250/549-5191 or 800/610-0805, www.silverstarclubresort.com), which offers standard hotel rooms and self-contained suites spread through three buildings. Guests enjoy use of all facilities at the nearby National Altitude Training Centre. Summer rates start at a reasonable $95 s or d, rising to $135 for a suite.

The Kootenays and B.C. Rockies

The wild and rugged Kootenays region of British Columbia lies east of the Okanagan Valley and south of the TransCanada Highway. It is bordered by the United States to the south and Alberta to the east. Three north-to-south-trending mountain ranges—the Monashees, Selkirks, and Purcells—run parallel to each other across the region, separated by lush green valleys and narrow lakes up to 150 kilometers (93 mi.) long. The snowcapped mountains and forested valleys abound with wildlife, including large populations of deer, elk, moose, black bear, and grizzly bear.

Recreational opportunities abound throughout the Kootenays in all seasons. In summer, anglers flock to the lakes and rivers for trout, char, kokanee salmon, freshwater cod, and bass. Other visitors enjoy canoeing, swimming, or sunbathing on the beaches, or take to the mountains

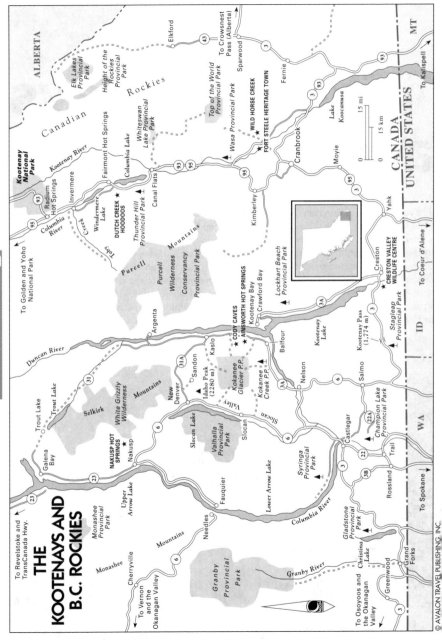

THE KOOTENAYS AND B.C. ROCKIES

© AVALON TRAVEL PUBLISHING, INC.

for hiking and wildlife-viewing. Much of the region's higher elevations are protected in rugged and remote parks, including the spectacular Valhalla, Kokanee Glacier, Top of the World, and Purcell Wilderness Conservancy Provincial Parks. In colder months the mountains of the Kootenays catch a phenomenal amount of snow, turning the whole region into a winter wonderland. You won't find any major resorts here; however, three small but legendary ski areas—Red Mountain, Whitewater, and Fernie—attract adventurous powderhounds with some of North America's highest snowfalls and steepest lift-served slopes.

West Kootenays

Clustered on the edge of the Monashee Range in the western Kootenays are several communities that seem a world away from the hustle and the bustle of the nearby Okanagan Valley. Grand Forks, Rossland, Trail, and Castlegar all boomed around the beginning of the 20th century, when thousands of gold-hungry prospectors descended on the slopes of Red Mountain. Today Red Mountain draws more powderhounds than prospectors, and lakes, rivers, parks, and peaks are the area's main attractions.

In addition to mining history, the West Kootenays are also known as the home of the Doukhobors, a religious sect of Russian immigrants who arrived in the early 1900s to till the land and practice their faith in peace. Aspects of their unique culture and lifestyle can be seen today in Grand Forks and elsewhere in the region.

GRAND FORKS AND VICINITY

Originally a mining town, Grand Forks (pop. 4,200) is home to descendants of the Doukhobors, a Russian religious sect who settled here in the early 1900s. Some still speak Russian, which is taught in local schools. Both the **Mountain View Doukhobor Museum** (Hardy Mountain Rd., 250/442-8855) and the **Doukhobor Heritage Centre** (6110 Reservoir Rd., 250/442-3523) catalog their history. Grand Forks also features a mix of impressive historic early-20th-century homes and restored civic buildings.

Practicalities

In a pleasant setting on the west edge of town, **Pinegrove Motel** (209 Central Ave., 250/442-

8203) offers rooms from $80 s, $90 d (with a huge discount for travelers aged 50 or older). Campers gravitate to the riverside **municipal campground** (end of 5th Street, $14–18), where showers and hookups are offered. Along the main street is the **Grand Forks Visitor Info Centre** (7362 5th St., 250/442-2833, www.boundary.bc.ca, Mon.–Fri. 9:30 A.M.–4:30 P.M.).

Christina Lake

This lake, 25 kilometers (15.6 mi.) east of Grand Forks along Highway 3, is a summer favorite for folks from throughout the West Kootenays, who come for the lake's warm waters and fishing for rainbow trout, bass, and kokanee. The best of many commercial campgrounds is **Cascade Cove RV Park** (1290 River Rd., 250/447-6662, $17–24).

ROSSLAND

Clinging to the slopes of an extinct volcanic crater deep in the tree-covered Monashee Mountains, Rossland (pop. 4,500) was once a gold-rush boomtown known as "The Golden City." The precious yellow metal was discovered on Red Mountain 1890, with the town's population peaking seven years later at 7,000. At that time, the city boasted four newspapers, 40 saloons, and daily rail service south to Spokane. By 1929, the mountain had yielded six million tons of ore worth $165 million. Today, tourism supplies the bulk of Rossland's gold.

Sights

Downtown Rossland is a picturesque place full of historic buildings and old-fashioned street lamps.

Pick up a "How to find your way around the twisting, hilly, scenic, tree-lined, and sometimes confusing (because it's situated on the side of a mountain—which is really what makes this place so great) streets and trails of Rossland" pamphlet from the museum, library, or downtown shops, and hit the streets. On the west side of downtown is the **Rossland Museum** (Hwy. 3B and Columbia Ave., 250/362-7722, summer daily 9 A.M.–5 P.M., adult $5, senior $4, child $2) at the entrance of the Le Roi mine. Exhibits catalog the area's lustrous geological and human history. To experience the day-to-day life of the early miners, take a mine tour—an introductory course in local geology, detailed explanations of how ore is mined, and more—for adult $10, senior $8, child $6.

Biking, Skiing, and Snowboarding

Each spring, Rossland comes alive with pedal power as mountain-bike enthusiasts take advantage of the maze of old logging and mining trails surrounding the city. Now known as the "Mountain Bike Capital of Canada," Rossland has hosted both the Canadian and North American championships. Rent bikes from **The Powderhound** (2040 Columbia Ave., 250/362-5311).

The site of what was once one of the world's richest gold mines is now part of **Red Mountain** (250/362-7700 or 800/663-0105, www.ski-red.com), an alpine resort offering some of North America's most challenging lift-served runs. The heart-stopping face of Red Mountain is the star of the show, but adjacent Granite Mountain offers a vertical rise of 880 meters (2,900 ft.) and almost unlimited intermediate, expert, and extreme skiing and snowboarding, mostly on unmarked trails through powder-filled glades. Lift tickets are adult $46, senior $30, child $25.

Accommodations

The **Ram's Head Inn** (250/362-9577 or 877/267-4323, www.ramshead.bc.ca), one of Canada's premier small lodges, lies in the woods at the base of Red Mountain. Primarily designed for wintertime, the inn offers 14 ultra-comfy guest rooms,

a dining area, game room, sauna, outdoor hot tub, and a spacious communal lounge with luxurious chairs and a large fireplace. Summer rates are $70–92 s or d, with winter packages averaging around $100–120 per person per night.

Food

Each morning, locals converge on the **Sunshine Café** (2116 Columbia Ave., 250/362-5070) for hearty cooked breakfasts from $6. The rest of the day, the café offers a diverse menu including Mexican and Indian dishes. **Goldrush Books and Espresso** (2063 Washington St., 250/362-5333) sets a few tables around bookshelves full of local and Canadian literature. On the ski hill access road, the **Rock Cut Neighbourhood Pub** (250/362-5814) is busiest in winter, but opens year-round. It offers typical pub fare, smartly presented and well priced. Enjoy the mountain surroundings by eating on the heated deck.

CASTLEGAR

Though endowed with the rich history of the Doukhobors, Castlegar (pop. 7,400) is not a particularly attractive place. Spread out along the barren Columbia River Valley, it's a real crossroads town. The area's first nonnative residents, the Doukhobors, arrived in 1908. These pacifist Russian immigrants planted orchards, built sawmills, and even operated a jam factory while living in segregated villages along the valley floor. Many of their descendants still live in the area.

Sights

Castlegar's major attraction is the **Doukhobor Village Museum** (east side of river along Hwy. 3A, 250/365-6622, open daily 9 A.M.–6 P.M., adult $5, child $2.50). The village allows a glimpse of the traditional lifestyle of these intriguing Russian immigrants. Admission includes a guided tour, led by Doukhobor descendants, through the main building and the simply furnished brick dwellings and outbuildings. While you're in a Russian frame of mind, visit the old **Doukhobor Bridge,** which crosses the Kootenay River along Highway 3A. It was built by the Doukhobors in the 1910s as a link from their community to

Nelson; none of them had any bridge-building experience, but the 100-meter (330-ft.) suspension bridge was used until 1968.

Practicalities

The comfortable and reasonably priced **Cozy Pines Motel** (2100 Crestview Cres., 250/365-5613, $55 s, $60 d) offers spotless rooms with kitchenettes. Campers should head north out of town toward Nelson and turn west off Highway 3A to **Syringa Provincial Park** ($17), on the banks of Lower Arrow Lake.

Castlegar Visitor Info Centre is off Columbia Avenue (1995 6th Ave., 250/365-6313, summer daily 8 A.M.–7 P.M., rest of year Mon.–Fri. 9 A.M.–5 P.M.).

THE SLOCAN VALLEY

The historically rich Slocan Valley, or "Silvery Slocan," nestles snugly between the Slocan and Valhalla Ranges of the Selkirk Mountains. In the 1890s the valley sprang into the limelight when silver was discovered at Sandon. It's much quieter today, offering many picturesque towns and an abundance of outdoor-recreation opportunities.

New Denver

Western gateway to "Silver Country," this picturesque town of 600 is on Slocan Lake, opposite Valhalla Provincial Park. Originally called Eldorado and renamed after Denver, Colorado, the town reached its mining peak in the 1890s.

Today the main street is lined with funky false-front stores and pioneer-style buildings left over from the prosperous silver days. Visit the **Silvery Slocan Museum** (6th St. and Bellevue Dr., 250/358-2201, July–early Sept.) to find out all about New Denver's heyday.

Down on the lake within easy walking distance of the main street, **Sweet Dreams Guesthouse** (702 Eldorado St., 250/358-2415, www.newdenverbc.com, $55 s, $70–90 d) offers large rooms and a cooked breakfast. Out of New Denver to the south, **Silverton Resort** (250/358-7157, www.silvertonresort.com, $85–150) takes advantage of its watery location with lakefront cottages and boat and kayak rentals.

SANDON, CAPITAL OF THE SILVERY SLOCAN

Once a silver-mining town of 5,000, Sandon was the original boomtown of the Slocan Valley. In its heyday Sandon boasted 24 hotels, 23 saloons, banks, general stores, mining brokers' offices, a newspaper, and a rail link to the outside world. It was incorporated as a city in 1908 and mining continued until 1955. In that year, the creek running through town flooded, sweeping away most of the city and leaving a ghost town.

Reached via an unpaved road that branches south of Highway 31A east of New Denver, today you could count the population of Sandon on two hands. Start a visit at the 1900 city hall, where the *Sandon Walking Tour Guide* is sold. The brochure details all the original structures—only a fraction of which remain—with a map that makes exploring on foot more enjoyable. Up the creek from city hall are **Sandon Museum** (250/358-7920), where exhibits bring the old town back to life, and **Silversmith Mine Powerhouse,** which still supplies power to the few remaining residents.

NAKUSP

Situated 48 kilometers (30 mi.) northwest of New Denver, Nakusp (pop. 1,800) was established during the mining-boom years. Today the small town is best known for its hot springs and its stunning location on Upper Arrow Lake at the foot of the Selkirk Mountains.

Nakusp Museum (6th Ave., July–Aug. daily 9 A.M.–5 P.M., $1) features an odd but intriguing collection of items, including predam photos of the towns now flooded beneath the Arrow Lakes. Take the signposted road one kilometer (0.6 mi.) north from town off Highway 23 to **Nakusp Hot Springs** (250/265-4528, summer daily 9:30 A.M.–10 P.M., rest of year daily 10 A.M.–9:30 P.M., adult $7, senior and child $6).

Practicalities

Kuskanax Lodge (515 Broadway, 250/265-3618 or 800/663-0100, $95 s or d) has 50 bright and breezily decorated rooms. A nearby resort with its own private hot springs is **Halcyon Hot Springs** (32 km/20 mi. north of Nakusp, 250/265-3554 or 888/689-4699, www.halcyon-hotsprings.com). Accommodations are in cabins, cottages (my favorite), chalets, or a luxury family-oriented Lodge Suite, with rates ranging $74–228 s or d. **Nakusp Village Campground** (8th St., 250/265-4019) has large shaded sites, coin-operated showers, and firewood within walking distance of the beach and the main street; unserviced sites are $16, hookups $19.

The place to be seen in Nakusp is the **Broadway Deli Bistro** (408 Broadway St. W, 250/265-3767, daily from 7 A.M.), where you'll find great coffee and a constant stream of muffins coming out of the oven.

Nelson and Vicinity

The elegant city of Nelson (pop. 9,700) lies in a picturesque setting on the West Arm of Kootenay Lake, 660 kilometers (410 mi.) east of Vancouver. Its relaxed pace, hilly tree-lined streets, and late-19th-century architectural treasures have helped attract an eclectic mix of jaded big-city types, artists, and counterculture seekers. But while the city itself is uniquely charming, the surrounding wilderness of the Selkirk Mountains is Nelson's biggest draw. The area's many lakes provide excellent fishing, sailing, and canoeing, as well as some of British Columbia's best inland beaches.

SIGHTS AND RECREATION

Nelson has 350 designated heritage buildings, more per capita than any other city in British Columbia save Victoria. Most can be viewed by walking around the downtown core between Baker and Vernon Streets. Pick up the detailed *Heritage Walking Tour* or *Heritage Motoring Tour* brochures from the information center. The walking-tour brochure includes the 1909 courthouse on Ward Street and the impressive stone-and-brick 1902 city hall on the corner of Ward and Vernon Streets.

Museums

Nelson's two museums are both worth visiting. **Nelson Museum** (402 Anderson St., 250/352-9813, summer Mon.–Sat. 1–6 P.M., rest of year Mon.–Sat. 1–4 P.M., $3) depicts local history, with displays covering native peoples, explorers, miners, traders, and the Doukhobors. It also contains the *Ladybird,* a record-breaking speedboat

designed prior to the advent of hydroplanes in the 1950s. The **Chamber of Mines Museum** (next to information center on Hall St., 250/352-5242, Mon.–Fri. 1–5 P.M.) concentrates on Nelson's mining history.

Kokanee Creek Provincial Park

This 257-hectare (640-acre) park 20 kilometers (12 mi.) northeast of Nelson features a great beach and one of the Kootenays' most popular campgrounds. The epicenter of the action occurs along the park's long sandy beach, backed by a shallow lagoon and a large grassed area dotted with picnic tables. Kokanee—landlocked salmon—spawn at the mouth of Kokanee Creek (access is from the visitors center) in

NELSON'S ARTWALK

Organized by the local arts council, Nelson's July–September Artwalk (250/352-2402) highlights the work of up to 100 local artists at venues across the city. Works are displayed citywide at restaurants, hotels, the theater building, art galleries, and even the local pool hall. On the last Friday of every month of the event, receptions are held at each of the venues. The receptions feature live entertainment, refreshments, and the artists themselves on hand to discuss their work. A brochure available at the information center and motels and galleries around town contains biographies of each featured artist, tells where his or her work is displayed, and provides a map showing you the easiest way to get from one venue to the next.

late summer. Instead of migrating in from the ocean like their anadromous cousins, kokanee spend their lives in the larger lakes of British Columbia's interior, spawning each summer in the rivers and streams draining into the lakes. A visitors center (250/825-4421, mid-June–mid-Sept. daily 9 A.M.–9 P.M.) holds displays on local ecosystems.

Kokanee Glacier Provincial Park

Straddling the highest peaks of the Selkirk Mountains, this 32,000-hectare (79,000-acre) mountain wilderness park can be seen from downtown Nelson. The steep and narrow gravel roads into the park are often impassable until

late June, and the hiking trails remain snow-covered even later. But don't let these things discourage you from visiting. This is one of B.C.'s premier provincial parks, filled with magnificent scenery and abundant wildlife and providing some unrivaled opportunities for backcountry travel. The park's environment is very different from the valley floor—dominated by barren peaks and, for a few short weeks in the middle of summer, meadows of lush subalpine wildflowers.

The main access is via an unsealed road that spurs off Highway 3A 20 kilometers (12 mi.) from Nelson and follows Kokanee Creek 16 kilometers (10 mi.) to **Gibson Lake**. A 2.5-kilometer

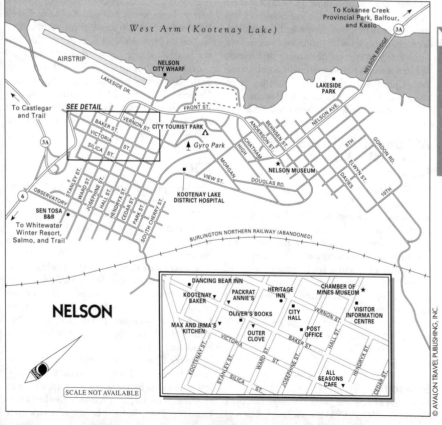

NELSON

SCALE NOT AVAILABLE

© AVALON TRAVEL PUBLISHING, INC.

BRITISH COLUMBIA

(1.6-mi.) trail circles the lake, but the best scenery is around **Kokanee Lake,** four-kilometers (2.5 mi.) away. Because of the park's remote location, it's vital to pick up information on road and hiking-trail conditions (in years of high snowfall, some hiking trails are impassable until late July) at the visitors center in Kokanee Creek Provincial Park.

Skiing and Snowboarding

Legendary powder and an off-the-beaten-path location makes **Whitewater Winter Resort** (250/354-4944 or 800/666-9420, www.skiwhite water.com) a hidden gem. The small resort 20 kilometers (12 mi.) south of Nelson sits beneath a string of 2,400-meter (7,900-ft.) peaks that catch an amazing amount of snow. Three double chairlifts access 18 marked trails (the Summit Chair opens up the best powder-packed slopes). The area's abundant snowfall makes for a long season, but conditions are best in February and March. Whitewater has no on-mountain accommodations—just the lifts and a day lodge with a cafeteria, rental shop, and ski/snowboard school. Lift tickets are adult $42, senior and youth $32.

ACCOMMODATIONS AND CAMPING

Under $50

The **Dancing Bear Inn** (171 Baker St., 250/352-7573 or 877/352-7573, www.dancingbearinn .com), right downtown, offers clean and comfortable accommodations at a very reasonable price. It features a cozy lounge area with a TV, reading material, information on local attractions and restaurants, and a cupboard full of board games. Other facilities include Internet access, kitchen, laundry, and lockers. The dorm-style rooms are spacious, with a maximum of six beds in each. A few doubles and a single room are also available. Members of Hostelling International pay $17 per night, nonmembers $20; private rooms are $40–46 d.

$50–100

Right downtown, the 1898 **Heritage Inn** (422 Vernon St., 250/352-5331, www.heritageinn.org) is a city landmark. It provides attractive, recently refurbished rooms, some with lake views, for $67–89 s, $77–99 d, including breakfast in the downstairs restaurant.

The pick of Nelson's many bed-and-breakfasts is **Sen Tosa B&B** (uphill from downtown at 402 Observatory St., 250/354-1993, $65 s, $75 d). It offers three comfortable guest rooms and particularly delicious breakfasts. Guests have use of a communal living area and a pleasant garden with an outdoor hot tub.

Campgrounds

City Tourist Park (corner High St. and Willow St., 250/352-9031, $16–22) downtown isn't particularly impressive. It's surrounded by houses and its sites are closely spaced. A much better choice is the lakeside **Kokanee Creek Provincial Park** (20 km/125 mi. northeast of Nelson on Hwy. 3A, 250/825-4421). Although the large park offers more than 100 sites, it's often full; the beautiful location makes this one of the Kootenays' most popular campgrounds. Unserviced sites are $22. If the park is full, continue eight kilometers (five mi.) farther northeast to Balfour, where you'll find two commercial campgrounds.

FOOD

The best place for breakfast is the **Heritage Inn** (422 Vernon St., 250/352-5331, daily 7:30 A.M.–8:30 P.M.). Cooked breakfasts are huge, especially the omelets (from $6.50), which come piled high with delicious hash browns. The counterculture of Nelson is evident at the café inside **Packrat Annie's** bookstore (411 Kootenay St., 250/354-4646), where a wide cross-section of the local community wanders in for herbal tea, muffins, or lunch. The **Kootenay Baker** (295 Baker St., 250/352-2274) offers a great selection of breads and cakes.

Outer Clove (536 Stanley St., 250/354-1667, Mon.–Sat. 11:30 A.M.–9:30 P.M.) is typical of Nelson's better restaurants, appealing to modern tastes but in a relaxed, low-key environment. The emphasis is on garlic (it's even an ingredient in a couple of the desserts), with tapas from $5 (you'd need three for a filling meal) and dinners $12–19. All lunch items are under $10. Tucked into a back alley behind the main street is **All Seasons Café** (620 Heritage Lane, 250/352-0101), a small yet stylish place known for its wine list. Lunch is well priced, but dinner is most popular, with a menu ranging from vegetarian Japanese to West Coast salmon. The best pizza in town comes straight from the wood-fired oven at **Max & Irma's Kitchen** (515 Kootenay St., 250/352-2332, daily 11 A.M.–8 P.M.). I had the Cajun Pacific Pizza followed by a slice of cheesecake and the bill came to around $20.

INFORMATION AND SERVICES

All the information you'll need on Nelson and the Kootenays is available at **Nelson Visitor Info Centre** (225 Hall St., 250/352-3433, www.discovernelson.com, summer Mon.–Fri. 8:30 A.M.–6 P.M. and Sat.–Sun. 10 A.M.–6 P.M., rest of year Mon.–Fri. 8:30 A.M.–4:30 P.M.). Search out local literature at **Oliver's Books** (398 Baker St., 250/352-7525).

Kootenay Lake District Hospital (3 View St., 250/352-3111) is east of downtown. The post office is at 514 Vernon Street. For quality arts and crafts, drop by the **Craft Connection** (441 Baker St., 250/352-3006, closed Sun.), a co-op owned and operated by local artists and craftspersons.

NELSON TO KASLO
Ainsworth Hot Springs

Overlooking Kootenay Lake from a hillside 40 kilometers (25 mi.) north of Nelson, these springs (summer 10 A.M.–9:30 P.M., shorter hours rest of year) were discovered in the early 1800s by local natives who found that the hot, odorless water (high in magnesium sulfate, calcium sulfate, and sodium carbonate) helped heal their wounds and ease their aches and pains. Today the springs have been commercialized and include a main outdoor pool, a hot tub, steam bath, and cold plunge pool.

Rates are $8 for a single entry or $13 per day. The adjacent **Ainsworth Hot Springs Resort** (250/229-4212 or 800/668-1171, www.hotnaturally.com) features exercise and massage rooms, a lounge, and a licensed restaurant overlooking the main pool and beautiful Kootenay Lake. Room rates are from $118 s or d, but you'll pay $138–158 for a lake view.

Kaslo

Tree-lined streets graced by elegant late-19th-century architecture, lake and mountain views from almost every street, and the world's oldest passenger sternwheeler tied up at the wharf make Kaslo, 70 kilometers (43 mi.) north of Nelson, a worthwhile stop. Another of the Kootenays' great boomtowns, Kaslo's population exploded to over 3,000 after the discovery of silver at Sandon in 1893. Drydocked by the lakefront is the **SS Moyie,** the last sternwheeler to splash up Kootenay Lake. Built in 1897, the grand old red and white vessel was used for transportation of passengers, freight, and mail right up until its retirement in 1957. Today the ship serves as a museum (summer daily 9:30 A.M.–5 P.M., adult $5, senior $4, child $3), containing a fine collection of photos, antiques, and artifacts of the region.

North of town, the **Lakewood Inn** (Kohle Rd., 250/353-2395, www.lakewoodinn.com) has been taking in guests since the 1920s. Lakefront cabins are $80–100, while campers pay from $17.50. **Kaslo Visitor Info Centre** (324 Front St., 250/353-2525) is open mid-May–mid-October daily 9 A.M.–8 P.M.

ACROSS KOOTENAY LAKE TO CRESTON

From **Balfour,** the world's longest free ferry ride takes you across Kootenay Lake to **Kootenay Bay.** No reservations are taken and the trip takes around 45 minutes.

Crawford Bay

Beyond the ferry dock is the artistically inclined community of Crawford Bay (pop. 200). On the left as you descend the hill is **North Woven Broom** (250/227-9245), western Canada's only traditional broom manufacturer. Stop in anytime and you're likely to find craftspeople hard at work and eager to share their knowledge of this lost art. The workshop is crammed with brooms of all shapes and sizes, and prices range $24–58. A little farther along is **Kootenay Forge** (250/227-9467), a traditional blacksmith shop where you can watch artisans practicing this ancient trade.

Also at Crawford Bay is **Kokanee Springs Golf Resort** (250/227-9226 or 800/979-7999, www.kokaneesprings.com, greens fee $60), one of the province's most picturesque courses. Featuring water views, forested fairways, huge greens, large elevation drops, and colorful flower beds around the tee boxes, it's not only a beautiful place to golf, it's also very challenging. Resort lodging—decorated in a stylish deep blue color, offset by the natural colors of wooden trim and furniture—is $130 s o r d, but most guests stay as part of a golfing package.

South Along Kootenay Lake

From Crawford Bay, it's 80 kilometers (50 mi.) of lake-hugging road to Creston. Along the way you'll pass small clusters of houses and a number of resorts. **Mountain Shores Marina & Resort** (13 km/eight mi. from Crawford Bay, 250/223-8258) is a lakefront resort with a pool and marina. Campsites are crowded, but the location is superb. Tent sites are $20, hookups $23–28.

CRESTON

In a wide, fertile valley at the extreme southern end of Kootenay Lake lies Creston, a thriving agricultural center of 5,000. Although the town is south of the Kootenays' most spectacular mountains, the scenery is still impressive; the Selkirk Mountains flank the valley to the west, while the Purcell Mountains do the same to the east.

Creston is home to the **Columbia Brewery** (1220 Erickson St., 250/428-9344), producer of British Columbia's popular Kokanee beer. Tours are offered in summer Monday–Friday at 9:30 A.M., 11:30 A.M., 1 P.M., and 2:30 P.M.

Creston Valley Wildlife Management Area

This 7,000-hectare (17,300-acre) wildlife reserve, 10 kilometer (6.2 mi.) west of Creston, is a haven for more than 250 species of birds, including a large population of osprey, a flock of the rare Forester's tern, and a nesting colony of western grebe. Start a visit at the park's wildlife center (250/428-3259, May–Aug. daily 8 A.M.–6 P.M., Apr. and Oct. Wed.–Sun. 9 A.M.–4 P.M., $5), where displays focus on the abundant birdlife, as well as on mammals and reptiles present in the reserve. From the center, hiking trails lead along areas of wetland to a bird-watching tower.

Information

Creston Visitor Info Centre (1711 Canyon St., 250/428-4342, summer daily 9 A.M.–6 P.M., rest of year weekdays 9 A.M.–4:30 P.M.) is at the east end of town.

East Kootenays

In the southeastern corner of the province, the East Kootenays encompass the Purcell Mountains and the upper reaches of the Columbia River, with the Rocky Mountains rising abruptly from the Columbia Valley to the Continental Divide and the British Columbia–Alberta border to the west. The crossroads of the region is the service center of Cranbrook; from there Highway 3 heads west to Fernie and the neighboring province of Alberta, and Highway 93/95 parallels the Columbia River northward through a region dotted with golf courses, hot springs, and many provincial parks.

EAST FROM CRESTON

From Creston, the Crowsnest Highway (Hwy. 3) crosses the Purcell Mountains and descends to Cranbrook, the region's largest town. The distance between the two towns is a little over 100 kilometers (62 miles).

Yahk

Yahk grew into a thriving lumber town in the 1920s but was abandoned by the 1930s. Today empty houses and hotels line the streets, but the **pioneer museum** keeps history alive with its displays of household artifacts and costumes from the past. Tiny **Yahk Provincial Park** lies beside the rushing Moyie River east of town. Fishing in the river is good for rainbow trout and Dolly Varden; the campground has only 26 sites ($14), so arrive in early afternoon to be assured of a spot.

Moyie

North from Yahk, Highway 3/95 parallels the Moyie River to its source at Moyie Lake, a deep-blue body of water backed by cliffs. Halfway along the lake, Moyie—once boasting a population of 1,500—today holds nothing more than a few historic buildings, a pub, and a small general store; the 1904 church on Tavistock Street and the fire hall beside the highway are among the original survivors. Miners working the nearby St. Eugene Mine for lead and silver

were the first settlers. The old mine is visible back up the hill by wandering down to the lakeshore, or take Queens Avenue east out of town and look for tailings.

Around 13 kilometers (eight mi.) north of town is 91-hectare (230-acre) **Moyie Lake Provincial Park**, which has a sandy swimming beach, short interpretive trails, and the chance to view kokanee spawning on gravel river beds. The large campground ($22) has semi-private sites, hot showers, and a weekend interpretive program.

CRANBROOK AND VICINITY

Crossroads of the eastern Kootenays, Cranbrook (pop. 19,000) nestles at the base of the Purcell Mountains 106 kilometers east of Creston and provides spectacular views eastward to the Canadian Rockies. The city itself has few tourist attractions, but with all the surrounding wilderness and nearby Fort Steele Heritage Town, it's a good base for further exploration. Cranbrook also claims to be British Columbia's sunniest town, with 2,224 hours of sunshine annually.

Canadian Museum of Rail Travel

Cranbrook's main attraction, this museum is on a siding of the main C.P.R. line directly opposite downtown (Van Horne St., 250/489-3918, April–mid-Oct. daily 10 A.M.–6 P.M., mid-Oct.–Mar. Tues.–Sat. noon–5 P.M.). Most of the displays are outdoors, spread along three sets of track, including the only surviving set of railcars from the Trans-Canada Limited, a luxury train (also called "The Millionaires' Train") built for the Canadian Pacific Railway in 1929. The dining, sleeping, and solarium lounge cars sport inlaid mahogany and walnut paneling, plush upholsteries, and brass fixtures. Restoration displays, a viewing corridor, a model railway display, a slide show, and a 45-minute guided tour of the interiors of cars are included in the price of the Grand Tour Ticket (adult $9, senior $8, child $4). After the tour, wander through the railway garden then head for the Argyle Dining Car to enjoy scones and tea (served

BRITISH COLUMBIA

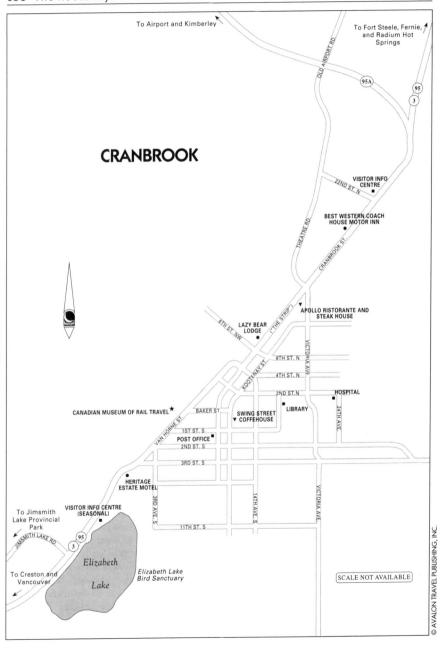

CRANBROOK

To Airport and Kimberley

To Fort Steele, Fernie, and Radium Hot Springs

OLD AIRPORT RD.

95A

95

3

22ND ST. N

VISITOR INFO CENTRE

BEST WESTERN COACH HOUSE MOTOR INN

THEATRE RD.

CRANBROOK ST.

6TH ST. NW

("THE STRIP")

LAZY BEAR LODGE

APOLLO RISTORANTE AND STEAK HOUSE

VICTORIA AVE.

6TH ST. N

4TH ST. N

KOOTENAY ST.

2ND ST. N

HOSPITAL

CANADIAN MUSEUM OF RAIL TRAVEL

BAKER ST.

SWING STREET COFFEEHOUSE

LIBRARY

24TH AVE.

VAN HORNE ST.

1ST ST. S

POST OFFICE

2ND ST. S

3RD ST. S

3RD AVE. S

HERITAGE ESTATE MOTEL

14TH AVE. S

VICTORIA AVE.

To Jimsmith Lake Provincial Park

VISITOR INFO CENTRE (SEASONAL)

11TH ST. S

JIMSMITH LAKE RD.

95

3

To Creston and Vancouver

Elizabeth Lake

Elizabeth Lake Bird Sanctuary

SCALE NOT AVAILABLE

BRITISH COLUMBIA

© AVALON TRAVEL PUBLISHING, INC.

Canadian Museum of Rail Travel

11:30 A.M.–2 P.M.) and to see, but not use, the railway's silver, china, and glassware collection.

Elizabeth Lake Bird Sanctuary

Beside the highway at the southern city limits (park at the information center), this large area of wetlands is a haven for many species of waterfowl, including Canada geese, teal, ringneck, scaup, redhead, bufflehead, goldeneye, and ruddy ducks. You can also see coots, grebes, black terns, and songbirds. Mammals present include muskrats, white-tailed deer, and occasionally moose.

Fort Steele

Once the social, administrative, and supply center for a gold mine at nearby Wildhorse Creek, **Fort Steele Heritage Town** (250/417-6000, May–mid-Oct., daily 9:30 A.M.–5 P.M., adult $8.50, senior $7.25, child $2.25), north of Cranbrook, re-creates the bustle of Fort Steele over 100 years ago. You'll see over 60 restored, reconstructed, fully furnished buildings, including log barracks, hotels, a courthouse, jail, museum, dentist's office, ferry office, printing office, and a general store crammed to the rafters with intriguing

historical artifacts. In summer, the park staff brings Fort Steele back to life with appropriately costumed workers. Hop on a stagecoach or a steam train, heckle a street politician, witness a crime and testify at a trial, watch a silent movie, and view operatic performances in the Opera House.

To get to the original **Wild Horse Creek** diggings, continue north from Fort Steele and take the logging road to Bull River. Fisherville—the first township in the East Kootenays and once home to over 5,000 miners—was established at the diggings in 1864 but was relocated upstream when it was discovered that the richest seam of gold was right below the main street.

Sam Steele Days

The annual four-day Sam Steele Days festival takes place on the third weekend in June and honors the commander of the first North West Mounted Police post in this region. Expect a huge parade, the Sweetheart Pageant, loggers' sports, bicycle and wheelchair races, a truck rodeo, sporting events, live theater, and whatever else the Sam Steele Society (250/426-4161, www.samsteele days.org) comes up with each year.

Accommodations

Most motels are along Highway 3 through town. The highway is known as Van Horne Street south of 4th Street North and Cranbrook Street to the north. On average, motel prices here are among the lowest in the province, making it a good spot to rest overnight.

The flower-basket-adorned **Heritage Estate Motel** (362 Van Horne St., 250/426-3862 or 800/670-1001) is definitely the best value-for-money choice. The rooms are spacious, and each contains complimentary tea and coffee. Rates are $48 s, $58 d in summer but drop as low as $40 s, $45 d the rest of the year. I'm not the only one who regards this place as a bargain, so you'll need to book ahead in summer. Continuing north, in the heart of the commercial strip, **Lazy Bear Lodge** (621 Cranbrook St., 250/426-6086 or 888/808-6086, $60 s, $65 d) is an old roadside motel snazzed up with log trim, beds of bright flowers, and a colorful coat of paint. The rooms remain basic but each has a coffeemaker, and some have a fridge and microwave. Out front is a small swimming pool for guest use.

Camping

One of the area's most attractive campgrounds is in **Jimsmith Lake Provincial Park,** four kilometers (2.5 mi.) off the main highway at the southern outskirts of the city. The park's wooded campsites are $14 per night. Downtown, **Mt. Baker RV Park** (14th Ave. and 1st St. S, 250/489-0056) provides grassy tent sites for $16 and hookups for $18–22.

North of town, near the entrance to Fort Steele, is **Fort Steele Resort and RV Park** (250/489-4268, www.fortsteele.com), which offers a heated pool, showers, laundry, and a barbecue and cooking facility. Unserviced sites are $20, serviced sites $27–35.

Food

For good coffee, fresh muffins, and light snacks head to **Swing Street Coffeehouse** (16 11th St. S, 250/426-5358, daily from 8:30 A.M.). Cranbrook lacks outstanding restaurants, but a few longtime favorites offer reliable food and service. One of these is **Apollo Ristorante and Steak House** (1012 Cranbrook St., 250/426-3721), with a salad bar, steaks, seafood, Italian dishes, and 25 varieties of pizza.

Information

Cranbrook has two information centers, one at each end of the city. The main **Cranbrook Visitor Info Centre** (2279 Cranbrook St. N, 250/426-5914 or 800/222-6174) is open in summer daily 8:30 A.M.–7 P.M., the rest of the year Monday–Friday 9 A.M.–5 P.M. At the southern entrance to the city is a seasonal center (July–Aug. daily 9 A.M.–5 P.M.).

FERNIE AND VICINITY

Fernie (pop. 5,200) nestles in the Elk Valley 100 kilometers (62 mi.) east of Cranbrook on Highway 3. The town itself is a coal-mining and forestry center offering little of visitor interest, but in winter one of British Columbia's great little alpine resorts comes alive nearby. Town center

is a couple of blocks south of the highway, holding the usual array of historic buildings and small-town shops. Look for an impressive red-brick courthouse on 4th Avenue and a good bakery on 2nd Avenue. About 12 kilometers (7.5 mi.) south of town is 259-hectare (640-acre) **Mount Fernie Provincial Park,** where hiking trails lead along a picturesque creek and to a waterfall.

Fernie Alpine Resort

This is another of British Columbia's legendary winter resorts, boasting massive annual snowfalls, challenging skiing and riding, and uncrowded slopes. Fernie (14 km/8.7 mi. south of town, 250/423-4655, www.skifernie.com) has long held a reputation throughout the west as a hidden gem. Lifts serve 1,215 hectares (3,000 acres) of fantastic terrain under a massive ridge that catches an incredible nine meters (30 ft.) of snow each year, filling a wide, open bowl with enough of the white fluffy stuff to please all powderhounds. A few runs are groomed, but the steeper stuff—down open bowls and through trees—is the main attraction. Lift tickets cost adult $58, senior $48, child $22. In July and August one chairlift operates, opening up hiking and mountain-biking terrain. Hikers pay $10 per ride, or $22 for a day pass. Use the lift to take the hard work out of mountain biking for $30 for a full day (rentals at base village).

Accommodations

Fernie has a variety of accommodation options, most offering packages through winter. The least expensive place to stay is **Raging Elk Hostel** (892 6th Ave., 250/423-6811, www.ragingelk.com). A converted motel, this hostel is an associate of Hostelling International, and although basic it provides all the usual hostelling facilities, including a communal kitchen and laundry. Each dormitory holds 4–10 beds and has its own bathroom ($15–18 per person). The few private rooms have twin beds or one double bed and also a TV ($25 s, $35 d). **Park Place Lodge** (742 Hwy. 3, 250/423-6871 or 888/381-7275, www.parkplacelodge.com) is a modern three-story hotel along the main road. Amenities include spacious and elegant rooms opening to an atrium, the River Rock Bistro, and a pub. Summer rates are from a reasonable $99 s, $109 d, with golf and ski packages starting from $85 per person.

Up at the resort, **Griz Inn** (250/423-9221 or 800/661-0118, www.grizinn.com) offers 45 kitchen-equipped suites, an indoor pool, hot tub, and restaurant. Through winter, room rates start at $105 s or d, while off-season rates (outside the busy winter season) drop as low as $70—excellent value.

The best bet for campers is 12 kilometers (7.5 mi.) south at Mount Fernie Provincial Park. Facilities are limited, but the treed setting more than makes up for it; $14 per night.

Other Practicalities

Jamochas Coffee House (851 7th Ave., 250/423-6977) is the pick of many local caffeine joints (and serves up some delicious homemade soups). Overlooking the Elk River at the west end of town, **Rip and Richard's Restaurant** (250/423-3002) serves standard fare, including hearty cooked breakfasts from $6, burgers from $6.50, and dinners from $10. From the deck, you'll enjoy panoramic views all the way across to the resort.

Fernie Visitor Info Centre (through town to the north, 250/423-6868) is open Monday–Friday 8:30 A.M.–4:30 P.M.

Sparwood and Vicinity

Northeast of Fernie 30 kilometers (18.6 mi.), Sparwood (pop. 4,000) began as three separate coal-mining towns: Michel, Middletown, and Natal. In the 1960s, a resurgence of civic pride saw the old towns demolished and replaced by the new center of Sparwood. The coal seams and part of the mining operations can be seen on the ridge high above Sparwood, but a more eye-catching element of the local industry is the world's largest truck, which sits beside Highway 3 in the center of town. Beside the truck is **Sparwood Visitor Info Centre** (250/425-2423), where you can arrange a tour of the mines. **Mountain Shadows Campground** (250/425-7815, $14–22) is set among trees immediately south of town and abuts the local golf course. Hot showers are provided.

Surrounded by towering peaks, the remote community of **Elkford** (pop. 3,000) lies 35 kilo-

meters (21.7 mi.) north of Sparwood on Highway 43. Continue through town for 87 kilometers (54 mi.) and you'll reach 17,245-hectare (42,600-acre) **Elk Lakes Provincial Park.** Abundant recreation opportunities in the area include fishing in the Elk River, wildlife viewing, and hiking and mountain biking on hundreds of kilometers of logging and mining roads are the main attraction for wilderness seekers. Get all the details at **Elkford Visitor Info Centre** (Highway 43 and Michel Rd., 250/865-4614 or 877/355-9453).

KIMBERLEY

Kimberley (pop. 7,000), 31 kilometers (19 mi.) north of Cranbrook on Highway 95A, is a charming little town, with no commercial strip or fast-food outlets, just streets of old stucco mining cottages with a downtown that's been "Bavarianized." In fact, Kimberley is also known as the "Bavarian City." Most of the local shops and businesses, and many of Kimberley's homes, have been decorated Bavarian-style with dark wood finish and flowery trim, steep triangular roofs, fancy balconies, brightly painted window shutters, and flower-filled window boxes.

Although named for a famous South African diamond mine, Kimberley boomed as a result of the silver and lead deposits unearthed on nearby North Star Mountain. The deposits were discovered in 1892, and by 1899 over 200 claims had been staked. As was so often the case, only operations run by larger companies proved profitable. The last of these, and one of the world's largest lead and zinc mines, Cominco's Sullivan Mine, closed in late 2001 as reserves became exhausted.

Bavarian Platzl

Strolling the Bavarian Platzl, you'll feel as though you've just driven into a village high in the Alps: Only the bell-wearing cows and brightly dressed milkmaids are missing. This is the focus of downtown—a cheerful, red-brick, pedestrian plaza complete with babbling brook, ornamental bridges, and the "World's Largest Cuckoo Clock" (Happy Hans pops out and yodels on the hour). Shops, many German restaurants, and delis line the plaza, selling European specialties. At the far end of the Platzl, **Kimberley Heritage Museum** (250/427-7510, summer Mon.–Sat. 9 A.M.–4:30 P.M., rest of year Mon.–Sat. 1–4 P.M.) houses mining-history exhibits, a stuffed grizzly bear, a hodgepodge of artifacts, and displays relating to all the locally popular outdoor sports.

Other Sights

Cominco Gardens, also known as Kimberley Gardens, enjoys a hilltop location (4th Ave., 250/427-2293, $3). Originally planted in 1927 to promote a fertilizer developed by Cominco, the one-hectare (2.5-acre) gardens now hold close to 50,000 flowers.

The **Bavarian City Mining Railway** (250/427-2929, adult $7, child $3) was constructed from materials salvaged from mining towns around the province. The seven-kilometer (4.3-mi.) track climbs a steep-sided valley, crosses a trestle bridge, and stops at particularly impressive mountain viewpoints, the original townsite, and the now-closed Sullivan mine entrance, before terminating near the base village of Kimberley Alpine Resort. The train operates up to six times daily through summer.

Kimberley Alpine Resort

From early December to early April, this resort (250/427-4881 or 800/258-7669, www.ski kimberley.com) provides great skiing and snowboarding on a wide variety of slopes four kilometers (2.5 mi.) west of downtown. Currently there are 67 named runs covering 738 hectares (1,800 acres), with a maximum vertical rise of 750 meters (2,460 ft.). Most beginners and intermediates will be content on the well-groomed main slopes, while more experienced skiers and snowboarders will want to head to the expert terrain served by the Easter Chair. Additional facilities at the resort include two snowboard parks, a cross-country ski area, an ice-skating rink, accommodations, and restaurants. Lift tickets are adult $48, senior $38, child $16. Summer activities include chairlift rides, hiking, mountain biking, and luge rides; head to the Adventure Desk in the Marriott Hotel (250/427-6743) for details.

Accommodations and Camping

If you plan on golfing or a winter vacation in Kimberley, contact **Kimberley Vacations** (250/427-4877 or 800/667-0871, www.kimberley vacations.bc.ca) for the best package deals. Otherwise contact one of the following choices.

If you don't mind being a couple of kilometers out of town, **Travellaire Motel** (toward Marysville at 2660 Warren Ave., 250/427-2252 or 800/477-4499) provides excellent value. It's only a small place, but it regularly revamped and decked out with new beds and furniture. There's also a barbecue area for guest use. Rates are $50 s, $58 d, or pay an extra $8 for a room with a small kitchenette. **Trickle Creek Residence Inn** is a Marriott affiliate at the base of Kimberley Alpine Resort (250/427-5175 or 877/282-1200, www.ski kimberley.com). This stunning log and stone structure holds 80 spacious rooms, each with a kitchen, balcony, and fireplace. Guest facilities include a fitness center and a year-round outdoor heated pool. Summer rates are $149 s or d for a studio room and $169 for a one-bedroom suite. Check the website for golf and ski packages.

Happy Hans Riverside RV Resort (250/427-2929, www.happyhans.com) is seven kilometers (4.3 mi) south of downtown on Highway 95A and then three kilometers (1.9 mi.) west along St. Mary's River Road. Tent sites are $18, hookups $24–28.

Food

European gourmet specialties, predominantly German, are available all around town. The **Gasthaus** (in the Platzl, 250/427-4851, daily except Tues. 11:30 A.M.–10 P.M.) features German lunches such as goulash ($7) and German dinner specialties such as bratwurst, rheinischer sauerbraten, wiener-schnitzel, and kassler rippchen ($11–17.50). Away from the Platzl, **Old Bauren Haus** (280 Norton Ave., 250/427-5133, dinner only, closed Tues.) features Bavarian specialties and plenty of atmosphere. It's in a post-and-beam building originally constructed about 350 years ago in southern Bavaria. The building was taken apart, shipped to Canada, and painstakingly rebuilt.

Garden Treasures (Cominco Gardens, 250/427-0501, mid-June–early Sept. daily

10 A.M.–6 P.M.) serves a classic afternoon tea, accompanied by desserts and delectables such as fresh-baked scones with jam. Prices are reasonable and the atmosphere, inside a real greenhouse, is delightful; the stunning pink-and-green interior is complemented by hanging plants, flowery tablecloths, and views of the distant mountains and gardens.

Information

For more information on Kimberley and the surrounding area, drop by **Kimberley Visitor Info Centre** (115 Gerry Sorensen Way, 250/427-3666, summer daily 9 A.M.–7 P.M., rest of year Mon.–Fri. 9 A.M.–5 P.M.).

CONTINUING NORTH TOWARD INVERMERE

This stretch of highway passes through a deep valley chock-full of commercial facilities like world-class golf courses, resorts, and hot springs. The low elevation makes for relatively mild winters and an early start to the summer season. And with the Purcell Mountains on one side and the Rockies on the other, the valley certainly doesn't lack for scenery.

Dutch Creek Hoodoos

Whiteswan Lake Provincial Park

North of Skookumchuck 28 kilometers (17.4 mi.), an unsealed logging road takes off east into the mountains, leading to 1,994-hectare (4,900-acre) Whiteswan Lake Provincial Park. Along the way, a trail leads down to **Lussier Hot Springs,** where two small pools collect the odorless water as it bubbles out of the ground. Within the park itself, the road closely follows the southern shoreline of first Alces Lake and then the larger Whiteswan Lake. The two lakes attract abundant birdlife: Loons, grebes, and herons are all common. They also attract anglers, who come for great rainbow trout fishing. Camping is at one of four campgrounds within the park; $14 per site.

Canal Flats

The small lumber-mill town of Canal Flats lies between the Kootenay River and Columbia Lake. In 1889 the two waterways were connected by a canal with a single lock, but the passage was so narrow and dangerous that only two steamboats ever got through.

North of Canal Flats, the highway passes 44-hectare (110-acre) **Thunder Hill Provincial Park,** which overlooks turquoise and blue **Columbia Lake,** then approaches and passes the weirdly shaped **Dutch Creek Hoodoos,** a set of photogenic rock formations carved over time by ice, water, and wind. To get a closer look, take the unpaved road to the left after crossing Dutch Creek northbound.

Fairmont Hot Springs

Kootenay natives used these springs as a healing source for eons prior to the arrival of Europeans, but they wouldn't recognize the place today. Surrounding the site is **Fairmont Hot Springs Resort** (250/345-6311 or 800/663-4979, www.fairmontresort.com), comprising a four-star resort, golf courses, a ski resort, and an airstrip long enough to land a Boeing 737. Despite all the commercialism, the hot springs (daily 8 A.M.–10 P.M. adult $8, child $6) are still the main attraction. Their appeal is simple; unlike most other springs, the hot water bubbling up from underground here contains calcium, not sulfur with its attendant smell. A lodge with upscale accommodations and a campground make up the rest of the resort complex. Rooms in the lodge are $159–265 s or d, the more expensive with a loft and kitchen. Discounted ski, golf, and spa packages are often available. In the off-season, rooms go for less than $100. Campers have a choice of over 300 sites spread around tree-shaded grounds, all just a one-minute stroll from the hot pools. Unserviced sites are $19, while hookups range $26–39 (no tents), discounted outside of summer and open year-round.

INVERMERE AND VICINITY

The next area to lure travelers off Highway 93/95 is **Windermere Lake.** Overlooking the lake, the town of Invermere (pop. 3,200) is the commercial center of the Columbia Valley. The lake and surrounding wilderness is a great spot for recreational activities, and is especially popular among landlocked Albertans. On the approach to town is **Windermere Valley Museum** (622 Third St., 250/342-9769), where the entire history of the valley is contained in seven separate buildings. The main street itself (7th Ave.) is lined with restored heritage buildings and streetlights bedecked with hanging baskets overflowing with colorful flowers.

Panorama Mountain Village

Panorama (250/345-6413 or 800/663-2929, www.panoramaresort.com) is a year-round resort village in the Purcell Mountains west of Invermere. Development includes a residential subdivision, an open-air gondola to move visitors between the two main villages, a year-round water park, and **Greywolf Golf Course,** where water comes into play on 14 of the 18 holes. During the warmer months, there are also white-water rafting and inflatable kayak trips down Toby Creek, horseback riding, and, in the village itself, tennis and a swimming pool. It was skiing that first put Panorama on the map, mainly because the resort boasts the third-highest vertical rise of all North American winter resorts (1,200 m/3,900 ft.), behind only Whistler/Blackcomb (also in British Columbia) and Big Sky, Montana. Despite the impressive relief, Panorama offers slopes suitable for all levels of expertise; adult $52, child $36.

Practicalities

Invermere holds motels, eateries, grocery stores, gas stations, a Greyhound bus depot, and a laundry. The motels downtown are a bit overpriced; the best option is **Delphine Lodge** (250/342-6851, mid-Jan.–Oct., $65–100 s or d) two kilometers (1.2 mi.) north in the historic village of Wilmer. Restored to its former glory, this 19th-century hotel has been converted to a boutique bed-and-breakfast. The rooms share bathrooms but are comfortable, and guests have the use of a private garden, lounge, and library.

At the turnoff to town is **Invermere Visitor Info Centre** (250/342-2844, July–Aug. daily 9 A.M.–5 P.M.). The website www.adventurevalley.com provides information about local recreational opportunities.

RADIUM HOT SPRINGS

The small service center of Radium Hot Springs (pop. 1,000), 140 kilometers (87 mi.) north of Cranbrook, enjoys a spectacular setting—the panorama across the braided Columbia River extends west to the Purcell Mountains while to the east are the Canadian Rockies and Kootenay National Park. As well as providing accommodations and other services for highway travelers, Radium is a destination in itself for many. The town is just three kilometers (two mi.) from the hot springs for which it's named, and boasts a wildlife-rich wetland on its back doorstep, two excellent golf courses, and many other recreational opportunities.

Columbia River Wetland

Radium sits in the Rocky Mountain Trench, which has been carved over millions of years by the Columbia River. From its headwaters south of Radium, the Columbia flows northward through a 180-kilometer-long (110 mi.) wetland to Golden, continuing north for a similar distance before reversing course and flowing south into the United States. The wetland by Radium holds international significance, not only for its size (26,000 hectares/64,250 acres), but also for the sheer concentration of wildlife it supports. Over 100 species of birds live among the sedges, grasses, dogwoods, and black cottonwoods surrounding the convoluted banks of the Columbia. Of special interest are blue herons in large numbers and ospreys in one of the world's highest concentrations.

The wetland also lies along the Pacific Flyway, so particularly large numbers of ducks, Canada geese, and other migratory birds gather here in spring and autumn. The northbound spring migration is celebrated with the **Wings over the Rockies Bird Festival,** (888/933-3311) which is held in the first week of May in conjunction with International Migratory Bird Day. The festival features a variety of ornithologist speakers, field trips on foot and by boat, workshops, and events tailored especially for children, all of which take place in Radium and throughout the valley.

Recreation

The 36-hole **Springs at Radium Golf Resort** (250/347-6200 or 800/667-6444) includes the 6767-yard Springs Course, generally regarded as one of British Columbia's top 10 resort courses. It lies between the town and steep cliffs that descend to the Columbia River far below. Immaculately groomed fairways following the land's natural contours, near-perfect greens, and over 70 bunkers filled with imported sand do little to take away from the surrounding mountainscape. Greens fees are $76 for 18 holes (discounted $5 after 2:30 P.M. and then to $54 after 4 P.M.).

White-water rafting trips are offered by **Kootenay River Runners** (250/347-9210 or 800/599-4399); from $68 for a half-day trip, $105 for a full day. This company also offers a more relaxing evening float through the Columbia River Wetland in large and stable Voyageur canoes. Horse fanciers can rent a ride at **Longhorn Stables** (one km/0.6 mi. north of town, 250/347-9755).

Accommodations

Radium, with a population of just 1,000, has over 30 motels, an indication of its importance as a highway stop for overnight travelers. Those that lie along the access road to Kootenay National Park come alive with color through summer as each tries to outdo the other with floral landscaping. At the top end of the motel strip,

closest to the national park, **Misty River Lodge** (also known as Radium International Hostel, 250/347-9912, www.radiumhostel.bc.ca) provides dormitory-style accommodations ($21 per person), as well as two private rooms ($60 s or d), a kitchen, a lounge stocked with reading material, and a bike workshop. An elevated deck provides the ideal location to watch the sun setting over the Purcell Mountains.

Kootenay Motel (250/347-9490 or 877/908-2020) is along Highway 93, up the hill from the junction of Highway 95. The rooms are very basic (but air-conditioned) and rent from $50 s, $58 d; $7 extra for a kitchenette. Also on-site are a barbecue area and a pleasant gazebo. Up the hill a little and across the road is **Black Bear's Inn** (250/347-9565 or 800/688-6138, www.black bearsinn.com), with a pleasant outdoor barbecue area; basic sleeping rooms are $69 s or d, or pay $99 for a room with a private balcony overlooking the valley.

South of town 3 kilometers (1.9 mi.), **Radium Resort** (250/347-9311 or 800/667-6444, www.radiumresort.com) is surrounded by an 18-hole golf course and holds a wide variety of facilities including a health club, indoor pool, restaurant, and lounge. Guest rooms overlook the golf course and are linked to the main lodge building by a covered walkway. Rack rates start at $160, but check the website (or the roadside board) for specials.

Within Kootenay National Park, but accessed from in town off Highway 93/95, is **Redstreak Campground**. The closest commercial camping is at **Canyon RV Resort,** nestled in its own private valley immediately north of the Highway 93/95 junction (250/347-9564, www.canyon rv.com, Apr.–Oct.). Treed sites are spread along a pleasant creek and all facilities are provided; $20–25 per night.

Food

For breakfast, head to the **Springs Course** restaurant (Stanley St., 250/347-9311, from 7 A.M.). The view from the deck, overlooking the Columbia River and Purcell Mountains, is nothing short of stunning. The food is good and remarkably inexpensive; in the morning,

BRITISH COLUMBIA

for example, an omelet with three fillings, hash browns, and toast is just $9.

Back in town, **Back Country Jack's** (Main St. W., 250/347-0097, 11 A.M.–11 P.M.) is decorated with real antiques and real hard bench seats in very private booths. There's a wide variety of platters to share, including Cowboy Caviar (nachos and baked beans) for $7.50, and a surprisingly good barbecued chicken soup ($5). Just around the corner is **Screamer's,** the place to hang out with an ice cream on a hot summer's afternoon.

The restaurant at the **Radium Resort** (three km/1.9 mi. south of town, 250/347-9311) caters mostly to resort guests, but everybody is welcome. Enjoy lunch on the outdoor patio for under $10, or dine on sea bass smothered with a fruit-filled salsa for $24 in the evening. Buffets are offered on Wednesday and Friday night from 6 P.M. ($20 pp).

Information
On the east side of the Highway 93/95 junction is **Radium Hot Springs Visitor Info Centre** (250/347-9331 or 800/347-9704, www.rhs.bc.ca, June–Sept. daily 9 A.M.–7 P.M.). This building is also home to the national park information center.

Kootenay National Park

Shaped like a lightning bolt, this narrow 140,600-hectare (34,700-acre) park lies northeast of Radium Hot Springs and is bordered to the east by Banff National Park (Alberta). Highway 93, extending for 94 kilometers (58 mi.) through the park, provides spectacular mountain vistas, and along the route you'll find many short and easy interpretive hikes, scenic viewpoints, hot springs, picnic areas, and roadside interpretive exhibits. The park isn't particularly noted for its day-hiking opportunities, but backpacker destinations such as Kaufmann Lake and the Rockwall rival almost any other area in the Canadian Rockies.

Day-use areas, a gas station and lodge, and three campgrounds are the only roadside services inside the park. The park is open year-round, although you should check road conditions in winter, when avalanche-control work and snowstorms can close Highway 93 for short periods of time.

NATIONAL PARK PASSES

Passes are required for entry into Kootenay and Yoho National Parks. Passes are interchangeable between parks—including adjacent Banff and Jasper—and are valid until 4 P.M. the day following purchase. The cost of a **National Parks Day Pass** is adult $7, senior $6, child $3.50. There is a maximum per-vehicle entry fee of double the adult (or senior) rate. An annual **National Parks of Canada Pass,** good for entry into all Canadian national parks for one year from the date of purchase, is adult $45, senior $38 to a maximum of $89 per vehicle ($76 for two or more seniors).

Passes can be purchased at the information centers in Radium and Field (Yoho National Park), at the park gates, or at similar facilities in Banff National Park.

THE LAND
Kootenay National Park lies on the western side of the Continental Divide, straddling the Main and Western Ranges of the Canadian Rockies. As elsewhere in the Canadian Rockies, the geology of the park is complex. Over the last 70 million years, these mountains have been pushed upward—folded and faulted along the way—by massive forces deep beneath the earth's surface. They've also been subject to erosion that entire time, particularly during the ice ages, when glaciers carved U-shaped valleys and high cirques into the landscape. These features, along with glacial lakes and the remnants of the glaciers themselves, are readily visible in the park today.

The park protects the upper headwaters of the **Vermilion** and **Kootenay Rivers,** which drain into the Columbia River south of the park.

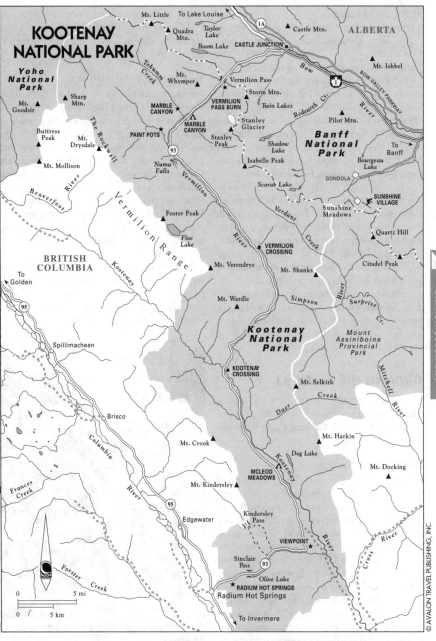

KOOTENAY NATIONAL PARK

Yoho National Park

Mt. Little
To Lake Louise
Quadra Mtn.
Taylor Lake
Boom Lake
CASTLE JUNCTION
Castle Mtn.
ALBERTA

Mt. Goodsir
Sharp Mtn.
Tokumm Creek
Mt. Whymper
Vermilion Pass
Storm Mtn.
Twin Lakes
Bow
Mt. Ishbel
BOW VALLEY PARKWAY

Buttress Peak
The Rockwall
MARBLE CANYON
VERMILION PASS BURN
Stanley Glacier
Redearth Cr.
Pilot Mtn.

Mt. Drysdale
MARBLE CANYON
PAINT POTS
Stanley Peak
Banff National Park
To Banff

Mt. Mollison
93
Numa Falls
Shadow Lake
Isabelle Peak
Bourgeau Lake
GONDOLA

Beaverfoot River
Vermilion Range
Foster Peak
Scarab Lake
Verdant
Sunshine Meadows
SUNSHINE VILLAGE

BRITISH COLUMBIA
Floe Lake
Creek
Quartz Hill

To Golden
95
Kootenay
Mt. Verendrye
VERMILION CROSSING
Mt. Shanks
Citadel Peak

Spillimacheen
Mt. Wardle
Simpson
Surprise Cr.
River

Kootenay National Park
Mount Assiniboine Provincial Park
Mitchell River

KOOTENAY CROSSING
Mt. Selkirk

Brisco
Daer
Creek

Columbia River
Mt. Crook
Dog Lake
Mt. Harkin
Mt. Docking

Frances Creek
MCLEOD MEADOWS
Kootenay

Mt. Kindersley
95
Edgewater
Kindersley Pass
VIEWPOINT
River
River
Cross

Sinclair Pass
93
Olive Lake
RADIUM HOT SPRINGS
Radium Hot Springs

Forster Creek
0   5 mi
0   5 km

To Invermere

© AVALON TRAVEL PUBLISHING, INC.

BRITISH COLUMBIA

Flora and Fauna

In the lowest areas of the park, in the Kootenay River Valley, **Douglas fir** and **lodgepole pine** find a home. Along the upper stretches of the Vermilion River Valley, where the elevation is higher, **Engelmann spruce** thrive, while immediately above lie forests of **subalpine fir.** The tree line in the park is at around 2,000 meters (6,560 ft.) above sea level. This is the alpine, where low-growing species such as **willow** and **heather** predominate. For a short period each summer, these elevations come alive with color as **forget-me-nots, avens,** and **avalanche lilies** flower.

Large mammals tend to remain in the Kootenay and Vermilion River Valleys. **White-tailed deer, mule deer, moose, black bears,** and **elk** live year-round at these lower elevations, as do **bighorn sheep,** which can be seen at mineral licks along Highway 93. The most common large mammal present in Kootenay is the **mountain goat,** but these flighty creatures stay at high elevations, feeding in alpine meadows through summer. **Grizzlies** number around 10 within the park; they range throughout the backcountry, and occasionally are sighted in spring high on roadside avalanche slopes.

DRIVING HIGHWAY 93

Climbing eastward from the town of Radium Hot Springs, Highway 93 enters the park just below narrow **Sinclair Canyon,** a natural gateway to the wonders beyond.

Radium Hot Springs

These hot springs (three km/1.9 mi. northeast of town, 250/347-9485, late June–early Sept. daily 9 A.M.–11 P.M., rest of year daily noon–9 P.M.) were a popular destination for the early Kootenay people, who, like today's visitors, came to enjoy the odorless mineral water that gushes out of the Redwall Fault at 44°C (111°F). Steep cliffs tower directly above the hot pool, whose waters are colored a milky blue by dissolved salts, which include calcium bicarbonate and sulfates of calcium, magnesium, and sodium. The main pool is particularly stimulating in winter, when it's edged by snow and covered in steam—your head is almost cold in the chill air, but your submerged body melts into oblivion. Admission is $6.25 for adults (day pass $9.25), $5.25 for seniors and children (day pass $8.25).

To Kootenay Valley

Leaving the hot springs, the road parallels Sinclair Creek to tiny **Olive Lake,** which is ringed with bright yellow wildflowers in summer, and **Sinclair Pass.** The highway then descends to the valley floor, passes two riverside picnic areas, and crosses the pretty **Kootenay River** at **Kootenay Crossing.** The highway then climbs a low saddle and descends to the Vermilion River. On the descent, you pass a particularly nice picnic spot at **Wardle Creek.** Across the river, the mountainside is scarred black, the result of a wildfire that devastated over 4,000 hectares (9,900 acres) of forest in the summer of 2001.

Continuing north, the highway passes **Kootenay Park Lodge** (lodging, food, gas, and an official park information center) then climbs through an area affected by a fire that swept through the entire valley in 2003.

Sinclair Canyon provides a natural gateway to Kootenay.

Paint Pots and Marble Canyon

A scenic one-kilometer (0.6-mi.) trail (20 minutes each way) leads over the Vermilion River to the Paint Points, a unique natural wonder: three circular ponds stained red, orange, and mustard yellow by oxide-bearing springs. The natives collected ochre from around the pools and mixed it with animal fat or fish oil then used it in ceremonial body and rock painting.

Just up the road, be sure to stop and take the enjoyable self-guided trail, one kilometer (0.6 mi.) each way, which leads along this ice-carved **Marble Canyon.** The walk takes only about 30 minutes or so, yet as one of several interpretive plaques says, it takes you back over 500 million years.

HIKING

Some 200 kilometers (124 mi.) of trails lace Kootenay National Park. Hiking opportunities range from short interpretive walks to challenging treks through remote backcountry. All trails start from Highway 93 on the valley floor, so you'll be facing a strenuous climb to reach the park's high alpine areas, especially those in the south.

Interpretive Trails and Easy Walks

The most popular trails in the park lead to the Paint Pots and through Marble Canyon. At the other end of the park, the area between Redstreak Campground and the hot springs is laced with trails. One particularly scenic loop is the **Juniper Trail** (3.2 km/2 mi.; one hour round-trip), which can be picked up just inside the park boundary. Named for the abundance of juniper berries, it provides good valley views with minimal exertion.

From McLeod Meadows Picnic Area, the **Dog Lake Trail** (2.6 km/1.6 mi.; 40 minutes one-way) is an easy walk that ends at a small lake hidden from the highway by a forested ridge.

On a sunny day, the trail to **Stanley Glacier** (4.2 km/2.6 mi.; 90 minutes one-way) is my favorite in the park. Beginning in the far north of the park, just seven kilometers (4.3 mi.) west of the Continental Divide, it climbs steadily

for two kilometers (1.2 mi.), then levels off and winds through a massive U-shaped glacial valley, with the sheer face of Mount Stanley rising 500 meters (1,640 ft.) above the forest to the west. Although the trail officially ends atop a moraine after 4.2 kilometers (2.6 mi.), it's worthwhile continuing 1.3 kilometers (0.8 mi.) to the tree-topped plateau visible higher up the valley. Surprisingly, once on the plateau, you'll find a gurgling stream, a healthy population of marmots, and incredible views west to Stanley Glacier and north back down the valley.

Full-Day Excursions

The elevation gain (1,050 m/3,445 ft.) on the strenuous hike to **Kindersley Summit** (10 km/6.2 mi.; four hours one-way) will be a deterrent for many, but views from the summit will make up for the pain endured along the way. From Highway 93, two kilometers (1.2 mi.) west of Sinclair Pass, the trail climbs through a valley, then switchbacks up across a number of avalanche paths and through more forest before emerging at an alpine meadow on Kindersley Pass. This is where the scenery makes the journey worthwhile, with views east to the Continental Divide and north over the Kootenay River Valley.

Of all the lakes in Kootenay National Park, none are as beautiful as **Floe Lake,** which, unfortunately, requires a strenuous day trip to reach (10.4 km/6.5 mi.; 3.5 hours one-way; elevation gain 730 m/2,395 ft.). From the trailhead eight kilometers (five mi.) north of Vermilion Crossing, the trail closely parallels Floe Creek almost the entire way. Nestled in a glacial cirque, the lake's aquamarine waters reflect the Rockwall, a sheer limestone wall rising 1,000 meters (3,280 ft.) above the far shore. In fall, stands of stunted larch around the lakeshore turn brilliant colors, adding to the incredible beauty.

PARK PRACTICALITIES

Accommodations

Most park visitors opt to stay in Radium Hot Springs, but there is one lodging within the park. **Kootenay Park Lodge** (Vermilion Crossing, 65 km/40 mi. from Radium Hot Springs,

403/762-9196, www.kootenayparklodge.com, mid-May–Sept.) dates from the 1920s. It consists of a main lodge with restaurant, 10 cabins, a restaurant, and a gas station/grocery store. The most basic cabins ($89 s or d) have a bathroom, small fridge, and coffeemaker, and rates rise to $129 for a cabin with cooking facilities and a fireplace.

Camping

The park's largest camping area is **Redstreak Campground** (mid-May–mid-Oct.) on a narrow plateau in the extreme southwest (vehicle access from Hwy. 93/95 on south side of Radium Hot Springs township), which holds 242 sites, plus showers and cooking shelters. In summer, free slide shows and talks are presented by park naturalists five nights a week at and typically feature topics such as wolves, bears, the park's human history, or the effects of fire. Tent sites are $22, hookups $26–30, and fire permits are $6. No reservations.

The park's two other campgrounds lie along Highway 93 and offer fewer facilities (no hookups or showers). The larger of the two is **McLeod Meadows Campground,** ($17) beside the Kootenay River 27 kilometers (16.8 mi.) from Radium Hot Springs. **Marble Canyon Campground** is farther north, across the highway from the natural attraction of the same name.

Information

Kootenay Park Information Centre (250/347-9615, June–Sept. daily 9 A.M.–7 P.M., rest of year Mon.–Fri. 9 A.M.–5 P.M.) is outside the park in the town of Radium Hot Springs. Here you can collect a free map with hiking trail descriptions, find out about trail closures and campsite availability, get the weather forecast, browse through a gift shop, and buy park passes. For further information click through the links at the Parks Canada website (www.pc.gc.ca).

Yoho National Park and Vicinity

Yoho, a Cree word of amazement, is a fitting name for this 131,300-hectare (324,450-acre) national park immediately north of Kootenay National Park and beside Banff National Park to the east. Although it's the smallest of four contiguous parks, its wild and rugged landscape holds spectacular waterfalls, extensive icefields, a lake to rival those in Banff, and one of the world's most intriguing fossil beds. In addition, you'll find some of the finest hiking in all of Canada on the park's 300-kilometer (186-mi.) trail system.

Within the park are four lodges, four campgrounds, and the small railway town of **Field,** where you'll find basic services. The park is open year-round, although road conditions in winter can be treacherous and occasional closures occur on Kicking Horse Pass. The road out to Takakkaw Falls is closed through winter, and it often doesn't reopen until mid-June.

From the park's western edge, Highway 1 follows the Kicking Horse River as it descends to the Columbia River Valley and the town of Golden.

THE LAND

The park extends west from the Continental Divide to the Western and Main Ranges of the Rocky Mountains. The jagged peaks along this section of the Continental Divide—including famous Mount Victoria, which forms the backdrop for Lake Louise—are some of the park's highest. But the award for Yoho's loftiest summit goes to 3,562-meter (11,686-ft.) **Mount Goodsir,** west of the Continental Divide in the Ottertail Range.

The park's only watershed is that of the **Kicking Horse River,** which is fed by the Wapta and Waputik Icefields. The Kicking Horse, wide and braided for much of its course through the park, flows westward, joining the mighty Columbia River at Golden.

HISTORY

The Kootenay and Shuswap tribes of British Columbia were the first humans to travel through the rugged area that is now the national park. It's believed the men hid their families in the mountains before crossing over to the prairies to hunt buffalo and to trade with other tribes. The first Europeans to explore the valley of the Kicking Horse River were members of the 1858 Palliser Expedition, who approached from the south and overnighted at Wapta Falls. It was here that the expedition geologist, Dr. James Hector, inadvertently gave the Kicking Horse River its name. While walking his horse over rough ground, he was kicked unconscious and took two hours to come to, by which time, so the story goes, other members of his party had begun digging his grave.

ROAD-ACCESSIBLE SIGHTS

As with all other parks of the Canadian Rockies, you don't need to travel deep into the backcountry to view the most spectacular features—many are visible from the roadside. The sights below are listed from east to west, starting at the park boundary (the Continental Divide).

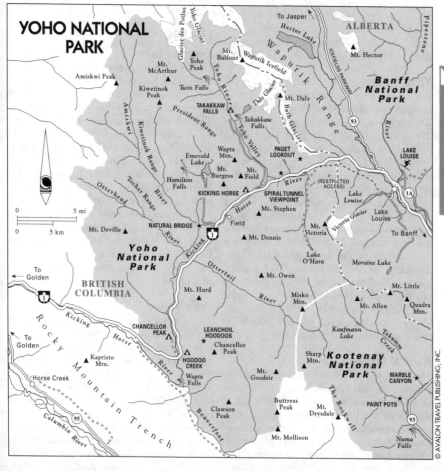

BRITISH COLUMBIA

Spiral Tunnel Viewpoint

The joy that C.P.R. president William Van Horne felt upon completion of his transcontinental rail line in 1886 was tempered by massive problems along a stretch of line west of Kicking Horse Pass. "Big Hill" was less than five kilometers (3.1 mi.) long, but its gradient was so steep that runaway trains, crashes, and other disasters were common. A trail from Kicking Horse Campground takes you past the remains of one of those doomed trains. Nearly a quarter-century after the line opened, railway engineers and builders finally solved the problem. By building two spiral tunnels down through two kilometers (1.2 mi.) of solid rock to the valley floor, they lessened the grade dramatically and the terrors came to an end. Along the way is a viewpoint with interpretive displays telling the fascinating story of Big Hill.

Yoho Valley

Fed by the Wapta Icefield in the far north of the park, the **Yoho River** flows through this spectacularly narrow valley, dropping more than 200 meters (660 ft.) in the last kilometer (0.6 mi.) before its confluence with the Kicking Horse River. The road leading up the valley passes the park's main campground, climbs a *very* tight series of switchbacks (watch for buses reversing through the middle section). The road ends 14 kilometers (8.7 mi.) from the main highway at **Takakkaw Falls,** the most impressive waterfall in the Canadian Rockies. Meaning "wonderful" in the language of the Cree, Takakkaw tumbles 254 meters (830 ft.) over a sheer rock wall at the lip of the Yoho Valley, creating a spray bedecked with rainbows. It can be seen from the parking lot, but it's well worth the easy 10-minute stroll over the Yoho River to appreciate the sight in all its glory.

Natural Bridge

Three kilometers (1.9 mi.) west of Field is the turnoff to famous Emerald Lake. On your way out to the lake, you'll first pass another intriguing sight. At Natural Bridge, two kilometers (1.2 mi.) down the road, the Kicking Horse River has worn a narrow hole through a limestone wall, creating a bridge. A trail leads to several viewpoints.

Emerald Lake

One of the jewels of the Canadian Rockies, the beautiful lake is surrounded by a forest of Engelmann spruce, as well as many peaks over 3,000 meters (9,800 ft.). It's covered in ice most of the year, but comes alive with activity for a few short months in summer when hikers, canoeists, and horseback riders take advantage of the magnificent surroundings. **Emerald Lake Canoe Rentals** (250/343-6000) rents canoes and small boats for $20 per hour, $35 for two hours, or $60 all day. **Emerald Lake Stables** (250/344-8982) takes visitors on a one-hour trail ride along the west shore of Emerald Lake for $35.

HIKING
Emerald Lake

One of the easiest yet most enjoyable walks in Yoho is the **Emerald Lake Loop** (5.2 km/3.2 mi.; 1.5 hours round-trip). The trail encircles the lake and can be hiked in either direction. The best views are from the western shoreline, where a massive avalanche has cleared away the forest of Engelmann spruce. The trail to **Emerald Basin** (4.5 km/2.8 mi.; 1.5–2 hours one-way) gains 280 meters (920 ft.) of elevation after leaving the lakeshore 1.5 kilometers (0.9 mi.) from the parking lot. The most impressive sight awaiting you in the basin is the south wall of the President Range, towering 800 vertical meters (2,625 ft.) above. The trail to **Hamilton Falls** (800 m/0.5 mi.; 40 minutes one-way) is an easy walk that begins from the Emerald Lake parking lot.

Yoho Valley

The valley for which the park is named lies north of the TransCanada Highway. As well as the sights already discussed, it provides many fine opportunities for serious day-hikers to get off the beaten track. The following day hikes begin from different trailheads near the end of the road up Yoho Valley. In each case, leave your vehicle in the Takakkaw Falls parking lot.

The trail to **Twin Falls** (8 km/5 mi.; 2.5 hours one-way) takes over where the road through the Yoho Valley ends, continuing in a northerly

LAKE O'HARA

Nestled in a high bowl of lush alpine meadows, Lake O'Hara, 11 kilometers (6.8 mi.) from the nearest road, is surrounded by dozens of smaller alpine lakes and framed by spectacular peaks permanently mantled in snow. As if that weren't enough, the entire area is webbed by a network of hiking trails. What makes this destination all the more special is that a quota system limits the number of visitors.

Hiking
The obvious trail is **Lake O'Hara Shoreline** (2.8 km/1.7 mi.; 40 minutes), which loops around the picturesque lake, passing a waterfall, and offering a myriad of different perspectives on the surrounding peaks. Many of the region's other hikes lead off the shoreline trail. Of these, the shortest is the **Lake Oesa Trail** (3 km/1.9 mi.; one hour one-way) which leads up and into a rocky, water-filled cirque surrounded by talus slopes and 3,000-meter (10,000-ft.) peaks. In the adjacent cirque, **Opabin Plateau** (5.9 km/3.7 mi. round-trip) can easily be reached in one hour, but it's easy to spend an entire day enjoying the numerous lakes and scrambling around the surrounding slopes. On the edge of the cirque, **Opabin Prospect** is one the most magnificent trail-accessible lookouts in all of western Canada. Other trails lead to **Lake McArthur** (3.5 km/2.2 mi.; 80 minutes one-way), a stunning deep-blue body of water edged by colorful alpine meadows, and **Cathedral Basin** (7.5 km/4.7 mi.; 2.5 hours one-way), which is a little farther so receives fewer visitors.

Book the Bus
It's possible to walk to Lake O'Hara, but the vast majority of visitors take the shuttlebus. The departure point is a signed parking lot 15 kilometers (9.3 mi.) east of Field. Buses for day visitors depart mid-June–early October at 8:30 A.M. and 10:30 A.M. returning at 3:30 P.M. and 6:30 P.M. To book a seat call the dedicated reservations line (250/343-6433) up to three months in advance. The reservation fee is $12 per booking and the bus fare is $15 per person round-trip. Six places are allotted for the following day on a first-come, first-served basis. Show up at the **Field Visitor Centre** the day *before* you want to go. Although the center officially opens at 9 A.M., staff come to the locked front door and take names at 8 A.M. Plan to arrive before 8 A.M. as there's usually a line for these last-minute seats. Cancellations are filled on standby basis by folks waiting around at the parking lot on the day of departure (generally, arrive around 7:30 A.M., head to the covered shelter, and you'll be the first in line). You have the best chance of snagging a seat if the weather is bad.

Accommodations and Camping
Spending a night at **Lake O'Hara Lodge** (250/343-6418, www.lakeohara.com) is a very special experience, and one that draws familiar faces year after year. The 15 cabins, each with a private bathroom, are spread around the lakeshore ($575–625 s or d) while within the main lodge are eight rooms, most of which are twins with share bathrooms ($420 s or d). Rates include all meals, taxes, gratuities, and transportation.

Just below the lake itself is a campground. Each of 30 sites has a tent pad, fire pit, and picnic table, while other facilities include pit toilets, two cooking shelters with woodstoves, and bear-proof food caches. Reservations for sites are made in conjunction with the bus trip. Sites are $8 per night.

direction up the Yoho River to Twin Falls, passing many other waterfalls along the way. At spectacular Twin Falls, water from the Wapta Icefield divides in two before plunging off an 80-meter-high (260 ft.) cliff.

One of the finest day hikes in all of the Canadian Rockies is the **Iceline** (6.4 km/4 mi.; 2.5 hours one-way), which gains a heart-thumping 690 meters (2,260 ft.) in elevation. The highlight is a four-kilometer (2.5-mi.) traverse of a moraine below Emerald Glacier. Views across the valley improve as the trail climbs to its 2,220-meter (7,283-ft.) crest. Many options present themselves along this trail, including continuing on to Twin Falls or backtracking and branching off west to **Yoho Lake** and **Yoho Pass**. As always, there's a Gem Trek map (*Lake Louise & Yoho*) to help sort out your options.

Burgess Shale

High on the rocky slopes above Field is a layer of sedimentary rock known as the Burgess Shale, which is famous worldwide, for it has unraveled the mysteries of a major stage of evolution. Encased in the shale, the fossils here are of marine invertebrates around 530 million years old. Generally fossils are the remains of vertebrates, but at this site some freak event—probably a mudslide—suddenly buried thousands of spineless animals (invertebrates), preserving them by keeping out the oxygen that would have decayed their delicate bodies.

Protected by UNESCO as a World Heritage Site, the two main fossil beds are open only to those accompanied by a licensed guide. The **Yoho–Burgess Shale Foundation** (250/343-6006 or 800/343-3006, www.burgess-shale.bc.ca) guides trips to both sites July through mid-September. The access to **Walcott's Quarry** is along a strenuous 10-kilometer (6.2-mi.) trail that gains 760 meters (2,490 ft.) in elevation; $55 per person. Trips to the more easily reached **Mt. Stephen Fossil Beds** gain 520 meters (1,700 ft.) of elevation in three kilometers (1.9 mi.); $25. The trails to both sites are unrelenting in their elevation gain—you must be fit. Schedules are posted on the foundation website.

PARK PRACTICALITIES

Accommodations

Hostelling International operates **HI–Whiskey Jack Wilderness Hostel** (403/670-7580 or 866/762-4122, mid-June–Sept., $17–21) in a meadow opposite Takakkaw Falls. Amenities include bunk beds, showers, and a communal kitchen.

In Field is the simple yet elegant **Kicking Horse Lodge** (100 Centre St., 250/343-6303 or 800/659-4944, www.kickinghorselodge.net, $130–140 s or d) with well-furnished rooms, a large comfortable lounge, and a restaurant (open in summer only). Rates are reduced greatly outside summer. In the same price range is **Cathedral Mountain Lodge and Chalets** (one km/0.6 mi. along Yoho Valley Road 250/343-6442, www.cathedralmountain.com). Older cabins are $140 s or d and have basic cooking facilities. Newer log cabins are $180–200.

Cilantro on the Lake, Emerald Lake Lodge

© ANDREW HEMPSTEAD

Emerald Lake Lodge (403/609-6150 or 800/663-6336, www.crmr.com) is a grand, luxury-class accommodation along the southern shore of one of the Canadian Rockies' most magnificent lakes. It boasts 85 units, as well as a hot tub and sauna, swimming pool, restaurant, lounge, and café. Guests can also go horseback riding, or go boating and fishing on Emerald Lake. The rooms are large and many of the more expensive ones are on the lakefront in cabin-style buildings. Rates range $335–700 s or d per night, with sharp discounts in the off-season (rates as low as $150 in Nov.).

Camping

The park's main camping area is **Kicking Horse Campground** (five km/three mi. northeast of Field along the road to Takakkaw Falls, mid-May–mid-Oct.). Facilities include coin showers ($1), flush toilets, and cooking shelters. All sites are $22 (no hookups). Back toward the Trans-Canada Highway, **Monarch Campground** ($14) offers more limited facilities and less private sites. **Hoodoo Creek Campground,** along the Trans-Canada Highway 23 kilometers (14 mi.) southwest of Field, provides 106 private sites among the trees for $17 per vehicle. Facilities include flush toilets, hot water, cooking shelters, and an interpretive program.

Food

Truffle Pigs Café (318 Stephen St., Field, 250/343-6462, summer daily 7:30 A.M.–10 P.M.) is one of those unexpected finds that makes traveling such a joy. It's contained at the back of a general store, with seating in a section off to the side or outside on a small patio. The best of the breakfast and lunch dishes are described on a massive blackboard, with freshly baked cookies and locally brewed coffee complementing sandwiches made to order from the glass-fronted deli. But it's in the evening that this place really shines, with dishes as adventurous as the Spinach Maple Pecan Salad ($11) and as simple as an Alberta-raised buffalo rib-eye steak served with a port-based jus and a baked potato ($25).

Overlooking Emerald Lake, **Cilantro on the Lake** is a casual café featuring magnificent views from tables inside an open-fronted, log chalet-style building or out on the lakefront deck. The menu is varied—you can sit and sip a coffee or have a full lunch or dinner. Appetizers—such as thick and creamy corn and potato chowder—are all under $10, while entrées range $22–$33 for extravagantly rich beef tenderloin served with a lobster and mushroom cream.

Information

The main source of information about the park is the **Field Visitor Centre** (Field, 250/343-6783, in peak season daily 9 A.M.–7 P.M.; rest of year, daily 9 A.M.–4 P.M., www.pc.gc.ca/yoho). Inside you'll find helpful staff, information boards, and interpretive panels. This is also the place to try and make a last-minute reservation

WHITE-WATER RAFTING

Anyone looking for white-water–rafting action will want to run the Kicking Horse River. The rafting season runs late May–mid-September, with river levels at their highest in late June. The Lower Canyon, immediately upstream of Golden, offers the biggest thrills, including a three-kilometer (1.9-mi.) stretch of continuous rapids. Upstream of here the river is tamer but still makes for an exciting trip, while even farther upstream, near the western boundary of Yoho National Park, it's more a float—a good adventure for the more timid visitor. The river is run by a number of companies, most of which offer the option of half-day ($60–80) or full-day ($90–105) trips. The cost varies with inclusions such as transportation from Banff and lunch. Golden-based companies include **Whitewater Voyageurs** (250/344-7335 or 800/667-7238), **Alpine Rafting** (250/344-6778 or 888/599-5299), and **Wet 'n' Wild Adventures** (250/344-6546 or 800/668-9119). Some operators offer bus transfers from Banff as an add-on while Lake Louise–based **Wild Water Adventures** (403/522-2211 or 888/647-6444) leads half-day trips down the river for $70, including a narrated bus trip to their put-in point 27 kilometers (17 mi.) east of Golden.

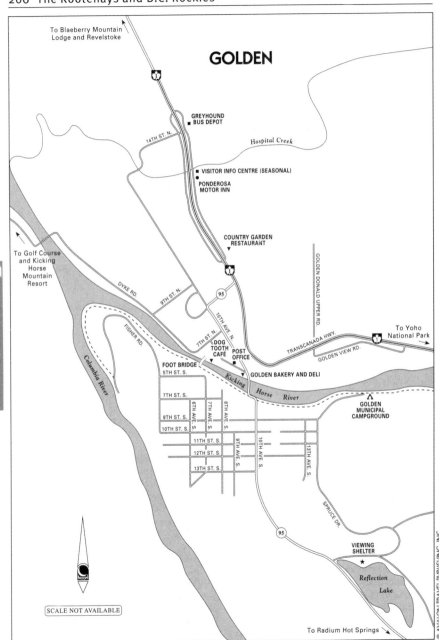

GOLDEN

To Blaeberry Mountain
Lodge and Revelstoke

GREYHOUND
BUS DEPOT

14TH ST. N.

Hospital Creek

VISITOR INFO CENTRE (SEASONAL)

PONDEROSA
MOTOR INN

COUNTRY GARDEN
RESTAURANT

To Golf Course
and Kicking
Horse
Mountain
Resort

GOLDEN DONALD UPPER RD.

DYKE RD.

9TH ST. N.

95

10TH AVE. N.

To Yoho
National Park

FISHER RD.

TRANSCANADA HWY.

7TH ST. N.

GOLDEN VIEW RD.

DOG
TOOTH
CAFÉ

POST
OFFICE

Columbia River

FOOT BRIDGE

5TH ST. S.

GOLDEN BAKERY AND DELI

Kicking Horse River

7TH ST. S.

6TH AVE. S.

7TH AVE. S.

8TH AVE. S.

GOLDEN
MUNICIPAL
CAMPGROUND

9TH ST. S.

10TH ST. S.

11TH ST. S.

9TH AVE. S.

10TH AVE. S.

13TH AVE. S.

12TH ST. S.

13TH ST. S.

SPRUCE DR.

95

VIEWING
SHELTER

★

*Reflection
Lake*

SCALE NOT AVAILABLE

To Radium Hot Springs

for the Lake O'Hara bus (see "Lake O'Hara" sidebar) and find out schedules for the interpretive programs.

GOLDEN

From the western boundary of Yoho National Park, the TransCanada Highway meanders down the beautiful Kicking Horse River Valley to the town of Golden (pop. 5,300), at the confluence of the Kicking Horse and Columbia Rivers. As well as being a destination in itself, Golden makes a good central base for exploring the region or as an overnight stop on a tour through the Canadian Rockies that takes in the national parks on the western side of the Continental Divide.

Kicking Horse Mountain Resort

Spread across the lower slopes of the Purcell Mountains (the runs are easily spotted across the valley as you enter town from the east) is Kicking Horse Mountain Resort (250/439-5400 or 866/754-5425, www.kickinghorseresort.com), a year-round resort with the Golden Eagle Express gondola transporting visitors high into the alpine late June–early September in just 12 minutes. The 360-degree panorama at the summit is equal to any other accessible point in the Canadian Rockies. Graded hiking trails lead from the upper terminal through a fragile, treeless environment, while mountain bikers revel in a challenging descent in excess of 1,000 meters (3,280 ft.). A single gondola ride is adult $17, senior $14, child $9 (ask about excellent breakfast and lunch deals at the Eagle's Eye Restaurant that basically equate to a free ride).

With a vertical rise of 1,260 meters (4,130 ft.), 50 percent of terrain designated for experts, lots of dry powder snow, and minimal crowds, Kicking Horse has developed a big reputation with skiers and snowboarders since opening for the 2000–2001 winter season. Lift tickets are adult $54, senior $42, child $24. To get to Kicking Horse, follow the signs from Highway 1 into town and take 7th Street N west from 10th Avenue N.; it's over the Columbia River and 13 kilometers (eight mi.) uphill from this intersection.

Accommodations

The distinctive two-story, lime-green **Ponderosa Motor Inn** (TransCanada Hwy. at 12th Ave., 250/344-2205 or 800/881-4233, www.ponderosa motorinn.bc.ca, $78 s, $88 d) is typical of Golden's many roadside motels, with comfortable rooms at a reasonable price. **Blaeberry Mountain Lodge** (250/344-5296, www.blaeberry mountainlodge.bc.ca) is set on a 62-hectare (150-acre) property among total wilderness. Rooms are in the main lodge or self-contained cabins, with plenty of activities available to guests. Standard rooms with shared bathroom are $65 and the large cabins, which feature a separate bedroom and full kitchen, are $145. Breakfast and dinner are offered for $12 and $22, respectively. To get there, drive nine kilometers (5.6 mi.) north of Golden along Highway 1 then seven kilometers (4.3 mi.) farther north along Moberly School Road.

Along Highway 1 back toward Yoho National Park, **Kicking Horse River Chalets** (2924 Kicking Horse Rd., 866/502-5171, www.kicking horseriverchalets.com) comprises luxurious peeled-log cabins, each with full kitchen and dishwasher, wood-burning fireplace, balcony, and loft. The rate is $200 per night for up to four people.

Camping

Continue south through the old part of town over the Kicking Horse River and take 9th Street S east at the traffic lights to reach **Golden Municipal Campground** (250/344-5412, mid-May–mid-Oct., $15–20). It's a quiet place, strung out along the river and two kilometers (1.2 mi.) from downtown along a riverfront walkway. Facilities include picnic shelters, hot coin-operated showers, and 70 sites with fire pits. Adjacent is a recreation center with a swimming pool and fitness facility.

Food

At an elevation of 2,347 meters (7,700 ft.), the **Eagle's Eye** is the crowning glory of Kicking Horse Mountain Resort and is Canada's highest restaurant. Access is by gondola from the resort's base village (13 km/eight mi. west of downtown,

250/439-5400). As you'd expect, the views are stunning, and are set off by a stylish timber and stonework interior, including a floor-to-ceiling fireplace and a wide wraparound deck protected from the wind by glass paneling. It's open daily at 8 A.M. for a simple cold and cooked breakfast buffet costing adult $18, child $12, which includes the gondola ride. Lunch is only a few bucks more, while for dinner (7–10 P.M.) the setting becomes more romantic and the food more adventurous. Dinner entrées range $25–40 and include such delights as salmon baked in a saffron-vanilla cream and served with strawberry salsa ($28). All evening diners enjoy a complimentary gondola ride.

Downtown at the **Golden Bakery & Deli** (419 9th Ave., 250/344-2928, Mon.–Sat. 6:30 A.M.–6 P.M.), the coffee is always fresh and the faces friendly. Baked goodies include breads, pastries, cakes, and meat pies, with inexpensive daily specials displayed on a blackboard in a seated section off to the side of the main counter. Tucked behind the row of shops along 9th Avenue is the funky little **Dog Tooth Café** (1007 11th Ave. S, 250/344-3660, Mon.–Sat. 7 A.M.–8 P.M., Sun. 9 A.M.–6 P.M.). Seating is indoors below the main service area or out back in an adobe-style terrace facing the pedestrian bridge over the Kicking Horse River. The menu includes basic café fare and specialties such as a huge serving of Thai noodle salad for just $7.

Information

The year-round **Golden Visitor Info Centre** is in the old railway station building (500 10th Avenue, 250/344-7125 or 800/622-4653, Mon.–Fri. 8:30 A.M.–4:30 P.M.). Back out on the highway is a seasonal information center (July–Aug. daily 9 A.M.–5 P.M.) beside the Ponderosa Motor Inn. In addition to all the regular brochure racks, it has public Internet access and a handy map of local bike trails.

Central British Columbia

Ranging from the western slopes of the Rocky Mountains to the Pacific Ocean, central British Columbia holds such varied natural features as the massive Fraser River, the lofty peaks of the Cariboo and Coast Mountains, and the deeply indented coastal fjords around Bella Coola.

The region's history is dominated by colorful sagas of Canada's biggest gold rush, when over 100,000 miners and fortune seekers passed through the area on their way to the goldfields. But the best-remembered man in these parts was an explorer, not a miner. In 1793, Alexander Mackenzie left the Fraser River for the final leg of his epic transcontinental journey. Fourteen days later he reached the Pacific Ocean, becoming the first person to cross the continent.

Today the most heavily traveled route through central British Columbia is the Trans-Canada Highway, which bisects Glacier National Park, a small but spectacular park of glaciers and towering peaks. Heading west from the park, the highway passes the heli-skiing hub of Revelstoke and Shuswap Lake before coming to the large population center of Kamloops.

BRITISH COLUMBIA

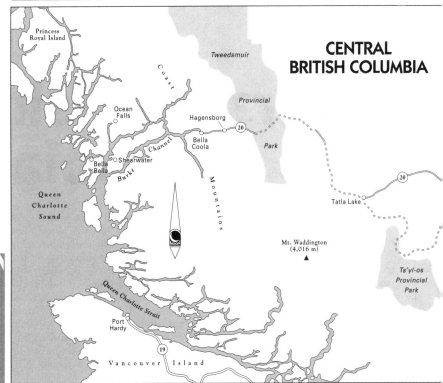

CENTRAL
BRITISH COLUMBIA

From Kamloops, two highways lead north. Highway 5 accesses Wells Gray and Mount Robson Provincial Parks, the former a vast forested wilderness and the latter named for one of the most spectacular mountain peaks in all of Canada. The other route, Highway 97, runs through Cariboo Country, best-known for the 1860s gold-rush town of Barkerville, now completely restored and one of the highlights of a trip north.

Golden to Kamloops

GLACIER NATIONAL PARK

Encompassing 135,000 hectares (333,590 acres) of the Selkirk Mountains west of the Rocky Mountain Trench, this park is a wonderland of jagged snowcapped peaks, extensive icefields, thundering waterfalls, steep-sided valleys, and fast-flowing rivers. The TransCanada Highway bisects the park, cresting at 1,327-meter (4,550 ft.) **Rogers Pass.** From this lofty summit, Golden is 80 kilometers (50 mi.) east and Revelstoke is 72 kilometers (45 mi.) west.

Those from south of the 49th parallel probably associate the park's name with the American national park in Montana. The two parks share the same name and glaciated environment, but the similarities end there. In the "other" park, buses shuttle tourists here and there and the backcountry is crowded with hikers. Here in the Canadian version, commercialism is almost

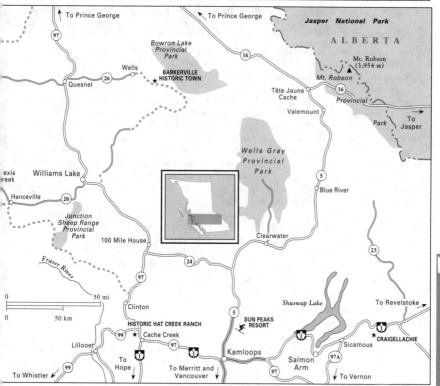

To Prince George

97

Bowron Lake Provincial Park

Wells

To Prince George

16

Jasper National Park

ALBERTA

▲ Mt. Robson (3,954 m)

BARKERVILLE HISTORIC TOWN

26

Quesnel

Mt. Robson

16

Tête Jaune Cache

Provincial

Valemount

To Jasper

Park

exis reek

Williams Lake

Wells Gray Provincial Park

Hanceville

20

5

Blue River

Junction Sheep Range Provincial Park

100 Mile House

Clearwater

Fraser River

24

23

97

0   50 mi

0   50 km

Clinton

5

Shuswap Lake

To Revelstoke

HISTORIC HAT CREEK RANCH

99   ★ Cache Creek

SUN PEAKS RESORT

★ **CRAIGELLACHIE**

Lillooet

97

Kamloops

Sicamous

97A

To Whistler

99

To Hope

To Merritt and Vancouver

Salmon Arm

97

To Vernon

© AVALON TRAVEL PUBLISHING, INC.

totally lacking and use of the backcountry is blissfully minimal.

The best place to start a visit to the park is **Rogers Pass Information Centre.** Looking south from the center, you can see the Illecillewaet, Asulkan, and Swiss Glaciers. As far as actual "sights" go, driving through the park you'll be surrounded by one of the most awe-inspiring panoramas visible from any Canadian highway. Each roadside viewpoint seems to outdo the last. You can also get out of the car and go hiking to get a better feeling for the park, but most of the trails here entail strenuous climbs.

Through-traffic excepted, permits are required for entry into Glacier National Park; they're available from the information center. A one-day permit is adult $5, senior $4.25, child $2.50 to a maximum of $10 per vehicle.

The Land

Regardless of whether you approach the park from the east or west, you'll climb over 700 vertical meters (2,300 ft.) to reach the summit of Rogers Pass. The pass is not particularly high, but it's impressive. Surrounding peaks, many topping 3,000 meters (9,800 ft.), rise dramatically from the pass, with heavy winter snows feeding more than 400 glaciers, some visible from the highway.

Flower lovers will be impressed by the 600 species of flowering plants that have been identified within the park. The best time to see wildflowers in the high meadows and forests is early August, though an amazing profusion of color sweeps through the lower-elevation forests starting in June, and in July the edge of the highway and avalanche paths turn bright yellow with wild lilies. The lower montane forest supports a lush

A RAILWAY AND A ROAD

In a scenario familiar throughout western Canada, the proclamation of Glacier National Park was influenced by the Canadian Pacific Railway's desire to see tourists use its rail line.

For C.P.R. engineers, finding a passable train route through the Columbia Mountains proved a formidable challenge. The major obstacle was not the elevation, but the threat of avalanches coupled with narrow valleys and steep approaches. After a route was chosen, workers toiled with picks and shovels for three years, completing the railbed on November 7, 1885. The last spike was driven into the ground at Craigellachie, 100 kilometers (62 mi.) to the west, and the transcontinental rail line was finally opened. Unfortunately, despite railway engineering ingenuity, frequent and devastating avalanches took their toll, killing over 200 workers in the first 30 years of operation. Forced to stop the carnage, the C.P.R. rerouted the line, tunneling under the actual pass in 1916.

In the 1950s, a team of engineers tackled the same problem that faced those on the railway—this time in an effort to build a highway across the pass. The tunnel approach that had worked for the railway was deemed impractical for a highway, so a new solution to the avalanche danger was required. In 1962 a route over the pass was completed—this time with the addition of concrete snowsheds over sections of the highway. At the same time, the world's largest mobile avalanche-control program was created to stave off danger. Experts constantly monitor weather and snow conditions so they can accurately predict when and where avalanches will occur. Then they close the highway and dislodge potential slides with mobile howitzers, thereby stabilizing the slopes.

---

variety of tree species, including mountain hemlock, subalpine fir, Engelmann spruce, western red cedar, and western hemlock.

The rugged terrain and long hard winters in Glacier National Park mean that resident mammals are a tough and hardy bunch. Healthy populations of both black and grizzly bears inhabit the park. The black bears often feed along the roadside in late spring. Grizzlies are less common and tend to remain in the backcountry, but early in the season, lingering snow can keep them at lower elevations; look for them on avalanche slopes.

Hiking

The park's 21 hiking trails cover 140 kilometers (87 mi.) and range from short interpretive walks to long, steep, difficult climbs. Aside from the interpretive trails, most gain a lot of elevation, rewarding hikers with outstanding views. Remember, many of the park's high-elevation trails are covered in snow until well into July.

Two short trails provide an introduction to the park: **Abandoned Rails Interpretive Trail** (one km/0.6 mi.; 20 minutes round-trip), which starts to the west of the information center, and the **Meeting of the Waters Trail** (one km/0.6 mi.; 25 minutes round-trip), which starts behind Illecillewaet Campground, four kilometers (2.5 mi.) south of the information center.

Are you feeling energetic? You'll need to be on the following two hikes, my favorites in the park. Starting from the **Illecillewaet Campground,** the **Avalanche Crest Trail** (4.2 km/2.6 mi.; 2.5 hours one-way; elevation gain 800 m/2,632 ft.) heads off to the left from the information board, climbing steeply through a subalpine forest for the first three kilometers (1.9 mi.), then leveling out and providing stunning views below to Rogers Pass and south to Illecillewaet and Asulkan Glaciers. While elevation on the **Asulkan Valley Trail** (6.5 km/four mi.; four hours one-way; elevation gain 930 m/3,059 ft.) is similar to others in the steep-sided Illecillewaet River Valley, it is gained over a longer distance, meaning a less strenuous outing. Nevertheless, a full day should be allowed roundtrip. From the back of Illecillewaet Campground, the trail follows Asulkan Brook through a valley of dense subalpine forest. Whereas other trails lead to panoramic overlooks, the highlight of this trail's final destination is a view of the immense icefield rising high above you.

© ANDREW HEMPSTEAD

The snowcapped peaks of Glacier National Park can be seen from the highway.

Accommodations and Camping

Don't expect any surprises at **Glacier Park Lodge** (at Rogers Pass, 250/837-2126 or 800/528-1234, www.glacierparklodge.ca), a Best Western affiliate and the only motel in the park. It offers 50 midsize rooms, a restaurant, a 24-hour café, and heated outdoor pool. Summer rates are from $135 s, $150 d; off-season rates are well under $100 d.

Illecillewaet Campground (all sites $17), four kilometers (2.5 mi.) south of the information center, is open late June–September. Facilities include cooking shelters, flush toilets, picnic tables, firewood, and an evening interpretive program. Sites are not particularly private, and the surrounding peaks and towering cedar trees mean little sunshine before noon, but the campground is the perfect base for exploring as it's the trailhead for the park's main concentration of hiking trails. Smaller **Loop Brook Campground** (July–Aug., $17) is three kilometers (1.9 mi.) beyond the Illecillewaet Campground toward Revelstoke, but holds just 20 sites. No reservations are taken.

With just 80 campsites in the entire park and no reservations taken, chances are good that both campgrounds will be full if you arrive late in the afternoon. If that's the case, plan on overnighting 40 kilometers (25 mi.) west at **Canyon Hot Springs Resort** (250/837-2420, www.canyonhotsprings.com, May–Sept., $20–27), where you'll find hot springs, showers, a laundry, and a restaurant.

Information

The **Rogers Pass Centre** (250/837-7500, www.pc.gc.ca/glacier, mid-June–Aug. daily 8 A.M.–7 P.M., Sept.–mid-June daily 9 A.M.–5 P.M.) is 1.2 kilometers (0.7 mi.) north of the actual pass and resembles the old-fashioned snowsheds that once protected the railroad from avalanches. The center's fascinating displays focus on the park's natural and human history. Videos on various aspects of the park are shown on the television and the center's theater shows *Snow War,* an award-winning documentary on avalanche protection. The center is also the only place in the park to buy park passes, necessary for those planning any hiking or camping. If you already have an annual pass, it must be presented for admission to the information center.

REVELSTOKE

Revelstoke (pop. 8,000) lies 72 kilometers (45 mi.) west of Rogers Pass at the confluence of the Illecillewaet River and the mighty Columbia, surrounded by mountains—the Monashees to the west and the Selkirks to the east. The setting couldn't be more spectacular. The town holds a couple of museums, but the main attractions are farther afield, including two massive dams, a national park on the back doorstep (see following section), and, in winter, great skiing and snowboarding at Powder Springs.

Sights

The TransCanada Highway makes a lazy loop around the back of Revelstoke, missing downtown completely. It's well worth the detour to downtown, not just for the best dining and accommodations, but to enjoy the laid-back atmosphere of a small city that has done an excellent job of preserving its heritage. The downtown core has been rejuvenated and centers around the appealing, all-brick **Grizzly Plaza.** Pick up the *Heritage Walking & Driving* brochure at the local information center for routes that take in the highlights of downtown's many old buildings.

Railway buffs shouldn't miss **Revelstoke Railway Museum** (Victoria Rd., 250/837-6060, July–Aug. daily 9 A.M.–7 P.M., Sept.–June Mon.–Fri. 1–4 P.M., adult $5, senior $4, child $2.50), a re-creation of an early C.P.R. station. Reflecting the importance of this mode of transportation in Revelstoke's history, the museum centers around a massive 1948 steam locomotive and Business Car No. 4, the ultimate in early rail-travel luxury. **Revelstoke Museum** (July–Aug. Mon.–Sat. 10 A.M.–5 P.M., Sept.–June Mon.–Fri. 1–4 P.M.), in an imposing two-story former post office building on the corner of Boyle Avenue and 1st Street, holds a great collection of historical black-and-white photos.

Dams

The 1,900-kilometer (1,180-mi.) **Columbia River,** North America's third-longest, is controlled by many dams. Four of these are in British Columbia and two are in the vicinity of Revelstoke. The dams also provide the necessary water for two massive hydroelectric operations. These two generating stations are each capable of producing 1,800 megawatts of electricity—or, combined, 30 percent of the province's needs.

Revelstoke Dam, eight kilometers (five mi.) north of the city on Highway 23, holds back a massive reservoir that stretches upstream 100 kilometers (62 mi.). Exhibits at the two-story **Revelstoke Dam Visitor Centre** (summer Mon.–Fri. 8 A.M.–7 P.M.), above the generating station, explain the valley's history and the operation and impact of the dams. From the center, a high-speed elevator whisks visitors to the top of the dam for an excellent view. Upstream of Revelstoke Dam, Mica Dam, 140 kilometers (87 mi.) by road to the north, is even larger.

Skiing and Snowboarding

The local downhill resort is **Powder Springs** (250/837-5151 or 800/991-4455, www.catpowder.com), on the lower slopes of Mount Mackenzie. The resort's chairlift and T-bar serve a vertical rise of 330 meters (1,000 ft.). Facilities include ski and snowboard rentals, a ski school, cafeteria, and bar.

It's possible to ski the mountain's higher slopes with **CAT Powder Skiing,** owned by the resort and based out of the day lodge. Packages include skiing, accommodations, and all meals, and cost around $1,050 for two days, $1,420 for three days.

Entertainment

In July and August, free entertainment takes place nightly at the **Grizzly Plaza bandshell** (bottom of Mackenzie Ave.). Whether it be comedy or country, crowds of up to a couple hundred gather, sitting in plastic chairs, snagging a table at a surrounding restaurant, or just standing in the background. For music and dancing of a more formal nature, the young crowd heads for **Big Eddy Inn** (2108 Big Eddy Rd., 250/837-9072). For a quieter evening, head to the **One Twelve Lounge** (in the Regent Inn at 112 1st St., 250/837-2107) or the poolside lounge

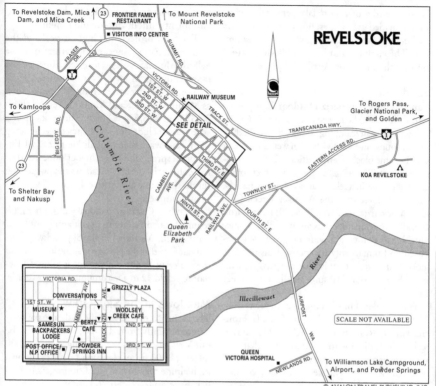

To Revelstoke Dam, Mica Dam, and Mica Creek

FRONTIER FAMILY RESTAURANT

To Mount Revelstoke National Park

VISITOR INFO CENTRE

REVELSTOKE

FRASER DR.

VICTORIA RD.

1ST ST. W
2ND ST. W
3RD ST. W

SUMMIT RD.

RAILWAY MUSEUM

TRACK ST.

SEE DETAIL

To Kamloops

BIG EDDY RD.

Columbia River

23

To Shelter Bay and Nakusp

CAMBELL AVE.

MACKENZIE

NINTH ST. E

RAILWAY AVE.

THIRD ST. E

TOWNLEY ST.

FOURTH ST. E

Queen Elizabeth Park

TRANSCANADA HWY.

To Rogers Pass, Glacier National Park, and Golden

EASTERN ACCESS RD.

KOA REVELSTOKE

Illecillewaet River

AIRPORT WA

SCALE NOT AVAILABLE

QUEEN VICTORIA HOSPITAL

NEWLANDS RD.

To Williamson Lake Campground, Airport, and Powder Springs

© AVALON TRAVEL PUBLISHING, INC.

Detail:

VICTORIA RD.

CAMBELL AVE.
MACKENZIE AVE.

GRIZZLY PLAZA

CONVERSATIONS

1ST ST. W

MUSEUM ★

WOOLSEY CREEK CAFE

SAMESUN BACKPACKERS LODGE

BERTZ CAFE

2ND ST. W

POST OFFICE/ N.P. OFFICE

POWDER SPRINGS INN

3RD ST. W

BRITISH COLUMBIA

at the **Sandman Inn** (on TransCanada Hwy., 250/837-5271).

Accommodations

How does free skiing and snowboarding sound? That's the reward for traveling to Revelstoke in winter and choosing one of the following two accommodations.

Samesun Backpacker Lodge (400 2nd St. W, 250/837-4050 or 877/562-2783, www.samesun .com) provides a true home away from home. This heritage house has been fully restored, complete with hardwood floors and comfortable beds with linen. The rooms share bathrooms, kitchen facilities, a laundry, free Internet access, and a game room. Summer rates start at $20 pp, but for winter travel check the website for what is probably the least expensive ski-and-stay package anywhere in North America ($30 per night).

Powder Springs Inn (200 3rd St. W, 250/837-5151 or 800/991-4455, www.catpowder.com) has regularly revamped motel rooms, a hot tub, and a restaurant/bar. The rooms are great value year-round; $70 s or d in summer ($79 d with breakfast) and $49 s or d in winter. This motel is owned by the downhill resort and winter packages equate to free skiing.

Camping

KOA Revelstoke (six km/3.7 mi. east of downtown, 250/837-2085 or 800/562-3905, mid-Apr.–mid-Oct.) is a well-kept facility with grassy sites, lots of trees, a swimming pool, a well-stocked store, free hot showers, laundry facilities, and a main lodge that looks like a Swiss chalet. Unserviced sites are $22, full hookups $27.

Quiet **Williamson Lake Campground** (250/837-5512 or 888/676-2267, $15.50–19) lies on the edge of a warm lake perfect for swimming. Shaded grassy sites, hot showers, a picnic shelter, and fire pits are all just above the shoreline. The campground is seven kilometers (4.3 mi.) south of town on Airport Way.

Food

Lunch is busiest at **Bertz Outdoor Equipment and Café** (217 Mackenzie Ave., 250/837-6575), a downtown café/camping combo. Expect healthy salads, soups, and sandwiches, all well under $10. On the same block, **Conversations** (205 Mackenzie Ave., 250/837-4772) serves up gourmet coffees and light meals in a relaxed atmosphere. Across the road from these two, the **Woolsey Creek Café** (212 Mackenzie St., 250/837-5500) has a warm, friendly atmosphere, but is always full and noisy with locals enjoying a wide range of well-prepared and remarkably inexpensive dishes. The globally inspired menu is very inexpensive, with breakfasts under $10 and all dinner entrées under $15.

For the sake of hurried highway travelers only, I'll include a spot out on the TransCanada. **Frontier Family Restaurant** (250/837-5119), a typical roadside diner with an atmosphere that lives up to its name. The wood interior is decorated with red and white checkered curtains, cowboy boots, hats, antlers, and cattle horns; the waitresses wear jeans; and a sign outside says "Y'all come back, y'hear!" On top of all that, the food is good and well priced.

Information

Revelstoke Visitor Info Centre (204 Campbell Ave., 250/837-5345 or 800/487-1493) is open June–early September daily 8 A.M.–7 P.M., the rest of the year Monday–Friday 8:30 A.M.–4:30 P.M. The website www.cityofrevelstoke.com has a load of local links. On the TransCanada Highway, in front of the Frontier Family Restaurant, is a **seasonal information center** (summer daily 7 A.M.–7 P.M.).

MOUNT REVELSTOKE NATIONAL PARK

The aptly named Meadows in the Sky Parkway allows visitors to this 26,000-hectare (64,200-acre) national park to experience a high alpine environment without any strenuous hiking.

The park protects the highest peaks of the Clachnacudiann Range, a northern arm of the Selkirk Mountains. The forested slopes of the range come to an icy apex around the Clachnacudiann Glacier and surrounding peaks, such as Mount Coursier and Mount Inverness, both 2,637 meters (8,674 ft.) high. The park's diverse vegetation includes forests of ancient cedar along the Illecillewaet River, subalpine forests of Engelmann spruce and fir on higher slopes, and finally, above the treeline, meadows of low-growing shrubs that come alive with color for a few weeks in midsummer.

As with all Canadian national parks, a permit is required for entry; in this case it applies only for travel on the Meadows in the Sky Parkway. Permits are issued at the park gate, at the lower end of the parkway. A one-day permit is adult $4, senior $3, child $2 to a maximum of $8 per vehicle.

Meadows in the Sky Parkway

The main access road into the park, the parkway climbs abruptly from the valley bottom, on the outskirts of Revelstoke, gaining nearly 1,500 meters (4,900 ft.) of elevation before reaching a high alpine meadow over 2,000 meters (6,600 ft.) above sea level after 26 kilometers (16 mi.). The road is very steep. It climbs relentlessly along seemingly endless hairpin bends through a subalpine forest of Engelmann spruce, hemlock, and the odd towering cedar. The summit area is snowed in until July, so try to plan your trip after this time. A shuttle bus runs the final kilometer (daily 10 A.M.–4:20 P.M.) to **Heather Lake.** It's also possible to walk this final stretch; the trail climbs 90 meters (300 ft.) in elevation and takes around 20 minutes each way. From the top, the panoramic view takes in the Columbia River Valley and the distant Monashee Mountains.

The park doesn't have an extensive network of hiking trails—just 10 marked trails totaling 65 kilometers (40 mi.) in length. Most take under an hour and are posted with interpretive panels. Heather Lake is the trailhead for the one-kilometer (0.6-mi.) **Meadows in the Sky Trail,** which features signs explaining the flora of the fragile alpine environment.

Mountain Bike Tours

Summit Cycle Tours (250/837-3734 or 888/700-3444, www.summitcycle.com) takes the hard part out of a mountain-biking trip through the national park. The company's tours start with a van ride to the summit of Meadows in the Sky Parkway, where you'll spend some time exploring the alpine environment. Then the tour proceeds downhill on a ride back to the valley floor. The four-hour tour costs $69 per person, and includes a picnic stop.

Park Information

The park's main gate is closed from 10 P.M. until 7 A.M., prohibiting access. No road-accessible campgrounds or services lie within the park. Revelstoke is home to the park's administration office, in the post office building (313 3rd St., 250/837-7500, Mon.–Fri. 8:30 A.M.–4:30 P.M.). Ask here about the park's evening interpretive program. Other sources of information are Rogers Pass Information Centre, in nearby Glacier National Park, and the website www.pc.gc.ca/revelstoke.

REVELSTOKE TOWARD SALMON ARM

Continuing west along the TransCanada Highway from Revelstoke, it's 104 kilometers (65 mi.) to the major center of Salmon Arm. Several commercial attractions along the way compete for your tourist dollar. They aren't the sort of thing you traveled to British Columbia for, but children will appreciate them.

On the shore of **Three Valley Lake** is **Three Valley Gap** (Apr.–mid-Oct. 8 A.M.–dusk, adult $8, child $4), a re-created "ghost town" and the **Three Valley Lake Chateau** (250/837-2109 or 888/667-2109, www.3valley.com, Apr.–mid-Oct., $115–150 s or d), a large motel (160 rooms) overlooking extensive gardens and the lake. Amenities include a café, restaurant, and indoor pool. Continuing west is **Enchanted Forest** (250/837-9477), where a trail through towering trees me-

anders past more than 250 handcrafted figurines to fairyland buildings, and **Beardale Castle Miniatureland** (250/836-2268), which takes miniature appreciators through several European towns and villages, into the world of nursery rhymes and fairy tales. Both are open May–September and charge around adult $7, child $3.50.

The Last Spike

At **Craigellachie,** signs point off the highway to the Last Spike. It was here on November 7, 1885 that a plain iron spike joined the last two sections of Canadian Pacific's transcontinental rail line, finally connecting Canada from sea to sea. A cairn with a plaque and a piece of railway line marks the spot. Nearby are picnic tables and Craigellachie Station, an information center open May–October.

Sicamous

This town of 3,000, 62 kilometers (39 mi.) west of Revelstoke, lies on the shore of **Shuswap Lake** and is known as the "Houseboat Capital of Canada." The lake itself is a convoluted body of water with four distinct arms, edged by secluded beaches, rocky coves, 25 marine parks, and more than 1,000 kilometers (620 mi.) of shoreline. Houseboating is the No. 1 activity in these parts, and Sicamous is headquarters to major agencies, including **Three Buoys Houseboat Vacations** (250/836-2403 or 800/663-2333, www.three buoys.com) and **Twin Anchors Houseboat Vacations** (250/836-2450 or 800/663-4026, www .twinanchors.com). Expect to pay from $150 per boat per day, more for those that sleep more than four people. The season runs May–October with peak season being summer school holidays.

SALMON ARM

Known as the "Gem of the Shuswap," Salmon Arm (pop. 15,000) lies along the Salmon Arm of Shuswap Lake, surrounded by lush farmland and forested hills.

Sights

From downtown, head toward the lake and **Marine Park,** where picnic tables dot the lawns and colorful flower boxes hang from the lampposts. The attractive **Salmon Arm Wharf,** the largest marina structure in British Columbia's interior, lures you out over the water, past a boat-launching area, a snack bar, and businesses renting motorboats and houseboats.

Two kilometers (1.2 mi.) east of Salmon Arm on Highway 97B, **R.J. Haney Heritage Park** (250/832-5243, summer daily 10 A.M.–5 P.M., $4.50) is home to the Salmon Arm Museum and Haney House, an early-20th-century farmhouse on beautiful, parklike grounds. Also in the park are a blacksmith's shop, an old fire hall, and a historic gas station.

Practicalities

ViewPoint Motel and RV Park (west of Salmon Arm toward Kamloops, 250/832-2833, www .viewpointmotel.bc.ca) enjoys a beautiful beachfront location, with plenty of amenities. Simple, self-contained cabins are older but well priced ($69–89 s or d), or you can camp for $16–24. The landscaped **KOA Salmon Arm** (just south of the TransCanada Hwy. along Hwy. 97B, 250/832-6489) features hot showers, a laundry, heated pool and hot tub, store, miniature golf, playground, and petting zoo. Tent sites are $23, full hookups $31, and rustic cabins $45.

ADAMS RIVER SOCKEYE

Roderick Haig–Brown Provincial Park, north of Squilax, protects the spawning grounds of North America's largest sockeye salmon run. The runs occur annually, but every four years (2006 is next up) a dominant run brings up to two million fish congregating in the river. They are present for the first three weeks of October, but numbers generally peak in the second week.

These salmon are near the end of their four-year life cycle, having hatched in the same section of the Adams River four years previously. After hatching, they spend up to two years of their life in Shuswap Lake before swimming out to the Pacific Ocean. It is estimated that in conjunction with dominant runs, 15 million Adams River sockeye enter the Pacific, with about 10 million running back toward their birthplace. Just one in five make it the full 500 kilometers (310 mi.).

Salmon Arm Visitor Info Centre (751 Marine Park Dr., 250/832-2230 or 877/725-6667, July–Aug. daily 9 A.M.–6 P.M., rest of year Mon.–Fri. 9 A.M.–5 P.M.) is in the heart of town, or check the website of **Tourism Shuswap** (www.shuswap.bc.ca) before leaving home.

Kamloops

Kamloops (pop. 80,000), 110 kilometers (68 mi.) west of Salmon Arm and 355 kilometers (220 mi.) northeast of Vancouver, is the largest city between Vancouver and Calgary. The city holds a few interesting sights but is certainly no scenic gem—the surrounding landscape is dominated by barren, parched, rolling hills. The downtown area, however, lies along the south bank of the Thompson River and is set off by well-irrigated parkland.

History

The Secwepemc, whose descendents are now known as Shuswap, were the first people to live in this region, basing their lifestyle on hunting and salmon fishing. The first non-native settlement occurred in 1812, when the North West Company established a fur-trading post at the confluence of the north and south branches of the Thompson River. Prospectors began arriving in 1858, followed by entrepreneurs who began setting up permanent businesses. Over the ensuing years all kinds of colorful characters have passed through or lived in Kamloops—fur traders, explorers, gold miners, cattle ranchers, railway builders, and farmers. After the C.P.R. line was completed in 1885, settlers began flooding in. Today the local economy revolves around the forest-products industry, copper mining, cattle and sheep ranching, and tourism.

SIGHTS AND RECREATION

Kamloops Museum

Excellent displays at Kamloops Museum (207 Seymour St., 250/828-3576, summer Mon.–Fri. 9 A.M.–8 P.M., Sat. 10 A.M.–5 P.M., and Sun. 1–5 P.M., rest of year Tues.–Sat. 9:30 A.M.–4:30 P.M.) cover local native culture, the fur trade (peek in the reconstructed fur trader's cabin), pioneer days, and natural history.

Secwepemc Museum & Heritage Park

A living-history museum dedicated to the Shuswap tribe, this cultural attraction (Hwy. 5 north, 250/828-9801, June–Aug. Mon.–Fri. 8:30 A.M.–8 P.M., Sat.–Sun. 10 A.M.–8 P.M., adult $6, senior and child $4) offers numerous exhibits focusing on the Shuswaps' traditions and rich mythology. Among the highlights are an archaeological site dating back 2,000 years, a re-created Shuswap winter village, a salmon-fishing station, a garden filled with native plants for food and medicinal purposes, and a re-creation of a traditional summer shelter.

Kamloops Wildlife Park

This nonprofit park (16 km/10 mi. east of Kamloops, 250/573-3242, July–Aug. daily 8:30 A.M.–8:30 P.M., rest of year 8 A.M.–4 P.M., adult $9, senior and child $8) is primarily a wildlife rehabilitation center, but among the more than 150 furry inhabitants are many species of mammals from western Canada, including a couple of grizzly bears, wolves, cougars, and lynx. Other attractions are a huge visitors center, a glass-walled beehive, and, for the kids, a petting zoo and miniature steam train.

River Cruise

One of the best ways to appreciate the city and some of its history is to take a two-hour cruise down the Thompson River in the *Wanda Sue* (250/374-7447, adult $13.50, senior $12.50, child $7.50), a reconstructed sternwheeler. The boat departs June–early September daily at 1:30 P.M. and weeknights at 6:30 P.M. from the terminal at the Old Yacht Club Public Wharf on River Street. Get your ticket from the wharf ticket office up to one hour before sailing.

Sun Peaks Resort

North of Kamloops off Highway 5, Sun Peaks (250/578-7222, www.sunpeaksresort.com) is another of British Columbia's fast-growing year-round resorts. In summer, the Sunburst Express lift takes the hard work out of reaching the alpine for hikers and bikers. From the top of the lift, a trail leads to the base village, while others continue higher, including to the high point of Mount Tod. Ride the lift all day for $15 ($30 with a mountain bike). Other activities include golfing ($44, rentals available), tennis, horseback riding, fishing, and swimming at the outdoor Sports Centre.

High season for the resort is winter, when skiers and snowboarders take to 1,500 hectares (3,700 acres) of lift-served terrain, including the newest face, Mt. Morrisey, which opened for the 2003–2004 season to rave reviews. Lift tickets are adult $55, senior $39, child $29; discounted multiday and half-day tickets available. On-mountain accommodations packages are good value—from $89 per person per night including a lift ticket. The central reservations number is 800/807-3257, or book online.

ACCOMMODATIONS AND CAMPING

Under $50

Built in 1909, the Old Courthouse is now home to **HI–Kamloops** (7 W. Seymour St., 250/828-7991). The building has been renovated to make hostellers feel a little more comfortable than the original "guests," yet the historic charm remains in the vaulted ceilings, winding staircases, and stained-glass windows. Upstairs in the main courtroom you can write a letter home in the witness stand, or relax in the jury seats. The original jail cells now hold bathrooms. And if you need to do any ironing, you'll be sent to solitary confinement—where the ironing board is. Dorm beds are $18 for members, $22 for nonmembers.

$50–100

Least expensive downtown is the **Fountain Motel**

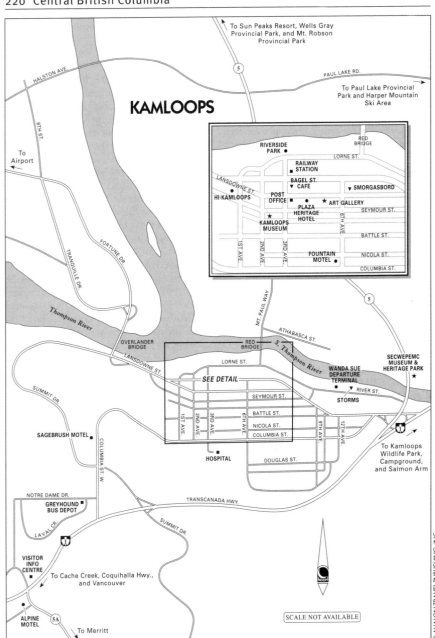

KAMLOOPS

To Sun Peaks Resort, Wells Gray
Provincial Park, and Mt. Robson
Provincial Park

PAUL LAKE RD.

To Paul Lake Provincial
Park and Harper Mountain
Ski Area

HALSTON AVE.

8TH ST.

To
Airport

RIVERSIDE
PARK

RED
BRIDGE

LORNE ST.

RAILWAY
STATION

LANSDOWNE ST.

HI-KAMLOOPS

BAGEL ST.
CAFÉ

SMORGASBORD

POST
OFFICE

PLAZA
HERITAGE
HOTEL

ART GALLERY

SEYMOUR ST.

6TH AVE.

KAMLOOPS
MUSEUM

BATTLE ST.

1ST AVE.

2ND AVE.

3RD AVE.

FOUNTAIN
MOTEL

NICOLA ST.

COLUMBIA ST.

FORTUNE DR.

TRANQUILLE DR.

Thompson River

OVERLANDER
BRIDGE

LANSDOWNE ST.

RED
BRIDGE

S. Thompson River

MT. PAUL WAY

ATHABASCA ST.

LORNE ST.

SEE DETAIL

SEYMOUR ST.

1ST AVE.

2ND AVE.

3RD AVE.

6TH AVE.

BATTLE ST.

NICOLA ST.

COLUMBIA ST.

9TH AVE.

12TH AVE.

WANDA SUE
DEPARTURE
TERMINAL

RIVER ST.

STORMS

SECWEPEMC
MUSEUM &
HERITAGE PARK

SUMMIT DR.

SAGEBRUSH MOTEL

COLUMBIA ST. W

HOSPITAL

DOUGLAS ST.

To Kamloops
Wildlife Park,
Campground,
and Salmon Arm

NOTRE DAME DR.

GREYHOUND
BUS DEPOT

LAVAL CR.

TRANSCANADA HWY.

SUMMIT DR.

VISITOR
INFO
CENTRE

To Cache Creek, Coquihalla Hwy.,
and Vancouver

ALPINE
MOTEL

5A

To Merritt

SCALE NOT AVAILABLE

BRITISH COLUMBIA

(506 Columbia St., 250/374-4451 or 800/253-1569, $60–72 s or d), which offers a higher standard of rooms than the exterior may suggest. Other similarly priced choices lie along a wide sweeping bend of Columbia Street W between the Trans-Canada Highway and downtown, including the **Sagebrush Motel** (660 Columbia St. W, 250/372-3151, $55 s, $60 d), which has a pool and restaurant. On the western approach to the city are many newer accommodations aimed at the passing highway traveler. These offer clean and comfortable no-frills accommodations but no particular bargains. Among them, **Alpine Motel** (1393 Hugh Allan Dr., 250/374-0034 or 800/270-1260) offers standard rooms from $78, or suites with kitchen and hot tub for a few dollars more.

$100–150
Right downtown is the **Plaza Heritage Hotel** (405 Victoria St., 250/377-8075 or 877/977-5292, www.plazaheritagehotel.com), which opened in 1928 as one of the Interior's finest accommodations. A massive restoration has seen its reincarnation as a boutique hotel. The 68 rooms feature rich woods, a heritage color scheme, and comfortable beds covered in plush duvets. At street level is the Heritage Restaurant and a stylish lounge bar. Standard rooms are $139 s or d, or pay $10 extra for a king-size bed.

Campgrounds
Heading out of Kamloops to the east, 16 kilometers (10 mi.) from downtown, **Kamloops Waterslide and RV Park** (9115 TransCanada Hwy., 250/573-3789, $18–27) offers full hookups, coin-operated showers, a laundry, hot tub, grocery store, and full hookups.

The city's most scenic campground is at **Paul Lake Provincial Park,** north of Kamloops five kilometers (3.1 mi.) on Highway 5, then 17 kilometers (10.6 mi.) east on Paul Lake Road. The quiet lakeside setting makes up for a lack of facilities (no hookups or showers). All sites are $14.

FOOD
Sitting on one of downtown's busiest streets is the **Bagel Street Café** (428 Victoria St., 250/372-9322). Bagels and other pastries and hearty soups can be enjoyed either inside in a welcoming environment or at sidewalk tables. Another good lunch spot is **Smorgasbord** (225 7th Ave., 250/377-0055, Mon.–Sat. 7 A.M.–5 P.M.), which is not a smorgasbord as the British know it, but a small café offering a wide range of soups, salads, and sandwiches, with a daily special offering the best value.

Beyond the *Wanda Sue* dock is **Storms** (1502 River St., 250/372-1522, daily for lunch and dinner), one of Kamloops' best restaurants. The elegant setting includes tables set on an outdoor deck overlooking the river. The menu features classic European and North American dishes, such as a succulent rack of lamb roasted in Dijon mustard and fresh rosemary for $23. Other entrées start at $14, or just soak up the river atmosphere with a platter of appetizers for $19.

INFORMATION
Kamloops Visitor Info Centre (at Hillside Rd. opposite Aberdeen Mall, 250/374-3377 or 800/662-1994, mid-June–mid-Sept. daily 8 A.M.–8 P.M., rest of year Mon.–Fri. 8:30 A.M.–4 P.M.) is beside the TransCanada Highway on the western outskirts of town. The local tourism association's website is www.adventurekamloops.com.

TRANSPORTATION
Kamloops Airport is on Airport Road, seven kilometers (4.3 mi.) northwest of city center; follow Tranquille Road through the North Shore until you come to Airport Road on the left. **Air Canada** offers scheduled flights between Kamloops and Vancouver. The railway station is right downtown at the north end of 3rd Avenue. **VIA Rail** (800/561-8630) runs scheduled service three times weekly west to Vancouver and east to Jasper. **Greyhound** provides daily service to most parts of the province from its Kamloops depot (725 Notre Dame Dr., off Columbia St. W, 250/374-1212).

Local bus transportation is provided by **Kamloops Transit System** (250/376-1216); adult fare is $2 per sector. Taxi companies include **Kami Cabs** (250/554-1377) and **Yellow Cabs** (250/374-3333).

Kamloops to Jasper

From Kamloops, Highway 5 follows the North Thompson River to Tete Jaune Cache on Highway 16. This stretch of highway is part of the most direct route between Vancouver and Jasper National Park, and is also worthwhile for two excellent provincial parks—Wells Gray, a vast wilderness of rivers and mountains, and Mount Robson, protecting a spectacular peak that is the highest point in the Canadian Rockies.

Clearwater

The small town of Clearwater (pop. 1,600), 125 kilometers (78 mi.) north of Kamloops, is the gateway to Wells Gray Provincial Park. A few motels, restaurants, gas stations, services, and an information center (250/674-2646, July–Aug. daily 8 A.M.–6 P.M., Sept.–May Mon.–Fri. 9 A.M.–5 P.M.) can be found roadside; the rest of the community is off the highway to the south.

Camping is most pleasant within the nearby provincial park. **Dutch Lake Resort** (361 Ridge Rd., 250/674-3351 or 888/884-4424, www.dutch lake.com, May–Oct.) also offers sites (tents $22, hookups $30), as well as a selection of lakeside cabin accommodations. The original log cabins have a kitchen a separate sleeping room ($79 s or d), or choose one of the modern cabins (up to $129) with private decks. The resort has good fishing and a restaurant.

WELLS GRAY PROVINCIAL PARK

Wells Gray Provincial Park is a must-see detour on the route between Kamloops and Jasper. Snow-clad peaks, and ancient lava flows, thundering waterfalls, bubbling mineral springs, flower-filled meadows, and fishing for rainbow trout and Dolly Varden are park highlights.

Sights and Hikes

The main access road into the 540,000-hectare (1.7 million-acre) park leads north from Clearwater for 36 kilometers (22 mi.) to the park

boundary. Just beyond this point, a short hiking trail leads to a colorful lava canyon where **Spahats Creek Falls** plummets over multicolored bedrock into a churning pool of water. Continuing through the park, take a signposted gravel road to the west to **Green Viewing Tower** atop Green Mountain. The viewpoint provides panoramic views of a volcanic cone and many spectacular, rugged peaks. Next up is **Dawson Falls,** four kilometers (2.5 mi.) into the park, where the Murtle River cascades over a 90-meter-wide (300 ft.) ledge. A little farther along the main road is the **Mush Bowl,** where the river has carved huge holes in the riverbed. But save some film for incredible **Helmcken Falls,** where the Murtle River cascades off a plateau in a sparkling, 137-meter-high (450 ft.) torrent to join the Clearwater River. In winter, the frozen falls create an enormous ice cone as tall as a 20-story building.

Continuing north, at road's end you'll soon come to Clearwater Lake, one of the park's six major lakes. In summer, **Clearwater Lake Tours** (250/674-2121) runs a four-hour motorboat cruise from Clearwater Lake Campground to the north end of the lake, where you'll have views of adjacent Azure Lake. Tours depart at 10 A.M. (adult $45, senior $36, child $28). The company also rents canoes ($35 a day or $160 a week) and provides wilderness drop-offs.

Accommodations and Camping

Between Clearwater and the park boundary, **Wells Gray Guest Ranch** (250/674-2792, www.wells grayranch.com, May–Oct.) is surrounded by grassy meadows full of wildflowers and grazing horses. Activities organized for guests include horseback riding, canoeing, white-water rafting, and fishing. Well-furnished, kitchen-equipped cabins rent for $125 per night, or you can camp for $14. The ranch also has a restaurant and saloon.

Each of the three campgrounds ($14) inside the park has drinking water, toilets, and picnic tables. Heading up the road from the village of

Elk are commonly spotted along the road between Kamloops and Jasper.

Clearwater, you'll pass, in order, **Dawson Falls Campground, Falls Creek Campground** (with spacious riverside sites), and finally **Clearwater Lake Campground,** which is almost at the end of the road, right on the lake, and is the first to fill each night.

CONTINUING TOWARD MOUNT ROBSON

Blue River

Home to one of the world's premier heli-ski operations, tiny Blue River lies right on busy Highway 5, 215 kilometers (134 mi.) north of Kamloops.

Mike Wiegele Resort (250/673-8381 or 800/661-9170, www.wiegele.com), at the north end of town, offers heli-skiing in the surrounding Monashee and Cariboo Mountains. The resort is a world leader in the sport and annual host of the Powder 8 World Championships. Check the website for all winter packages and rates (from $3,200 for three days). During summer, the resort is a base for heli-hiking, glacier-based heli-skiing, heli-fishing, heli-biking, and boring old flightseeing. Other summer activities centered

at the lodge include mountain biking, fishing, and tennis. In the height of summer, luxurious motel-style rooms are a steal at $110 s or d, while freestanding, self-contained lakeside chalets are $200–300. The main lodge holds the Powder Max Dining Room as well as a health club. **Glacier Mountain Lodge** (250/673-2393, www.glaciermountainlodge.com) is another stylish Blue River accommodation, this one offering 33 well-appointed guest rooms. Rates of $89–130 s, or d make this place a good value also. Outside of summer, rates start at $65 s or d.

Valemount and Vicinity

North of Blue River, Highway 5 follows the North Thompson River through the Cariboo Mountains to Valemount, 30 kilometers (18.6 mi.) south of the Yellowhead Highway.

From the Yellowhead Highway junction north of Valemount, Prince George is 270 kilometers (168 mi.) to the west, and the British Columbia–Alberta border is 77 kilometers (48 mi.) east. Eastbound, a worthwhile stop before reaching Mount Robson Provincial Park is **Rearguard Falls,** reached via a one-kilometer (0.6-mi.) hike (20 minutes each way) from the highway.

BERG LAKE TRAIL

This is the most popular overnight hike in the Canadian Rockies, but don't let the crowds put you off—the hike is well worth it. Beautiful aqua-colored **Berg Lake** lies below the north face of Mount Robson, which rises 2,400 meters (7,880 ft.) directly behind the lake. Glaciers on the mountain's shoulder regularly calve off into the lake, resulting in the icebergs that give the lake its name.

The trail itself is spectacular, following a fast-flowing river for much of the way, then passing through the steep-sided Valley of a Thousand Falls. The first glimpses of Mount Robson come soon after reaching the head of this valley. Although the panorama at Berg Lake is stunning, most hikers who have come this far will want to spend some time exploring the area, climbing farther to Toboggan Falls or the head of Robson Glacier.

The return journey to Berg Lake requires at least one night in the backcountry. Book early, as the limited number of campsites fills quickly. If the uphill walk in seems too ambitious, contact **Robson Helimagic** (250/566-4700 or 877/454-4700, www.robsonhelimagic.com), which makes helicopter drop-offs at Robson Pass from Valemount every Monday and Friday; $175 per person (minimum four).

- **Trailhead**: two kilometers (1.2 mi.) north of Mount Robson Visitor Centre
- **Length**: 19.5 kilometers (12 mi.); eight hours one-way
- **Elevation gain**: 725 meters (2,380 ft.)
- **Trail reservations**: 604/689-9025 or 800/689-9025

MOUNT ROBSON PROVINCIAL PARK

Spectacular 224,866-hectare (555,650-acre) Mount Robson Provincial Park was created in 1913 to protect a vast wilderness of steep canyons and wide forested valleys; icy lakes, rivers, and streams; and rugged mountain peaks permanently blanketed in snow and ice. The park lies along the Continental Divide, adjacent to Jasper National Park (Alberta), and home to magnificent 3,954-meter (12,970-ft.) **Mount Robson,** the highest peak in the Canadian Rockies.

Highway 16 splits the park in two, and many sights of interest are visible from the highway. But you'll have to leave the car behind to experience one of the park's biggest draws: The famous Berg Lake Trail is strictly for hikers.

Cariboo Country

The wild, sparsely populated Cariboo region extends from Kamloops north to Prince George and west to the Pacific Ocean. Its most dramatic natural features are the mountain ranges rising like bookends to either side. In the west, the **Coast Mountains** run parallel to the coast and rise to a height of 4,016 meters (13,175 ft.) at **Mount Waddington.** In the east, the **Cariboo Mountains** harbor numerous alpine lakes, high peaks, and several provincial parks. Between the two ranges flows the Fraser River, which is flanked to the west by expansive plateaus home to British Columbia's biggest ranches. This was once gold-

rush country—most of the region's towns began as stopping places along the Gold Rush Trail.

CACHE CREEK

A town born with the fur trade at a spot where traders cached furs and food supplies, Cache Creek was once the largest town between Vancouver, 337 kilometers (209 mi.) to the south, and Kamloops, 80 kilometers (50 mi.) to the east. But since the new Coquihalla Highway opened, bypassing the town, Cache Creek has become but a shadow of its former self. The surrounding desertlike climate is intriguing; sagebrush and cacti grow on the relatively barren volcanic landscape, and tumbleweeds blow through town. Due to the town's former highway prominence, the main drag is lined with motels, roadside diners, and gas stations.

Historic Hat Creek Ranch

Between 1885 and 1905, the Cariboo Wagon Road bustled with stagecoaches and freight wagons. One of the few sections of the original road still open to the public is at Hat Creek Ranch (250/457-9722, mid-May–mid-Oct. daily 10 A.M.–6 P.M.), 11 kilometers (6.8 mi.) north of Cache Creek on Highway 97. Many of the original buildings—some dating as far back as 1861—still stand, and visitors can watch the blacksmith at his forge, appreciate a collection of antique farm machinery, enjoy a picnic lunch in the orchard, or take a guided tour of the ranch house. Admission to the ranch is free, but a donation is requested after touring the house.

LILLOOET

This historic town of 2,100 was founded as Mile 0 of the 1858 Cariboo Wagon Road—also known as the Gold Rush Trail—which led north to the Barkerville and Wells goldfields. Several towns along the Gold Rush Trail—70 Mile House, 100 Mile House, and 150 Mile House, among them—were named for their distance up the wagon road from Lillooet.

With thousands of prospectors passing through in the mid-1800s, Lillooet was the scene of its own gold rush. By this time the city held some 16,000 residents, making it the second-largest population center north of San Francisco and west of Chicago. But as in all other boomtowns, the population explosion was short-lived. Once all the most productive local goldfields were worked dry, the prospectors moved on.

A row of rusty farming relics out front marks **Lillooet Museum** (Main St. at 8th Ave., 250/256-4308, May–mid-Oct. daily 11 A.M.–4 P.M.). Inside are ore samples and details about the one-time boomtown's mining history and growth. Then saunter along wide Main Street and pretend you're

back in the gold-rush era—which won't be hard if you happen to be here in June during **Only in Lillooet Days.** During this weeklong celebration, the town re-creates the Old West with all sorts of entertaining events.

Practicalities

One block up the hill from the museum, **4 Pines Motel** (108 8th Ave., 250/256-4247 or 800/753-2576, www.4pinesmotel.com) charges a very reasonable $52 s, $64 d for modern rooms, some with cooking facilities. **Cayoosh Creek Campground** ($12–18) is a barren spot near the south end of town, where Cayoosh Creek drains into the much larger Fraser River. Facilities include hot showers and hookups.

CLINTON TO 100 MILE HOUSE
Clinton

Originally called 47 Mile House, the old-fashioned town of Clinton lies 40 kilometers (25 mi.) north of Cache Creek on Highway 97. **South Cariboo Historical Museum** (Highway 97, 250/459-2442, summer Mon.–Fri. 10 A.M.–6 P.M.) occupies an old brick schoolhouse and contains pioneer belongings, guns, historical photos, native and Chinese artifacts, freight wagons, and all sorts of items from the gold-rush days. A nearby natural attraction worth seeing is **Painted Chasm,** in **Chasm Provincial Park,** eight kilometers (five mi.) north of town. Glacial meltwater has carved a deep box canyon out of mineral-laden volcanic bedrock. It's quite a spectacle when the sunlight brings out the color and sparkle of the minerals.

The huge log structure on the main street is **Cariboo Lodge Resort** (250/459-7992 or 877/459-7992, www.cariboolodgebc.com). The restaurant here provides hearty cooking (dinner entrées $12–17), while the adjacent pub has western-style decor. The motel rooms ($80s or d) are clean and comfortable, but not as interesting as the exterior of the building may suggest.

Echo Valley Ranch & Spa

Deep in the heart of Cariboo Country, Echo Valley Ranch & Spa (250/459-2386 or 800/

© ANDREW HEMPSTEAD

honeymoon cabin, Echo Valley Ranch & Spa

253-8831, www.evranch.com) provides the opportunity to immerse yourself in western culture while indulging in the luxury of an upscale lodge. The emphasis is on horseback riding, with lessons and guided rides scheduled each day, but there are plenty of other things to do, such as four-wheel-driving, watching a falcon trainer at work, and learning about native culture. The centerpiece of the sprawling property is an impressive main lodge, built entirely of glistening spruce logs. Inside is a comfortable lounge area, the communal dining room overlooking an open kitchen, and a downstairs billiards and TV room. Adjacent is an impressive Baan Thai structure, with full spa services, and the Pavilion, for quiet contemplation. Rooms in the main lodge are beautifully furnished, and each has a private balcony, while the honeymoon cabin sits high above a deep ravine and has a wraparound deck complete with hot tub. Dining is ranch style, at a couple of long tables with plenty of interaction between guests, but the food is anything but chili and beans: It's prepared by a one-time chef to European royalty. As you'd expect, staying at Echo Valley isn't cheap (from $300 pp per night), but it is one of the most special places I have ever visited.

North to 100 Mile House

North of Clinton, a gravel road leads west off the highway into the ranch country of the Fraser Plateau. Up this road about 40 kilometers (25 mi.) is **Big Bar Lake** which offers fishing for rainbow trout and camping ($14) in a provincial park. Also in the vicinity is the enormous **Gang Ranch.** Started in the 1860s, the ranch was at one time North America's largest and today spreads over 400,000 hectares (1,000,000 acres).

Back on the main highway, between 70 Mile House and 100 Mile House are several turnoffs leading to hundreds of lakes, big and small. All information centers in Cariboo Country stock the invaluable *Cariboo-Chilcotin Fishing Guide* with essential fishing information (where, when, and with what) for many of the local lakes, plus maps, camping spots, and even recipes for the ones that didn't get away.

Passing through 100 Mile House, it's difficult to miss the **South Cariboo Visitor Info Centre** (250/395-5353 or 877/511-5353, Mon.–Fri. 8:30 A.M.–4:30 P.M.). Look for the world's largest cross-country skis out front. A small wetland lies directly behind the information center, with signage depicting the many species that are often present. At the north end of town, one of the original Cariboo stagecoaches is on display.

WILLIAMS LAKE

The largest city in the Cariboo region is Williams Lake (pop. 11,500), an important ranching and forestry center 95 kilometers (59 mi.) north of 100 Mile House.

Sights and Recreation

The highlight of the large **Museum of the Cariboo Chilcotin** (113 4th Ave. N, 250/392-7404, summer Mon.–Sat. 10 A.M.–4 P.M., the rest of the year Tues.–Sat. 11 A.M.–4 P.M., $3) is the **BC Cowboy Hall of Fame** and associated rodeo, ranching, and Stampede displays. Other exhibits include historical photos, remains of the Chinese settlement at Quesnel Forks, and all kinds of picks, pans, and axes from the gold-mining days.

One of many stores in town selling the painting, pottery, weaving, photography, and jewelry of ocal artisans is **Station House Gallery** (1 Mackenzie Ave. N, 250/392-6113). On the eastern outskirts of the city, **Scout Island Nature Centre** (250/398-8532, June–mid-Sept. Mon.–Fri. 9 A.M.–4 P.M., Sun. 1–4 P.M.) is surrounded by wetlands that serve as a staging area for migratory waterfowl. Colorful displays inside the center catalog the surrounding ecosystem, but the idea is to get out into the wetlands. Wander along one of the short hiking trails or climb the observation tower for a bird's-eye view of the wild landscape.

The region's diverse waterways provide plenty of opportunities for taking to the water. Numerous gently flowing streams and serene lakes make perfect spots for canoe and kayak discovery trips, while the Fraser River provides opportunities for exciting rafting trips. **Chilko River Expeditions** (395 North 1st Ave., 250/398-6711 or 800/967-7238, www.chilkoriver.com) offers a full-day trip in rafts and inflatable kayaks for $110 per person, as well as overnight trips. Fishing in local waters is rewarding, yielding a variety of trout, steelhead, Dolly Varden, and kokanee (although the fishing in Williams Lake itself is poor).

Williams Lake Stampede

On the first weekend of July, the town comes alive as the best cowboys in the land compete in the Williams Lake Stampede (250/392-6585, www.williamslakestampede.com), one of Canada's largest rodeos. The highlight of each day's action is the rodeo, when cowboys compete for big bucks in bareback riding, saddle-bronc riding, calf-roping, steer-wrestling, chuckwagon racing, and the crowd favorite, bull riding. Scheduled around these traditional rodeo events are cow-milking contests, barrel racing, tractor pulls, cattle penning, chariot races, raft races, a parade, barn dances, all-you-can-eat breakfasts and steak-outs, and a host of other decidedly western-flavored activities.

Stampede headquarters is below the main grandstand. This is where you can purchase tickets and Stampede memorabilia; many of the event posters have become collectors' items.

Accommodations and Camping

The least expensive motels are along Highway 97 on the city's northeastern and western outskirts. Off the highway at the north end of town is **Jamboree Motel** (845 Carson Dr., 250/398-8208, $55 s, $60 d).

If a ranching vacation is more your style, consider **Springhouse Trails Ranch** (20 km/12 mi. southwest of town on Dog Lake Rd., 250/392-4780, www.springhousetrails.com). The basic but comfortable rooms are $62 s, $74 d, and all-inclusive package deals are available from $130 per person per day, including accommodations, meals, and riding. You can also camp here for $24 a night, with hookups.

The best campground in the area is **Wildwood Campsite** (13 km/eight mi. north of city center, 250/989-4711, $16–22). Facilities include full hookups, washrooms and showers, a laundry, and a general store.

Food

Williams Lake lacks outstanding eateries but has no shortage of typical family-style restaurants. One of these is the **Great Cariboo Steak Company** (Fraser Inn, 285 Donald Rd., 250/398-7055, Mon.–Fri. from 6 A.M., Sat. from 7 A.M., Sun. from 8 A.M.). Breakfast ranges $5–10; all-you-can-eat lunch buffets are $10; sandwiches, croissants, and burgers run $6.50–9; and dinner prices range from $8.50 for the all-you-can-eat salad bar to $14–21 for steak, prime rib, chicken, seafood, and pasta dishes. On the northern edge of town, the **Laughing Loon Neighbourhood Pub** (1730 S. Broadway, 250/398-5666) offers a wide-ranging menu of beef, chicken, and pork dishes in a welcoming atmosphere.

Information

As you enter town from the south, make your first stop the **Williams Lake Visitor Info Centre** (1148 Broadway, 250/392-5025, June–Aug. daily 8 A.M.–6 P.M., rest of year Mon.–Fri. 9 A.M.–5 P.M.).

HIGHWAY 20

Highway 20 west of Williams Lake leads 485 kilometers (301 mi.) to Bella Coola, the only road-accessible town along the 500 kilometers (311 mi.) of coastline between Powell River and Prince Rupert. The highway is paved less than half its length;

the rest of the way it's mostly all-weather gravel and can be slow going in spots. But experiencing the vast and varied wilderness of the Chilcotin Coast is worthy of as much time as you can afford. Once at the end of the road, you can jump aboard a BC Ferries service to Port Hardy (Vancouver Island), or of course return to Williams Lake.

West from Williams Lake

The first worthwhile detour along Highway 20 is **Junction Sheep Range Provincial Park,** which lies at the end of a 20-kilometer (12-mi.) un-paved road that branches south off Highway 20 at Riske Creek, 47 kilometers (29 mi.) west of Williams Lake. The triangular park protects 4,573 hectares (11,300 acres) of mostly semi-arid grasslands between the Fraser and Chilcotin Rivers. The confluence of these two major rivers forms the southern tip of the park and can be reached on foot in well under one hour from the end of the access road. The park is also home to around 600 bighorn sheep.

Back on Highway 20, the first community with services is **Alexis Creek,** 114 kilometers (71 mi.) west of Williams Lake. Beside the Chilcotin River, 10 kilometers (6.2 mi.) west of Alexis Creek, is **Bull Canyon Provincial Park,** with campsites for $14 a night. Continuing west, the highway follows the Chilcotin River for 60 kilometers (37 mi.) to Chilanko Forks; here a spur road leads 10 kilometers (6.2 mi.) north to **Puntzi Lake.** At this picturesque body of water are a number of low-key fishing resorts, including **Poplar Grove Resort** (250/481-1186 or 800/578-6804, www .poplargroveresort.com), which features small lakeside cabins, each with basic cooking facilities and shared washrooms ($48–62), guest rooms in a main lodge ($65–90), or you can camp for $18 per night. The lodge rents motor boats ($42 per day), perfect for chasing the lake's large population of kokanee.

Chilko Lake

The road narrows and turns to gravel, passing the small community of **Tatla Lake,** and con-tinues westward, climbing steadily to **Nimpo Lake,** where **Stewart's Lodge** (250/742-3388 or 800/668-4335, www.stewartslodge.com) offers

cabins of varying standards ($65–165 s or d), as well as "outpost" cabins at remote lakes through-out the Chilcotin region.

From this point, it's 40 kilometers (25 mi.) to 1,524-meter (5,000-ft.) **Heckman Pass** over the Coast Mountains. Continuing west across the pass, you face with "The Hill." This infa-mous descent from Heckman Pass to the Bella Coola Valley drops nearly to sea level in less than 10 kilometers (6.2 mi.).

BELLA COOLA

The urge to see what's at the end of the road brings many travelers over The Hill and down to Bella Coola (pop. 800). Here the Bella Coola River drains into North Bentinck Arm, a gateway to the Inside Passage and the Pacific Ocean. On July 22, 1793, Alexander Mackenzie reached the coast here, becoming the first cross continental North America, earning him a place in history as one of the world's greatest explorers.

Sights and Recreation

Bella Coola Museum (250/799-5767, June–mid-Sept. Mon.–Sat. 10 A.M.–5 P.M., $2), housed in a schoolhouse and surveyor's cabin, concentrates on the story of early settlers, a group of Norwegians who were reminded of their homeland by the sur-rounding fjord and snowcapped peaks. They set-tled 15 kilometers (9.3 mi.) inland at a spot on the river they named Hagensborg. Today, many hand-hewn timber buildings still standing are testament to the construction skills of these early settlers.

Bella Coola has plenty of outdoor recreation to keep visitors busy. Unfortunately, most of the action is out on the water and requires the services of a boat charter company (not cheap). Fishing is the most popular activity; expect to pay from $75 per hour for four persons. Those with a sense of history will want to visit Mackenzie Rock, in the Dean Channel, where Alexander Mackenzie, in his own words, "mixed up some vermillion and melted grease and inscribed in large characters on the face of the rock on which we slept last night, this brief memorial: Alexander Mackenzie, from Canada, by Land, the Twenty Second of July, One Thousand Seven Hundred and Ninety Three." For charter information, call **Bella Coola Outfitting** (250/799-0066).

Practicalities

Right on the river is **Bella Coola Motel** (Clayton St., 250/799-5323, $85 s, $90 d), whose clean and comfortable rooms each have a full kitchen. In Hagensborg, **Bay Motor Hotel** (250/982-2212 or 888/982-2212, $70 s, $75 d) has a restaurant and bar. Bella Coola's only campground is in Hagensborg: **Gnome's Home Campground and RV Park** (250/982-2504) has unserviced sites for $14 and serviced sites for $18–23.

Discovery Coast Passage

Between early June and early September, **BC Ferries** (250/386-3431 or 888/223-3779, www .bcferries.com) operates the *Queen of Chilliwack* twice weekly between Bella Coola and Port Hardy, on Vancouver Island. The trip takes 22 hours, with stops made at a number of remote coastal communities. One-way fares are adult $110, child 5–11 $55, vehicle $220.

QUESNEL

Back inland, Highway 97 north from Williams Lake takes you to Quesnel. The town (pop. 8,500) began during the Barkerville gold rush of the 1860s. Prospectors traveling north on the Fraser River disembarked at the confluence of the Fraser and Quesnel Rivers, and a town sprang up on the site.

Sights

At **Heritage Corner** (Carson Ave. and Front St.) you can see the Old Fraser Bridge, the remains of the steamer *Enterprise,* a Cornish waterwheel used by gold miners, and the original Hudson's Bay Store. To learn all about Alexander Mackenzie or the gold-rush days, head to **Quesnel and District Museum** (Highway 97 at Carson Ave., 250/992-9580, June–mid-Sept. daily 8 A.M.–4:30 P.M., $4).

Eight kilometers (five mi.) west of Quesnel on Baker Drive are the geologically intriguing, glacially eroded hoodoos at the small, day-use **Pinnacles Provincial Park.**

Billy Barker Days

The main event in Quesnel is the **Billy Barker Days** celebration (250/992-1234), named for the prospector who made the first gold strike in the Cariboo. Over the third weekend of July, downtown streets are closed to traffic in favor of an outdoor crafts fair, parade, and dancing. Residents casually stroll around town in period costumes from the gold-mining days—men in cowboy hats, women in slinky long dresses with brightly feathered hats. The Quesnel Rodeo is one of some 150 events staged during the festival.

Accommodations and Camping

Right downtown is the **Cariboo Hotel** (254 Front St., 250/992-2333 or 800/665-3200). Built in 1896, this historic inn has been restored with modern furnishings; rates of $60 s, $65 d include a continental breakfast. North of downtown is the **Talisman Inn** (753 Front St., 250/992-7247 or 800/663-8090, www.talismaninn.bc.ca). Most of the 86 rooms are of a standard quality for the price ($70 s, $80 d), although the larger rooms, with more modern furnishings, seriously spacious bathrooms, a microwave, a toaster, and high-speed Internet access are the best value ($90 s, $100 d). A light breakfast is included in all rates.

For campers, the best bet is to head north 11 kilometers (6.8 mi.) to **Ten Mile Lake Provincial Park,** where sites are $17 a night.

Food

For a full meal or just a coffee and cake, head to the **Heritage House Restaurant** (102 Carson Ave., 250/992-2700), in a historic log building that dates from 1867, when it was used as a Hudson's Bay Company trading post. Prices are right, and everything served is fresh and healthy. A popular coffeehouse is **Granville's** (383 Reid St.), open daily from 8 A.M.

Information

Quesnel Visitor Info Centre is beside Lebourdais Park (705 Carson Ave., 250/992-8716 or 800/992-4922, www.city.quesnel.bc.ca) and is open in summer daily 8 A.M.–8 P.M. and the rest of the year Monday–Friday 8:30 A.M.–4:30 P.M.

EAST FROM QUESNEL

Cottonwood House

About 28 kilometers (17 mi.) east of Quesnel on Highway 26, Cottonwood House (250/992-3997, early June–mid-Sept. daily 8 A.M.–8 P.M.) is a roadhouse built in 1864. In addition to the old guesthouse, structures at the site include a barn, stable, and other outbuildings. You'll also find an interpretive center and displays of old farming equipment. In summer, carriage rides are a main attraction.

Wells

A few kilometers before reaching Barkerville Historic Town, Highway 26 passes the village of Wells, which offers accommodations, a restaurant, a pub, and a general store. Life in the village revolves around the historic 1933 **Wells Hotel** (2341 Pooley St., 250/994-3427 or 800/860-2299, www.wellshotel.com, $70–130 s or d) and there's nowhere better to relax than around the log fire in the hotel's comfy sitting room. Guest rooms are in the original hotel or in a new wing, but all are warmly furnished. Some share bathrooms but rates include a hearty continental breakfast.

Barkerville

In 1862 Billy Barker struck gold on Williams Creek, in the north of Cariboo Country, 88 kilometers (55 mi.) east of Quesnel. One of Canada's major gold rushes followed, as thousands of prospectors streamed into what soon became known as Barkerville. The area turned out to be the richest of the Cariboo mining districts, yielding over $40 million in gold. By the mid-1860s Barkerville's population had peaked at over 10,000. But fortunes began to fade after the beginning of the 20th century. The town was rebuilt after a 1916 fire, but the gold played out soon thereafter, and many of the miners lost interest and moved on.

Today **Barkerville Historic Town** (250/994-3332, year-round daily 8 A.M.–8 P.M., adult $9, senior $8, child $2.50) holds over 120 authentically restored buildings. Historic reenactments take place throughout summer, when the town's shops, stores, and restaurants all operate in a century-old time warp. Highlights include the town bakery, which sells some of the most mouthwatering baked goods in the province; the stagecoach rides, a big hit with the kids; and the musical comedy performances at the

Coyotes are common throughout Cariboo Country.

© ANDREW HEMPSTEAD

Theatre Royal, presented two to three times daily (adults $10).

Bowron Lake Provincial Park

Best known for its wilderness canoe circuit, Bowron Lake Provincial Park encompasses 121,600 magnificent hectares (300,500 acres) of forests, lakes, and rivers in the Cariboo Mountains. To get there, take Highway 26 east of Quesnel toward Barkerville, but just past Wells take a signposted gravel road to the north.

The park boundary follows a chain of six major lakes—**Indianpoint, Isaac, Lanezi, Sandy, Spectacle,** and **Bowron**—and some smaller lakes and waterways that form a roughly diamond-shaped circuit. Campsites, cabins, and cooking shelters are strategically spaced along the way. To circumnavigate the entire 116-kilometer (72-mi.) route takes 7–10 days of paddling and requires seven portages. Before setting out on the circuit, paddlers must obtain a permit from the BC Parks Registration Centre (May 15–Sept. 30 daily 7 A.M.–8 P.M.) at the end of the park access road. Permits cost $150 per canoe. A limited number of persons are permitted on the circuit at any given time. Reserve a spot by calling 250/387-1642 or 800/435-5622 as far in advance as possible.

Northern British Columbia

Wild, remote northern British Columbia extends from the Yellowhead Highway (Hwy. 16) north to the 60th parallel. Its mostly forested landscape is broken by two major mountain ranges—the Rockies and the Coast Mountains—and literally thousands of lakes, rivers, and streams. Wildlife is abundant here; the land is home to moose, deer, black and grizzly bears, elk, Dall's sheep, and mountain goats. The region's largest city is Prince George, from where the Yellowhead Highway runs west all the way to the Pacific Ocean at Prince Rupert, a busy coastal city at the north end of the BC Ferries network and a stop on the Alaska Marine Highway. Off the coast from

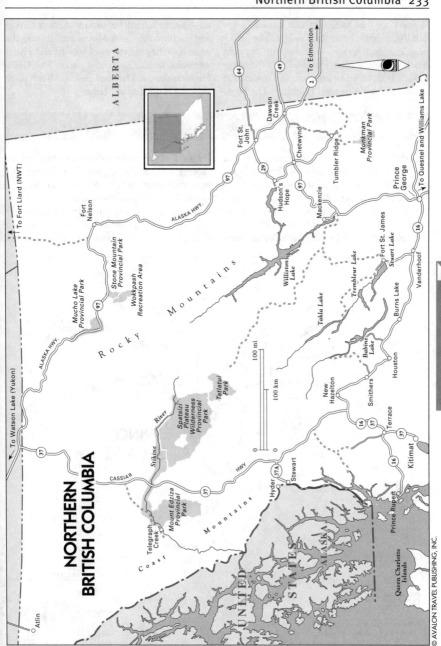

NORTHERN BRITISH COLUMBIA

ALBERTA

To Edmonton

To Quesnel and Williams Lake

Fort St. John

Dawson Creek

Chetwynd

Tumbler Ridge

Monkman Provincial Park

Prince George

Hudson's Hope

Mackenzie

Fort Nelson

ALASKA HWY.

To Fort Liard (NWT)

Stone Mountain Provincial Park

Wokkpash Recreation Area

Muncho Lake Provincial Park

ALASKA HWY.

To Watson Lake (Yukon)

Rocky   Mountains

Williston Lake

Fort St. James

Stuart Lake

Vanderhoof

16

Takla Lake

Trembleur Lake

Babine Lake

Burns Lake

Houston

Smithers

Stikine River

Spatsizi Plateau Wilderness Provincial Park

Tatlatui Park

100 mi

100 km

New Hazelton

16

37

Terrace

37

Kitimat

16

CASSIAR   HWY.

37

Mount Edziza Provincial Park

Telegraph Creek

Coast   Mountains

Hyder

Stewart

37A

Prince Rupert

UNITED   STATES

ALASKA

Queen Charlotte Islands

Atlin

BRITISH COLUMBIA

© AVALON TRAVEL PUBLISHING, INC.

"Rupert" are the Queen Charlotte Islands, part of British Columbia yet entirely unique. The islands beckon adventure, with legendary fishing, great beachcombing, ancient Haida villages, and a typical laid-back island atmosphere. Two routes head north off the Yellowhead Highway. The Stew-art–Cassiar Highway begins west of Prince George and parallels the Coast Mountains, passing the turnoff to the twin towns of Stewart and Hyder and some remote provincial parks. The Alaska Highway starts in Dawson Creek and heads up to the great northland of Alaska.

Prince George

British Columbia's seventh-largest city, Prince George (pop. 78,000) lies roughly at the geographical center of the province, at the confluence of the historically important Fraser and Nechako Rivers, where Simon Fraser constructed a post in 1807. The railroad reached the area in 1908, and in 1915 the Grand Trunk Pacific Railway plotted the townsite of Prince George south of the original Fort George. The new town went on to become a major logging, sawmill, and pulp-mill town, the center of the white spruce industry in British Columbia's central interior. Hundreds of sawmills started cutting local timber, and Prince George be-

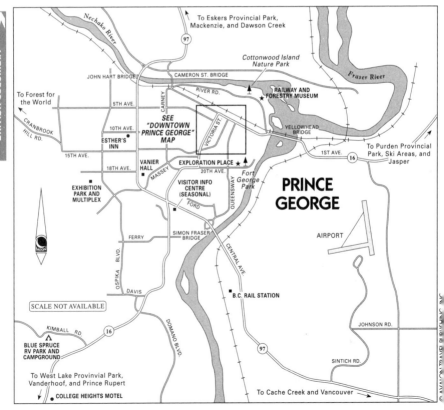

came the self-proclaimed "Spruce Capital of the World." The city has continued from strength to strength, and has grown to become northern British Columbia's economic, social, and cultural center.

SIGHTS

The best place to start a Prince George sightseeing trip is the top of **Connaught Hill,** which affords a panoramic view of the city. To get there from downtown, take Queensway Street south, turn right on Connaught Drive, then right again on Caine Drive. At the summit are grassy tree-shaded lawns, picnic spots, and several well-kept gardens bursting with color in summer.

Downtown

The site where Simon Fraser established Fort George, at the east end of 20th Avenue, is today preserved as **Fort George Park.** Trails lead through the park along the Fraser River and to the Indian Burial Grounds. Also in the park is the **Exploration Place** (250/562-1612, July–Aug. daily 10 A.M.–5 P.M., Sept.–May Wed.–Sun. 10 A.M.–5 P.M., adult $9, senior $7, child $5), which combines kid-friendly attractions with History Hall, an excellent place to discover the human history of Prince George dating back to the indigenous Carrier tribe. Among the items on display are two towering grizzly bears in the foyer. In front of the museum is the original Fort George Railway Station

DOWNTOWN PRINCE GEORGE

BRITISH COLUMBIA

NATIVE FRIENDSHIP GALLERY
VIA RAIL STATION
3RD AVE.
4TH AVE.
5TH AVE.
6TH AVE.
7TH AVE.
8TH AVE.
9TH AVE.
10TH AVE.
11TH AVE.
1ST AVE.
2ND AVE.
BRUNSWICK ST.
QUEBEC ST.
DOMINION ST.
GEORGE ST.
SCOTIA
WINNIPEG ST.
VANCOUVER ST.
VICTORIA ST.
POST OFFICE
WADDLING DUCK
RAMADA HOTEL
MOSQUITO BOOKS
COAST INN OF THE NORTH
CITY HALL
RCMP
CIVIC PLAZA
COLISEUM
LIBRARY
BUS DEPOT
PATRICIA BLVD.
HOSPITAL
VISITOR INFO CENTRE
15TH AVE.
16
CONNAUGHT DR.
Connaught Hill
QUEENSWAY ST.
SCALE NOT AVAILABLE

© AVALON TRAVEL PUBLISHING, INC.

and an old schoolhouse (peek in through the window at row after row of old-fashioned desks).

The architecturally stunning **Two Rivers Gallery** (725 Civic Plaza, 250/614-7800, Tues.–Sat. 10 A.M.–5 P.M., Sun. noon–5 P.M., adult $5, senior $4, child $2) is a cultural icon in Northern British Columbia. The large permanent collection is the main draw, but temporary shows that change every four to five weeks are included in the admission fee. It's also a good place to buy high-quality local artwork at a reasonable price. Look for paintings, sculpture, pottery, beadwork, woven and painted silk items, and jewelry.

Around Town

Prince George Railway and Forestry Museum (River Rd., 250/563-7351, mid-June–Aug. daily 9 A.M.–5 P.M., Sept. Wed.–Sun. 10 A.M.–4 P.M., adult $6, senior $5, child $3) catalogs Prince George's industrial history. Take a self-guided tour through some of the antiquated railway cars and buildings, clamber on retired railway equipment, and chug back in time via the black-and-white photo displays and assorted memorabilia. Continue beyond the museum to **Cottonwood Island Nature Park,** one of Prince George's 16 city parks and a beautiful spot for a quiet stroll or picnic. The park lies beside the Nechako River, which overflows each spring; over time, sediment from the overflow has built up an island. The park's dominant feature is an extensive forest of northern black cottonwood trees. In spring sticky buds cover the cottonwoods, and in summer the air is thick and the ground white with seed-bearing tufts of fluff.

ACCOMMODATIONS AND CAMPING

Under $50

Prince George holds just one accommodation that falls into this price range. It's the **College Heights Motel** (five km/3.1 mi. west of downtown along Hwy. 16, 250/964-4708). It has no toll-free number, no website, not even cable TV, but for $38 s, $42 d in high season, what do you expect?

$50–100

Along the Highway 97 bypass west of downtown, **Esther's Inn** (1151 Commercial Cres., 250/562-4131 or 800/663-6844, www.esthersinn.bc.ca) is big and flashy, although the rooms are a little dated. This is reflected in the prices—a reasonable $69 s or d for a large room (the small rooms are very small) or take the King Bridal Suite for under $100. Rooms surround a lush tropical atrium packed with palms and philodendrons, waterfalls, Polynesian artifacts, swimming pools, a water slide, and a thatched-roof restaurant.

Over $100

The 193-room **Coast Inn of the North** (770 Brunswick St., 250/563-0121 or 800/663-1144, www.coasthotels.com) has a smallish fitness room, an indoor pool, a sauna, and three in-house eateries (including a Japanese restaurant). The contemporary rooms are as nice as any in Prince George and come with a coffeemaker, work desk, and high-speed Internet. Request a corner room and you'll get a balcony. Rack rates are a scary $185 s, $195 d, but you'd be crazy to pay this much; call or check the website, and you should be able to find a room for under $150, *including* breakfast.

Campgrounds

Privately operated **Blue Spruce RV Park and Campground** (Kimball Rd., five km/3.1 mi. west on Hwy. 16 from junction of Hwy. 97, 250/964-7272, Apr.–mid-Oct.) is a popular spot, filling up each night during the busy summer months. Each site has a picnic table and a barbecue grate, and the facilities include spotlessly clean heated bathrooms, a coin-operated laundry, a swimming pool, minigolf, and a playground. Unserviced sites are $17, hookups $20–24.50.

FOOD

An excellent place for lunch is **Papaya Grove** in Esther's Inn (1151 Commercial Cres., 250/562-4131). You can choose from three different seating areas: under a thatched roof, around the pool, or in the lounge. All are enclosed within a massive tropical indoor atrium. A set menu is offered, but the buffet is the most popular choice. The daily lunch buffet (11 A.M.–2 P.M.) is $12, with a different theme each day. Sunday brunch is particularly good; for $18 you get all the usual breakfast choices, along with salmon, prawns, roast beef, and a staggering number of desserts. The dinner buffet is $18 Sunday–Thursday, $21 on Friday and Saturday when prime rib is served.

With its thoughtful menu and casually elegant setting, the **Waddling Duck** (1157 5th Ave., 250/561-5550, daily 11 A.M.–11 P.M.) stands out as the restaurant of choice for a nice night out in Prince George. The setting is a big old stone and brick building, with lots of exposed beams and polished wood throughout. The food blends western Canada produce with cooking styles from around the world: You find entrées ($11–28) like broiled bison with braised asparagus and grilled halibut in a lemon-thyme demiglace mixing it up with favorites like pasta primavera. I'm not usually a fan of tiramisu, but the Waddling Duck's version ($7) was delectable.

INFORMATION AND SERVICES

Tourism Prince George (250/562-3700 or 800/668-7646, www.tourismpg.com) operates two information centers. The main one is in the VIA Rail station at 1300 1st Ave. (year-round Mon.–Fri. 8:30 A.M.–5 P.M.). The other one is at the corner of Highways 16 and 97, handy if you're coming into the city from the south or west (July–early Sept. daily 9 A.M.–8 P.M.).

Prince George Public Library (887 Dominion St., 250/563-9251, Mon.–Thurs. 10 A.M.–9 P.M., Fri.–Sat. 10 A.M.–5:30 P.M.) has a good display of native art and artifacts. **Mosquito Books** (1600 15th Ave., 250/563-6495, closed Sun.) features a great selection of local and northern British Columbia literature, as well as major Canadian newspapers.

The main post office is on the corner of 5th Avenue and Quebec Street. For emergencies, contact **Prince George Regional Hospital** (2000 15th Ave., 250/565-2000) or the **RCMP** (250/562-3371).

TRANSPORTATION

The airport is about 18 kilometers (11.2 mi.) east of town and is served by **Air Canada** (888/247-2262) and **WestJet** (800/538-5696) with daily flights from Vancouver. The **Airporter** (250/563-2220) meets all flights.

The downtown **Greyhound** bus depot (1566 12th Ave., 250/564-5454) is the terminus for services from Vancouver and along the Yellowhead Highway.

The **Prince George Transit System** (250/563-0011) operates buses throughout the city daily except Sunday. For a cab call **Prince George Taxi** (250/564-4444). Car-rental agencies in town include **Budget** (250/563-2662), **National** (250/564-4847), and **Thrifty** (250/564-3499).

BRITISH COLUMBIA

West from Prince George

VANDERHOOF AND VICINITY

The first town west of Prince George is Vanderhoof (pop. 4,500), a service center for the Nechako Valley and British Columbia's geographical center (the exact spot is marked by a cairn five km/3.1 mi. east of town).

Vanderhoof Heritage Museum

The 1914 building at the corner of Highway 16 and Pine Avenue houses **Vanderhoof Heritage Museum** (250/567-2991, May–early Sept. daily 10 A.M.–5 P.M., $3), with mounted birds and animals, blacksmithing tools, and a rock collection. A dozen other historic buildings surround the museum, among them a jail, a 1922 schoolhouse, and a restored gambling room. Also in the village is the **OK Café** (8:30 A.M.–8 P.M.), where you can tuck into hearty homemade soup and rolls, salads, and tasty pie and ice cream. It's inside a heritage-style building decorated with old-fashioned wallpaper and frilly curtains.

Vanderhoof's town symbol is the Canada goose. You can see these beautiful birds and other waterfowl in spring and fall at their transient home, Nechako Bird Sanctuary, along the banks of the Nechako River. Access it via the wooden bridge at the north end of Burrard Avenue, the town's main street.

Practicalities

Inexpensive accommodations are available at the **Coachlight Motel** (Hwy. 16 at the east side of town, 250/567-2296, $60 s, $70 d), with RV hookups for $16. Similarly priced, but right downtown is the **North Country Inn** (2575 Burrard Ave., 250/567-3047). The rooms are just your run-of-the-mill roadside motel variety, but the attached restaurant has a distinct alpine feel. Breakfasts are hearty and cost from $5; lunch is mostly burgers and sandwiches ranging $5–9. In the evening the soup and salad bar is $8, and steak, seafood, and pasta dinners run $10–29. Try the delicious chicken lasagna. **Riverside Park Campground** (250/567-4710, $16) enjoys a pleasant setting beside the Nechako River. To get there, turn north off Hwy. 16 onto Burrard Avenue and continue through town; the campground is on the west side of Burrard Avenue. Showers and firewood are supplied.

Vanderhoof Visitor Info Centre (2353 Burrard Ave., 250/567-2124 or 800/752-4094) is open July–early September daily 8:30 A.M.–6 P.M., the rest of the year Monday–Friday 9 A.M.–5 P.M.

Fort St. James National Historic Site

A sealed road leads 60 kilometers (37 mi.) north from Vanderhoof to Fort St. James (pop. 2,200), the earliest nonnative settlement in northern British Columbia. In the early 1800s, Fort St. James was the chief fur-trading post and capital of the large and prosperous district of New Caledonia—the name originally given to central British Columbia by Simon Fraser. Today the beautifully restored fort forms the centerpiece of Canada's largest collection of original fur-trade buildings. Enter the fort through the Visitor Reception Centre (250/996-7191, mid-May–Sept. daily 9 A.M.–5 P.M., adult $6, senior $5, child $3), which holds displays on pioneer explorers, fur traders, and the indigenous Carrier people. In July and August, characters dressed in pioneer garb lurk in the log-constructed general store, the fish cache, the single men's bunkhouse, the main house, and the veggie garden. You're actively encouraged to get into the spirit of things and play along. Tell them you've just arrived by canoe, want to stay the night in the men's house, and need a good horse and some provisions . . . then see what happens!

VANDERHOOF TO SMITHERS

Heading west from Vanderhoof, the Yellowhead Highway passes through low rolling terrain to **Fort Fraser,** one of the province's oldest communities; Simon Fraser established the former fur-trading post in 1806.

FISH FANTASIES

More than 300 lakes dot the high country between Burns Lake and Houston, with many renowned for fishing. Common species are rainbow, eastern brook, and cutthroat trout, as well as kokanee, chinook salmon, steelhead, and lake char. To even mention all the lakes and their fishing possibilities would take a whole other book. Instead, here are a few places I've had success dangling a line over the years:

Babine Lake, north of Topley, is British Columbia's largest natural lake and is known for its trophy-size rainbow trout as well as steelhead runs in the Babine River. Stay at the well-priced **Grande Isles Resort** (250/697-6322, www .grandeislesresort.com).

Francois Lake, south of Burns Lake, is the place to troll for lake char to nine kilograms (20 lbs.), as well as kokanee and rainbow trout. Stay the night and cook your catch at the lakefront **Birch Bay Resort** (250/699-8484, www.birch bay.ca), where you can choose between camping and cabins.

Morice River, west of Houston (south at the Northwood Pulp Mill sign), combines accessibility and reliability to make it a favorite steelhead fishing spot.

Fraser Lake

Where the highway crosses the wide Nechako River, a short spur leads to 191-hectare (470-acre) **Beaumont Provincial Park,** on the shore of Fraser Lake. Camping (May–Oct.) is $17 per night.

The town of Fraser Lake (pop. 1,400), 60 kilometers (37 mi.) west of Vanderhoof, lies on a chunk of land sloping gently down to its namesake lake. In winter, trumpeter swans settle in at each end of the lake. In summer, a salmon run on the Stellako River—a short stretch of water between Fraser and Francois Lakes—draws scores of eager anglers. Overlooking Fraser Lake, **Piper's Glen Resort** (250/690-7565, www.pipersglenresort.com) features a grassy lakeshore camping area with full hookups and showers ($15–18 per site) and basic self-contained cabins ($40). The good prices continue through to canoe rentals ($15 per half-day) and motor boats ($40 per day).

Burns Lake

The first thing you see when you enter Burns Lake is an enormous chainsaw-carved trout with the inscription "Three Thousand Miles of Fishing!" That pretty much sums up what attracts visitors to the town and surrounding **Lakes District.** Continue west along the highway through town to reach the green and white **Heritage Centre** (summer daily 1–5 P.M., $2), comprising a museum and the local information center. The museum is housed in a 1919 home whose furnished rooms contain an odd assortment of articles, including memorabilia from an old ship (viewed through a porthole) and typewriters that have seen better days. For a wonderful view of the area, follow 5th Avenue up the hill out of town, and then take the turnoff to Boer Mountain Forestry Lookout.

KOA Burns Lake (Freeport Rd., seven km/4.3 mi. east of Burns Lake, 250/692-3105, $18–24) has picturesque tent sites in a forested area while RVers hook up to full services in an open area. Amenities include free showers, a launderette, and a convenience store.

Houston

Like Burns Lake, Houston's welcoming sign also proudly bears a carved fish—this time a steel-head. Houston calls itself "Steelhead Country," for the only species of trout that migrates to the ocean. This forestry town of 4,000 lies at the confluence of the Bulkley and Morice Rivers, with the Telkwa and Babine Ranges for a backdrop.

Motels in town include **Houston Motor Inn** (250/845-7112 or 800/994-8333) and **Pleasant Valley Motel** (250/845-2246 or 888/311-7766). Both are on the highway, and both charge from $60 s, $65 d.

Houston Visitor Info Centre (Highway 16 at Benson Ave., 250/845-7640, summer daily 9 A.M.–5 P.M.) is difficult to miss—look for the huge fishing rod in the parking lot.

Telkwa

As you continue west, the scenery just keeps getting better. You'll pass open fields and rolling, densely forested hills, all the while surrounded by mountains. The neat little village of Telkwa lies at the confluence of the Bulkley and Telkwa Rivers. Its streets are lined with many historic buildings, some restored, others not, but all described in the *Walking Tour Through Historic Telkwa,* available at many local businesses.

On the highway through town, the **Douglas Motel** (250/846-5679, $75–85 s, $95 d) is one of the best places to stay between Prince George and the coast. It offers a beautiful setting, surrounded by gardens that run right down to the Buckley River. Rooms are $70 s, $75 d, while self-contained log cabins, complete with fireplaces, are $85 s, $95 d. Nearby **Tyhee Lake Provincial Park** has a good swimming beach, picnic facilities, and a campground with hot showers (May–Sept., $20).

SMITHERS

The Coast Mountains surround the town of Smithers (pop. 5,800), while the splendid 2,560-meter (8,400-ft.) **Hudson Bay Mountain** towers directly above. It's a mid-size town with a small-town feel, a vibrant community with some excellent accommodations, fine restaurants, and interesting arts-and-crafts shops. In winter, the town is a base for skiers and snowboarders from throughout the north who flock to the slopes of **Ski Smithers** (250/847-2550, www.skismithers.com).

Sights

The grand old 1925 courthouse, at the junction of the Yellowhead Highway and Main Street, is home to **Bulkley Valley Museum** (250/847-5322, summer Mon.–Sat. 11 A.M.–5 P.M.), whose displays spotlight the valley's history with plenty of black-and-white photos and pioneer equipment.

Driftwood Canyon Provincial Park

This park, 17 kilometers (10.6 mi.) northeast of town (take Hwy. 16 three km/1.9 mi. east, head north on Old Babine Lake Rd., left on Telkwa High Rd., and then right on Driftwood Rd.), protects fossil beds laid down millions of years ago. A short walk from the road leads to a viewing platform over the east bank of Driftwood Creek, where interpretive panels describe the site's significance. Excavated specimens can be viewed in the Bulkley Valley Museum.

Accommodations and Camping

Because skiers and snowboarders from throughout the north flock to the slopes of Hudson Bay Mountain when the snow falls, the local lodgings are apt to be as busy in winter as in summer. The upscale **Stork Nest Inn** (1485 Main St., 250/847-3831, www.storknestinn.com) features comfortable, air-conditioned rooms with high-speed Internet access. Breakfast and a daily paper are included in the rates of $70 s, $75 d. Save a few bucks by staying at the **Florence Motel** (4160 Hwy. 16, 250/847-2678, $48 s, $53 d), but it's a bit rough around the edges.

The premier accommodation in this region is the **Logpile Lodge** (3105 McCabe Rd., 250/847-5152, www.logpilelodge.com, $85–135 s or d), north of town (call for directions) and surrounded by a magnificent mountain panorama. Guest rooms on the upper floor have vaulted ceilings, while exposed log walls dominate those on the lower floor. All seven rooms have a solid log bed and a private balcony. A big breakfast, cooked to order, will set you up for an activity-filled day (horseback riding, canoeing, fishing, and more) with local operators.

Riverside Park Municipal Campsite (May–Oct., $14) is beside the Bulkley River north of town, providing shaded sites and river fishing only minutes from downtown. Facilities include showers and a kitchen shelter but no hookups. **Riverside Golf Course** (Yellowhead Hwy., east of town, 250/847-3229, $16–23) has hookups.

Food

Mountainside Café (3763 Fourth Ave., 250/847-3455) is a funky little space with a stylish yet uncomplicated decor. The varied menu includes everything from fish and chips to a Thai curry ($14). Expect live music on Thursday evening. At **Schimmels Fine Pastries** (1172 Main St., 250/847-9044, Tues.–Sat. from 5:30 A.M.) enjoy a range of delicious cakes and pastries, or enjoy a bowl of homemade soup ($3–5) with a sandwich ($4–7) made to order.

Information and Services

Tourism Smithers (www.tourismsmithers.com, 250/847-5072 or 800/542-6673) operates the **Smithers Visitor Info Centre,** upstairs in the museum building at the corner of Main Street and the Yellowhead Highway (summer daily 9 A.M.–6 P.M., the rest of the year Mon.–Fri. 8:30 A.M.–4:30 P.M.). A good source of northern literature is **Mountain Eagle Books** (1237 Main St., 250/847-5245). Check your email at **BC Web** (1188 Main St., 250/877-6228).

Smithers Airport, right beside Highway 16, four kilometers (2.5 mi.) west of town, is served by **Air Canada** (888/247-2262). The **Greyhound** bus depot (250/847-2204) is on Highway 16, west of the information center. **Thrifty** (250/847-3332) has a limited number of rental vehicles at the airport.

Continuing West from Smithers

About eight kilometers (five mi.) west of Smithers on the Yellowhead Highway, take the Hudson Bay Mountain Lookout turnout for magnificent views of the mountain and the quickly receding **Kathlyn Glacier** on its north face.

The next place to stop and stretch your legs is the viewpoint at **Moricetown Canyon,** where the **Bulkley River** funnels and roars its way down through a 15-meter-wide (50 ft.) canyon. Salmon desperately hurl themselves up these spectacular rapids in autumn. Below the canyon the river pours into a large pool. The canyon is part of Moricetown Indian Reserve, which recognizes an area that has been a Carrier village site for more than 5,000 years. Villagers still fish the canyon using traditional spears and nets; look for the locals congregated around the canyon in summer.

NEW HAZELTON AND VICINITY

It's easy to be confused by the three Hazeltons—**Hazelton, New Hazelton,** and **South Hazelton**—situated at the most northerly point on the Yellowhead Highway. As usual, the arrival of the Grand Trunk Pacific Railway caused the confusion. The original Hazelton (called "Old Town") was established 50 years or so before the railway came. The other two Hazeltons were founded because each of their respective promoters thought he owned a better spot for a new railway town. Today the largest of the three small communities is New Hazelton (pop. 900), a service center watched over by spectacular Mount Rocher Deboule. Make your first stop the **Hazelton Visitor Info Centre** (Hwy. 16 and Hwy.62, 250/842-6071, June–Sept., daily 8 A.M.–7 P.M.).

Hazelton

From New Hazelton, Highway 62 leads about eight kilometers (five mi.) northwest to Hazelton. Along the way it crosses the one-lane **Hagwilget Suspension Bridge,** high above the turbulent Bulkley River. Stop and read the plaque about the original footbridge—made from poles and cedar rope—that once spanned the gorge here (you'll be glad you live in modern times).

At the junction of the Bulkley and Skeena Rivers, Hazelton has retained its unique 1890s-style architecture and pioneer-settlement atmosphere. Along the waterfront sit a museum (open daily 10 A.M.–5 P.M.), a landing with river views, and a café.

'Ksan Historical Village and Museum

'Ksan, which means "between the banks," is an authentically reconstructed Gitksan village

on the outskirts of Hazelton (Apr.–Sept. daily 9 A.M.–5 P.M., Oct.–Mar. 9:30 A.M.–4:30 P.M.). In the main building is a museum, featuring cedar boxes and cedar-bark mats, woven and button blankets, masks, and an art gallery with changing exhibitions. Beyond the museum is the village proper. Access to the three main longhouses is on a guided tour (departures on the hour). You get to visit the burial house, food cache, smokehouse, community houses, and the 'Ksan artists' carving shop and studio. You'll see traditional northwest coast carved interiors, paintings and painted screens, totem poles, and fine examples of native artifacts, arts and crafts, tools and implements, and personal possessions. Admission to the museum is $2, but I highly recommend taking the full tour (adult $10, senior $8.50, child free).

TERRACE AND VICINITY

Terrace (pop. 13,500) lies on the Yellowhead Highway, 580 kilometers (360 mi.) west of Prince George and 146 kilometers (91 mi.) east of Prince Rupert. The city is built on a series of steep terraces along the beautiful **Skeena River** and is surrounded by mountains.

History buffs will find plenty of interest at **Heritage Park** (4113 Sparks St., 250/615-3000, June–Aug. Wed.–Sun. 10 A.M.–6 P.M., adult $4, senior $2.50), but it is the mix of intriguing natural attractions and outstanding recreation opportunities surrounding Terrace that are the main draw.

Nisga'a Memorial Lava Bed Provincial Park

Protecting Canada's youngest lava flow, this park's fascinating landscape is unique within western Canada. The flow is about 18 kilometers (11 mi.) long and three kilometers (1.9 mi.) wide. Experts estimate the molten rock spewed through the earth's crust between 1650 and 1750. You can see all different types of lava, as well as crevasses, spiky pinnacles, sinkholes, craters, and bright blue pools where underground rivers have risen to the surface. Explore the lava with caution—in some parts the surface may be unstable, and it's very hard on footgear. The only facilities are a day-use area and a couple of short hiking trails.

To get to the park, take Highway 16 west out of town for three kilometers (1.9 mi.), then head north around the back of the sawmill on Kalum Lake Drive. The park is 78 kilometers (48 mi.) along this road (watch for logging trucks). The information center in Terrace has an interesting brochure on the lava beds.

Hiking

For an easy stroll, take the three-kilometer (1.9-mi.) path (50 minutes or less) around **Ferry Island,** in the middle of the Skeena River east of downtown (reached via Hwy. 16). More demanding is **Terrace Mountain Nature Trail,** a five-kilometer (3.1-mi.) trail providing great views of the city and the surrounding area from the lower slopes of the mountain. It takes about two hours round-trip. The trailhead is at Halliwell Avenue and Anderson Street (by Heritage Park). Farther afield, **Clearwater Lakes Trail,** which begins from Highway 37, 27 kilometers (16.7 mi.) south of Terrace, leads 1.8 kilometers (1.1 mi.) to Little Clearwater Lake, then another 700 meters (0.4 mi.) to Big Clearwater Lake. A shallow creek links the two lakes, lined by pretty picnic spots and berries to pick in season.

Fishing and Swimming

Anglers flock to the **Skeena River** April–May and August–October for some of the world's best steelhead fishing. Chinooks make their upstream migration in late May and again July through August. Coho salmon run from August to early fall. You can pick up a list of local guides and outfitters from the information center.

Lakelse Lake Provincial Park, at the north end of beautiful Lakelse Lake, offers swimming, a sandy beach, fishing, and a hiking trail through an old-growth forest of towering spruce, cedar, and hemlock. To get there, take Highway 37 south toward Kitimat for 26 kilometers (16 mi.).

Kitimat

Continue south from Lakelse Lake to reach Kitimat (pop. 12,000), 62 kilometers (38 mi.) south of Terrace. When developed in the 1950s, it was

Canada's largest industrial endeavor ever. It included one of the world's largest aluminum smelters, a company town to serve the workers, and a massive hydroelectric scheme. **Smelter tours** (250/639-8259) are offered summer weekdays, but there are also natural attractions, such as the province's largest living tree, a 500-year-old Sitka spruce. For a list of local services, check the website www.visitkitimat.com or drop by **Kitimat Visitor Info Centre** (2109 Forest Ave., 250/632-6294 or 800/664-6554) at the north entrance to town.

Accommodations

The less expensive motels are strung out along Highway 16 on the eastern and western outskirts of the city. To the west, your best bet is **Cedars Motel** (4830 Hwy. 16, 250/635-2258), which is nothing special but charges only $52 s, $58 d. On the other side of town is **Copper River Motel** (three km/1.9 mi. east at 4113 Hwy. 16, 250/635-6124 or 888/652-7222, $70 s, $75 d), set up for anglers, with fishing supplies and guides, 4WD rentals, and free ice. Rooms are clean and have coffee- and tea-making appliances. On the down side are the paper-thin walls. RV parking is $22.

Right downtown is the upmarket **Coast Inn of the West** (4620 Lakelse Ave., 250/638-8141 or 800/663-1144, www.coasthotels.com), where each of the 60 air-conditioned rooms is decorated in stylish pastel colors. Facilities include a restaurant (daily 6:30 A.M.–10 P.M.), a lounge, and room service. Rack rates are $145 s, $155 d, but check the website for discounts.

Camping

On Ferry Island in the Skeena River, just over three kilometers (1.9 mi.) east of downtown, **Ferry Island Campground** (250/615-3000, $14–18) offers sheltered sites among birch and cottonwood trees, berry bushes, and wildflowers. A few sites have excellent views of the river and mountains, and a hiking trail runs through the woods and around the island. There are no showers and only a few powered hookups.

A short drive from Terrace, the following provincial parks have campgrounds: **Kleanza Creek Provincial Park** ($14), 20 kilometers (12 mi.) east of Terrace on Highway 16; **Exchamsiks River Provincial Park** ($14), 50 kilometers (31 mi.) west on Highway 16; and **Lakelse Lake Provincial Park** ($20), 16 kilometers (10 mi.) south of Terrace along Highway 37, offering a sandy beach, safe swimming, an interpretive amphitheatre, hot showers, and flush toilets.

Food

One of the most popular places to go for breakfast is the **Bear Restaurant** (Northern Motor Inn, on Hwy. 16 just east of Terrace, 250/635-6375, daily 6 A.M.–11 P.M.). Large omelets, hash browns, toast, and coffee run around $9. At **Don Diego's** (3212 Kalum St., 250/635-2307, Mon.–Sat. 11 A.M.–9 P.M., Sun. 10 A.M.–2 P.M. and 5–9 P.M.) you can get all the Mexican usuals, as well as delicious pastas (made in-house), Thai-influenced stir-fries, and freshly prepared seafood from down the road in Prince Rupert (entrées $11–18). Try and save room for a bowl of homemade ice cream. The food alone stands this restaurant apart from others in town, but the setting is also pleasant, with lots of plants and Mexican wall hangings, and outdoor tables to catch the evening sun.

Information

The **Terrace Visitor Info Centre** (4511 Keith Ave., 250/635-2063 or 800/499-1637, www .terracetourism.bc.ca, summer Mon.–Fri. 8:30 A.M.–8 P.M. and Sat.–Sun. 9 A.M.–8 P.M., rest of year Mon.–Fri. 9 A.M.–5 P.M.) is beside Highway 16 on the east side of town. The helpful staff will happily load you down with brochures and pamphlets and tell you everything there is to do in the area. For local literature and a good selection of Canadiana, head downtown to **Misty River Books** (4710 Lakelse Ave., 250/635-4428, Mon.–Sat. 9 A.M.–6 P.M.).

West Toward Prince Rupert

The 146-kilometer (91-mi.) stretch of the Yellowhead Highway between Terrace and Prince Rupert rivals any stretch of road in the province for beauty. For almost the entire distance, the highway hugs the north bank of the beautiful **Skeena River** (Skeena is a Gitksan word meaning "river of mist"). On a fine day, views from the road are stunning—snow-dusted mountains, densely forested hillsides, ponds covered in yellow water lilies, and waterfalls like narrow ribbons of silver snaking down vertical cliffs from the snow high above. In some sections the highway shrinks to two extremely narrow lanes neatly sandwiched between the railway tracks and the river—drive defensively.

At **Exchamsiks River Provincial Park,** 50 kilometers (31 mi.) west of Terrace, you'll find camping for $14 and a grassy picnic area where the deep-green Exchamsiks River drains into the much larger Skeena River. Continuing westward, the Skeena widens and becomes a tidal estuary. Keep an eye out for bald eagles on the sandbars or perched in the trees above the highway.

Prince Rupert

Prince Rupert (pop. 18,000) lies on hilly Kaien Island 726 kilometers (451 mi.) west of Prince George. Life at this bustling port city revolves around the ocean. The city boasts a large fishing fleet and is a major water transportation hub; from here you can catch ferries south to Vancouver Island, west to the Queen Charlotte Islands, or north to Alaska. The city itself holds an odd but intriguing mixture of cultural icons—Pacific Northwest native totem poles, old English street names, modern high-rise hotels and civic buildings—all crammed together on the edge of the Pacific Ocean.

History

For at least 5,000 years, Kaien Island and the vicinity have been inhabited by the Coast Tsimshian, whose lives were traditionally dominated by fishing and food gathering. They followed the spring and summer salmon and oolichan runs, returning every season to the same village sites. Trade networks were established, artistic traditions emerged, and a class system evolved. Before 1790 the region was among the most heavily populated areas on British Columbia's coastline.

BRITISH COLUMBIA

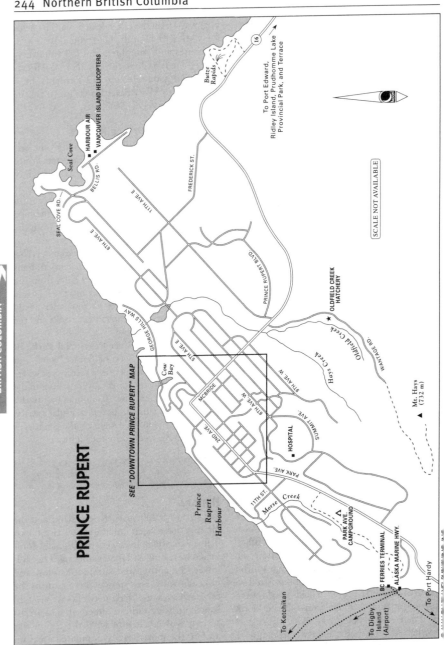

PRINCE RUPERT

Prince Rupert Harbour

SEE "DOWNTOWN PRINCE RUPERT" MAP

Seal Cove

■ HARBOUR AIR
■ VANCOUVER ISLAND HELICOPTERS

SEAL COVE RD.

BELL'S RD.

8TH AVE E

11TH AVE E

FREDERICK ST.

PRINCE RUPERT BLVD

GEORGE HILLS WAY

Butze Rapids

16

To Port Edward, Ridley Island, Prudhomme Lake Provincial Park, and Terrace

SCALE NOT AVAILABLE

★ OLDFIELD CREEK HATCHERY

Oldfield Creek

WANTAGE RD.

Hays Creek

▲ Mt. Hays (732 m)

5TH AVE E

Cow Bay

McBRIDE

9TH AVE W

8TH AVE W

2ND AVE

SUMMIT AVE.

■ HOSPITAL

PARK AVE.

11TH ST.

Morse Creek

△ PARK AVE. CAMPGROUND

■ BC FERRIES TERMINAL
■ ALASKA MARINE HWY.

To Ketchikan

To Digby Island (Airport)

To Port Hardy

European Prince Rupert was the brainchild of Charles M. Hays, general manager of the Grand Trunk Pacific Railway. In 1902, Hays devised a plan to build a rail line from North Bay, Ontario, to a new port on the central B.C. coast—a port he hoped would rival Vancouver and become the Pacific port for Canada. In the early 1900s fishing and fish processing became important parts of the city's economy, and during World War II Prince Rupert became a shipbuilding center and an American army base.

SIGHTS AND RECREATION
Museum of Northern British Columbia

You can easily spend several hours at this fascinating museum, which occupies a distinctive post-and-beam building overlooking the water (1st Ave. W and McBride St., 250/624-3207, June–Aug. Mon.–Sat. 9 A.M.–8 P.M., Sun. 9 A.M.–5 P.M., Sept.–May Mon.–Sat. 9 A.M.–5 P.M., adult $5, child $1). Exhibits trace the history of Prince Rupert from 5,000-year-old Tsimshian settlements through fur-trading days to the founding of the city. Many of the most fascinating displays spotlight the Coast Tsimshian natives—their history, culture, traditions, trade networks, and potlatches. Among the Tsimshian artifacts on display are totem poles, pots, masks, beautiful wooden boxes, blankets, baskets, shiny black argillite carvings, weapons, and petroglyphs. Admission includes a museum tour and evening slide slow, or join a town walking tour for $2.

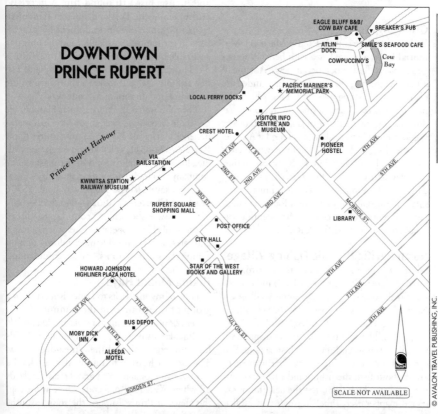

DOWNTOWN PRINCE RUPERT

EAGLE BLUFF B&B/ COW BAY CAFE
BREAKER'S PUB
ATLIN DOCK
SMILE'S SEAFOOD CAFE
COWPUCCINO'S
Cow Bay
PACIFIC MARINER'S MEMORIAL PARK
LOCAL FERRY DOCKS
VISITOR INFO CENTRE AND MUSEUM
CREST HOTEL
PIONEER HOSTEL
Prince Rupert Harbour
VIA RAILSTATION
KWINITSA STATION RAILWAY MUSEUM
RUPERT SQUARE SHOPPING MALL
LIBRARY
POST OFFICE
CITY HALL
HOWARD JOHNSON HIGHLINER PLAZA HOTEL
STAR OF THE WEST BOOKS AND GALLERY
BUS DEPOT
MOBY DICK INN
ALEEDA MOTEL
1ST AVE.
1ST ST.
2ND ST.
2ND AVE.
3RD ST.
3RD AVE.
4TH AVE.
5TH AVE.
MCBRIDE ST.
6TH AVE.
7TH AVE.
8TH AVE.
1ST AVE.
7TH ST.
8TH ST.
9TH ST.
FULTON ST.
BORDEN ST.

SCALE NOT AVAILABLE

© AVALON TRAVEL PUBLISHING, INC.

BRITISH COLUMBIA

Wander down to the docks and hop aboard a water taxi for an inexpensive harbor tour.

Other Sights

Right by the museum is **Pacific Mariner's Memorial Park,** a grassed area with benches strategically placed for the best ocean views. A statue of a mariner staring out to sea is surrounded by plaques remembering those lost at sea. Also in the park is the *Kazu Maru,* a small fishing boat that drifted across the Pacific from Japan after its owner was lost. From here, walk south along 1st Avenue, then head to the foot of 2nd Street, which ends harborside. Here you'll find the **Kwinitsa Station Railway Museum** (250/627-1915, June–Aug. daily 9 A.M.–noon and 1–5 P.M.), housed in a small railway station—one of only four such buildings that remain of the chain of 400 identical stations along the Grand Trunk Railway.

North Pacific Historic Fishing Village

South of Prince Rupert (take the first road to the right after leaving Kaien Island) in Port Edward is the oldest remaining cannery village on North America's west coast (250/628-3538, 15 May–Sept. daily 9 A.M.–6 P.M., adult $12, senior $9, child under 6 free). Dating from 1889, the village is now classified as a historic site. You can find out everything you've ever wanted to know about fish, the fishing industry, and canning—even which fish tastes the best (locals say it's red snapper every time). You're free to stroll at your own pace along the boardwalk through the riverside cannery settlement with its many original buildings, but a variety of guided tours are offered and included in the admission charge. Also included is the *Skeena River Story,* a live performance and slide show presented five times daily.

Hitting the Harbor

The best way to see the harbor is naturally from water level. All sorts of shuttle services run around the harbor to communities with no road connections. Times vary. Head down to the small docks at the bottom of McBride Street for route and schedule information, or call 250/624-3337. The shortest trip is a 15-minute run to **Dodge Cove** on **Digby Island.** There's not much to do on the island, but it's a nice cruise there and back, and it costs just $10 round-trip. A ferry also cruises along the Portland Inlet to **Kincolith** (pop. 400), one of four traditional Nisga'a villages in the remote Nass Valley, and the only one accessible by boat. The *Centurion IV* (250/624-5411) departs Prince Rupert Monday and Friday at 8:30 A.M. and makes a short stop before returning midafternoon; $15 one-way.

The calm waters of Prince Rupert Harbour are perfect for kayaking. Even if you have had no experience in a kayak, **Eco-treks Adventures** (Cow Bay, 250/624-8311) will take you on an easy paddle along the shoreline for $40 per person. The company also leads harbor tours in Zodiacs ($25) and rents kayaks (single $50 per day, double $70). **Seashore Charters** (250/624-5645 or 800/667-4393, www.seashorecharter.com) keeps a list of all the local charter operators, their vessels, tours, and rates, and can provide more information on fishing tours, harbor tours, and adventure tours.

Hiking Mount Hays

On one of my first visits to Prince Rupert, I led a group of three others to the summit of 732-meter (2,400-ft.) Mount Hays via an old gondola cut line. Halfway up we got tangled up in head-high undergrowth and then knee-deep snow. Therefore, I heartily recommend you take the more conventional route, a gravel road that leads off where Wantage Road ends. Once at the top, the views of Prince Rupert, the sound, southeastern Alaska, and bald eagles soaring through updrafts are second to none.

ACCOMMODATIONS AND CAMPING

Prince Rupert has a great campground within easy walking distance of the ferry terminals. On the other hand, motel accommodations are generally overpriced and need to be booked well in advance during the busy summer months.

Under $50

The **Pioneer Hostel** (167 3rd Ave. E, 250/624-2334 or 888/794-9998) fills with "steadies" in winter, but in summer daily rates are a reasonable $22 pp for a dorm bed and $43 d for a private room (that shares a bathroom).

$50–100

My favorite Rupert accommodation is **Eagle Bluff Bed and Breakfast** (201 Cow Bay Rd., 250/627-4955 or 800/833-1550). The house is built out over the water, overlooking the marina and harbor, and lies within easy walking distance of cafés and restaurants. Rates are $50 s, $60 d for a shared bath; $60 s, $70 d for a private bath; and $90 for

Eagle Bluff Bed and Breakfast

a large suite sleeping five. A cooked breakfast—complete with freshly baked muffins—is included.

Check the website of the local tourist office (www.tourismprincerupert.com) for a rundown on all Prince Rupert motels. A bunch of them fall into this price range, but none stand out as being anything more than a bed and a room. Least expensive is the **Aleeda Motel** (900 3rd Ave. W, 250/627-1367 or 888/460-2023, www.aleeda motel.bc.ca, $60 s, $70 d), and the **Moby Dick Inn** (935 2nd Ave. W, 250/624-6961 or 800/663-0822, www.mobydickinn.com, $84 s, $94 d) has the nicest rooms.

$100–150

The massive building right downtown is the 15-story **Howard Johnson Highliner Plaza Hotel** (815 1st Ave. W, 250/624-9060 or 888/561-7666, www.hojoprincerupert.com, from $120 s or d), which has a downstairs restaurant and many rooms with balconies and harbor views.

In a prime harborside location, the full-service **Crest Hotel** (222 1st Ave. W, 250/624-6771 or 800/663-8150, www.cresthotel.bc.ca) holds a glass-enclosed waterfront café, a restaurant, and a lounge with nightly entertainment. Rates for the warmly decorated rooms—some with water views, all with niceties like cordless phones and big TVs—range $145–250 s or d.

Campgrounds

Like the rest of Rupert's accommodations, **Park Avenue Campground** (1750 Park Ave., 250/624-5861 or 800/667-1994) fills and empties daily with the arrival and departure of the ferries. If you know when you're arriving in the city, phone ahead to avoid any hassles. The campground is a one-kilometer (0.6-mi.) walk from both the city center and ferry terminals. Facilities include hot showers, cooking shelters, a mail drop, and visitor information. Grassed tent sites are $14, full hookups $26.

FOOD

Breakfast

Most of Rupert's larger motels have restaurants, but the place to head for substantial and inexpensive breakfasts is the **Moby Dick Inn** (935 2nd Ave. W, 250/624-6961, daily from 7 A.M.). You can order anything from a bowl of fruit and a muffin ($4) to eggs, bacon, and toast ($5) or steak and eggs ($8). It's always crowded, and service can be slow.

Cow Bay Cafés

East of downtown is Cow Bay, originally a fishy-smelling, rough-and-tumble part of town home to a large fishing fleet. The boats are still there, moored in a marina, and a few old buildings still stand. But for the most part, the bay is a changed place. Rowdy dives have been replaced by trendy art and crafts shops, restaurants, and two of the city's best cafés.

Cowpuccino's (25 Cow Bay Rd., 250/627-1395, daily 7:30 A.M.–10 P.M.) is a great little coffeehouse with freshly brewed coffee, delicious desserts, newspapers and magazines to read, and a laid-back atmosphere. Right on the water is **Cow Bay Café** (205 Cow Bay Rd., 250/627-1212, Tues.–Sun. 11 A.M.–8 P.M.), where you can sit at an outside table and take in the smells of the ocean, or stay inside and enjoy the greenery. Good home-cooked meals, including vegetarian dishes, and daily specials start at $7.

Seafood

Ask a local where to go for good seafood and the answer is invariably **Smile's Café** (113 Cow Bay Rd., 250/624-3072, summer daily 9 A.M.–10 P.M., Sept.–June 11 A.M.–8 P.M.), a venerable institution that has been serving up uncomplicated seafood since 1934. This diner-style café, decorated with black-and-white fishing photos and colored-glass floats, is always busy, mobbed by local fishermen, residents, and visitors no matter what the time of day. The extensive menu includes seafood salads and sandwiches, burgers, fish and chips, shellfish, and seafood specialties. Prices range $6–25 per plate.

The harbor views alone at the **Waterfront Restaurant** (Crest Hotel, 222 1st Ave. W, 250/624-6771) would be reason enough to dine

TO OR FROM PRINCE RUPERT BY FERRY

Prince Rupert is the northern terminus of the BC Ferries network and the only Canadian stop on the Alaska Marine Highway. The two terminals sit side by side two kilometers (1.2 mi.) from downtown.

All ferries are modern vessels with day rooms, sleeping cabins, shower facilities, food service, and plenty of room to sit back and relax. Summer demand means you should book as far in advance as possible if you're transporting a vehicle or would like a cabin.

BC Ferries

BC Ferries (250/386-3431 or toll-free in B.C. 888/223-3779, www.bcferries.com) offers thrice-weekly (once a week outside summer) service between Port Hardy (Vancouver Island) and Prince Rupert. The 440-kilometer (273-mi.) journey on the well equipped *Queen of the North* takes 15 hours.

One-way fares are: adult $106, child 5–11 $53, vehicle $245, cabin $50–60, three-meal dining package $45. Fares are discounted 20 percent outside summer and B.C. seniors ride for half-price year-round.

Alaska Marine Highway

The Alaska Marine Highway (907/465-3941 or 800/642-0066, www.alaska.gov/ferry) operates an extensive network of ferries through southeastern Alaska, with Prince Rupert a major stop. The first port north from Prince Rupert is Ketchikan (adult US$58, child 5–11 US$27, vehicle up to 15 feet US$140), six hours away, with vessels continuing north to Juneau and Skagway (adult US$180, child 5–11 US$90, vehicle up to 15 feet US$344). Renting a cabin for the Prince Rupert–Skagway trip, with, for example, an en suite, costs US$125. Check-in time is three hours ahead of sailing time—it takes up to two hours to go through Customs and one hour to load up. Foot passengers must be there one hour ahead of sailing.

here, but the food is also excellent. The menu concentrates on local seafood—think smoked steelhead ($11) to start, followed by rich seafood pasta ($23), delicate halibut cheeks ($24), Alaska king crab ($34), or a seafood hotpot ($30). The wine list (lots of Pacific Northwest wines) is the best in town.

INFORMATION AND SERVICES

Prince Rupert Visitor Info Centre (250/624-5637 or 800/667-1994, www.tourismprince rupert.com, June–Aug. Mon.–Sat. 9 A.M.–8 P.M., Sunday 9 A.M.–5 P.M., Sept.–May Mon.–Sat. 9 A.M.–5 P.M.) is in the museum complex at 1st Avenue and McBride Street. It's one of the best information centers around, with a knowledgeable staff and lots of printed material on Prince Rupert sights, walking tours, restaurants, services, and ferry schedules.

The **library** (McBride Ave. at 101 6th Ave., 250/627-1345, Mon.–Fri. 9 A.M.–9 P.M., Sat. 9 A.M.–6 P.M.) is the place to go on a rainy day to catch up on your emailing or to read up on local history. If you're looking to buy books, especially on B.C. native art or history, spend some time at **Star of the West Books and Gallery** (518 3rd Ave. W, 250/624-9053). A gallery in the back of the store features local wildlife, native art, and photography.

Prince Rupert Regional Hospital (1305 Summit Ave., 250/624-2171) is south of downtown. The post office is on 2nd Avenue at 3rd Street. Launderettes are at 226 7th Street and 745 2nd Avenue W.

TRANSPORTATION
Getting There

Prince Rupert Airport is west of town on Digby Island, linked to the city by a ferry that takes buses and foot passengers only—no vehicles. Airlines provide free bus transportation between the airport and downtown via the ferry, but bus passengers must pay the ferry fare ($15 per person). **Air Canada** (888/247-2262) provides daily flights between Vancouver and Prince Rupert via Terrace. **Hawk Air** (800/487-1216) flies between Vancouver International Airport's South Terminal and Prince Rupert, as well as to other northern towns. This company offers significant discounts for advance bookings.

Prince Rupert is the western terminus of Canada's transcontinental rail system, which runs east from here to Prince George, Edmonton, and beyond. **VIA Rail** (250/627-7589) trains to Price Rupert run three times weekly, terminating down on the waterfront.

Buses from Prince George terminate at the **Greyhound** depot (822 3rd Ave. W, 250/624-5090).

Getting Around

Local bus service along four routes is provided by **Prince Rupert Transit System** (250/624-3343). Adult fare starts at $2, exact change only. All-day passes cost $3 and are available from the driver. The only car-rental agencies in town are Budget (250/627-7400) and National (250/624-5318). For a cab call Skeena Taxis (250/624-2185).

Queen Charlotte Islands

Wild. Quiet. Mysterious. Primordial. The Queen Charlotte Islands spread like a large upside-down triangle approximately 100 kilometers (62 mi.) off the northwest coast of mainland British Columbia. Of the chain's 150 mountainous and densely forested islands and islets, the main ones are **Graham Island** to the north and **Moresby Island** to the south, separated by narrow Skidegate Channel. The islands stretch 290 kilometers (180 mi.) from north to south and up to 85 kilometers (53 mi.) across at the widest spot. Wildlife is abundant, including the world's largest black bears, estimated to number almost 10,000. Stare out to sea to spot killer whales, dolphins, seals, sea lions, otters, and tufted puffins. If you visit between late April and June, you might spot gray whales feeding in Hecate Strait on their way from Mexico to Alaska. The best place to whale-watch is along Skidegate Inlet near the museum or at the northernmost tip of Rose Spit.

Life on the islands is very different from elsewhere in the province. Isolated from the mainland by stormy Hecate Strait, the 4,500 residents share an island camaraderie and laid-back, away-from-it-all temperament. Visitors can expect a friendly reception and adequate services. Motel-style accommodations are available in each town, but bed-and-breakfasts provide a closer glimpse of the island lifestyle. Groceries are also available, though choices can be limited. Gasoline is slightly more expensive than on the mainland, and raging nightlife is nonexistent.

THE HAIDA

The Haida people have lived on the Queen Charlottes since time immemorial. Fearless warriors, expert hunters and fishermen, and skilled woodcarvers, they owned slaves and threw lavish potlatches. Living in villages scattered throughout the Queen Charlotte Islands, they hunted sea otters for their luxuriant furs, fished for halibut and Pacific salmon, and collected chitons, clams, and seaweed from tidepools.

After contact with Europeans, diseases ravaged the Haida population, and by the 1830s when nonnatives began settling the islands, their traditional lifestyle came to a sudden end as they abandoned village sites and were forced onto reserves at Skidegate and Masset.

Today totem poles are rising once again on the Queen Charlottes, as a renewed interest in Haida art and culture is compelling skilled elders to pass their knowledge on to younger generations. **Gwaii Haanas National Park Reserve** protects the sites of their abandoned villages and **Ninstints** is preserved as a UNESCO World Heritage Site.

GETTING TO THE ISLANDS
By Air
The main gateway is Sandspit, where the small air terminal holds car rental agencies (book ahead) and an information center, and across the road is the Sandspit Inn. **Air Canada** (888/247-2262) flies daily between Vancouver and Sandspit while **Hawk Air** (800/487-1216) flies in from Prince Rupert. The **Airporter** bus meets all Sandspit flights and transports passengers to Queen Charlotte City for $15.

By Ferry
In summer, **BC Ferries** (250/386-3431 or toll-free in B.C. 888/223-3779, www.bcferries.com) operates the *Queen of Prince Rupert* between Prince Rupert and Skidegate five or six times a week in summer, less frequently the rest of the year. Departure times vary, but most often it's 11 A.M. from Prince Rupert (arriving Skidegate at 5:30 P.M.) and 11 P.M. from Skidegate (arriving Prince Rupert at 6 A.M.). Peak one-way fares are adult $24.25, child 5–11 $12.25, vehicle $89.50. Cabins cost $40–45. B.C. seniors get a discount, as do all travelers outside the peak summer season (early June–mid-Sept.) Cabins are available for $32–45.

The ferry terminal is five kilometers (3.1 mi.) east of Queen Charlotte City at Skidegate.

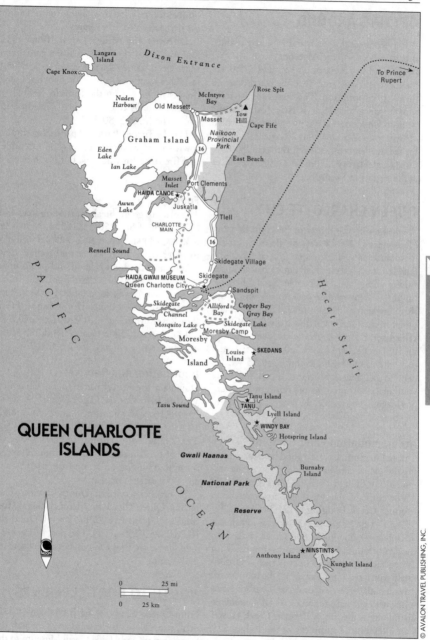

QUEEN CHARLOTTE
ISLANDS

© AVALON TRAVEL PUBLISHING, INC.

GETTING AROUND

A ferry connects Graham and Moresby Islands, departing hourly in each direction 7 A.M.–10 P.M.; peak round-trip fare is adult $5, child $2.50, vehicle $12.50. Apart from that, the islands have no public transportation. The least expensive car rentals are available at **Rustic Car Rentals** (Queen Charlotte City, 250/559-4641), which charges from $55 a day plus 20 cents a kilometer for the smallest vehicles. Both **Budget** (250/637-5688) and **Thrifty** (250/637-2299) have offices at the airport in Sandspit.

QUEEN CHARLOTTE CITY

Perched along the shores of Bearskin Bay, five kilometers (3.1 mi.) west of the dock for the mainland ferry, picturesque Queen Charlotte City is not really a city at all but a small laid-back fishing village of 1,100 people. Several heritage buildings in town date back to 1909; most of them are along the main road. The town is also home to the Queen Charlotte division of **Weyerhaeuser,** a logging giant that leases much of the land on Graham Island. In summer, the company runs a five-hour bus tour (250/557-4212) detailing all stages of logging. If you don't have your own transportation and don't mind a bit of pro-logging propaganda, the tour is a good way to see some of Moresby Island.

Accommodations and Camping

Queen Charlotte City is a good base for exploring the islands and has a wide variety of accommodations. Built in 1910, the old Premier Hotel has been totally renovated and now operates as **Premier Creek Lodging** (3101 3rd Ave., 250/559-8415 or 888/322-3388, www.qcislands .net/premier), offering beds to suit all budgets. In the main lodge, single "sleeping rooms" with shared facilities cost $35 per person, but definitely worth the extra money are the rooms with private bathrooms, balconies, and harbor views (some with kitchens) for $65 s, $75 d. Behind the main lodge is the simple **Premier Creek Hostel** (same telephone numbers as the lodge, $19 per night). It has two four-bed dorms and one

double room, a kitchen, living room, laundry, gas barbecue, and bike rentals.

Dorothy and Mike's Guest House (3125 2nd Ave., 250/559-8439,) features gardens and water views, use of a kitchen, and a cooked breakfast. One room has its own kitchen, but I prefer the ocean view from the Kumdis Room, furnished in boldly colored fabrics. Rates are $45 s (shared bath), $65–80 d.

Haydn Turner Park ($9 per night) through town to the west, has toilets, picnic tables, and fire rings for campers, but no showers or hookups.

Food

The place to go for breakfast is **Margaret's Café** (3223 Wharf St., 250/559-4204, Mon.–Sat. 6:30 A.M.–3 P.M., Sun. 8 A.M.–3 P.M.). In addition to water views, this place has a bustling atmosphere, and the food is good and plentiful for the price (cooked breakfasts from $6.50), but be prepared to wait for a table. For something more substantial, head to **Hummingbird Café** (Sea Raven Motel at 3301 3rd Ave., 250/559-8583). Specializing in local seafood, the Hummingbird is open nightly from 6 P.M.

Information and Services

Down on the waterfront, **Queen Charlotte Visitor Info Centre** (3220 Wharf St., 250/559-8316, www.qcinfo.ca, June–Aug. daily 10 A.M.–7 P.M., May and Sept. daily 10 A.M.–2 P.M.) offers natural history displays, a wide variety of brochures and information on everything that's going on around the islands, and current weather forecasts.

Emergency services in Queen Charlotte City include **Queen Charlotte Islands General Hospital** (3209 3rd Ave., 250/559-4300) and the **RCMP** (250/559-4421). The post office and a launderette are in the City Centre Building off 2nd Avenue.

NORTH TO PORT CLEMENTS

From Queen Charlotte City, Graham Island's main road follows the eastern coastline past the ferry terminal and Haida Gwaii Museum to the

Haida community of Skidegate Village, from where it's a pleasant 65-kilometer (40 mi.) coastal drive to Port Clements.

Haida Gwaii Museum

While totem poles and other ancient Haida art can be seen in various places around the islands, this museum (250/559-4643, summer Mon.–Fri. 10 A.M.–5 P.M., Sat.–Sun. 1–5 P.M., adult $6, child $3) on the north side of the Skidegate Landing ferry terminal allows visitors the opportunity to see a variety of such art under one roof. Inside are striking Haida wood and argillite carvings, pioneer artifacts, a beautiful woven blanket, jewelry, historic black-and-white photos, stunning prints by Haida artist Robert Davidson, ancient totems from Tanu and Skedans dating to 1878, the skull of a humpback whale, shells galore, and a collection of stuffed birds.

Between late April and early June, migrating **gray whales** rest and feed on shallow gravel bars of Skidegate Inlet in front of the museum on their annual 15,000-kilometer (9,321 mi.) odyssey between Mexico and Alaska.

Skidegate Village and Vicinity

Continuing north from the museum you'll soon come to Skidegate Village, a Haida reserve of 700 residents. A weathered totem pole, over 100 years old, still stands here, and a new totem—this one carved by Haida artist Bill Reid—stands in front of the longhouse facing the beach. The longhouse is the Skidegate Haida Band Council House, where local artisans fashion miniature totem poles, argillite ornaments, and jewelry in traditional designs.

From Skidegate, the road follows the shoreline of Hecate Strait, past driftwood-strewn beaches, an attractive old graveyard, and Balance Rock, one kilometer (0.6 mi.) north of Skidegate Village. A highway sign and turnout mark the start of a short trail down to the rock. Sandwiched between the Tlell River and the beach, **Tlell** is a haven for artisans; look for signs pointing the way to their outlets, which are concentrated on Richardson Road off Wiggins Road.

Naikoon Provincial Park (Southern End)

Just north of Tlell is the southern tip of Naikoon Provincial Park. While the park's main entrance is farther north out of Masset, this section has camping (**Misty Meadows Campground,** $14) and beachwalking. For a solid half-day hike, the wreck of the *Pezuta,* nine kilometers (5.6 mi.) north of the day-use area, is a good turnaround point; allow five hours for the round-trip.

MASSET AND VICINITY

Masset (pop. 900) is the oldest town on the Queen Charlottes. It was founded in 1909, just east of a Haida community named Massett. Over time, Massett became known as Old Massett and the new town was incorporated as Masset (with one *t*).

As you enter town from the south, make a stop at the **Masset Visitor Info Centre** (250/626-3982, mid-May–mid-Sept. daily 9 A.M.–4 P.M.), then cross Delkatla Inlet for downtown Masset and Old Massett or continue straight ahead for Naikoon Provincial Park.

Sights

Masset makes a good base from which to explore the beautiful surrounding area and Naikoon Provincial Park, but there's not much to do in town except wander down to the wharf, where some interesting activity is almost always going on: boats coming and going, fishermen loading supplies or unloading their catch.

Bordering Masset to the east is **Delkatla Wildlife Sanctuary,** where you can observe Canada geese, sandhill cranes, trumpeter swans, great blue herons, many varieties of ducks, and other waterfowl resting during migration. Access is along a hiking trail from town, or along Tow Hill Road toward Naikoon Provincial Park, turning left at the sanctuary sign onto Masset Cemetery Road.

If you're in search of Haida treasures, head for the village of **Old Massett,** also known as Haida. Go as far as the road takes you and you'll end up at the old blue schoolhouse, now **Ed Jones Haida Museum** (summer Sat.–Sun. 9 A.M.–5 P.M., donation). Exhibits include a large collection of fascinating old photographs showing how the villages used to look, Haida art and prints, and some of the original totem poles from around the Queen Charlottes. Many locals sell jewelry and art work in local outlets; look for signs through the village.

Accommodations and Camping

Several B&Bs in Masset provide lodgings and local flavor. **Harbourview Lodging** (1608 Delkatla St., 250/626-5109 or 800/661-3314) has pleasant guest rooms (one with a view of the fishing pier) and a sauna, communal kitchen, and laundry. Rooms with shared bathrooms are $55 s or d, en suites $80, including a light breakfast. Separated from the water only by a colorful flower garden, **Copper Beech House** (1590 Delkatla Rd., 250/626-5441, www.copperbeechhouse.com, $60 s, $80 d) offers three guest rooms, crammed with eclectic collections of sea treasures and original artwork. Enthusiastic host David Phillips is renowned for his island-style breakfasts, included in the rates.

Alaska View Lodge (Tow Hill Rd., 250/626-3333 or 800/661-0019, www.alaskaviewlodge.com) is right on the beach and backed by dense temperate rainforest. Accommodations in the main building share bathrooms and range $50–60 s, $70–80 d, depending on the view. Closer to the beach, two rooms in the Guesthouse feature practical beach furniture and a joined deck; $70 s and $90 d. Breakfast is included.

The **Village of Masset RV Site and Campground** (Tow Hill Rd., two km/1.2 mi. north of Masset) features large, fairly private campsites with tables among the trees, and washrooms with coin-operated hot showers. Unserviced sites are $12, powered sites $18.

Food

Even though Masset has a large fishing fleet, most of the catch ends up in mainland canneries. Your best choice for seafood is **Café Gallery** (Collison Ave. and Orr St., 250/626-3672, Mon.–Sat. 8:30 A.M.–9 P.M.), where the daily lunch specials are around $9 and dinner entrées range $14–20.

NAIKOON PROVINCIAL PARK

This spectacular park encompasses some 72,640 hectares (179,000 acres) along the northeast tip of Graham Island. Tlell marks the park's southern boundary, while access to the northern reaches is via the road out to Tow Hill, 26 kilometers (16 mi.) east of Masset. The park's dominant features are its beaches, almost 100 kilometers (62 mi.) of them, bordering Hecate Strait on the east and the turbulent Dixon Entrance on the north. Dolphins, orcas, harbor porpoises, and hair seals swim offshore year-round, and northern fur seals and California gray whales migrate north past the park in May and June. Land mammals are also abundant, with concentrations of black-tailed deer, black bear, marten, and river otter.

Sights and Hikes

The drive out to the park from Masset is superb, passing through moss-draped trees and forests of spruce before reaching **Tow Hill.** This strip of sand north from Tow Hill is a beachcomber's delight, as it's strewn with shells, driftwood, and shiny, sea-worn pebbles of every color under the sun. Around three kilometers (1.9 mi.) along the beach, look for semiprecious agate among piles of

a victim of the sea, Naikoon Provincial Park

pebbles that become exposed at low tide. Known to the Haida as Naikoon, meaning "long nose," a narrow five-kilometer (3.1-mi.) point of land separates the waters of Hecate Strait and Dixon Entrance. From Tow Hill, it's about 10 kilometers (6.2 mi.; three hours) one-way to the spit.

Practicalities

At **Agate Beach Campground,** near Tow Hill, campsites are spread along the beach and offer outstanding views. A shelter and pit toilets are provided, but no showers. In summer you need to nab a spot early in the day—by late afternoon they're all taken; $14 per night.

SANDSPIT AND VICINITY

Across Skidegate Channel from Queen Charlotte City, Sandspit (pop. 450) is the only community on Moresby Island. It occupies a low-lying, windswept spit overlooking Shingle Bay, 15 kilometers (9.3 mi.) east of the ferry dock. The rest of the island is wilderness. The northern half is largely given over to logging and holds remote logging camps. The southern half and over 100 outlying islands fall within Gwaii Haanas National Park Reserve, which protects a high concentration of abandoned Haida villages.

Those determined to tour the forests in their own vehicle can make an enjoyable loop trip south out of Sandspit. Logging roads lace the forest, leading to beaches strewn with driftwood, streams alive with salmon and steelhead, and beautiful **Skidegate** and **Mosquito Lakes** (good trout fishing). Free campgrounds are available at Gray Bay and Mosquito Lake.

Accommodations and Camping

Sandspit lacks the appeal of communities on Graham Island, but services are available. Friendly **Moresby Island Guest House** (385 Beach Rd., 250/637-5300, www.moresbyisland-bnb.com) is a popular kayakers' hangout offering rooms with shared baths and kitchens; $30 s, $65–70 d, including a light breakfast and use of a kitchen and laundry. **Sandspit Inn** (250/637-5334) across from the airport charges from $80 s, $90 d, and has Sandspit's only restaurant and bar.

Campgrounds are at **Gray Bay** and **Mosquito Lake** (named after the Mosquito airplane, not the pesky insects), both on the logging roads detailed above.

GWAII HAANAS NATIONAL PARK RESERVE

World-renowned for its ancient Haida villages dotted with totem poles, this park encompasses the southern half of Moresby Island as well as 137 smaller islands in the south of the archipelago. It's a remarkable place. Ancient brooding totems and remnants of mighty Haida longhouses stand against a backdrop of lush wilderness—dense trees, thick spongy moss, and rock-strewn beaches with incredibly clear water. Colonies of nesting seabirds and an abundance of marinelife—killer and minke whales, sea lions, tufted puffins—all add to the atmosphere.

Jointly managed by Parks Canada and the Haida nation, the park protects the homeland of seafaring Haida, who lived here for almost 10,000 years. **Ninstints,** on tiny Anthony Island near the south end of the park, is the world's best-preserved totem village. Anthony Island was declared a UNESCO World Heritage Site in 1981, just 97 years after the last Haida families had abandoned their remote home. **Hotspring Island,** site of another village, holds hot springs and unique flora.

Park Practicalities

The only access to the park is by air or sea. Most visitors travel as part of a guided tour. **Moresby Explorers** (250/637-2215 or 800/806-7633, www.moresbyexplorers.com) and **Queen Charlotte Adventures** (250/559-8990 or 800/668-4288, www.qcislands.net/qciadven) both offer guided boat and kayak trips and can also provide transfers and kayak rentals for those heading into the park unguided. Costs range from $150 per person for a boat trip to Skedans to $1,500 for an eight-day trip to Ninstints. **Oceanlight II Adventures** (604/328-5339, www.oceanlight2.bc.ca) has been conducting sailing trips through the south end of the archipelago since well before the proclamation of a park. Board the company's

71-foot *Ocean Light II* for eight days of sailing, visiting all the best-known abandoned Haida villages, exploring the waterways, and searching out land and sea mammals. All meals and accommodations aboard the boat are included in the rate of $3,050 per person.

South Moresby Air Charters (Queen Charlotte City, 250/559-4222, www.qcislands.net/smoresby) offers flightseeing trips to the park, including visits to Skedans ($480 for 1–4 peo-ple includes one hour on the ground) and Ninstints ($1,800).

If you're not planning on traveling with a commercial operator, you must register and pay a user fee ($10 per day). Once you arrive on the islands, take the orientation session (held at Queen Charlotte and Sandspit Visitor Info Centres), and you're ready to go. The Parks Canada website (www.pc.gc.ca) has all the details, as well as a list of all outfits licensed to operate in the park.

The Stewart–Cassiar Highway

An alternative to the Alaska Highway, this route turns off the Yellowhead Highway 45 kilometers (28 mi.) west of New Hazelton and leads north to the Yukon, joining the Alaska Highway just west of Watson Lake. The route opens up a magnificent area of northern wilderness that in many ways rivals that along the more famous Alaska Highway. It's a remote, rugged region, with few services but plenty to see and do. The highway is mainly paved. On sections of improved gravel, be prepared for washboard conditions, especially after heavy rain. The highlight is the side trip to the twin coastal villages of Stewart and Hyder. Total length of the trip between the Yellowhead and Alaska Highways is 733 kilometers (455 mi.), or 863 kilometers (536 mi.) with a jaunt out to Stewart.

FROM YELLOWHEAD HIGHWAY TO MEZIADIN JUNCTION

Tree-covered hills, dense patches of snow-white daisies, banks of pink-and-white clover and purple lupine, craggy mountains and distant peaks, beautiful lakes covered in yellow water lilies, and lots of logging trucks flying along the road—these are images of the 155 kilometers (96 mi.) between the Yellowhead Highway and Meziadin Junction, the turnoff to Stewart.

Kitwanga
This small village just north of the Yellowhead Highway is home to **Kitwanga Fort National Historic Site,** on the site of Battle Hill, where 200 years ago a native warrior named Nekt fought off attacks from hostile neighbors. A trail leads from the parking lot down to the flat area around the bottom of the hill, where you can read display panels describing the hill's history.

Meziadin Junction
At the junction is a gas station and a small information center. Just south of the junction is **Meziadin Lake Provincial Park,** with a campground (June–mid-Sept., $14) sloping down to the water's edge.

STEWART (AND HYDER) SIDE TRIP

From Meziadin Junction, Stewart is 65 kilometers (40 mi.) west along a spectacular stretch of highway that crosses the glaciated Coast Mountains. After 35 kilometers (21.7 mi.), all uphill, a string of glaciers sitting like thick icy slabs atop almost-vertical mountains come into view, and then eggshell-blue **Bear Glacier** bursts into view. From Bear Glacier it's downhill all the way to Stewart. Keep an eye out for three mighty waterfalls on the north side of the highway, one after another. One plummets down into a large buildup of ice, complete with blue ice cave.

Stewart
The twin towns of Stewart, British Columbia, and Hyder, Alaska, straddle the international boundary at the headwaters of **Portland Inlet,**

HYDER (POP. 90)

Continue through Stewart along the Portland Canal, and next thing you know you've crossed an international border and you're in Hyder, Alaska—without all the formalities and checkpoints you'd expect at an international border.

The "Friendliest Little Ghost Town in Alaska" is a classic end-of-the-road town, with unpaved roads and a motley assortment of buildings. Local residents send their kids to school in Canada and use the Canadian phone system. Everyone sets their clocks to Pacific Standard Time, except the postmaster, who's on Alaska Time. Prices are quoted in Canadian dollars, except for that same postmaster, who only accepts U.S. currency. Finally, no one ever has to wait for a drink—Hyder has one bar for every 30 residents.

Soak up the historic charm of Hyder by wandering the main street and poking your nose in the few remaining businesses. Join the tradition and tack a bill to the wall of the **Glacier Inn** to ensure that you won't return broke, then toss back a shot of 190-proof, pure grain alcohol in one swallow to qualify for your "I've Been Hyderized" card. At the end of the main drag, head left out to the wharf, where the mountain panorama extends for 360 degrees. Head right and you're on the way to **Fish Creek,** the most accessible place in all of North America to watch bears feasting on salmon (late July–Sept.).

If you want to stay the night in Hyder, chose between basic rooms at the **Sealaska Inn** (250/636-2486, $38–48 s, $45–55 d) or pull up your rig at the campground next door. If you want to stay forever, marry a local.

the world's fourth-longest fjord. Canada's most northerly ice-free port, Stewart (pop. 800) enjoys a stunning setting; snowcapped peaks rise over 2,000 meters (6,600 ft.) from the surrounding fjord.

After a 1910 gold strike, Stewart's population mushroomed to 10,000. The main street was lined with busy shops, the city had four daily newspapers, and at least every second day a steamer loaded with new arrivals and supplies would dock at one of two long wharves. But the boom was short-lived and by the end of World War I the population had dwindled to just 20. A nearby copper mine, in Canada, but only accessible through Hyder, kept the town alive, but what's left of a local economy today revolves around the timber industry, which uses the local port facilities to transport logs to southern markets.

To get the lowdown on the town's interesting past, head to **Stewart Historical Society Museum** in the original city hall (Columbia St. between 6th St. and 7th St., 250/636-2568, July–Aug. daily 9:30 A.M.–4:30 P.M.).

Practicalities

Four historic buildings holding over 30 rooms are all centrally located to downtown. One is an old hotel, another was once home to a brothel, another is above the Bitter Creek Café. All rooms have modern bathrooms and most are in a contemporary style. Check in is at the **Ripley Creek Inn** (250/636-2344, www.ripleycreekinn.homestead.com) just off the main street. Rates range $59–99 s, $59–120 d. **King Edward Hotel & Motel** (5th Ave., 250/636-2244 or

800/663-3126, www.kingedwardhotel.com) has a café (the local gathering spot for breakfast), restaurant, and bar. Choose between air-conditioned guest rooms in the hotel, or motel rooms with kitchens, which are across the road. Either way, you have to pay more than they're worth—$79 s, $89 d for those in the hotel and $99 s, $109 d in the motel. Nestled at the base of a steep-sided forest at the back of Stewart is **Rainey Creek Campground** (8th Ave., 250/636-2537, May–Sept., $15–20). Facilities are basic, and you need quarters for the showers.

Along the main street, the **Bitter Creek Café** (311 5th Ave., 250/636-2166, daily for lunch and dinner) mixes small-town friendliness with contemporary cooking. Choose from seafood chowder ($7), vegetable stir-fry topped with a handful of prawns ($20), halibut done multiple ways ($20), or something as global as single-serve gourmet pizza ($13). It's definitely the best food in town. Next door, the small but ever-busy **Brothers Bakery** sells delicious cakes and breads at reasonable prices.

Staff at **Stewart Visitor Info Centre** (north end of 5th Ave., 250/636-9224 or 888/366-5999, mid-May–mid-Sept. daily 8:30 A.M.–7 P.M.) are a wealth of local information. Ask for road conditions out to Salmon Glacier, hard-to-find trail-heads, and history sheets.

The Road to Salmon Glacier

Continuing beyond Hyder, the unpaved road follows Fish Creek and then the Salmon River, passing an abandoned mining operation and then the ruins of a covered bridge. From this point the road narrows considerably and becomes increasingly steep (travel is not recommended for RVs), crossing back into Canada and looping through abandoned mine buildings. It continues climbing steeply, with Salmon Glacier first coming into view 25 kilometers (15.5 mi.) from Hyder. The road parallels the glacier and climbs to a high point after another 10 kilometers (6.2 mi.), where the best lookout point is. This glacier, one of Canada's largest and most accessible, is one of British Columbia's most awesome sights, snaking for many

kilometers through the highest peaks of the Coast Mountains.

NORTH OF MEZIADIN JUNCTION

Meziadin to Dease Lake

For the first 200 kilometers (124 mi.) north from Meziadin Junction, the Cassiar Highway follows a valley bordered by the Coast Mountains to the west and the Skeena Mountains to the east. Around 100 kilometers (62 mi.) from Meziadin, **Bell II Lodge** (250/558-7980 or 888/655-5566, www.bell2lodge.com) comes into view. Fishing is the biggest attraction here, especially through summer for chinook salmon and in early fall for steelhead. The lodge sells all the tackle you'll need, rents belly boats, and offers a variety of guiding services ($250 for a full day). The lodge itself holds comfortable rooms for $119 s or d, a restaurant (open daily 7 A.M.–10 P.M.), and a bar. Tent camping is $12 and RVs and trailers pay $17.

At the 200-kilometer (124-mi.) mark is 1,800-hectare (4,400-acre) **Kinaskan Lake Provincial Park,** known for its hungry rainbow trout. In the south of the park, a trail leads one kilometer (0.6 mi.) to great fishing at Natadesleen Lake, then a similar distance to beautiful, tiered Cascade Falls. Camping is $14 a night.

The small Tahltan town of **Iskut** has a post office, gas station, and grocery store. North of Iskut is **Bear Paw Ranch Resort** (250/234-3005), where cabins are $65 s or d and lodge-style rooms are $95 s or d. The resort offers horseback riding, fishing, canoe trips, and amenities including a restaurant, lounge, hot tub, and sauna.

North of Iskut, the Cassiar Highway passes through **Stikine River Provincial Park.** The bridge over the Stikine River is used as a pull-out point for canoe trips that start in **Spatsizi Plateau Wilderness Provincial Park,** farther east. Downstream from the bridge, the river flows in a torrent of white water through the **Grand Canyon of the Stikine,** an 85-kilometer (53-mi.) defile.

Dease Lake

The small community of Dease Lake, on the shores of its namesake lake 65 kilometers (40 mi.) north of Iskut, provides basic tourist services. Accommodations are at the **Northway Motor Inn** (250/771-5341, $70 s, $74 d) and the closest camping is 10 kilometers (6.2 mi.) south, where the highway crosses the Tanzilla River. The best place to eat is the **Boulder Café** (daily 8 A.M.–9 P.M.), where an always-busy waitress will serve you breakfast (around $8), lunch, or dinner (burgers $7, main dishes from $10) while you admire the old photographs lining the walls.

Telegraph Creek

From Dease Lake a gravel road leads 119 kilometers (74 mi.) west along the Tanzilla River to Telegraph Creek (pop. 300), overlooking the Stikine River. The road passes through the Stikine River Recreation Area, where it drops over one incredibly steep and scary section. The hamlet boasts friendly people, gorgeous scenery, and heritage buildings dating back to the 1860s. Jet boat trips are a good way to travel even farther into the wilderness—by the hour or day, or right through to Wrangell, Alaska (book through Stikine Riversong Lodge). Originally a Hudson's Bay Company store, the **Stikine Riversong Lodge** (250/235-3196, www.stikineriversong .com) has a café, general store, gas station, and comfortable rooms for $60 s, $65 d.

Continuing to the Alaska Highway

As you continue north from the turnoff to Telegraph Creek, the road parallels the east shore of Dease Lake. Good campsites are found by the lake, along with the occasional chunk of jade on the lakeshore—the area has been called the jade capital of the world. From Dease Lake to the Alaska Highway it's clear sailing for 235 kilometers (140 mi.) along the northern slopes of the Cassiar Mountains.

Cassiar, 115 kilometers (71 mi.) north of Dease Lake, was once a company town for an asbestos mine, complete with a thousand residents, a grocery store, liquor store, bank, supermarket, and a multimillion-dollar school. But when the mine closed in 1992 the buildings were auctioned off right down to the last fence post. A 16-kilometer (10-mi.) spur leads to the ex-townsite. Continuing north is **Boya Lake,** clear, icy cold, well stocked with fish, and ringed by white claylike beaches. Campsites are $14 per night.

From Boya Lake, the highway continues north, paralleling the Dease River for around 20 kilometers (12 mi.) and traversing the Liard Plain across the border and into the Yukon. From the border it's another four kilometers (2.5 mi.) to the junction of the Alaska Highway, then 21 kilometers (13 mi.) east to Watson Lake or 423 kilometers (263 mi.) west to Whitehorse.

North from Prince George

The landscapes and lifestyles in the area northeast of Prince George are closely aligned with neighboring northwest Alberta. The region's dominant natural feature, the Peace River, flows east from British Columbia's northern Rockies across the border into Alberta, lacing the two provinces together both topographically and economically. Rich farmland flanks the river on both sides of the border, creating a common agricultural zone whose hub is Grande Prairie, Alberta. This region of British Columbia also shares Alberta's mountain time zone.

PRINCE GEORGE TO CHETWYND

Heading north out of Prince George, Highway 97 climbs through low rolling hills to the Nechako Plateau before descending alongside the Crooked River to massive Williston Lake.

Carp Lake Provincial Park

This 38,612-hectare (95,000-acre) park lies 140 kilometers (87 mi.) north of Prince George on Highway 97, then 32 kilometers (20 mi.) west along a sometimes rough unsealed road. Carp

Lake is a picturesque body of water dotted with islands and filled with fish, although you won't catch carp (the lake was named by explorer Simon Fraser, who noted Carrier Indians journeyed to the lake for fish "of the carp kind"). You really need a watercraft of some kind to truly appreciate the many coves and islands and to take advantage of the rainbow trout fishing opportunities. Still, if you're boatless and camping, the detour is worthwhile. Hiking trails follow part of a trail taken by early explorers and trappers, while another leads one kilometer (0.6 mi.) to Rainbow Lake. Campsites ($14) are spread along the lakeshore.

Mackenzie

The forestry town of Mackenzie (pop. 6,200) lies 180 kilometers (112 mi.) north of Prince George on the southern arm of massive **Williston Lake,** a reservoir created by the **W. A. C. Bennett Dam.** At the town's entrance is the world's largest tree crusher, used during the logging operation that took place in anticipation of the dam construction.

Tourist facilities in town are limited. The nicest place to stay, catering mostly to business travelers, is the **Alexander Mackenzie Hotel** (Mackenzie Blvd., 250/997-3266, $80 s or d). All 99 rooms are air-conditioned, and the complex includes a pub and restaurant. On the town's southern outskirts, **Mackenzie Municipal RV Park** is little more than a gravel parking lot, but it holds a few grassy tent sites. Picnic tables, firewood, hot showers, and hookups are all supplied for $12–16 a night.

Powder King

Continuing east toward Chetwynd, the landscape becomes more dramatic as the highway climbs steadily up the western slopes of the Rocky Mountains to **Pine Pass.** Near the pass, and right beside the highway, is Powder King (250/962-5899, www.powderking.com), another of British Columbia's legendary ski destinations. It's best known for its incredible snowfall—over 12 meters (41 ft.) annually. One triple chair and two surface lifts serve a vertical rise of 640 meters (2,100 ft.). At the base area is a self-contained village, with rentals, a café and restaurant, and limited dorm beds. Lift tickets are adult $40, senior $32, child $20. The lifts run late November–April, Thursday–Sunday only.

Chetwynd

Chetwynd (pop. 3,200) lies at the relatively busy junction of Highways 97 and 29. The community was first established in 1912, when it was known as "Little Prairie." The one main road through town is lined with services. The best option for campers is to head 29 kilometers (18 mi.) north to **Moberly Lake Provincial Park** ($14).

Make a stop at **Chetwynd Visitor Info Centre** (250/788-1943, July–early Sept. daily 8:30 A.M.–6 P.M.), in a railway caboose beside the highway, and then decide whether you want to continue east to Dawson Creek or cut off the first section of the Alaska Highway by jogging north through Hudson's Hope.

TUMBLER RIDGE

Tumbler Ridge, 94 kilometers (58.4 mi.) south of Chetwynd, is a modern boomtown that sprang up much the same way gold-rush towns did a hundred years ago. Back in the early 1980s the provincial government struck a deal with several coal companies, agreeing to improve regional infrastructure in return for the companies developing a mine and a township at the site of the rich Northeast Coal Deposits. Tumbler Ridge, now with a population of 4,000, was created virtually overnight. From the start it held all the creature comforts, services, and recreational facilities you'd expect in a long-established town.

The mining operation here is massive. The Quintette Mine moves 120 million tons of earth annually, from which 4.3 million tons of coal are extracted. From the mine, a 13-kilometer (eight-mi.) conveyor belt transports raw coal to a processing plant and railhead from where it's shipped to the port city of Prince Rupert. If you're interested in touring the mine (July and Aug. only), contact the **Tumbler Ridge Visitor Info Centre** (250/242-4702, Mon.–Fri. 8:30 A.M.–4:30 P.M.).

HUDSON'S HOPE

This small town of 1,000 is the only settlement between Chetwynd and Fort St. John. Founded as a fur-trading post in 1805, it is a picturesque spot, with the two nearby dams attracting the most attention.

W. A. C. Bennett and Peace Canyon Dams

These two dams are the area's main attractions, their sheer size an awe-inspiring sight. Together the two facilities generate almost 40 percent of the hydroelectricity used in the province.

Larger of the two, the W. A. C. Bennett Dam, seven kilometers (4.3 mi.) west of town, is one of the world's largest earth-filled structures. The 183-meter-high (600 ft.) structure backs up **Williston Lake,** British Columbia's largest lake, which extends more than 300 kilometers (186 mi.) along three flooded valleys. At the top of the dam's control building is **Bennett Dam Visitor Centre** (888/333-6667, summer daily 9 A.M.–6 P.M.), where displays catalog the construction tasks, a film celebrates the dam's opening, and the uses of electricity are detailed.

The much smaller Peace Canyon Dam is downstream from Bennett Dam, five kilometers (3.1 mi.) south of Hudson's Hope. **Peace Canyon Dam Visitor Centre** (250/783-9943, summer daily 8 A.M.–4 P.M.) focuses on more than just the dam, with displays telling the story of the fossilized plesiosaur, a marine reptile, that was discovered during dam construction, along with dozens of dinosaur footprints.

Practicalities

Neither of the town's two accommodations is outstanding. The choices are **Peace Glen Hotel** (Dudley Dr., 250/783-9966 or 877/783-5520) and **Sportsman Inn** (10501 Carter Ave., 250/783-5523). Both have an in-house pub and restaurant and charge from $70 s or d a night. The town's three municipal campgrounds each charge $9 per night. Closest to civilization is **King Gething Campground,** on the south end of town, which has flush toilets, coin-operated showers, and plenty of firewood.

Hudson's Hope Visitor Info Centre (10507 105th Ave., 250/783-9154, mid-June–early Sept. daily 9 A.M.–6 P.M.) provides brochures on nearby hiking opportunities. (The trails are enjoyable but not well marked.)

The Alaska Highway

In the early days, driving the Alaska Highway (or Alcan) was notoriously difficult. Travelers returned with tales of endless mud holes and dust, washed-out bridges, flat tires, broken windshields and smashed headlights, wildlife in the road, mosquitoes the size of hummingbirds, and sparse facilities. But they also sported "I drove the Alaska Highway" bumper stickers as though they'd won a prize. Nowadays the route doesn't require quite the bravado—it's paved most of the way, has roadside lodges fairly frequently, and can easily be driven in three days, or two at a pinch. What hasn't changed is the scenery. You'll still see mile after mile of unspoiled wilderness, the majestic peaks of the northern Canadian Rockies, abundant wildlife, and gorgeous rivers and streams (and you can still buy the stickers).

Although official signage along the Alaska Highway is in kilometers, many services are marked in miles, a legacy of imperial measurement. This only becomes confusing when you consider that highway improvements have shortened the original route. For example, Liard River Hot Springs is still marked as Mile 496, though it's now only 754 kilometers (462 mi.) from Dawson Creek.

DAWSON CREEK

Although Dawson Creek (pop. 11,700) marks the southern end of the Alaska Highway, it's still a long way north—over 400 kilometers (248 mi.) northeast of Prince George and 1,200 kilometers (746 mi.) north of Vancouver. While the

NORTH TO ALASKA

When the Japanese threatened invasion of North America during World War II, the Alaska Highway was quickly built to link Alaska with the Lower 48. It was the longest military road ever constructed in North America—an unsurpassed road-construction feat stretching 2,288 kilometers (1,421 mi.) between Dawson Creek, B.C., and Delta Junction, Alaska.

Construction began March 9, 1942, and was completed, incredibly, on November 20 that same year. In less than nine months troops had bulldozed a rough trail snaking like a crooked finger through almost impenetrable muskeg and forest, making literally hundreds of detours around obstacles and constructing 133 bridges. The highway was the major contributing factor to the growth of northern British Columbia in the 1940s. At the height of construction, the region's population boomed. Dawson Creek's population alone rose from 600 to over 10,000, and Whitehorse replaced Dawson City as a more convenient capital of the Yukon.

city thrives on its historic location at Mile Zero, it's also an important service center whose economy is more closely tied to neighboring Alberta than to British Columbia.

Northern Alberta Railway (N.A.R.) Park

This park, on the corner of Highway 2 and the Alaska Highway, makes a good first stop in town. Here you'll find Dawson Creek Visitor Info Centre, an art gallery, and the **Station Museum** (250/782-9595, June–Aug. daily 8 A.M.–7 P.M., rest of year Tues.–Sat. 10 A.M.–noon and 1–4 P.M., $3). This marvelous and curious museum, housed in the original 1931 N.A.R. station, offers exhibits on a wide variety of topics, including construction of the Alaska Highway, the area's railroad history, pioneer life, and local flora and fauna.

In the towering grain elevator adjacent to the museum is **Dawson Creek Art Gallery** (250/782-2601, summer daily 9 A.M.–5 P.M., rest of year Tues.–Sat. 10 A.M.–5 P.M.). The elevator itself is

fascinating. It was saved from demolition and redesigned with a spiral walkway around the interior walls to make the most of the building's height.

Mile Zero

In front of N.A.R. Park is the Alaska Highway's official starting point, marked by a cairn. The original marker, a one-meter (three-ft.) post, was mowed down by a car in the 1940s. Despite the cairn's official status, the Mile Zero signpost in the center of 102nd Avenue at 10th Street is more often photographed. It reads "May the highway continue to be a road to friendship" and notes the following distances: Fort St. John, 48 miles; Fort Nelson, 300 miles; Whitehorse, 918 miles; and Fairbanks, 1,523 miles.

Accommodations and Camping

Dawson Creek's oldest and most colorful accommodation is the downtown **Alaska Hotel** (10209 10th St., 250/782-7998, www.alaska hotel.com, $65 s, $75 d). Known as the Dew Drop Inn when it first opened in 1928, the guest rooms remain basic (no televisions or phones and shared bathroom facilities) but are decorated in a cheerful pink and pastel color scheme. Rooms at the **Super 8 Motel** (1440 Alaska Ave., 250/782-8899 or 800/800-8000, www.super8.com, $84 s or d) are exactly what you always get at this reliable chain—clean, comfortable, and practically furnished, with a light breakfast thoughtfully thrown in to help you avoid the local diners.

Mile Zero RV Park and Campground (250/782-2590) isn't at Mile Zero of the famous highway—it's about one kilometer (0.6 mi.) north from downtown—but it's the pick of Dawson Creek's numerous campgrounds. Sites sit around a large shaded grassy area, and each one has a picnic table. Facilities include hot showers and a laundry. Rates are $12–19 a night.

Food

The best-known eatery in town is the **Alaska Café** (Alaska Hotel, 10209 10th St., 250/782-7040). What originally opened as a candy store in the 1930s is today colorfully decorated in an old-fashioned style and serves everything from

DAWSON CREEK

To Fort St. John and
Delta Junction, Alaska

MILE ZERO RV PARK
AND CAMPGROUND

97 ALASKA HWY

MILE ZERO
CAFE

97 HART HWY.

To Chetwynd
and Prince George

SUPER 8 MOTEL

ALASKA AVE.

GREYHOUND
BUS DEPOT

CITY HALL

102ND AVE.

NORTHERN ALBERTA
RAILWAY PARK

MILE ZERO
SIGNPOST

MILE ZERO CAIRN

ALASKA
HOTEL/
CAFE

POST OFFICE

49

To Peace River
(Alberta)

108TH AVE.

SCALE NOT AVAILABLE

108TH AVE.

110TH AVE.

HOSPITAL

2

To Bear Mountain Ski Area

To Airport and Grande Prairie (Alberta)

© AVALON TRAVEL PUBLISHING, INC.

BRITISH COLUMBIA

standard pub fare like beef dip ($4) to a steak
and Alaska king crab combo. Entrées range
$10–22, with the 12-ounce T-bone ($19) the
perfect way to kick off a trip up the Alaska
Highway.

Information

An almost obligatory stop for travelers heading
north on the famous highway is the **Dawson
Creek Visitor Info Centre** (N.A.R. Park,
Alaska Ave., 250/782-9595, June–Aug. daily
8 A.M.–7 P.M., rest of year Tues.–Sat. 10 A.M.–noon
and 1–4 P.M.). **Tourism Dawson Creek** (866/
645-3022, www.tourismdawsoncreek.com) is a
good source of pretrip information.

FORT ST. JOHN

As the second-largest community along the
Alaska Highway (only Whitehorse, Yukon, is
larger), Fort St. John (pop.15,100) is an important service center for local industries, including oil, gas, and coal extraction; forestry; and
agriculture.

Sights

Fort St. John–North Peace Museum (9323 100th
St., 250/787-0430, June–July daily 8 A.M.–8 P.M.,
Aug.–May Mon.–Sat. 11 A.M.–4 P.M., adult $4.50,
senior $3.50, child $2.50) is difficult to miss as you
drive though town—look for the outside exhibits,

including a skyscraping 40-meter-high (130 ft.) oil derrick. Inside, local history springs to life with reconstructed historical interiors of a trapper's cabin and other furnished rooms. Don't miss the fur press, the birchbark canoe, and the grizzly bear with claws big enough to send shivers up your spine.

On the north side of town, **Charlie Lake** is a remnant of an enormous lake that covered this area more than 10,500 years ago. At Charlie Lake Cave, animal bones and artifacts such as stone tools, a fluted spear point, and a handmade stone bead—the oldest found in North America—were discovered, leading archaeologists to postulate that this area was one of the earliest North American sites occupied by humans. Modern human visitors come for the fishing (trout, arctic grayling, walleye, and northern pike) or strolling the trails in **Beatton Provincial Park.**

Accommodations and Camping

Plan on arriving in Fort St. John mid-afternoon, visit the museum or go for a hike in Charlie Lake, and then check into one of the motels lining the Alaska Highway. Ramada, Best Western, and Super 8 are all represented in town, but the amenities and standard of rooms are best at **Quality Inn Northern Grand** (9830 100th Ave., 250/787-0521 or 800/663-8312, www.qualityinnnortherngrand .com, $109 s, $119 d). Don't be perturbed by the bland, boxy exterior. Inside is a comfortable alpine-style sitting area, and indoor pool and exercise room, a restaurant, and stylish mid-size guest rooms with niceties like high-speed Internet access and heated bathroom floors.

Fort St. John Centennial RV Park (9323 100th St., 250/785-3033, $14–23) is close to the museum, but it's small and doesn't offer much shade. Facilities include showers, a laundry, and hookups. Sites are $14–23 per night. A more pleasant option would be either one of the two provincial parks north of town on Charlie Lake (all sites $14).

Information

Fort St. John Visitor Info Centre (9923 96th Ave., 250/785-3033, www.fortstjohnchamber .com) is a year-round facility (Mon.–Fri. 8 A.M.–5 P.M.) with extended summer hours (daily 8 A.M.–8 P.M.).

TO FORT NELSON

The 374-kilometer (232-mi.) stretch of the Alaska Highway between Fort St. John and Fort Nelson passes through boreal forest and a landscape that becomes more and more mountainous.

From **Wonowon,** the highway climbs steadily to **Pink Mountain,** at Mile 147. Numerous services perch on the low summit, where snow can fall year-round. On the west side of the highway, **Pink Mountain Campsite** (250/772-3234) provides tent and RV sites for $16 (no hookups) and rustic cabins that share bathrooms for $35 s, $45 d (showers are an extra $2.50). Beyond the summit is **Mae's Kitchen** (250/772-3215, daily 7 A.M.–10 P.M.), where breakfasts are huge and the pancakes ($6) and blueberry muffins ($3) are especially good. For lunch, try the house special buffalo burger, complete with fries and salad for $8.50. Continuing northward, look for the "maintained" airstrip to the west—how would you like to land on that one?

Sikanni Chief to Prophet River

Twenty kilometers (12 mi.) north from Sikanni Chief you'll pass **Buckinghorse River Provincial Park,** which offers camping ($14 a night) and good river fishing. From here north, a scenic stretch of the highway runs through Minaker River Valley then parallels the Prophet River, passing a rustic campground (open May–Sept., $8) where a hiking trail leads down to the river.

FORT NELSON

At Mile 300 of the Alaska Highway, Fort Nelson (pop. 4,100) is the largest town between Fort St. John and the Yukon. The Muskwa, Prophet, and Sikanni Chief Rivers all flow together here to create the large Fort Nelson River, which in turn flows into the even larger Liard River.

Sights

Fort Nelson Historical Museum (north end of town, 250/774-3536, summer daily 8:30 A.M.–7:30 P.M., adult $5, senior or child $3.50) contains a great collection of Alaska Highway construction items and native and pioneer artifacts. An interesting 30-minute movie, shown throughout the day, uses footage taken during the construction of the highway to effectively convey what a mammoth task the project was. At the end of Mountain View Drive is the **Native Trail,** a four-kilometer (2.5-mi.) self-guided interpretive trail that passes two native-style shelters and holds signs describing native foods, local wildlife, and trapping methods. Allow at least one hour round-trip.

Accommodations and Camping

Fort Nelson has many hotels and motels spread out along the Alaska Highway. The nicest is **Blue Bell Inn** (4103 50th Ave., 250/774-6961) a modern two-story lodging with comfortable air-conditioned rooms, a laundry, and an adjacent 24-hour restaurant. Rates are $65 s, $75 d, kitchens an extra $10.

Beside the museum is **Westend Campground** (250/774-2340, Apr.–Oct., $15–21), where you can choose from tent sites in an open area or individual sites surrounded by trees. Facilities include coin-operated showers, a launderette, grocery store, and free firewood. On either side of town along the Alaska Highway, the closest camping is 20 kilometers (12 mi.) south at Andy Bailey Provincial Recreation Area or 77 kilometers (48 mi.) west at Tetsa River Provincial Park.

Food

As you enter town from the south, modern **Dan's Neighbourhood Pub** (4204 50th Ave. N, 250/774-3929, daily 11 A.M.–midnight) wouldn't look out of place in Vancouver—and it's always busy. All the usual fare is offered, with entrées under $12.

Information

At Mile 300.5 of the Alaska Highway is **Fort Nelson Visitor Info Centre** (250/774-6868, summer daily 8 A.M.–8 P.M.).

CONTINUING TO WATSON LAKE

Awaiting the traveler on this 525-kilometer (326-mi.) portion of the Alaska Highway are Rocky Mountain peaks, glacial lakes, mountain streams, provincial parks with some great scenery, and the mighty Liard River.

Soon after leaving Fort Nelson, the Alaska Highway climbs the lower slopes of **Steamboat Mountain,** which, with a certain amount of imagination, resembles an upturned boat. Here you'll have tremendous views of the Rocky Mountains and the valley below.

Summit Lake and Vicinity

This lake, 140 kilometers (87 mi.) west of Fort Nelson, is a popular stopping point for travelers. It lies at the north end of 25,690-hectare (63,500-acre) **Stone Mountain Provincial Park,** a vast wilderness of jagged peaks, lakes, and rivers. At Summit Lake's eastern end is an exposed campground ($14 a night) with pit toilets and picnic tables. The **Summit Café** (daily 7 A.M.–10 P.M.) is a popular truck stop.

Just beyond the lake, the highway crosses 1,295-meter (4,250-ft.) **Summit Pass,** highest point along the Alaska Highway. From this lofty summit, the highway continues to **One-fifteen Creek Provincial Park,** where a short trail leads to huge beaver dams. Camping in the park is $14.

Muncho Lake Provincial Park

Lying among mountains and forested valleys at the north end of the Canadian Rockies, this 88,420-hectare (218,500-acre) park surrounds stunning **Muncho Lake,** one of the highlights of the Alaska Highway. Upon entering the park from the east, the park's namesake lake will grab your attention. The magnificent, 12-kilometer-long (7.5 mi.) body of water is encircled by a dense spruce forest, which gives way to barren rocky slopes at higher elevations. North of the lake, natural mineral licks attract Stone sheep and woodland caribou to the roadside.

The small community of Muncho Lake spreads out along the eastern banks of the lake, providing services for park visitors. If you plan to overnight here, try to book ahead; motel rooms

BRITISH COLUMBIA

and campgrounds all fill up well in advance in July and August. **J & H Wilderness Resort** (250/776-3453) offers basic motel rooms ($68 s or d) and campsites ($18–27) with clean and modern facilities, including free hot showers. The resort's restaurant (daily 7 A.M.–10 P.M.) is particularly good, and portions are served with the traveler's hearty appetite in mind. The most pleasant camping is found at the two campgrounds in the provincial park itself, north of the town. Sites at these two campgrounds are all $14 a night, but with only 15 sites in each one, they fill up fast.

Liard River Hot Springs Provincial Park

One of the most wonderful places to stop on the whole highway is this 1,082-hectare (2,700-acre) park, 40 kilometers (25 mi.) north of Muncho Lake. Most travelers understandably rush to soak their tired, dusty limbs in the hot pools. But the rest of the park is also worth exploring. The hot springs have created a microclimate around the overflow area. Over 80 of the plant species here are found nowhere else in northern British Columbia. Also inhabiting the area are many species of small fish, plus mammals such as moose, woodland caribou, and black bear. A 500-meter (0.3-mi.) boardwalk leads to Alpha Pool, where water bubbles up into a long, shallow manmade pool surrounded by decking. A rough trail leads farther to undeveloped Beta Pool, which is cooler, much deeper, and not as busy.

At the entrance to the hot springs is a campground providing toilets and showers. Sites are $17 May–August and $10 the rest of the year. The sites are often full by noon. Gates to the hot springs and campground are locked between 11 P.M. and 6 A.M.

Opposite the park entrance, at Mile 497, is **Trapper Ray's Lodge** (250/776-7349), which has rooms for $70 s or $75 d, campsites for $14–18, a small café, some grocery supplies, and gas.

To Watson Lake

Anglers will find good fishing for grayling in the Liard River below Smith River Falls, 30 kilometers (18.6 mi.) or so northwest of the hot springs. Canyon and river views dot the highway heading north and west, and visitor services are available at Coal River and Fireside. The highway crosses the 60th parallel and enters the **Yukon** just before Contact Creek Lodge (all services). It then meanders back and forth across the border six times before reaching the final crossing, 57 kilometers (35 mi.) farther west.

Alberta

The prosperous province of Alberta, the heart of western Canada, lies between the mountains of British Columbia to the west and the prairies of Saskatchewan to the east. Its total area is 661,185 square kilometers (255,000 sq. mi.) and holds a population of 3 million. **Edmonton,** the capital, is a modern, livable city boasting some of Canada's finest cultural facilities, as well as the world's largest shopping and amusement mall. Calgary, meanwhile, is home to the world-famous **Calgary Stampede**—a Western wingding of epic proportions. But for most visitors to Alberta, the great outdoors, not the big cities or the fast bucks, is the main draw. The stunning mountain playgrounds of **Banff** and **Jasper National Parks** show off the **Canadian Rockies** at their best, with pristine glaciers, rushing rivers, and snowcapped peaks reflected in hundreds of high-country lakes. The parks, and much of the rest of the province, are home to an abundance of wildlife such as moose, elk, bighorn sheep, wolves, bears, and an amazing array of birds. Ancient wildlife thrived here, too—one of the world's greatest concentrations of dinosaur bones continues to be unearthed in the Red Deer River Valley outside **Drumheller.**

Note: Please see front color map **Alberta.**

Calgary

Calgary's nickname, "Cowtown," is cherished by the city's 1,000,000 residents, who prefer that romantic vision of their beloved home to the city's more modern identity as a world energy and financial center. The city's rapid growth, from a North West Mounted Police (NWMP) post to a large and vibrant metropolis in little more than 100 years, can be credited largely to the effects of resource development, particularly oil and natural gas.

Once run by gentlemen who had made their fortunes in ranching, Calgary is still an important cattle market. But the oil and gas bonanzas of the 1940s, 1950s, and 1970s changed everything. The resources discovered throughout western Canada brought enormous wealth and growth to the city, turning it into the headquarters for a burgeoning energy industry. With the city's rapid growth came all the problems plaguing major cities around the world, with one major exception—the distinct lack of manufacturing and industrial sites means there is little pollution.

Downtown is a massive cluster of modern steel-and-glass skyscrapers, the legacy of an explosion of

ALBERTA

112TH AVE. NE

To Drumheller and Edmonton

52ND ST. NE

McKNIGHT BLVD.

To Dinosaur Provincial Park and Medicine Hat

MEMORIAL DR.

52ND ST. SE

36TH ST. NE

36TH ST. SE

1A

72

C-TRAIN

17TH AVE. SE

BARLOW TRAIL

CALGARY INTERNATIONAL AIRPORT

32ND AVE. NE

16TH AVE. NE

BARLOW TRAIL

Inglewood Bird Sanctuary

2

Nose Creek

DEERFOOT TRAIL

CALGARY ZOO

FISH HATCHERY

2

EDMONTON TRAIL

STAMPEDE PARK AND SADDLEDOME

Nose Creek

BEDDINGTON BLVD.

64TH AVE. NW

CENTRE ST.

SEE "CALGARY CITY CENTER" MAP

River

West Nose Creek

BEDDINGTON TRAIL

4TH ST. NW

16TH AVE.

9TH AVE. SW

12TH AVE. SW

14TH ST. NW

14TH ST. NW

Nose Hill Park

33RD AVE.

SYMONS VALLEY RD.

BANFF TRAIL

JUBILEE AUDITORIUM

MEMORIAL DR.

BUS DEPOT

CROWCHILD T

COUNTRY HILLS BLVD.

C-TRAIN

MOTEL VILLAGE

40TH AVE. NW

UNIVERSITY OF CALGARY

McMAHON STADIUM

BOWNESS RD.

BOW TRAIL

EDGEMONT BLVD

JOHN LAURIE BLVD.

CROWCHILD TRAIL

53RD ST. NW

17TH AVE. SW

SARCEE TRAIL

112TH AVE.

NOSE HILL DR

53RD ST. NW

1A

Bow River

SARCEE TRAIL

CALGARY

8

BOW VALLEY TRAIL

STONEY TRAIL

TRANSCANADA HIGHWAY

CANADA OLYMPIC PARK

OLD BANFF COACH RD.

563

To Cochrane

To Banff

KOA CALGARY WEST

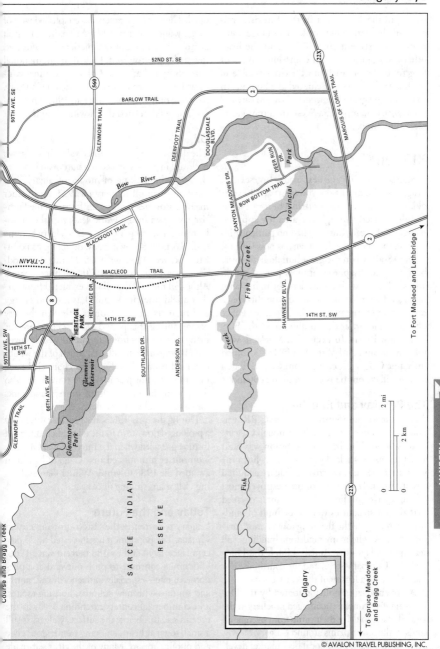

ALBERTA

wealth in the 1970s. Set in this futuristic mirage on the prairie are banks, insurance companies, investment companies, and the head offices of hundreds of oil companies. But not forgetting its roots, each July the city sets aside all the material success it's achieved as a boomtown to put on the greatest outdoor show on earth—the Calgary Stampede, a Western extravaganza second to none.

HISTORY

In addition to being one of Canada's largest cities, Calgary is also one of the youngest; at 130 years old, it has a heritage rather than a history. Native peoples moved through the area for approximately 2,000 years, but they had no particular interest in the direct vicinity of what is now Calgary. In the 1860s, when the great buffalo herds were beginning to disappear, hunters moved north, and so did the whiskey traders, bringing with them all the problems associated with this illegal trade. In 1875, the North West Mounted Police established a fort at the confluence of the Bow and Elbow Rivers. Inspector J.F. Macleod, who took over command of the fort in 1876, coined the name Calgary. It comes from Calgary Bay, a remote village on the Isle of Mull in Scotland.

The Railway and Ranching

As soon it was announced that the C.P.R. was building its transcontinental line through Calgary, settlers flooded in. In 1883, a station was built and a townsite was laid out around it. Just nine years after the railway arrived, Calgary acquired city status. In 1886, a major fire destroyed most of the town's buildings. City planners decreed that all new structures were to be built of sandstone, which gave the fledgling town a more permanent look. The many sandstone buildings still standing today—the Palliser Hotel, the Hudson's Bay Company store, and the courthouse, for example—are a legacy of this early bylaw.

An open grazing policy initiated by the Dominion Government encouraged ranchers in the United States to drive their cattle from overgrazed lands to the fertile plains around Calgary. Slowly, a ranching industry and local beef market devel-

oped. The first large ranch was established west of Calgary, and soon many NWMP retirees, English aristocrats, and wealthy American citizens had invested in nearby land. Linked to international markets by rail and sea, Calgary's fortunes continued to rise with those of the ranching industry, receiving only a minor setback in 1905 when Edmonton was declared the provincial capital.

Oil

The discovery of oil at Turner Valley in Calgary's backyard in 1914 signaled the start of an industry that was the making of modern Calgary. The opening of an oil refinery in 1923 and further major discoveries nearby transformed a medium-size cowtown into a world leader in the petroleum and natural gas industries. Calgary became Canada's fastest-growing city, doubling its population between 1950 and 1975. During the worldwide energy crisis of the 1970s, oil prices soared. Although most of the oil was extracted from farther afield, the city boomed as a world energy and financial center. Construction in the city center during this period was never-ending, as many corporations from around the world moved their headquarters to Alberta. Much of the wealth obtained from oil and gas was channeled back into the city, not just for office towers but also for sporting facilities, cultural centers, and parks for citizens and visitors alike to enjoy.

During the early 1980s, the province was hit by a prolonged downturn in the oil market. But good fortune prevailed when the International Olympic Committee announced that Calgary had been awarded the **1988 Olympic Winter Games,** leaving Calgarians smiling once again.

Today and the Future

Calgary is currently the fastest-growing city in Canada. The population has increased by 25 percent since 1994 and by 188 percent since 1966. City limits continue to push outward at a phenomenal rate—especially in the northwest, north, and south—with new suburbs, housing estates, and commercial centers extending as far as the eye can see. But below the surface, Calgary is still a small town at heart, enjoying tremendous civic and public support. Many of the city's self-made millionaires bequeath their money to the city, and residents in their thousands are always willing to volunteer their time at events such as the Calgary Stampede. This civic pride makes the city a great place to live and an enjoyable destination for the millions of tourists who visit each year.

Sights

DOWNTOWN

The downtown core is a mass of modern steel-and-glass high-tech high-rises built during the oil boom of the 1970s and early 1980s. Many historic buildings were knocked down during this development, but the last few years has seen a subtle change in direction, with developers incorporating historic buildings in new projects, especially along Stephen Avenue Walk.

Crisscrossing downtown is the Plus 15 walkway system—a series of interconnecting, enclosed sidewalks elevated at least 4.5 meters (15 ft.—hence the name) above road level. In total, 47 bridges and 12 kilometers (7.5 mi.) of public walkway link downtown stores, four large malls, hotels, food courts, and office buildings to give pedestrians protection from the elements. All walkways are well marked and wheelchair accessible. The following sights can be visited separately or seen on a walking tour (in the order presented).

Stephen Avenue Walk

The traditional center of the city is 8th Avenue, between 1st Street SE and 3rd Street SW—a traffic-free zone known as Stephen Avenue Walk. This bustling, tree-lined pedestrian mall has fountains, benches, cafés, restaurants, and souvenir shops. In summer, the mall is full of shoppers and tourists, and at lunchtime, thousands of office workers descend from the buildings above. Many of Calgary's earliest sandstone buildings still stand along the mall on the block between 1st and 2nd Streets SW. On the corner of 1st Street SW is the **Alberta Hotel,** one of the city's most popular meeting places until Prohibition in 1916.

At the east end of the walk is **Olympic Plaza,** used during the 1988 Olympic Winter Games for the nightly medal-presentation ceremonies (plaques commemorate medal winners). Today, it's a popular summer lunch spot for office workers,

and in winter the frozen wading pool is used as an ice-skating rink. Across 2nd Street SE from the plaza is **City Hall,** built in 1911. It still houses some city offices, although most have moved next door to the modern **Civic Complex.**

Glenbow Museum

Adjacent to Stephen Avenue Walk, this excellent museum (130 9th Avenue SE, 403/268-4100, Mon.–Sat. 9 A.M.–5 P.M., Sun. noon–5 P.M., adult $11, senior $8.50, child $7) chronicles the entire history of western Canada through three floors of informative exhibits and well-displayed artifacts. Second floor galleries display the museum's permanent collections of contemporary and Inuit art. The third-floor Nitsitapiisinni Gallery is the best part of the museum. Developed under the

Calgary's historic City Hall

5TH AVE. NW

4TH AVE. NW

3RD AVE. NW

7TH ST. NW

1ST AVE. NW

2ND AVE. NW

8TH ST. NW

11TH ST. NW

10TH ST. NW

9TH ST. NW

MEMORIAL DR.

C. TRAIN

Prince's Island Park

RIVER CAFÉ

Footbridge

KENSINGTON RD.

EAU CLAIRE MARKET

EAU CLAIRE AVE.

CHINESE CULTURAL CENTRE ★

2ND AVE. SW

7TH ST. SW

6TH ST. SW

2ND ST. SW

3RD AVE. SW

INTERNATIONAL HOTEL

CAESAR'S STEAKHOUSE

HY'S STEAKHOUSE

4TH AVE. SW

HAWTHORN HOTEL & SUITES

5TH AVE. SW

3RD ST. SW

5TH ST. SW

BOW VALLEY SQUARE

To Bus Depot

6TH AVE. SW

7TH AVE. SW

CALGARY SCIENCE CENTRE ★

DEVONIAN GARDENS ★

STEPHEN AVENUE WALK

JAMES JOYCE IRISH PUB

11TH ST. SW

10TH ST.

9TH ST. SW

8TH ST. SW

8TH AVE. SW

THE BAY

THE PALACE ▼

9TH AVE. SW

COWBOYS ▼

BANKERS HALL

POST OFFICE

CO RC

MOUNTAIN EQUIPMENT CO-OP

ALBERTA BOOT CO.

FAIRMONT PALLISER

10TH AVE. SW

BUZZARD'S COWBOY CUISINE

VISTEK

BONTERRA RESTAURANT

THAI SA-ON ▼

12TH ST. SW

11TH AVE. SW

8TH ST. SW

7TH ST. SW

6TH ST. SW

5TH ST. SW

4TH ST. SW

2ND ST. SW

1ST ST. SW

12TH AVE. SW

13TH AVE. SW

10TH ST. SW

9TH ST.

BEST WESTERN SUITES DOWNTOWN

14TH AVE. SW

15TH AVE. SW

16TH AVE. SW

NELLIE'S ▼

KAO'S JAZZ AND BLUES BISTRO ▼

17TH AVE. SW

MERCURY ▼

18TH AVE. SW

18TH AVE. SW

19TH AVE. SW

ROYAL AVE.

20TH AVE. SW

DURHAM AVE.

ALBERTA

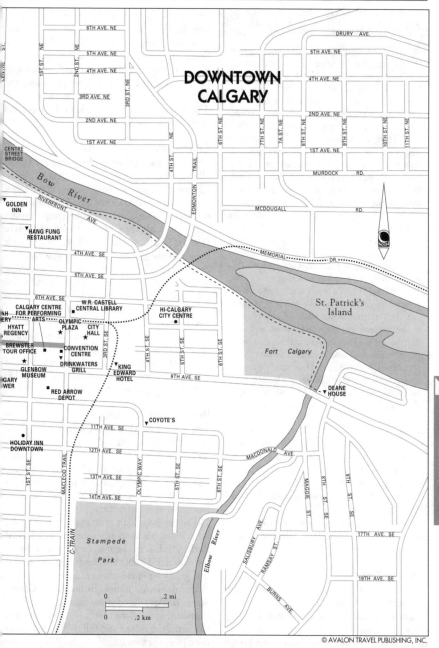

DOWNTOWN CALGARY

6TH AVE. NE
5TH AVE. NE
4TH AVE. NE
3RD AVE. NE
2ND AVE. NE
1ST AVE. NE

DRURY AVE.
5TH AVE. NE
4TH AVE. NE
2ND AVE. NE
1ST AVE. NE

MURDOCK RD.

CENTRE STREET BRIDGE

Bow River

RIVERFRONT AVE.

MCDOUGALL RD.

MEMORIAL DR.

GOLDEN INN

HANG FUNG RESTAURANT

4TH AVE. SE
5TH AVE. SE
6TH AVE. SE

W.R. CASTELL CENTRAL LIBRARY

HI-CALGARY CITY CENTRE

St. Patrick's Island

CALGARY CENTRE FOR PERFORMING ARTS

OLYMPIC PLAZA   CITY HALL

Fort Calgary

HYATT REGENCY

BREWSTER TOUR OFFICE

CONVENTION CENTRE

DRINKWATERS GRILL

KING EDWARD HOTEL

9TH AVE. SE

GLENBOW MUSEUM

RED ARROW DEPOT

DEANE HOUSE

COYOTE'S

11TH AVE. SE

MACDONALD AVE.

HOLIDAY INN DOWNTOWN

12TH AVE. SE
13TH AVE. SE
14TH AVE. SE

MAGGIE ST.

17TH AVE. SE

C-TRAIN

Stampede Park

Elbow River

SALISBURY AVE.

RAMSAY ST.

BURNS AVE.

19TH AVE. SE

0   .2 mi
0   .2 km

ALBERTA

© AVALON TRAVEL PUBLISHING, INC.

GETTING ORIENTED

The TransCanada Highway (Hwy. 1) passes through the city north of downtown and is known as **16th Avenue North** within the city limits. Highway 2, Alberta's major north–south highway, is known as **Deerfoot Trail** within city limits. Many major arteries are known as **trails;** The main route south from downtown is **Macleod Trail,** a 12-kilometer (7.5-mi.) strip of malls, motels, restaurants, and retail stores. If you enter Calgary from the west and are heading south, a handy bypass to take is **Sarcee Trail,** then **Glenmore Trail,** which joins Highway 2 south of the city. **Crowchild Trail** starts downtown and heads northwest past the university to Cochrane.

The street-numbering system is divided into four quadrants—northwest, northeast, southwest, and southeast. Each street address has a corresponding abbreviation tacked onto it (NW, NE, SW, and SE). The north–south division is the Bow River. The east–west division is at Macleod Trail and north of downtown at **Centre Street.** Streets run north to south and avenues from east to west. Both streets and avenues are numbered progressively from the quadrant divisions (e.g., an address on 58th Ave. SE is the 58th street south of the Bow River, is east of Macleod Trail, and is on a street that runs east to west).

watchful eye of Blackfoot elders, it details the stories and traditions of native peoples, through interpretive panels and displays of ceremonial artifacts, jewelry, and a full-size teepee. The third floor also presents historical displays on each aspect of the Canadian West—the fur trade, the North West Mounted Police, pioneering settlers, ranching, and the oil industry. On the fourth floor is a collection of military paraphernalia and mineralogy displays (including a meteorite).

Calgary Tower
Built in 1968, the Calgary Tower (9th Ave. and Centre St., 403/266-7171, 6:30 A.M.–11 P.M.) is now only Calgary's fourth-highest building, but the ride to the top is still a worthwhile introduction to the city. The Observation Terrace

affords a bird's-eye view of the Canadian Rockies and the ski-jump towers at Canada Olympic Park to the west, the Olympic Saddledome (in Stampede Park) to the south, and the city below. The non-reflective glass is perfect for photography, binoculars are available for guest use, and audio-visual terminals describe the sights below. The one-minute elevator ride to the top costs adult $10, senior $7, child $5.

Chinatown
At the east end of town on 3rd Avenue is a small Chinatown of approximately 2,000 residents. Chinese immigrants came to Calgary in the 1880s to work on the railroads and stayed to establish exotic food markets, restaurants, and import stores here. The **Calgary Chinese Cultural Centre** (197 1st St. SW, 403/262-5071, 9 A.M.–9 P.M.) is one of the largest such centers in Canada. The centerpiece of its intricate interior is a glistening golden dragon hanging 20 meters (66 ft.) above the floor. Head up to the 3rd floor for the best views, passing a mural along the way. At street level is a store selling traditional Chinese medicines and on the lower level is a small museum and gallery (11 A.M.–5 P.M.) displaying the cultural history of Calgarians of Chinese descent. One of the museum's most intriguing pieces is the world's first seismograph, which dates from A.D. 132.

West on First Avenue
Eau Claire Market at the north end of 3rd Street SW is a colorful indoor market filled with stalls selling fresh fruit from British Columbia, seafood from the Pacific, Alberta beef, bakery items, and exotic imports. Under the same roof are specialty shops, an IMAX and regular theaters, and nine restaurants.

The northern limit of downtown is along the Bow River, where picturesque **Prince's Island Park** is linked to the mainland by a bridge at the end of 3rd Street SW. Jogging paths, tables, and grassy areas are scattered among the trees of this manmade island. To the east is **Centre Street Bridge,** guarded on either side by large (restored) stone lions. For a good view of the city, cross the bridge and follow the trail along the cliff to the west.

Devonian Gardens

The C-train will whisk you from the Calgary Science Centre back into the heart of the city to Devonian Gardens. A glass-enclosed elevator rises to the 4th floor of Toronto Dominion Square (8th Ave. and 3rd St. SW, 403/221-4274, daily 9 A.M.–9 P.M.), where a one-hectare (2.5-acre) indoor garden features 16,000 subtropical plants and 4,000 local plants—138 species in all. Within the gardens are waterfalls, fountains, pools, and bridges. Lunchtime entertainers and art exhibits can often be enjoyed in this serene environment. Admission is free, and it's open year-round.

HISTORIC PARKS

Fort Calgary Historic Park

In 1875, with the onset of a harsh winter, the newly arrived NWMP built Fort Calgary at the confluence of the Bow and Elbow Rivers in less than six weeks. The original fort is long gone—instead the 16-hectare (40-acre) site has been transformed into a two-part historic park (750 9th Ave. SE, 403/290-1875, May–early Oct. daily 9 A.M.–5 P.M., adult $8, senior $7, child $5). Most of the focus is on the interpretive center, housed in a replica of 1888 barracks, complete with volunteer RCMP veterans on hand to answer questions. Inside, the lives of Canada's famous "Mounties," the legacy of natives, hardy pioneers, and the wild frontier they tamed all are re-created by convincingly costumed interpreters. History comes alive through a variety of activities and programs, including working carpenters, a room especially for kids and filled with games of a bygone era, and a canteen selling meals that I imagine are more appealing than the those the original officers enjoyed. Beside the barracks is an exact replica of the original fort, built using tools and techniques that are more than 100 years old. Tours of the fort (included in general admission) leave at regular intervals through the day

CALGARY FOR KIDS

Calgary offers plenty of distractions for children. **Calgary Zoo** and **Heritage Park** (detailed in the main text) mix kid-friendliness with enough of interest to keep grown-ups busy as well. Here are a few other suggestions to keep the young ones occupied.

Calgary Science Centre

This downtown complex (701 11th St. SW, 403/268-8300, summer 9:30 A.M.–5 P.M., rest of year Tues.–Sun. 10 A.M.–5 P.M., adult $11, senior $9, child $8) is a wonderful facility chock-a-block with hands-on science exhibits. WOWtown is especially for the under-seven crowd—a working crane model, playground and maze, microscopes, optical illusions, and even a "quiet room." In the **Discovery Dome,** dynamic audiovisuals are projected onto a massive concave screen.

Out and About

Kids will be kids, so plan on taking a break from Calgary's regular attractions and head 10 kilometers (6.2 mi.) west of the city limits to **Calaway Park** (TransCanada Hwy., 403/240-3822, May–June Sat.–Sun. 10 A.M.–8 P.M., July–Aug. daily 10 A.M.–8 P.M., Sept.–mid-Oct. Sat.–Sun. 11 A.M.–6 P.M.), with 27 rides including a double-loop roller coaster. Other attractions include an enormous maze, Western-themed minigolf, a zoo for the kids, a trout-fishing pond, and live entertainment in the Western-style "Showtime Theatre." Everything except food is included in the admission charge of $21 for those aged 7–49 and $15 for those aged 3–6, free for all others.

The **City of Calgary** (403/268-2489) operates nine outdoor pools (open June–early Sept.) and 12 indoor pools (open year-round). Facilities at each vary. The outdoor pools in **Fish Creek Provincial Park** are among the most popular while the nearby **Family Leisure Centre** (11150 Bonaventure Dr. SE, 403/278-7542, daily 9 A.M.–9 P.M.) has a lot more to offer than just swimming. Entry of $8 includes use of regular pools as well as a giant indoor water slide, a wave pool, and even a skating rink.

from the main lobby of the barracks. To get to Fort Calgary, either walk along the river from downtown or hop aboard bus no. 1 (Forest Lawn) or no. 14 (East Calgary) from 7th Avenue.

Heritage Park

This 27-hectare (66-acre) park (1900 Heritage Dr. SW, 403/268-8500, mid-May–Aug. daily 9 A.M.–5 P.M., Sept.–early Oct. Sat.–Sun. only 9 A.M.–5 P.M.) is on a peninsula jutting into Glenbow Reservoir southwest of downtown. More than 100 buildings and exhibits help re-create an early-20th-century pioneer village. Many of the buildings have been moved to the park from their original locations. Highlights include a Hudson's Bay Company fort, a two-story outhouse, a working blacksmith's shop, an 1896 church, a tepee, and an old schoolhouse with original desks. A boardwalk links stores crammed with antiques, and horse-drawn buggies carry passengers along the streets. You can also ride in authentic passenger cars pulled by a steam locomotive or enjoy a cruise in a paddlewheeler on the reservoir. A traditional bakery sells cakes and pastries, and full meals are served in the Wainwright Hotel. Park admission only adult $13 ($22 with all rides), child $8 ($17 with all rides). A pancake breakfast is offered free for visitors arriving before 10 A.M. To get there, take the C-train to Heritage Station and transfer to bus no. 502 (weekends only).

CANADA OLYMPIC PARK

This 95-hectare (235-acre) park beside the Trans-Canada Highway on the western outskirts of the city was developed for the 1988 Olympic Winter Games and is now a legacy Calgarians get to enjoy year-round. Olympic events held here were ski-jumping, luge, bobsled, and freestyle skiing. I doubt that many people remember the winner, but the memories of a bobsled team from Jamaica and the antics of English plumber/ski-jumper "Eddie the Eagle" will be etched in the minds of everyone who watched for years to come.

Olympic Hall of Fame

This is North America's largest museum devoted to the Olympic Games. Three floors catalog the entire history of the Olympic Winter Games through more than 1,500 exhibits, interactive video displays, costumes and memorabilia, an athletes timeline, a bobsled and ski-jump simulator, and highlights from the last four Olympic Winter Games held at Albertville (France), Lillehammer (Norway), and Nagano (Japan), and Salt Lake City (United States), including costumes worn by Jamie Sale and David Pelletier during their infamous silver-then-gold-medal–winning final skate. Most visitors pass through the museum (summer 8 A.M.–8 P.M., rest of year 9 A.M.–5 P.M., $4.50) as part of the Olympic Odyssey Tour.

Ski-Jumping, Luge, and Bobsled Facilities

Visible from throughout the city are the 70- and 90-meter ski-jump towers, synonymous with the Olympic Winter Games. A glass-enclosed elevator rises to the observation level. The jump complex has three additional jumps of 15, 30, and 50 meters, which are used for junior competitions and training. All but the 90-meter jump have plastic-surfaced landing strips and are used during summer. At the western end of the park are the luge and bobsled tracks. A complex refrigeration system keeps the tracks usable even on relatively hot days (up to 28°C/80°F). At the bottom of the hill is the Ice House, home to the National Sliding Centre, the world's only year-round facility where athletes can practice their starts for luge, bobsled, and skeleton. You can too—it costs just $5 per "start." Additionally, summer rides on a real luge along a lower section of the track cost $20, or the really adventurous can ride the **Road Rocket** ($55), North America's only summer bobsled ride, which reaches speeds of up to 100 kph (62 mph).

Practicalities

An **Olympic Odyssey Tour** package that includes admission to the Hall of Fame, a trip to the observation deck of the 90-meter ski-jump tower, a visit to the luge and bobsled tracks, and a movie showing highlights from the 1988 Olympic Winter Games, is $15, or take a self-guided tour for $10. Once the official tour is done, head back over to the Ice House to try your hand at the luge or bobsled, rent a mountain bike ($20 for two hours) and ride the trails ($9 includes un-limited chairlift rides), or just relax on the sun-drenched deck with lunch from the cafeteria. Summer hours for the guest services window are 8 A.M.–9 P.M. For general information on the park, call 403/247-5452, www.coda.ab.ca.

OTHER PARKS
Calgary Zoo
The Calgary Zoo (1300 Zoo Rd. NE, 403/232-9300, year-round 9 A.M.–5 P.M., adult $15, senior $13, child $6.50) is one of Canada's finest zoos. Unique viewing areas have been designed to allow visitors the best look at the zoo's 1,000-plus animals. For example, in Destination Africa, giraffes tower over a huge glass-walled pool that provides a home to two hippos while a massive building re-creates a rainforest, with gorillas and monkeys absolutely everywhere. Other high-lights include a section on Australia's nocturnal animals (lights are turned on at night, reversing night and day and allowing visitors to watch nocturnal animals during their active periods), ex-otic mammals such as lions and tigers, and con-servatories filled with tropical flowers and birds. One of the largest display areas is Canadian Wilds, devoted to the mammals you may or may not see on your travels through Alberta. Nature Tales is a daily interpretive program that takes in everything from trained elephants strutting their stuff to grizzly bear feeding. The main park-ing lot is off Memorial Drive east of downtown, or jump aboard the 202 Whitehorn C-train run-ning east along 7th Avenue.

Sam Livingston Fish Hatchery
Pearce Estate Park, a pleasant spot for a picnic, is home to this hatchery (403/297-6561, Mon.–Fri. 10 A.M.–4 P.M., Sat.–Sun. 1–5 P.M.; rest of year weekdays only). The facility produces approxi-mately 2.5 million trout per year, which are used to stock 300 lakes and rivers throughout the province. A self-guided tour (grab a brochure at the main of-fice) leads through the hatchery, from the incu-bation room to holding tanks and an area containing various displays. In summer the hatch-ery is open. To reach the park and hatchery, take 17th Avenue east from the city and turn north onto 17th Street SE.

Inglewood Bird Sanctuary
More than 250 species of birds have been noted in this 32-hectare (79-acre) park on the bank of the Bow River, east of downtown. The land was orig-inally owned by a member of the NWMP and was established as a park in 1929. Walking trails are open year-round, but before heading out, it's worth dropping by the interpretive center (403/221-4500, May–Sept. 10 A.M.–5 P.M., Oct.–Apr. Tues.–Sat. 10 A.M.–4 P.M.) to learn more about the urban ecosystem and pick up a bird list. To get there, take 9th Avenue SE to Sanctuary Road, and follow the signs to a parking area on the south bank of the river.

Fish Creek Provincial Park
At the southern edge of the city, this 1,170-hectare (2,900-acre) park is one of the largest urban parks in North America. Many prehistoric sites have been discovered on its grounds, including camp-sites and buffalo jumps. Three geographical re-gions meet in the area, giving the park a diversity of habitat. Stands of aspen and spruce predominate, but a mixed-grass prairie, as well as balsam, poplar, and willow can be found along the floodplains at the east end of the park. The ground is carpeted with 364 recorded species of wildflowers, and wildlife is abundant—mule deer and ground squirrels are common, and white-tailed deer, coyotes, and beavers are also present. The easiest access to the heart of the park is to turn east on Canyon Meadows Drive from Macleod Trail, then south on Bow River Bot-tom Trail. Once you've walked the short interpre-tive trail beginning from the end of the road, plan on taking lunch at the **The Ranche** (Bow Bottom Trail, 403/225-3939, Mon.–Fri. 11:30 A.M.–9 P.M., Sat. 5–10 P.M., Sun. 10:30 A.M.–9 P.M.). While this beautifully restored ranch house is old-style stately, the food is anything but, serving elk, buf-falo, and beef combined with organic vegetables and other local ingredients to create an imaginative menu that is among the best in the city. Expect to pay $15–24 for a lunch entrée, or $26–32 at din-ner. For Sunday brunch, the eggs Benedict with Canadian back bacon ($10) is an easy choice.

ALBERTA

Recreation

OUTDOOR ACTIVITIES

The **City of Calgary** (403/268-2489, www.calgary.ca) operates a wide variety of recreational facilities, including swimming pools and golf courses, throughout the city.

Walking and Biking

A good way to get a feel for the city is by walking or biking along the 210 kilometers (130 mi.) of paved trails within the city limits. The trail system is concentrated along the Bow River as it winds through the city; other options are limited. Along the riverbank, the trail passes through numerous parks and older neighborhoods to various sights such as Fort Calgary and Inglewood Bird Sanctuary. From Fort Calgary, a trail passes under 9th Avenue SE and follows the Elbow River, crossing it several times before ending at Glenmore Reservoir and Heritage Park. Ask at tourist information centers for a map detailing all trails. The ski slopes at **Canada Olympic Park** (west of downtown along the TransCanada Hwy., 403/247-5452) are the perfect place to hone your downhill mountain-bike skills. Bike rental is $20 for two hours while a day pass for the chairlift is $9.

Golf

More than 40 public, semiprivate, and private golf courses are located in and around the city limits. Many courses begin opening in April for a season that extends for up to seven months. The City of Calgary (403/268-2489, www.calgary.ca) operates a handful of public courses, but the semiprivate courses are less crowded and more of a challenge. Three personal favorites are **Springbank Links** (125 Hackamore Trail NW, Springbank, 403/202-2000, $60), mixing target golf with links-style; **Elbow Springs Golf Club** (southwest of the city along Highway 8, 403/246-2800, $58), a relatively easy 27-hole layout unique for its water hazards stocked with rainbow trout; and 27-hole **Heritage Pointe Golf and Country Club** (south of downtown on Dunmore Rd., 403/256-2002, $110 includes a power cart), generally regarded as one of Canada's best courses that allows public play.

Winter Activities

When Calgarians talk about going skiing or snowboarding for the day, they're usually referring to the five world-class winter resorts in the Rockies, a short drive to the west. The city's only downhill facilities are at **Canada Olympic Park** (403/247-5452), which has three chairlifts and a T-bar serving a vertical rise of 150 meters (500 ft.). Although the slopes aren't extensive, on the plus side are a long season (mid-Nov.–late March), night skiing (weeknights until 9 P.M.), extensive lodge facilities including rentals, and excellent teaching staff. Lift tickets can be purchased on an hourly basis ($22 for four hours) or $28 for a full day. Seniors pay just $14 for a full day on the slopes.

SPECTATOR SPORTS

Rodeo and, surprisingly to many out-of-towners, show-jumping, attract huge crowds of spectators in Calgary (both are covered in the Festivals and Events section). The city is also home to the **Stampeders** (403/289-0205, www.stampeders.com), a franchise in the Canadian Football League that competes in a July–November season.

Hockey

There's no better way to spend a winter's night in Calgary than by attending a home game of the **Calgary Flames** (403/777-2177, www.calgaryflames.com), the city's National Hockey League franchise. On these nights, the Saddledome in Stampede Park fills with 20,000 ice-hockey fans who follow every game with a passion. Once one of the most competitive NHL franchises (they last won the Stanley Cup in 1989), the drop in exchange rates has made it difficult for the Flames to compete with the U.S. teams when it comes to top-dollar player salaries. The season runs October–April, and games are usually held in the early evening (7 P.M. weeknights, 8 P.M. Saturday, 6 P.M. Sunday). Tickets start at $22 for nosebleed seats, but if you want to be rink-side, expect to pay up to $160 for the best seats in the house.

ARTS AND ENTERTAINMENT

Calgary Straight (www.calgarystraight.com) and *ffwd* (www.ffwdweekly.com) are weekly magazines available freely throughout the city that list theater events, cinema screenings, and art displays, to keep everyone abreast of the local music scene. Tickets to major concerts, performances, and sporting events are available in advance from **Ticketmaster** (403/777-0000, www.ticketmaster.ca).

Art Galleries

It may put a dent in Calgary's cowtown image, but the city does have a remarkable number of galleries displaying and selling work by Albertan and Canadian artisans. Unfortunately, they are not concentrated in any one area, and most require some effort to find. The **Micah Gallery** is the exception. It's right downtown on Stephen Avenue Walk (110 8th Ave. SW, 403/245-1340). Across the river from downtown, Kensington Road is dotted with galleries. Most affordable is **Galleria Arts & Crafts** (1141 Kensington Rd., 270-3612), with two stories of shelf space stocked with paintings, etchings, metal sculptures, jewelry, and wood carvings. Another cluster of galleries lies along 17th Avenue SW. Here, **Collectors Gallery** (829 17th Ave. SW, 403/245-8300) sells the work of prominent 19th- and 20th-century Canadian artists.

Theater

Calgary's Western image belies a cultural diversity that goes further than being able to get a few foreign beers at the local saloon bar. In fact, the city has 10 professional theater companies, an opera, an orchestra, and a ballet troupe. The main season for performances is September–May. **Alberta Theatre Projects** (403/294-7475, www.atplive .com) is a well-established company based in the downtown Calgary Centre for Performing Arts (205 8th Ave. SE). Usual performances are of contemporary material. Expect to pay under $20 for matinees and up to $66 for the very best evening seats. **Lunchbox Theatre** (2nd Fl., Bow

Valley Sq., 205 5th Ave. SW, 403/265-4292, www.lunchboxtheatre.com) runs especially for the lunchtime crowd September–early May. Adults pay $15, seniors $10 for usually comedy content. For adult-oriented experimental productions, head to **One Yellow Rabbit** (225 8th Ave. SW, 403/264-3224, www.oyr.org).

Theatersports is a concept of improvisation-comedy theater developed at the University of Calgary in the 1970s. The original performances led to the formation of the **Loose Moose Theatre Company** (403/265-5682, www.loosemoose .com), which today offers this lighthearted form of entertainment Friday and Saturday nights. The company was looking for a new venue at the time of publication.

Music and Dance

Calgary Opera (403/262-7286, www.calgary opera.com) performs at the Jubilee Auditorium (1415 14th Ave. NW) October–April. Tickets range from $22–88. The Jack Singer Concert Hall at the Calgary Centre for Performing Arts is home to the **Calgary Philharmonic Orchestra** (403/571-0270, www.cpo-live.com), one of Canada's top orchestras. **Alberta Ballet** (403/245-4222, www.albertaballet.com) performs at locations throughout the city.

Cinemas

Most major shopping malls—including Eau Claire Market, closest to downtown—have a **Cineplex Odeon** cinema. For information, call the 24-hour film line (403/263-3166). Also in Eau Claire Market is an **IMAX Theatre** (403/974-4629), with a screen that's five-and-a-half stories tall. Tickets are $7.25, or $10.50 for a double feature. **Uptown Stage & Screen** (612 8th Ave. SW, 403/265-0120) is a restored downtown theater that has a reputation for alternative, art, and foreign films. Over the Bow River from downtown, the 1935 **Plaza Theatre** (1133 Kensington Rd. NW, Kensington, 403/283-3636) shows everything from art house to Hindu.

Boot Scootin' Bars

With a nickname like "Cowtown," it's not surprising that some of Calgary's hottest nightspots

ALBERTA

play country music. **Ranchman's** (9615 Macleod Trail SW, 403/253-1100) is *the* place to check out first, especially during Stampede Week. Some of country's hottest stars have played this authentic honky-tonk. Food is served at a bar out front all day, then at 7 P.M. the large dance hall opens with a band keeping the crowd boot scootin' most nights. The hall is a museum of rodeo memorabilia and photographs, with a chuck wagon hanging from the ceiling. Glitzy **Cowboy's** (826 5th St. SW, 403/265-0699) has a Western theme but attracts a young crowd with country and rock bands, promotions, and a perky wait staff. A few blocks east, the peanut shells have been swept off the floor at the old Dusty's saloon, which has been reincarnated as hip **Coyote's** (1088 Olympic Way SE, 403/770-2200). The crowd is urban-slick, but when country music plays, the fancy-dancing crowd seems to know every word.

Other Bars and Nightspots

One of the best options for a quiet downtown drink is the **Sandstone Lounge** (Hyatt Regency, 700 Centre St., 403/717-1234), which stands out for its central location (off Stephen Ave. Walk), classy surroundings, and extensive drink selection. Also on Stephen Avenue Walk, in an old bank building, **James Joyce Irish Pub** (114 8th Ave. SW, 403/262-0708) has Guinness beer on tap and a menu of traditional British dishes.

If you're looking to dance the night away (without doing it in a line), there are a number of non-country alternatives. Downtown in a grandly restored theater, **The Palace** (219 8th Ave. SW, 403/263-9980) has a large dance floor and big-time lighting and sound systems. **Mercury** (801 17th St. SW, 403/541-1175) attracts a young, hip crowd for its cocktail-bar ambience. One of Calgary's most infamous nightspots is the **Back Alley** (4630 Macleod Trail SW, 403/287-2500), which is far from refined, but probably deserves a mention as it's outlasted the other flash-in-the-pans.

Jazz and Blues

One of the most popular jazz clubs in town is **Kao's Jazz and Blues Bistro** (718 17th Ave. SW,

403/228-9997), which brings in good bands Wednesday–Sunday. It also has a small patio. **Beat Niq** (at the lower level of 811 1st St., 403/263-1650) is a New York–style jazz club that welcomes everyone.

When it comes to live blues (and occasionally jazz), the **King Edward Hotel** (438 9th Ave. SE, 403/262-1680) is the genuine item. This place has hosted all of the legends—including Buddy Guy and Junior Well—but sometimes the most memorable performances take place during the Sunday night jam, when an unknown musician lets loose with a cool piano riff.

SHOPPING

The largest shopping center downtown is **Calgary Eaton Centre,** on Stephen Avenue Walk at 4th Street SW. This center is linked to other plazas by the Plus 15 Walkway system. The other major downtown shopping complex is **Eau Claire Market,** at the entrance to Prince's Island Park, where the emphasis is on fresh foods and trendy boutiques.

Camping Gear and Western Wear

Mountain Equipment Co-op (830 10th Ave. SW, 403/269-2420) is Calgary's largest camping store. The store is a cooperative owned by its members, similar to the American R.E.I. stores. Across the road, a similar supply of equipment is offered at **Coast Mountain Sports** (817 10th Ave. SW, 403/264-2444). The selection may be smaller than at MEC, but many name-brand items are perpetually sale priced.

Alberta Boot Co. (614 10th Ave. SW, 403/263-4605), within walking distance of downtown, is Alberta's only Western boot manufacturer. This outlet shop has thousands of pairs for sale in all shapes and sizes, all made from leather. Boots start at $250 and go all the way up to $1,700 for alligator hide. You'll find **Lammle's Western Wear** outlets in all the major malls and at Calgary International Airport. Another popular Western outfitter is **Riley & McCormick** on Stephen Avenue Walk (220 8th Ave. SW, 403/262-1556).

Festivals and Events

CALGARY STAMPEDE

Every July, the city's perennial rough-and-ready Cowtown image is thrust to the forefront when a fever known as Stampede hits town. For 10 days, Calgarians let their hair down—business leaders don Stetsons, bankers wear boots, half the town walks around in too-tight denim outfits, and the rate of serious crime drops. For most Calgarians, it is known simply as The Week (always capitalized). It is a celebration of the city's past—of endless sunny days when life was broncos, bulls, and steers, of cowboys riding through the streets, and saloons on every corner. But it isn't just about the past. It's the Cowtown image Calgarians cherish and the frontier image that visitors expect. On downtown streets, everyone is your neighbor. Flapjacks and bacon are served free of charge around the city; normally staid citizens shout "Ya-HOO!" for no particular reason; Indians ride up and down the streets on horseback; and there's drinking and dancing until dawn every night.

Stampede Highlights

The epicenter of the action is **Stampede Park,** immediately south of the city center, but the action kicks off downtown with the **Stampede Parade** (second Fri. in July). The approximately 150 floats include close to 4,000 people and 700 horses, and the procession takes two hours to pass any one point. It features an amazing array of floats, each cheered by 250,000 people who line the streets up to 10 deep. The loudest "Ya-HOOs" are usually reserved for Alberta's oldest residents and Stampede royalty, but this is the Stampede, so even politicians and street sweepers elicit enthusiastic cheers.

Rodeo: The pinnacle of any cowboy's career is walking away with the $50,000 winner-take-all on the last day of competition in the Calgary Stampede. For the first eight days, heats are held each

STAMPEDE TICKETING AND INFORMATION

Advance tickets for the afternoon rodeos and evening chuck wagon races/grandstand shows go on sale nearly one year ahead of time. The good seats are sold out well in advance. The grandstand is divided into sections, each with a different price tag. The best views are from the A section, closest to the infield yet high enough not to miss all the action. To either side are the B and C sections, also with good views. Above the main level is the Clubhouse level, divided into another four sections, all enclosed by glass and air-conditioned. Ticket prices for the first eight days of rodeo competition range $24–49 ($45 for section A). The evening chuck wagon races/grandstand shows run $29–65 ($58 for section A).

If you didn't purchase tickets in advance, you'll need to pay the **general admission** at the gate ($12), then you can purchase "rush seating" tickets for the afternoon's rodeo ($10) or the chuck wagon race/grandstand show ($15) from the booths in front of the grandstand. With this ticket you'll have access only to either an area of the infield with poor views or seats well away from the action. Purchasing tickets in advance is *definitely* the preferred option. Order by phone (403/269-9822 or 800/661-1767) or online (www.calgarystampede.com).

Information

Check either of Calgary's daily newspapers for a daily pullout section with a schedule of events at Stampede Park and throughout the city. At Stampede Park, schedule and maps are widely available at distinctive **Howdy Folk Chuckwagons** topped with cowboy hats and staffed by friendly volunteers.

Upcoming dates for the Calgary Stampede include July 9–18, 2004; July 8–17, 2005; and July 7–16, 2006.

ALBERTA

afternoon from 1:30 P.M., with finals held the last Saturday and Sunday. Although Stampede Week is about a lot more than the rodeo, everyone loves to watch this event. Cowboys compete in bronc riding, bareback riding, bull riding, calf roping, and steer wrestling, and cowgirls compete in barrel racing. Wild cow milking, a wild horse race, bull fighting, and nonstop chatter from hilarious rodeo clowns all keep the action going between the more traditional rodeo events.

Chuck Wagon Races: The **Rangeland Derby** chuck wagon races feature nine heats each evening starting at 8 P.M. At the end of the week, the top four drivers from the preliminary rounds compete in a winner-take-all, $50,000 dash-for-the-cash final. Chuck wagon racing is an exciting sport any time, but at the Stampede the pressure is intense as drivers push themselves to stay in the running. The grandstand in the infield makes steering the chuck wagons through an initial figure eight difficult, heightening the action before they burst onto the track for what is known as the Half Mile of Hell to the finish line. The first team across the finish line doesn't always win the race; drivers must avoid 34 penalties, ranging from 1 to 10 seconds added to their overall time.

Other Stampede Park Attractions: At the **Indian Village** the five nations who signed Treaty Seven 100 years ago—the Blackfoot, Blood, Piegan, Sarcee, and Stoney—set up camp for the duration of the Stampede. Each tepee has its own colorful design. Behind the village is a stage where native dance competitions are held. The cavernous **Roundup Centre** holds various commercial exhibits and a showcase of Western art and photography. **Centennial Fair** is an outdoor stage with events for children such as duck races and magicians. In the **Agricultural Building,** livestock is displayed, and next door in the **John Deere Show Ring,** the World Blacksmith's Competition and horse shows take place. A **midway** takes center stage through the western edge of the park with the thrills and spills of rides such as the reverse bungee drawing as many spectators as paying customers.

Rope Square: During the Stampede, downtown's Olympic Plaza is known as Rope Square. Every morning, 8:30–10:30 A.M., free pancake breakfasts are served from the back of chuck wagons. For the rest of the morning, the square is the scene for a variety of entertainment, which might include country-music bands, native dance groups, marching bands, or mock gunfights. West along Stephen Avenue Walk, square dancing takes place each morning at 10 A.M. Also at 10, horse-drawn carriages leave the Fairmont Palliser for an hour-long tour through town.

SPRUCE MEADOWS

It is somewhat ironic that a city known around the world for its rodeo is also home to the world's premier show-jumping facility, **Spruce Meadows** (Spruce Meadows Way, 403/974-4200, www.sprucemeadows.com). Ever-encroaching residential developments do nothing to take away from the wonderfully refined atmosphere within the white picket fence that surrounds the sprawling 120-hectare (300-acre) site. The facility comprises six grassed outdoor rings, two indoor arenas, seven stables holding 700 horse stalls, 90 full-time employees (and many thousands of volunteers), and its own television station that broadcasts to 90 countries. In Europe, the world of show-jumping can be very hoity-toity. At Spruce Meadows, the atmosphere couldn't be more different, which makes it a wonderful place to spend a day—even for non–horse lovers. Visitors spread out picnic lunches on grassy embankments, wander through the stables, and watch the superstars of the sport up-close and personal. During the major tournaments, browsing through the on-site agricultural fair, art and craft booths, and a large marketplace promoting Alberta attractions will round out a busy day of following the competitions from ring to ring.

Tournaments and Tickets

Spruce Meadows hosts a packed schedule of tournaments that attract the world's best riders, which in turn attracts up to 50,000 spectators a day. The four big ones are the **National,** the first week of June; **Canada One,** the last week of June; the **North American,** the first week of July; and the **Masters,** the first week of September. The Masters is the world's richest show-

The Calgary Stampede is western Canada's best-known event.

jumping tournament, with $1,000,000 up for grabs on the Sunday afternoon ride-off.

General admission is a bargain at just $5 per person and except on the busiest of days, this will get you a prime viewing position at any of the rings. The exception is tournament weekends, when covered reserved seating ($20–25) is the best way to watch the action.

To get to Spruce Meadows on tournament weekends, take C-train south to Fish Creek–Lacombe Station, and from there bus transfers to the grounds are free. Driving, take Macleod Trail south to Highway 22X, and turn right toward the mountains along Spruce Meadows Way.

OTHER FESTIVALS
Spring
In conjunction with **Roughstock,** Calgary's rodeo season kicks off with **Rodeo Royal** (403/261-0101) at the Saddledome on the third weekend of March. **Calgary International Children's Festival** (403/294-7414, www.calgarychildfest.org) is the third week of May. Events include theater, puppetry, and performances by musicians from around the world. It's held in Jack Singer Concert Hall and Olympic Plaza. Stephen Avenue Walk and Olympic Plaza come alive with the sights, sounds, and tastes of the Caribbean in mid-June for **Carifest** (www.carifest.ca).

Summer
Jazz Festival Calgary (403/249-1119, www.jazz festivalcalgary.ca) features various jazz and blues artists at clubs and concert halls throughout the city during the last week of June. **Canada Day** is celebrated on July 1 in Prince's Island Park, Fort Calgary, the zoo, and Heritage Park. The **Calgary Folk Music Festival** (403/233-0904, www .calgaryfolkfest.com), during the last week of July, is an indoor and outdoor extravaganza of Canadian and international performers that centers on Prince's Island Park. The second week of August is **Afrikadey!** (403/234-9110, www.afrikadey.com), with performances and workshops by African-influenced musicians and artists, and screenings of African-themed films.

Fall
In October, hockey and skiing and snowboarding fever hits the city as the **NHL Calgary Flames** start their season and the first snow flies. Late September–early October sees movie screenings during the **Calgary International Film**

ALBERTA

Festival (403/283-1490, www.calgaryfilm.com) at the historic Uptown Stage & Screen and Plaza theaters. This is followed by **Wordfest** (403/294-7492, www.wordfest.com) where authors talk about their books, workshops are given, and many readings take place at venues throughout the city and in Banff. A good place for kids on Halloween is Calgary Zoo (403/232-9300), where **Boo at the Zoo** celebrations take place.

Accommodations and Camping

Accommodations in Calgary vary from campgrounds, a hostel, and budget motels to a broad selection of upscale hotels catering to business travelers. Most downtown hotels offer drastically reduced rates on weekends—Friday and Saturday nights might be half the regular room rate. During Stampede Week, prices are higher than the rest of the year and accommodations are booked months in advance. Rates quoted below are for a double room in summer, but outside of Stampede week.

The bed-and-breakfast scene in Calgary is alive and well. The **Bed & Breakfast Association of Calgary** (www.bbcalgary.com) represents around 40 of these homes offering rooms to visitors. The association doesn't offer a reservation service, but is simply a grouping of properties that meet certain standards.

DOWNTOWN
Under $50
HI–Calgary City Centre (520 7th Ave. SE, 403/670-7580 or 888/762-4122, www.hihostels.ca) is an excellent choice for budget travelers, both for its convenient location and wide variety of facilities. It has 110 beds, most in eight-bed dormitories, but with one private room. Other amenities include a fully equipped kitchen, laundry facilities, a large common room, an outdoor barbecue, a game room, a snack bar, lockers, and a summer activity program that includes city walking tours. Members of Hostelling International pay $22 for a dorm bed ($26 for nonmembers) or $46 s or d ($54 for nonmembers) in the private room. It's one block east of the City Hall C-train station and the Airport Shuttle Express stops out front ($15 one-way).

$50–100
The most central bed-and-breakfast is **Inglewood B&B** (1006 8th Ave. SE, 403/262-6570, www.inglewoodbedandbreakfast.com), named for the historic neighborhood in which it lies. Its location is excellent—close to the river and Stampede Park, as well as a 10-minute stroll from downtown. The three rooms, each with private facilities, range $85–135 s or d, depending on the room configuration. Rates include a cooked breakfast of your own choosing.

Least expensive of Calgary's downtown hotels is the **Regis Plaza Hotel** (124 7th Ave. SE, 403/262-4641, www.regisplazahotel.com, $79–84 s or d). It's one of the few old hotels that has survived Calgary's ongoing construction boom. Of the 100 rooms, only 30 have en suite bathrooms—the rest share bathroom facilities—but all have televisions and a zippy 1970s decor.

$100–150
Across the railway tracks from downtown, the **Best Western Suites Downtown** (1330 8th St. SW, 403/268-6900 or 800/981-2555, www.bestwesterncalgary.com) features more than 120 self-contained units, each with contemporary styling, a kitchen, and air-conditioning. Rates for a standard suite start at $125 s or d, but an upgrade to a king-size bed and jetted tub is usually only around $20 extra.

$150–200
Holiday Inn Calgary Downtown (119 12th Ave. SW, 403/266-4611 or 800/661-9378, www.holidayinn-calgary.com) is a newish 12-story, 188-room accommodation on the south side of the railway tracks, within easy walking distance of Stampede Park. Rooms are reliable and practical, and each has a small balcony. Downstairs is a

fitness room, an outdoor heated pool, a restaurant, and a lounge. Summer rates are $159 s or d, but rooms go for around $100 with 21-day advance purchase—an excellent deal.

$200–250

Least expensive of the hotels right downtown is the **Hawthorn Hotel and Suites** (618 5th Ave. SW, 403/263-0520 or 800/661-1592, www.hawthorn calgary.com). Although the 300 rooms are unremarkable, bonuses include full kitchens, free hot buffet breakfast, and an outdoor pool. Rack rates are $210–260, but check the website and save at least $60 in any number of ways.

The **International Hotel of Calgary** (220 4th Ave. SW, 403/265-9600 or 800/661-8627, www.internationalhotel.ca) features 250 one- and two-bedroom suites, an indoor pool, a fitness room, and a restaurant. Regular rates are $229–269, with seniors enjoying a solid discount.

Over $250

Kensington Riverside Inn (1126 Memorial Dr. NW, Kensington, 403/228-4442 or 877/313-3733, www.kensingtonriversideinn.com, $259–319 s or d) is the city's only boutique hotel. Each of the 19 guest rooms has a slightly different feel and layout—from bold contemporary to warmly inviting; some have a private balcony, others have a gas fireplace or jetted tub, but it's in-room niceties such as Egyptian cotton sheets and heated towel racks that make this lodging special. A coffee tray and morning paper left by your door, followed by a gourmet breakfast served in the downstairs dining room are included in the rates. The inn is across the Bow River from downtown in Kensington, one of Calgary's hippest neighborhoods.

One block north from the Calgary Tower is the **Hyatt Regency Calgary** (700 Centre St., 403/717-1234 or 800/233-1234, www.hyatt .com). Incorporating a historic building along Stephen Avenue Walk in its construction, this 21-story hotel features an indoor swimming pool, a refined lounge, and a renowned restaurant specializing in Canadian cuisine. The hotel's Stillwater Spa is the premier spa facility in Calgary—spend any time here and you'll forget you're

in a city hotel. The up-to-date guest rooms won't take your breathe away, but have a wide range of amenities and luxurious bathrooms; from $270 s or d weeknights and $150 on weekends. Parking is an additional $16.

Easily Calgary's best-known hotel, the gracious **Fairmont Palliser** (133 9th Ave. SE, 403/263-0520 or 800/661-1592, www.fairmont.com, from $280 s or d) was built in 1914 by the C.P.R. for the same clientele as the company's famous properties in Banff and Jasper. The rooms may seem smallish by modern standards, and the hotel lacks certain recreational facilities, but the elegance and character of the grande dame of Calgary accommodations are priceless.

MACLEOD TRAIL

A string of hotels along Macleod Trail south of downtown pick up highway traffic as it enters the city. Most mid-priced chains are represented, with the following just a sampling.

$50–100

Southernmost of the motels on Macleod Trail is the **Stetson Village Inn** (10002 Macleod Trail SW, 403/271-3210 or 888/322-3210, $73 s, $77 d), an older-style place tucked between shopping malls. Local calls are free and the adjoining restaurant and lounge open nightly. The rates could be lower, but it's a prime spot for getting out of the city to begin your exploration of Southern Alberta.

Most of the chain motels along Macleod Trail fall into this price category. Book in advance or online and you should pick up rates around or a little under $100 a night.

The **Best Western Calgary Centre Inn** (3630 Macleod Trail SW, 403/287-3900 or 877/287-3900, www.bwcalgarycentre.com, $110 s or d) may be close to the geographical center of the city, but it's not downtown as the name suggests. Each of the rooms is decorated in a bright and breezy color scheme, and comes stocked with amenities such as a hairdryer and coffeemaker. On the premises are an indoor pool and a fitness center. Rates include a continental breakfast.

WEST OF DOWNTOWN

Motel Village—bordered by 16th Avenue NW, Crowchild Trail, and Banff Trail—is Calgary's main concentration of moderately priced motels. From the adjacent Banff Trail station, downtown is a short, safe ride away on the C-train. Farther west along 16th Avenue NW is another string of reasonably priced motels.

$50–100

The **Red Carpet Inn** (4635 16th Ave. NW, 403/286-5111) doesn't look anything special from the outside. Nothing will change your opinion inside the 35 air-conditioned guest rooms—this motel is simply a good, clean choice for travelers looking for somewhere to spend the night before heading off to the mountains. Summer rates are $79 s, $89 d, discounted to $47 s, $52 d through a generous off-season that extends from September to May.

$100–150

The **Comfort Inn** (2363 Banff Trail NW, Motel Village, 403/289-2581 or 800/228-5150, www .comfortinncalgary.com) combines a wide range of amenities with reasonable rates to be my pick of Motel Village accommodations. All rooms have a simple yet snazzy contemporary look, along with high-speed Internet, a coffeemaker, a hairdryer, and an ironing facility. Other features include an indoor pool and waterslide complex. Rates starting at $104 s or d include a light breakfast (or upgrade to a King Suite for $164).

Directly opposite Canada Olympic Park is the **Four Points by Sheraton Calgary West** (8220 Bow Ridge Crescent NW, 403/288-4441 877/288-4441, www.fourpointscalgarywest.com, $139 s, $149 d), a real standout on this side of the city. The 118 rooms are big and bright and each has a balcony (ask for one with a view of Canada Olympic Park). Along with city-hotel luxuries like high-speed Internet and room service, other amenities include an indoor pool and water slide, a fitness center, the Mountain Oasis Retreat spa facility, and a restaurant and lounge. Check the hotel website for rates discounted well under $100 and for suites for less than the rack rate. Some packages include airport shuttles—perfect if you're renting from Hertz, which has a desk in the lobby.

NORTHEAST (AIRPORT)

The many hotels that lie in the northeast quadrant of the city have airport shuttles and most can be contacted directly by courtesy phone from the airport.

$50–100

Check hotel websites listed below for rooms around the $100 mark, or take the easy way out and book your stay at the no-frills **Pointe Inn** (1808 19th St. NE, 403/291-4681 or 800/661-8164, www.pointeinn.com, $70 s, $80 d). Facilities include a launderette, a café, a restaurant, and a lounge. Request a nonsmoking room.

$100–150

Holiday Inn Calgary Airport (1250 McKinnon Dr. NE, 403/230-1999 or 800/465-4329, www .hicalgaryairport.com, $149–169 s or d) is a little farther from the airport than the other choices, but with a free shuttle that's of little consequence. The rooms are exactly what you expect from Holiday Inn, the restaurant has surprisingly good city views, and the indoor pool is the perfect place to take a dip after a long flight.

Similarly priced is the **Radisson Hotel Calgary Airport** (2120 16th Ave. NE, 403/291-4666 or 800/333-3333, www.radisson.com), which features 185 comfortable rooms, a large lobby filled with greenery and comfortable seating, an indoor pool, a fitness center, spa services, and a Western-style saloon. Standard rooms are $145, or upgrade to Business Class for $165 and enjoy better views, an evening turndown service, and breakfast.

Over $150

Delta Calgary Airport Hotel (403/291-2600 or 877/814-7706, www.deltahotels.com, $199 s or d) is the only accommodation right at the airport. The main terminal is linked to the hotel lobby by a walkway. The medium-size rooms come with luxuries like down duvets and plush bathrobes, each has a writing desk, and most importantly, they are well sound-proofed. Hotel amenities include two restaurants, a lounge, an indoor pool, and a business center. Delta properties across Canada fill the upper niche of the travel market, but they also offer some great bargains—this property is no different, so check the website before being perturbed by the price tag.

CAMPGROUNDS

No camping is available within the Calgary city limits, although campgrounds can be found along all major routes into the city. Shuttle buses run to and from campgrounds into Stampede Park during the Calgary Stampede. Reservations are necessary for this week.

West

Calgary West K.O.A. (221 101st St. SW, 403/288-0411 or 800/562-0842, www.koa.com, mid-Apr.–mid-Oct.) is on a north-facing hill on the west side of Canada Olympic Park. The modern facilities include showers, a laundry room, an outdoor heated pool, a game room, and a grocery store. Around 350 sites are laid out on terraces, so no one misses out on the views. Unserviced sites are $27, hookups $29–37.

Calaway Park (10 km/6.2 mi. west of city limits, 403/249-7372, June–Aug.) is farther out along the TransCanada Highway. Trees are scarce, but on clear days the view of the Canadian Rockies is spectacular. The toilets, showers, and laundry room are in a trailer but are of reasonable standards. Tent sites $17, powered sites $25, and full hookups $28.

North

Whispering Spruce Campground (403/226-0097, www.whisperingspruce.com, Apr.–Oct.) is on the west side of Highway 2, 10 kilometer (6.2 miles) north of the airport. Facilities include showers, a small grocery store, a laundry, a games room, and horseshoe pits. Tent sites are $19, hookups $23–26.

East

Mountain View Farm Campground, three kilometers (1.9 mi.) east of the city limits on the TransCanada Highway (403/293-6640, www.calgarycamping.com) doesn't have a view of the mountains, but it does have a small petting farm, minigolf, and hay rides. The sites are very close together. Facilities include showers, a grocery store, and a laundry room. Tent sites are $21, hookups $25–27.

South

South of Calgary on the Highwood River is **Nature's Hideaway Family Campground** (403/938-8185, www.natureshideaway.com, mid-Apr.–Oct., $21–30). Although farther out than all of the others, it's in a densely wooded floodplain where birds are abundant and deer and coyotes are seen often. The facilities are a little tired, but on the plus side, there's no end of things to do—swimming, fishing, and trail rides. To get there, head south on Highway 2, then take Highway 552 east for 12 kilometers (7.5 mi.), then go north for one kilometer (0.6 mi.), then east for two kilometers (1.2 miles) more.

Food

Calgary may lack the cultural trappings that Alberta's capital, Edmonton, boasts, but it gives that city a run for its money in the restaurant department. South of downtown, along 17th Avenue and 4th Street, a once-quieter part of the city has been transformed into a focal point for Calgary's restaurant scene, with cuisine to suit all tastes. Familiar North American fast-food restaurants line Macleod Trail south of the city center.

DOWNTOWN

Cheap and Cheerful

All of the major high-rise buildings have plazas with inexpensive food courts, coffeehouses, and cappuccino bars—the perfect places for people-watching. One place that tries harder to be different is **Sunterra Village Marche** (Plus 15 Level, TransCanada Tower, 450 1st St. SW, 403/262-8240, Mon.–Fri. 6 A.M.–8 P.M.), set up to represent a French streetscape, complete with a patisserie, carvery, salad counter, deli, wine bar, and juice joint. Meals can be packaged to go, but plan on "eating in" at a wide variety of seating styles, including outdoors. On the north side of downtown, **Eau Claire Market** combines a food court with restaurants. Somewhere between the two is **Good Earth Market Café** (403/237-8684, daily 6:30 A.M.–10 P.M.) for healthy snacks and a wide variety of teas and coffees.

Built in 1906 for the superintendent of Fort Calgary, **Deane House** (806 9th Ave., 403/269-7747, Mon.–Fri. 11 A.M.–3 P.M., Sat.–Sun. 10 A.M.–3 P.M.) is a casual dining room surrounded by carefully tended gardens that re-create those laid out 100 years ago. The menu offers a wide choice of simple, healthy lunchtime fare, mostly under $12, making it the perfect place to head after spending the morning at adjacent Fort Calgary.

Canadian

Thomsons (112 Stephen Ave. Walk, 403/537-4449, 6:30 A.M.–9:30 P.M.) is in a historic sandstone building cleverly integrated with a modern Hyatt hotel, but it's not aimed at the hotel

crowd. First off, the buffet breakfast ($16) is as good as it gets, with omelets made to order and real maple syrup to douse your pancakes. The rest of the day, the menu is dominated by Canadian game and seafood (entrées $28–34). Just make sure to leave room for the smoothest crème brûlée ($7) in the city.

Walk north from Eau Claire Market to reach the **River Café** (Prince's Island, 403/261-7670, Mon.–Fri. 11 A.M.–11 P.M., Sat.–Sun. 11 A.M.–10 P.M.), a cozy, rustic dining room that will surprise you with some of Calgary's finest cooking. More of a restaurant than a café, it features extensive use of produce and ingredients sourced from across Canada. Standouts include the buffalo, Alberta beef, and salmon dishes, with the latter often incorporating maple syrup.

Drinkwaters Grill (237 Stephen Ave. Walk, 403/264-9494, Mon.–Fri. 11:30 A.M.–2 P.M., daily 5:30–11 P.M.) is in a 1913 red brick building that has had a funky makeover—from the hand-painted floor to an elaborate high ceiling. Canadian produce rules the menu. Lunchtime choices may include a warm beef tenderloin salad ($17) while in the evening the slow-roasted prime rib ($26–42) shines.

GOOD OL' ALBERTA BEEF

Although Alberta isn't renowned for its culinary delights, flavor-filled and tender Alberta beef is a provincial highlight. It's served at most Calgary restaurants, but only a few restaurants specialize in it. The following are my favorites.

Not much has changed at **Hy's Steakhouse** (316 4th Ave. SW, 403/263-2222, Mon.–Fri. 11:30 A.M.–2:30 P.M., Mon.–Sat. 5–11 P.M.) since its opening in 1956, but no one seems to mind. It's the perfect place to dig into perfectly prepared steaks ($30–42) or sample smaller portions at lunch (mostly under $20) in the atmosphere of a refined gentlemen's club.

Caesar's Steak House (512 4th Ave. SW, 403/264-1222, Mon.–Fri. 11 A.M.–midnight, Sat. 4:30 P.M.–midnight) hasn't been around for as long as Hy's, but 30 years is still a long time in the

restaurant business. The elegant room has a Roman-style decor with dark wood, leather seating, and dim lighting—just what you expect from a steakhouse. Although the menu includes ribs and seafood, it's juicy prime cuts of Alberta beef ($25–40) that this place is known for.

The food at **Buzzard's Cowboy Cuisine** (140 10th Ave., 403/264-6959, daily 11 A.M.–11 P.M.) doesn't come close to competing with the above two steakhouses, but that's not why I've included it. Buzzard's is fun. It's what everyone wants to think Calgary used to be like, but is about as authentic as downtown bankers wearing blue jeans for Stampede. Choices range from steak burgers for under $10 to charbroiled buffalo for $24 and it wouldn't be a complete meal at Buzzard's without sharing a platter of prairie oysters ($8) to start.

Asian

Chinatown, along 2nd and 3rd Avenues east of Centre Street, naturally has the best assortment of Chinese restaurants. **Hang Fung Restaurant** (119 3rd Ave. SE, 403/269-4646), tucked behind a Chinese grocery store of the same name, doesn't try to be anything it's not. Local Chinese come here for simple inexpensive meals, mostly under $7. Just as inexpensive is **Golden Inn Restaurant** (107 2nd Ave. SE, 403/269-2211), which is popular with the local Chinese as well as with professionals, and late-shift workers appreciate its long hours (open until 4 A.M.).

On the south side of the rail line, **Thai Sa-On** (351 10th Ave. SW, 403/264-3526, dinner nightly) is a small space that's big on the tastes of Thailand. The menu offers a great variety of red and green curries, but I tried the red snapper, medium spiced, baked, and served whole and couldn't have been happier. The prices? For downtown dining, the food is ridiculously inexpensive, with the snapper costing $17.

South American

It's impossible not to get caught up in the lively atmosphere at **The Conga Room** (109 Stephen Ave. Walk, 403/262-7248, 11:30 A.M.–midnight), where the noise level increases as the sangria flows. So much so that wait staff blow whistles to ensure clear passage when loaded down with dishes like El Gaucho, a platter of Brazilian delicacies for two, or a spit-roasted chicken to be carved at the table. If that's not enough live entertainment for you, dine on the weekend, when a Latin band plays.

SOUTH OF THE RAILWAY TRACK

The area immediately south of downtown offers a diverse choice of dining options. The major concentrations of restaurants are along 4th Street and 17th Avenue. Find your way to the intersection of these two streets and walk south along 4th or west along 17th and take your pick. What follows are a few favorites.

Breakfast

Nellie's (738 17th Ave. SW, 403/244-4616, daily 8 A.M.–3 P.M.), in the heart of Calgary's trendiest dining strip, is a pleasant surprise. It's a small, outwardly low-key place with a big reputation (so much so that it's now one of five Nellie's restaurants in the city). Service is fast and efficient and, most importantly, the food's great. Breakfasts claim the spotlight—if you're hungry, don't bother with the menu, just order the Belly Buster ($9).

Canadian

Formerly a brewpub, **Wildwood** (2417 4th Ave., 402/228-0100) has evolved into a respected restaurant serving up a wide selection of Canadian cuisine. Still, its roots show through in the fish chowder, which uses ale as a base ($6). For an entrée, go healthy with a fruity spinach salad ($9) or bring back childhood memories with a meatloaf ($11) that's as good as your mother ever made. Friday and Saturday between 4 P.M. and 7 P.M. oysters are a "Buck a Shuck."

European

Few restaurants in the city are as popular as **Chianti** (1438 17th Ave. SW, 403/229-1600, daily for lunch and dinner until midnight). More than 20 well-prepared pasta dishes are featured on the menu, and all of the pasta is made daily on the premises. Among many specialties are an antipasto platter ($14.50 for two) and frutti di mare, a spicy seafood combination served on a bed of pasta; at $17, it's the most expensive entrée. All regular pasta entrées are less than $12. The restaurant is dark and noisy in typical Italian style. The owner often sings with an accordionist on weekends.

Closer to downtown, **Bonterra Restaurant** (1016 8th St. SW, 403/262-8480) is a stylish dining room with a vaulted ceiling and lots of exposed woodwork. Tables out on the Mediterranean-style patio are in great demand through summer. The menu is modern Italian, with pastas $13–17 and the seafood lasagna a worthwhile splurge at $24. The nationalistic wine list has only a few bottles under $30.

Information and Services

INFORMATION

Information Centers

Tourism Calgary (403/263-8510 or 800/661-1678, www.tourismcalgary.com) promotes the city to the world. The organization also operates four **Visitor Service Centres.** The one that greets visitors arriving by air is across from Carousel 4 at Calgary International Airport (year-round, daily 6 A.M.–11 P.M.). Two other centers staffed by Tourism Calgary staff are in Riley & McCormack stores on the 200 block of Stephen Avenue Walk (daily 9:30 A.M.–5:30 P.M.) and in Eau Claire Market (daily 10 A.M.–5 P.M.). For highway travelers entering Calgary from the south, a Visitor Service Centre is in the Chase Cattle Company Western wear store in Willow Park Village (10816 Macleod Trail, daily 10 A.M.–6 P.M.).

Bookstores

McNally Robinson (120 Stephen Ave. Walk, 403/538-1797 or 866/798-1797, www.mcnallyrobinson.com, Mon.–Thurs. 9 A.M.–9 P.M., Fri.–Sat. 9 A.M.–10 P.M., Sun. 11 A.M.–5 P.M.) fills two stories of a heritage building and comes complete with a full-service restaurant. Set around a central atrium is a large collection of books sensibly cataloged in easy-to-find sections. One of the largest areas is devoted to Canada and another to children's literature. Also downtown, the **Book Company** in Bankers Hall (315 8th Ave. SW, 403/237-8344) is another good place to find books on western Canada as well as general travel writing and nonfiction works.

For topographic, city, and wall maps, as well as travel guides and atlases, **Map Town** (400 5th Ave. SW, 403/266-2241 or 877/921-6277, www.maptown.com, Mon.–Fri. 9 A.M.–6 P.M., Sat. 10 A.M.–5 P.M.) should have what you're looking for.

The suburb of Kensington, immediately northwest of downtown, has a variety of new and used bookstores, including **Pages** (1135 Kensington Rd. NW, 403/283-6655, Mon.–Sat.

10 A.M.–5:30 P.M., Thurs.–Fri. until 9 P.M., and Sun. noon–5 P.M.), which offers a thoughtful selection of Canadian fiction and nonfiction titles.

Indigo/Chapters has 15 stores across Calgary, including one **Chapters** megastore in Chinook Centre (6455 Macleod Trail, 403/212-0090) and another farther south (9631 Macleod Trail, 403/212-1442), and an **Indigo** store in Signal Hill Centre (Sarcee Trail SW, 403/246-2221). The company also operates stores in major malls and Calgary International Airport under the **Coles** name.

Used Books

Fair's Fair (1609 14th St. SW, 403/245-2778) is the biggest of many secondhand and collector bookstores along 17th Avenue SW. Surprise, surprise, it's remarkably well organized, with a solid collection of well-labeled Canadiana filling more than one room. **Author Author** (223 10th St. NW, 403/283-9521) and **Annie's Book Company** (912 16th Ave. NW, 403/282-1330) are two of a group of similar stores along 16th Avenue NW between 6th and 9th Streets. Both these stores also stock a good range of western Canada nonfiction.

Libraries

The Calgary Public Library Board's 16 branch libraries are scattered throughout the city. The largest is **W.R. Castell Central Library** (616 Macleod Trail SE, 403/260-2600, www.calgarypubliclibrary.com, Mon.–Thurs. 10 A.M.–9 P.M., Fri.–Sat. 10 A.M.–5 P.M., Sun. 1:30–5 P.M.). Four floors of books, magazines, and newspapers from around the world are enough to keep most people busy on a rainy afternoon.

SERVICES

The downtown post office is at 207 9th Avenue SW. All city libraries provide free Internet access, or you can head to the **Hard Disk Café** (638 11th Ave. SW, 403/261-5686) for some online surfing. Most major banks carry U.S. currency and can handle basic foreign-exchange transactions, or head to **Calforex** (304 8th Avenue SW, 403/290-0330).

I've been trusting my photographic needs to **Vistek** (1231 10th Ave. SW, 403/244-0333 or 800/561-0333, Mon.–Fri. 8:30 A.M.–6 P.M., Sat. 9:30 A.M.–5 P.M.) for many years. Turnaround time on print film is one hour; on slide film it's overnight.

Handy self-service launderettes are **14th Street Coin Laundry** (1211 14th St. SW, 403/541-1636, daily 7 A.M.–11 P.M.), which has washers big enough to handle sleeping bags and blankets, and **Heritage Hill Coin Laundry** (8228 Heritage Hill Rd. SE at the corner of Macleod Trail and Heritage Dr., 403/258-3946).

Emergency Services

For medical emergencies, call 911 or contact one of the following hospitals: **Foothills Hospital** (1403 29th Ave. NW, 403/670-1110), **Rockyview General Hospital** (7007 14th St. SW, 403/943-3000), or **Alberta Children's Hospital** (1820 Richmond Rd. SW, 403/229-7211). For the **Calgary Police,** call 911 in an emergency or 403/266-1234 for nonurgent matters.

Transportation

GETTING THERE

By Air

Calgary International Airport (YYC; www.calgaryairport.com) is within the city limits northeast of downtown. It is served by more than a dozen scheduled airlines and used by seven million passengers each year. **Arrivals** is on the lower level, where passengers are greeted by White Hat volunteers, dressed in traditional Western attire and ready to answer any questions you may have. Across from the baggage carousels are an information desk (open daily 7 A.M.–10 P.M.) and a bank of computer terminals linked to hotels and other tourist services. The desks for all major rental car outlets are across the road.

A cab to downtown runs approximately $30, or take the **Airport Shuttle Express** (403/291-1991, www.airportshuttleexpress.com) to major downtown hotels for $14 per person one-way. This service runs daily 5:30 A.M.–1 A.M.

For details of airlines flying into Calgary, see the Transportation section of the On the Road chapter or click through the links on the airport website.

By Bus

The **Greyhound** bus depot (850 16th St. SW, 403/265-9111 or 800/661-8747) is two blocks away from the C-train stop ($2 into town), or you can cross the overhead pedestrian bridge at the terminal's southern entrance and catch a transit bus. The cavernous depot has a restaurant, a cash machine, information boards, and lockers large enough to hold backpacks ($2). Buses connect Calgary daily with Edmonton (3.5 hours), Banff (two hours), Vancouver (15 hours), and all other points within the province. No reservations are taken. Just turn up, buy your ticket, and hop aboard. If you buy your ticket seven days in advance, discounts apply. If you plan to travel extensively by bus, the Canada Coach Pass is a good deal.

From their offices near the Calgary Tower, **Red Arrow** (205 9th Ave. SE 403/531-0350) shuttles passengers between Calgary and downtown Edmonton with some services continuing to Fort McMurray in northern Alberta.

GETTING AROUND

Bus

You can get just about everywhere in town by using **Calgary Transit** (403/262-1000, www.calgarytransit.com), which combines two light-rail lines with extensive bus routes. Buses are

ALBERTA

adult $2, child $1.25 one-way to all destinations—deposit the exact change in the box beside the driver and request a transfer (valid for 90 minutes) if you'll be changing buses. A day pass, which is valid for unlimited bus and rail travel, is adult $5.60, $3.60. If you're downtown, the best place for information and schedules is the **Calgary Transit Customer Service Centre** (244 7th Ave. SW, Mon.–Fri. 8:30 A.M.–5 P.M.)

C-Train

C-train, the light-rail transit system, has two lines that total 40 kilometers (25 mi.) of track and 36 stations. Both converge on 7th Avenue, running parallel for the entire distance through downtown. From here, the 202 (also known as Whitehorn) runs past the zoo and the Max Bell Theatre to suburban Whitehorn. The other line (101) starts in the northwest at surburban Dalhousie with stops at the university and Banff Trail (Motel Village). On the south side of the city, stations include two for Stampede Park and a bunch along Macleod Trail before ending in the far south of the city at Somerset-Bridlewood. C-train travel is free along 7th Avenue and $2 to all other destinations.

Passengers with Disabilities

All C-trains and stations are wheelchair accessible. Low-floor buses are employed on many bus routes; call ahead for a schedule. **Calgary Handi-bus** (403/537-7770) provides wheelchair-accessible transportation throughout the city. A book of eight tickets is $12, but visitors receive free service for a limited length of time.

Taxi

The flag charge for a cab in Calgary is $2.75, and then $1.45 for every kilometer. Taxi companies include **Advance** (403/777-1111), **Associated Cabs** (403/299-1111), **Checker Cabs** (403/299-9999), **Red Top** (403/974-4444), and **Yellow Cab** (403/974-1111).

Car Rental

If you're planning on starting your Alberta travels from Calgary and need a rental car, make reservations as far in advance as possible to secure the best rates. Rentals beginning from the airport incur additional charges, so consider renting from downtown or one of the many hotels that have representatives based in their lobbies. Rental agencies and their local numbers include: **Avis** (403/269-6166), **Budget** (403/226-1550), **Discount** (403/299-1224), **Dollar** (403/221-1888), **Economy** (403/291-1640), **Enterprise** (403/263-1273), **Hertz** (403/221-1300), **National** (403/221-1690), **Rent-A-Wreck** (403/287-1444), and **Thrifty** (403/262-4400).

Tours

Brewster (403/221-8242, www.brewster.ca) runs a Calgary City Sights tour lasting 3.5 hours. Included on the itinerary are downtown, various historic buildings, Canada Olympic Park, and Fort Calgary. The tours run June–early October and cost adult $47, child $43.50. Pickups are at most major hotels. Brewster also runs day tours departing Calgary daily to Banff, Lake Louise, and the Columbia Icefield. The latter is a grueling 15-hour trip that departs at 6 A.M. Brewster's downtown office is located on Stephen Avenue Walk at the corner of Centre Street.

ALBERTA

Banff National Park

This 6,641-square-kilometer (2,564-sq.-mi.) national park encompasses some of the world's most magnificent scenery. The snowcapped peaks of the Canadian Rockies form a spectacular backdrop for glacial lakes, fast-flowing rivers, endless forests, and two of North America's most famous resort towns, Banff and Lake Louise. The park's vast wilderness is home to deer, moose, elk, mountain goats, bighorn sheep, black and grizzly bears, wolves, and cougars. Many of these species are commonly sighted from roads in the park, others forage within town, and some remain deep in the backcountry. The human species is concentrated mainly in the picture-postcard town

BANFF NATIONAL PARK

Bigham R.

To Rocky Mountain House

Coral Creek

Abraham Lake

(11)

Obstruction Mountain ▲

White

Goat

Wilderness

A L B E R T A

Mt. Cline ▲

Jasper National Park

Cirrus Mountain ▲

Nigel Peak ▲

Sunwapta Pass

HILDA CREEK HOSTEL ●

Parker's Ridge

Mt. Wilson ▲

RAMPART CREEK HOSTEL ●

THE CROSSING ●

ICEFIELD CENTRE

To Jasper

(93)

Mt. Andromeda ▲

Mt. Athabasca ▲

Saskatchewan Glacier

North Saskatchewan River

(93)

RAMPART CREEK ⛺

SASKATCHEWAN RIVER CROSSING

(11)

(93)

Snow Dome ▲

Columbia Icefield

Castleguard Mountain ▲

Watchman Peak ▲

Mt. Saskatchewan ▲

Alexandra River

Mt. Amery ▲

Banff National Park

Mt. Eramus ▲

Mt. Sarbach ▲

Mt. Columbia ▲

Mt. Lyell ▲

Glacier Lake

Rostrum Peak ▲

Lyell Glacier

Mt. Forbes ▲

Mt. Outram ▲

ALBERTA

© AVALON TRAVEL PUBLISHING, INC.

ALBERTA

BANFF NATIONAL PARK (cont'd)

Wapiti Mtn.

Barrier Mtn.

Red Deer River

Bare Range

Panther River

Panther Mtn.

Ghost River Wilderness

Mt. Oliver

Mt. Aylmer

Palliser Range

Vermilion Range

Douglas Lake

Cascade River

ALBERTA

SKI BANFF @ NORQUAY

Mt. St. Bride

Skoki Lakes

Sawback Range

Johnston Creek

CASTLE MOUNTAIN CHALETS

CASTLE MOUNTAIN

Castle Mtn.

CASTLE MOUNTAIN WILDERNESS HOSTEL

JOHNSTON CANYON

1A

PARKWAY

To Jasper

ICEFIELDS PARKWAY

LAKE LOUISE

Lake Louise

BAKER CREEK CHALETS

1A

PROTECTION MOUNTAIN

93

BOW

VALLEY

Kicking Horse Pass

Lake Louise

LAKE LOUISE

Mt. Temple

Moraine Lake

Boom Lake

Storm Mtn.

Redearth Creek

Yoho National Park

To Golden

Kootenay

National

Park

Vermilion Pass

93

Stanley Peak

Isabelle Peak

Shadow Lake

To Radium Hot Springs

10 mi

10 km

0

0

© AVALON TRAVEL PUBLISHING, INC.

ALBERTA

of Banff, 128 kilometers (80 mi.) west of Calgary. Northwest of Banff, along the TransCanada Highway, is Lake Louise, regarded as one of the seven natural wonders of the world, rivaled for sheer beauty only by Moraine Lake, just down the road. Just north of Lake Louise, the Icefields Parkway begins its spectacular course alongside the Continental Divide to Jasper National Park.

One of Banff's greatest draws is the accessibility of its natural wonders. Most highlights are close to the road system. For more adventurous travelers, an excellent system of hiking trails leads to alpine lakes, along glacial valleys, and to spectacular viewpoints where crowds are scarce and human impact has been minimal. Summer in the park is busy. In fact, the park receives nearly half of its four million annual visitors in just two months—July and August.

Park Entry

Permits are required for entry into Banff National Park. A National Parks Day Pass is adult $7, senior $6, child $3.50 to a maximum of $14 per vehicle ($12 for seniors). It's interchangeable between parks and is valid until 4 P.M. the day following its purchase. Passes can be bought at the eastern park gate on the TransCanada Highway, the park information centers in Banff and Lake Louise, and campground kiosks.

THE LAND

Banff National Park lies within the main and front ranges of the Rocky Mountains, a mountain range that extends the length of the North American continent. The **front ranges** lie to the east, bordering the foothills. These geographically complex mountains are made up of younger bedrock that has been folded, faulted, and uplifted. The **main ranges** are older and higher, lying mainly horizontal and not as severely disturbed as the front ranges. Here the pressures have been most powerful and the results most dramatic; these mountains are characterized by castlelike buttresses and pinnacles and warped waves of stratified rock. Most glaciers are found among these mighty peaks. Along the spine of the main range is the **Continental Divide.** To the east of the divide, all waters flow to the Atlantic Ocean, while those to the west flow into the Pacific.

Many factors combine to make these mountains so beautiful. They are distinctive because the layers of drastically altered sediment are visible from miles away, especially when accentuated by the angle of sunlight or a light fall of snow. Cirques, gouged into the mountains by glacial action, fill with glacial meltwater each spring, turning them their trademark translucent green color.

Flora

Almost 700 species of plants have been recorded in the park, each falling into one of three distinct vegetation zones. **Montane-zone** vegetation is usually found at elevations below 1,350 meters (4,430 ft.). Because fires often affect this zone, lodgepole pine is the dominant species; its tightly sealed cones open only with the heat of a forest fire, thereby regenerating the species quickly after a blaze. Dense forests of white and Engelmann spruces typify the **subalpine zone.** White spruce dominates to 2,100 meters (6,890 ft.); to 2,400 meters (7,870 ft.), Engelmann spruce is most prevalent. Subalpine fir grows above 2,200 meters (7,550 ft.) and is often stunted in growth, affected by the high winds experienced at such lofty elevations. The transition from subalpine to alpine is gradual and usually occurs at approximately 2,300 meters (7,560 ft.). The **alpine zone** has a severe climate, with temperatures averaging below 0°C (32°F). Low temperatures, strong winds, and a very short summer force alpine plants to adapt by growing low to the ground with long roots. Mosses, mountain avens, saxifrage, and an alpine dandelion all thrive in this environment. The best place to view the brightly colored carpet of alpine flowers is Sunshine Meadows or Parker's Ridge.

Fauna

Viewing the abundant and varied wildlife is one of the park's most popular activities. During summer, with the onslaught of millions of visitors, many of the larger mammals tend to move away from the more heavily traveled areas. It then becomes a case of knowing when and where to look for them. Spring and fall are the best times of year for wildlife viewing. The big-game animals have

WHERE CAN I GO TO SEE A BEAR?

This commonly asked question doesn't have an exact answer, but the exhilaration of seeing one of these magnificent creatures in its natural habitat is unforgettable.

From the road, you're most likely to see **black bears,** which range in color from jet black to cinnamon brown. They are often sighted along the Bow Valley Parkway at dawn or late in the afternoon, most commonly in spring. Farther north, watch for black bears along the Icefields Parkway, especially in the vicinity of Cirrus Mountain.

Grizzly bears spend most of the year in remote valleys, often on south-facing slopes. During late spring, they are occasionally seen in the area of Bow Pass. In recent years, a grizzly has taken up residence in the Bow Valley between the town of Banff and Lake Minnewanka. The one place I can guarantee you'll see a grizzly is the Lake Louise Visitor Centre. She's stuffed (literally), but gives you a good idea just how big these magnificent creatures are.

The chance of encountering a bear face-to-face in the backcountry is remote. To lessen chances even further, several simple precautions should be taken. Never hike alone or at dusk, always make lots of noise when passing through heavy vegetation, keep a clean camp, and read the pamphlets available at all park visitors centers. If you're in a vehicle and spot a bear, stay there. Visitors centers in Banff and Lake Louise compile lists of all recent bear sightings.

moved below the snow cover of the higher elevations, and the crowds have thinned out. Winter also has its advantages. Although bears are hibernating, a large herd of elk winters in the town of Banff, coyotes are often seen roaming around town, bighorn sheep have descended from the heights, and wolf packs are occasionally sighted along the Bow Valley Corridor.

Few visitors leave Banff without having seen elk, which are easily distinguished by their white rumps. In summer, look for them in open meadows along the Bow Valley Parkway, along the road to Two Jack Lake, or at Vermilion Lakes. In fall, you'll find hundreds of elk grazing on the golf course until the first snow flies. Fall is rutting season, and the horny bull elk become dangerous as they gather their harems. In winter, small herds find a home on the edge of town. Bighorn sheep are also common. Look for them at the south end of the Bow Valley Parkway, between switchbacks on the Mt. Norquay Road, and between Lake Minnewanka and Two Jack Lake. Moose were once common around Vermilion Lakes, but competition from the expanding elk population caused their numbers to decline—now fewer than 100 live in the park. Search them out along the Icefields Parkway near Waterfowl Lakes. Mule deer, named for their large ears, are most common in the southern part of the park. Watch for them along the Mt. Norquay Road and Bow Valley Parkway. White-tailed deer are much less common but are seen occasionally at Saskatchewan River Crossing. Mountain goats occupy all mountain peaks in the park, living almost the entire year in the higher subalpine and alpine regions. The most accessible place to view these high-altitude hermits is along Parker's Ridge in the far northwestern corner of the park.

Wolves had been driven close to extinction by the early 1950s, but today at least six wolf packs have been reported in the park. One pack winters close to the town and is occasionally seen on Vermilion Lakes during this period.

Birds

Although more than 240 species of birds have been recorded in the park, most are shy and live in heavily wooded areas. One species that definitely isn't shy is the fearless gray jay, which haunts all campgrounds and picnic areas. Similar in color, but larger, is the Clark's nutcracker, which lives in higher, subalpine forests. Woodpeckers live in subalpine forests. Most common of the grouses is the downy ruffled grouse, seen in montane forest. The blue grouse and spruce grouse are seen at higher elevations, as is the white-tailed ptarmigan, which lives above the treeline (watch for them in Sunshine Meadows or on the Bow Summit Loop). Although raptors are not common in the park, bald eagles and golden eagles are present part of the year, and the great horned owl, Alberta's provincial bird, lives in the park year-round.

HISTORY

On November 8, 1883, three young railway workers—Franklin McCabe and William and Thomas McCardell—went prospecting for gold on their day off from working on the transcontinental rail line. They traced a warm stream to its source and found something that would prove to be even more precious than gold—a hot mineral spring that in time would attract wealthy customers from around the world. A small reserve was established around the springs on November 25, 1885, and two years later the reserve was expanded and renamed **Rocky Mountains Park.** It was primarily a business enterprise centered around the unique springs and catering to wealthy patrons of the railway. Luxurious hotels such as the Banff Springs were constructed, and a golf course, the hot springs themselves, and manicured gardens were developed. The park soon became Canada's best-known tourist resort, attracting visitors from around the world.

Town of Banff

Many visitors to the national park don't realize that the town of Banff is a bustling commercial center with 7,700 permanent residents. The town's location is magnificent. It's spread out along the Bow River, extending to the lower slopes of Sulphur Mountain to the south and Tunnel Mountain to the east. In one direction is the towering face of Mount Rundle, and in the other, framed by the buildings along Banff Avenue, is Cascade Mountain. Some people are happy walking along the crowded streets or shopping in a truly unique setting, but those visitors who are more interested in some peace and quiet can easily slip into pristine wilderness just a five-minute walk from town.

History

After the discovery in 1883 of the Cave and Basin just a few kilometers from the railway line, many commercial facilities sprang up along what is now Banff Avenue. Enterprising locals soon realized the area's potential and began opening restaurants and offering guided hunting and boating trips. By 1900, the bustling community of Banff had eight hotels. It was named after Banffshire, the Scottish birthplace of George Stephen, the C.P.R.'s first president.

After a restriction on automobiles in the park was lifted in 1916, Canada's best-known tourist resort also became its busiest. More and more commercial facilities sprang up, offering luxury and opulence amid the wilderness of the Canadian Rockies. Calgarians built summer cottages, and the town began advertising itself as a year-round destination.

For most of its existence, the town of Banff was run as a service center for park visitors by the Canadian Parks Service in Ottawa—a government department with plenty of economic resources but little idea about how to handle the day-to-day running of a mid-size town. Any inconvenience this arrangement caused park residents was offset by cheap rent and subsidized services. In June 1988, Banff's residents voted to sever this tie, and on January 1, 1990, Banff officially became an incorporated town, no different from any other in Alberta.

SIGHTS AND DRIVES

Banff Park Museum

Although displays of stuffed animals are not usually associated with national parks, the Banff Park Museum (93 Banff Ave., 403/762-1558, summer daily 10 A.M.–6 P.M., rest of year daily 1–5 P.M., adult $4, senior $3.50, child $3) provides an insight into the park's early history. Visitors during the Victorian era were eager to see the park's animals without actually having to venture into the bush. A lack of roads and scarcity of

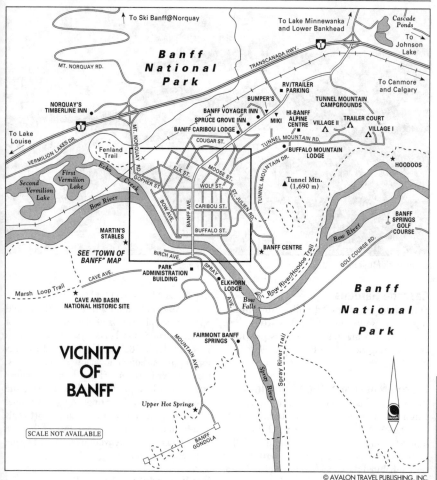

Labels within the map:

↑ To Ski Banff@Norquay

To Lake Minnewanka and Lower Bankhead

Cascade Ponds

To Johnson Lake

Banff National Park

MT. NORQUAY RD.

TRANSCANADA HWY.

RV/TRAILER PARKING

To Canmore and Calgary

NORQUAY'S TIMBERLINE INN

BUMPER'S

TUNNEL MOUNTAIN CAMPGROUNDS

BANFF VOYAGER INN
SPRUCE GROVE INN
BANFF CARIBOU LODGE

MIKI

HI-BANFF ALPINE CENTRE

VILLAGE II

TRAILER COURT

VILLAGE I

To Lake Louise

VERMILION LAKES DR.

MT. NORQUAY RD.

COUGAR ST.

TUNNEL MOUNTAIN RD.

BUFFALO MOUNTAIN LODGE

HOODOOS

Fenland Trail

Echo Creek

GOPHER ST.

ELK ST.

MOOSE ST.

WOLF ST.

ST. JULIEN RD.

TUNNEL MOUNTAIN DR.

Tunnel Mtn. (1,690 m)

First Vermilion Lake

Second Vermilion Lake

Bow River

BOW AVE.

BANFF AVE.

CARIBOU ST.

BUFFALO ST.

Bow River

BANFF SPRINGS GOLF COURSE

MARTIN'S STABLES ★

SEE "TOWN OF BANFF" MAP

BIRCH AVE.

BANFF CENTRE ★

Bow River/Hoodos Trail

GOLF COURSE RD.

Marsh Loop Trail

CAVE AVE.

PARK ADMINISTRATION BUILDING

SPRAY AVE.

ELKHORN LODGE

Bow Falls

Banff National Park

CAVE AND BASIN NATIONAL HISTORIC SITE ★

VICINITY OF BANFF

MOUNTAIN AVE.

FAIRMONT BANFF SPRINGS

Spray River

Spray River Trail

Upper Hot Springs ★

SCALE NOT AVAILABLE

BANFF GONDOLA

NOON

M

large game due to hunting meant that the best places to see animals, stuffed or otherwise, was this museum, which was built in 1903.

Whyte Museum of the Canadian Rockies

The highlight of a visit to this, Banff's premier museum (111 Bear St., 403/762-2291, daily 10 A.M.–5 P.M., adult $6, senior and child $3.50) is the photography of Byron Harmon, whose black-and-white studies of mountain geography have shown people around the world the beauty of the Canadian Rockies. Included in the archives are over 4,000 volumes, tape recordings of early pioneers and outfitters, antique postcards, old cameras, manuscripts, and a large photography collection. Behind the museum are a number of heritage homes formerly occupied by local pioneers. Don't miss this one. The Whyte Museum hosts a variety of interesting walking tours through summer. The most popular of these is the **Historic Banff Walk,** which departs from the museum daily at 11 A.M. and 3 P.M., taking around 90 minutes.

Banff Park Museum

Cascade Gardens

Surrounding the **Park Administration Building,** on the south side of the Bow River, these immaculately manicured gardens provide a commanding view along Banff Avenue to Cascade Mountain.

Luxton Museum of the Plains Indian

Across from Cascade Gardens, this museum (1 Birch Ave., 403/762-2388, summer daily 10 A.M.–6 P.M., rest of year 11:30 A.M.–4:30 P.M., adult $6, senior $4, child $2.50) is dedicated to the heritage of the natives who once inhabited the Canadian Rockies and adjacent prairies. On the site of a trading post operated by Norman Luxton, this museum contains memorabilia from his 60-year relationship with the Stoney, as well as an elaborately decorated tepee, hunting equipment, a few stuffed animals, a realistic diorama of a buffalo jump, peace pipes, and traditional clothing. The adjacent Indian Trading Post is now one of Banff's better gift shops and is definitely worth a browse.

Cave and Basin National Historic Site

At the end of Cave Avenue is this historic site (403/762-1566, summer daily 9 A.M.–6 P.M., rest of year Mon.–Fri. 11 A.M.–4 P.M., Sat.–Sun. 9:30 A.M.–5 P.M., adult $4, senior $3.50, child $3), the birthplace of Banff National Park and of the Canadian national parks system. Bathhouses were installed in 1887, and bathers paid 10 cents for a swim. Although now closed to swimmers, the complex is still one of Banff's most popular attractions. Interpretive displays describe the hows and whys of the springs. A narrow tunnel winds into the dimly lit cave, and short trails lead from the center to the entrance of the cave and through a unique environment created by the hot water from the springs.

Banff Gondola

The easiest way to get high above town without raising a sweat is on the Banff Gondola (Mountain Ave., 403/762-2523, summer 7:30 A.M.–9 P.M., shorter hours rest of year, closed first two weeks of Jan., adult $20, child $10), rising 700 meters (2,300 ft.) in eight minutes to the summit of 2,285-meter (7,500-ft.) **Sulphur Mountain.** From the observation deck at the upper terminal, the breathtaking view includes the town below, the Bow Valley, Cascade Mountain, Lake Minnewanka, and the Fairholme Range. Bighorn sheep often hang around the upper terminal. The short

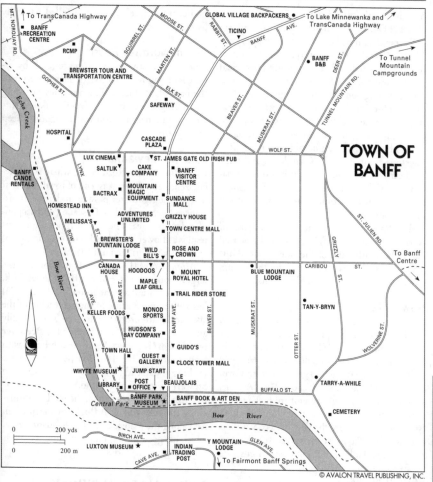

TOWN OF BANFF

© AVALON TRAVEL PUBLISHING, INC.

Vista Trail leads along a ridge to a restored weather observatory. **Summit Restaurant** serves mediocre food, inexpensive breakfasts, and priceless views. From downtown, the gondola is three kilometers (1.9 mi.) along Mountain Avenue. In summer, **Brewster** (403/762-6717) provides shuttle service to the gondola from downtown hotels ($25 includes gondola ride).

Fairmont Banff Springs

On a terrace above the Bow River is the **Fairmont Banff Springs,** (403/762-2211) one of the largest, grandest, and most opulent mountain-resort hotels in the world. "The Springs," as it's best known, has grown with the town and is an integral part of local history. Built by the C.P.R., it opened on June 1, 1888, and was the largest hotel in the world, with 250 rooms beginning at $3.50 per night including meals. Overnight, the quiet community of Banff became a destination resort for wealthy guests from around the world. Additions made over the years were never able to keep up with demand, and in 1911 construction of the hotel that stands today began—reminiscent of a

Scottish castle mixed with a French country chateau. Don't let the hotel's opulence keep you from spending time here. Visit the hotel between 11:30 A.M. and 1:30 P.M., and enjoy a huge buffet lunch combined with a 30-minute **Historical Hotel Tour** for $24.95 per person. Otherwise wander through on your own, admiring the 5,000 pieces of furniture and antiques (most "antiques" in public areas are reproductions), paintings, prints, tapestries, and rugs. Take in the medieval atmosphere of Mt. Stephen Hall with its lime flagstone floor, enormous windows, and large oak beams; take advantage of the luxurious spa facility (see Willow Stream under Other Recreation, later in this chapter), or relax in one of 12 eateries or four lounges.

The hotel is a 15-minute walk southeast of town, either along Spray Avenue or via the trail along the south bank of the Bow River. **Banff Transit** buses leave Banff Avenue for the Springs twice an hour; adult $1, child 50 cents.

Bow Falls

Small but spectacular, Bow Falls is situated below the Fairmont Banff Springs, only a short walk from downtown. The falls are most impressive in late spring when the entire Bow Valley watershed is filled with meltwater. To get there from town, cross the bridge at the south end of Banff Avenue, scramble down the grassy embankment to the left, and follow a pleasant trail along the Bow River to a point above the falls. This easy walk is one kilometer (0.6 mi.) each way. By vehicle, cross the bridge and follow the Golf Course signs.

Vermilion Lakes

This series of shallow lakes forms an expansive wetland supporting a variety of mammals and over 200 species of birds. Vermilion Lakes Drive, paralleling the TransCanada Highway immediately west of Banff, provides the easiest access to the area. The level of **First Vermilion Lake** was once controlled by a dam. Since the removal of the dam, the level of the lake has dropped. This is the beginning of a long process that will eventually see the area evolve into a floodplain forest such as is found along the Fenland Trail. **Second** and **Third Vermilion Lakes** have a higher water level that is controlled naturally by beaver dams.

Mount Norquay Road

One of the best views of town accessible by vehicle is on this road, which switchbacks steeply to the base of the local skiing and snowboarding area. On the way up are several lookouts, including one near the top where bighorn sheep often graze.

Lake Minnewanka

Lake Minnewanka Road begins where Banff Avenue ends at the northeast end of town. The first road to the right after passing under the Trans-Canada Highway leads to **Cascade Ponds,** a popular day-use area. The next turnout along this road is at **Lower Bankhead,** site of a mining operation that continued to 1922.

Minnewanka (Lake of the Water Spirit) is the largest body of water in Banff National Park. **Lake Minnewanka Boat Tours** (403/762-3473) has a 90-minute cruise to the far reaches of the lake. It departs from the dock 3–5 times daily and costs adults $26, children $11. **Brewster** (403/762-6717) offers this cruise combined with a bus tour from Banff for $41 per person. Easy walking trails lead along the western shore to **Stewart Canyon** and beyond.

From Lake Minnewanka, the road continues along the reservoir wall (bighorn sheep often feed along the roadside here) to **Johnson Lake,** which has good fishing and swimming, as well as lakeside picnic facilities.

BOW VALLEY PARKWAY

Two roads link Banff to Lake Louise. The Trans-Canada Highway is the quicker route, more popular with through traffic. The other is the more scenic 56-kilometer (35-mi.) Bow Valley Parkway, which branches off the TransCanada Highway five kilometers (3.1 mi.) west of Banff. Cyclists appreciate this road's two long, divided sections and low speed limit (60 kph/37 mph). As you enter the parkway, you pass the quiet **Fireside** picnic area beside a creek and an interpretive display describing how the Bow Valley was formed.

Johnston Canyon

Johnston Creek drops over a series of spectacular waterfalls here, deep within the chasm it has carved into the limestone bedrock. The canyon is 30 meters (100 ft.) at its deepest, with a raised catwalk leading through the depths of the canyon to the first waterfall. The lower falls are one kilometer (0.6 mi.) from Johnston Canyon Resort while the equally spectacular upper falls are 1.6 kilometers (one mi.) farther upstream.

Johnston Canyon to Castle Junction

At the west end of **Moose Meadows,** a small plaque marks the site of Silver City. At its peak in the 1870s, this boomtown had five mines and a population of 2,000. When it was discovered that the original claim had been salted, investment ceased, the mines closed, and everyone left.

Beyond Moose Meadows, the aptly named **Castle Mountain** comes into view. It's one of the park's most recognizable peaks and most interesting geographical features. The mountain consists of very old rock (approximately 500 million years old) sitting atop much younger rock (200 million years old). This unusual situation occurred as the mountains were forced upward by pressure below the earth's surface, thrusting the older rock up and over the younger rock in places. The road skirts the base of the mountain, passes **Castle Mountain Junction** (gas, groceries, and accommodations), and climbs a small hill to **Storm Mountain Viewpoint,** which provides more stunning views and a picnic area. The next commercial facility is **Baker Creek Chalets and Bistro,** an excellent spot for a meal, then another viewpoint at **Morant's Curve,** from which **Temple Mountain** is visible. After passing another picnic area and a chunk of Precambrian shield, the road rejoins the TransCanada Highway at Lake Louise.

HIKING

Although many natural landmarks can be seen from the roadside, to really experience the park's personality, you'll need to go for a hike. One of the best things about Banff's approximately 80 hiking trails is their variety. From short interpretive walks originating in town and easy hikes rewarded by spectacular vistas, to a myriad of overnight backcountry opportunities, Banff's trails offer something for everyone. Before attempting any hikes, however, you should visit the **Banff Visitor Centre** (224 Banff Ave., 403/762-1550), where staff can advise you on the condition of trails and closures.

From Town

The **Fenland Trail** (two km/1.2 mi.; 30 minutes) is a nice easy walk that will give you a taste of the Bow Valley ecosystem. From the Forty Mile Creek Picnic Area, along Mt. Norquay Road just beyond the rail crossing, the trail dives headfirst into a transitional area between wetland and floodplain forest. This fen environment is prime habitat for many species of birds. The work of beavers can be seen along the trail, and elk are here during winter.

The trail to the top of **Tunnel Mountain** (2.3 km/1.4 mi.; 30–60 minutes one-way) gains 300 meters (990 ft.) of elevation from St. Julien Road, 350 meters (0.2 mi.) south of Wolf Street. It ascends the mountain's western flank through a forest of lodgepole pine, switchbacking past some viewpoints before reaching a ridge just below the summit. Here the trail turns northward, climbing through a forest of Douglas fir to the summit (which is partially treed, preventing 360-degree views).

From a viewpoint famous for the Fairmont Banff Springs outlook, the **Bow River/Hoodoos Trail** (4.8 km/three mi.; 90 minutes one-way) passes under the sheer east face of Tunnel Mountain and follows the river into a meadow where deer and elk often graze. The trail ends at hoodoos, strange limestone-and-gravel columns jutting mysteriously out of the forest. An alternative to returning the same way is to catch the **Banff Transit** bus from Tunnel Mountain Campgrounds. It leaves every half hour ($1).

Sundance Canyon (4.4 km/2.7 mi.; 90 minutes one-way) is a wonderful walk, especially on a sunny afternoon, as much of the trail is along an open riverbank. The trail begins at the Cave and Basin National Historic Site and follows a paved path for the first three kilometers (1.9 mi.), then enters the forest and ends at a shaded picnic area from which the 2.4-kilometer (1.5-mi.) Sundance Loop begins.

Sunshine Meadows

Sunshine Meadows, straddling the Continental Divide, is a unique and beautiful region of the Canadian Rockies. It's best known as home to Sunshine Village, a self-contained alpine resort accessible only by gondola from the valley floor. But for a few short months each summer, the area is clear of snow and becomes a wonderland for hiking. Large amounts of precipitation create a lush cover of vegetation—over 300 species of wildflowers alone have been recorded here. The most popular destination is **Rock Isle Lake,** an easy 2.5-kilometer (1.6-mi.) jaunt from the upper village that crosses the Continental Divide while only gaining 100 meters (330 ft.) of elevation. From the lakeside viewing platform, a variety of options present themselves, include a loop around Larix Lake and a traverse along Standish Ridge.

It's possible to walk the six-kilometer (3.7-mi.) restricted-access road up to the meadows, but a more practical alternative is to take the Sunshine Meadows Shuttle along a road closed to public traffic. This service is operated by **White Mountain Adventures** (403/678-4099 or 800/408-0005, www.canadiannatureguides.com). The round-trip fare from Banff is adult $35, child $20, Check their website for a schedule.

Hikes Between Banff and Lake Louise

The easiest hike between Banff and Lake Louise is along Johnston Canyon, but there are also some more challenging options. The following three are my favorites.

Cory Pass (5.8 km/3.6 mi.; 2.5 hours one-way) is a long, hard slog from the Fireside Picnic Area (the elevation gain is 920 m/3,020 ft.), but once at the objective, a wild, windy, desolate area surrounded in jagged peaks, the view of dogtoothed Mount Louis is worth every bit of energy expended.

Rockbound Lake is a delightful little body of water tucked behind Castle Mountain. The trail (8.4 km/5.2 mi.; 2.5 hours one-way) itself is unremarkable, but crowds will be minimal and the lake is surrounded by impressive peaks. The

trail begins at Castle Mountain Junction, 30 kilometers (18.6 mi.) west of Banff.

From a signed parking lot along the TransCanada Highway three kilometers (1.9 mi.) west of Sunshine Village Junction, the trail to **Bourgeau Lake** gains 730 meters (2,400 ft.) over 7.6 kilometers (4.7 mi.). Hikers are rewarded with the spectacle of a small subalpine lake nestled at the base of an impressive limestone amphitheater. Allow 2.5 hours each way.

OTHER RECREATION
Mountain Biking

Whether you have your own bike or you rent one from the many bicycle shops in town, everyone can enjoy cycling in the park. Loop roads through the golf course and past Lake Minnewanka and the Bow Valley Parkway are all popular, while Mt. Norquay Road is a steep grunt favored by local

HOOKED ON FISHING

The finest fishing in Banff National Park is in **Lake Minnewanka,** where lake trout as large as 15 kilograms (33 lbs.) have been caught. One way to ensure a good catch is through **Lake Minnewanka Boat Tours** (403/762-3473), which offers 3.5-hour guided fishing expeditions in a heated cabin cruiser, at $240 for one or two persons. Fishing boats and tackle are also for rent at the lake.

The most experienced of local guides is Dan Bell of **Upper Bow Fly Fishing** (403/760-7668, www.upperbowflyfishing.com). Bell has been fishing and guiding in the Banff area for over 20 years, and has represented Canada as a member of the National Fly Fishing Team on multiple occasions. His purpose-built drift boats are perfect for chasing brown trout along the **Bow River,** with regular stops made for fly-casting from the banks. Rates start at $175 per person for a half-day on the river and include guiding, gear, and lessons.

Before fishing anywhere in the park, you need a National Park fishing license ($7 per week, $20 per year), available from the Banff Visitor Centre and sport shops around town.

riders for the exercise. Several routes into the backcountry have been designated as mountain-bike trails. These include Sundance (3.7 km/2.3 mi. one-way), Rundle Riverside to Canmore (15 km/9.3 mi. one-way), and Spray River Loop (via Goat Creek; 48 km/30 mi. round-trip). **Bactrax** (225 Bear St., 403/762-8177) and **Adventures Unlimited** (211 Bear St., 403/762-4554) rent front- and full-suspension mountain bikes for $6–10 per hour and $22–40 per day. Rates include a helmet, lock, and biking map. Bactrax also offers mountain-bike tours, including to Vermilion Lakes and along Sundance Canyon. Tours cost $15 per person per hour.

Horseback Riding

Warner Guiding & Outfitting (www.horseback .com) offers a great variety of trips. Their main office is downtown in the **Trail Rider Store** (132 Banff Avenue, 403/762-4551), although trips depart from either **Martin's Stables** (403/762-2832), behind the recreation grounds on Birch Avenue, or **Banff Springs Corral** (403/762-2848) along Spray Avenue. One-hour rides are $27, two hours $40, or join the three-hour Mountain Morning Breakfast Ride for $61.

Rafting and Canoeing

Anyone looking for white-water rafting action will want to run the Kicking Horse River in neighboring British Columbia (see the Golden section of The Kootenays and British Columbian Rockies chapter). **Rocky Mountain Raft Tours** (403/762-3632) offers one-hour ($28) and two-hour ($42) float trips down the Bow River, beginning just below Bow Falls.

  Banff Canoe Rentals (corner of Wolf St. and Bow Ave., 403/762-3632) rents canoes for use on the Bow River or Vermilion Lakes; $18 per hour or $50 for a full day.

Golf

Sandwiched between the Bow River and Mount Rundle is the **Banff Springs Golf Course,** considered one of the world's most scenic. Designed in 1928 by Stanley Thompson, not only is the course breathtakingly beautiful, but it's also challenging for all levels of golfers. Pick up a copy of the book *The World's Greatest Golf Holes,* and you'll see a picture of the fourth hole on the Rundle Nine. It's a par three, over Devil's Cauldron 70 meters (230 ft.) below, to a small green backed by the sheer face of Mount Rundle rising vertically more than 1,000 meters (3,280 ft.) above the putting surface. Another unique feature of the course is the abundance of wildlife. There's always the chance of seeing elk feeding on the fairways, or coyotes, deer, or black bears scurrying across in front of you as you putt. Greens fee is $180 for 18 holes including a cart (through the first and last months of operation, May and mid-Sept.–mid-Oct., greens fee is reduced to $70). The Tunnel 9 offers the same spectacular challenges as Thompson's original layout, but lacks the history; nine holes is $50, or play twice for $75. Free shuttle buses run from the Fairmont Banff Springs to the clubhouse, where you'll find club rentals ($40), three putting greens, a driving range, a pro shop, a café, and a restaurant. Booking tee times well in advance is essential (403/762-6801).

Spas and Hot Springs

The luxurious **Willow Stream** spa facility (403/762-2211, 6 A.M.–10 P.M.) in the Fairmont Banff Springs is the place to pamper yourself. The epicenter of the facility is a circular mineral pool capped by a high glass-topped ceiling and ringed by floor-to-ceiling windows on one side and on the other by hot tubs fed by cascading waterfalls of varying temperatures. Other features include outdoor saltwater hot tubs, private solariums, steam rooms, luxurious bathrooms, a café featuring light meals, and separate male and female lounges complete with fireplaces and complimentary drinks and snacks. A great variety of other services are offered, including facials, body wraps, massage therapy, salon services, and hydrotherapy. General admission is $50 per day (book in advance), with almost 100 services available at additional cost (most of these include general admission, so, for example, you can spend the day at Willow Stream and receive a one-hour massage for $129).

  The **Upper Hot Springs** (Mountain Ave., 403/762-1515, 10 a.m.–10 P.M., $7.50) were developed in 1901 as an alternative to those at the Cave and Basin and are still run by Parks Canada.

Most folks come for a relaxing soak, but massages are available for an additional charge.

WINTER RECREATION

Of Alberta's six world-class alpine resorts, three are in Banff National Park. Apart from an abundance of snow, the resorts have something else in common—spectacular views—which are worth the price of a lift ticket alone. In fact, the entire park is covered in an impossibly white blanket of snow from November until May. You'll always find something to do: cross-country skiing, ice-skating, or snowshoeing. Crowds are nonexistent, and hotels reduce rates by up to 70 percent (except Christmas holidays), which is reason enough to venture into the mountains. Lift and lodging packages begin at $80 per person.

Ski Banff @ Norquay

Visible from town, the steep eastern slopes of Mount Norquay are home to a small resort (403/762-4421; www.banffnorquay.com) with a big reputation. The resort combines the expert-only runs off the North American Chair with intermediate cruising runs out of sight from town. Snowboarders congregate at a half-pipe and terrain park. A magnificent post-and-beam day lodge nestled below the main runs is surrounded on one side by a wide deck that catches the afternoon sun while inside is a cafeteria, restaurant, and bar. Lift tickets are adult $49, senior $38, child $16; lift, lesson, and rental packages cost about the same. A shuttlebus does pickups from Banff hotels for the short, six-kilometer (3.7-mi.) ride up to the resort; $5.

Sunshine Village

The skiing and snowboarding at Sunshine (403/762-6500 or 877/542-2633, www.skibanff .com) has lots going for it—over six meters (20 ft.) of snow annually (no need for snowmaking up here), wide-open bowls, a season stretching for nearly 200 days, skiing and snowboarding in two provinces, and the only slope-side accommodations in the park. A gondola whisks skiers and snowboarders six kilometers (3.7 mi.) from the valley floor to the alpine village while eight high-speed quads (including the world's fastest) open up an amazing amount of terrain. The total vertical rise is 1,070 meters (3,510 ft.) and the longest run (down to the lower parking lot) is eight kilometers (five mi.). Lift tickets are $56 per day, seniors $46, child $20, and those under six ride free. Two days of skiing or boarding and one night's lodging at slopeside **Sunshine Inn** costs from $155 per person per day. The inn has a restaurant, lounge, game room, and hot tub. Transportation from Banff, Canmore, or Lake Louise to the resort is $10 roundtrip; check the website or inquire at major hotels for the timetable.

Rentals and Sales

Each resort has ski and snowboard rental and sales facilities, but getting your gear down in town is often easier. **Monod Sports** (129 Banff Ave., 403/762-4571) has been synonymous with Banff and the ski industry for over half a century. **Rude Boys Snowboard Shop** (downstairs in Sundance Mall, 215 Banff Ave., 403/762-8480) has only been around since the 1980s, but is *the* snowboarder hangout. Other shops with sales and rentals include **Abominable Ski & Sport** (229 Banff Ave., 403/762-2905), **Ski Stop** (Fairmont Banff Springs, 403/762-5333), and **Snow Tips** (225 Bear St., 403/762-8177). Basic rental packages—skis, poles, and boots (or snowboard and boots)—are $20–25 per day, while high performance packages range $30–45.

Other Winter Activities

No better way of experiencing the park's winter delights exists than skiing through the landscape on cross-country skis. Many summer hiking trails are groomed for winter travel. The most popular areas around the town are Johnson Lake, Golf Course Road, Spray River, and Sundance Canyon. The booklet *Cross-Country Skiing—Nordic Trails in Banff National Park,* is available from the visitors center. Rental packages ($12–20 per day) are available from **Performance Sports** (208 Bear St., 403/762-8222), **Snowtips** (225 Bear St., 403/762-8177), and **Mountain Magic Equipment** (224 Bear St., 403/762-2591).

Ice-Skating rinks are located on the **Bow River** along Bow Street; and on the golf course side of the **Fairmont Banff Springs.** The latter rink is lit after dark, and a raging fire is built beside it—the perfect place to enjoy a hot chocolate. Early in the season (check conditions first), skating is possible on **Vermilion Lakes** and **Johnson Lake.** Rent skates from the **Ski Stop** (Fairmont Banff Springs, 403/762-5333) for $5 per hour. **Warner Guiding and Outfitting** (403/762-4551) offers sleigh rides on the frozen Bow River throughout winter ($18 per person).

NIGHTLIFE

Similar to other resort towns around the world, Banff has more than its fair share of bars and nightclubs. At **Wild Bill's** (upstairs at 201 Banff Ave., 403/762-0333) bands usually play a bit of everything, but generally expect alternative music early in the week and rock or country Thursday–Sunday. The food here is excellent. Across the road from Wild Bill's is the **Rose and Crown** (202 Banff Ave., 403/762-2121), an English-style pub serving British beers and typical pub meals. It also features a rooftop patio and rock and roll bands a few nights a week. **St. James Gate Old Irish Pub** (207 Wolf St., 403/762-9355) is a large Irish-style bar with a reputation for excellent British-style meals and occasional appearances by Celtic bands. Away from busy Banff Avenue is **Melissa's** (218 Lynx St., 403/762-5776) which is a long-time favorite drinking hole for locals. It has a small outdoor patio, a long evening happy hour, pool, and multiple TVs.

Banff has two nightclubs. Cavernous **Aurora,** downstairs in the Clock Tower Mall (110 Banff Ave., 403/760-5300), was formerly an infamous gathering place known as Silver City, but after renovations in the late 1990s added some class to Banff's clubbing scene (and is respectable early in the evening), but becomes one obnoxiously loud, over-priced, smoky, pick-up joint after midnight. The other option is **Hoodoos** (137 Banff Ave., enter from Caribou St., 403/762-8434).

Police patrol Banff all night, promptly arresting anyone who even looks like trouble, including anyone drunk or drinking in the streets.

SHOPPING
Canadiana and Clothing

Few companies in the world were as responsible for the development of a country as was the **Hudson's Bay Company** in Canada. From 1670 onward, the company established trading posts across the country, with stores today continuing their traditional role of providing a wide range of goods, in towns big and small across the country. In Banff, the Hudson's Bay Company store (403/762-5525) is at 125 Banff Avenue. Another Canadian store, this one famous for its fleeces, sweaters, and leather goods, is **Roots** (227 Banff Ave., 403/762-9434). For Western clothing and accessories, check out the **Trail Rider Store** (132 Banff Ave., 403/762-4551). Pick up your Canadian-made Tilley Hat from **Piccatilley Square** (Main Fl. Cascade Plaza, 317 Banff Ave., 403/762-0302).

Camping and Outdoor Gear

Inexpensive camping equipment and supplies can be found in **Home Hardware** (208 Bear St., 403/762-2080) and **The Hudson's Bay Company** (125 Banff Ave., 403/762-5525). More specialized needs are catered to at **Mountain Magic Equipment** (224 Bear St., 403/762-2591).

Gifts and Galleries

Banff's numerous galleries display the work of mostly Canadian artists. **Canada House** (201 Bear St., 403/762-3757) features a wide selection of Canadian landscape and wildlife works and native art. **Quest Gallery** (105 Banff Ave., 403/762-2722) offers a diverse range of affordable Canadian paintings and crafts as well as more exotic pieces such as mammoth tusks from prehistoric times and Inuit carvings from Nunavut. Across the Bow River from downtown, browse through traditional native arts and crafts at the **Indian Trading Post** (1 Birch Ave., 403/762-2456).

FESTIVALS AND EVENTS
Spring

Most of the major spring events take place at local alpine resorts, including a variety of snowboard competitions that make for great spectator viewing. One long-running spring event is the **Slush Cup,** which takes place at Sunshine Village in late May. Events include kamikaze skiers and boarders who attempt to jump an ice-cold pit of water.

Summer

Summer is a time of hiking and camping, so festivals are few and far between. The main event is the **Banff Arts Festival** (403/762-6214 or 800/413-8368, www.banffcentre.ca), a three-week (mid-July–early Aug.) extravaganza presented by professional artists studying at the Banff Centre. They perform dance, drama, opera, and jazz for the public at locations around town.

On July 1, Banff celebrates **Canada Day** with a pancake breakfast, a parade down Banff Avenue, and then an afternoon of fun and frivolity in Central Park that includes events such as a stupid pet tricks competition.

Fall

Fall is the park's quietest season, but busiest in terms of festivals and events. First of the fall events, on the last Saturday in September, **Melissa's Mini-marathon** attracts over 2,000 runners in 3-, 10-, and 22-kilometer races.

One of the year's biggest events is the **Banff Mountain Film Festival,** held on the first full weekend of November. Mountain-adventure filmmakers from around the world submit films to be judged by a select committee. Films are then shown throughout the weekend to an enthusiastic crowd of thousands. Exhibits and seminars are also presented, and top climbers and mountaineers from around the world are invited as guest speakers. Tickets for daytime shows start at $40 (for up to 10 films). Night shows are from $30, and all-weekend passes cost around $140 (weekend passes with two nights accommodations and breakfasts start at a reasonable $250). Films are shown in the two theaters of the Banff Centre. For more information, call the festival office (403/762-6675); for tickets, call the Banff Centre box office (403/762-6301 or 800/413-8368, www.banffcentre.ab.ca). Run in conjunction with the film festival is the **Banff Mountain Book Festival,** which showcases the work of

publishers, writers, and photographers whose work revolves around the world's mountains.

ACCOMMODATIONS

Finding a room in Banff in summer (July–Aug.) is nearly as hard as trying to justify its price. By late afternoon just about every room and campsite in the park will be occupied. The park's off-season is from October to May, and hotels offer huge rate reductions during this period. Shop around and you'll find many bargains.

All rates quoted below are for a standard room in the high season (June–early September.).

Under $50

HI–Banff Alpine Centre (403/762-4123, www.banffalpinecentre.ca) is just off Tunnel Mountain Road three kilometers (1.9 mi.) from downtown. Book this and all other Canadian Rockies hostels through Hostelling International's reservation service (403/670-7580 or 866/762-4122, www.hihostels.ca). This large, modern hostel sleeps 216 in small two-, four-, and six-bed dormitories. The large lounge area has a fireplace, and other facilities include a recreation room, public Internet access, bike and ski/snowboard workshop, large kitchen, self-service café, and laundry. In summer, members pay $27.50 per person per night (nonmembers $31.50) for a dorm bed or $78 s or d ($90 for nonmembers) in a private room.

Along the main strip of accommodations and a 10-minute walk to downtown, is **Global Village Backpackers** (449 Banff Ave., 403/762-5521 or 888/844-7875, www.globalbackpackers.com). They're converted motel rooms, so each small dormitory has its own bathroom. Guest amenities include a hot tub, sauna, communal kitchen, games room with a pool table, TV room, activities desk, bike rentals, quiet courtyard, and laundry. Dorm beds are $30 per person, with a number of "semiprivate" rooms for $65 s or d.

Y Mountain Lodge (102 Spray Ave., 403/762-3560 or 800/813-4138 www.ymountainlodge.com, $24 per person) is another option for budget travelers.

$50-100

Accommodations in this price range are limited to private rooms at the backpacker lodges detailed above and a few bed-and-breakfasts. One such establishment is **Tan-Y-Bryn** (118 Otter St., 403/762-3696). Mrs. Cowan has been offering budget accommodation at this 1926 residence for many years, and although furnishings are sparse at best and bathrooms shared, the price is unequalled in town: $50–65 s, $55–75 d includes a light breakfast.

Blue Mountain Lodge (137 Muskrat St., 403/762-5134, www.bluemtnlodge.com, $85–110 s, $90–110 d) is a rambling, older-style lodge with 10 guest rooms, each with a private bath, TV, and telephone. Guests have use of shared kitchen facilities, a lounge, and Internet access while enjoying an expansive cold buffet breakfast each morning.

$100-150

Most Banff bed-and-breakfasts fall into this price range. The website of the Banff/Lake Louise Tourism Bureau (www.banfflakelouise.com) has detailed listings of all private homes registered to take guests. At the lower end of this price range, **Banff B&B** (440 Muskrat St., 403/762-8806, www.banffbb.com, $100–125 s or d) is as good a choice as any. The owners have created a home-away-from-home atmosphere in a modern home set in a residential street yet just a short walk from Banff Avenue.

Elkhorn Lodge (124 Spray Ave., 403/762-2299 or 877/818-8488) is halfway up the hill to the Fairmont Banff Springs. The four small sleeping rooms are $105 s or d, while larger rooms with fridges are $155.

Two blocks off Banff Avenue, the **Homestead Inn** (217 Lynx St., 403/762-4471 or 800/661-1021, www.homesteadinnbanff.com) is a fairly basic hostelry with a faux-Tudor exterior and 27 guest rooms. High-season rates are $140–150 s or d, discounted well below $100 outside of summer.

$150-200

Dating from 1917, **Tarry-A-While** (117 Grizzly St., 403/762-0462, www.tarry.ca) was built for one of the Canadian Rockies' most famous residents, Mary Schäffer. Guests choose from three rooms, each with its own character. The simply furnished Wild Horse Room upstairs is particularly appealing. It features fir-paneled walls, a solid pine bed, and a claw-foot tub in the en suite bathroom. Summer rates are $140 s, $150 d (from $90 s, $100 d rest of year), which includes an expansive breakfast spread and use of an upstairs sitting room piled high with local literature.

The days of Banff motel rooms under $100 disappeared in 2001 when bulldozers took to the town's last remaining park-at-your-door motel, now replaced by the **Spruce Grove Inn** (545 Banff Ave.), a modern mountain-style lodge. Rooms are spacious and a relatively good value at $160 s or d. At the time of writing, reservations and check-in are made at the adjacent Banff Voyager Inn (403/762-3301 or 800/879-1991, www.banffvoyagerinn.com).

$200-250

The famous Brewster brothers guided the first guests through the park, and their descendants are still actively involved in the tourist industry, opening Banff's most central and stylish accommodations in 1996. **Brewster's Mountain Lodge** (208 Caribou St., 403/762-2900 or 888/762-2900, www.brewsteradventures.com) features an eye-catching log exterior with an equally impressive lobby in a prime downtown location. The Western theme is continued in the 77 upstairs rooms. Superior rooms feature two queen-size beds or one king-size bed ($220), deluxe rooms offer a private balcony ($240), and loft suites have hot tubs (from $270). Rates here in the off-season are slashed up to 50 percent.

Within easy walking distance of downtown is **Banff Caribou Lodge** (521 Banff Ave., 403/762-5887 or 800/563-8764, www.banffcaribouproperties.com). Its 200 bright, airy rooms featuring handcrafted log furniture go for $220 s or d. Facilities include a guest shuttlebus, a family-style steakhouse, and a whirlpool tub and sauna. The impressive log entrance is not easily missed.

$250-300

In the heart of downtown Banff, the venerable

Mount Royal Hotel (138 Banff Ave., 403/762-3331 or 800/267-3035, www.mountroyalhotel.com) is a distinctive red-brick building where guests are offered 60 tastefully decorated rooms with high-speed Internet access and the use of a large health club with hot tub. Rates are from $260 s or d, but are discounted as low as $110 in the shoulder season.

The first things you'll notice at **Buffalo Mountain Lodge** (15-min. walk from town on Tunnel Mountain Rd., 403/762-2400 or 800/661-1367, www.crmr/bml, from $295 s or d) are the impressive timber-frame construction and the lobby with its vaulted ceiling and eye-catching fieldstone fireplace. The rooms, chalets, and bungalows all have fireplaces, balconies, large bathrooms, and comfortable beds topped by feather-filled duvets; many have kitchens. And you won't need to go to town to eat—one of Banff's best restaurants, Cilantro Mountain Café, is adjacent to the main lodge.

Over $300

The 770-room **Fairmont Banff Springs** (403/762-2211 or 800/257-7544, www.fairmont.com), one of the world's great mountain resort hotels, has undergone massive renovations in recent years, cementing its position as Banff's premier accommodation. Even though the rooms have been modernized, many date from the 1920s, and as is common in older establishments, these are small. But room size is only a minor consideration when staying in this historic gem. With 12 eateries, a luxurious spa facility, a huge indoor pool, an elegant library, a 27-hole golf course, tennis courts, horseback riding, and enough twisting, turning hallways, boardwalks, towers, and shops to warrant a detailed map, you'll not be wanting to spend time in your room. Through summer, guests have a choice of two packages—the **Castle Experience** ($1,039 d) and the **Canadian Rockies Experience** ($1,179 d). The Castle Experience includes golfing and golf lessons, horseback riding, guided hiking and climbing, tennis, mountain bike rental, canoeing, unlimited entry to Willow Stream spa facilities and one spa treatment, tennis, and three meals daily in any of hotel restaurants. The Canadian Rockies Ex-

Fairmont Banff Springs

perience includes additional activities, such as guided fishing (from $1,179 d). Between mid-September and mid-June, rooms are sold separately, or on a bed-and-breakfast basis, and prices start at $260 s, $300 d, but you may find cheaper deals at the Fairmont website.

ACCOMMODATIONS ALONG THE BOW VALLEY PARKWAY

The Bow Valley Parkway is the original route between Banff and Lake Louise. It's a beautiful drive in all seasons and along its length are a hostel and three lodges, each a viable alternative to staying in Banff.

Under $50

HI–Castle Mountain Wilderness Hostel, 32 kilometers (20 mi.) from Banff along the Bow Valley Parkway, is near a number of interesting hikes and across the road from a general store with basic supplies. This hostel sleeps 28 and has a kitchen, common room, hot showers, and bike rentals. Check-in is 5–11 P.M. Members of Hostelling International pay $19, nonmembers $23. Make bookings through the association's reservation line (403/670-7580 or 866/762-4122, www.hihostels.ca).

$100–150
Johnston Canyon Resort (403/762-2971 or 888/378-1720, www.johnstoncanyon.com, mid-May–early Oct.) is 26 kilometers (16 mi.) west of Banff at the beginning of a short trail that leads to the famous canyon. The rustic cabins are older, and some have kitchenettes. On the grounds are tennis courts, a barbecue area, and general store. Resort dining options are as varied as munching on a burger and fries at the counter of an old-time cafeteria to enjoying oriental-style Chilean sea bass in a dining room that oozes alpine charm. Basic two-person cabins are $119, two-person cabins with a fireplace are $159, and they rise in price all the way to $268 for a "Classic" cabin complete with cooking facilities, and luxurious heritage-style furnishings.

$150–200
Baker Creek Chalets (403/522-3761, www .bakercreek.com) lies along the Bow Valley Parkway 43 kilometers (27 mi.) northwest of Banff and just 12 kilometers (7.5 mi.) from Lake Louise. Each of the log cabins has a kitchenette, fireplace, and outside deck (complete with cute woodcarvings of bears climbing over the railings). Basic one-room cabins are $165 for two; one-bedroom cabins with loft (sleeps six) are $185; two bedroom cabins (sleeps six) are $240. A newer lodge wing has eight luxurious suites, each with richly accented log work, a deck, a microwave and fridge, and a deluxe bathroom; $195 s or d, $215 with a double jetted-tub, and $275 with a loft. Check the website for great off-season deals. The restaurant here is highly recommended.

Over $200
At Castle Junction, 32 kilometers (20 mi.) northwest of Banff, is **Castle Mountain Chalets** (403/762-3868, www.castlemountain.com), home to 21 magnificent log chalets. Each has high ceilings, beautifully handcrafted log interiors, at least two beds, a stone fireplace, full kitchen with dishwasher, a bathroom with hot tub, and satellite TV. Rates range $250–330 s

or d. Part of the complex is a grocery store, barbecue area, library, and the only gas between Banff and Lake Louise. The nearest restaurants are located at Baker Creek and Johnson Canyon.

CAMPGROUNDS
Although the town of Banff has seven campgrounds with approximately 1,500 sites in its immediate vicinity, all of them fill by early afternoon. The best way to ensure a site is to arrive in the morning, when other campers are leaving. When the main campgrounds fill, visitors unable to secure a site are directed to an "overflow" area, which provides few facilities and no hookups but at less cost. Except during fire bans, open fires are permitted in designated areas throughout all campgrounds, but you must purchase a Fire Permit ($6 per site per night) to burn wood, which is provided at no cost.

In 2005, Parks Canada will implement a reservation system for national park campgrounds. Check the website (www.pc.gc.ca) for details. For general camping information, stop by the Banff Visitor Centre (224 Banff Ave., 403/762-1550).

Near the Town of Banff
The three largest campgrounds in the vicinity of Banff are strung out over 1.5 kilometers (0.9 mi.) along Tunnel Mountain Road, with the nearest sites 2.5 kilometers (1.6 mi.) from town.

Closest to town are **Tunnel Mountain Village II** and **Tunnel Mountain Trailer Court** (both $26–30 per night). The former has electrical hookups and is the only campground near Banff open year-round. The latter has full hookups and is open mid-May–September. Both have hot showers but little privacy between sites. No tents are allowed (except when Tunnel Mountain Village I is closed).

Less than one kilometer (0.6 mi.) farther along Tunnel Mountain Road is the park's largest campground (622 sites), **Tunnel Mountain Village I** (mid-May–early Sept., $22). Each site has a fire ring and picnic table, and other amenities include drinking water, hot showers, and cooking shelters, but no hookups.

Along the Lake Minnewanka Road northeast of town are two campgrounds offering less services than those detailed above, but with sites that offer more privacy. The pick of the two is **Two Jack Lakeside Campground** (June–mid-Sept., $22), with 80 sites spread tucked into trees at the south end of Two Jack Lake, an extension of Lake Minnewanka. Facilities include hot showers, cooking shelters, drinking water, and flush toilets. It's just over six kilometers (3.7 mi.) from the TransCanada Highway underpass. The much larger **Two Jack Main Campground** (mid-June–mid-Sept., $17) is a short distance farther along the road, with 381 sites spread through a shallow valley. It offers the same facilities as Two Jack Lakeside, but has no showers. The overflow camping area ($8) for these and the three Tunnel Mountain campgrounds is at the beginning of the Lake Minnewanka Road loop, a short walk along Cascade River from a picturesque picnic area.

Bow Valley Parkway

Along Bow Valley Parkway between the town of Banff and Lake Louise are three campgrounds. Closest to Banff is **Johnston Canyon Campground** (early June–mid-Sept., $22), between the road and the rail line 26 kilometers (16 mi.) west of Banff. It's the largest of the three campgrounds, with 140 sites, and has hot showers but no hookups. Almost directly opposite is Johnston Canyon Resort, with groceries and a restaurant, and the beginning of a trail to the park's best-known waterfalls.

Continuing eight kilometers (five mi.) toward Lake Louise, **Castle Mountain Campground** (early June–early Sept., $17) is also within walking distance of a grocery store (no restaurant), but has just 44 sites and no showers. Services are limited to flush toilets, drinking water, and cooking shelters.

Protection Mountain Campground ($17) another 14 kilometers (8.7 mi.) west and just over 20 kilometers (12.5 mi.) from Lake Louise, opens as demand dictates, usually by late June. It offers 89 sites, along with flush toilets, drinking water, and stove-equipped cooking shelters.

FOOD

Banff has more than 100 dining establishments—more per capita than any town or city across Canada. From lobster to linguini, alligator to à la carte, and fajitas to fudge, anyone who spends time in the park will find something that suits his or her taste and budget.

In July and August, the most popular restaurants don't take reservations and you can expect a wait.

Groceries

Banff has two major grocery stores. In addition to a wide selection of basic groceries, **Keller Foods** (122 Bear St., 403/762-3663, 7 A.M.–10 P.M.) has a good deli with premade salads and sandwiches, preheated soup, and hot chickens. At the other end of downtown, **Safeway** (318 Marten St., 403/762-5329) is open 8 A.M.–11 P.M.

Coffee Shops

The **Cake Company** (220 Bear St., 403/762-2330) serves great coffee, as well as a delicious variety of pastries, muffins, and cakes baked daily on the premises. **Evelyn's Coffee Bar** (Town Centre Mall, Banff Ave., 403/762-0352) has good coffee and huge sandwiches. The few outside tables—on the busiest stretch of the busiest street in town—are perfect for people-watching. **Jump Start** (opposite Central Park at 206 Buffalo St., 403/762-0332) has a wide range of coffee concoctions as well as delicious homemade soups (from $5.50) and sandwiches ($7).

Steak

Even though **Bumper's** (603 Banff Ave., 403/762-2622, 4:30–10 P.M.) is away from the center of Banff, it's worth leaving the shopping strip and heading out to this popular steak house. Large cuts of Alberta beef, an informal atmosphere, efficient service, and great prices keep people coming back. Favorite choices are the slabs of roast prime rib of beef, in four different-sized cuts and cooked to order. Prices range from $18 for the "Ladies" cut to $29 for the "Man Mountain" cut, which includes unlimited trips to a small salad bar.

Banff's most fashionable steak house is **Saltlik** (221 Bear St., 403/762-2467, from 11 A.M.). It's big and bold and the perfect choice for serious carnivores with cash to spare. The concrete-and-steel split-level interior is complemented with modish wood furnishings. Facing the street, glass doors fold back to a terrace for warm-weather dining. The specialty is AAA Alberta beef, finished with grain feeding to enhance the flavor, then flash-seared at 650°C (1,200°F) to seal in the juices, and served with a side platter of seasonal vegetables. Entrées are priced comparable to a city steak house ($18–35), but the cost creeps up as you add side dishes.

Other Canadian

Of the many Banff drinking holes that offer predictable pub-style menus, **Wild Bill's** (201 Banff Ave., 403/762-0333, daily from 11 A.M.) is a standout. Named for one of Banff's most famed mountain men, the decor is suitably Western, with a menu to match. The nachos grande ($9.50) with a side of guacamole ($3) is perfect to share. Later in the day, steaks and spit-roasted chicken are traditional favorites ($15–26).

A town favorite that has faithfully served locals for many years is **Melissa's** (218 Lynx St., 403/762-5511, 7:30 A.M.–10 P.M.). Breakfast is busiest, while lunch and dinner are casual affairs—choose from a wide variety of generously sized burgers, freshly prepared salads, and mouthwatering Alberta beef.

Occupying the prime position on one of Banff's busiest corners is **Maple Leaf Grill** (137 Banff Ave., 403/760-7680, 11 A.M.–11 P.M.) featuring dramatic Canadian-themed decor such as exposed river stone, polished log work, and a two-story interior waterfall (check out the massive moose head in the small room beyond the bar). The cooking uses modern styles with an abundance of Canadian game and produce.

The **Buffalo Mountain Lodge Restaurant** (Tunnel Mountain Rd., 403/762-2400, 7 A.M.–10 P.M.) has a distinctive interior of hand-hewn cedar beams and old-world elegance—complete with stone fireplace and a chandelier made entirely from elk antlers. The featured cuisine is referred to as "Rocky Mountain," reflecting an abundance of Canadian game and seafood combined with native berries and fruits. Dinner entrées range $24–33, and include fare like elk sirloin that's given an exotic touch by accompanying quince compote.

The signature restaurant at the Fairmont Banff Springs is the **Banffshire Club** (Spray Ave., 403/662-6860), which seats just 76 diners and requires that men wear a jacket. This fine-dining restaurant is a bastion of elegance, which begins as a harp player serenades you through a gated entrance. Inside, extravagantly rich wood furnishings, perfectly presented table settings, muted lighting, and kilted staff create an atmosphere as far removed from the surrounding wilderness as is imaginable. Most diners choose one of four table d'hôte menus, which range from $75 per person for two courses to $175 for nine courses accompanied by specially selected wines. It's open daily 6–10 P.M.

Out of Town Canadian

The first of two noteworthy restaurants along the Bow Valley parkway is **Bridges,** at Johnston Canyon Resort (26 km/16 mi. from Banff, 403/762-2971). With a historic atmosphere and views out to a creek, it opens nightly at 6 P.M. for a wide-ranging menu that includes a jambalaya pasta served with a generous quantity of shrimp ($13–21).

A further 17 kilometers (10.6 mi.) along the parkway is **Baker Creek Bistro** (at Baker Creek Chalets, 403/522-2182). Dining is in a small room that exemplifies the term "mountain hideaway," in an adjacent lounge bar, or out on a small deck decorated with pots of colorful flowers. Cooked breakfasts are served in summer, but it's the evening menu that draws the biggest raves. The menu isn't large, but dishes feature lots of Canadian game and produce, with favorites like medallions of venison served with an orange and gin sauce ($29). It's open in summer daily 8 A.M.–9:30 P.M., the rest of the year, Wednesday–Sunday 5–9:30 P.M. (closed Apr.); reservations are recommended for dinner.

European

Most of Banff's many European restaurants have

been around for decades, predating the new wave of eateries featuring Canadian cuisine. A longtime favorite with the casual crowd is **Guido's** (upstairs at 116 Banff Ave., 403/762-4002, from 5:30 P.M.). Prices are a little higher than they should be for the dated surroundings, but diners return here for the homemade pasta cooked to perfection in a variety of classic Italian sauces, rather than for the ambience.

Ticino (415 Banff Ave., 403/762-3848) is an ever-popular Banff institution reflecting the heritage of early mountain guides with lots of log work, and old wooden skis, huge cowbells, and an alpenhorn decorating the walls. It's named for the southern province of Switzerland, where the cuisine has a distinctive Italian influence. The Swiss chef is best known for a wild mushroom soup, unique to the region, his beef and cheese fondues ($16–24 per person), and varied presentations of veal. I couldn't fault the pork tenderloin, baked with gruyere cheese and an apricot paste ($24). Ticino is open daily from 7 A.M. for a hot and cold buffet breakfast and daily for dinner 5–11 P.M.

The **Grizzly House** (207 Banff Ave., 403/762-4055, 11:30 A.M.–midnight) provides Banff's most unusual dining experience. The decor is, to say the least, eclectic (many say eccentric). Each table has a phone for across-table conversation, or you can call your waiter, the bar, a cab, diners in the private booth, or even those who spend too long in the bathroom. Through all this, the food is good and the service as professional as anywhere in town. The menu hasn't changed in decades, and this doesn't displease anyone. Most dining revolves around traditional Swiss fondues, but with nontraditional dipping meats such as buffalo, rattlesnake, alligator, shark, ostrich, venison, and shrimp. Four-course table d'hôte fondue dinners are $32–48 per person.

You'll think you've swapped continents when you step into **Le Beaujolais** (212 Buffalo St., 403/762-2712, from 6 P.M.), a Canadian leader in French cuisine. With crisp white linens, old-style stately decor, and immaculate service, this elegant room has been one of Banff's most popular fine-dining restaurants for 20 years. Its 2nd-floor location ensures great views of Banff, especially from window tables. The dishes feature mainly Canadian produce, prepared and served with a traditional French flair. Entrées begin at $31, but the extent of your final tab depends on whether you choose à la carte items or one of the three- to six-course table d'hôte menus ($55–85)—and also on how much wine you consume. Nationalism shows in the 10,000-bottle cellar, with lots of reds from the Bordeaux and Burgundy regions of France.

Asian
My favorite Japanese restaurant in Banff is **Miki** (600 Banff Ave., 403/762-4581, from 6 P.M.), away from downtown at the far end of the motel strip. Due mostly to its location, getting a table (even one with mountain views) is easy. Daily combo specials provide the best value (around $25 for five courses), or choose from the usual array of sushi, prepared in sight of diners.

INFORMATION
Banff Visitor Centre
Once you've arrived in town, make your first stop the Banff Visitor Centre (224 Banff Ave., mid-June–Aug. daily 8 A.M.–8 P.M., mid-May–mid-June and Sept. daily 8 A.M.–6 P.M., rest of year daily 9 A.M.–5 P.M.). On the right-hand side is a row of desks manned by **Parks Canada** (403/762-1550, www.pc.gc.ca/banff) staff, there to answer hiking questions. Also here, you can pick up the brochure *Banff and Vicinity Drives and Walks* (a compact guide to things to see and do around Banff). Across the floor from Parks Canada, is a desk for the **Banff/Lake Louise Tourism Bureau** (403/762-0270, www.banfflakelouise.com). This organization represents businesses and commercial establishments in the park. Here you can find out about accommodations and restaurants and have any other questions answered. To answer the most-often-asked question, the washrooms are downstairs. Also in the center is a **Friends of Banff National Park** shop, which stocks a good variety of park-related literature, and houses a small theater.

Banff Public Library
Banff's library (101 Bear St., 403/762-2661,

Mon.–Thurs. 10 A.M.–8 P.M., Fri. 10 A.M.–6 P.M., Sat. 11 A.M.–6 P.M., and Sun. 1–5 P.M.) has a solid collection of nonfiction books, many about the park and its environs, and free Internet access.

Bookstores

Banff Book & Art Den (94 Banff Ave., 403/762-3919, www.banffbooks.com, 9 A.M.–9 P.M.) is the largest bookstore in the Canadian Rockies, with reading material spread over a split-level hardwood floor. It stocks a large collection of park literature, wilderness guides, coffee-table books, travel guides, and the entire range of Gem Trek maps.

SERVICES

The post office (Mon.–Fri. 9 A.M.–5:30 P.M.) is on the corner of Buffalo and Bear Streets opposite Central Park. A separate line for General Delivery lessens the wait for other services. Send and receive email and surf the Internet for free at **Banff Public Library** or at **Cyber-web** (Sundance Mall, 215 Banff Ave., 403/762-9226, daily 9 A.M.–midnight), a full-service Internet café.

Major banks can be found along Banff Avenue and are generally open 9 A.M.–3:30 P.M. The **Bank of Montreal** (107 Banff Ave.) allows cash advances with MasterCard, while the **C.I.B.C.** (98 Banff Ave.) accepts Visa. **Freya's Currency Exchange** (108 Banff Ave., 403/762-5111) is in the Clock Tower Mall.

The only downtown launderette is **Cascade Coin Laundry** (lower level of Cascade Plaza, 7:30 A.M.–10 P.M.). **Chalet Coin Laundry** (8 A.M.–10 P.M.) is on Tunnel Mountain Road at the Douglas Fir Resort.

Along Banff Avenue you'll find a handful of one-hour photo places; check around for the cheapest, as many have special offers. The most competitive and reliable is the **Film Lab** (202 Banff Ave., 403/762-2126), or save a few bucks with the overnight service offered at **Keller Foods** (122 Bear St., 403/762-3663).

Mineral Springs Hospital (403/762-2222) is at 301 Lynx Street. **Cascade Plaza Drug** (317 Banff Avenue, 403/762-2245), on the lower level of the Cascade Plaza, is open until 9 P.M. For the **RCMP,** call 403/762-2226.

TRANSPORTATION

Getting There

Calgary International Airport, 128 kilometers (80 mi.) east, is the closest airport to Banff National Park. **Brewster** (403/762-6767, www.brewste.ca) is one of many companies offering shuttles between the airport and Banff hotels ($44 one way). The main depot is the **Brewster Tour and Transportation Centre** (100 Gopher St., 7:30 A.M.–10:45 P.M.), a five-minute walk from downtown Banff. Here you'll find a ticket office, lockers, a café, and gift shop. Other airport buses are **Banff Airporter** (403/762-3396, www.banffairporter.com) and **Rocky Mountain Sky Shuttle** (403/762-5200, www.rockymountainskyshuttle.com). The advantage of traveling with these two companies is that they offer door-to-door-service for around the same price as Brewster. Adjacent desks at the airport's Arrivals level take bookings, but reserve a seat by booking over the phone or online in advance.

Greyhound (403/762-1092) offers scheduled service from the Calgary bus depot at 877 Greyhound Way SW, five times daily to the Brewster Tour and Transportation Centre. Greyhound

THE BREWSTER BOYS

Few guides in Banff were as well known as Jim and Bill Brewster. In 1892, aged 10 and 12, respectively, they were hired by the Banff Springs Hotel to take guests to local landmarks. As their reputation as guides grew, they built a thriving business. By 1900, they had their own livery and outfitting company, and soon expanded operations to Lake Louise. Other early business interests of the Brewsters included a trading post, the original Mt. Royal Hotel, the first ski lodge in the Sunshine Meadows, and the hotel at the Columbia Icefield.

Today, a legacy of the boys' savvy, **Brewster,** a transportation and tour company, has grown to become an integral part of many tourists' stays. The company operates some of the world's most advanced sightseeing vehicles, including a fleet of Snocoaches on Athabasca Glacier.

buses also leave Vancouver from the depot at 1150 Station Street, three times daily for the scenic 14-hour ride Banff.

Getting Around

Most of the sights and many trailheads are within walking distance of town. **Banff Transit** (403/760-8294) operates bus service along two routes through the town of Banff: one from the Fairmont Banff Springs to the RV and trailer parking area at the north end of Banff Avenue; the other from the Fairmont Banff Springs to the Tunnel Mountain Campgrounds. Mid-May–September, buses run twice an hour between 7 A.M. and midnight. October–December, the two routes are merged as one, with buses running hourly midday–midnight. Travel costs $1 per sector.

Cabs around Banff and Lake Louise are reasonably priced—flag drop is $3, then it's $1.65 per kilometer. From the Banff bus depot to Tunnel Mountain accommodations will run around $7, same to the Fairmont Banff Springs, more after midnight. Companies are **Banff Taxi** (403/762-4444), **Legion Taxi** (403/762-3353), and **Taxi Taxi** (403/762-8000).

Plan on renting a vehicle before you reach the park. In addition to high pricing for walk-in customers, the main catch is that no local companies offer unlimited mileage. The most you'll get is a free 150 kilometers (93 mi.), and then expect to pay $.25 cents per kilometer (0.6 mi.). **Banff Rent-a-car** (230 Lynx St., 403/762-3352) rents used cars for $60 per day with 150 free kilometers. Other agencies are **Avis** (403/762-3222), **Budget** (403/762-4565), **Hertz** (403/762-2027), and **National** (403/762-2688). Reservations for cars in Banff should be made well in advance.

Tours

Brewster (403/762-6717 or 877/791-5500) is the dominant tour company in the area. Their three-hour Discover Banff bus tour takes in downtown Banff, Tunnel Mountain Drive, the hoodoos, the Cave and Basin, and Banff Gondola (gondola fare not included). This tour runs in summer only and departs from the bus depot daily at 8:30 A.M.; call for hotel pickup times. Adult fare is $43, children half price. During summer, the company also offers tours from Banff to Upper Hot Springs ($21; includes pool admission), Banff Gondola ($29; includes gondola ride), Lake Minnewanka ($46; includes two-hour boat cruise), and Columbia Icefield ($95; Snocoach extra).

Discover Banff Tours (Sundance Mall, 215 Banff Ave., 403/760-1299 or 877/565-9372) is a smaller company, with smaller buses and more personalized service. Their tour routes are similar to Brewster's: A three-hour Discover Banff tour visits Lake Minnewanka, the Cave and Basin, and the hoodoos for adult $45, child $25; a full day trip to the Columbia Icefield is adult $90, child $50; and a two-hour evening Wildlife Safari is adult $35, child $20.

Lake Louise

As the first flush of morning sun hits Victoria Glacier, and the impossibly steep northern face of Mount Victoria is reflected in the sparkling emerald-green waters of Lake Louise, you'll understand why this lake is regarded as one of the world's seven natural wonders. Overlooking the lake is one of the world's most photographed hotels, Fairmont Chateau Lake Louise. Apart from staring, photographing, and videoing, the area has plenty to keep you busy. Some of the park's best hiking, canoeing, and horseback riding are nearby. And only a short distance away is Moraine Lake, not as famous as Lake Louise but rivaling it in beauty.

Lake Louise is 56 kilometers (35 mi.) northwest of Banff along the TransCanada Highway, or a little bit farther if you take the quieter Bow Valley Parkway. The hamlet of Lake Louise, composed of a small mall, hotels, and restaurants, is in the Bow Valley, just west of the TransCanada Highway. The lake is 200 vertical meters (660 ft.) above the valley floor, along a winding four-kilometer (2.5-mi.) road.

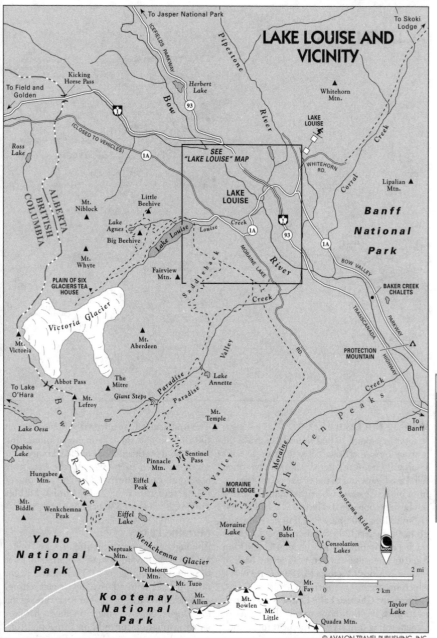

LAKE LOUISE AND VICINITY

To Jasper National Park

To Skoki Lodge

ICEFIELDS PARKWAY

Pipestone River

Bow

Kicking Horse Pass

Herbert Lake

93

Whitehorn Mtn.

To Field and Golden

LAKE LOUISE

Corral Creek

(CLOSED TO VEHICLES)

WHITEHORN RD.

Ross Lake

1A

SEE "LAKE LOUISE" MAP

Lipalian Mtn.

ALBERTA

BRITISH COLUMBIA

Mt. Niblock

Little Beehive

LAKE LOUISE

Banff

Lake Agnes

Lake Louise

Louise Creek

1A

National

Big Beehive

93

Mt. Whyte

MORAINE LAKE

River

Park

Fairview Mtn.

Saddleback

BOW VALLEY

PLAIN OF SIX GLACIERS TEA HOUSE

Creek

1A

Victoria Glacier

Mt. Aberdeen

Valley

BAKER CREEK CHALETS

TRANSCANADA

Mt. Victoria

Abbot Pass

The Mitre

Paradise

Lake Annette

PROTECTION MOUNTAIN

HIGHWAY

To Lake O'Hara

Giant Steps

Mt. Lefroy

Paradise

Mt. Temple

RD.

To Banff

Lake Oesa

Bow

Range

Opabin Lake

Pinnacle Mtn.

Sentinel Pass

Larch Valley

Moraine

Creek

Hungabee Mtn.

Eiffel Peak

MORAINE LAKE LODGE

Valley of the Ten Peaks

Panorama Ridge

Mt. Biddle

Wenkchemna Peak

Eiffel Lake

Moraine Lake

Mt. Babel

Consolation Lakes

2 mi

Yoho National Park

Neptuak Mtn.

Wenkchemna Glacier

0

2 km

Deltaform Mtn.

Mt. Tuzo

Moraine Lake Lodge

Mt. Fay

0

Kootenay National Park

Mt. Allen

Mt. Bowlen

Mt. Little

Quadra Mtn.

Taylor Lake

ALBERTA

© AVALON TRAVEL PUBLISHING, INC.

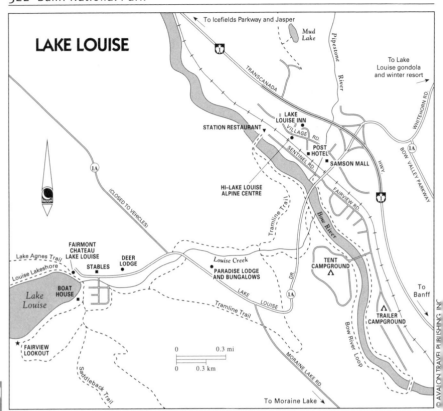

Visiting the Lake

In summer, around 10,000 visitors a day make the journey from the Bow Valley floor up to Lake Louise. By noon the tiered parking lot is often full. Paved trails lead to the lake's eastern shore, in front of the Chateau, where the dramatic setting can be fully appreciated. The lake is 2.4 kilometers (1.5 mi.) long, 500 meters (1,640 ft.) wide, and up to 90 meters (295 ft.) deep. Its cold waters reach a maximum temperature of 4°C (39°F) in August. The snow-covered peak at the back of the lake is **Mount Victoria** (3,459 m/11,350 ft.), which sits on the Continental Divide.

Fairmont Chateau Lake Louise is a tourist attraction in itself. No one minds the hordes of camera-toting tourists who traipse through each day—and there's really no way to avoid them.

The immaculately manicured gardens between the chateau and the lake make an interesting foreground for the millions of Lake Louise photographs taken each year. At the lakeshore boathouse, canoes are rented for $30 per hour, or take a trail ride from **Lake Louise Stables** (403/522-3511) for $30 per hour.

Moraine Lake

Although less than half the size of Lake Louise, Moraine Lake is worthy of just as much film. It's at the end of a winding road 13 kilometers (eight mi.) off Lake Louise Drive. Its rugged setting, nestled in the Valley of the Ten Peaks among the towering mountains of the main ranges, has provided inspiration for millions of people from around the world since Walter Wilcox became

LAKE OF LITTLE FISHES

During the summer of 1882, Tom Wilson, an outfitter, was camped near the confluence of the Bow and Pipestone Rivers when he heard the distant rumblings of an avalanche. He questioned Stoney Indian guides and was told the noises originated from the "Lake of Little Fishes." The following day, Wilson, led by a native guide, hiked to the lake to investigate. He became the first white man to lay eyes on what he named Emerald Lake. Two years later, the name was changed to Lake Louise, honoring Princess Louise Caroline Alberta, daughter of Queen Victoria. In 1890, a modest two-bedroom wooden hotel replaced a crude cabin that had been built on the shore of the lake, as word of its beauty spread. After many additions, a disastrous fire, and the addition of a concrete wing in 1925, the chateau of today took shape, with the most recent addition being a conference center in early 2004.

© ANDREW HEMPSTEAD

the first white man to reach its shore in 1899. Wilcox's subsequent writings—such as "no scene has given me an equal impression of inspiring solitude and rugged grandeur . . ."—guaranteed the lake's future popularity. The lake often remains frozen until June, and the access road is closed all winter. A trail leads along the lake's northern shore, and canoes are rented for $28 per hour from the lakeside concession.

Lake Louise Sightseeing Gondola

During summer the Friendly Giant at Lake Louise winter resort (403/522-3555) whisks visitors up the face of Mount Whitehorn to Whitehorn Lodge in either open chairs or enclosed gondola cars. The view from the top—across the Bow Valley, Lake Louise, and the Continental Divide—is among the most spectacular in the Canadian Rockies. Short trails lead through the forests, across open meadows, and, for the energetic, to the summit of Mount Whitehorn, over 600 vertical meters (1,970 ft.) above. Visitors are free to walk these trails, but guided walks are complimentary and leave regularly from the Interpretation Cen-

tre. The lift operates mid-May–mid-September daily 8:30 A.M.–6 P.M.; adult $18.95, senior $16.95, child $8.95.

HIKING

The variety of hiking opportunities in the vicinity of Lake Louise and Moraine Lake is surely equal to that in any area on the face of the earth. Head out early in the morning to miss the prams, high heels, dogs, and bear-bells that you'll surely encounter during the busiest periods.

Two trails lead from the village to the chateau (a pleasant alternative to driving the steep and very busy Lake Louise Dr.). Shortest is the 2.7-kilometer (1.7-mi.) **Louise Creek Trail.** It begins on the downstream side of the point where Lake Louise Drive crosses the Bow River, crosses Louise Creek three times, and ends at the Lake Louise parking lot. The other trail, **Tramline,** is 4.5 kilometers (2.8 mi.) longer but not as steep. It begins behind the railway station and follows the route of a narrow-gauge railway that once transported guests from the C.P.R. line to Fairmont Chateau Lake Louise.

ALBERTA

Lake Louise

Drive four kilometers (2.5 mi.) from the Trans-Canada Highway up to Lake Louise to access the following trails. Probably the busiest trail in all of the Canadian Rockies is the **Louise Lakeshore Trail** (two km/1.2 mi.; 30 minutes one-way), which follows the north shore of Lake Louise to the west end of the lake. Here numerous braided glacial streams empty their silt-filled waters into Lake Louise. Along the trail's length are benches to sit and ponder what English mountaineer James Outram once described as "a gem of composition and of coloring. . . perhaps unrivalled anywhere." Continue beyond the end of the lake to reach **Plain of the Six Glaciers** (5.3 km/3.3 mi.; two hours), which is a little more strenuous (370-m/1,215-ft. elevation gain), where you can reward yourself with a snack from the teahouse.

The trail to **Lake Agnes** (3.6 km/2.2 mi.; 90 minutes one-way) is a short, steep ascent to another teahouse (homemade soups, healthy sandwiches, and hot drinks), this one picturesquely sited on the edge of an alpine lake. From the teahouse, a one-kilometer (0.6-mi.) trail leads to **Little Beehive** and impressive views of the Bow Valley. Another trail leads around the northern shore of Lake Agnes, climbing to the **Big Beehive,** a total of five kilometers (3.1 mi.) from the chateau. This is a great place to admire the uniquely colored waters of Lake Louise directly below.

Paradise Valley

This aptly named valley lies between Lake Louise and Moraine Lake; access is from Moraine Lake Road, 3.5 kilometers (2.2 mi.) from Lake Louise Drive. You can hike as far up the valley as you like, but the most popular loop is 18 kilometers (11.2 mi.), which will take you around six hours, sans stops. The trail crosses Paradise Creek numerous times in the first five kilometers (3.1 mi.), then divides, following either side of the valley to form a loop. **Lake Annette** is 700 meters (0.4 mi.) along the left fork. It's a typical subalpine lake in a unique setting—nestled against the near-vertical 1,200-meter (3,940-ft.) north face of snow- and ice-capped **Mount Temple.** Those continuing farther will be rewarded with views across the valley and a series of waterfalls known as the **Giant Steps.**

Moraine Lake

Before heading off into the hills, make sure you savor the beauty of Moraine Lake from two spots—from the top of the high rock pile at the lake's outlet and from along the paved lakeshore trail. Now you're ready to tackle one of the many surrounding trails, such as to **Larch Valley** (2.9 km/1.8 mi.; 60 minutes one-way), which gains 400 meters (1,300 ft.) of elevation from just beyond the canoe dock. In fall, when the larch trees have turned a magnificent gold and the sun is shining, few spots in the Canadian Rockies can match the beauty of this valley. But don't expect to find much solitude (and don't be too disappointed if trail restrictions are in place due to wildlife movement). Although the most popular time for visiting the valley is fall, it's a worthy destination all summer, when the open meadows are filled with colorful wildflowers. The trail to **Eiffel Lake** branches off the Larch Valley Trail after 2.4 kilometers (1.5 mi.), by which time most of the elevation gain has already been made. The lake itself soon comes into view. It's small, and looks even smaller in its rugged and desolate setting, surrounded by the famed Valley of the Ten Peaks. Total trail length from the parking lot is 5.6 kilometers (3.5 mi.); allow two hours each way.

WINTER RECREATION

Lake Louise is an immense winter wonderland offering one of the world's premier alpine resorts, unlimited cross-country skiing, ice-skating, and sleigh rides, and nearby heli-skiing. Between November and May, accommodation prices are reduced by up to 70 percent (except Christmas holidays).

Lake Louise

Canada's answer to U.S. megaresorts such as Vail and Killington is Lake Louise (403/522-3555 or 877/253-6888, www.skilouise.com). The nation's second-largest winter resort (behind only Whistler/Blackcomb) comprises gentle trails, mogul fields, long cruising runs, steep chutes, and vast bowls filled with famous Rocky Mountain powder.

The resort is made up of four distinct faces that total some pretty impressive numbers: a 990-meter (3,250-ft.) vertical rise, 1,700 hectares (4,200 acres) of patrolled terrain, and over 100 named runs. The four back bowls alone are each as big as many mid-size resorts and are all well above the treeline. Lift tickets are $59 per day, seniors $47, and children under 12 $15. The season runs mid-November–early May. Free shuttle buses run regularly from Lake Louise accommodations to the hill. From Banff you pay $15 round-trip for transportation to Lake Louise.

Other Winter Activities

The most popular **cross-country skiing** areas are on Lake Louise, along Moraine Lake Road, and in Skoki Valley at the back of the Lake Louise ski area. For details and helpful trail classifications, pick up a copy of *Cross-Country Skiing—Nordic Trails in Banff National Park,* from the Lake Louise Visitor Centre.

Of all the **skating** rinks in Canada, the one on frozen Lake Louise, in front of the Chateau, is surely the most spectacular. Spotlights allow skating after dark, and on special occasions hot chocolate is served. Skates are available in the chateau at **Monod Sports** (403/522-3837); $12 for two hours. Also from the front of the chateau, **Brewster Lake Louise Sleigh Rides** (403/522-3511) offers rides in traditional horse-drawn sleighs along the shores of Lake Louise (adult $20, child $14)

ACCOMMODATIONS AND CAMPING

In summer, accommodations at Lake Louise are even harder to come by than in Banff, so it's essential to make reservations well in advance. Any rooms not taken by early afternoon will be the expensive ones.

Under $50

With beds for $100 less than anyplace else in the village, the **HI–Lake Louise Alpine Centre** (Village Rd., 403/522-2200 or central reservations 403/670-7580 or 866/762-4122, www.hihostels.ca) is understandably popular. Of log construction, with large windows and high vaulted ceilings, the lodge holds an inexpensive restaurant, a large lounge area and guide's room (a quiet place to plan your next hike or browse through the large collection of mountain literature), and rooms spread through two buildings. Members of Hostelling International pay $34 per person per night (nonmembers $38) for a dorm bed or $99 s or d ($112 for nonmembers) in a private room. The hostel is open year-round, with check-in after 3 P.M.

$150–200

Not right in the village, but a good deal for families, small groups, and those who like privacy, **Paradise Lodge and Bungalows** (403/522-3595, www.paradiselodge.com, mid-May–mid-Oct.) provides excellent value in a wonderfully tranquil setting. Spread around well-manicured gardens are 21 attractive cabins. Each has a rustic, yet warm and inviting interior, with comfortable beds, separate sitting areas, and well-appointed bathrooms. The least expensive cabins are $165, or pay just $10 extra for a one-bedroom cabin with a fully equipped kitchen ($185 for two bedrooms). Luxury suites, each with a fireplace and TV, start at $235.

Historic **Deer Lodge** (403/609-6150 or 800/661-1595, www.crmr.com/dl) dates from the 1920s, with many additions made through the years. Facilities include a rooftop hot tub, games room, restaurant, and bar. The least expensive rooms ($165 s or d) are small and don't have phones. Rooms in the $200–250 range are considerably larger, or pay $260 for a heritage-themed tower room. It's along Lake Louise Drive, up the hill from the village, and just a five-minute walk from the lake itself.

Over $200

In the village, the **Post Hotel** (403/522-3989 or 800/661-1586, www.posthotel.com) may lack views of Lake Louise, but it enjoys a riverside setting and is as elegant, in a modern, woodsy way, as the Chateau. Each bungalow-style room is furnished with Canadian pine and

ALBERTA

has a balcony. Many have whirlpool tubs and fireplaces, while some have kitchens. Other facilities include an indoor pool, steam room, and library. Summer rates start at $310 s or d.

Fairmont Chateau Lake Louise (506/863-6310 or 800/257-7544, www.fairmont.com), a historic 500-room hotel on the shore of Lake Louise, has views equal to any mountain resort in the world. But all this historic charm and mountain scenery comes at a price. During the summer season (late June–mid-Oct.), rooms must be booked as a Canadian Rockies Experience package, costing from $600 per person for accommodations, a wide range of activities, and all meals. This rate is for a standard room, with the cost rising exponentially for lakeside rooms and suites. Official rates drop as low as $200 s, $250 d outside of summer, with accommodation and lift packages often advertised for around $200 d.

Campgrounds

Exit the TransCanada Highway at the Lake Louise interchange, 56 kilometers (35 mi.) northwest of Banff, and take the first left beyond Samson Mall and under the railway bridge to reach **Lake Louise Campground,** within easy walking distance of the village. Just under 200 serviced (powered) sites are grouped together at the end of the road. In addition to hookups, this section ($26) has showers and flush toilets. Across the river are 216 unserviced sites ($23), each with a fire ring and picnic table. Other amenities include cooking shelters and a modern bathroom complex complete with hot showers. The serviced section of this campground is open year-round, the unserviced section mid-May–September. If this campground is full, you'll be directed to an area set aside for overflow camping south along Highway 1 ($8).

FOOD AND DRINK
Breakfast
Laggan's Mountain Bakery (Samson Mall, 403/552-2017, daily 6 A.M.–8 P.M.) is *the* place to hang out with a coffee and one of their delicious freshly baked goodies. My favorite combo is hot chocolate, a sausage roll, and a slice of chocolate brownie, which comes to around $6 (or $8 if

I go for two slices of brownie). If the tables are full, order takeout and enjoy your feast on the grassy bank behind the mall.

If you made the effort to rise early and experienced the early-morning tranquility of Moraine Lake, the perfect place sit back and watch the tour bus crowds pour in is from the dining room of **Moraine Lake Lodge** (403/522-3733, June–Sept. from 7:30 A.M.). Staying overnight at the lodge may be an extravagant splurge, but breakfast isn't. A simple, well-presented continental buffet is just $12.50, while the hot version is a reasonable $15.

Lake Louise Station Restaurant
Choose between dining in a restored railway station or adjacent rail cars at the only restaurant in Lake Louise not affiliated with a hotel (200 Sentinel Rd., 403/522-2600, lunch from 11:30 A.M., dinner from 6 P.M.). Although the menu is not extensive, it puts an emphasis on creating imaginative dishes with a combination of Canadian produce and Asian ingredients. Lighter lunches include a Caesar salad topped with roasted garlic dressing—perfect for those planning an afternoon hike. In the evening, expect appetizers such as red shrimp and scallops with a mild Indonesian orange cream sauce ($10) and entrées like a memorable baked sea bass ($28).

Fairmont Chateau Lake Louise
Within this famous hotel are a choice of eateries and an ice-cream shop. The **Poppy Brasserie** has obscured lake views and is the most casual place for a meal. Breakfasts are offered buffet-style, either continental ($18) or cooked ($25), from 7 A.M. Lunch and dinner are à la carte. It's open until 8:30 P.M. **Walliser Stube** is an elegant two-story wine bar decorated with rich wood paneling and solid-oak furniture. It offers a simple menu of German dishes from $17.95 as well as cheese fondue. The **Fairview Dining Room** has a lot more than just a fair view. As the chateau's signature dining room, it enjoys the best views and offers the most elegant setting. Appetizers start at $7, while entrées ($24–37) combine Canadian produce with contemporary cooking styles. For all reservations, call 403/522-3511.

Post Hotel

Although the dining room at the Post Hotel (Village Rd., 403/522-3989, 11:30 A.M.–2 P.M., 6–8:30 P.M.) isn't cheap it's a favorite of locals and visitors alike. The chef specializes in European cuisine, preparing a number of Swiss dishes (such as veal zurichois) to make owner George Schwarz feel homesick. But he's also renowned for his presentation of Alberta beef, Pacific salmon, and Peking duck. Main courses start at $25.

INFORMATION AND SERVICES

Lake Louise Visitor Centre (beside Samson Mall on Village Rd., 403/522-3833, mid-June–Aug. daily 8 A.M.–8 P.M., mid-May–mid-June and Sept. daily 8 A.M.–6 P.M., rest of year daily 9 A.M.–4 P.M.) is an excellent Parks Canada facility filled with interpretive exhibits and slide and video displays.

Woodruff & Blum (Samson Mall, 403/522-3842, 9 A.M.–10 P.M.) offers an excellent selection of books on the natural and human history of the park, as well as animal field guides, hiking guides, and general western Canadiana. In the Fairmont Chateau Lake Louise, **Mountain Lights** (403/522-3734) has a similar, albeit smaller collection.

A small **postal outlet** in Samson Mall also serves as a bus depot and car rental agency. Although Lake Louise has no banks, there's a currency exchange in the Fairmont Chateau Lake Louise and a cash machine in the grocery store. The mall also holds a busy **Laundromat. Pipe-**

stone Photo (403/522-3617, 9 A.M.–7 P.M.) has a range of photographic supplies unequaled in all of the Canadian Rockies. It's relatively well priced, and has one-hour photo developing.

TRANSPORTATION

Calgary International Airport is the closest airport to Lake Louise. **Brewster** (403/762-6767, www.brewster.ca) operates a bus service leaving the airport four times daily, stopping at Banff, Samson Mall, and the chateau. Calgary to Lake Louise is $49.

The only car rental agency in the village is **National** (403/522-3870). The agency doesn't have many vehicles (you'd be better off picking one up at Calgary International Airport). **Lake Louise Taxi & Tours** (Samson Mall, 403/522-2020) charges $2.50 for flag drop, then $1.60 per kilometer. From the mall to Fairmont Chateau Lake Louise runs around $11, to Moraine Lake $20, and to Banff $110. **Wilson Mountain Sports** (Samson Mall, 403/522-3636) has mountain bikes for rent from $15 per hour or $35 per day (includes a helmet, bike lock, and water bottle).

Tours

No tours of the area are offered for visitors staying in Lake Louise. For those staying in Banff, **Brewster** (403/762-6717) has a nine-hour tour departing select Banff hotels daily for $78. In winter this tour departs Tuesday and Friday morning, runs five hours, and includes Banff sights; $55.

Icefields Parkway — Banff

The 230-kilometer (143-mi.) Icefields Parkway, between Lake Louise and Jasper, is one of the most scenic, exciting, and inspiring mountain roads ever built. From Lake Louise, it parallels the Continental Divide, following in the shadow of the highest, most rugged mountains in the Canadian Rockies. The first 122 kilometers (76 mi.) to Sunwapta Pass (the boundary between Banff and Jasper National Parks) can be driven in two hours, and the entire parkway in four. But you'll probably want to spend at least one day,

and probably more, stopping at each of the 13 viewpoints, hiking the trails, watching the abundant wildlife, and just generally enjoying one of the world's most magnificent landscapes. Along the section within Banff National Park are two lodges, three hostels, three campgrounds, and one gas station.

The parkway remains open year-round, although winter brings with it some special considerations. The road is often closed for short periods for avalanche control, so check road conditions in Banff or Lake Louise before setting out. And fill up with gas because no services are available between November and April.

SIGHTS

The impressive scenery begins immediately after the Icefields Parkway forks right from the Trans-Canada Highway just north of Lake Louise. Just three kilometers (1.9 mi.) from the junction is **Herbert Lake,** a perfect place for early morning or evening photography when the **Waputik Range** and distinctively shaped **Mount Temple** are reflected in its waters.

Hector Lake Viewpoint is 16 kilometers (10 mi.) from the junction. Although the view is partially obscured by trees, the emerald-green waters nestled below a massive wall of limestone form a breathtaking scene.

Crowfoot Glacier

The aptly named Crowfoot Glacier can best be appreciated from north of Bow Lake. From the viewpoint, 17 kilometers (10.6 mi.) north of Hector Lake, it's easy to see how this and other glaciers are formed. It sits on a wide ledge near the top of Crowfoot Mountain, from where its glacial "claws" cling to the mountain's steep slopes. The retreat of this glacier has been dramatic. Only 50 years ago, two of the claws extended to the base of the lower cliff.

Bow Lake

The sparkling, translucent waters of Bow Lake are among the most beautiful that can be seen from the Icefields Parkway. The lake was created when moraines, left behind by retreating glaciers, dammed subsequent meltwater. At the southeast end of the lake is a day-use area with waterfront picnic tables and a trail that leads to a swampy area at the lake's outlet. At the upper end of the lake is a lodge and the trailhead for a walk to Bow Glacier Falls.

The road leaves Bow Lake and climbs to **Bow Summit.** Looking back, the true color of Bow Lake becomes apparent, and the Crowfoot Glacier reveals its unique shape. At an elevation of 2,069 meters (6,790 ft.), this pass is one of the highest points crossed by a public road in Canada. It is also the beginning of the Bow River, the one you camped beside at Lake Louise, photographed flowing through the

Mount Chephren provides a dramatic backdrop to Lower Waterfowl Lake.

town of Banff, and strolled along in downtown Calgary.

Peyto Lake

From the parking lot at Bow Summit, a short, paved trail leads to one of the most breathtaking views you could ever imagine. Far below the viewpoint is Peyto Lake, an impossibly intense green-colored lake whose hues change as the concentration of glacial run-off increases over summer. The lake is one of many park landmarks named for early outfitter Bill Peyto. In 1898, he was part of an expedition camped at Bow Lake. Seeking solitude (as he was reportedly wont to do), he slipped off during the night to sleep near this lake. Other members of the party coined the name "Peyto's Lake," and it stuck.

To Saskatchewan River Crossing

From Bow Pass, the parkway descends to a viewpoint directly across the Mistaya River from **Mount Patterson** and the **Snowbird Glacier,** clinging precariously to the mountain's steep northeast face. **Mistaya Lake** is a three-kilometer-long (1.9 mi.) body of water that sits at the bottom of the valley between the road and the divide, but it can't be seen from the parkway. The best place to view this panorama is from the **Howse Peak Viewpoint** at Upper Waterfowl Lake. From here, the high ridge that forms the Continental Divide is easily distinguishable. Numerous trails lead around the swampy shores of **Upper** and **Lower Waterfowl Lakes,** providing one of the park's best opportunities to view moose, which feed on the abundant aquatic vegetation that grows in Upper Waterfowl Lake.

From a parking lot 14 kilometers (8.7 mi.) northeast of Waterfowl Lake Campground, a short trail descends into the montane forest to **Mistaya Canyon.** Here, the effects of erosion can be appreciated as the Mistaya River leaves the floor of Mistaya Valley, plunging through a narrow-walled canyon into the North Saskatchewan Valley. The area is scarred with potholes where boulders have been whirled around by the action of fast-flowing water, carving deep depressions into the softer limestone bedrock below.

Saskatchewan River Crossing to Sunwapta Pass

On the north side of the North Saskatchewan River, the Icefields Parkway follows the base of **Mount Wilson.** A pullout just past Rampart Creek Campground has good views of Mount Amery to the west and Mounts Sarbach, Chephren, and Murchison to the south. Beyond here is the **Weeping Wall,** a long cliff of gray limestone where a series of waterfalls tumbles more than 100 meters (330 ft.) down the steep slopes of **Cirrus Mountain.** In winter, this wall of water freezes, becoming a popular spot for ice climbers to test their skills. Before ascending to Sunwapta Pass, the road makes a sweeping curve over an alluvial plain of the North Saskatchewan River. Halfway up to the pass is a viewpoint well worth stopping for. From here, views extend down the valley to the slopes of Mount Saskatchewan and, on the other side of the parkway, Cirrus Mountain. Another viewpoint, farther up the road, has the added attraction of **Panther Falls** across the valley. A cairn at **Sunwapta Pass** (2,023 m/6,640 ft.) marks the boundary between Banff and Jasper National Parks. It also marks the divide between the North Saskatchewan and Sunwapta Rivers, whose waters drain into the Atlantic and Arctic Oceans, respectively.

HIKING

The trail to **Bow Glacier Falls** (3.4 km/2.1 mi.; one hour one-way) gains minimal elevation, making it enjoyable for everyone. It begins by skirting one of the most beautiful lakes in the Canadian Rockies before ending at a narrow but spectacular waterfall. The trailhead is Num-ti-jah Lodge, 36 kilometers (22.3 mi.) northwest from the Trans-Canada Highway. A further 20 kilometers (12 mi.) is Waterfowl Lakes Campground, the starting point of a trail to **Chephren Lake** (four km/2.5 mi.; 60–90 minutes one-way). A minimal output of energy (the elevation gain is just 100 m/330 ft.) is amply rewarded—the lake is a beauty and crowds are minimal.

Take advantage of a high point along the Icefields Parkway, four kilometers (2.5 mi.) south of

ALBERTA

Sunwapta Pass, to climb even higher, to **Parker's Ridge** (2.4 km/1.5 mi.; one hour one-way). This trail climbs through a fragile alpine environment to the summit of a ridge form where the panorama extends across two-kilometer-wide (1.2 mi.) Saskatchewan Glacier to Castleguard Mountain.

ACCOMMODATIONS AND CAMPING

Under $50

Five hostels are spread along the Icefields Parkway north of Lake Louise, three of which are in Banff National Park. Facilities are limited and beds should be reserved (403/670-7580 or 866/762-4122, www.hihostels.ca) as far in advance as possible. Rates are $19 per night for members of Hostelling International; nonmembers pay $23. Check-in at all three is 5–10 P.M. The first, 24 kilometers (15 mi.) from Lake Louise, is **HI–Mosquito Creek Wilderness Hostel,** which is near good hiking and offers accommodations for 32 in four cabins. Facilities include a kitchen, wood-heated sauna, and large common room with fireplace. With similar facilities is **HI–Rampart Creek Wilderness Hostel,** a further 64 kilometers (40 mi.) along the parkway, and **HI–Hilda Creek Wilderness Hostel,** at the top of Sunwapta Pass.

$50–100

The Crossing (403/761-7000, www.thecrossing resort.com, mid-March–November, $95–110 s or d) is a large complex 87 kilometers (54 mi.) north of Lake Louise and 45 kilometers (28 mi.) south of Columbia Icefield. The guest rooms offer a good combination of size and value, but lack the charm of those at Num-ti-jah to the south and the views enjoyed by those at the Columbia Icefield Centre to the north. Each of the 66 units has a phone and television. In addition to overnight rooms, The Crossing has the only gas between Lake Louise and Jasper, a self-serve cafeteria, a restaurant, a pub, and a large gift shop.

Over $100

Simpson's Num-ti-jah Lodge (403/522-2167, www.num-ti-jah.com, closed Nov.), on Bow Lake 40 kilometers (25 mi.) north of Lake Louise, dates to 1920. With a rustic mountain ambience that has changed little over time, an overnight stay at Num-ti-jah is a memorable experience. Just don't expect the conveniences of a regular motel. Under the distinctively red, steep-pitched roof of the main lodge are 25 rooms, some of which share bathrooms, and there's not a TV or phone in sight. Downstairs, guests soak up the warmth of a roaring log fire while mingling in a comfortable library filled with historic mountain literature. A dining room lined with historic memorabilia is open throughout the day, serving up a breakfast buffet and evening delicacies such as shellfish fettuccini ($20). Rates are $165–180 s or d for a room with shared bath, $180–240 s or d for an en suite. Rates are reduced 40 percent outside of summer.

Campgrounds

Beyond Lake Louise, the first camping along the Icefields Parkway is at **Mosquito Creek Campground** (year-round, $13), 24 kilometers (15 mi.) from the TransCanada Highway. Don't be perturbed by the name, the bugs here are no worse than anywhere else. The 32 sites are nestled in the forest, with a tumbling creek separating the campground from a hostel. Each site has a picnic table and fire ring, while other amenities include pump water, pit toilets, and a cook shelter with an old-fashioned woodstove.

Waterfowl Lake Campground (late June–mid-Sept., $17) is 33 kilometers (20 mi.) north along the Icefields Parkway from Mosquito Creek. It features 116 sites between Upper and Lower Waterfowl Lakes, with a few sites in view of the lower lake. Facilities include pump water, flush toilets, and cooking shelters with wood-burning stoves.

Continuing toward Jasper, the Icefields Parkway passes The Crossing, a good place to gas up and buy last minute groceries before reaching **Rampart Creek Campground** (late June–early Sept., $13), 31 kilometers (19 mi.) beyond Waterfowl Lake and 88 kilometers (55 mi.) from Lake Louise. With just 50 sites, this campground fills early. Facilities include cooking shelters, pit toilets, and pump water.

Jasper National Park

Snowcapped peaks, vast icefields, beautiful glacial lakes, soothing hot springs, thundering rivers, and the most extensive backcountry trail system of any Canadian national park make Jasper a stunning counterpart to its sister park, Banff. A 3.5-hour drive west of Alberta's provincial capital of Edmonton, Jasper extends from the headwaters of the Smoky River in the north to the Columbia Icefield (and Banff National Park) in the south. To the east are the foothills, and to the west is the Continental Divide, which marks the Alberta–British Columbia border. This 10,900-square-kilometer (4,208-sq.-mi.) wilderness is a haven for wildlife; much of the park is traveled only by wolves and grizzlies.

JASPER NATIONAL PARK

To Grande Cache

To Edmonton

Hinton

ALBERTA

Brûlé

Brûlé Lake

POCAHONTAS

Fiddle River

MIETTE HOT SPRINGS

Utopia Mtn.

Moosehorn Creek

Mt. Aeolus

Mt. Roche Ronde

Mt. Roche Miette

Celestine Lake

Rocky R.

Snake Indian Falls

Jasper Lake

Talbot Lake

Snake Indian River

Willmore Wilderness Park

Jasper National Park

The Ranee

Whitecap Mtn.

SNARING RIVER

Pyramid Mtn.

Pyramid

Blue Creek

Snaring River

Snaring Mtn.

Azure Lake

Topaz Lake

Snake Indian Mtn.

Mt. Bridgeland

Miette River

Yellowhead Lake

Mt.

Twintree Lake

Swoda Mtn.

Calumet Glaciers

Calumet Peak

Resthaven Mtn.

Resthaven Icefield

Mt. Chown

Mt. Bess

Smoky River

Mt. Robson

Reef Icefield

Mt. Robson Provincial Park

Moose Lake

Fraser River

To Valemount and Prince George

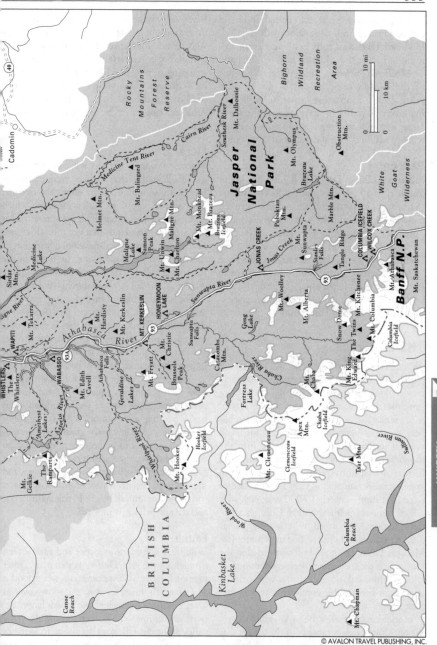

ALBERTA

© AVALON TRAVEL PUBLISHING, INC.

The park's most spectacular natural landmarks can be admired from two major roads. The **Yellowhead Highway** runs east–west from Edmonton to British Columbia through the park. The **Icefields Parkway,** which is regarded as one of the world's great mountain drives, runs north–south, connecting Jasper to Banff. The main service center in the park is the town of Jasper, a smaller, less-commercial version of Banff, where you'll find several motels and restaurants.

Park Entry

A **National Parks Day Pass** is adult $7, senior $6, child $3.50 to a maximum of $14 per vehicle ($12 for seniors). It's interchangeable between parks and is valid until 4 P.M. the day following its purchase. Passes can be purchased at the park information center, at the booth along the Icefields Parkway a few kilometers south of the town of Jasper, and at campground kiosks. If you're traveling north to Jasper along the Icefields Parkway, you'll be required to stop and purchase a park pass just beyond Lake Louise.

THE LAND

Although the peaks of Jasper National Park are not particularly high, they're among the most spectacular along the entire Continental Divide. Approximately 100 million years ago, layers of sedimentary rock—laid down here up to one billion years ago—were forced upward, folded, and twisted under tremendous pressure into the mountains seen today. The land's contours were further altered during four ice ages that began approximately one million years ago. The last ice age ended approximately 10,000 years ago, with a final remnant being the huge Columbia Icefield. Debris left behind by retreating glacier blocked valleys and created bodies of water like **Maligne Lake.** The glacial silt suspended in the lake's waters produces amazing emerald, turquoise, and amethyst colors; early artists who painted these lakes had trouble convincing people that their images were real.

In addition to creating the park's gemlike lakes, the retreating glaciers carved out the valleys that they ever-so-slowly flowed through. The Athabasca

River Valley is the park's largest watershed, a typical example of a U-shaped, glacier-carved valley. Another beautiful aspect of the park's scenery is its abundance of waterfalls. They vary from the sparkling tumble of Mountain Creek as it cascades down a limestone cliff into a picturesque pool at Punchbowl Falls, to the roar of the Athabasca Falls where the river is forced through a narrow gorge.

Flora

Vegetation zones in the park range from montane in the valleys, through subalpine evergreen forests higher up, to alpine tundra above the treeline. Only a small part of the park is montane, which is characterized by stands of Douglas fir, as well as savannahlike grasslands that occur on drier sites in valley bottoms. Well-developed stretches of montane can be found along the floors of the Athabasca and Miette River Valleys, providing winter habitat for larger mammals such as elk.

The subalpine zone, heavily forested with evergreens, extends from the lower valley slopes up to the treeline. The dominant species in this zone is lodgepole pine, although Engelmann spruce, alpine fir, poplar, and aspen grow here. The treeline in Jasper lies at an elevation of between 2,050 and 2,400 meters (6,700 and 7,900 ft.) above sea level. Above this point is the alpine zone, where the climate is severe; the average yearly temperature is below freezing, and summer is brief. The zone's plant species grow low to the ground, with extensive root systems to protect them during high winds and through the deep snow cover of winter. During the short summer, these open slopes and meadows are carpeted with a profusion of flowers such as golden arnicas, bluebells, pale columbines, and red and yellow paintbrush.

Fauna

Wildlife is abundant in Jasper and can be seen throughout the year. During winter, many larger mammals move to lower elevations where food is accessible. By June, most of the snow cover at lower elevations has melted, the crowds haven't arrived, and animals can be seen feeding along the valley floor. In fall, tourists move to warmer climates, the rutting season begins, bears go into hibernation, and a herd of elk moves into the town of Jasper for the winter.

Five species of deer inhabit the park. The large-eared mule deer is commonly seen around the edge of town or grazing along the road. White-tailed deer can be seen throughout the park. A small herd of woodland caribou roams throughout the park; they're most commonly seen during late spring, feeding in river deltas. The town of Jasper is in the home range of approximately 500 elk, which can be seen most of the year around the town or along the highway northeast and south of town. Moose, although not common, can be seen along the major drainage systems feeding on aquatic plants.

In summer, mountain goats can often be seen feeding in alpine meadows. A good place for goat-watching is Goat Lookout on the Icefields Parkway. Unlike most of the park's large mammals, these surefooted creatures don't migrate to lower elevations in winter but stay sheltered on rocky crags, where wind and sun keep the vegetation snow free. Often confused with the goat is the darker bighorn sheep. The horns on the males of this species are very thick and often curl 360 degrees. Bighorns are the most common of all large mammals in the park; look for them in the east of the park at Disaster Point.

Black bears number approximately 80 in the park. They are most commonly seen along the Icefields Parkway in spring, when they first come out of hibernation. Grizzly bears are occasionally seen crossing the Icefields Parkway at higher elevations early in summer. For the most part,

they remain in remote mountain valleys, and if they do see, smell, or hear you, they'll generally move away. Read the pamphlet *Keep the Wild in Wildlife,* which is available at campgrounds and information centers throughout the park, before setting out into the woods.

HISTORY

The first white man to enter the Athabasca River Valley was David Thompson, one of Canada's greatest explorers. He was looking for a pass through the mountains to use as access to the Pacific Ocean. The gap he eventually found—**Athabasca Pass,** south of Mount Edith Cavell—became famous as the route used by the North West and Hudson's Bay companies to cross the Rockies. Meanwhile, the North West Company built a post named Jasper's House near the present town of Jasper. In time, an easier passage through the mountains was discovered farther north (at what is now called **Yellowhead Pass**), displacing Thompson's original, more difficult route to the south.

At the start of the 20th century, only seven homesteaders lived in the valley, but the Grand Trunk Pacific Railway was pushing westward, bringing with it the possibility of multitudes of settlers coming to live there. In 1907, the federal government officially declared the boundaries of Jasper Forest Park. Jasper was officially designated as a national park in 1930. This was followed by the construction of many roads, including the Icefields Parkway, which opened in 1940.

Icefields Parkway—Jasper

Sunwapta Pass (2,040 m/6,690 ft.), four kilometers (2.5 mi.) south of the Columbia Icefield, marks the boundary between Banff and Jasper National Parks.

The following sights along the Icefields Parkway are detailed from south to north, from the Icefield Centre to the town of Jasper, a distance of 105 kilometers (65 mi.). The scenery along this stretch of road is no less spectacular than the other half through Banff National Park, and it's easy to spend at least a full day en route.

No gas is available along this stretch of the Icefields Parkway. The nearest gas stations are at Saskatchewan River Crossing (Banff National Park) and in the town of Jasper, a total distance of 150 kilometers (93 mi.), so keep your tank topped up to be safe.

COLUMBIA ICEFIELD

The largest and most accessible of 17 glacial areas along the Icefields Parkway is 325-square-kilometer (125-sq.-mi.) Columbia Icefield, at the south end of the park, 105 kilometers (65 mi.) south from Jasper and 132 kilometers (82 mi.) north from Lake Louise. It's a remnant of a major glaciation that covered most of Canada 20,000 years ago. It has survived because of its elevation at 1,900–2,800 meters (6,230–9,190 ft.) above sea level, cold temperatures, and heavy snowfalls. From the main body of the ice cap, which sits astride the Continental Divide, six glaciers creep down three main valleys. Of these, **Athabasca Glacier** is the most accessible and can be seen from the Icefields Parkway; it's one of the few glaciers in the world that you can drive right up to. It's an impressive 600 hectares (1,480 acres) in area and up to 100 meters (330 ft.) deep.

Icefield Centre

The magnificent Icefield Centre (mid-April–mid-Oct. daily 10 A.M.–9 P.M., extended to 9 A.M.–11 P.M. in July–Aug.) overlooks the Athabasca Glacier from across the Icefields Parkway. This is the staging point for Snocoach tours,

but before heading out on to the icefield, don't miss the **Glacier Gallery** on the lower floor. This large display area details all aspects of the frozen world, including the story of glacier formation and movement. Back on the main floor of the center you'll find a Parks Canada desk (780/852-6288)—a good source of information for northbound visitors—the Snocoach ticketing desk, restrooms, and the obligatory gift shop. Upstairs is an overpriced café (daily 9 A.M.–6 P.M.) and a passable restaurant (daily 7–10 A.M. and 6–9:30 P.M.). The only redeeming feature of these dining options has nothing to do with the food—the view both from inside and out on the massive deck is stupendous.

COLUMBIA ICEFIELD TO JASPER

Sunwapta Lake, at the toe of the Athabasca Glacier, is the source of the **Sunwapta River,** which the Icefields Parkway follows for 48 kilometers (30 mi.) to Sunwapta Falls. Eight kilometers (five mi.) north from the Icefield Centre, the road descends to a viewpoint for **Stutfield Glacier.** Six kilometers (3.7 mi.) farther down the road is **Tangle Ridge,** a grayish-brown wall of limestone over which Beauty Creek cascades. At this point the Icefields Parkway runs alongside the Sunwapta River, following its braided course through the **Endless Range,** the eastern wall of a classic glacier-carved valley. A further 41 kilometers (25 mi.) along the road a 500-meter (0.3-mi.) spur at Sunwapta Falls Resort leads to **Sunwapta Falls.** Here the Sunwapta River changes direction sharply and drops into a deep canyon. The best viewpoint is from the bridge across the river, but it's also worth following the path on the parking lot-side of the river downstream along the rim of the canyon.

Goat Lookout

After following the Athabasca River for 17 kilometers (11 mi.), the road ascends to a lookout with picnic tables offering panoramic river views. Below the lookout is a steep bank of exposed glacially ground material containing natural

EXPLORING THE COLUMBIA ICEFIELD

From the Icefields Parkway, an unpaved road leads down through piles of till left by the retreating Athabasca Glacier to Sunwapta Lake, from where a short path leads up to the toe of the glacier. (Along the access road, look for the small markers showing how far the toe of the glacier reached in years gone by; the furthermost marker is across the highway beside the stairs leading up to the Icefield Centre.)

Taking the Snocoach

The icefield can be very dangerous for unprepared visitors. The safest way to experience the glacier firsthand is on a Snocoach (780/852-3332, www.brewster.ca), a big-wheeled vehicle developed especially for glacial travel. The tour, which begins with a bus ride from the Icefield Centre and includes time spent walking on the surface of the Athabasca Glacier, costs adult $28, child $14, and operates mid-April–mid-October 9 A.M.–5 P.M. (try to plan your tour for after 3 P.M., when the tour buses have departed for the day). The ticketing office is on the main floor of the Icefield Centre (no reservations are taken).

HIKES ALONG ICEFIELDS PARKWAY

The trail to **Wilcox Pass** (four km/2.5 mi.; 90 minutes one-way), beginning from the Wilcox Creek Campground, three kilometers (1.9 mi.) south of the Icefield Centre, is moderately strenuous. On the plus side, the elevation gain (340 m/1,115 ft.) allows panoramic views of the valley, Columbia Icefield, and surrounding peaks, with the flower-filled alpine meadows only adding to the appeal.

Continue along Highway 93A one kilometer (0.6 mi.) beyond Athabasca Falls and take the 5.5-kilometer (3.4-mi.) Geraldine Fire Road to access the trail to **Geraldine Lakes** (five km/3.1 mi.; 2 hours one-way). The first of four lakes is an easy two-kilometer (1.2-mi.) walk. From the back of the lake, the trail climbs steeply past a scenic 100-meter-high (330 ft.) waterfall, and traverses some rough terrain where the trail becomes indistinct; follow the cairns. At the end of the valley is another waterfall. The trail climbs east of the waterfall to a ridge above the second of the lakes, five kilometers (3.1 mi.) from the trailhead. Two other lakes, accessible only by bush bashing, are located farther up the valley.

ICEFIELDS PARKWAY ACCOMMODATIONS AND CAMPING

Two lodges and two hostels lie along the Icefields Parkway proper. A number of other accommodations and the park's main campgrounds are along the parkway, but within close proximity to the town of Jasper. These are covered in the following Town of Jasper section.

Under $50

Beauty Creek Hostel (17 km/10.5 mi. north of Columbia Icefield, May–Sept.) is nestled in a small stand of Douglas fir between the Icefields Parkway and the Sunwapta River. Each of its separate male and female cabins sleeps 12 and has a woodstove. A third building holds a well-equipped kitchen and dining area. **Athabasca Falls Hostel** (32 km/20 mi. south of Jasper town,

deposits of salt. The local mountain goats spend most of their time on the steep slopes of Mount Kerkeslin, to the northeast, but occasionally cross the road and can be seen searching for the salt licks along the riverbank, trying to replenish lost nutrients.

Athabasca Falls

Nine kilometers (5.6 mi.) beyond Goat Lookout and 32 kilometers (20 mi.) south of Jasper, the Icefields Parkway divides when an old stretch of highway (Hwy. 93A) crosses the Athabasca River and continues along its west side for 25 kilometers (15.5 mi.) before rejoining the parkway seven kilometers (4.3 mi.) south of the town. At the southern end of this loop the Athabasca River is forced through a narrow gorge and over a cliff into a cauldron of roaring water below. Trails lead from a day-use area to various viewpoints above and below the falls.

year-round) is larger and has electricity. In both cases, members of Hostelling International pay $13, nonmembers $18 and check-in is 5–11 P.M. Reservations can be made for these hostels by calling Jasper International Hostel (780/852-3215 or 877/852-0781).

$150–200
Historic **Sunwapta Falls Resort** (780/852-4852 or 888/828-5777, www.sunwapta.com, May–mid-Oct.) is 55 kilometers (34 mi.) south of the town of Jasper and within walking distance of the picturesque waterfall for which it is named. It features 52 units, all with televisions and some with kitchenettes, fireplaces, and balconies. Rates are $169 s or d, reduced to $95 outside of the busy July–mid-September period. In the main lodge is a lunchtime self-serve restaurant popular with passing travelers. In the evening this same room is transformed into the Endless Chain Restaurant, featuring simply prepared Canadian game and seafood in the $18–26 range and a delectable wild berry crumble for $6.

Columbia Icefield Chalet (780/852-6550 or 877/423-7433, www.brewster.ca, June–mid-Oct., $185–205), the top story of Columbia Icefield Centre, lies in a stunning location high above the treeline and overlooking the Columbia Icefield, 105 kilometers (65 mi.) south of the town of Jasper and 132 kilometers (82 mi.) north of Lake Louise. It features 29 standard rooms, 17 of which have glacier views, and three larger, more luxurious corner rooms. All units have satellite TV and phones.

Campgrounds
Aside from Whistlers and Wapiti Campgrounds at the top end of the Icefields Parkway, there are four other campgrounds along this stretch of road. **Wilcox Creek** and **Columbia Icefield Campgrounds** are within two kilometers (1.2 mi.) of each other at the extreme southern end of the park, just over 100 kilometers (62 mi.) south of the town of Jasper and around 125 kilometers (78 mi.) north of Lake Louise. Both are primitive facilities with pit toilets, cooking shelters, and fire rings; all sites are $13. Continuing north is **Jonas Creek** and then **Honeymoon Lake** and **Mt. Kerkeslin Campgrounds.** All cost $13 per night and have only primitive facilities.

Town of Jasper

ALBERTA

Jasper is the wonderfully underrated counterpart to its neighbor, Banff—it has half Banff's population, and it's also less commercialized and its streets are a lot quieter. Part of the town's charm is its location at the confluence of the Athabasca and Miette Rivers, surrounded by the rugged, snowcapped peaks of Jasper National Park. Edmonton, Alberta's capital, is a 3.5-hour drive to the east while the town of Banff is 280 kilometers (174 mi.) to the southeast.

Connaught Drive, the town's main street, parallels the rail line as it curves through town. Along here, you'll find the Park Information Centre, the bus depot, the rail terminal, restaurants, motels, and a series of parking lots. Behind Connaught Drive is Patricia Street (one-way northbound), which has more restaurants and services and leads to more hotels and motels on Geikie Street. Behind this main commercial core are rows of neat houses—much less pretentious than those in Banff—and all the facilities of a regular town, including a library, a school, a swimming pool, a hospital, and a new emergency services building, the latter a priority after incorporation.

SIGHTS AND DRIVES
With all the things to do and see in the park, it's amazing how many people hang out in town. The best way to avoid the problem is to avoid town during the middle of day. The Park Information Centre, on Connaught Drive, is the only real reason to be in town. The shaded park in front of the center is a good place for people-watching. Try for a parking spot in the lot along the railway line.

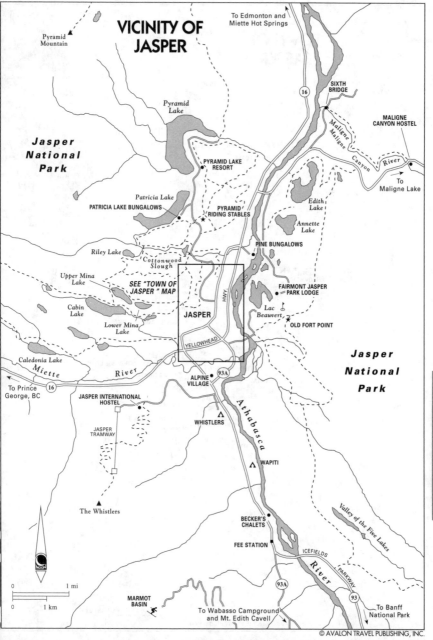

VICINITY OF JASPER

Pyramid Mountain

To Edmonton and Miette Hot Springs

16

SIXTH BRIDGE

MALIGNE CANYON HOSTEL

Pyramid Lake

Maligne Maligne Canyon River

To Maligne Lake

Jasper National Park

PYRAMID LAKE RESORT

Patricia Lake

Edith Lake

PATRICIA LAKE BUNGALOWS

PYRAMID RIDING STABLES

Annette Lake

Riley Lake

PINE BUNGALOWS

Cottonwood Slough

SEE "TOWN OF JASPER" MAP

Upper Mina Lake

FAIRMONT JASPER PARK LODGE

Cabin Lake

JASPER

Lac Beauvert

OLD FORT POINT

Lower Mina Lake

YELLOWHEAD

Caledonia Lake

Miette River

16

To Prince George, BC

JASPER INTERNATIONAL HOSTEL

ALPINE VILLAGE

93A

Jasper National Park

JASPER TRAMWAY

WHISTLERS

Athabasca

The Whistlers

WAPITI

Valley of the Five Lakes

BECKER'S CHALETS

0   1 mi

FEE STATION

ICEFIELDS PARKWAY

River

0   1 km

93A

To Banff National Park

93

MARMOT BASIN

To Wabasso Campground and Mt. Edith Cavell

ALBERTA

© AVALON TRAVEL PUBLISHING, INC.

TOWN OF JASPER

To Pyramid Lake

To Highway 16

To Maligne Canyon and Miette Hot Springs

Pyramid Benchland Trail

SAWRIDGE INN

TONQUIN INN

JUNIPER

CONNAUGHT DR.

16

Athabasca River

JASPER INN

BEAR HILL LODGE

PYRAMID LAKE RD.

BONHOMME ST.

ASPEN AVE.

GEIKIE ST.

PATRICIA ST.

ACTIVITY CENTRE

JASPER-YELLOWHEAD MUSEUM

JASPER AQUATIC CENTRE

CEDAR AVE.

BEAR'S PAW BAKERY

YELLOWHEAD HWY.

To Mina Lakes

TOTEM SKI SHOP

SOURCE FOR SPORTS

JASPER CAMERA & GIFT

ELM AVE.

PARK INFORMATION CENTRE

LIBRARY

POST OFFICE

WHISTLERS INN

VIA RAIL STATION/BUS DEPOT

ATHABASCA HOTEL

HOSPITAL

ON-LINE SPORT & TACKLE

CHABA THEATRE

MOUNTAIN FOODS & CAFÉ

MALIGNE AVE.

ANDY'S BISTRO

PATRICIA CENTRE

FIDDLE RIVER

MIETTE AVE.

MALIGNE TOURS

CONNAUGHT SQUARE

FREEWHEEL CYCLE

JASPER MARKETPLACE

SOFT ROCK CAFE

VILLA CARUSO

ALBERTA

CABIN CREEK RD.

WILLOW AVE.

PINE AVE.

CONNAUGHT DR.

To Old Fort Point

93

16

93A

TEKARRA LODGE

Miette River

To Prince George, BC

To Icefields Parkway and Banff (Banff National Park)

MOON

SCALE NOT AVAILABLE

Museums

Jasper has two museums—one worth visiting, the other maybe so, just for a laugh. At the back of town is the excellent **Jasper-Yellowhead Museum and Archives** (400 Pyramid Lake Rd., 780/852-3013, mid-June–Sept. daily 10 A.M.–9 P.M., rest of year Thurs.–Sun. 10 A.M.–5 P.M., adult $3.50, child $2), filled with exhibits that take visitors along a timeline of Jasper's human history through the fur trade, the coming of the railway, and the creation of the park. The **Wildlife Museum,** in the darkened bowels of the Whistlers Inn (Connaught Dr. and Miette Ave., 780/852-3361, year-round, daily 9 A.M.–10 P.M.), is a throwback to a bygone era, when displays of stuffed animals were considered the best way to extol the wonders of nature. "See animals in their natural setting" cries museum advertising, but the shrubbery looks suspiciously like fake Christmas trees and the bull elk seems to be screaming "Get me out of here!" Yep, they even charge you for it—exchange $3 for a token at the Whistlers' reception desk.

Patricia and Pyramid Lakes

A winding road heads through the hills at the back of town to these two picturesque lakes, formed when glacial moraines dammed shallow valleys. The first, to the left, is Patricia; the second, farther along the road, is Pyramid, backed by **Pyramid Mountain** (2,765 m/9,072 ft.). Both lakes are popular spots for picnicking, fishing, and boating. Boat rentals are available at **Pyramid Lake Boat Rentals** (780/852-4900). Canoes, rowboats, paddleboats, and kayaks are $25 for the first hour and $15 for each additional hour. Motorboats are $35 per hour.

Jasper Tramway

This tramway (780/852-3093, July–Aug. daily 8:30 A.M.–10 P.M., shorter hours Apr.–June and Sept.–Oct., adult $18, child $9) climbs more than 1,000 vertical meters (3,280 ft.) up the steep north face of **The Whistlers.** From the upper terminal, a 1.4-kilometer (0.9-mi.) trail leads to the true summit. The view is breathtaking; to the south is the Columbia Icefield, and on a clear day you can see Mount Robson (3,954 m/12,970 ft.) to the northwest—the highest peak in the

Canadian Rockies. Free two-hour guided hikes leave the upper terminal for the true summit at regular intervals through the day. The tramway is three kilometers (1.9 mi.) south of town on Highway 93 (Icefields Pkwy.) and then a similar distance up Whistlers Road.

Mount Edith Cavell

To reach the base of Jasper's most distinctive peak, take Highway 93A south from town and take the 14.5-kilometer (nine-mi.) spur that ends at a parking lot below the mountain's northeast face. Mount Edith Cavell (3,363 m/11,000 ft.) can be seen from many vantage points in the park—including the town and the golf course—but none is more impressive than directly below it. From the parking area, the **Path of the Glacier Trail** (one hour round-trip) traverses moraines deposited by the receding Angel Glacier and leads to some great viewpoints.

Edith and Annette Lakes

These two lakes along the road to Jasper Park Lodge—across the Athabasca River from town—are perfect for a picnic, a swim, or a pleasant walk. They are remnants of a much larger lake that once covered the entire valley floor. The lakes are relatively shallow; therefore, the sun warms the water to a bearable temperature. In fact, they have the warmest waters of any lakes in the park. The 2.5-kilometer (1.6-mi.) **Lee Foundation Trail** encircles Lake Annette and is wheelchair accessible. Both lakes have day-use areas with beaches and picnic areas.

Maligne Canyon

To get here, head northeast from town and turn right onto Maligne Lake Road. The canyon access road veers left 11 kilometers (6.8 mi.) from Jasper. This unique geological feature has been eroded out of the easily dissolved limestone bedrock by the fast-flowing Maligne River. The canyon is up to 50 meters (160 ft.) deep, yet so narrow that squirrels often jump across. At the top of the canyon, opposite the teahouse, are large potholes in the riverbed. These potholes are created when rocks and pebbles become trapped in what begins as a shallow depression, and under the force of the rushing water the rocks carve jug-shaped hollows into the soft bedrock.

An interpretive trail winds down from the parking lot, crossing the canyon six times. The most spectacular sections of the canyon can be seen from the first two bridges, at the upper end of the trail. To avoid the crowds at the upper end of the canyon, an alternative is to park at Sixth Bridge, near the confluence of the Maligne and Athabasca Rivers, and walk *up* the canyon.

Medicine Lake

From the canyon, Maligne Lake Road climbs to Medicine Lake, which does a disappearing act each year. The water level fluctuates because of an underground drainage system known as *karst*. At the northwest end of the lake, where the outlet should be, the riverbed is often dry. In fall, when runoff from the mountains is minimal, the water level drops, and by November the lake has almost completely dried up. Early Indians believed that spirits were responsible for the phenomenon, hence the name.

Maligne Lake

Continue beyond Medicine Lake to reach Maligne Lake (48 km/30 mi. from Jasper), one of the world's most-photographed lakes. It's also the largest glacier-fed lake in the Canadian Rockies and second-largest in the world. The most popular tourist activity at the lake is a 90-minute narrated cruise on a glass-enclosed boat up the lake to oft-photographed **Spirit Island.** Cruises leave June–August, every hour on the hour 10 A.M.–5 P.M., with fewer sailings in May and September; adult $32, child $15.50. Rowboats and canoes can be rented at the 1929 **Boat House** ($15 per hour or $60 per day). The lake also has excellent trout fishing (see Other Recreation). All commercial operations associated with the lake are operated by **Maligne Tours** (627 Patricia St., Jasper, 780/852-3370, www.malignelake.com). This company also runs the **Maligne Lake Shuttle** from the downtown office and major hotels to the lake eight times daily through summer (four times daily in spring and fall). The first shuttle leaves for the lake each morning at 8:30 A.M.

Miette Hot Springs

Miette Hot Springs Road branches south from the highway 43 kilometers (27 mi.) east of Jasper. One kilometer (0.6 mi.) along Miette Hot Springs Road, a short trail leads to photogenic **Punchbowl Falls.** After curving, swerving, rising, and falling many times, the road ends 18 kilometers (11 mi.) from Highway 16 at Miette Hot Springs (780/866-3939, mid-May–mid-Oct., 10:30 A.M.–9 P.M., extended summer hours 8:30 A.M.–10:30 P.M.), the warmest springs in the Canadian Rockies. Water that flows into the pools is artificially cooled from 54°C (128°F) to a soothing 39°C (100°F). Adjacent to the main pools is a cool "plunge pool." Admission is $6 for a single swim or $8.25 for the day (discounted for seniors to $5 and $7.25 respectively). Many hiking trails begin from the hot springs complex; the shortest is from the picnic area to the source of the springs (allow five minutes each way).

HIKING

The 1,200 kilometers (745 mi.) of hiking trails in Jasper are significantly different from those in the other mountain national parks. The park has an extensive system of interconnecting backcountry trails that, for experienced hikers, can provide a wilderness adventure rivaled by few areas on the face of the earth. I'll leave descriptions of these longer trails to experts Brian Patton and Bart Robinson, authors of *The Canadian Rockies Trail Guide,* and concentrate on the best day hikes.

Before setting off on any hike, whatever the length, go to the **Park Information Centre** in downtown Jasper for trail maps, trail conditions, and trail closures.

Around Town

Numerous official and unofficial hiking trails weave across the benchland immediately west of the town of Jasper, many branching out from beside the museum. To get a taste of this accessible section of the park, plan on taking the **Pyramid Benchland Trail** (seven km/4.3 mi.; 5 hours round-trip), which climbs onto the bench before emerging at a bluff overlooking the Athabasca River Valley. In the vicinity, two kilometers (1.2

mi.) along Pyramid Lake Road, the **Patricia Lake Circle** (five km/3.1 mi.; 90 minutes round-trip) doesn't actually encircle Patricia Lake, but instead just passes along a portion of its southern shoreline, with good chances of spying beaver in the adjacent Cottonwood Slough.

Feeling energetic? Continue to the end of Pyramid Lake Road and lace up for the trail to **The Palisade** (11 km/6.8 mi.; four hours one-way), gaining 850 meters (2,790 ft.) of elevation along the way.

Near Mount Edith Cavell

Cavell Road begins 13 kilometers (eight mi.) south from town along Highway 93A and ends after 14.5 kilometers (nine mi.) at the trailhead for the **Cavell Meadows Trail** (four km/2.5 mi.; 1.5 hours one-way)—one of most scenic in the park. The trail starts out following the paved Path of the Glacier Loop, then branches left, climbing steadily through a subalpine forest of Engelmann spruce and then stunted subalpine fir to emerge facing the northeast face of Mount Edith Cavell and Angel Glacier. The view of the glacier from this point is nothing less than awesome, as the ice spills out of a cirque, clinging to a 300-meter-high (980 ft.) cliff face. The trail continues to higher viewpoints and an alpine meadow that, by mid-July, is filled with wildflowers.

The trail into the **Tonquin Valley** is one of the overnight treks that I'd said earlier was beyond the scope of this book, but this one is just too good to pass by. The easiest of two approaches begins opposite the hostel on Cavell Road and follows the **Astoria River** (19 km/11.8 mi.; 6–7 hours one-way) for much of the way. Amethyst Lakes and the 1,000-meter (3,280-ft.) cliffs of the Ramparts first come into view after 13 kilometers (eight mi.). At the 17-kilometer (10.5-mi.) mark the trail divides. To the left it climbs into Eremite Valley, where there's a campground. The right fork continues following Astoria River to Tonquin Valley, Amethyst Lakes, and a choice of four campgrounds and two lodges (see Accommodations).

Maligne Lake Area

Hikes in the vicinity of Maligne Lake, 48 kilo- meters (30 mi.) from the town of Jasper, provides many opportunities to view the lake and explore its environs. To get there, take Highway 16 east for four kilometers (2.5 mi.) from town and turn south on Maligne Lake Road.

The **Lake Trail (Mary Schäffer Loop)** (3.2 km/two mi.; one hour round-trip) is the easiest local trail, but also offers the most spectacular views. From the boat house, follow the lakeshore through an open area of lakeside tables to a point known as **Schäffer Viewpoint,** named for the first white person to see the valley. Across the lake are the aptly named Bald Hills, the Maligne Range, and to the southwest, the distinctive twin peaks of Mount Unwin and Mount Charlton. After dragging yourself away from the spectacular panorama, continue along a shallow bay before following the trail into a forest of spruce and subalpine fir, then looping back to the middle parking lot.

The loop trail through the **Opal Hills** (8.2 km/5.1 mi.; three hours round-trip) begins from the upper parking lot, climbing a total of 455 meters (1,500 ft.) to the high alpine meadows.

The **Bald Hills Trail** (5.2 km/3.2 mi.; two hours one-way) gains 495 meters (1,620 ft.) along an old fire road that leads to the site of a fire lookout. The 360-degree view takes in the jade-green waters of Maligne Lake, the Queen Elizabeth Ranges, and the twin peaks of Mount Unwin and Mount Charlton. The trail begins from the picnic area at the very end of Maligne Lake Road.

OTHER RECREATION

A number of booking agents represent the many recreation-tour operators in Jasper. The **Jasper Adventure Centre** (Chaba Theatre, 604 Connaught Dr., 780/852-5595, www.jasperadventure centre.com) takes bookings for all the activities below, as well as for accommodations and for transportation to various points in the park and beyond. **Maligne Tours** (627 Patricia St., 780/852-3370, www.malignelake.com) operates all activities in the Maligne Lake area, including the famous lake cruise.

Mountain Biking

In addition to the paved roads, many unpaved

ALBERTA

GLORIOUS GOLF

Even if your game's not on, it's difficult not to enjoy walking the fairways of **Jasper Park Lodge Golf Course** (780/852-6090), consistently ranked as one of the top 10 courses in Canada. Designed by renowned golf-course architect Stanley Thompson, the course opened in 1925 after 200 men had spent an entire year clearing trees and laying out the holes to Thompson's design.

The 18-hole, 6,670-yard course takes in the contours of the Athabasca River Valley as it hugs the banks of turquoise-colored Lac Beauvert. It's a true test of accuracy, and with holes named The Maze, The Bad Baby, and The Bay, you'll need lots of balls. Greens fees for 18 holes vary with the season: $125 mid-June–September, under $100 mid-May–mid-June, and under $80 in early May and from October 1 through to closing (usually mid-Oct.). An electric cart is $32 per round. Golfing after 5 P.M. is $79 with a cart—a great deal during the long days of June and July. Other facilities include a driving range, club rentals ($28–42), a restaurant, and a lounge.

© ANDREW HEMPSTEAD

designated bicycle trails radiate from the town. One of the most popular is the **Athabasca River Trail,** which begins at Old Fort Point and follows the river to a point below Maligne Canyon. Rental outlets include **On-line Sport & Tackle** (600 Patricia St., 780/852-3630), **Source for Sports** (406 Patricia St., 780/852-3654), and **Freewheel Cycle** (618 Patricia St., 780/852-3898). Expect to pay $5–8 per hour or $22–35 for any 24-hour period. Freewheel Cycle leads a five-hour bike tour along Maligne Lake Road, but most of the hard work is done for you, as transportation is provided to the lake, allowing a two-hour downhill run on the bikes; $95 per person.

Horseback Riding

On the benchlands immediately behind the town of Jasper is **Pyramid Riding Stables** (Pyramid Lake Rd., 780/852-7433), where one-, two-, and three-hour guided rides are $28, $48, and $70, respectively. The one-hour trip follows a ridge high above town, providing excellent views of the Athabasca River Valley. **Skyline Trail Rides** (Jasper Park Lodge, 780/852-4215) offers a one-hour guided ride around Lake Annette ($25 per

person) and a 4.5-hour ride to Maligne Canyon ($70 per person).

White-Water Rafting

On the Athabasca River, the Mile 5 Run is an easy two-hour float that appeals to all ages. The boulder-strewn rapids of the Sunwapta River offer more thrills and spills—these trips are for the more adventurous and last around three hours. Most companies run both rivers and provide transportation to and from downtown hotels. Expect to pay $45–55 for trips on the Athabasca and $60 for the Sunwapta. The following companies run at least one of the two rivers: **Maligne Rafting Adventures** (780/852-3370), **Raven Adventures** (780/852-4292), **Rocky Mountain River Guides** (780/852-3777), and **White Water Rafting** (780/852-7238 or 800/557-7238).

ALBERTA

If white-water rafting sounds a little too adventurous for your liking, consider an easy float down the Athabasca River in a historic 10-meter (33-ft.) **voyageur canoe.** These large, stable craft were developed over 200 years ago specifically for travel along Canadian waterways. The voyageur canoes used by **Rocky Mountain Voyageur** (780/852-3343, www.jaspercanoes .com) are an exact replica in size and shape of the original design. Costumed guides—complete with plaid shirts and sashes—point out prominent natural features and relate historic tales as these canoes and up to 12 passengers float gently down the Athabasca River for around one hour from Old Fort Point. No rapids are encountered and unless it's raining, you won't get wet. The cost is adult $45, child $26, which includes round-trip transfers from downtown Jasper.

Fishing

Fishing in the many alpine lakes—for rainbow, brook, Dolly Varden, cutthroat, and lake trout, as well as pike and whitefish—is excellent. Many outfitters offer guided fishing trips. Whether you fish with a guide or by yourself, you'll need a national park fishing license ($7 per week, $20 per year), available from the Park Information Centre.

Stable 5.5-meter (18-ft.) Freighter canoes with a small electric motor are the preferred boat on Maligne Lake for chasing lake trout. They're available at the lakeside **Boat House** (780/852-3370, June–mid-Sept. daily 8:30 A.M.–6:30 P.M.) for $90 per day, with rod and reel rentals extra. Guided fishing trips also originate at the Boat House; half-day $125 per person for two people, full day $170 per person for two. **Currie's Guiding** (780/852-5650) offers trips to Maligne Lake (full day $190 per person) and to lakes requiring a 30–60 minute hike to access (from $150 per person for a half-day). These rates include equipment and instruction. **Source for Sports** (406 Patricia St., 780/852-3654) and **On-line Sport & Tackle** (600 Patricia St., 780/852-3630) sell and rent fishing tackle and also have canoe and boat rentals.

WINTER RECREATION

Winter is certainly a quiet time in the park, but that doesn't mean there's a lack of things to do. Marmot Basin offers world-class alpine skiing; many snow-covered hiking trails are groomed for cross-country skiing; portions of Lac Beauvert and Pyramid Lake are cleared for ice-skating; horse-drawn sleighs travel around town; and Maligne Canyon is transformed into a magical, frozen world. Hotels reduce rates by 40–70 percent through winter and many offer lodging and lift tickets for under $70 per person.

Marmot Basin

The best terrain for adventurous skiers and snowboarders at Marmot Basin (780/852-3816 or 800/363-3078, www.skimarmot.com) is Charlie's Basin and the open bowls and lightly treed glades off the summit of Eagle Ridge. Marmot Basin has seven lifts servicing 600 hectares (1,500 acres) of terrain and a vertical rise of 900 meters (2,940 ft.). Marmot doesn't get the crowds of the three resorts in Banff National Park, so lift lines are uncommon. Lift tickets are $50 for adults, $40 for seniors, $20 for children. Rentals are available at the resort or in town at **Totem Ski Shop** (408 Connaught Dr., 780/852-3078).

Cross-Country Skiing

For many, traveling Jasper's hiking trails on skis is just as exhilarating as on foot. An extensive network of 300 kilometers (185 mi.) of summer hiking trails is designated for skiers, with around 100 kilometers (62 mi.) groomed. The four main areas of trails are along Pyramid Lake Road, around Maligne Lake, in the Athabasca Falls area, and at Whistlers Campground. A booklet available at the Park Information Centre details each trail and its difficulty. Rental packages, repairs, and sales are available from **Source for Sports** (406 Patricia St., 780/852-3654), a rental shop at **Jasper Park Lodge** (780/852-3433), and **Totem Ski Shop** (408 Connaught Dr., 780/852-3078).

Maligne Canyon

By late December, the torrent that is the Maligne River has frozen solid. Where it cascades down

ALBERTA

through Maligne Canyon the river is temporarily stalled for the winter, creating remarkable formations through the deep limestone canyon. **Maligne Tours** (627 Patricia St., 780/852-3370) offers exciting three-hour guided tours into the depths of the canyon throughout winter, daily at 9 A.M., 1 P.M., and 6 P.M.; adult $24, children $12.50.

ENTERTAINMENT AND EVENTS
Bars and Nightclubs
The most popular nightspot in town is the **Atha-b,** in the Athabasca Hotel (510 Patricia St., 780/852-3386, minimal cover charge), where bands play some nights. It gets pretty rowdy with all the seasonal workers, but it's still enjoyable. This hotel also has a large lounge and a bar with a pool table and a popular 5–7 P.M. happy hour. **Pete's** (upstairs at 614 Patricia St., 780/852-6262) has a jam on Tuesday night and bands playing Friday–Sunday. The music varies—it could be blues, rock, or Celtic. Escape these smoky bar scenes at the **Downstream Bar** (620 Connaught Dr., 780/852-9449), a nonsmoking place that opens at 4 P.M. and has live music Friday and Saturday.

Festivals and Events
Canada Day (July 1) celebrations begin with a pancake breakfast and progress to a flag-raising ceremony (in front of the information center) and a parade along Connaught Drive. Live entertainment and a fireworks display end the day. The **Jasper Lions Pro Indoor Rodeo,** on the second weekend of August, dates from 1933 and attracts pro cowboys from across Canada. Apart from the traditional rodeo events, the fun includes a mechanical bull, a children's rodeo, a casino, pancake breakfasts, and the ever-popular stick-pony parade. Most of the action takes place in the arena at the Jasper Activity Centre (Pyramid Lake Rd., 780/852-4622).

ACCOMMODATIONS
In summer, motel and hotel rooms here are expensive. Most of the motels and lodges are within walking distance of town and have indoor pools and restaurants. Luckily, alternatives to staying in $200-plus hotel rooms do exist. The best alternatives are the lodges scattered around the edge of town. Open in summer only, each offers a rustic yet distinct style of accommodation in keeping with the theme of staying in a national park. Additionally, many private residences have rooms for rent in summer, three hostels are close to town, and there's always camping in the good ol' outdoors.

Under $50
On the road to the Jasper Tramway, seven kilometers (4.3 mi.) south from town off the Icefields Parkway, is **Jasper International Hostel** (780/852-3215 or 877/852-0781, www.hihostels .ca), which has 84 beds in men's and women's dorms, a large kitchen, a common room, showers, public Internet access, an outdoor barbecue area, and mountain-bike rentals. Members of Hostelling International pay $20, nonmembers $25. In the summer months this hostel fills up every night. The front desk is open daily noon–midnight. Cab fare between downtown Jasper and the hostel is $18. **Maligne Canyon Hostel** (closed Wed. Oct.–Apr.) is along Ma-

PRIVATE HOME ACCOMMODATIONS

At last count, Jasper had over 100 residential homes offering accommodations. Often they supply nothing more than a room with a bed, but the price is right—$50–100 s or d. Use of a bathroom may be shared with other guests or the family; few have kitchens and only a few supply light breakfast. In most cases, don't expect too much with the lower-priced choices. The positive side, apart from the price, is that your hosts are usually knowledgeable locals and downtown is only a short walk away. For a full listing that includes the facilities at each approved property, check the Jasper Home Accommodation Association website (www.stayinjasper.com). The Park Information Centre has a board listing private-home accommodations with rooms available for the upcoming night.

ligne Lake Road, beside the Maligne River and a short walk from the canyon. **Mt. Edith Cavell Hostel** (mid-June–Oct.) offers a million-dollar view for the price of a dorm bed. It's 13 kilometers (eight mi.) up Cavell Road off Highway 93A, and because of the location there's usually a spare bed. Rates at both these hostels are $13 for members, $18 for nonmembers and check-in is between 5 P.M. and 11 P.M. Make reservations through the main Jasper hostel.

$50–100

Jasper's least expensive hotel rooms can be found right downtown in the historic **Athabasca Hotel** (510 Patricia St., 780/852-3386 or 877/542-8422, www.athabascahotel.com). The cheapest of its 61 rooms share bathrooms and are above a noisy bar, but the price is right ($75–89 s or d). This hotel also has more expensive rooms, each with a private bathroom ($118–154 s or d).

Typifying a bungalow camp of the 1950s, **Pine Bungalows** (780/852-3491, May–mid-Oct.) lies on a secluded section of the Athabasca River opposite the northern entrance to town. Sparse but comfortable motel-style units with kitchenettes are $90 s or d, individual wooden cabins with kitchens and fireplaces begin at $120 (most cabins face the river but Nos. 1 and 3 enjoy the best views). Modern two-bedroom log cabins are $155.

$100–150

Bear Hill Lodge (100 Bonhomme St., 780/852-3209, www.bearhilllodge.com, mid-Apr.–mid-Oct.) is the only "summer only" cabin accommodation right in the town of Jasper. The original cabins are basic, but each has a TV, bathroom, gas fireplace, and coffeemaker ($135 s or d; $155 with a kitchenette). Chalet Rooms are larger and more modern, and each has a wood-burning fireplace, but no kitchen ($155). Colin Rooms are more spacious still; each has a jetted tub, gas fireplace, and limited cooking facilities ($175).

Becker's Chalets (780/852-3779, www.beckers chalets.com, May–early Oct.) is spread along a picturesque bend on the Athabasca River six kilometers (3.7 mi.) south of town. Moderately priced chalets each with kitchenette, gas fireplace, and double bed ($125, or $155 for those on the riverfront), are an excellent deal. Premium log duplexes featuring all the modern conveniences, including color TV, range $170–220. Also available are a limited number of one-bed sleeping rooms ($85). Becker's also boasts one of the park's finest restaurants.

$150–200

Appealing **Tekarra Lodge** (Hwy. 93A, 780/852-3058 or 888/404-4540, www.tekarralodge.com, May–early Oct.) is on a plateau above the confluence of the Miette and Athabasca Rivers, 1.5 kilometers (0.9 mi.) south of downtown Jasper. En suite rooms in the main lodge are $154 s or d, but it's in the historic self-contained cabins that Tekarra really shines. Each has been totally modernized yet retains a cozy charm, with comfortable beds, fully equipped kitchenettes, wood-burning fireplaces, and smallish but adequate bathrooms. Also on site are a restaurant open for breakfast and dinner, bike rentals, and a laundry.

the view from Becker's Chalets

Continuing a short distance south along Highway 93A from Tekarra Lodge, at the junction of the Icefields Parkway three kilometers (1.9 mi.) south of town, is **Alpine Village** (780/852-3285, www.alpinevillagejasper.com, late Apr.–mid-Oct.). Across from the Athabasca River, this resort is laid out across well-manicured lawns, and all buildings surrounded by colorful gardens of geraniums and petunias. The older "sleeping cabins" have been renovated ($150 s or d, $170 with a kitchen and fireplace), while the newer deluxe one-bedroom log cabins feature stone fireplaces and modern furnishings ($190).

This is the price range that most downtown Jasper hotel rooms fall within. One of the best values among these is the **Tonquin Inn** (Juniper St., 780/852-4987 or 800/661-1315, www .tonquininn.com), where guests enjoy luxurious rooms, a beautiful indoor pool, an outdoor hot tub, and a steakhouse. Even standard rooms have king-size beds ($179 s or d; $10 extra for air-conditioning) and some have kitchens ($205).

$200–250
Jasper Inn (98 Geikie St., 780/852-4461 or 800/661-1933, www.jasperinn.com) is a modern chateau-style lodging of brick and red cedar. Many rooms have private balconies and over 100 are self-contained suites with kitchenettes and fireplaces. Other features include a large indoor pool, and a sundeck overlooking a Japanese rock garden. Rates start at $213 s or d, with kitchen units starting at $218. The Upper Loft suites, complete with a kitchen and fireplace are a much better deal at $225 s or d (from $99 outside of summer).

Over $250
Historic **Jasper Park Lodge** (780/852-3301 or 800/257-7544, www.fairmont.com) lies along the shore of Lac Beauvert across the Athabasca River from downtown. It has four restaurants, three lounges, horseback riding, tennis courts, a championship golf course, and Jasper's only covered shopping arcade. The 446 rooms vary in configuration and are spread out over the expansive property. The least expensive units ($549 s or d) are smallish, hold two twin beds, and offer no

views. Fairmont Deluxe Rooms ($559 s or d) have water views, while Jasper Premier Rooms ($629 s or d) have a distinct country charm, each with either a sitting room or patio and lake views. The vast majority of guests don't pay the summer rack rates quoted above. Most often the cost of lodging is included in one of the plethora of packages offered, such as the Grand Canadian Lodge Experience, which includes golf, meals, taxes, and gratuities and brings the cost of a standard room down to well under $400 per night.

CAMPGROUNDS
Jasper's 10 campgrounds (780/852-6176) have always filled on a first-come, first-served basis, but in 2005 a percentage of sites will be reservable for a fee of $11 per booking. See the Parks Canada website (www.pc.gc.ca) for information. When the main campgrounds fill, campers are directed to overflow areas ($8 per vehicle). Campgrounds in Jasper begin opening in mid-June and all but Wapiti are closed by mid-October. All campsites have a picnic table and fire ring, with a fire permit costing $6 (includes firewood).

Near the Town of Jasper
Whistlers Campground (May–mid-Oct.), at the base of Whistlers Road, three kilometers (1.9 mi.) south of town, has 781 sites, making it the largest campground in Alberta. Prices vary with the services available—walk-in sites $19, unserviced sites $22, powered sites $26, full hookups $30. Each section has showers. A further two kilometers (1.2 mi.) south along the Icefields Parkway is **Wapiti Campground,** which offers 366 sites and has showers; unserviced sites $22, powered sites $26. This is the park's only campground open year-round, with powered winter sites at $17 per night. Whistlers and Wapiti are the only two campgrounds with powered sites, and therefore they're in great demand. A line usually forms well before the official check-out time of 11 A.M.

Sites at **Wabasso Campground** ($17 per night) along Highway 93A 16 kilometers (10 mi.) south of town, are set among stands of spruce and aspen.

East Along Highway 16

East of town, along Highway 16, are two smaller, more primitive campgrounds. **Snaring River Campground** (Celestine Lake Rd., $13), 17 kilometers (11 mi.) from Jasper, and **Pocahontas Campground** ($17) 45 kilometers (28 mi.) northeast. Both are open mid-May–early September.

FOOD

It's easy to find a good, or even great, meal in Jasper. Connaught Drive and Patricia Street are lined with cafés and restaurants. Considering this is a national park, menus are reasonably well priced. You should expect hearty fare, with lots of beef, game, and a surprising selection of seafood.

Coffeehouses and Cafés

The **Soft Rock Café** (632 Connaught Dr., 780/852-5850, 8 A.M.–10 P.M.) occupies a sunny spot along Jasper's main thoroughfare. It's one of the most popular places in town to start the day. Seating is inside or out and you should order at the counter. Breakfast options include omelets and skillet dishes (all under $10). If the cinnamon buns are still in the oven, you'll have to come back later in the day—they're gigantic! Back toward the heart of downtown, **Mountain Foods & Café** (606 Connaught Dr., 780/852-4050) offers a full cooked breakfast for $6 and healthy wraps, rolls, and sandwiches the rest of the day. At the northern end of the downtown core, the **Bear's Paw Bakery** (4 Cedar Ave., 780/852-3233, daily from 7 A.M.) offers a great range of European-style breads as well as cakes and pastries.

Canadian

One of Jasper's best restaurants, **Becker's Gourmet Restaurant** (780/852-3535, daily 5:30 A.M.–9 P.M.), is six kilometers (3.7 mi.) south of town along the Icefields Parkway. From this cozy dining room where the atmosphere is intimate or the adjacent enclosed conservatory, the views of Mount Kerkeslin and the Athabasca River are inspiring. This restaurant is a throwback to days gone by, with an ever-changing menu of seasonal game and produce that includes a daily

wild game special. Hot and cold appetizers range $9–13 while no entrée is over $30. Becker's is also open for breakfast 8–11 A.M.; the buffet costs $11.50.

Walter's Dining Room (Sawridge Inn, 780/852-5111, daily from 5 P.M.) is surrounded by the greenery of a four-story atrium. The cooking is contemporary, but distinctly Canadian. You could start with the venison pâté, followed by maple-glazed salmon, spending a little over $30 for the two courses. The adjacent lounge has the same pleasant setting and a smaller, less-expensive menu.

With a lofty upstairs setting, **Villa Caruso** (640 Connaught Dr., 780/852-3920, 11 A.M.–midnight) offers a lucky few diners outdoor table settings with great valley views. The restaurant itself has a modern, Western-style decor, with lots of polished log work and elegant table settings. Look for a wide variety of Alberta beef dishes including a massive 16-ounce T-bone for $31.

Seafood

Fiddle River Seafood Restaurant (upstairs at 620 Connaught Dr., 780/852-3032) is a long way from the ocean and not particularly coastal in feel, but offers a wide variety of seafood. The striking decor matches dark polished wood with forest-green furnishings, and large windows provide mountain views (reservations are needed for windowside tables). Trout, arctic char, red snapper, ahi tuna, and halibut all make regular appearances on the blackboard menu. Expect to pay around $40 per person for a three-course meal.

European

Andy's Bistro (606 Patricia St., 780/852-4559, daily from 5 P.M.) is an elegantly casual eatery offering a wide range of uncomplicated dishes using Canadian game and produce prepared with Swiss-influenced cooking styles. Start with a plate piled high with Prince Edward Island steamed mussels ($12, but enough for two people), then chose from among dishes such as vegetarian gnocchi ($18) or lake trout served with chanterelle mushrooms and a peppercorn sauce ($22). Andy's has an extensive cellar of wines, but no official wine list. Instead, diners are encouraged to choose from red wines set along the bar and white wines from the fridge. In a town of seasonal workers, the experienced and knowledgeable staff at Andy's are notable.

Miss Italia Ristorante (upstairs at 610 Patricia St., 780/852-4002, 8 A.M.–10 P.M.) features a bright and breezy interior decor with tables also set on a narrow terrace bedecked with pots of colorful flowers. Pastas made fresh daily average $15, a baked filet of Atlantic salmon is $16, and souvlaki with a side of salad and pita bread is just $16.

Jasper Park Lodge

Jasper's premier accommodation, across the river from downtown, offers a choice of casual or elegant dining in a variety of restaurants and lounges. Across from the reception area is a dedicated dining reservation desk (780/852-6052, 11 A.M.–8 P.M.).

The **Emerald Lounge** takes pride of place in the expansive lobby of the main building. Tables are inside and out, along a terrace with uninterrupted lake and mountain views. Both lunch and dinner menus feature imaginative modern Canadian cuisine, but dinner (from 5:30 P.M.) is decidedly more expensive.

The **Beauvert Dining Room** is a casual 500-seat eatery. The breakfast buffet (6–9 A.M.) is $19, while in the evening (6–8 P.M.), diners pay $57 per person for an à la carte entrée—which includes a mouthwatering hickory-smoked Alberta prime rib dish—along with unlimited visits to appetizer "stations" and a dessert buffet.

The **Edith Cavell Room** is seriously cultured dining, unequaled in Jasper. With an emphasis on local produce and Canadian game and seafood, the classic cuisine is served with a French flair. Prices for two-, three-, and four-course table d'hôte combos are a relatively reasonable $50, $65, and $75, respectively. Dinner is served 6–10 P.M. Dress code is resort casual: no T-shirts or jeans and a jacket and tie "recommended but not required."

INFORMATION AND SERVICES

Park Information Centre

A beautiful old stone building dating from 1913, the residence of Jasper's first superintendent is now used by Parks Canada as the Park Information Centre. It's right downtown on Connaught Drive (780/852-6176, summer daily 8 A.M.–7 P.M., rest of year daily 9 A.M.–5 P.M.). In the same building is the **Parks Canada Trail Office** (780/852-6177), which handles questions for those going into the backcountry. **Jasper Tourism and Commerce** (780/852-3858) also has a desk in this building, and the friendly staff never seems to tire of explaining that all the rooms in town are full. Beside the main Parks Canada desk is the **Friends of Jasper National Park** outlet selling topographic maps, books, and local publications. Look for notices posted out front with the day's interpretive programs.

Other Sources of Information

Jasper's weekly newspaper, *The Booster,* is available throughout town on Wednesday. As well as newsworthy stories, it includes a list of upcoming events, trail reports, and a town map with funky little symbols highlighting the location of various "crimes."

For more information on the park, check the Parks Canada website (www.pc.gc.ca). For general tourist information, contact **Jasper Tourism and Commerce** (780/852-3858, www.jaspercanadian rockies.com). The official Town of Jasper website (www.jasper-alberta.com), with lists of current events, current weather conditions, and loads of helpful links, is also worth checking out.

Books and Bookstores

Housed in Jasper's original Royal Canadian Mounted Police detachment building, small **Jasper Municipal Library** (Elm Ave., 780/852-3652, Mon.–Thurs. 11 A.M.–9 P.M., Fri.–Sat. 11 A.M.–5 P.M.) holds just about everything ever written about the park.

Head to the **Friends of Jasper** store in the Park Information Centre or the **museum** for a good selection of books on the park's natural and human history. A larger selection of literature, including lots of western Canadiana, can be found at **Jasper Camera and Gift** (412 Connaught Dr., 780/852-3165, daily 9 A.M.–10 P.M.). **Counter Clockwise** (Jasper Marketplace, 627 Patricia St., 780/852-3152) has a similar selection. **Maligne**

Lake Books (Jasper Park Lodge, 780/852-4779) has a good selection of coffee-table books.

Services

The post office (502 Patricia St.) is behind the Park Information Centre. Mail to be picked up here should be addressed to General Delivery, Jasper, AB T0E 1E0.

More than Mail (620 Connaught Dr., 780/852-3151) offers a wide range of communication services including regular post, public Internet access, fax and copying facilities, a work area for laptops, international calling, and currency exchange.

The two **Laundromats** on Patricia Street are open 6 A.M.–11 P.M. and offer showers that cost $2 for 10 minutes (quarters).

In an emergency contact the **hospital** (518 Robson St., 780/852-3344) or the **RCMP** (780/852-4848).

TRANSPORTATION

Getting There

Getting to Jasper by public transportation is easy, although the closest airport handling domestic and international flights is at Edmonton, 360 kilometers (224 mi.) to the east. The **VIA rail station** and the **bus depot** (used by both Greyhound and Brewster) are in the same building, central to town at 607 Connaught Drive. The building is open 24 hours daily in summer, shorter hours the rest of the year. Jasper is on the VIA's "Canadian" route. Another rail option is offered by **Rocky Mountaineer Railtours** (800/665-7245). This company operates a luxurious summer-only rail service between Vancouver and Jasper with an overnight in Kamloops (British Columbia).

Greyhound buses (780/852-332) depart Jasper for all points in Canada (except Banff), including Vancouver (three times daily, 12–13 hours) and Edmonton (five times daily, 4.5 hours). The only buses between Jasper and Banff are operated by **Brewster** (780/852-3332), with buses continuing on from Banff to Calgary International Airport. Buses depart the airport May–October daily at 12:30 P.M. ($80 one-way to Jasper), pick up passengers in Banff at 2:30 P.M. ($57 one-way), and Lake Louise at 4:15 P.M. ($49 one-way), and arrive in Jasper at 8 P.M. The return service departs daily from Jasper Park Lodge at 12:50 P.M. and from the downtown bus depot at 1:30 P.M., arriving at Calgary airport at 9:30 P.M. Brewster also runs a nine-hour (one-way) tour between Banff and Jasper departing daily mid-April–mid-October from the Banff and Jasper depots at 8 A.M. The tour costs $95 one-way, $133 round-trip. The round-trip requires an overnight in Jasper.

Getting Around

The **Maligne Lake Shuttle** (780/852-3370) runs out to Maligne Lake May–September, 4–6 times daily ($28 round-trip) from its depot at 627 Patricia Street. Stops are made at Maligne Canyon and Maligne Canyon Hostel.

Rental cars start at $65 per day with 100 free kilometers (62 mi.). The following companies have agencies in town: **Avis** (780/852-3970), **Budget** (780/852-3222), **Hertz** (780/852-3888), and **National** (780/852-1117).

Cabs in town are not cheap. Most drivers will take you on a private sightseeing tour or to trailheads if requested; try **Jasper Taxi** (780/852-3600).

Tours

Brewster (780/852-3332) offers a four-hour Discover Jasper Tour taking in Patricia and Pyramid Lakes, Maligne Canyon, Maligne Lake, and Jasper Tramway (ride not included in fare). It departs April–October daily at 8:30 A.M. from the railway station; adult $41, child $20.50. **Maligne Tours** (627 Patricia St., 780/852-3370, www.malignelake.com) schedules a variety of tours, including one to Maligne Lake ($62, includes cruise). **Jasper Adventure Centre** (604 Connaught Dr., 780/852-5595, www.jasperadventurecentre.com) operates a number of well-priced tours, including the following: Mount Edith Cavell (departs 2 P.M.; three hours; $45), Maligne Valley (departs 9:30 A.M.; five hours; $70), and Miette Hot Springs (departs 6 P.M.; four hours; $49). They also offer similarly priced tours taking in historical sites and local wildlife.

ALBERTA

Southern Alberta

Southern Alberta is bordered to the east by Saskatchewan, to the south by Montana (U.S.), and to the west by British Columbia, and, for the purpose of this book, bordered to the north by the TransCanada Highway. In other words, this chapter covers the region south of Calgary.

From Calgary, a good option is to loop through southern Alberta by first heading west along the TransCanada Highway to the booming mountain town of Canmore, then south through Kananaskis Country. A more direct route is Highway 2 south through Fort Macleod to Alberta's third-largest city, Lethbridge. From this point, to the east is an area of prairie deemed "unsuitable for agriculture" by early explorer John Palliser, while to the west is Waterton Lakes National Park, comparable to Banff and Jasper scenery-wise, but without the crowds.

Southern Alberta reveals plentiful evidence of its history and prehistory. Thousands of years of

wind and water erosion have uncovered the world's best-preserved dinosaur eggs near Milk River and have carved mysterious-looking sandstone hoodoos farther downstream at Writing-On-Stone Provincial Park—named for the abundant rock carvings and paintings created there by ancient artists. Head-Smashed-In Buffalo Jump, west of Fort Macleod, was used by native peoples for at least 5,700 years to drive massive herds of buffalo to their deaths.

COCHRANE

The foundation of Alberta's cattle industry was laid down here in the 20th century, when Senator Matthew Cochrane established the first of the big leasehold ranches in the province. Today's town of Cochrane, 38 kilometers (24 mi.) northwest of downtown Calgary along Highway 1A, has seen its population increase by over 10 percent annually since the mid 1990s, now sitting at over 12,000. Although ranching is still important to the local economy, Cochrane is growing as a "bedroom" suburb of Calgary. The business district, in the older section of town between Highway 1A and the rail line, is a delightful pocket of false-fronted buildings holding cafés, restaurants, and specialty shops.

Cochrane Ranche

To prevent the lawlessness that existed across the U.S. west from extending into Canada, the government began granting huge grazing leases across the prairies. One of the original takers was Matthew Cochrane, who established the first real ranch west of Calgary, bringing herds of cattle from Montana to his 76,500-hectare (189,000-acre) holding in 1881. After two harsh winters, he moved his herds south again. A small piece of Cochrane's holding is now preserved as Cochrane Ranche Provincial Historic Site. Almost completely surrounded by development, the 61-hectare (150-acre) site straddles Big Hill Creek one kilometer (0.6 mi.) west of downtown along Highway 1A. A short trail leads up to a bluff and the *Men of Vision* statue of a rider and his horse looking over the foothills. An old log cabin by the parking lot is used as an interpretive center

(403/932-1193, mid-May–Sept. 9 A.M.–5 P.M.), and picnic tables dot the grounds.

Cowboy for a Day

Immerse yourself in the Western lifestyle at **Griffin Valley Ranch** (403/932-7433), one of the few places in Alberta that allows unguided horseback riding. Trails lead through this historic 1,800-hectare (4,500-acre) ranch along creeks, through wooded areas and open meadows, and to high viewpoints where the panorama extends west to the Canadian Rockies. Horse rentals are similarly priced to trail riding (one hour $30, two hours $50, three hours $70); the catch is that at least one member of your party must be a "member" of the ranch (simply sign a waiver and pay the $50 annual fee). To get to the ranch, follow Highway 1A west from Cochrane for 18 kilometers (11 mi.), take Highway 40 north, and then follow the signs.

Accommodations and Camping

The best local lodging is **Big Springs Estate Bed & Breakfast** (403/948-5264 or 888/948-5851, www.bigsprings-bb.com, $109–199 s or d), 16 kilometers (10 mi.) northeast along Highway 22, then east along Highway 567 beyond the entrance to Bill Hill Springs Provincial Park. Set on 14 hectares (35 acres), this luxurious accommodation comprises five comfortable guest rooms, a cheerful breakfast room, a large sitting area, and extensive gardens. All rates include a gourmet breakfast, evening snacks, and other niceties such as slippers and robes. Back in town, you'll find Western style on a budget at the **Rocky View Hotel** (1st St. and 2nd Ave. W, 403/932-2442, $40–65 s or d). Rooms are very basic, with shared bathroom facilities and no phones.

Two kilometers (1.2 mi.) south of downtown off Griffin Road is **River's Edge Campground** (500 River Ave., 403/932-4675, mid-Apr.–mid-Oct.), which has showers and charges $12 for unserviced sites, $20 for powered sites.

Food

Cochrane Coffee Traders (114 2nd Ave., 403/932-4395) is as good as any place to start the day. Choose from a wide range of specialty

ALBERTA

Canmore

Banff

National

Park

Peter Lougheed Provincial Park

Height of the Rockies P.P.

Elk Lakes P.P.

Whiteswan Lake Provincial Park

BRITISH COLUMBIA

ROCKY MOUNTAINS

Cochrane

Airdrie

Irricana

CALGARY

Strathmore

Kananaskis

Country

Okotoks

Turner Valley

Longview

Wyndham-Carseland Provincial Park

Mt. Livingstone

Livingstone Falls

FORESTRY

TRUNK RD.

Chain Lakes Provincial Park

Nanton

Vulcan

McGregor Lake

Little Bow River

Travers Reservoir

Little Bow Provincial Park

Carmangay

Claresholm

Barons

Keno Lake

Oldman

Park Lake Provincial Park

Crowsnest Mountain

River

HEAD-SMASHED-IN BUFFALO JUMP

Fort Macleod

Lethbridge

Crowsnest Pass (1,396 m)

Coleman

Lundbreck

OLDMAN DAM

Cowley

Turtle Mountain

Beaver Mines

Pincher Creek

Beauvais Lake Provincial Park

Waterton River

Belly R.

St. Mary Reservoir

St. Mary R.

Raym

Magra

Castle R.

Continental Divide

Cardston

Woolford Provincial Pa

0   20 mi
0   20 km

Waterton Lakes National Park

Akamina-Kishinena P.P.

Waterton

Mountain View

Police Outpost Provincial Park

Aetna

Carway

Piegan

De Bon

MONTANA

Glacier National Park

Chief Mountain (2,756 m)

N. Milk R.

Milk

22 1A 2 9 21 66 40 22 7 547 24 22 2 23 533 23 519 520 520 520 517 3 810 507 2 5 6 507 505 800 774 5 820 5 506 501 17 93 93 93 22X

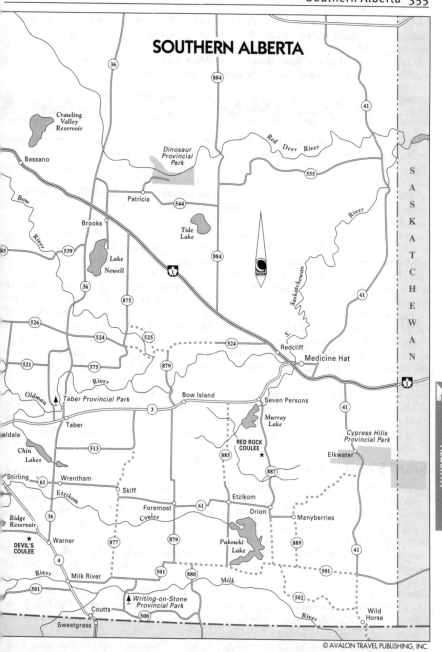

SOUTHERN ALBERTA

coffees and sweet treats, as well as a healthy selection of sandwiches. Back on 1st Street is the two-story wooden-fronted Rocky View Hotel, which houses the **Canyon Rose Restaurant** (403/932-2442), a popular all-day dining spot,

and the **Stageline Saloon.** Of the many eateries lining Cochrane's downtown 1st Street, none is more popular on a hot summer's afternoon than **Mackay's** (403/932-2455), an ice cream parlor dating from 1948.

Canmore

Canmore (pop.11,000) is nestled below the distinctive peaks of the Three Sisters in the Bow Valley between Calgary (103 km/64 mi. to the east) and Banff (28 km/17 mi. to the west), and on the northern edge of Kananaskis Country. Long perceived as a gateway to the mountain national parks, the town is very much a destination in itself these days. Its ideal mountain location and the freedom it enjoys from the strict development restrictions that apply in the nearby parks have made Canmore the one of Canada's fastest-growing communities, its population having tripled in the last 20 years.

The surrounding wilderness, much of it protected by 32,600-hectare (80,550-acre) **Bow Valley Wildland Provincial Park,** provides Canmore's best recreation opportunities. If you think the scenery around Canmore looks familiar, it may be because you've seen it on the big screen—the area has featured in *Shanghai Noon, Mystery Alaska, The Edge, Wild America, The Last of the Dogmen, Legends of the Fall, Snow Dogs,* and the 2003 Kevin Costner film *Open Range.*

SIGHTS AND RECREATION

Canmore is spread across both sides of the Trans-Canada Highway, with downtown Canmore occupying an island in the middle of the Bow River. Although development sprawls in all directions, large tracts of forest remain intact, including along the river, where you'll finding paths leading beyond built-up areas and into natural areas.

Downtown

The oldest part of the town, on the southwestern side of the TransCanada Highway, retains its original charm. To get there from the TransCanada Highway, take Railway Avenue from High-

way 1A and drive down Eighth Street, the main drag (parking is easiest one street back along 7th St., where one parking lot—at 6th Ave.—is designated for RVs). At the east end of Eighth Street is Canmore's original **North West Mounted Police post** (403/678-1955, summer, daily 9 A.M.–6 P.M., rest of year Mon.–Fri. noon–4 P.M., free), built in 1892. It's one of the few such posts still in its original position. The interior is decorated with period furnishings, while out back is a thriving garden filled with the same food crops planted by the post's original inhabitants. Around the corner from the 1891 **Canmore Hotel** are the **Town Hall** and the **Canmore Museum and Geoscience Centre** (403/678-2462, summer daily 9 A.M.–6 P.M., rest of year Wed.–Sun. 10 A.M.–5 P.M., donation), highlighting the valley's rich geological history and its importance to the growth of the town and related industries. Geological formations along three local hikes are described, which—along with a small fossil display, microscopes, and computer resources—makes this facility an interesting rainy day diversion.

Hiking

Paved paths around town are suitable for walking and biking. They link Policeman's Creek with the golf course, Nordic center, and Riverview Park on the Bow River. To explore the surrounding wilderness, consider one of the following longer walks.

The historic **Grassi Lakes Trail** (two km/1.2 mi.; 40 minutes one-way) begins from just off Spray Lakes Road, one kilometer (0.6 mi.) beyond the Nordic center. Around 150 meters (0.1 mi.) from the parking lot, take the left fork. From this point, the trail climbs steadily to stairs cut into a cliff face before leading up to a bridge over Canmore Creek and to the two small lakes. With

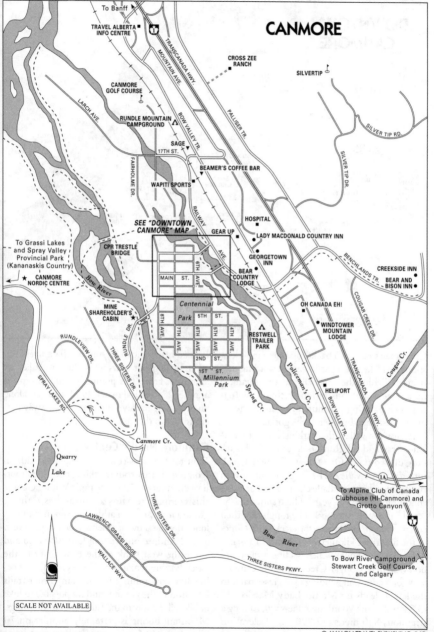

CANMORE

To Banff

TRAVEL ALBERTA
INFO CENTRE

CROSS ZEE
RANCH

SILVERTIP

CANMORE
GOLF COURSE

TRANSCANADA HWY.

MOUNTAIN AVE.

BOW VALLEY TR.

PALLISER TR.

SILVER TIP RD.

LARCH AVE.

RUNDLE MOUNTAIN
CAMPGROUND

SAGE
17TH ST.

BEAMER'S COFFEE BAR

FAIRHOLME DR.

WAPITI SPORTS

SILVER TIP DR.

RAILWAY

HOSPITAL

SEE "DOWNTOWN
CANMORE" MAP

GEAR UP

LADY MACDONALD COUNTRY INN

To Grassi Lakes
and Spray Valley
Provincial Park
(Kananaskis Country)

CPR TRESTLE
BRIDGE

GEORGETOWN
INN

BENCHLANDS TR.

CREEKSIDE INN

CANMORE
NORDIC CENTRE

6TH AVE.

BEAR
COUNTRY
LODGE

BEAR AND
BISON INN

MAIN ST.

AVE.

COUGAR CREEK DR.

Bow River

MINE
SHAREHOLDER'S
CABIN

Centennial

OH CANADA EH!

Park

RUNDLEVIEW DR.

8TH AVE.

5TH ST.

WINDTOWER
MOUNTAIN
LODGE

7TH
AVE.

6TH
AVE.

5TH
AVE.

4TH
AVE.

RESTWELL
TRAILER
PARK

Policeman's Cr.

TRANSCANADA HWY.

Cougar Cr.

THREE SISTERS DR.

BUNDLE DR.

2ND ST.

1ST ST.

Millennium
Park

Spring Cr.

BOW VALLEY TR.

HELIPORT

SPRAY LAKES RD.

Canmore Cr.

Quarry
Lake

1A

LAWRENCE GRASSI RIDGE

THREE SISTERS DR.

To Alpine Club of Canada
Clubhouse (HI-Canmore) and
Grotto Canyon

WALLACE WAY

Bow River

To Bow River Campground,
Stewart Creek Golf Course,
and Calgary

THREE SISTERS PKWY.

MOON

ALBERTA

SCALE NOT AVAILABLE

© AVALON TRAVEL PUBLISHING, INC.

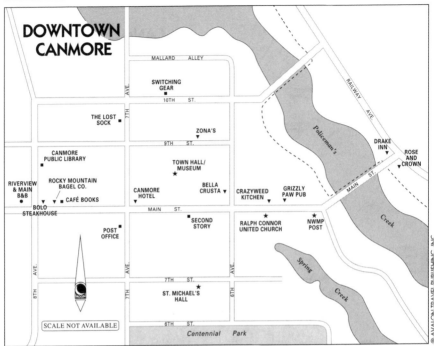

DOWNTOWN CANMORE

MALLARD ALLEY

SWITCHING GEAR

10TH ST.

THE LOST SOCK

ZONA'S

9TH ST.

CANMORE PUBLIC LIBRARY

TOWN HALL/ MUSEUM

ROCKY MOUNTAIN BAGEL CO.

CANMORE HOTEL

BELLA CRUSTA

CRAZYWEED KITCHEN

GRIZZLY PAW PUB

RIVERVIEW & MAIN B&B

CAFÉ BOOKS

BOLO STEAKHOUSE

MAIN ST.

SECOND STORY

RALPH CONNOR UNITED CHURCH

NWMP POST

POST OFFICE

7TH ST.

ST. MICHAEL'S HALL

6TH ST.

Centennial Park

MALLARD AVE.

7TH AVE.

8TH AVE.

7TH AVE.

6TH AVE.

RAILWAY AVE.

DRAKE INN

ROSE AND CROWN

MAIN ST.

Policeman's Creek

Spring Creek

SCALE NOT AVAILABLE

© AVALON TRAVEL PUBLISHING, INC.

Chinaman's Peak as a backdrop, these gin-clear, spring-fed lakes are a particularly rewarding destination. Behind the upper lake, an easy scramble up a scree slope leads to four pictographs (native rock paintings) of human figures. They're on the first large boulder in the gorge.

Across the valley, the parking lot at Benchlands Trail and Elk Run Boulevard is the beginning of two trails. One follows **Cougar Creek** into a narrow valley. The first section of trail runs alongside a manmade channel that acts as a conduit for run-off in years of high snowfall (the "creek" is dry all summer). The rough trail then enters a canyon and crosses the creekbed 10 times in the first three kilometers (1.9 mi.) to a major fork (allow one hour), which is a fine turnaround point. Where Cougar Creek exits the canyon, look for a faint trail winding up a grassy bank to the left. It leads up **Mount Lady Macdonald** (3.5 km/2.1 mi.; 90 minutes one-way), gaining a strenuous 850 meters (2,790 ft.) of elevation along the way. The distance given is to a disused

helipad below the main summit. It's a steep, unrelenting slog, but views across the Bow Valley are stunning. From this point, the true summit is another 275 vertical meters (900 ft.) away, along an extremely narrow ridge that drops away precipitously to the east.

Canmore Nordic Centre

Built for the cross-country skiing and biathlon (combined cross-country skiing and rifle shooting) events at the 1988 Olympic Winter Games, this complex remains a world-class training ground for Canadian athletes. Even in summer, long after the snow has melted, the place is worth a visit. An interpretive trail leads down to and along the west bank of the Bow River to the barely visible remains of Georgetown, a once-bustling coal-mining town. Many other trails lead around the grounds and it's possible to hike or bike all the way to the Fairmont Banff Springs. Mountain biking is extremely popular on 70 kilometers (43.5 mi.) of trails. Bike rentals are available at **Trail Sports** (below the day lodge, 403/678-6764) for $8 per hour and $30 per day for a front-suspension bike. The day lodge has a lounge area, a café, and an information desk (403/678-2400, daily 8 A.M.–4:30 P.M.).

Golf

Canmore has three golf courses. As with golfing elsewhere in the Canadian Rockies, book all tee times well in advance. **SilverTip** (403/678-1600 or 877/877-5444, www.silvertipresort.com, greens fee $145) is set on a series of wide benches between the valley floor and the lower slopes of Mount Lady Macdonald. It boasts a Slope Rating of 153, making it the hardest-ranked course in mainland North America. Needless to say, the layout is very challenging, its most distinct feature being elevation changes of up to 40 meters (130 ft.) on any one hole, and a total 200-meter (656-ft.) elevation difference between the lowest and highest points on the course. **Stewart Creek Golf Club** (403/609-6099 or 877/993-4653, www.stewartcreekgolf.com) lies across the valley in the Three Sisters Mountain Village development. It's shorter than SilverTip, but still measures over 7,000 yards from the back tees. The fairways are relatively wide, but positioning of tee shots is important, and the course is made more interesting by hanging greens, greenside exposed rock, and historic mine shafts. Greens fees are $135, with twilight rates of $85. At both courses, rates include use of a power cart and practice facility. **Canmore Golf Course** (403/678-4784, $50) is a staid old semiprivate layout at the north end of 8th Avenue. It's an interesting layout, with scenic mountain panoramas and water on many holes.

Horseback Riding

Nestled on a wide bench on the northeastern side of town, **Cross Zee Ranch** (403/678-4171) has been guiding visitors through the valley since the 1950s. From expansive stables, riders are presented with a variety of options that pass through thickly wooded areas, colorful meadows, and to high lookouts. Options include Ranger Ridge and Bone Gully (one hour; $25 per person), Sunny Bench (90 minutes; $36), and the Great Aspens ride (two hours; $44).

ENTERTAINMENT AND EVENTS

Nightlife

Canmore doesn't have anywhere near the number of bars that nearby Banff is so famous for, but no one ever seems to go thirsty. The **Sherwood House** (838 Eighth St., 403/678-5211) has a beer garden that catches the afternoon sun and is especially busy on weekends. At the other end of the main street is the **Drake Inn** (909 Railway Ave., 403/678-5131), with a small patio and a nonsmoking section with comfortable lounges. Along the main street, **Grizzly Paw Brewing Company** (622 Eighth St., 403/678-9983) brews its own beer, with six ales produced in-house (look for special winter brews around Christmas).

Oh Canada, Eh!

Popularized across the country at Niagara Falls, this musical dinner show (125 Kananaskis Way off Bow Valley Trail, 403/609-0004 or 800/773-0004, performances nightly through summer at 6:30 P.M., rest of year Fri. and Sat. only) provides a rip-roaring evening of fun and food in a modern building decorated as a cavernous log cabin. It's unashamedly cheesy, but the parade of costumed Canadian characters—such as lumberjacks, natives, Mounties, and even Anne of Green Gables—will keep you laughing as they sing and dance across the floor. The food is surprisingly good, with Canadian favorites such as Alberta beef, salmon, and maple chocolate cake served buffet-style.

Festivals and Events

Canmore's small-town pride lives on through a busy schedule of festivals and events, which are nearly always accompanied by parades of flag-waving kids, free downtown pancake breakfasts, and an evening shindig somewhere in town. **Canada Day** (July 1) is celebrated with a pancake breakfast, parade, various activities in Centennial Park, and fireworks. Canmore Nordic Centre hosts a variety of mountain-biking events each summer, highlighted by a stop on the **24 Hours of Adrenalin** tour, in which racers complete as many laps as they can in a 24-hour period.

On the first weekend of August, Canmore hosts a **Folk Music Festival** (403/678-2524). This event, which attracts over 10,000 fans, features national and international acts performing in Centennial Park, musical workshops, and a free pancake breakfast beside the post office. The first Sunday of September is the **Canmore Highland Games** (403/678-9454), a day of dancing, eating, and caber tossing, culminating in a spectacular and noisy parade of pipe bands through the grounds of Centennial Park that attracts upwards of 10,000 spectators. In the evening (buy tickets at the gate), a *ceilidh* celebration involving lots of loud beer-drinking and foot-stomping Celtic music takes place under a big top.

ACCOMMODATIONS AND CAMPING

Under $50

On a bench along the lower slopes of Grotto Mountain, **HI–Canmore** (Bow Valley Trail, 403/678-3200, www.alpineclubofcanada.ca) is within the building that houses the Alpine Club of Canada headquarters. It has a kitchen, an excellent library, a laundry, bar, sauna, and a lounge area with a fireplace. Rates in a dorm are $19 per night for HI or Alpine Club members, $23 otherwise. Head southeast along Bow Valley Trail from town; it's signposted to the left, 500 meters (0.3 mi.) after passing under the TransCanada Highway.

$50–100

With around $100 budgeted for a room, it's hard to go past **Riverview and Main** (918 8th St., 403/678-9777, www.riverviewandmain.com, $85–120 s or d), centrally located half a block beyond the end of the downtown core. The rooms are decently sized and brightly decorated and each has access to a deck. The guest lounge centers on a riverstone wood-burning fireplace. Rates include a selection of hot and cold breakfast items.

The **Gateway Inn** (403/678-5396 or 877/678-1810, www.gatewayinn.ca), eight kilometers (five mi.) west of Canmore in Harvie Heights has standard motel rooms ($75–89 s or d) and self-contained cabins, each with a kitchenette and adjacent firepit (from $89 s or d).

$100–150

Named for one of the valley's original coal-mining communities, the **Georgetown Inn** (1101 Bow Valley Trail, 403/678-3439 or 800/657-5955, www.georgetowninn.ab.ca) is run by a friendly English couple who have set the place up as a country inn of times gone by. Each of the 25 rooms has its own individual charm, with a modern twist on decor that features lots of English antiques. Best value are Superior Rooms, each with a separate sitting area and electric fireplace ($149). Complimentary nonalcoholic drinks and a delicious cooked breakfast are included in rates ranging $129–189 s or d (from $89 in winter).

Windtower Mountain Lodge (160 Kananaskis Way, 403/609-6600 or 866/609-6600, www.windtowermountainlodge.com) provides hotel and suite accommodation within a condominium development. Complex facilities include a picnic and barbecue area, fitness center, outdoor hot tub, a café, and underground parking. Choose from hotel-style rooms ($109–149 s or d) or suites with separate sleeping rooms, a full kitchen, private balcony, laundry, and large well-equipped living area ($179–279 s or d).

Deadman's Flats, seven kilometers (4.3 mi.) east of Canmore along the TransCanada Highway, is home to the alpine-style **Kiska Inn** (110 1st Ave., 403/678-4041 or 866/678-4041, $105–120 s or d, includes breakfast). Each guest room is spacious and subtly themed (the Canmore Room is particularly appealing). Guest amenities include a shared kitchen, a comfortable lounge room, a barbecue area, and Internet access.

$150–200

The quality of accommodations in this category far exceeds that of similarly priced options down the road in Banff.

Lady Macdonald Country Inn (1201 Bow Valley Trail, 403/678-3665 or 800/567-3919, www.ladymacdonald.com, $155–225 s or d) exudes a welcoming atmosphere and personalized service. Its 12 rooms are all individually furnished, with the smallest, the Palliser Room, featuring elegant decor and a magnificent wrought-iron bed. The largest of the rooms is the Three Sisters, which has bright, welcoming decor, a king-

Lady Macdonald Country Inn

size bed, two-way gas fireplace, hot tub, and uninterrupted views of its namesake. Rates include a hearty hot breakfast.

Creekside Country Inn (709 Benchlands Trail, 403/609-5522 or 866/609-552, www.creeksidecountryinn.com, $159–179, discounted to $79–129 outside of summer) is a modern, mountain-style lodge featuring lots of exposed timber. The 12 rooms are elegant in their simplicity; eight have lofts. Facilities include a lounge with roaring log fire, a small exercise room, a whirlpool tub, and a steam room. Rates include a gourmet continental breakfast that will set you up for a day of hiking.

$200–250

The **Bear and Bison** (705 Benchlands Trail, 403/678-2058, www.bearandbison.com, $245 s or d) is an elegant lodging with nine guest rooms in three different themes. Timber and stone surroundings are complemented by rich heritage tones throughout. Each room has a king-size four-poster bed, a jetted tub, a fireplace, and a private balcony or patio. The lounge has a high, vaulted ceiling, a welcoming open fire, and panoramic picture windows. Guests also enjoy an inviting library and a private garden complete

with an oversized hot tub. Rates include baked goods upon arrival, predinner drinks, and a gourmet breakfast.

Campgrounds

Restwell Trailer Park (off 8th St. in downtown Canmore, 403/678-5111, www.restwelltrailer park.com) is mostly filled with permanent residents, and doesn't try to be anything it's not. Overnight travelers are welcome, and the best sites along a stretch of grass that parallels Policeman's Creek. Unserviced sites are $26, hookups $29–39.

East of Canmore are three government campgrounds operated by Bow Valley Campgrounds (403/673-2163,). Each has pit toilets, cooking shelters, and firewood for sale at $6 per bundle. **Bow River Campground** is three kilometers (1.9 mi.) east of Canmore at the Three Sisters Parkway overpass; **Three Sisters Campground** is accessed from Deadman's Flats, four kilometers (2.5 mi.) farther east, but has a pleasant treed setting; while **Lac des Arcs Campground** slopes down to the edge of a large lake of the same name another seven kilometers (4.3 mi.) toward Calgary. These campgrounds are open May–mid-September and all sites are $17.

ALBERTA

FOOD

The restaurant scene has come a long way in Canmore in the last few years. While you can still get inexpensive bar meals at each of the many pubs, other choices run the gamut, from the lively atmosphere of dining on funky fusion food in the front yard of a converted residence to an upmarket French restaurant.

Cafés, Coffee, and Other Goodies

The **Rocky Mountain Bagel Company** (830 8th St., 403/678-9978, 6:30 A.M.–11 P.M.) is a popular, centrally located gathering spot. It's the perfect place to start the day with a good strong coffee and fruit-filled muffin. Out on the Bow Valley Trail (between Dairy Queen and Boston Pizza) is **Beamer's Coffee Bar** (403/678-3988, daily from 7 A.M.). Always busy, this place has a huge following due to great coffee, a friendly owner, and a long comfortable couch wrapped around a fireplace—the perfect place to relax with one of Beamer's complimentary daily papers.

Crazyweed Kitchen (626 8th St., 403/609-2530, 11 A.M.–7 P.M.) dishes up creative culinary fare such as Thai chicken wraps or curried seafood. Healthy portions are served at tables inside or out, or packed to go. Around the corner, **Bella Crusta** (702 6th Ave., 403/609-3366) are purveyors of the best gourmet pizza in the Bow Valley. Heated slices to go are $5, or pay $12–15 for a family-sized version and heat it yourself on a barbecue, as the friendly staff recommend.

Casual Canadian

Tucked away behind the main street is **Zona's** (710 9th St., 403/609-2000, daily 11 A.M.–2 A.M.), a great little bistro with a laid-back atmosphere. Earthy tones, hardwood floors, rustic furniture, bamboo blinds, and kiln-fired clay crockery create an inviting ambience unequalled in Canmore. The menu takes ideas from around the world, with an emphasis on healthy eating and freshly prepared Canadian produce. Chose from dishes such as Moroccan molasses lamb curry ($14) or a filet of salmon baked in a maple and whiskey sauce ($18).

Beyond the crowded deck, a fine little restaurant within the **Bolo Steakhouse** (838 8th St., 403/678-5211, 7 A.M.–9:30 P.M.) oozes historic mountain charm. Creative appetizers are all $10 along with Rocky Mountain specialties such as buffalo rib steak, scalloped venison, nut-crusted salmon, and charbroiled Alberta beef, all in the $15–29 price range. Leave room for a generous slice of mixed berry cheesecake.

In a two-story log structure with inside, deck, and rooftop table settings, **Sage** (1712 Bow Valley Trail, 403/678-4878) offers interesting and creative food using lots of Canadian game. For lunch, chose trout crêpes ($10), venison meatloaf ($10), or eggs Benedict Alberta-style—with beef substituting for ham. The drink list is extensive, with specialty teas on a separate menu and refreshing choices such as thyme lemonade.

INFORMATION AND SERVICES

The best source of pretrip information is **Tourism Canmore** (www.tourismcanmore.com). At the western entrance to town (Banff side) the **Travel Alberta Information Centre** (403/678-5277, May–Sept. 8 A.M.–8 P.M., and Oct. 9 A.M.–6 P.M.) provides plenty of information on the town. **Canmore Public Library** (700 9th St., 403/678-2468) is open Monday–Thursday 11 A.M.–8 P.M., Friday–Sunday 11 A.M.–5 P.M. At the top end of the main street, **Café Books** (826 Main St., 403/678-0908, Mon.–Sat. 9:30 A.M.–9 P.M., Sun. 10:30 A.M.–5:30 P.M.) stocks an excellent selection of Canadiana, including hiking guides, coffee-table-style pictorials, Rocky Mountain cookbooks, and calendars, as well as nonfiction by local authors.

The post office is on Seventh Avenue, beside Rusticana Grocery. **The Lost Sock** launderette (8 A.M.–9:30 P.M.) is in the small mall on Seventh Avenue at 10th Street. **Canmore Hospital** (403/678-5536) is along Bow Valley Trail. For the **RCMP,** call 403/678-5516.

Kananaskis Country

During Alberta's oil-and-gas boom of the 1970s, oil revenues collected by the provincial government were channeled into various projects aimed at improving the lifestyle of Albertans. One lasting legacy of the boom is Kananaskis (Can-AN-a-skiss) Country, a sprawling 4,250-square-kilometer (1,640-sq.-mi.) area west of Calgary that has been developed with an emphasis on providing recreation opportunities for as many people as possible.

Within the area are two distinct ecosystems: the high peaks of the Continental Divide to the west, and the lower, rolling foothills to the east. The glacier-carved **Kananaskis Valley** separates the two. Although Kananaskis Country lacks the famous lakes and glaciated peaks of Banff and Jasper National Parks, in many ways it rivals them. Wildlife is abundant, and opportunities for observation of larger mammals are superb. The region has large populations of moose, mule and white-tailed deer, elk, black bears, bighorn sheep, and mountain goats. Wolves, grizzly bears, and cougars are present, too, but are less likely to be seen.

The main access to Kananaskis Country is 80 kilometers (50 mi.) west of Calgary and 23 kilometers (14.3 mi.) east of Calgary. Other points of access are south from Canmore, at Bragg Creek on the region's northeast border, west from Longview in the southeast, or along the Forestry Trunk Road from the south. For more information, contact the regional Parks and Protected Areas division of the provincial government (Provincial Building, 800 Railway Ave., Canmore, 403/678-5508; www.cd.gov.ab.ca), or see the Preserving Alberta section of their website. Another good source of information is **Friends of Kananaskis Country** (www.kananaskis.org), a nonprofit organization that sponsors educational programs, is involved in a variety of hands-on projects, and promotes Kananaskis Country in partnership with the government.

Bow Valley Provincial Park

This park, at the north end of Kananaskis Country, sits at the confluence of the Kananaskis and Bow Rivers and extends as far south as Barrier Lake. The entrance to the park is four kilometers (2.5 mi.) west of Highway 40 (the main access into Kananaskis Country). To the casual motorist driving along the highway, the park seems fairly small, but more than 300 species of plants have been recorded, and 60 species of birds are known to nest within its boundaries. The abundance of wildflowers, birds, and smaller mammals can be enjoyed along four short interpretive trails. Other popular activities in the park include fishing for brook and brown trout and whitefish in the Bow River, bicycling along the paved trail system, and attending interpretive programs presented by park staff.

Facilities at the two campgrounds (403/673-2163, www.bowvalleycampgrounds.com) within the park, **Willow Rock** and **Bow Valley,** are as good as any in the province. Both have showers, flush toilets, and cooking shelters. Willow Rock also has powered sites and a coin laundry and is open for winter camping. Unserviced sites are $17–20, powered sites $20–23; both campgrounds take reservations.

A **Visitor Information Centre** (summer Mon.–Fri. 8 A.M.–8 P.M., rest of year Mon.–Fri. 8:15 A.M.–4:30 P.M.) is at the park entrance on Highway 1X. It offers general information on the park and Kananaskis Country, as well as interpretive displays. A 2.2-kilometer (1.4-mi.) hiking trail also begins here.

KANANASKIS VALLEY

This is the most developed area of Kananaskis Country, yet summer crowds are minimal compared to Banff. Highway 40 follows the Kananaskis River through the valley between the TransCanada Highway and Peter Lougheed Provincial Park.

Sights and Drives

The following sights are along Highway 40 and are detailed from the TransCanada Highway in the north to Peter Lougheed Provincial Park in the south.

ALBERTA

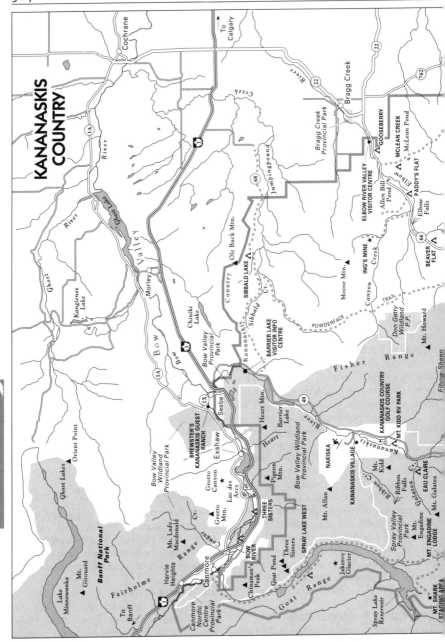

KANANASKIS COUNTRY

ALBERTA

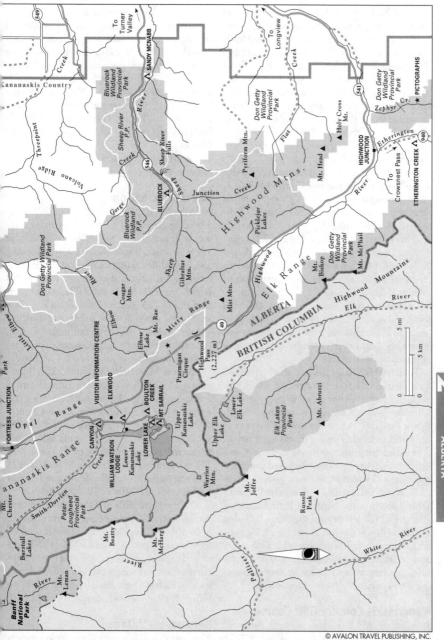

ALBERTA

© AVALON TRAVEL PUBLISHING, INC.

From the TransCanada Highway, Highway 40 branches south across open rangeland. The first worthwhile stop along this route is **Canoe Meadows,** a large day-use area above the sparkling Kananaskis River. Below the picnic area, whitewater enthusiasts use a short stretch of river as a slalom course. Manmade obstacles and gates challenge recreational and racing kayakers, while upstream (around the first bend), the manmade Green Tongue creates a steep wave, allowing kayakers to remain in one spot, spinning and twisting while water rushes past them.

South from Canoe Meadows, stop at **Barrier Lake Visitor Information Centre** (403/673-3985, June–mid-Sept., daily 9 A.M.–6 P.M., rest of year daily 9 A.M.–4 P.M.). Nestled between Highway 40 and the Kananaskis River, riverside trails lead in both directions, including two kilometers (1.2 mi.) downstream to Canoe Meadows. Barrier Lake itself is farther along Highway 40, dominated to the south by the impressive peak of Mount Baldy (2,212 m/7,257 ft.). The lake is manmade, but still a picture of beauty. From the south end of Barrier Lake, Highway 40 continues south to a spot that will be of particular interest to anglers, **Mt. Lorette Ponds,** stocked annually with rainbow trout.

Kananaskis Village lies just off Highway 40 four kilometers (2.5 mi.) south of the ponds. The village, the epicenter of action during the 1988 Olympic Winter Games, sits on a high bench below Nakiska—where the downhill events of the games were held—and overlooks a golf course. The village comprises two hotels, restaurants, and other service shops set around a paved courtyard complete with waterfalls and trout-stocked ponds.

From the village, it's 15 kilometers (9.3 mi.) farther south to the border of Peter Lougheed Provincial Park. Just beyond the village is **Wedge Pond,** originally dug as a gravel pit during golf-course construction, and now filled with water and encircled by a one-kilometer (0.6-mi.) trail offering fantastic views across the river to towering 2,958-meter (9,700-ft.) Mount Kidd.

Kananaskis Country Golf Course

Regularly voted "Best Value in North America" by *Golf Digest,* this 36-hole layout (403/591-7272

or 877/591-2525, www.kananaskisgolf.com) is bisected by the Kananaskis River and surrounded by magnificent mountain peaks. It comprises two 18-hole courses: **Mt. Kidd,** featuring undulating terrain and an island green on the 197-yard fourth hole, and the shorter (which is a relative term—both courses measure over 7,000 yards from the back markers) **Mt. Lorette,** where water comes into play on 13 holes. Greens fees are $70 (Alberta residents pay $55) and a cart is an additional $14 per person. Golfers enjoy valet parking and use of the driving range, as well as a restaurant and bar with awesome mountain views.

Winter Recreation

Nakiska (403/591-7777; 800/258-7669, www .skinakiska.com) is a state-of-the-art alpine resort built to host the alpine skiing events of the 1988 Olympic Winter Games. Great cruising and fast fall-line skiing on runs cut specially for racing will satisfy the intermediate-to-advanced crowd. The resort has a total of 28 runs and a vertical rise of 735 meters (2,410 ft.). Lift tickets are $46 for adults, $36 for seniors and students, $15 for children. Kids five and under ski free. Check the website for accommodation packages and transportation schedules from Canmore.

Fortress Mountain (403/264-5825, Snowphone 403/244-6665, www.skifortress.com) is a sleeping giant as alpine resorts go. It's a 30-minute drive farther into Kananaskis Country than Nakiska but the rewards are uncrowded slopes, more snow, on-hill accommodations, and spectacular views. Lift tickets are $35 per day or $27 for the afternoon; seniors and students $25 ($20 after noon). On-hill lodging is at **Fortress Lodge** (403/591-7108 or 800/258-7669).

The most accessible of Kananaskis Country's 200 kilometers (124 mi.) of cross-country trails are in the Ribbon Creek area. Most heavily used are those radiating from Kananaskis Village and those around the base of Nakiska. Most trails are easy to intermediate, including a five-kilometer (3.1-mi.) track up Ribbon Creek. Rentals are available in the Village Trading Post in Kananaskis Village.

Kananaskis Village

This modern mountain village 90 kilometers

(56 mi.) from Calgary was built for the 1988 Olympic Winter Games. It was again in the world spotlight when eight of the world's most powerful men met here for the 2002 G8 Summit.

The village is home to two resortlike hotels, both open year-round. Don't be too perturbed by the rates quoted below—check the websites for packages and deals offering discounts of up to 50 percent. The 321-room **Delta Lodge at Kananaskis** (403/591-7711 or 800/778-5050, www.deltahotels.com) is part of an up-scale Canadian hotel chain. In the main lodge are 251 moderately large Delta Rooms, many with mountain views, balconies, and fireplaces (from $210 s or d). Connected by a covered walkway are 70 Signature Club rooms, each boasting elegant Victorian-era charm, a mountain view, a luxurious bathroom complete with bathrobes, extra-large beds, and many extras, such as CD players (from $305 s or d). All guests have use of spa and fitness facilities. The other accommodation is the more intimate **Kananaskis Resort and Conference Centre** (403/591-7500 or 888/591-7501, www.kananaskisresort.com). Some of the 90 guest rooms are bedroom lofts with gas fireplaces, kitchenettes, large bathrooms, and sitting rooms ($290 s or d); the others are standard hotel rooms that begin at $230. The inn also offers the Mountain Spa facility, a fitness center, and an indoor pool.

The Delta property contains four restaurants and two bars. For a warm, relaxed atmosphere, head to the **Bighorn Lounge** (open daily from 11 A.M.) near the arcade's main entrance. The bistro-style menu is highlighted by a wide variety of appetizers perfect for sharing, such as cheese platters. The casual **Fireweed Grill** (open daily 6 A.M.–10 P.M.) offers floor-to-ceiling windows and an adjoining outdoor patio used during summer. Country-style **Brady's Market** features seasonal produce prepared in traditional European dishes. **Seasons Dining Room** (403/591-7711), in the Signature Club wing, is the village's most elegant restaurant. French-Canadian cuisine is served on sterling silver, as a pianist plays in the background. It's open for dinner only; expect to pay $18–30 for an entrée.

Camping

Mount Kidd RV Park (403/591-7700, www.mountkiddrv.com) is arguably the finest RV park in Canada. It's nestled below the sheer eastern face of Mount Kidd along Highway 40 south of Kananaskis Village. The campground's showpiece is the Campers Center (yes, the American spelling). Inside is the main registration area and all the usual bathroom facilities as well as whirlpool baths, saunas, a wading pool, game room, lounge, groceries, a concession, and laundry. Outside are two tennis courts, picnic areas by the river, and many paved biking and hiking trails. Most of the 229 campsites are hookups, but the few tenting sites are a good value at $20 per night. Hookups are $26–32. It's open year-round, with reservations for less than four nights taken from 8 A.M. up to one calendar month in advance.

Those who can survive without such luxuries should continue 6.5 kilometers (four mi.) beyond Mount Kidd RV Park to **Eau Claire Campground** (403/591-7226, www.kananaskiscamping.com, June–mid-Sept.), where each site has a picnic table and firepit.

PETER LOUGHEED PROVINCIAL PARK

This park is a southern extension of the Kananaskis Valley and protects the upper watershed of the Kananaskis River. It is contained within a high mountain valley and dominated by two magnificent bodies of water—**Upper** and **Lower Kananaskis Lakes.**

Highway 40 is the main route through the park. The most important intersection to make note of is five kilometers (3.1 mi.) along Highway 40 from the park's north boundary. At this point, Kananaskis Lakes Road branching off to the west, accessing Upper and Lower Kananaskis Lakes. These two lakes are the center of boating and fishing in the park and opportunities abound for hiking and camping nearby.

Highwood Pass

In the southeastern corner of the park, Highway 40 climbs to Highwood Pass (2,227 m/7,310 ft.), the highest road pass in Canada. The pass is right at the treeline, one of the most accessible alpine areas in all of western Canada. Simply step out of your vehicle and follow the interpretive trails through the **Highwood Meadows.** In the vicinity, the **Rock Glacier Trail,** two kilometers (1.2 mi.) north of Highwood Pass, leads 150 meters (0.1 mi.) to a unique formation of moraine rock.

From the pass, Highway 40 descends into the Highwood/Cataract Creek areas of Kananaskis Country (Highwood Junction is 35 km/22 mi. from the pass). Highwood Pass is in critical wildlife habitat and is closed December 1–June 15.

Hiking

The park offers a number of interesting interpretive trails and more strenuous hikes. Most trailheads are along Kananaskis Lakes Road, a paved road that leads off Highway 40 to Upper and Lower Kananaskis Lakes. **Rockwall Trail,** from the Visitor Information Centre, and **Marl Lake Trail,** from Elkwood Campground, are wheelchair accessible and barrier-free, respectively. The **Boulton Creek Trail** (4.9 km/three mi.; 90 minutes round-trip) is an easy loop that begins from Boulton Bridge, 10 kilometers (6.2 mi.) from Highway 40. A booklet, available at the trailhead, corresponds with numbered posts along this interpretive trail.

From the Upper Lake day-use area, at the very end of Kananaskis Lakes Road, the trail to **Rawson Lake** (3.5 km/2.2 mi.; 1.5 hours one-way) begins by following the lakeshore for just over one kilometer (0.6-mi.). Just beyond the small waterfall it begins an uphill climb (305 m/1,000 ft.), ending at a picturesque subalpine lake surrounded by a towering yet magnificently symmetrical headwall. The setting of **Elbow Lake** (1.3 km/0.8 mi.; 30 minutes one-way) is almost as spectacular as Rawson, but the trail is shorter (and therefore busier). The trailhead is the Elbow Pass day-use area, beside Highway 40, 13 kilometers (eight mi.) south of Kananaskis Lakes Road. Continue south along Highway 40 to Highwood Pass (four km/2.5 mi.) to the **Ptarmigan Cirque Trail** (5.6 km/3.5 mi.; 2 hours round-trip), a steep (elevation gain is 230 m/750 ft.) interpretive walk that climbs high into the treeless alpine zone. Along way you're likely to see numerous small mammals—Columbian ground squirrels, pikas, least chipmunks, and hoary marmots are all common.

Other Recreation

The **Bike Trail** is a 20-kilometer (12.5-mi.) paved trail designed especially for bicycles that begins behind the Visitor Information Centre and follows Lower Kananaskis Lake to Mount Sarrail Campground. Many other trails are designated for mountain-biking use; inquire at the Visitor Information Centre (403/591-6344). **Boulton Creek Trading Post** (403/591-7058) rents mountain bikes during summer ($8 per hour, $32 per day). Upper and Lower Kananaskis Lakes have fair fishing for a variety of trout and whitefish. A nightly interpretive program takes place in campground amphitheaters throughout the park. Look for schedules posted on bulletin boards, or check with the Visitor Information Centre.

Camping

Within the park are six auto-accessible campgrounds that hold a total of 507 sites. All are on Kananaskis Lakes Road and are linked by bicycle and hiking trails. **Boulton Creek Campground** ($17) has coin-operated showers just beyond the registration gate, flush toilets, a few of 118 sites with power, and an interpretive amphitheater, and is within walking distance of a restaurant and grocery store. **Elkwood Campground** ($17) is the largest of the park's campgrounds, with 130 sites. It offers showers ($1 for five minutes) along each of four loops, flush toilets, a playground, and an interpretive amphitheater. **Canyon, Lower Lake,** and **Interlakes Campgrounds** ($17) are more rustic, with only pit toilets, pump water, and picnic tables (Interlakes has some great water views). **Mt. Sarrail Campground** ($15) is described as a "walk-in" campground for tenters, but some sites are right by the main parking lot. All campgrounds in Peter Lougheed Provincial Park are operated by Kananaskis Camping Inc. (403/591-7226, www.kananaskiscamping.com).

Information and Services

At the excellent **Visitor Information Centre** (four km/2.5 mi. along Kananaskis Lakes Road from Highway 40, 403/591-6322, summer daily

9 A.M.–7 P.M., rest of year Mon.–Fri. 9 A.M.–5 P.M. and weekends 9 A.M.–5 P.M.) explore the natural and cultural history of the park through photographs, videos, and hands-on displays. The knowledgeable staff hides hordes of literature under the desk—you have to ask for it. A comfortable lounge area overlooking the valley is used mainly in winter by cross-country skiers but is always open for trip planning or relaxing.

Located along Kananaskis Lakes Road, 10 kilometers (6.2 mi.) south of Highway 40, **Boulton Creek Trading Post** (mid-May–mid-Oct. 9 A.M.–6 P.M. extended to 10 P.M. in July and Aug.) is the park's only commercial center. It sells groceries, basic camping supplies, fishing tackle and licenses, propane, and firewood. The store also rents bikes.

SPRAY VALLEY PROVINCIAL PARK

The creation of 35,800-hectare (88,460-acre) Spray Valley Provincial Park in 2001 provided the final link in continuous protection between bordering Peter Lougheed Provincial Park in the south and Willmore Wilderness Park beyond the northern reaches of Jasper National Park in the north. The park's dominant feature is **Spray Lake Reservoir,** a 16-kilometer-long (10 mi.) body of water that provides a variety of recreational opportunities.

The **Smith-Dorrien/Spray Trail** is the only road through the park. This 60-kilometer (37-mi.) unpaved (and often dusty) road links Peter Lougheed Provincial Park in the south to Canmore in the north. From the south, the road climbs up the Smith-Dorrien Creek watershed, passing Mud Lake and entering the Spray Valley Provincial Park just south of Mt. Engadine Lodge. Around three kilometers (1.9 mi.) farther north is **Buller Pond** (on the west side of the road), from which the distinctive "Matterhorn" peak of Mount Assiniboine can be seen on a clear day. The road then parallels the eastern shoreline of Spray Lake for over 20 kilometers (12.5 mi.), passing three lakefront picnic areas. Beyond the north end of Spray Lake, the road passes **Goat Pond** and the Goat Creek trailhead, then descends steeply into the Bow Valley and Canmore.

Accommodations and Camping

Mount Engadine Lodge (403/678-4080, www .mountengadine.com, mid-June–mid-Oct. and early Feb.–mid-Apr.) is set on a ridge overlooking an open meadow and small creek at the turnoff to the Mount Shark staging area. The main lodge has a dining room, a comfortable lounge area, and a beautiful sundeck holding a hot tub. Breakfast is served buffet style, lunch can be taken at the lodge or packed for a picnic, and dinner is served in multiple courses of European specialties. Rates for lodge rooms range from $115 per person for a room with a shared bathroom to $140 for a private bathroom and fireplace. Cabins are $125 per person. All meals are included in these nightly rates.

The park's only campground is **Spray Lake West** ($14), a rustic facility spread out along the western shoreline of Spray Lake. Many of the 50-odd sites are very private, but facilities are limited to picnic tables, fire pits, and pit toilets. Firewood is $6 per bundle.

OTHER REGIONS OF KANANASKIS COUNTRY

Sibbald

The Sibbald Creek Trail (Hwy. 68) traverses the rolling foothills of the Sibbald and Jumpingpound Valleys and is accessible from the Trans-Canada Highway, intersecting Highway 40 south of the Barrier Lake Visitor Information Centre. Fishing is popular in **Sibbald Lake** and **Sibbald Meadows Pond.** A couple of short trails begin at the picnic area at Sibbald Lake, including the 4.4-kilometer (2.7-mi.) **Ole Buck Loop,** which climbs a low ridge.

Sibbald Lake Campground ($17) offers 134 sites spread around five loops (Loop D comes closest to the lake). Amenities include pit toilets, drinking water, and a nightly interpretive program. For camping information contact Elbow Valley Campgrounds (403/949-3132, www.evcamp.com).

Elbow River Valley

The main access road into the Elbow River Valley is Highway 66 west from Bragg Creek. It

ALBERTA

BIGHORN SHEEP

Bighorn sheep are the most distinctive of the hoofed mammals in western Canada. Easily recognized by their impressive horns, they're often seen grazing on grassy mountain slopes or at salt licks beside the road. The color of their coat varies with the season; in summer it's a brownish gray with a cream-colored belly and rump, turning lighter in winter. Males can weigh up to 120 kilograms (265 lbs.). Females generally weigh around 80 kilograms (180 lbs.). Both sexes possess horns, rather than antlers like moose, elk, and deer. Unlike antlers, horns are not shed each year and can grow to astounding sizes. The horns of rams are larger than those of ewes and curve up to 360 degrees. The spiraled horns of an older

ram can measure over one meter (three ft.) and weigh as much as 15 kilograms (33 lbs.). In fall, during the mating season, a hierarchy is established among them for the right to breed ewes. As the males face off against each other to establish dominance, their horns act as both a weapon and a buffer against the head-butting of other rams. The skull structure of the bighorn, rams in particular, has become adapted to these clashes, preventing heavy concussion.

These animals are particularly tolerant of humans and often approach parked vehicles; although they are not dangerous, as with all mammals in the park, you should not approach or feed them.

climbs steadily along the Elbow River, passing **McLean Pond** and **Allen Bill Pond** (both are stocked with rainbow trout) and six-meter-high (20-ft.) **Elbow Falls,** before climbing through an area devastated by wildfire in 1981 and then descending to a campground, 42 kilometers (26 mi.) from Bragg Creek.

Five campgrounds, with a combined total of 551 sites, lie along the Elbow River Valley. The most developed of the five is **McLean Creek Campground,** 12 kilometers (7.5 mi.) west of Bragg Creek. At the campground entrance is the Camper Centre with groceries, coin showers, and firewood ($6 per bundle). Unpowered sites are $20 per night, powered sites $23. For reservations contact Elbow Valley Campgrounds (403/949-3132, www.evcamp.com). The other campgrounds and their distances from Bragg Creek are **Gooseberry** (10 km/6.2 mi.), **Paddy's Flat** (20 km/12.4 mi.), **Beaver Flat** (30 km/18.6 mi.), and, at the very end of the road, **Little Elbow** (50 km/31 mi.). Each of these campgrounds has only basic facilities—pit toilets and hand-pumped drinking water—but, still, sites are $17 per night.

Bragg Creek

Bragg Creek is rural retreat beside the Elbow River, just outside the Kananaskis Country boundary. Many of Bragg Creek's 1,000 residents commute daily to nearby Calgary (40

km/25 mi. east). The ideal location and quiet lifestyle have attracted artists and artisans—the town claims to have more painters, potters, sculptors, and weavers than any similarly sized town in Alberta. Arriving along Highway 22 from either the north or south, you'll be greeted upon arrival in Bragg Creek by a slightly confusing four-way stop intersection with a treed triangle of land in the middle. Take the option along the north (right) side of the distinctive polished-log Bragg Creek Trading Post II to access the main shopping center, a Western-themed collection of basic town services interspersed with craft shops and cafés. White Avenue, also known as **Heritage Mile** and originally the main commercial strip, has more of the same and leads through an appealing residential area. This road continues southwest to 122-hectare (300-acre) **Bragg Creek Provincial Park,** a day-use area alongside the Elbow River. With a basket of goodies from one of Bragg Creek's many food outlets, leave the main parking lot behind to enjoy a picnic lunch on one of the many riverside picnic tables.

Best of a bunch of bed-and-breakfasts is **Countryside Inn** (call for directions, 403/949-2805), a large country-style house nestled among stands of trees within walking distance of both the river and village. The home has three comfortable guest rooms—one with its own hot tub—a spacious sitting room, a billiards room, and an outdoor hot tub. A hearty breakfast is included in the rates of $100 s, $125 d.

Bragg Creek Shopping Centre holds a wide variety of eateries as well as most services. At the east end, **Pies Plus** (403/949-3450) specializes in meat and fruit pies at reasonable prices, but doesn't open until 10 A.M. and is closed Monday. Early risers should head to the opposite end of the parking lot to **Bragg Creek Coffee Company** (403/949-3251), which opens weekdays at 6 A.M. and on weekends at 8 P.M. Join locals for an early morning coffee or head here for the daily $7 soup-and-sandwich lunch special. The **Steak Pit** (43 White Ave., 403/949-3633, daily from 11:30 A.M.) is a fantastic restaurant. The decor is early Canadian, yet realistic and elegant. The dining room, decorated with hand-hewn cedar furniture, is only a small part of the restaurant, which also has a café, lounge, sports bar, and gift shop. Eating here isn't cheap but *is* comparable to Calgary restaurants. The menu sets out to prove that great steaks don't need fancy trimmings, and does so with the best cuts of Alberta beef and great spuds.

Sheep River Valley

The Sheep River Valley lies immediately south of the Elbow River Valley, in an area of rolling foothills between open ranchlands to the east and the high peaks bordering **Elbow-Sheep Wildland Provincial Park** to the west. Access is from the town of Turner Valley (take Sunset Blvd. west from downtown), along Highway 546. The highway passes through **Sheep River Provincial Park** (which protects the wintering ground of bighorn sheep), then **Sheep River Falls,** and ends at a campground 46 kilometers (29 mi.) west of Turner Valley.

Along Highway 546, west from Turner Valley, are two campgrounds. **Sandy McNabb Campground,** the larger of the two, is a short walk from the river right by the entrance to Kananaskis Country. All sites are $17 per night. Both facilities are operated by High Country Camping (403/558-2373 or 866/366-2267, www.camping alberta.com). All sites are filled on a first-come, first-served basis.

Highwood/Cataract Creek

The Highwood/Cataract Creek areas stretch from Peter Lougheed Provincial Park to the southern border of Kananaskis Country. This is the least developed area in Kananaskis Country. The jagged peaks of the Highwood Mountains, mostly protected by remote **Don Getty Wildland Provincial Park** are the dominant feature; high alpine meadows among the peaks are home to bighorn sheep, elk, and grizzlies. Lower down, spruce and lodgepole pine forests spread over most of the valley, giving way to grazing lands along the eastern flanks. The main access from the north is along Highway 40, which drops 600 vertical meters (1,970 ft.) in the 35 kilometers (22 mi.) between **Highwood Pass** and **Highwood Junction.** From the east, Highway 541 west from Longview joins Highway 40 at Highwood Junction.

Open May–November, **Etherington Creek** is seven kilometers (4.3 mi.) south of Highwood Junction, while **Cataract Creek** is five kilometers (3.1 mi.) farther south and is open mid-May–early September. Both offer primitive facilities including water, pit toilets, firewood, fire pits, and picnic tables; $17 per night.

ALBERTA

Calgary to Lethbridge

The trip between Calgary and Lethbridge takes about two hours nonstop, but there are many tempting detours in between, including the ranching country southwest of Calgary, the Porcupine Hills west of Claresholm, historic Fort Macleod, and Head-Smashed-In Buffalo Jump, one of the best-preserved sites of its type in North America.

OKOTOKS AND VICINITY

The fast-growing town of Okotoks is in the Sheep River Valley 34 kilometers (21 mi.) south of Calgary and just minutes from Highway 2 to the east. It's the largest population base between Calgary and Lethbridge, and many of its 11,000 residents commute into Calgary to work. Take Elizabeth Street east from Highway 2A and continue through downtown to reach **Okotoks Visitor Information Centre** (53 N. Railway St., 403/938-3204, May–early Aug. daily 9 A.M.–5 P.M.). Staff and local businesses have put together the **Okotoks Art Walk,** which links downtown businesses displaying the works of local artists.

Practicalities

The best accommodations in town are provided at **Okotoks Country Inn** (on Hwy. 2A, 403/938-

1999 or 877/938-3336), which features 40 climate-controlled rooms, modern facilities, and rates of $82 s, $92 d that include a light breakfast. Municipally operated **Sheep River Campground** has a delightful riverside location just a short walk from town off Highway 2A; tents $18, hookups $21–30.

The **Ginger Room Restaurant and Gift Shop** (43 Riverside Dr., 403/938-2907, daily 10 A.M.–8 P.M.) is a large Victorian-style mansion that has become a local landmark. Inside it's crammed with two floors of crafts and antiques. At the back is a tearoom that is always busy.

Black Diamond

This town of 1,700 on the banks of the Sheep River, west of Okotoks along Hwy. 7, was named for the coal once mined nearby. Town center is a bustling little strip along Centre Avenue. At the main intersection is the **Black Diamond Hotel** (403/933-4656), which has been modernized on the outside, but on the inside retains a classic small-town pub atmosphere that rocks with country music each weekend. Three blocks south, the **Triple "A" Motel** (322 Government Rd., 403/933-4915) has basic rooms for $40 single, $50 double. **Lions Campground** (access via 5th St. off Centre Street), in Centennial Park, is a great little spot by the Sheep River. It has showers, a kitchen shelter, and firewood; unserviced sites $12, powered sites $14–18.

Wonders (130 Government Rd., 403/933-2347, July–Aug. 6:30 A.M.–10 P.M.), a small gift shop, is the unofficial tourist information center, but it's worth dropping by just to enjoy coffee on the outdoor deck.

Turner Valley

Linked to Black Diamond by a four-kilometer (2.5-mi.) riverside path, Turner Valley is synonymous with the oil-and-gas industry in Alberta as, in 1914, Canada's first major crude-oil discovery was made here. Natural gas has been burned off ever since at an area known as Hell's Half Acre, on the eastern edge of town. Cross

THE BIG ROCKS

The name Okotoks came from the Blackfoot word *okatak* (rock), probably in reference to the massive boulders seven kilometers (4.3 mi.) west of town along Highway 7. Known as *erratics,* they are the largest such geological formations of their type in the world. During the last ice age, a sheet of ice up to one kilometer (0.6 mi.) thick crept forward from the north. A landslide in what is now Jasper National Park deposited large boulders on top of the ice. The ice continued moving south, carrying the boulders with it. Many thousands of years later, as temperatures warmed and the ice melted, the boulders were deposited far from their source (hence the name "erratic").

the Sheep River southeast of downtown to watch the gas flares that still burn 24 hours a day. Although it's protected as a National Historic Site, the **Turner Valley Gas Plant** is not set up as a tourist attraction. Instead, join a tour run by the local information center (Main St., 403/933-4944; departures daily 10 A.M.–5 P.M.).

Just west of Turner Valley's only traffic light is the Quonset-shaped **Chuckwagon Café** (105 Sunset Blvd., 403/933-0003). It's a typical small-town diner, with the $3.99 breakfast special an especially good value, although the portion isn't huge (the record of three servings in one sitting is currently held by Ian Wallace of Canmore). The rest of the day, well-priced Canadian and Chinese fare is served.

Bar U Ranch National Historic Site

Established in 1882, the Bar U Ranch (31 km/19 mi. south of Black Diamond, 403/395-2212 or 800/568-4996, June–mid-Oct. Mon.–Fri. 10 A.M.–6 P.M., until 8 P.M. on weekends, adult $6.50, senior $5.50, child $3) was one of western Canada's top ranches in the late 19th century. Like most of the big ranches in North America, the Bar U was broken up over time, but a 145-hectare (360-acre) parcel of the original spread has been preserved, with hundreds of Percherons running free through its rolling fields. Many of the old buildings have been restored; there's an interpretive center, a small theater, a blacksmith's shop, and a general store. In the **Roadhouse Restaurant,** the menu reflects the food that ranch hands of days gone by would have enjoyed after a long day in the saddle: buffalo burgers, sourdough breads, hearty soups, and stew are all offered.

HIGH RIVER TO FORT MACLEOD

High River

In the heart of the province's ranching country, 45 kilometers (28 mi.) south of Calgary, the town of High River has grown steadily from its beginnings as a fording spot along its namesake. From Highway 2, take 12th Avenue west to the downtown precinct, a compact collection of staid old

buildings on the west side of the railway tracks. Housed in a restored C.P.R. station, the **Museum of the Highwood** (406 1st St. W, 403/652-7156, summer Mon.–Sat. 10 A.M.–5 P.M., Sunday 1–5 P.M., $2) is chock-full of displays portraying early Western life. Of particular interest is the exhibit cataloging chuck wagon racing, a sport that has special significance to locals as the area boasts many champions. Better still, if you're visiting in mid-June, plan on attending the **North American Chuckwagon Championships** at the fairgrounds. In a rail car beside the museum is the **Whistle Stop Café** (1st St. SW, 403/652-7026, Monday 10 A.M.–2 P.M., Tues.–Sat. 10 A.M.–4 P.M., Sunday 11 A.M.–4 P.M.). You won't find anything too fancy here, just salads and sandwiches under $8 and slices of delicious berry pie for $3.50.

The local campground is in **George Lane Memorial Park** (west along 5th Ave. SW, 403/652-2529, May–Oct.), within walking distance of downtown. Sites are well spaced and some enjoy riverside positioning. Facilities include showers and cooking shelters; unserviced sites $14, powered sites $20.

Nanton

A couple of attractions make this ranching town 70 kilometers (43 mi.) south of Calgary a worthwhile stop. Firstly, beside the southbound lane of Highway 2 is the **Nanton Lancaster Society Air Museum** (Hwy.2 southbound, 403/646-2270, June–Aug. 9 A.M.–5 P.M., Sept.–May Sat.–Sun. 10 A.M.–4 P.M.), home to one of the few Lancaster bombers still in existence. Secondly, Nanton is home to a number of fine antiques shops. The best of these are along the northbound lane through town. Also northbound is an early-20th-century schoolhouse that functions as the local **information center** (403/646-5933, July–Aug. daily 9 A.M.–5 P.M.).

South of Nanton and 14 kilometers (8.7 mi.) west of the traffic roar on Highway 2, a short stretch of tree-lined Willow Creek is protected by **Willow Creek Provincial Park.** Generations of native tribes hunted and camped in the area; just outside the park you can find a buffalo jump and tepee rings well hidden in the grass. Visitors today swim in the creek and camp here. Up

ALBERTA

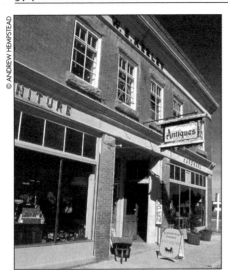

Antique shoppers will appreciate the many antique shops in Nanton.

on the benchland is a campground with limited services; $15 per night.

Claresholm

Most people stop at Claresholm (pop. 3,600), 100 kilometers (62 mi.) south of Calgary, just long enough to fill up with gas, grab a burger, and stretch their legs. But it's worth more than a quick stop—allow at least enough time to pop into the museum and then do a lap of the downtown core and its many historic buildings (those facing Hwy. 2 are the oldest). **Claresholm Museum** (5126 Railway Ave., 403/625-3131, mid-May–Aug. daily 9:30 A.M.–5 P.M., $1), in the C.P.R. station, holds an array of historical displays, including a dental clinic and a railway ticket office.

The nicest motel rooms (by far) between Calgary and Fort Macleod are at the **Bluebird Motel** (403/625-3395 or 800/661-4891, www.bluebird motel.ab.ca, $62–72 s, $72–82 d) at the north end of town. All rooms are air-conditioned and feature coffeemakers and large TVs; most also have refrigerators, and the more expensive ones have cooking facilities.

Centennial Park (4th St. W, north off Highway 520, 403/625-2751) is in a residential area close to the golf course. It offers powered sites, showers, and cooking shelters; unserviced sites $13, powered sites $17.

HEAD-SMASHED-IN BUFFALO JUMP

Archaeologists have discovered dozens of buffalo jumps across the North American plains. The largest, oldest, and best preserved is Head-Smashed-In, which is along a weathered sandstone cliff in the Porcupine Hills, 14 kilometers (8.7 mi.) west of Highway 2, just north of the junction with Highway 3. At the base is a vast graveyard with thousands of years worth of bones from butchered bison piled 10 meters (33 ft.) high. The jump represents an exceptionally sophisticated and ingenious bison-hunting technique used by Plains natives at least 5,700 years ago—possibly up to 10,000 years ago. Several methods were used to kill the bison, but by far the most successful method was to drive entire herds over a cliff face. To the west is a large basin of approximately 40 square kilometers (15 sq. mi.) where bison grazed. They were herded from the basin east along carefully constructed stone cairns that led to a precipice where the stampeding bison, with no chance of stopping, plunged to their deaths below.

HEAD-SMASHED-IN WHAT?

The name Head-Smashed-In has no connection to the condition of the bison's heads after tumbling over the cliff. It came from a Blackfoot legend: About 150 years ago, a young hunter wanted to watch the buffalo as they were driven over the steep cliff. He stood under a ledge watching as the stampeding beasts fell in front of him, but the hunt was better than usual, and as the animals piled up, he became wedged between the animals and the cliff. Later his people found him, his skull crushed under the weight of the buffalo—hence the name Head-Smashed-In.

Although a small section of the hill has been excavated, most of it appears today the same as it has for thousands of years. The relative height of the cliff, however, drastically decreased with the buildup of bones. Along with the bones are countless numbers of artifacts such as stone points, knives, and scrapers used to skin the fallen beasts. Metal arrowheads found in the top layer of bones indicate that the jump was used up until the coming of whites in the late 1700s. Recognizing the site's cultural and historical importance, UNESCO declared the jump a World Heritage Site in 1981.

Interpretive Centre

As you approach the jump site along Spring Point Road, the Head-Smashed-In Interpretive Centre (403/553-2731, www.head-smashed-in.com, summer daily 9 A.M.–6 P.M., rest of year daily 10 A.M.–5 P.M., adult $8.50, senior $7, child $4) doesn't become visible until you've parked your car and actually arrived at the entrance. The center—disguised in the natural topography of the landscape—is set into a cliff. A series of ramps and elevators marks the beginning of your tour as you rise to the roof, and from there a trail leads along the clifftop to the jump site. It isn't hard to imagine the sounds and spectacle of thousands of bison stampeding over the rise to the north and tumbling to their deaths below. Back inside you walk down floor by floor, passing displays and films explaining in an interesting and informative way the traditional way of life that existed on the prairies for nearly 10,000 years, as well as the sudden changes that took place when the first white men arrived. Outside the center is another trail that leads along the base of the cliff for a different perspective. Here a large aluminum building covers a recent dig site; the ground is littered with shattered bones. The center also has a gift shop and café selling, of all things, buffalo burgers.

FORT MACLEOD

Southern Alberta's oldest permanent settlement is Fort Macleod (pop. 3,200), 172 kilometers (107 mi.) south of Calgary and 44 kilometers (27 mi.) west of Lethbridge.

It was the site of a post established by Colonel James F. Macleod, who had been sent west with orders to curb the whiskey trade. These first troops of the NWMP eventually put an end to the illicit whiskey trade, and with the help of Métis scout Jerry Potts—who ironically didn't mind a drop of the hard stuff himself—they managed to restore peace between the warring tribes. Potts stayed at Fort Macleod until he died, and is buried in the local cemetery.

Historic Downtown

While nearby Head-Smashed-In Buffalo Jump gets all the attention, the downtown core of Fort Macleod is one of western Canada's finest remaining examples of an early 1900s streetscape. In 1906, a fire destroyed most of the wooden buildings, so a bylaw was passed requiring any new structures to be built of brick or stone. Many buildings along Col. Macleod Boulevard (the main street) function as they did during the town's boom years: the **Queen's Hotel** has rooms, the **Empress Theatre** (235 Col. Macleod Blvd., 403/553-4404, www.empresstheatre.ab.ca) is the oldest operating theater in the province, and the town office is contained in the only remaining courthouse that dates from Alberta's days as part of the North-West Territories. Throughout summer, guided walking tours of town leave regularly from the Fort. Or you can get the walking-tour brochure and do it at your own pace.

The original fort on the Oldman River would have looked much like the **replica fort** (219 25th St., 403/553-4703, July–Aug. daily 9 A.M.–8 P.M., May–June and Sept. daily 9 A.M.–5 P.M., rest of year weekdays 9:30 A.M.–4 P.M., adult $7.50, senior $7, child $4.50) just off the main street. Inside, a museum details the history of the NWMP and the early days of settlement in southern Alberta, while other buildings facing the central courtyard reflect varying aspects of frontier life. In the arena during summer, riders dress in period costume and perform a scaled-down version of the famous **Mounted Police Musical Ride**—a spectacular display of precision riding—four times daily at 10 A.M., 11:30 A.M., 2 P.M., and 3:30 P.M.

ALBERTA

Practicalities

Local motel rooms fill up fast every afternoon in summer, so book ahead or check in early. None of the motels offer rooms with kitchens, but all have air-conditioned rooms—a definite plus to combat the summer heat. At the **Kosy Motel** (433 Col. Macleod Blvd., 403/553-3115), the 12 rooms are clean and comfortable and priced at a reasonable $50 s, $60 d. One step up is the **Red Coat Inn** (359 Col. Macleod Blvd., 403/553-4434 or 800/423-4434, www.redcoat inn.com, $64 s, $70 d, $90 kitchenette), offering an indoor pool. **Daisy May Campground** (249 Lyndon Rd., 403/553-2455, May–Sept.) is be-side the oldest golf course west of Winnipeg and within walking distance of downtown. It provides showers, a camp kitchen, a heated pool, laundry facilities, and a game room. Tent sites cost $17, sites with hookups $22–27.

In the heart of historic downtown, the **Town Bake Shop** (220 Col. Macleod Blvd., 403/553-4124, Mon.–Sat. 5:30 A.M.–6 P.M.) offers tasty cooked breakfasts from $4.50 and similarly priced sandwiches and bagels the rest of the day.

The **Tourist Information Centre** (east end of town on Hwy. 3, 403/553-4955, www.fort macleod.com) is open mid-May–Aug. daily 9 A.M.–5 P.M.

Lethbridge and Vicinity

An urban oasis on the prairies, this city of rich ethnic origins has come a long way since the 1860s when Fort Whoop-Up, the most notorious whiskey-trading fort in the West, was the main reason folks came to town. Today, Lethbridge (pop. 70,000) is an important commercial center serving the surrounding ranch and farm country. The city is also a transportation hub, with Highways 3, 4, and 5 converging here. Calgary is 216 kilometers (134 mi.) to the north, Medicine Hat 168 kilometers (104 mi.) to the east, Waterton Lakes National Park 130 kilometers (81 mi.) to the west, and the United States border 105 kilometers (65 mi.) to the south.

Native History

This area was the territory of various tribes of the powerful Blackfoot Confederacy. They sheltered from the extreme winters at a site in the Oldman River Valley known to them as *Sik-ooh-kotoks* (black rocks). The first white traders to the area arrived in the 1850s. Soon after came the whiskey traders who had been forced north by the U.S. Army. Fort Whoop-Up, built on the east bank of the Oldman River, became the most notorious of approximately 50 whiskey posts in southern Alberta. The arrival of whiskey on the plains coincided with a smallpox epidemic and the dislocation of the Cree, who had been forced by the arrival of European settlers into the terri-tory of the Blackfoot, their traditional enemies. These factors combined to create a setting for the last great intertribal battle to be fought in North America. At dawn on October 25, 1870, a party of approximately 800 Cree warriors attacked a band of Blood Blackfoot camping on the west bank of the Oldman River. Unknown to the Cree, a large party of Peigan Blackfoot was camped nearby. Alerted by scouts, the Peigan crossed the river and joined the fray, forcing the Cree back into what is now known as Indian Battle Park. More than 300 Cree and approximately 50 Blackfoot were killed.

SIGHTS

Downtown Lethbridge is relatively compact and parking is easy to come by. It's possible to walk from here to the sights and parks along the valley bottom, but then you're left with an uphill trek back to your vehicle.

Downtown

Housed in a former hospital, the **Sir Alexander Galt Museum** (5th Ave. S off Scenic Dr., 403/320-4248, daily 10 A.M.–4:30 P.M., free) is considered one of the best small-city museums in the country. The main gallery provides a view across the valley—in effect a panorama of the city's past. From this vantage point, you can see the

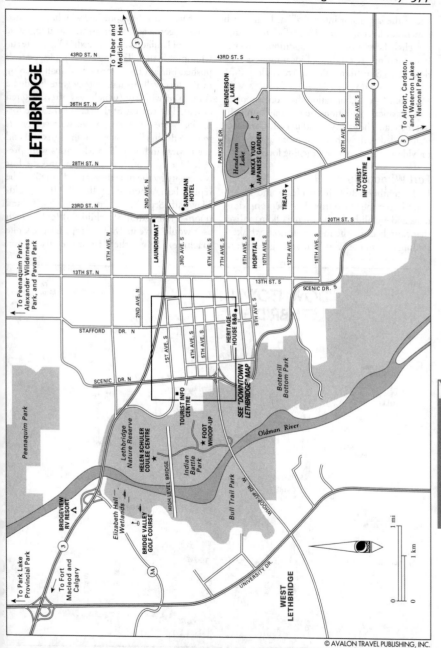

LETHBRIDGE

To Taber and Medicine Hat

43RD ST. N
36TH ST. N
28TH ST. N
23RD ST. N
13TH ST. N

43RD ST. S

HENDERSON LAKE
Henderson Lake
NIKKA YUKO JAPANESE GARDEN
PARKSIDE DR.

To Airport, Cardston, and Waterton Lakes National Park

TOURIST INFO CENTRE

To Peenaquim Park, Alexander Wilderness Park, and Pavan Park

2ND AVE. N
5TH AVE. N
LAUNDROMAT
SANDMAN HOTEL

3RD AVE. S
6TH AVE. S
7TH AVE. S
9TH AVE. S
HOSPITAL
10TH AVE. S
12TH AVE. S
16TH AVE. S
20TH AVE. S
23RD AVE. S
20TH AVE. S

TREATS

20TH ST. S
13TH ST. S
SCENIC DR. S

STAFFORD DR. N
2ND AVE. N
1ST AVE. S
4TH AVE. S
5TH AVE. S
9TH AVE. S

HERITAGE HOUSE B&B

SEE "DOWNTOWN LETHBRIDGE" MAP

SCENIC DR. N

Botterill Bottom Park

TOURIST INFO CENTRE

Peenaquim Park

Lethbridge Nature Reserve
HELEN SCHULER COULEE CENTRE

FOOT WHOOP-UP

Indian Battle Park

Oldman River

BRIDGEVIEW RV RESORT

To Park Lake Provincial Park

To Fort Macleod and Calgary

Elizabeth Hall Wetlands

BRIDGE VALLEY GOLF COURSE

HIGH LEVEL BRIDGE

Bull Trail Park

WHOOP-UP DR. N

UNIVERSITY DR.

WEST LETHBRIDGE

ALBERTA

1 mi
1 km

© AVALON TRAVEL PUBLISHING, INC.

site of the last major intertribal battle in North America, old coal mines, Fort Whoop-Up, and the High Level Bridge. Two additional galleries have rotating art exhibits of local interest. The downtown **Southern Alberta Art Gallery** (601 3rd Ave. S, 403/327-8770, Tues.–Sat. 10 A.M.–5 P.M., Sun. 1–5 P.M., donation) has contemporary and historical exhibitions that change throughout the year. The gallery is within **Galt Gardens** a well-tended park with lots of nice big trees that provide a shaded spot for lunching locals.

Fort Whoop-Up

In December 1869, John Healy and Alfred Hamilton came north from Fort Benton, Montana, and established a fort on the Oldman River that soon became the most notorious whiskey-trading post in the West. The story goes that its name was coined by someone who had returned to Fort Benton and, when asked how things were going at Hamilton's Fort, replied, "Oh, they're still whoopin' it up." Trading was simple. Natives pushed buffalo hides through a small opening in the fort wall. In return they were handed a tin cup of whiskey (which was often watered down). The success of the trade led to the formation of the NWMP, who rode west with orders to close down all whiskey-trading forts and end the lawless industry. The Mounties were preceded by word of their approach, and the fort was empty by the time they arrived in 1874. The replica Fort Whoop-Up (403/329-0444, mid-May–early Sept. Mon.–Sat. 10 A.M.–6 P.M., Sun. noon–5 P.M., adult $5, child $4) looks much as it would have in 1869 (except for the Coke machine). To get there from the city center,

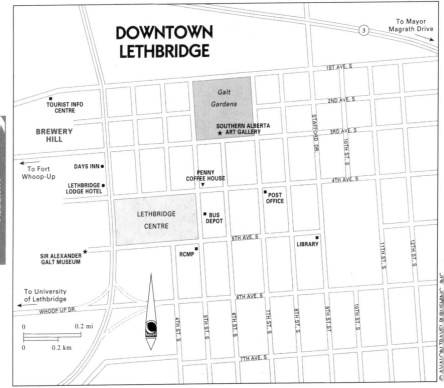

DOWNTOWN LETHBRIDGE

Fort Whoop-Up is a great place to soak up Lethbridge's less-than-savory past.

turn west onto 3rd Avenue S and follow it down into the coulee.

Other Oldman River Valley Sights

High Level Bridge spans 1.6 kilometers (one mi.) and towers 100 meters (330 ft.) above the Oldman River Valley—once the longest and highest trestle-construction bridge in the world. It was built by the C.P.R. for $1.3 million in 1909, replacing 22 wooden bridges. Of the many views of the bridge available along the valley, none is better than standing directly underneath it (walk down from the Tourist Information Centre on Brewery Hill).

Lethbridge is unique in that it's built on the prairie benchlands and not beside the river that flows so close to town. The largely undisturbed Oldman River Valley has been developed into reserves and parks, including **Lethbridge Nature Reserve,** an 82-hectare (202-acre) area of floodplain and coulees below the High Level Bridge. Here, the **Helen Schuler Coulee Centre** (403/320-3064, June–Aug. Sun.–Thurs.

10 A.M.–8 P.M., Fri.–Sat. 10 A.M.–6 P.M., rest of year Tues.–Sun. 1–4 P.M.) offers interpretive displays and is the starting point for three short trails.

Nikka Yuko Japanese Garden

This garden (Henderson Lake Park, Mayor Magrath Dr., 403/328-3511, mid-May–mid-Oct. daily 10 A.M.–4 P.M., until 8 P.M. July–Aug., adult $5, senior $4, child $3) has been designed as a place to relax and contemplate, with no bright flowers, only green shrubs and gardens of rock and sand. The main pavilion is of traditional design, housing a *tokonoma* or tea ceremony room. Japanese women in traditional dress lead visitors through the gardens and explain the philosophy behind different aspects of the design. A short trail leads around the main body of water to the bell tower, whose gentle "gong" signifies good things happening in both countries simultaneously. A special presentation is made Sunday at 1:30 P.M., which may be anything from a bonsai-pruning demonstration to a traditional Japanese sword fight.

ALBERTA

ACCOMMODATIONS AND CAMPING

$50–100

Heritage House B&B (1115 8th Ave. S, 403/328-3824) is an excellent alternative to the motels. The 1937 home is considered one of the finest examples of international art deco design in the province. Its two guest rooms are spacious and tastefully decorated, a hearty breakfast is served downstairs in the dining room, and town is only a short walk along the tree-lined streets of Lethbridge's most sought-after suburb. The bathroom is shared, but for $50 s, $65 d, that's of little consequence.

The downtown **Days Inn** (100 3rd Ave. S, 403/327-6000 or 800/661-8085, from $79 s or d) offers full-on consistency and plenty of amenities at a reasonable price. Rates include continental breakfast, in-room coffee, a daily paper, and use of an indoor pool and exercise room.

Over $100

Inside the nine-story **Sandman Hotel Lethbridge** (421 Mayor Magrath Dr. S, 403/328-1111 or 800/726-3626, www.sandmanhotels.com), all 139 rooms are tastefully decorated and air-conditioned. Also in the hotel is an indoor pool, a business center, and a 24-hour restaurant. Standard rooms are $109, or upgrade to a king suite for $129.

Lethbridge Lodge Hotel (320 Scenic Dr. S, 403/328-1123 or 800/661-1232, www.lethbridgelodge.com) is a modern, full-service hotel with a prime downtown location. The 191 big, bright rooms come in five configurations. Some have views of the Oldman River Valley, the others of an enclosed tropical atrium. Amenities include a café, a restaurant, a lounge, and an indoor pool. Rack rate is $159 s or d, but check the website for rates discounted to around $100.

Campgrounds

Henderson Lake Campground (7th Ave. S in Henderson Lake Park, 403/328-5452) has full hookups, showers, a laundry room, groceries, firewood, and fire rings. The serviced section is little more than a paved parking lot, but tenters and those with small vans enjoy the privacy afforded by trees at the back of the campground. Unserviced sites cost $18; those with hookups are $23–28. **Bridgeview RV Resort** (on west bank of Oldman River at 910 4th Ave. S, 403/381-2357, May–Sept., $23–32) has similar facilities to Henderson Lake Campground, as well as a heated pool and a restaurant, but the nearby highway can be noisy.

FOOD

Downtown

Lethbridge has some fine coffee shops; the pick of the bunch is **Penny Coffee House** (331 5th St. S, 403/320-5282, Mon.–Fri. 7:30 A.M.–10 P.M., Sat. 7:30 A.M.–5:30 P.M., Sun. 10 A.M.–5 P.M.), where coffee is under $2, refills are free, and a nice, thick, healthy sandwich with soup is $6.50.

Bontanica (Lethbridge Lodge Hotel, 320 Scenic Dr. S, 403/328-1123 daily 6:30 A.M.–10 P.M.) is a cool, clean space with lots of healthy choices. Breakfast is especially good and prices all day are surprisingly inexpensive. At the entrance is a coffee bar. In the same hotel is **Anton's,** as close as it gets to fine dining in southern Alberta. The menu features a lot of steak and seafood prepared with European flair. The table d'hôte ($30) is the best way to enjoy a meal without breaking the budget.

Mayor Magrath Drive

As well as having the bulk of Lethbridge's accommodations, this road has many fast-food and family restaurants. **Treats Eatery** (1104 Mayor Magrath Dr. S, 403/380-4880, Mon.–Sat. 11 A.M.–10 P.M., Sun. 4–10 P.M.) is a Western-style family-dining restaurant. It has an enormous gold-rimmed wagon wheel hanging from the ceiling—ask to sit away from it if you like. The menu is straightforward, basically burgers and beef, but is well priced, with steaks $16–20.

INFORMATION AND SERVICES

Lethbridge has two information centers. The biggest is the **Mayor Magrath Tourist Information Centre** (2805 Scenic Dr., 403/320-1222, summer daily 9 A.M.–8 P.M., rest of year daily 9 A.M.–5 P.M.), on the south side of the city where Magrath Drive and Scenic Drive meet. The second, **Brewery Gardens Tourist Information Centre** (403/320-1223, mid-May–Sept. daily 9 A.M.–8 P.M., Sept.–Oct. Tues.–Sat. 9 A.M.–5 P.M.), is on the western edge of downtown. If you're traveling in from the west (Fort Macleod), take the 1st Avenue S exit as Highway 3 climbs from the Oldman River Valley; it's straight after the High Level Bridge on the right.

Lethbridge Public Library (810 5th Ave. S, 403/380-7310, Mon.–Fri. 9:30 A.M.–9 P.M., Sat. 9:30 A.M.–5:30 P.M., Sun. 1:30–5:30 P.M.) is an excellent facility with a wide range of literature.

The post office (704 4th Ave. S) is in a historic stone building. Make a rainy day of it at **Family Coin Laundry** (128 Mayor Magrath Dr. N, daily 7:30 A.M.–8:30 P.M.), one block north of the highway, where there's a lounge, a TV, and free coffee. Contact **Lethbridge Regional Hospital** (9th Ave. and 18th St. S, 403/382-6111) or the **RCMP** (403/329-5010) for emergency services or police assistance.

TRANSPORTATION

Lethbridge Airport is eight kilometers (five mi.) south of town on Highway 5. It's served by **Air Canada** connectors (888/247-2262) from Calgary 4–7 times daily. Major motels and car-rental companies—**Budget** (403/328-6555), **Hertz** (403/382-3470), and the like—have courtesy phones at the airport. A cab to downtown is approximately $20. Buses leave daily from the **Greyhound** bus depot (411 5th St. S, 403/327-1551 or 800/661-8747) for Fort Macleod and Calgary.

LA Transit (403/320-3885) buses run throughout the city at $2 per sector. For a taxi, call **Lethbridge Cabs** (403/327-4005).

CARDSTON AND VICINITY

Cardston (population 3,500), 76 kilometers (47 mi.) southwest of Lethbridge and 35 kilometers (22 mi.) north of the U.S. border, has a richly religious heritage and a fine carriage museum.

The town was founded in 1887 by Charles Ora Card of the Church of Jesus Christ of Latter-Day Saints (better known as the Mormon Church), after he led 11 families north from Utah in covered wagons. The small cabin he built still stands on its original location (337 Main St., June–Aug. Mon.–Sat. 1:30 A.M.–5 P.M.).

Remington-Alberta Carriage Centre

This world-class museum (623 Main St., 403/653-5139, May 15–Aug. 9 A.M.–6 P.M., rest of year 10 A.M.–5 P.M., adult $6.50, senior $5.50, child $1.50) focusing on the era of horse-drawn transportation, holds North America's largest collection of carriages, buggies, and wagons—more than 210 at last count. The main exhibit galleries tell the story of the horse-and-buggy era through a life-sized early-20th-century townscape. You can transport yourself through time by watching blacksmiths at work in the carriage factory, listening to deals being made at the carriage dealer, or wandering over to the racetrack, where the rich liked to be seen in their elegant carriages.

Alberta Temple

While living in simple log cabins, the early Mormon pioneers started planning the construction of the first Mormon temple built outside of the United States. The Cardston Alberta Temple of the Church of Jesus Christ of Latter-Day Saints, to give its full name, is a grandly symmetrical marble and granite structure that is visible from just about everywhere in town. Only members of the Mormon faith in good standing may enter the temple itself, although a visitors center (348 3rd St. W, 403/653-1696, May–Sept. 9 A.M.–9 P.M.) beside the main entrance is open to the public.

Nearby Parks

Original surveys of the area show what is now **Woolford Provincial Park** as an island in the St. Mary River. A stand of large cottonwood trees here provides a pleasant, shaded area surrounded by prairie. The campground is small, and facilities are limited to picnic tables, firewood, and pit toilets. Sites are $13 per night.

To reach the park, travel three kilometers (1.9 mi.) northeast of Cardston on Highway 3, then southeast for 13 kilometers (eight mi.) along a gravel road.

South of Cardston is the Old Mormon Trail that settlers from Utah used on their way north. The town of **Aetna,** just off Highway 2, was once a thriving Mormon community with a cheese factory, a school, and a store. A worthwhile stop in Aetna is **Jensen's Trading Post,** a general store with an interesting collection of antiques.

Beyond the turnoff to Aetna, Highway 2 continues south to **Police Outpost Provincial Park,** on a small lake beside the International Boundary. The police outpost that gave the lake and park their name was set up in 1891 to control smuggling of whiskey north across the border, but the remote location led to its closure soon after. The park's campground ($17) has pit toilets and picnic tables.

Accommodations

The choices are simple here—good-value motel rooms or camping downtown or in one of the nearby provincial parks. Least expensive of Cardston's motels is the **Flamingo Motel** (848 Main St., 403/653-3952 or 888/806-6835, $65 s, $75 d), two blocks up the hill from the Remington-Alberta Carriage Centre. The 38 rooms each have a fridge and microwave while other amenities include a small outdoor pool, barbecue area, and coin laundry.

Within walking distance of the Remington-Alberta Carriage Centre is **Lee Creek Campground** (at end of 7th Ave. W, off Main St., 403/653-3734, May–Sept., $15–20), with full hookups and showers.

Information

The **Tourist Information Centre** (621 Main St., 403/653-3787, mid-May–Aug. daily 8 A.M.–8 P.M.) is in a big open-plan building at the entrance to the carriage museum. **Cardston Book Shop** (226 Main St., 403/653-4222, Mon.–Sat. 9 A.M.–6 P.M.) has an interesting selection of religious books and texts, as well as small selection of general Canadiana.

SOUTHEAST FROM LETHBRIDGE ON HIGHWAY 4

From Lethbridge, it's a fast 105 kilometers (65 mi.) to the Coutts–Sweetgrass border crossing, which leads into Montana. Hopefully you're not planning on leaving Alberta just yet, because along the way are two out-of-the-way attractions well worth your attention.

The dominate feature of the barren landscape south of Lethbridge is the **Milk River.** This waterway is unique among western Canada's river systems in that it is the only one that flows south to the Missouri River, eventually draining into the Gulf of Mexico.

Devil's Coulee

On May 14, 1987, Wendy Slobada, an amateur paleontologist, was exploring the coulees near her family's ranch outside of Milk River when she discovered some fossilized eggshells. The find

Cut across Highway 61 to Medicine Hat and you'll pass by a collection of windmills at Etzikom.

sent waves of excitement around the scientific world, and the site became known as **Devil's Coulee Dinosaur Egg Site.** What she had found were clutches of eggs that had been laid by hadrosaurs approximately 75 million years ago. Each prehistoric egg was about 20 centimeters (eight in.) long and contained the perfectly formed embryonic bones of unhatched dinosaurs. No other find in the entire world has taught scientists more about this part of the dinosaur's life cycle.

Devil's Coulee Dinosaur Heritage Museum (403/642-2118, www.devilscoulee.com, late May–Aug. daily 9 A.M.–5 P.M.) is in the village of Warner, on Highway 4, 66 kilometers (41 mi.) southeast of Lethbridge. It's only a small facility, but a display reconstructs the site. Tours to the actual site leave from the museum daily throughout summer at 10 A.M. and 2 P.M. Tour cost is $15 per person and advance reservations are required.

Writing-On-Stone Provincial Park

This park, off Highway 501 43 kilometers (27 mi.) east of the town of Milk River, has the largest concentrations of petroglyphs and pictographs found in North America. But that's only one of the reasons to venture out into this remote part of the province: a warm river for swimming, great canoeing, intriguing rock formations, and abundant wildlife round out one of Alberta's premier nonmountain parks. The park protects a stretch of the Milk River that has cut a deep valley into the rolling shortgrass prairie. Soft sandstone and shale cliffs are capped with harder, iron-rich sediments. Years of wind and water erosion have carved out the softer, lower rock, leaving mushroom-shaped pinnacles and columns called **hoodoos.**

Writing-On-Stone was a place of great spiritual importance to generations of natives, a place for contact with the supernatural. They attempted to interpret previous carvings and paintings, added their own artwork to the rock, and left gifts of tobacco and beads as a way of communicating with the spirits of the dead. Much of the cliff art remains visible today, providing clues to the region's early inhabitants. Artifacts excavated from below the cliffs suggest that the area had been inhabited for at least 3,000 years, but any rock art

of that age would have been destroyed by erosion long ago. Of the carvings visible today, the earliest are thought to be the work of the Shoshoni, created approximately 700 years ago. During the 1730s, the Shoshoni were driven into the mountains by the Blackfoot. The valley's strange rock formations led the Blackfoot to believe that the area was a magical place—a place to be respected and feared—and that existing carvings were created by the spirits. The Blackfoot added their own artistry to the rocks, and many of the Blackfoot carvings are panels that tell a story. The **Hoodoo Interpretive Trail** is a two-kilometer (1.2-mi.) hike along the cliffs, with numbered posts that correspond to a trail brochure available from the information center. Along the way are some examples of petroglyphs and pictographs (including the famous battle scene) that have been ravaged by time and vandals.

The park has an excellent campground nestled below the hoodoos in a stand of cottonwood trees. Adjacent is a beach with canoe rentals, and an interpretive program is operated in conjunction with park staff. Services such as showers and firewood sales ($5 per bundle) are available April–mid-September, but the campground is open year-round. Unserviced sites are $16, powered sites $20. Reservations are taken (403/647-2877 or 877/877-3515). For more information on the park, call 403/647-2364.

HIGHWAY 3 EAST FROM LETHBRIDGE
Coaldale

The first town east of Lethbridge on Highway 3 is Coaldale, with a population of 7,200. The main reason to leave the highway here is to visit the **Alberta Birds of Prey Centre** (north of Hwy. 3 at 20th St., then left on 16th Ave., 403/345-4262, mid-May–mid-Oct. daily 9:30 A.M.–5 P.M.). The aim of this off-the-beaten-path center is to ensure the survival of birds of prey such as hawks, falcons, eagles, and the great horned owl, Alberta's provincial bird. Many of the birds are brought to the center injured or as young chicks. They are nurtured at the center until they are strong enough to be released back into the wild. The interpretive building features the works of various wildlife artists and has displays cataloging the human fascination with birds of prey through thousands of years. Behind the building, trails lead past birds that are recovering from injury, tame birds, and a cage where birds fly free. Visitors are invited to watch daily "flying programs" and the opportunity to be photographed with a falcon. Entry to the main building is free, but it costs adult $7, senior $6 to enter the compounds and take part in interpretive programs.

Taber

Taber, 51 kilometers (32 mi.) east of Lethbridge, is most famous for its deliciously sweet **Taber corn.** Long hot days and cool nights bring out a sweetness that isn't found in regular corn. August and early September is the best time to look for corn vendors along the road. Or find corn, along with other fresh local produce, each Thursday at the farmers market in the Taber Agriplex. On the last weekend of August, when the corn has ripened, the town's **Cornfest** celebration takes place, with a pancake breakfast, a midway, hot-air-balloon flights, a classic-car show, and, of course, plenty of corn to taste.

Taber Provincial Park (May–Sept., $17), on a floodplain above the Oldman River two kilometers (1.2 mi.) west, then three kilometers (1.9 mi.) north of town, is a welcome relief from the surrounding prairie. Campsites are situated near a stand of large cottonwood trees.

Calgary to Medicine Hat

The TransCanada Highway heads out of Calgary in a southeasterly direction. It passes through Bassano, and then Brooks, gateway to Dinosaur Provincial Park (see Drumheller and Vicinity in the Central Alberta chapter) before reaching Medicine Hat after 300 kilometers (186 mi.).

STRATHMORE AND VICINITY

From Calgary, the TransCanada Highway parallels the Bow River (although it's never in sight) 100 kilometers (62 mi.) to Bassano. The only town along the way is Strathmore, home to the large **Calgary Stockyards** (west side of town, 403/240-7694, www.teamcsy.com). Livestock auctions take place throughout summer and fall; if you're interested in attending, check the website for a schedule.

Wyndham-Carseland Provincial Park

Visit this 178-hectare (440-acre) park for the fishing and bird-watching. Rainbow and brown trout, up to 60 centimeters (24 in.) long, are caught in the Bow River where it flows through the park; the best fishing is in the deeper main channel. Also within the park is a large population of white pelicans, as well as prairie falcons, Canada geese, kingfishers, and great blue herons.

A 200-site campground is spread out along the river, and all sites are $17. The park is about 30 kilometers (19 mi.) south of Strathmore via Highway 24 or 817.

BASSANO

Bassano is on the TransCanada Highway midway between Calgary and Medicine Hat. It's a thriving agricultural town of 1,200 people.

Bassano Dam

The biggest local attraction is this dam, nine kilometers (5.6 mi.) south of Highway 1. To get there, follow the signs through town, along the rail line, and through the fields (if you cross a single-lane bridge, you're on the right road). The dam combines a 2.3-kilometer (1.4-mi.) earthen embankment with a spillway at a sharp bend in the Bow River. Water is diverted from behind the spillway into a 4,500-kilometer (2,800-mi.) system of gravity-fed canals supplying water to the 100,000-hectare (250,000-acre) **Eastern Irrigation District,** land that would otherwise be agriculturally worthless. Built by the C.P.R. between 1910 and 1914, the dam was known as the most important structure of its type in the world because of its great length and unique foundations.

RED ROCK COULEE

South of Seven Persons, the last community on Highway 3 before Medicine Hat, is a small area of badlands on a gentle rise in the surrounding plains. The bedrock here is relatively close to the surface, and wind and water erosion have cut through the topsoil to expose it. In some places, the erosion has extended into the bedrock itself, revealing varicolored strata laid down millions of years ago. This strange landscape is dotted with red boulder-shaped concretions measuring up to 2.5 meters (eight ft.) across. These intriguing rock formations formed under the surface of a prehistoric sea, when sand, calcite, and iron oxide collected on a nucleus of shells, bones, and corals. They became part of the bedrock as layers of sediment were laid down, but as erosion took its course, the surrounding bedrock disappeared and the concretions emerged. The formations here are believed to be the largest of their type in the world. To get there, follow Highway 887 south from Seven Persons for 23 kilometers (14 mi.). Where the road curves sharply to the east (left), continue straight ahead uphill on an unsealed road and park at the lone picnic table. The boulders are laid out below and to the south.

BROOKS

Brooks (pop. 10,000) is in the heart of Alberta's extensive irrigated farmlands, 160 kilometers (100 mi.) southeast of Calgary. The town began as a railway stop in the 1880s, thriving when the Canadian Pacific Railway completed the irrigation system centered on Bassano Dam. Today, it's 30,000 oil and gas wells and one of Canada's largest meat packing plants that keep the local economy rolling. For visitors, Brooks offers all tourist services and is a good base for exploring Dinosaur Provincial Park (see Drumheller and Vicinity in the Central Alberta chapter).

Sights

Brooks Aqueduct, seven kilometers (4.3 mi.) southeast of town, was a vital link within the Eastern Irrigation District until decommissioned in the 1970s. It carried water across a shallow valley to dry prairie on the other side, opening up a massive chunk of otherwise unproductive land to farming. At the time of its completion in 1914, the 3.2-kilometer (two-mi.) aqueduct was the longest concrete structure of its type in the world. Although now replaced by an earth-filled canal, the impressive structure has been preserved as a National Historic Site. Admission to the small interpretive center (403/362-4451, mid-May–Aug., 10 A.M.–6 P.M.) is free.

Budding gardeners won't want to miss the **Crop Diversification Centre** (two km/1.2 mi. east of town, 403/362-3391, summer Mon.–Fri. 9 A.M.–4 P.M., Sat.–Sun. 1–5 P.M., free), where research is done on greenhouse crops, various fruits, ornamental flowers, vegetables, oil seeds, and weed control. The grounds are an oasis of flowerbeds and experimental plots, many of which are open to the public.

Part of **Kinbrook Island Provincial Park,** 13 kilometers (eight mi.) south of Brooks, is an island in **Lake Newell,** the largest manmade body of water in Canada. Although the lake was developed as a constant source of water for Eastern Irrigation District farmland, it's swimming, fishing, and boating that draws the summertime crowds. The campground has showers, a laundry, firewood sales, and picnic shelters, and a concession with bike rentals operates during summer. Unserviced sites are $17, powered sites $20.

ALBERTA

Practicalities

As usual, the **Super 8 Motel** (Cassils Rd., 403/362-8000 or 800/800-8000, www.super8 .com, $89 s, $95 d) is a reliable mid-priced choice. At the eastern access to town, this location features 61 air-conditioned rooms, each with a microwave. A continental breakfast is included in the rates. **Kiwanis Campground** (Cassils Rd. by eastern access, $7–10) has a few pull-through powered sites and a handy highway location, but better options exist out of town. Halfway between Brooks and Tilley is **Tille-**

brook RV Park and Campground (403/362-4525, Apr.–Oct., tenting $17, hookups $20–23), an excellent base for exploring Dinosaur Provincial Park and Lake Newell, one of the province's best-developed parks. It has powered sites, enclosed shelters with gas stoves, showers, a launderette, summer interpretive programs, and a trail to the aqueduct.

Coming from the west, take the second Brooks exit from the TransCanada Highway to reach **Brooks Information Centre** (Cassils Rd., 403/362-6881, Wed.–Sun. 11 A.M.–6 P.M.).

Medicine Hat and Vicinity

The prosperous industrial city of Medicine Hat (pop. 52,000) sits on some of western Canada's most extensive natural-gas fields, 168 kilometers (104 mi.) east of Lethbridge and 40 kilometers (25 mi.) west of the Saskatchewan border. Known as "The Hat" to locals, the city straddles the South Saskatchewan River along which many areas are protected as parkland. The city also holds interesting attractions such as the remains of Canada's once-thriving pottery industry and an archeological site regarded as one of the most extensive and richest finds from the late-prehistoric period of native history. Travelers keeping an eye on their spending will also appreciate Medicine Hat—it's home to some of western Canada's cheapest motels and consistently has Canada's cheapest gas prices.

The Name Medicine Hat

Many tales describe how the name Medicine Hat evolved. One of the most popular legends tells the story of the Cree chief who led his people to the cliffs above the South Saskatchewan River. Here, the Great Serpent told him that he must sacrifice his wife to the river in exchange for a *saamis* (medicine hat). This would give him magical powers and allow him to defeat the Blackfoot when they attacked later that night. Another story tells of how the Blackfoot were forced into the waters of the South Saskatchewan River by the Cree, who then fired an arrow into the heart of the Blackfoot medicine man. As he slowly sank below the water's surface, his hat was swept away into the

hands of the Cree. The Blackfoot saw this as a terrible omen and retreated.

SIGHTS AND RECREATION

Saamis Tepee

As the location of Medicine Hat's main information center, it makes sense that you stay on the TransCanada Highway (approaching from either direction) and take the signposted exit (South Ridge Dr.) to the Saamis Tepee. Besides, standing more than 20 stories high beside the TransCanada Highway, with a base diameter of 50 meters (160 ft.) and made entirely of steel (it weighs 1,000 tons), this is one sight you don't need detailed directions to find. It overlooks Seven Persons Creek Coulee, an archaeological site used in late prehistoric times as a native camp where buffalo were dried and processed. A self-guided interpretive trail, beginning at the tepee, leads to a bluff and into the valley where the camp was located.

Downtown

Many early-20th-century buildings located in the downtown area are still in active use, including private homes, churches, and businesses. The availability of local clay led to thriving brick-manufacturing plants here during the late 1800s; many original buildings still stand in mute testimony to the quality of the bricks. Because of the abundance of natural gas in the area, city officials in the early days found it cheaper to leave the city's gas

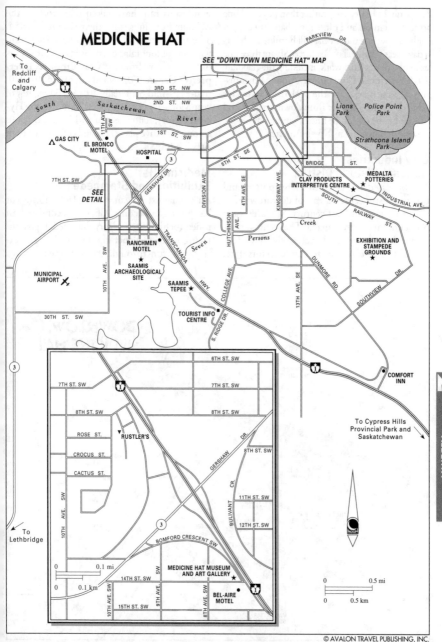

MEDICINE HAT

SEE "DOWNTOWN MEDICINE HAT" MAP

SEE DETAIL

To Redcliff and Calgary

South Saskatchewan River

Parkview Dr.

3RD ST. NW
2ND ST. NW

11TH AVE. SW
1ST ST. SW

GAS CITY
EL BRONCO MOTEL
HOSPITAL

7TH ST. SW

GERSHAW DR.

5TH ST. SE

BRIDGE ST.

Lions Park
Police Point Park
Strathcona Island Park

MEDALTA POTTERIES
CLAY PRODUCTS INTERPRETIVE CENTRE

INDUSTRIAL AVE.

DIVISION AVE.
4TH AVE. SE
KINGSWAY AVE.
HUTCHINSON AVE.

SOUTH RAILWAY ST.

Seven Persons Creek

RANCHMEN MOTEL
SAAMIS ARCHAEOLOGICAL SITE
SAAMIS TEPEE

TRANSCANADA HWY.

COLLEGE AVE.

EXHIBITION AND STAMPEDE GROUNDS

DUNMORE RD.
SOUTHVIEW DR.
13TH AVE. SE

MUNICIPAL AIRPORT

30TH ST. SW

TOURIST INFO CENTRE

S. RIDGE DR.

10TH AVE. SW

To Lethbridge

COMFORT INN

To Cypress Hills Provincial Park and Saskatchewan

6TH ST. SW
7TH ST. SW
7TH ST. SW

8TH ST. SW
8TH ST. SW

ROSE ST.
RUSTLER'S
CROCUS ST.
CACTUS ST.

GERSHAW DR.

8TH ST. SW

11TH ST. SW
12TH ST. SW

10TH AVE. SW

BULIVANT CR.

BOMFORD CRESCENT SW

MEDICINE HAT MUSEUM AND ART GALLERY

BEL-AIRE MOTEL

14TH ST. SW
15TH ST. SW

9TH AVE. SW
8TH AVE. SW
10TH AVE. SW

0   0.1 mi
0   0.1 km

0   0.5 mi
0   0.5 km

MOON

ALBERTA

lamps on 24 hours a day rather than pay someone to turn them on and off. More than 200 copper replicas now line the streets, still burning 24 hours a day. Near City Hall on 1st Street SE are three fine examples of this brickwork, including the elaborate 1919 **Provincial Courthouse.** Among other historical landmarks are the 1913 **St. Patrick's Church** (across the river from downtown on 2nd St.), said to be one of the finest examples of Gothic Revival architecture in North America.

Clay Industries
National Historic District

Nearby clay deposits led to a large pottery and brick industry centered east of downtown. For the first 50 years of last century, **Medalta** was a household name in Canada. Their china, popular in homes and used exclusively by C.P.R.-owned hotels, is now prized by collectors. Fire,

wind, and rain have taken their toll on the Medalta buildings since their closure in 1954. The site is currently undergoing restoration, with one of four kilns open for inspection. Tours of the site leave from the **Clay Products Interpretive Centre** (703 Wood St., 403/529-1070, mid-May–mid-Sept. daily 10 A.M.–5 P.M., rest of year Mon.–Fri. 9 A.M.–4 P.M.) in the nearby **Hycroft** factory, renowned for its 1950s and 1960s commemorative plates. A combo ticket for both sites is adult $8, senior $6.

Medicine Hat
Exhibition and Stampede

An annual extravaganza since 1887, this event has grown to become Alberta's second-richest rodeo (behind the Calgary Stampede), guaranteeing knuckle-clenching, bronc-riding, foot-stompin' fun through the last week of July.

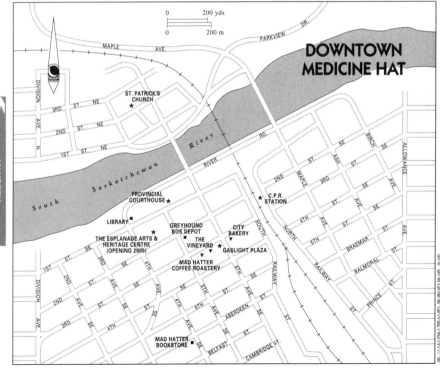

Various events are held throughout the city, culminating with the weekend rodeo and chuck wagon races. The stampede also features many exhibitors displaying their wares, as well as a midway, a Pioneer Village, a trade show, and lots of free entertainment. A top country act is the Saturday night feature. For more information, contact the stampede office (403/527-1234, www.mhstampede.com).

ACCOMMODATIONS AND CAMPING

Under $50

Medicine Hat is one of the only places in western Canada with a *choice* of motels offering rooms less than $50. Most are bunched together along the downtown side of the TransCanada Highway around Gershaw Drive. The best value is the **Bel-Aire Motel** (633 14th St. SW, 403/527-4421, $38 s, $46 d). The 12 rooms are cooled by noisy air-conditioners and each has a small fridge. Rooms at the others aren't as nice (obviously, this is relative) as at the Bel-Aire, but they're as cheap as you'll find on your travels. Try the **Ranchmen Motel** (1617 Bomford Cres., 403/527-2263, $40 s, $44 d), which has a tired-looking minigolf course.

$50–100

Rising from an area of strip malls beside the TransCanada Highway, the **Comfort Inn** (2317 TransCanada Hwy., 403/504-1700 or 800/228-5150) is easily recognized by its modern lines and burgundy and yellow color scheme. The sharp design is carried through into the 100 guest rooms, each which comes loaded with amenities. Other features are an indoor pool, business center, and fitness room. Local calls and a big continental breakfast are included in the rates of $90 s or d (reduced to $70 outside of summer), making it an excellent choice for a mid-priced stay in Medicine Hat.

Campgrounds

Gas City Campground (403/528-8158, May–Sept.) is on the edge of town, has nearly 100 sites, and is far enough away from the highway to be relatively quiet. From the back of the campground, a

trail heads along the river and into town. At night, this is a good spot from which to view the illumination of Medicine Hat's industrial core. Tent sites are $16, hookups $24–30. Good hot showers, laundry facilites, groceries, and full hookups make this the place to try first. To get there, turn off the highway at 7th Street SW and follow the signs down 11th Avenue.

OTHER PRACTICALITIES

Food

Mad Hatter Coffee Roastery (513 3rd St. SE, 403/529-2344, Mon.–Fri. 7 A.M.–5:30 P.M., Sat. 8 A.M.–5:30 P.M., Sun. 10 A.M.–5 P.M.) is a funky little space with a few tables out front. Coffee is just $1. **City Bakery** (317 6th Ave. SE, 403/527-2800, Mon.–Fri. 7:30 A.M.–5:30 P.M.) has lots of old-fashioned cakes and pastries, while sandwiches and bagels are made to order. The mocha slushie machine looks a little out of place in this traditional bakehouse, but the resulting drink is delicious.

Medicine Hat's best dining is at **The Vineyard** (579 3rd St. SE, 403/528-2666, daily 11 A.M.–2 P.M. and dinner from 5 P.M.). Reserve a table or arrive early to snag a table in the courtyard. The menu has something to suit all tastes, with everything from buffalo burgers to burritos on a menu that ranges $15–24 for entrées. Service is as professional as you'll find in southern Alberta.

If you're staying in one of the cheap highway motels, money is obviously important to you. If that's the case, you'll want to head to **Rustler's** (901 8th St. SW, 403/526-8004, daily 6 A.M.–11 P.M.) for a meal. It's one of the city's oldest eating establishments and because of its history (see the menu for its amusing history), a real Wild West atmosphere prevails. Seating is out back in the tavern or in a restaurant section where set out under the glass top of one table is a poker game complete with gun and bloodstained playing cards. The place is popular all day, but breakfast is especially crowded. Large portions of eggs, bacon, and hash browns begin at $5, omelets at $5.50. For the rest of the day, it's hard to beat the beef. Last time through I enjoyed the Alberta ribeye with roast potatoes and vegetables ($12–18 depending on the cut). The vegetables were ordinary, but the steak was exactly as I ordered it.

Information

To get to the **Tourist Information Centre** (8 Gehring Rd. SE, 403/527-6422 or 800/481-2822, mid-June–Aug. daily 8 A.M.–7 P.M., rest of year Mon.–Fri. 9 A.M.–5 P.M., Sat. 10 A.M.–3 P.M.), take the Southridge Drive exit from the Trans-Canada Highway just east of the big tepee. A good city website is www.city.medicine-hat.ab.ca.

Up the hill from downtown, **Mad Hatter Bookstore** (399 Aberdeen St. SE, 403/526-8563, Mon.–Fri. 9:30 A.M.–5:30 P.M., Sat. 9 A.M.–5 P.M.) has thousands of used books in relatively well-organized categories. The large **Medicine Hat Public Library** (414 1st St. SE, 403/502-8527, Mon.–Thurs. 10 A.M.–9 P.M., Fri.–Sat. 10 A.M.–5:30 P.M., Sun. 1–5:30 P.M.) overlooks the river and has a free paperback exchange.

CYPRESS HILLS PROVINCIAL PARK

Covering an area of 200 square kilometers (77 sq. mi.), Cypress Hills occupies a small section of an upland plateau that extends well into Saskatchewan, with the entire area protected as **Cypress Hills Provincial Park.** The hills rise as high as 500 meters (1,640 ft.) above the surrounding grasslands, and at their highest elevation (1,466 m/4,800 ft., the same as the town Banff), they are the highest point between the Canadian Rockies and Labrador. The French word for lodgepole pine is *cyprès,* which led to the hills being named Les Montagnes de Cyprès, and thus Cypress Hills, when in fact cypress trees have never grown in the park.

The park is 70 kilometers (43 mi.) southeast of Medicine Hat along Highway 41. It offers good hiking, fishing, or just plain relaxing and is popular as a place to escape the high summer temperatures of the prairies. The only commercial facilities are in the townsite of **Elkwater,** which sits in a natural amphitheater overlooking **Elkwater Lake.** The facilities are limited (no bank, one restaurant, one motel, one gas station), so come prepared.

Flora and Fauna

The park supports more than 400 recorded plant species in four ecological zones: **prairie, parkland, foothills,** and **boreal forest.** The best way to view the flora of the park is on foot; many trails pass through two or three zones in the space of an hour's walking. Sixteen species of orchid are found in the park—some are very common, whereas others, such as the sparrow's egg lady's slipper, are exceedingly rare.

The unique environment of the hills provides a favorable habitat for 37 species of mammals, 400 species of birds, and a few turtles. Big game was once common throughout the hills, but in 1926 the last remaining large mammal—a wolf—was shot. Soon thereafter, elk were reintroduced to the park and now number more than 200. Moose, never before present in the park, were introduced in the 1950s and now number about 60.

Exploring the Park

Various roads link the townsite of Elkwater to lakes and viewpoints within the park. To access the center of the park, take Reesor Lake Road east from Highway 41, passing a viewpoint with spectacular vistas of the transition from grassland to boreal forest. The road then descends steeply to **Reesor Lake,** which has a campground, a picnic area, a short hiking trail to a viewpoint, and excellent fishing for rainbow trout. Bull Trail Road off Reesor Lake Road leads to **Spruce Coulee** and a reservoir stocked with eastern brook and rainbow trout.

Just east of the marina, **Elkwater Boat & Bike Rentals** (403/893-3835) rents mountain bikes ($5 per hour, $25 per day), canoes ($8 per hour, $40 per day), motorboats ($16 per hour), and personal watercraft ($55 per hour).

Practicalities

Green Tree Motel (401 4th St., 403/893-3811) is the only motel in the park. The 13 basic motel rooms ($60 s or d) have TVs but no phones. Larger log cabins are self-contained; each has a kitchen and fireplace ($80).

Within the park are more than 500 campsites in 12 campgrounds. The main camping season is mid-May–mid-September, although some campgrounds remain open year-round with limited services. Closest to Elkwater are **Beaver Creek Campground** ($24) with full hookups and **Elkwater Campground** ($17–24) with unserviced and serviced sites. Both have showers. Of the other campgrounds, you'll find the most solitude at **Reesor Lake Campground** ($15, no showers or hookups)—except for the bugling elk in fall.

The large **Cypress Hills Visitor Centre** (403/893-3833, mid-May–Aug. daily 9 A.M.–5 P.M.) overlooks Elkwater Lake, a short walk from the townsite campgrounds. Audiovisual programs explain the natural history and archaeological and historical resources of the park and a nightly interpretive program operates during July and August. The website www.cypresshills.com is a good source of general park information.

Waterton Lakes National Park

Everybody traveling to this rugged 526-square-kilometer (203-sq.-mi.) park does so by choice. It's not on the way to anywhere else or on a major highway, but is tucked away in the extreme southwestern corner of Alberta. The park is bounded to the north and east by the rolling prairies covering southern Alberta; to the south by the U.S. border and Glacier National Park in Montana; and to the west by the Continental Divide, which forms the Alberta–British Columbia border. The natural mountain splendor, a chain of deep glacial lakes, large and diverse populations of wildlife, and an unbelievable variety of day hikes make this park a gem that shouldn't be missed.

The route to Waterton is almost as scenic as the park itself. From whichever direction you arrive, the transition from prairie to mountains is abrupt, almost devoid of the foothills that characterize other areas along the eastern slopes of the Canadian Rockies. From the park gate, two roads penetrate the mountains to the west. One ends at a large glaciated lake, the other at a spectacular canyon.

Park Entry

All visitors to Waterton Lakes are required to stop at the park entrance and buy a permit. Park entry for one day is adult $5, senior $4, to a maximum of $10 per vehicle ($8 for seniors traveling together).

THE LAND

About 1.9 million years ago, glaciers from the sheet of ice that once covered most of Alberta crept through the mountains. As these thick sheets of ice advanced and retreated with climatic changes, they gouged out valleys such as the classically U-shaped **Waterton Valley.** The three Waterton Lakes are depressions left at the base of the steep-sided mountains after the ice had completely retreated 11,000 years ago. The deepest lake is 150 meters (500 ft.). **Cameron Lake,** at the end of the Akamina Parkway, was formed when a moraine—the pile of rock that accumulates at the foot of a retreating glacier—dammed Cameron Creek. From the lake, Cameron Creek flows through a glaciated valley before dropping into the much deeper Waterton Valley at **Cameron Falls,** behind the town of Waterton. The town itself sits on an alluvial fan composed of silt and gravel picked up by mountain streams and deposited in Upper Waterton Lake.

Flora and Fauna

Botanists have recorded 1,200 species of plants growing within the park's several different vegetation zones. In the northeastern corner, near the park gate, a region of **prairies** is covered in semi-arid vegetation such as fescue grass. As Highway 5 enters the park it passes Maskinonge Lake, a **wetlands** area of marshy ponds where aquatic plants flourish. **Montane** forest covers most mountain valleys and lower slopes—mainly lodgepole pine and Douglas fir shading a forest floor covered with wildflowers and berries. An easily accessible section of this habitat is along the lower half of Bertha Lake Trail. Above the montane forest is the **subalpine** zone, which rises as far as the timberline. These distinct forests of larch, fir, Engelmann spruce, and whitebark pine can be seen

ALBERTA

ALBERTA

WATERTON LAKES NATIONAL PARK

5 mi

5 km

To Cardston

Paine Lake

River

Belly

INTERNATIONAL HWY.

CUSTOMS

To U.S. Highway 89 and Saint Mary, MT

17

BELLY RIVER

North Fork

CANADA

UNITED STATES

Glacier National Park

MONTANA

CROOKED CREEK

Crooked Creek

WATERTON RIVERSIDE

CHIEF MOUNTAIN

Lewis Range

Sofa Mtn.

5

6

WATERTON SPRINGS

To Pincher Creek

6

Waterton River

Brook

Galwey

Dungarvan Creek

Sofa Creek

Crypt Lake

Mt. Boswell

Vimy Peak

Hell Roaring Falls

PARK GATE

Lower Waterton Lake

5

PASS CREEK

Middle Waterton Lake

Upper Waterton Lake

Waterton Lakes National Park

Mt. Crandell

WATERTON VISITOR CENTRE

Waterton Townsite

Blakiston Creek

Crandell Lake

Bertha Lake

Campbell Mtn.

CRANDELL MOUNTAIN

Mt. Dungarvan

Mt. Galwey

Mt. Glendowan

Carthew Creek

Mt. Alderson

Creek

Boundary

Lake Wurderman

RED ROCK CANYON PKWY.

Red Rock Canyon

Blakiston Falls

Mt. Carthew

Carthew Lakes

Newman Peak

Goat Lake

Anderson Peak

Mt. Blakiston

Cameron Creek

AKAMINA PKWY.

Lineham Creek

Mt. Lineham

Rowe Lakes

Cameron Lake

Mt. Custer

Bauerman Creek

Blakiston Creek

Lone Mtn.

Lineham Lakes

Lineham

Akamina Pass

Forum Lake

Lost Lake

Twin Lakes

Akamina-Kishinena Provincial Park

Wall Lake

Forum Peak

ALBERTA

BRITISH COLUMBIA

Akamina Creek

© AVALON TRAVEL PUBLISHING, INC.

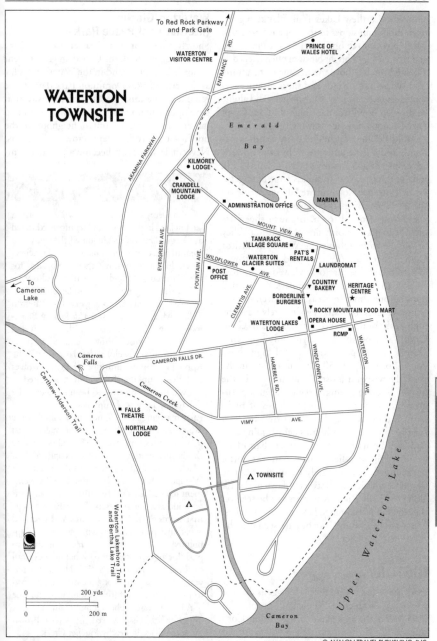

WATERTON TOWNSITE

To Red Rock Parkway and Park Gate

WATERTON VISITOR CENTRE

PRINCE OF WALES HOTEL

ENTRANCE RD.

AKAMINA PARKWAY

Emerald Bay

KILMOREY LODGE

CRANDELL MOUNTAIN LODGE

ADMINISTRATION OFFICE

MARINA

MOUNT VIEW RD.

EVERGREEN AVE.

FOUNTAIN AVE.

WILDFLOWER AVE.

TAMARACK VILLAGE SQUARE

WATERTON GLACIER SUITES

PAT'S RENTALS

LAUNDROMAT

POST OFFICE

CLEMATIS AVE.

COUNTRY BAKERY

HERITAGE CENTRE

BORDERLINE BURGERS

ROCKY MOUNTAIN FOOD MART

WATERTON LAKES LODGE

OPERA HOUSE

RCMP

WATERTON AVE.

To Cameron Lake

Cameron Falls

CAMERON FALLS DR.

HAREBELL RD.

WINDFLOWER AVE.

Carthew-Alderson Trail

Cameron Creek

FALLS THEATRE

NORTHLAND LODGE

VIMY AVE.

TOWNSITE

Waterton Lakeshore Trail and Bertha Lake Trail

Upper Waterton Lake

ALBERTA

0   200 yds
0   200 m

MOON

Cameron Bay

© AVALON TRAVEL PUBLISHING, INC.

along the Carthew Lakes Trail. Blanketing the open mountain slopes in this zone is bear grass, which grows up to one meter (3.3 ft.) in height and is topped by a bright blossom often likened to a lighted torch. Above the treeline is the **alpine** zone where harsh winds and short summer seasons make trees a rarity. Only lichens and alpine wildflowers flourish at these high altitudes. Crypt Lake is a good place for viewing this zone.

Wildlife viewing in the park requires patience and a little know-how, but the rewards are ample, as good as anywhere in Canada. Elk inhabit the park year-round. A large herd gathers by Entrance Road in late fall, wintering on the lowlands. By early fall many mule deer are wandering around town. Bighorn sheep are often seen on the north side of Blakiston Valley or on the slopes above the Waterton Visitor Centre; occasionally they end up in town. White-tailed deer are best viewed along Red Rock Canyon Parkway. The park has a small population of moose occasionally seen in low-lying wetlands. Mountain goats rarely leave the high peaks of the backcountry, but from Goat, Crypt, and Bertha Lakes you might catch a glimpse of one perched on a cliff high above you. Approximately 50 black bears live in the park. They spend most of the summer in the heavily forested montane regions. During August and September, scan the slopes of Blakiston Valley, where they can often be seen feasting on saskatoon berries before going into winter hibernation. Much larger than black bears are the grizzlies, which roam the entire backcountry but are rarely encountered. The best time for viewing beavers is dawn and dusk along the Belly River. Muskrats can be seen on the edges of Maskinonge Lake eating bulrushes. Mink also live in the lake but are seen only by those with patience.

HISTORY

Evidence found within the park suggests that the Kootenai (also spelled "Kootenay") people who lived west of the park made trips across the Continental Divide approximately 8,400 years ago to hunt bison on the plains and fish in the lakes.

Waterton-Glacier International Peace Park

Shortly after Montana's Glacier National Park was created in 1910, the Canadian government set aside an area of land in the Waterton Valley as Waterton Lakes Dominion Park (later to be renamed a national park). The townsite that developed had no rail link, so unlike Banff and Jasper—its famous mountain neighbors to the north—it didn't draw large crowds of tourists. Nevertheless, it soon became a popular sum-

"KOOTENAI" BROWN

John George "Kootenai" Brown was born in England in the 1840s and reputedly educated at Oxford University. He joined the army and went to India, later continuing to San Francisco. Then, like thousands of others, he headed for the Cariboo goldfields of British Columbia, quickly spending any of the gold he found. After a while he moved on, heading east into Waterton Valley, where his party was attacked by Blackfoot. He was shot in the back with an arrow and pulled it out himself. Brown acquired his nickname through his close association with the Kootenai people, hunting buffalo and wolves with them until they had all but disappeared.

Even though Brown had been toughened by the times, he was a conservationist at heart. After marrying in 1869, he built a cabin by the Waterton Lakes and became the valley's first permanent resident. Soon he started promoting the beauty of the area to the people of Fort Macleod. One of his friends, local rancher F. W. Godsal, began lobbying the federal government to establish a reserve. In 1895, an area was set aside as a Forest Reserve, with Brown as its first warden. In 1911, the area was declared a national park, and Brown, age 71, was appointed its superintendent. He continued to push for an expansion of park boundaries until his final retirement at age 75. He died a few years later. His grave along the main access road to the townsite is a fitting resting place for one of Alberta's most celebrated mountain men. His Waterton cabin is preserved at Kootenai Brown Pioneer Village in nearby Pincher Creek.

mer retreat with a hotel, a restaurant, and a dance hall. The Great Northern Railway decided to operate a bus service from its Montana rail line to Jasper, with a stop at Waterton Lakes. This led to the construction of the **Prince of Wales Hotel** and summer boat cruises back across the U.S. border and into Glacier National Park. This brought the two parks closer together, and in 1932 Waterton-Glacier International Peace Park was created, the first of its kind in the world. The parks are administered separately but cooperate in preserving this pristine mountain wilderness through combined wildlife management, interpretive programs, and search-and-rescue operations. Peace Park celebrations take place each year, and the **Peace Park Pavilion** by the lake is dedicated to this unique bond. In 1979, UNESCO declared the park a **Biosphere Reserve,** only the second such reserve in Canada. The park gained further recognition in 1995, when, along with Glacier National Park, it was declared a **World Heritage Site** by UNESCO.

SCENIC DRIVES

Make your first stop the **Waterton Visitor Centre** (403/859-2445, June–Aug. 9 A.M.–8 P.M., May and early Sept. 9 A.M.–5 P.M.) on the slight rise before descending to the village. Friendly park staff will supply maps, trail descriptions, and detail any area closures.

Akamina Parkway

This road starts in the townsite and switchbacks up into Cameron Creek Valley, making an elevation gain of 400 meters (1,310 ft.) before ending after 16 kilometers (10 mi.) at Cameron Lake. The viewpoint one kilometer (0.6 mi.) from the junction of the park road is on a tight curve, so park off the road. From this lookout, views extend over the entire valley. This section of the road is also a good place to view bighorn sheep. From here to Cameron Lake are a number of picnic areas and stops of interest, including the site of Alberta's first producing oil well, and a little farther along the road, the site of **Oil City,** home of the first producing oil well in western

Canada; all that remains are the ill-fated hotel foundations and some depressions in the ground.

Cameron Lake, at the end of the road, is a 2.5-kilometer-long (1.5 mi.) subalpine lake that reaches depths over 40 meters (130 ft.). It lies in a large cirque carved around 11,000 years ago by a receding glacier. Mount Custer at the southern end of the lake is in Montana. To the west (right) of Custer is **Forum Peak** (2,225 m/7,300 ft.), whose summit cairn marks the boundaries of Alberta, Montana, and British Columbia. Beside the lakeshore are enclosed information boards and concession selling light snacks and renting canoes, rowboats, and paddleboats ($20 for the first hour; $15 for additional hours). A narrow trail leads along the lake's west shoreline, ending after two kilometers (1.2 mi.; 40 minutes each way).

Red Rock Canyon Parkway

The best roadside wildlife viewing within the park is along this 13-kilometer (eight-mi.) road that starts near the golf course and finishes at **Red Rock Canyon.** The transition between rolling prairies and mountains takes place abruptly as you travel up the Blakiston Valley. Black bears (and very occasionally grizzly bears) can be seen feeding on saskatoon berries along the open slopes to the north. **Mount Blakiston** (2,920 m/9,580 ft.), the park's highest summit, is visible from a viewpoint three kilometers (1.9 mi.) along the road. The road passes interpretive signs, picnic areas, and Crandell Mountain Campground. At the end of the road is Red Rock Canyon, a water-carved gorge where the bedrock, known as argillite, contains a high concentration of iron. The iron oxidizes and turns red when exposed to air—literally going rusty. A short interpretive trail leads along the canyon.

HIKING

Although the park is relatively small, its trail system is extensive; 224 kilometers (140 mi.) of well-maintained trails lead to alpine lakes and lofty summits affording spectacular views. One of the most appealing aspects of hiking in Waterton is that with higher trailheads than other parks

ALBERTA

in the Canadian Rockies, the treeline (and the best views) is reached quickly.

From Town

The trail up to the summit of **Bear's Hump** (1.2 km/0.7 mi.; 40 minutes one-way) is one of the most popular short hikes in the park, and although steep, it affords panoramic views of the Waterton Valley. From the back of the visitors center parking lot, the trail switchbacks up the northern flanks of the Bear's Hump, finishing at a rocky ledge high above town.

The trail to **Bertha Lake** (5.8 km/3.6 mi.; 2 hours one-way) follows Upper Waterton Lake for 1.5 kilometers (0.9 mi.), then branches right and climbs steadily through a montane forest to Lower Bertha Falls. From here, the trail passes another waterfall and switchbacks steeply to its maximum elevation on a ridge above the hanging valley in which Bertha Lake lies. The trail gains 460 meters (1,510 ft.) of elevation, so you should at least have a mid-level of fitness to attempt it.

Don't let the length of the **Waterton Lakeshore Trail** (14 km/8.7 mi.) put you off—it's easy walking the entire way. Most hikers take the Waterton Cruise Company's **MV *International*** one way ($14; call 403/859-2362) and hike back to town, spending about four hours on the trail.

Other Hikes

Arguably one of the most spectacular day hikes in Canada is the **Crypt Lake Trail** (8.7 km/5.4 mi.; 3–4 hours one-way). Access to the trailhead is aboard the Crypt Lake Shuttle (403/859-2362, $14 round-trip), which departs the Waterton marina daily at 9 A.M. and 10 P.M. for Crypt Landing, returning at 4 P.M. and 5:30 P.M. From Crypt Landing, the trail switchbacks for 2.5 kilometers (1.6 mi.) past a series of waterfalls and continues steeply up to a small green lake before reaching a campground. The final ascent to Crypt Lake from the campground causes the most problems, especially for those who suffer from claustrophobia. A ladder on the cliff face leads into a natural tunnel that you must crawl through on your hands and knees. The next part of the trail is along a narrow precipice with a cable for support. The lake at the end of the trail, nestled in a

hanging valley, is no disappointment. Its dark green waters are rarely free of floating ice, and the steep walls of the cirque rise over 500 meters (1,640 ft.) above the lake on three sides.

Crandell Lake (2.4 km/1.5 mi.; 40 minutes one-way) may be an anticlimax if you've already hiked up to Crypt Lake, but it's an easy destination for families and handy for campers at Crandell Campground, which is also the trailhead.

OTHER RECREATION
Cruising to Goat Haunt, Montana

This is the most popular activity in Waterton. From the marina downtown, **Waterton Inter-Nation Shoreline Cruise Company** (403/859-2362) runs scheduled cruises across the International Boundary to Goat Haunt, Montana, at the southern end of Upper Waterton Lake. The 45-minute trip along the lakeshore passes spectacular mountain scenery and usually wildlife. A half-hour stopover is made at Goat Haunt, which lies in a remote part of Glacier National Park and consists of little more than a dock and interpretive displays. You can return on the same boat or go hiking and return later in the day. Another option is to take an early boat trip and walk back to town on the **Waterton Lakeshore Trail.** Boats leave the Waterton marina five times daily (from 9 A.M.) during summer. Fewer trips are made during June and September. The cruises operate until the end of September. Tickets cost $25 round-trip, $14 one-way, and you'll need to book ahead in summer.

Golf

The rolling fairways and spectacular mountain backdrop of **Waterton Lakes Golf Course** (403/859-2114) can distract even the keenest golfer's attention. The 18-hole course, designed by Stanley Thompson and dating from 1929, isn't particularly long (6,103 yds.) or difficult, but the surrounding mountains and unhurried pace of play make for a pleasant environment. The course is four kilometers (2.5 mi.) north of the townsite on the main access road and is open June–early October. Its facilities include a rental shop, clubhouse, and restaurant serving sandwiches and snacks. A round of costs $33 during the day, or $19 for twilight golf. Club rentals are $10 and a power cart is an additional $27.

NIGHTLIFE

Interpretive programs are held nightly during the summer in Crandell Campground and at the **Falls Theatre** opposite Cameron Falls. Programs begin at 8:30 P.M., with guest speakers appearing at the Falls Theatre Saturday night. Ask at the Waterton Visitor Centre or call 403/859-2445 for a schedule.

Being the biggest and most central bar in town, the **Thirsty Bear Saloon** (Waterton Ave., 403/859-2211, 11 A.M.–2 A.M.) gets crowded. It pours happy hour daily 3–6 P.M., and a band plays two or three nights a week. The **Rams Head Lounge** (Kilmorey Lodge, Mount View Rd., 403/859-2334) has a rustic mountain ambience centered around a wood-burning fireplace. Outside is a deck with views of the lake. In the Prince of Wales Hotel, the staid **Windsor Lounge** (403/859-2231) has panoramic views across the lake and live entertainment most nights.

ACCOMMODATIONS AND CAMPING

Waterton has a limited number of accommodations. Most start opening in May and will be full every night during July and August. By mid-October many are closed, with only the HI–Waterton Alpine Centre, Kilmorey Lodge, Crandell Mountain Lodge, and Waterton Glacier Suites open year-round. All accommodations are within the townsite, so walking to the marina and shops isn't a problem.

Under $50

HI–Waterton Alpine Centre is in a wing of Waterton Lakes Lodge (corner of Windflower Ave. and Cameron Falls Rd., 403/859-2151 or 888/985-6343, www.watertonlakeslodge.com). A total of 21 beds are spread through six rooms, with a maximum of four beds in any one room. Guests have use of all lodge facilities, including the Waterton Spa and Recreation Centre (for a small fee), tennis, and bike rentals, as well as a common lounge area, shared kitchen, and bathrooms. Beds are $31 for members of Hostelling International, $35 for nonmembers—a great deal for those travelers willing to share living facilities. Check-in is after 4 P.M. Unlike the main lodge, the hostel is open year-round.

$50–100

If hostelling it or camping aren't your style, but you don't want to spend more than $100 for accommodations, consider **Northland Lodge** (Evergreen Ave., 403/859-2353, www.northlandlodgecanada.com), a converted house backing onto the woods. A large lounge with a TV and fireplace, and a large balcony create a convivial atmosphere between budget-conscious guests. The two rooms that share a bathroom are $85 s or d while the remainder are $110–155 s or d; rates include tea, coffee, and muffins in the morning.

$100–150

Kilmorey Lodge (Mount View Rd., 403/859-2334 or 888/859-8669, www.kilmoreylodge.com), a historic 1920s inn on the shores of Emerald Bay, provides excellent value for money. Victorian furnishings, lots of exposed timber, squeaking floorboards, and historic photographs add to the charm. From the lobby a narrow stairway leads up to 23 rooms tucked under the eaves, many of which have lake views. Each is furnished with antiques, and the beds have down comforters to ensure a good night's sleep. Downstairs is one of the town's finest restaurants, along with a lounge and gazebo for enjoying a quiet drink on those warm summer nights. Standard rooms during summer start at $113 s or d, rising to $213 for the spacious Deluxe King.

Across the road from the Kilmorey Lodge is **Crandell Mountain Lodge** (Mount View Rd., 403/859-2288 or 866/859-2288, www.crandellmountainlodge.com), a centrally located country-style inn. Each of the 17 rooms has a private bath and is beautifully finished with country-style furnishings (no phones), and out

© ANDREW HEMPSTEAD

Prince of Wales Hotel

ALBERTA

back is a private garden area. Two rooms are wheelchair-accessible. The smallest rooms are $129 s or d, most—with a choice of fireplace or kitchenette—are $159–199, and the largest suite is $199.

$150–200
At **Waterton Glacier Suites** (Windflower Ave., 403/859-2004 or 866/621-3330, www.waterton suites.com) each of 26 units features stylish, modern decor, is air-conditioned, and offers a fridge, microwave, and gas fireplace. Two-bedroom suites are $169 s or d, units with a jetted tub are $225, and spacious loft units are $259. Rates range $125–175 in the off-season.

Waterton Lakes Lodge (corner Windflower Ave. and Cameron Falls Rd., 403/859-2151 or 888/985-6343, www.watertonlakeslodge.com, May–late Oct.) is set on a 1.5-hectare (3.7-acre) site in the heart of town. All 80 rooms are large and modern, and each has mountain-themed decor and mountain views. Amenities include air-conditioning, a TV/VCR combination, Internet access, and a coffeemaker. The lodge complex also holds Waterton Spa and Recreation Centre (free entry for guests), a restaurant, small café, and lounge. Standard rooms are $215 s or d, while those with kitchenettes are

$240–260; check the website for steeply discounted off-season rates.

Over $200
Waterton's best-known landmark is the **Prince of Wales Hotel** (403/859-2231 or 406/892-2525, www.glacierparkinc.com, mid-May–late Sept.), a seven-story gabled structure built in 1927 on a hill overlooking Upper Waterton Lake. It was another grand mountain resort financed by the railway, except, unlike those in Banff and Jasper, it had no rail link and has always been U.S.-owned. Rates for the smallest (and they're small) "Value Rooms" are $265–276 s or d, depending on the view. Standard rooms start at $293, rising to $347 for those with a lake view. The opulence and history of this hotel is unequalled in Waterton, but don't expect the facilities of a similarly priced city hostelry: Rooms have no television and some have no elevator access.

Park Campgrounds
Waterton Lakes National Park has three campgrounds holding a total of 391 campsites. They're open only May–October with winter camping permitted at Pass Creek, along the park access road. No reservations are taken, so to ensure a site, try to time your arrival to check-out time, which is 11 A.M. **Townsite Campground** enjoys a prime lakeside location within walking distance of many trailheads, restaurants, and shops. Many of its over 238 sites have power, water, and sewer hookups. The campground also offers showers and cooking shelters. Walk-in tent sites are $19, unserviced sites $22, hookups $30. **Crandell Campground** is 10 kilometers (6.2 mi.) from the townsite on Red Rock Canyon Parkway. It has 129 unserviced sites ($17), flush toilets, and cooking shelters. Pleasant Crandell Lake is an easy 2.4-kilometer (1.5 mi.) walk from the southwest corner of the campground. **Belly River Campground,** 26 kilometers (16 mi.) from the townsite on Chief Mountain International Highway, is the smallest (24 sites) and most primitive of the park's three developed campgrounds. It has pit toilets and cooking shelters; sites are $13 per night. The latter two campgrounds supply firewood but charge $6 per site to burn it.

Commercial Campgrounds

Outside of the park, three private campgrounds take up the nightly overflow. **Waterton Springs Campground** (three km/1.9 mi. north of the park gate on Hwy. 6, 403/859-2247 or 866/859-2247, www.watertonsprings.com, June–Sept.) centers on a large building holding modern bathroom facilities, a lounge, a general store, and a laundry. Also on-site is a fishing pond stocked with rainbow trout. Tent sites are $17, trailers and RVs pay $22–26.

On Highway 5, five kilometers (3.1 mi.) east of the park gate, **Waterton Riverside Campground** (403/653-2888, June–Sept.) has powered sites and showers. Tent sites are $16, powered sites $22. Continuing east, **Crooked Creek Campground** (403/653-1100, mid-May–Sept.) charges $11 for tents and $16 for sites with power and water.

FOOD

Restaurants in the park offer a range of fare—from pizza and fast food to elegant dining. If you plan on cooking your own food, stock up before you get to the park. Groceries are available at the **Rocky Mountain Food Mart** on Windflower Avenue (open 8 A.M.–10 P.M.) and in the Tamarack Village Square on Mount View Road. The Food Mart sells hot chickens—an easy and inexpensive camping or picnicking meal.

Cafés and Cheap Eats

For everything from vegetarian pitas to buffalo burgers head to **Borderline Burgers** (305 Windflower Ave., 403/859-2284), where the indoor/outdoor tables are always busy. Next door, the **Country Bakery** (403/859-2181) opens daily at 6 A.M. serving breakfast, meat and fruit pies, a range of pastries, and packed lunches for hungry hikers.

Dining Rooms

Dinner at the **Lamp Post Dining Room** (Kilmorey Lodge, Mount View Rd., 403/859-2334, daily 7:30 A.M.–10 P.M.) is a wonderful way to spend the evening after a day exploring Water-ton. It has all the charm of the Prince of Wales Hotel but with a more casual atmosphere and lower prices to match. The game-oriented menu offers mouthwatering mains like grilled caribou doused in a blueberry cognac sauce ($29.95). Leave room to finish with a delicious piece of saskatoon berry pie ($5). An impressive wine list is dominated by Canadian offerings. Breakfast choices include granola ($4) made in-house or delicious oatmeal with a warmed bagel on the side ($5), as well as all the cooked usuals ($7–10).

The **Royal Stewart Dining Room** is a formal restaurant in the Prince of Wales Hotel (403/859-2231). Its high ceiling, views of the lake through large windows, and old-world elegance create a first-class ambience that is overshadowed only by the quality of the food. Prices are similar to any big-city restaurant of the same standard—expect to pay around $100 for two with a bottle of wine. If you're going to splurge, do it here. A large breakfast buffet every morning (6:30–9:30 A.M.; $22 per person) is worth trying if you won't be coming for dinner. Lunch is served 11:30 A.M.–2 P.M.; dinner 5–9:30 P.M. Reservations are required.

INFORMATION AND SERVICES

On the main access road opposite the Prince of Wales Hotel, the **Waterton Visitor Centre** (403/859-5133, June–Aug. 9 A.M.–8 P.M., May and Sept. 9 A.M.–5 P.M.) provides general information on the park, keeps current trail and weather reports, and sells fishing licenses. The park's **administration office** (Mount View Rd., 403/859-2224, year-round Mon.–Fri. 8 A.M.–4 P.M.) offers the same services as the Visitor Centre. As always, start your planning by visiting the Parks Canada website (www.pc.gc.ca) and click through the relevant links. For general tourist information, the local **chamber of commerce** website (www.watertonchamber.com) provides plenty of current information and links to accommodations.

Books

The **Waterton Natural History Association,** based in the Waterton Heritage Centre (117

Waterton Ave., 403/859-2624, May–Sept., 10 A.M.–5 P.M., longer hours July–Aug.), offers a variety of educational programs and stocks every book ever written about the park, as well as many titles pertaining to western Canada in general. Also here are a display area with exhibits telling the story of park's natural and human history, and a small gallery of paintings by local artists.

Shopping and Services

The numerous tourist-oriented gift shops along Waterton Avenue are worth browsing through when the weather isn't cooperating. In the **Tamarack Village Square** (Mount View Rd.), you'll find a bookshop, a currency exchange, and a sports store selling camping gear and fishing tackle. Waterton has no banks, but cash machines are scattered through town, including at Pat's Waterton on Mount View Road. The post office is beside the fire station on Fountain Avenue. **Itussiststukiopi Coin-Op Launderette** (301 Windflower Ave.) is open daily 8 A.M.–10 P.M.

TRANSPORTATION

The nearest commercial airport is at Lethbridge, 140 kilometers (87 miles) away. Cars can be rented at the airport. The closest that **Greyhound** buses come to the park is Pincher Creek, 50 kilometers (31 miles) away. From the depot (1015 Hewetson St., 403/627-2716), you'll need to get a cab, which will cost around $65; call **Crystal Taxi** (403/627-4262).

The **Park Transport Company,** (Tamarack Village Sq., Mount View Rd., 403/859-2378) operates hiker shuttle services to various trailheads within the park. Cameron Lake, the starting point for the Carthew-Alderson Trail (which heads back in town), is a popular drop-off point; $8 one-way. You could take one of these shuttles, then return on the bus later in the day if driving the steep mountain roads doesn't appeal to you. The company also offers two-hour tours ($28 per person) through the park and runs a local taxi service.

Pat's Waterton (Mount View Rd., 403/859-2266) rents mountain bikes (from $6 per hour, $30 per day) and motorized scooters ($20 per hour, $65 per day).

Crowsnest Pass

The Municipality of Crowsnest Pass is along Highway 3 between Pincher Creek and the Continental Divide in the southwestern corner of the province. It encompasses a handful of once-bustling coal-mining communities, including Bellevue, Hillcrest, Frank, Blairmore, and Coleman. Many topographic features in the area are named "Crowsnest," including a river, a mountain, and the actual pass (1,396 m/4,580 ft.) on the Continental Divide. From Pincher Creek, it's 62 kilometers (39 mi.) to the pass. The area is worth exploring for its natural beauty and recreation opportunities alone; the Crowsnest River reputedly offers some of Canada's best trout fishing. But a trip through this area wouldn't be complete without visiting the historic towns and mines along the route.

PINCHER CREEK AND VICINITY

The town, in a shallow valley 211 kilometers (131 mi.) south of Calgary, is surrounded by some of the country's best cattle land and is reputed to be the windiest spot in Alberta. The NWMP established a horse farm at what is now known as Pincher Creek in 1876. They found that oats and hay, the horses' main source of sustenance, grew much better here in the foothills than at their newly built post at Fort Macleod. The story goes that a member of the detachment found a pair of pincers near the river—lost many years earlier by prospectors from Montana—and the name stuck. Word of this fertile agricultural land quickly spread, and soon the entire area was settled.

Kootenai Brown Pioneer Village

This historic park (1037 Bev McLachlin Dr., 403/627-3684, June–Aug. daily 8 A.M.–8 P.M., Sept.–May Mon.–Fri. 8:30 A.M.–4:30 P.M., adult $6, senior $4, child $3) houses many displays associated with early pioneers of the region, including extensive archives, and a gift shop in the main log building by the entrance.

Oldman River Dam

The Oldman River Dam, north of Pincher Creek below the confluence of the Crowsnest, Castle, and Oldman Rivers is the latest attempt to irrigate regions of southern Alberta not normally able to produce crops. The 25-kilometer-long (15.5 mi.) reservoir is held back by one of Alberta's highest dam walls (76 m/250 ft.); Highway 785, which branches north from Highway 3 three kilometers (1.9 mi.) east of the Pincher Creek turn-off, crosses the wall and allows access to the base of the spillway, where there's camping, excellent fishing for rainbow trout, and a specially built kayaking course. The reservoir above is also a popular recreation spot for windsurfing, boating, and fishing.

Beauvais Lake Provincial Park

Deep in the foothills 24 kilometers (15 mi.) southwest of Pincher Creek, Beauvais Lake Provincial Park is a wilderness area with a rich history of early settlement. Foundations of buildings are all that remain of the first homesteaders' efforts to survive in what was then a remote location. The park's most famous settler was James Whitford, one of General Custer's scouts at the famous Battle of Little Bighorn. He is buried at Scott's Point. A reservoir (Beauvais Lake) in the southeast corner of the park is stocked annually with rainbow and brown trout. This area of the park is a maze of hiking trails, many beginning from the campground ($15), which has limited services. If you're tent camping, continue along the north side of the lake to a group of walk-in sites.

Accommodations and Camping

The **Parkway Motel** (1070 Waterton Ave., 403/627-3344 or 888/209-9902, www.parkway motel.ca, $65–95 s or d) is the best of a bunch of motels along the eastern edge of town. The mid-size rooms are comfortable and in-room coffee is supplied. The **Heritage Inn** (919 Waterton Ave., 403/627-5000 or 888/888-4374, www.heritageinn.net, $85 s, $95 d) has the nicest rooms in town, although they could be a little less expensive. It has a restaurant and lounge, as well as room service.

Pincher Creek Municipal Campground (May–Oct., tents $12, powered sites $15) is in a residential area on Wentworth Avenue, just off Highway 6. It has no services but is central to town. A short path leads to Kootenai Brown Pioneer Village. Much nicer if you don't need hookups is the **Cottonwood Campground,** 500 meters (0.3 mi.) downstream of the Oldman River Dam 10 kilometers (6.2 mi.) northeast of town. The 82 sites are spread throughout stands of towering cottonwood trees and all have easy river access. Fishing for rainbow trout is great in the river, but there's also a stocked trout pond. Camping is $15 per night.

Food

The **Swiss Alpine Restaurant** (988 Main St. at Waterton Ave., 403/627-5079, 11 A.M.–10 P.M.) is a long-time favorite with locals and savvy travelers in the know. The lounge displays lots of taxidermy and a Western-style atmosphere, and the dining area has good food, including Alberta beef and lamb, delicious salads (the Alpine salad is especially good), and traditional Swiss dishes such as fondue. Most entrées are more than $12, but portions are generous.

Information

Pincher Creek Tourist Information Centre (1037 Bev McLachlin Dr., 403/627-5855 or 888/298-5855, www.pincher-creek.com, June–Aug. daily 8:30 A.M.–8 P.M., Sept.–May Mon.–Fri. 8:30 A.M.–4:30 P.M.) is within Kootenai Brown Pioneer Village.

PINCHER CREEK TO LEITCH COLLIERIES

The first worthwhile stop as Highway 3 begins its westward climb to the Crowsnest Pass from Pincher Creek is **Lundbreck Falls** (signposted from the highway), where the Crowsnest River plunges 12 meters (40 ft.) into the canyon below. From the falls, Highway 3 passes the junction of Highway 22, which heads north to Kananaskis Country and Calgary. The next community west on Highway 3 is **Burmis,** which is well known for the **Burmis Tree,** a photogenic limber pine situated beside the highway on the west side of town.

Leitch Collieries

At the beginning of the 20th century, Leitch Collieries was the largest mining and coking operation in Crowsnest Pass, and in 1915 it became the first operation to cease production. Now it's a series of picturesque ruins with one of the most informative interpretive exhibits in the area. A boardwalk through the mine ruins leads to "listening posts" (where recorded information is played) and interpretive signs. The site is open year-round, with guided tours running daily 9 A.M.–5 P.M. in summer.

HILLCREST

Named after one of the pass's earliest prospectors, Hillcrest is best remembered for Canada's worst mine disaster. The Hillcrest Coal and Coke Company began operations in 1905 and shortly thereafter laid out a townsite. Before long, the town had its own railway spur, school, hotel, and store. Then disaster struck. At 9:30 A.M. on June 19, 1914, with 235 men working underground, an explosion tore apart the tunnels of the Hillcrest Mine. Many of those who survived the initial explosion were subsequently asphyxiated by the afterdamp (residual carbon monoxide and carbon dioxide). The final death toll was 189. The mine reopened and produced 250,000 tons of coal annually until closing in 1939 for economic reasons.

Many of the original miner residences still stand in Hillcrest, which is now a quiet town with a population of 1,000. The town has no services but two historically interesting sights. The **Hillcrest Mine** is accessible along a rough, unpaved road that branches left off 230th Street beyond the trailer court (it's easy to miss—the

road runs along the trailer court's back fence). The ruins are extensive—look for the sealed mine entrance at the rear of the ruins, half hidden by trees. Through town to the west (this road joins back up to Hwy. 3) is **Hillcrest Cemetery,** off 8th Avenue. Many of the mine-disaster victims could not be identified. They were wrapped in white cloth and buried in the cemetery one foot apart in mass graves.

FRANK

Frank is probably the most famous (or infamous) town in the Crowsnest Pass area. In 1901, two Americans acquired mineral rights to the area directly below Turtle Mountain. Within months, their company, the Canadian-American Coal and Coke Company, had established a mine and laid out the townsite of Frank. The mine, when operational, became the first to sell coal in the pass and continued to thrive along with the town of Frank, whose population swelled to 600.

April 29, 1903

It was before dawn. Everything in town was quiet, and the night shift was hard at work deep inside Turtle Mountain. Then, without warning, a gigantic chunk of the north face of the mountain sheared off, thundering into the valley below and burying part of Frank. It was the world's most destructive rockslide, burying 68 of the town's residents. (Amazingly, none of the 20 working coal miners were killed. After being trapped for 14 hours, they dug themselves out.) Looking at the north face of Turtle Mountain will give you an idea of the slide, but the full extent doesn't become apparent until you actually drive through the slide area or view the fan of limestone boulders that spread more than three kilometers (1.9 mi.) from the base of the mountain and more than two kilometers (1.2 mi.) to the east and west. Today, Turtle Mountain is monitored daily with some of the world's most advanced seismographic equipment but has shown no sign of moving since.

Sights

The original townsite of Frank is now an industrial

park. To get to it, cross the rail line at 150th Street (just west of the turn-off for the interpretive center). Take the first left and look for a rusty fire hydrant to the right. This landmark, which once stood on Dominion Avenue, Frank's main street, is all that remains of the ill-fated town. Directly behind it was the grand Imperial Hotel, which is now just a depression in the ground with a tree growing in it. This road then continues across Gold Creek and into the slide area. A memorial was erected here by Delbert Ennis, whose entire family survived the slide. This road was the main route through the area before the slide and has since been cleared. It eventually joins up with the Hillcrest access road.

Frank Slide Interpretive Centre (403/562-7388, mid-May–mid-Sept. 9 A.M.–6 P.M., rest of year 10 A.M.–5 P.M., adult $6, senior $5, child $4), on a slight rise at the northern edge of the slide area, is an excellent place to learn more about the history of the valley, its settlers, and its tragedies. The audiovisual presentation *In the Mountain's Shadow* is a particularly moving ac-

count of the terrible working and social conditions in the valley. A 1.5-kilometer (0.9-mi.) self-guided trail leads down into the slide. Better still, scramble up the slope behind the parking lot and walk along the ridge for a view of the entire slide area.

No tourist services are available in Frank, but who wants to camp under Turtle Mountain anyway?

BLAIRMORE AND VICINITY

With a population of 1,800, Blairmore is the largest of the Crowsnest Pass communities. The town had only a small mine itself, but when the Frank Mine opened in 1901, Blairmore thrived. Real estate brokers, insurance agents, doctors, and barristers all made their homes here, and in 1907, West Canadian Collieries—which owned the Lille and Bellevue mines—relocated its offices to Blairmore. A brickyard opened, and many of the wooden-front buildings along the main street were replaced by impressive brick structures that remain to this day.

Practicalities

The historic **Cosmopolitan Hotel** (13001 20th Ave., 403/562-7321, $50 s, $70 d) has 16 guest rooms that have recently been renovated. They're still basic, and some share bathrooms, but the price is right. You'll find the nicest rooms at the **Best Canadian Motor Inn,** right on the Crowsnest River at the far west end of town (11217 21st Ave., 403/562-8851 or 888/700-2264, www.bestcdn.com, $89 s, $94). It has a sauna, hot tub, coin-laundry, and restaurant. **Lost Lemon Campground** (403/562-2932, April–Oct.) is a private facility across the railway tracks at the west end of town. It has showers, a swimming pool, and a laundry room and is situated right beside the Crowsnest River, making it the perfect overnight stop for anglers; tent sites are $18, hookups $22–26.

The best place in Blairmore for a meal is the **Rendezvous Restaurant** (13609 20th Ave., 403/564-0000, Mon.–Sat. 6 A.M.–10:30 P.M., Sunday 7:30 A.M.–9 P.M.), which overlooks the Crowsnest River at the east entrance to town. It's open throughout the day, with a typical

Frank Slide

Canadian menu offered. The bar in the **Cosmopolitan Hotel** is always busy, although a little rough around the edges—don't ask for an umbrella in your drink and you should be all right.

COLEMAN AND VICINITY

Westernmost of the Crowsnest Pass communities is Coleman, which is 15 kilometers (nine mi.) from the British Columbia border. The town expanded rapidly at the end of the 19th century and by 1904 it had two hotels, two churches, and several stores along Main Street. When the Coleman Colliery closed in 1983, many of the town's miners joined the ranks of the unemployed, some found work in the British Columbia mines, and others packed up their belongings and left the pass completely. A walk down Coleman's 17th Avenue is like what walking down the main street of Bellevue, Frank, Passburg, and Lille must have looked like after their respective mines had closed.

Downtown

Located in the old Coleman High School building is the **Crowsnest Museum** (7701 19th Ave., 403/563-5434, summer 10 A.M.–6 P.M., rest of year Mon.–Fri. 10 A.M.–noon and 1–4 P.M., adult $6, senior $5, child $4). With two floors crammed full of exhibits and artifacts from throughout the region, allow at least an hour here. The adjacent schoolyard has displays of farming, mining, and firefighting equipment. Across the street is the *Coleman Journal* building. The *Coleman Journal* was a Pulitzer Prize–winning weekly newspaper that was published until 1970. After extensive restoration, the building has been opened to the public. Interpretive panels explain the slow process involved in early newspaper publishing. It's open the same hours as the museum. Many other buildings that remain are of historical significance and across the railway tracks at the west end of 17th Avenue are the remains of the coke ovens, the most complete in the pass.

Accommodations and Food

The **Stop Inn Motel** (on Hwy. 3 above downtown, 403/562-7381, $48 s, $52 d) has clean, basic rooms each with cable TV and a small fridge. Also on the highway, the newer **Valley View Motel** (403/563-5600, $66 s, $68 d) has 25 small but modern rooms, some of which are air-conditioned. On Crowsnest Lake 12 kilometers (7.5 mi.) west of town is **Kosy Knest Kabins** (403/563-5155, $50 s, $58 d), where all 10 units have kitchenettes and TVs.

Continuing West Along Highway 3

From Coleman, the British Columbia border is only 15 kilometers (9.3 mi.) away. It's impossible to miss the distinctive **Crowsnest Mountain** on the north side of the highway. One of the best vantage points is the **Travel Alberta Information Centre** (403/563-3888, mid-May–mid-June 10 A.M.–6 P.M. and mid-June–Aug. 9 A.M.–6 P.M.). The center is difficult to see coming from the east—look for a blue roof on the south side of the road opposite Crowsnest Lake. From here, Highway 3 crosses Island Lake and passes a small residential community known as **Crowsnest** before crossing the Continental Divide and entering the Kootenays region of British Columbia.

Central Alberta

The central sector of the province is a diverse region extending from the peaks of the Canadian Rockies in the west through the foothills and aspen parkland to the prairies in the east. East of Calgary, the Red Deer River flows through some of the world's richest dinosaur fossil beds; hundreds of specimens from the Cretaceous period—displayed in museums throughout the world—have been unearthed along a 120-kilometer (75-mi.) stretch of the river valley. One spot, Dinosaur Provincial Park, is the mother lode for paleontologists. This UNESCO World Heritage Site includes a "graveyard" of more than 300 dinosaurs of 35 species, many of which have been found nowhere else in the world (for comparison, Utah's Dinosaur Natural Monument has yielded just 12 species). The valley has more than just dinosaur skeletons, though; paleontologists have unearthed skin impressions, eggshells, dung, and footprints, as well as fossilized insects, fish, amphibians, crocodiles, pterodactyls, and reptiles. And the valley's landforms are as enthralling as the prehistoric artifacts they entomb—spectacular badland formations make for a sight not easily forgotten.

CENTRAL ALBERTA

Willmore
Wilderness
Park

Grande
Cache

Smoky River

40

40

Continental
Divide

Jasper

16

Jasper

Mt. Robson
Provincial
Park

5

93

93A

93

National

Park

Columbia
Icefield

Kinbasket
Lake

Saskatchewan River
Crossing

Mt. Revelstoke
National Park

Glacier
National
Park

1

Columbia

BRITISH

COLUMBIA

0   20 mi
0   20 km

43

32

Whitecourt

River

32

Edson

16

22

Hinton

16

FORESTRY

40

Pembina

Drayton Valley

Brazeau
Reservoir

Alder
Flats

Brazeau   River

River

Nordegg

TRUNK

N. Saskatchewan
River

22

Crescent
Falls

11

Nordegg

Abraham Lake

Rocky Mountain
House

White Goat
Wilderness

Mt. Michener
(2,337 m)

R.

Siffleur
Falls

Ram

RD.

Caroli

Siffleur
Wilderness

Clearwater
River

584

Sur

Yoho
National
Park

93

Banff

Red Deer
River

940

Wat
Vall

1

National

Park

Little
Deer F

Kootenay

1A

Banff

Canmore

1A

National

95

Park

Mt.
Assiniboine
P.P.

66

93

40

Kananaskis
Country

95

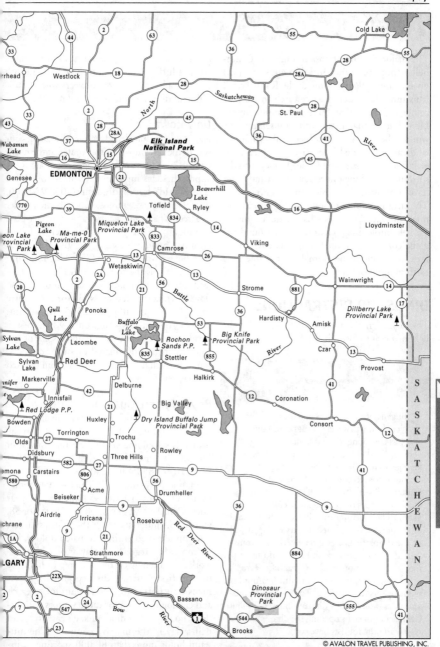

Drumheller and Vicinity

The major city in "Dinosaur Valley" is Drumheller (pop. 6,600), 138 kilometers (86 mi.) northeast of Calgary, home to the Royal Tyrrell Museum. The museum is a research and display center with more than 50 full-size dinosaurs exhibited, more than in any other museum in the world. The city is set in a spectacular lunarlike landscape in the Red Deer River Valley. Ancient glacial meltwaters gouged a deep valley into the surrounding rolling prairie, and wind and water have continued the erosion process ever since. The city's proximity to some of the world's premier dinosaur fossil beds has made it a mecca for paleontologists. Scientists from around the globe come to Drumheller and its environs to learn more about the animals that roamed the earth millions of years ago.

DINOSAUR DISTRACTIONS

The Royal Tyrrell Museum is definitely the highlight of a visit to Drumheller, but there are many

THE GREAT DINOSAUR RUSH

For generations, natives had regarded the ancient bones that were always common in the valley as belonging to giant buffalo. During early geographical surveys of southern Alberta by George Mercer Dawson, the first official dinosaur discovery was recorded. In 1884, one of Dawson's assistants, Joseph Burr Tyrrell, collected and sent specimen bones to Ottawa for scientific investigation. Their identification initiated the first real dinosaur rush. For the first century of digging, all of the dinosaur bones uncovered were transported to museums around the world for further study. Just more than 100 years after Tyrrell's discovery, a magnificent museum bearing his name opened in the valley. The idea of the museum was promoted by dinosaur hunter Dr. Phil Currie, and since its opening the dinosaurs have stayed and the tourists have come.

other diversions along the valley. Downtown itself is a little rough around the edges, but has been bought to life in recent years with the addition of dinosaur sculptures and murals.

Downtown

Start your Drumheller adventure by making your way to the downtown visitors center, at the north end of 2nd Street W and signposted along all approaches. It's impossible to miss—out front is the **world's largest dinosaur** (403/823-8100, daily 9 A.M.–6 P.M., admission $2, children under five free). The *Tyrannosaurus rex* would have been intimidating enough towering over its fellow creatures millions of years ago. But this one is even bigger—at 26 meters (85 ft.) high, it's four times as big as the real thing. A flight of stairs leads up to a viewpoint in its open mouth. Also downtown is the **Badlands Historical Centre** (335 1st St. E, 403/823-2593, May–Sept. 10 A.M.–6 P.M., July–Aug. until 9 P.M., $4), a small museum with an interesting display of privately owned and donated prehistoric pieces, most of which have been collected from the Red Deer River Valley.

Royal Tyrrell Museum

So many of the world's great museums are simply showcases for natural history, yet nestled in the badlands six kilometers (3.7 mi.) northwest of Drumheller, the Royal Tyrrell Museum (403/823-7707 or 888/440-4240, www.tyrrelluseum.com, mid-May–Aug. daily 9 A.M.–9 P.M., Sept.–mid-Oct. daily 10 A.M.–5 P.M., rest of year Tues.–Sun. 10 A.M.–5 P.M., adult $10, senior $8, youth $6, under six free), the world's largest museum devoted entirely to paleontology, is a lot more. It integrates display areas with fieldwork done literally on the doorstep (it lies close by that first "official" discovery), with specimens transported to the museum for research and cataloging. Even for those visitors with little or no interest in dinosaurs, it's easy to spend half a day in the massive complex. The museum holds more than 80,000 specimens, in-

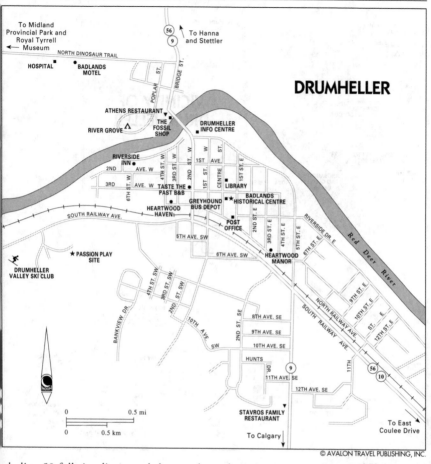

To Midland Provincial Park and Royal Tyrrell Museum

To Hanna and Stettler

NORTH DINOSAUR TRAIL

HOSPITAL

BADLANDS MOTEL

POPLAR ST.

BRIDGE ST.

DRUMHELLER

ATHENS RESTAURANT

THE FOSSIL SHOP

RIVER GROVE

DRUMHELLER INFO CENTRE

RIVERSIDE INN

2ND AVE. W

3RD AVE. W

1ST AVE. W

2ND ST. W

3RD ST. W

4TH ST. W

6TH ST. W

1ST AVE.

1ST ST. W

CENTRE ST.

1ST ST. E

1ST AVE. E

LIBRARY

TASTE THE PAST B&B

BADLANDS HISTORICAL CENTRE

GREYHOUND BUS DEPOT

HEARTWOOD HAVEN

SOUTH RAILWAY AVE.

POST OFFICE

2ND ST. E

3RD ST. E

4TH ST. E

5TH ST. E

6TH ST. E

RIVERSIDE DR. E

Red Deer River

5TH AVE. SW

PASSION PLAY SITE

6TH AVE. SW

HEARTWOOD MANOR

DRUMHELLER VALLEY SKI CLUB

BANKVIEW DR.

4TH ST. SW

3RD ST. SW

2ND ST. SW

10TH AVE. SW

8TH AVE. SE

9TH AVE. SE

10TH AVE. SE

2ND ST. SE

NORTH RAILWAY AVE.

SOUTH RAILWAY AVE.

9TH ST. E

10TH ST. E

ST. E

12TH ST. E

HUNTS DR.

11TH AVE. SE

11TH

STAVROS FAMILY RESTAURANT

12TH AVE. SE

To Calgary

To East Coulee Drive

0   0.5 mi
0   0.5 km

© AVALON TRAVEL PUBLISHING, INC.

M

ALBERTA

cluding 50 full-size dinosaur skeletons, the world's largest such display.

Beyond the lobby is a massive, slowly revolving model of the Earth set against a starry night—a perfect introduction to the place this planet has in the universe. Beyond the globe, a timeline of exhibits covers 3.8 billion years of life on this planet, beginning with early life forms and the development of Charles Darwin's theory of evolution. Before the age of the dinosaurs, the Precambrian and Paleozoic eras saw life on Earth develop at an amazing rate. These periods are cataloged through numerous displays, such as the one of British Columbia's Burgess Shale,

where circumstances allowed the fossilization of a community of soft-bodied marine creatures 530 million years ago. But the museum's showpiece is Dinosaur Hall, a vast open area where reconstructed skeletons and full-size replicas of dinosaurs are backed by realistic dioramas of their habitat. The museum also a major research center; a large window into the main preparation laboratory allows you to view the delicate work of technicians as they clear the rock away from newly unearthed bones. The badlands surrounding the complex can be explored along two short trails, or join a guide at 3 P.M. for a Discover the Badlands hike.

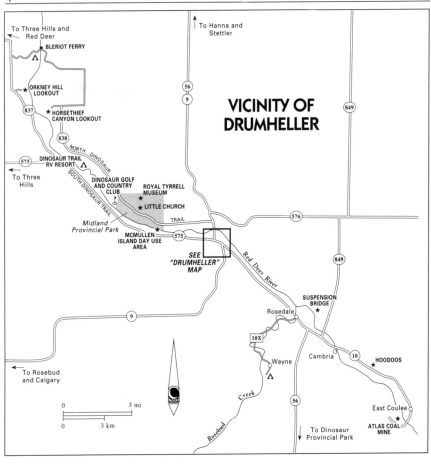

Dinosaur Digs

Become involved in the actual digging of dinosaur bones by participating in a field trip with the Royal Tyrrell Museum (403/823-7707 or 888/440-4240, www.tyrrellmuseum.com). The most popular activity is the **Day Dig.** These digs take place at a site close to Royal Tyrrell Museum, just outside of Drumheller. The adventure begins at 8:30 A.M. with a behind-the-scenes look at specimens already collected by museum staff, then it's out to the dig site. After a brief lesson in excavation techniques, the day is spent digging up dinosaur bones under the guidance of museum paleontologists. Lunch is provided, and

you're returned to the museum by 4 P.M., free to wander around the displays. The work is not particularly strenuous, but it gets hot in the badlands, so bring plenty of sunscreen and a hat. Cost is adult $90, child $60. Trips run June–September. Three times daily, those who just want to watch the digging are taken out to the site; $12 per person.

For those with more time, **Field Experience** trips allow interested parties to totally immerse themselves in the world of paleontology. These weeklong programs take place within Dinosaur Provincial Park. The week is spent prospecting for new finds, engaging in excavation work, and preparing specimens for further study. The program runs June–August, beginning each Sunday. The cost is $1,200 per person, which includes accommodations in trailers and all meals.

SCENIC DRIVES

Dinosaur Trail

This 56-kilometer (35-mi.) circular route to the west of Drumheller starts and finishes in town and passes many worthwhile stops, including two spectacular viewpoints. After passing the access road to Royal Tyrrell Museum, the road climbs steeply out of the valley onto the prairie benchland. Take the first access road on the left—it doubles back to **Horsethief Canyon Lookout,** where you can catch spectacular views of the badlands and the multicolored walls of the canyons. The halfway point of the trail is the crossing of the Red Deer River on the eight-vehicle **Bleriot Ferry** (Apr.–Nov. 8 A.M.–10:40 P.M.), one of the few remaining cable ferries in western Canada. On the return journey to Drumheller, the road continues along the top of the valley to **Orkney Hill Lookout** for more panoramic views across the badlands and the lush valley floor below. A "buffalo jump," where Indians once stampeded great herds of bison off the edge of the cliff, was located nearby, but centuries of erosion have changed the clay and sandstone landscape so dramatically that the actual position of the jump is now impossible to define.

East Coulee Drive

This 25-kilometer (15.5-mi.) road, southeast from Drumheller, passes three historic coal-mining communities in an area dotted with mine shafts and abandoned buildings. The first town along this route is **Rosedale,** where a suspension bridge crosses the river and is safe for those who want to venture across it.

A worthwhile detour from Rosedale is to **Wayne,** an almost–ghost town tucked up a valley alongside Rosebud Creek. It is nine kilometers (5.6 mi.) south along Highway 10X, with 11 creek crossings along the way. In its heyday early last century, Wayne had 1,500 residents, including a healthy population of moonshiners who operated in the surrounding hills, safe from the nearest RCMP patrol in Drumheller. By the time the mine closed in 1962, the population had dipped to 250 and then as low as 15 in the early 1990s, but now the population stands at approximately 50. The oldest operating business in the sleepy hamlet is the 1913 **Rosedeer Hotel** (403/823-9189) and its **Last Chance Saloon,** where the walls are lined with memorabilia from the town's glory days. It opens daily at noon, just in time for a lunchtime buffalo burger.

From Rosedale, Highway 10 continues southeast, crossing the Red Deer River at the abandoned mining town of Cambria and passing **hoodoos** to the left. These strangely shaped rock formations along the river valley have been carved by eons of wind and rain. The harder rock on top is more resistant to erosion than the rock beneath it, resulting in the odd, mushroom-shaped pillars.

Across the river from **East Coulee** is the **Atlas Coal Mine** (403/823-2220, mid-May–June 9:30 A.M.–5:30 P.M., July–Aug. 9:30 A.M.–8:30 P.M., $5, under six free). A wooden ore-sorting

© ANDREW HEMPSTEAD

Hoodoos are a highlight along East Coulee Drive.

ALBERTA

tipple—the last one standing in Canada—towers above the mine buildings. It's a great place to just walk around, or you can take the guided tour to learn more about the mining process.

RECREATION
Golf
Dinosaur Golf and Country Club (403/823-5622) is undoubtedly one of the most interesting in Alberta, with the back nine holes of lush fairways and greens winding through arid badlands, on high ridges, and through narrow coulees. It is located past the Royal Tyrrell Museum; greens fees are $39 (Mon.–Thurs. seniors pay $28) and a power cart with GPS is $30.

Canadian Badlands Passion Play
This Canadian version of the theatrical production of the life of Jesus Christ tells the story of his birth, his death, and his resurrection. The production is an enormous affair, with a cast of hundreds in a natural amphitheater with bench seating set among the badlands. It takes place nine times through the month of July. Tickets (403/823-2001) are adult $25, child $12.50. To get to the site, take South Dinosaur Trail west from downtown and follow the signs south on 17th Street.

Rosebud Theatre
Students in residence showcase their performance skills at the Rosebud Theatre (403/677-2001 or 800/267-7555, www.rosebudtheatre.com) in the hamlet of **Rosebud,** 35 kilometers (22 mi.) southwest of Drumheller. The fun actually starts across the road from the theater in the restored Mercantile Building, where the actors and actresses serve up a buffet meal. Then everyone heads over to the 220-seat theater for a lively production, always lighthearted and often with a rural theme. Popular with day-trippers from Calgary, the daytime show (Wed.–Sun., $41) begins with lunch at 11 A.M. followed by the performance at 1:30 P.M. In the evening (Thurs.–Sat., $46), plan on be seated by 6 P.M. for dinner, with the show starting at 8:30 P.M.

ACCOMMODATIONS AND CAMPING
During summer, demand outstrips supply, so it's *imperative* you make accommodation reservations as far in advance as possible. The Best Western and Super 8 chains are represented, along with the following options.

$50–100
Right on the main thoroughfare through town, **Taste the Past B&B** (281 2nd St. W, 403/823-5889, $75–90 s or d) occupies a 100-year-old coal baron's home. Guests choose between three simple rooms, but no one chooses to miss the full-cooked breakfast served in the sunny dining room. Period furnishings decorate public areas, including the living room, which is laid out around a fireplace. Outside, the well-tended garden is dotted with fossils.

Compared to other places in town, the rooms at **Badlands Motel** (toward museum at 801 N. Dinosaur Trail, 403/823-5155, $70 s, $80 d, $90 kitchenette) are a steal. Decor is a little plain, but rooms are spacious and air-conditioned. Part of the complex is a pancake house that is busy from 6 A.M. when the doors first open for breakfast.

$100–150
Within walking distance of downtown is **Heartwood Manor** (320 N. Railway Ave., 403/823-6495 or 888/823-6495, www.innsatheartwood.com, $110–180 s or d), a classic country inn that looks a little out of place surrounded by older homes. You can splurge on the Main Turret room with a carriage bed, a fireplace, a jetted tub, and separate sitting area. Or chose one of six other rooms, all with a cozy Victorian feel thanks to antiques and plush duvets. All rooms have en suite baths, but only some have televisions and phones. Rates include breakfast, served bedside if requested. Make reservations for **Heartwood Haven** (356 4th St.) through the Inn at Heartwood. In the heart of downtown, this building has undergone massive renovations to provide five guest rooms of varying configurations in the same price range. Breakfast is not supplied.

The perfect choice for those taking in a performance at the Rosebud Theatre is **Rosebud Country Inn** (403/677-2211 or 866/677-2211, www.rosebudcountryinn.com; $115–135 s or d), 35 kilometers (22 mi.) southwest of Drumheller. Some of the 12 rooms are on the small side, but all are charmingly decorated, with the central feature being a sleigh bed. Also on the plus side is air-conditioning. Rooms also have private bathrooms and televisions, but no phones, and one is wheelchair accessible. Keep an eye on goings-on in the village from the sunny verandah. Breakfast, presented buffet style, is included in the rates. With advance reservations, dinner is served to both guests and nonguests.

Campgrounds

A personal favorite is **Dinosaur Trail RV Resort** (11 km/7 mi. along Dinosaur Trail N, 403/823-9333, www.dinosaurtrailrv.com, May–Sept.), an oasis of green between the river and the badlands five kilometers (3.1 mi.) beyond the Tyrrell Museum. After a day exploring the region, back at the campground there's the option of casting a line from the riverbank for goldeye, floating downriver in a canoe (staff provide the upstream drop-off), cooling off in the outdoor pool, or exploring the adjacent badlands on foot. Other facilities include horseshoe pits, a playground, a grocery store, and a laundry. A number of serviced sites are laid out along the river, but most are dotted around the immaculately manicured grounds, shaded by rows of mature trees. Sites range from $25 for tenting to $35 for a full hookup.

Closer to town is **River Grove Campground** (25 Poplar St., 403/823-6655, May–Sept.), in a well-treed spot beside the Red Deer River. Serviced sites are semiprivate; tenters have more options and are able to disappear among the trees. The campground offers a nice stretch of sandy beach (by Albertan standards), minigolf, and an arcade, and town is just a short stroll away. Tent sites are $22, hookups $25–30.

OTHER PRACTICALITIES

Food

Out toward the museum, **Whif's Flapjack House** (801 N. Dinosaur Trail, 403/823-5155, 6 A.M.–9 P.M.) serves up a continuous flow of pancakes ($5–8) from when the doors first open each morning. It's your regular small-town burger joint the rest of the day. All dishes at the **Athens Restaurant** (71 Bridge St. N, 403/823-9400, 11 A.M.–10 P.M.) are made from scratch, and everything is excellent. Appetizers are $4–8; try the lemon soup or large Greek salad. Greek entrées start at $12. The house specialty is *klefti-iko*, juicy spring lamb baked with herbs and spices; have it with the Greek salad for the full effect, or try the generous portion of moussaka. The small dining room is lively and informal, an abundance of greenery hangs from the ceiling, and later in the evening the chef can often be seen chatting with satisfied patrons. At the Best Western Jurassic Inn, **Stavros Family Restaurant** (1103 Hwy. 9, 403/823-7700) has a clean, cool, and comfortable setting. The menu mixes European staples with familiar North American dishes, all for well under $20 per entrée.

Information

Drumheller Information Centre (corner of Riverside Dr. and 2nd St. W, 403/823-8100 or 866/823-3100, www.canadianbadlands.com, 9 A.M.–6 P.M., until 9 P.M. Fri.–Sat. during summer) is in the local chamber of commerce building beside the Red Deer River. You can't miss it—look for the seven-story *Tyrannosaurus rex* in front. **Drumheller Public Library** (224 Centre St., 403/823-5382, Tues.–Thurs. 11 A.M.–8 P.M., Fri.–Sat. 11 A.M.–5 P.M., Sun. 1–5 P.M.) has public Internet access.

DINOSAUR PROVINCIAL PARK

Now that you've been through the Royal Tyrrell Museum, you'll want to get out in the field and explore the area where many of the actual dinosaurs have been found. This region is protected by 7,330-hectare (18,000-acre) Dinosaur Provincial Park, which lies 120 kilometers (75 mi.) downstream of Drumheller. It's possible to get there by road from Drumheller—east on Highway 570 then south on Highway 36—but, from Calgary, the direct route is 200 kilometers (124 mi.) east along the TransCanada Highway.

Thirty-five species of dinosaurs—from every known family of the Cretaceous period—have been unearthed here, along with the skeletal remains of crocodiles, turtles, fish, lizards, frogs, and flying reptiles. Not only is the diversity of specimens great, but so is the sheer volume; more than 300 museum-quality specimens have been removed and are exhibited in museums around the world. The Royal Tyrrell Museum operates a field station in the park, where many of the bones are cataloged and stored. The displays, films, and interpretive programs offered at the center will best prepare you to begin your visit to the park.

Fieldwork in the Park

Each summer, paleontologists from around the world converge on the park for an intense period of digging that starts in late June and lasts for approximately 10 weeks. The earliest dinosaur hunters simply excavated whole or partial skeletons for museum display. Although the basic excavation methods haven't changed, the types of excavation have. "Bonebeds" of up to one hectare are painstakingly excavated over multiple summers. Access to much of the park is restricted in order to protect the fossil beds. Digging takes place within the restricted areas. Work is often continued from the previous season, or new sites are commenced, but there's never a lack of bones. New finds are often discovered with little digging, having been exposed by wind and rain since the previous season.

Excavating the bones is an extremely tedious procedure; therefore, only a few sites are worked on at a time, with preference given to particularly important finds such as a new species. Getting the bones out of the ground is only the beginning of a long process that culminates with their scientific analysis and display by experts at museums around the world.

Interpretive Programs and Tours

Even though much of the actual digging of bones is done away from public view, the **Field Station of the Royal Tyrrell Museum** (403/378-4342,

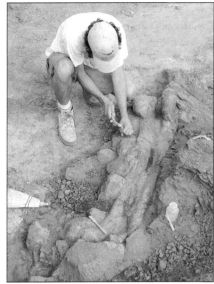

The Royal Tyrrell Museum is a world leader in dinosaur research, with much of the fieldwork taking place in Dinosaur Provincial Park.

July–Aug. daily 8:30 A.M.–9 P.M., Sept.–mid-Oct. daily 9 A.M.–5 P.M., and rest of year weekdays 9 A.M.–4 P.M., $3, seniors $2.50) organizes enough interesting activities and tours to keep you busy for at least a full day.

The **Badlands Bus Tour** takes you on a two-hour ride around the public loop road with an interpretive guide who will point out the park's landforms and talk about its prehistoric inhabitants. The **Centrosaurus Bone Bed Hike** takes visitors on a 2.5-hour guided hike into a restricted area where more than 300 centrosaurus skeletons have been identified. The **Camel's End Coulee Hike** is an easy 2.5-kilometer (1.5-mi.) guided walk to discover the unique flora and fauna of the badlands. Finally, a tour of the Field Station Laboratory is offered daily at 1:30 P.M. Space on all of these tours is limited. The laboratory tour is $2. Each of the other tours costs $6.50. The tours are *very* popular, and this is reflected in the procedure for purchasing tickets (403/310-0000 May–Aug. Mon.–Fri. 9 A.M.–4 P.M.). Tour tick-

DINOSAURS OF ALBERTA

Dinosaur bones found in the Red Deer River Valley play an important role in the understanding of our prehistoric past. The bones date from the late Cretaceous period, around 70 million years ago, when the area was a low-lying subtropical forest at the mouth of a river flowing into the ocean, and dinosaurs flourished.

Around this time, great quantities of silt and mud were flushed downriver, building up a delta at the edge of the sea. In time, this delta hardened, and the countless layers formed sedimentary rock, trapping the remains of fallen dinosaurs. As the Red Deer River curves through central Alberta, it cuts deeply into the ancient river delta, exposing the layers of sedimentary rock and revealing the once-buried fossil treasures.

The bones of 35 dinosaur species—around 10 percent of all those currently known—have been discovered in Alberta. Like today's living creatures, they are classified in orders, families, and species. Of the two orders of dinosaurs, both have been found in the Red Deer River Valley. The bird-hipped dinosaurs (order Ornithischia) were herbivores, while the lizard-hipped dinosaurs (order Saurischia) were omnivores and carnivores.

Apart from their sheer bulk, many herbivores lacked any real defenses. Others developed their own protection; the chasmosaurus had a bony frill around its neck, the pachycephalosaurus had a 25-centimeter-thick (10-in.) dome-shaped skull cap fringed with spikes, and the ankylosaurus was an armored dinosaur whose back was covered in spiked plates.

Among the most common herbivores that have been found in the valley are members of the family of duck-billed hadrosaurs. Fossilized eggs of one hadrosaur, the hypacrosaurus, were unearthed still encasing intact embryos. Another common herbivore in the valley was a member of the horned ceratops family; over 300 specimens of the centrosaurus have been discovered in one "graveyard."

Of the lizard-hipped dinosaurs, the tyrannosaurs were most feared by herbivores. The 15-meter (49-ft.) *Tyrannosaurus rex* is most famous among *Homo sapiens,* but the smaller albertosaurus, a remarkably agile carnivore weighing many tons, was the most common tyrannosaur found in the valley.

ets go on sale May 1 and must be picked up 30 minutes before the departure time. Some tickets are reserved for the day of the tour and sold as "rush" tickets (be at the Field Station when it opens at 8:30 A.M. to ensure that you get a ticket). Finally, if seats become available through no-shows, you may snag a seat at the last minute.

Documentaries are shown at the Field Station in the evenings, and special events are often staged somewhere in the park. The entire interpretive program operates in summer only, with certain tours offered in late May and September.

Exploring the Park

Much of the park is protected as a Natural Preserve. It's off-limits to unguided visitors as a way to protect the bonebeds and the valley's fragile environment. It also keeps visitors from becoming disoriented in the uniform landscape and ending up spending the night among the bobcats and rattlesnakes. The area is well marked and should not be entered except on a guided tour. One other important rule: *Surface collecting and digging for bones anywhere within the park is prohibited.*

You may explore the area bounded by the public loop road and take three short interpretive trails on your own. The **loop road** passes through part of the area where bones were removed during the Great Canadian Dinosaur Rush. Of special interest are two dinosaur dig sites excavated earlier this century, one of which contains a still-intact skeleton of a duck-billed hadrosaur.

The **Badlands Trail** is a 1.3-kilometer (0.8-mi.) loop that starts just east of the campground and passes into the restricted area. The **Coulee Viewpoint Trail,** which begins behind the Field Station, climbs steadily for 500 meters

ALBERTA

(1,650 ft.) to a high ridge above Little Sandhill Creek. This one-kilometer (0.6-mi.) trail takes 20 minutes. It's easy to ignore the nearby floodplains, but the large stands of cottonwoods you'll see were a contributing factor to the park being designated as a UNESCO World Heritage Site.

Camping

The park's campground is in a low-lying area beside Little Sandhill Creek. It has 128 sites, pit toilets, a kitchen shelter, and a few powered sites. Unserviced sites cost $17, powered sites $20. The campground fills up by early afternoon. To book a site, call 403/378-3700. Alternatives are detailed under the Brooks section of this chapter.

West-Central Alberta

Highway 2 is the most direct route between Alberta's two largest cities, Calgary and Edmonton. More than 100 kilometers (62 mi.) to the west, dominating the horizon, are the Canadian Rockies. Between the highway and mountains are the foothills. These hills rise gradually, eventually reaching the lofty peaks of the front ranges. Many rivers—the North Saskatchewan, Red Deer, Clearwater, and Brazeau—slice through the foothills on their cascading descent from sources high in the Canadian Rockies. Rocky Mountain House, located on the bank of the North Saskatchewan River, is the largest town in the region and a good base for exploring.

CALGARY TO RED DEER

The main route out of Calgary is the Deerfoot Trail, which becomes Highway 2 as it heads through outlying suburbs and onto the prairies. Follow Highway 2A to reach the following attractions, or stay on Highway 2 and look for well-marked exits.

Carstairs

Carstairs is a small farming, dairy, and ranching center 67 kilometers (42 mi.) north of Calgary. The town's tree-lined streets are dotted with grand old houses, and the grain elevators associated with all prairie towns stand silhouetted against the skyline. The main local attraction is **PaSu Farm** (10 km/6.2 mi. west of town, 800/679-7999, Tues.–Sat. 10 A.M.–5 P.M., Sun. noon–5 P.M.), a working farm with a dozen breeds of sheep. It also displays a wide variety of sheepskin and wool products, as well as weavings from Africa. The

farm's restaurant serves scones, homemade apple pie, and various teas each afternoon, along with a Sunday (noon–2:30 P.M.) carvery. Much of the wool from PaSu Farm is sold to **Custom Woollen Mills** (403/337-2221, Mon.–Fri. 8 A.M.–3 P.M.), on the other side of Carstairs, 20 kilometers (12.5 mi.) east on Highway 581 and 4.5 kilometers (2.8 mi.) north on Highway 791. At this working museum, the raw wool is processed on clunky-looking machines—some of which date from the 1880s—into wools and yarns ready for knitting (and sale). A self-guided tour is offered.

Red Lodge Provincial Park

This small park is 14 kilometers (8.7 mi.) west of **Bowden** on the **Little Red Deer River.** An English settler built a large log house on the river's edge and then painted the logs red, hence the name. The park is situated within a heavily wooded strip of land that extends east from the foothills well into central Alberta, an ideal habitat for deer and moose. The campground ($17) has a kitchen shelter, coin-operated showers, and firewood sales, and the river is good for swimming and fishing. It gets busy on summer weekends.

Innisfail

Innisfail Historical Village (in fairgrounds at 42nd St. and 52nd Ave., 403/227-2906, daily summer 11 A.M.–5:30 P.M.) has re-created historic buildings, including a stopping house, a school, a store, a C.P.R. station, and a blacksmith's shop, on a one-hectare (1.5-acre) site. Dog lovers will want to make a detour to RCMP **Dog Training Kennels,** four kilometers (2.5 mi.) south of town on the east side of the highway. Canine cops receive training here in obedience, agility, and criminal apprehension. Tours (403/227-3346) of the facility are given year-round, weekdays 1–3 P.M.; book in advance.

Markerville

This hamlet, 16 kilometers (10 mi.) west then three kilometers (1.9 mi.) north of Innisfail, was originally settled by Icelandic people in the 1880s. Today, around 100 people—most that trace their heritage back to the original settlers—call Markerville home. It's a pretty village, with smartly painted homes and well-kept gardens. The main attraction is **Markerville Creamery** (403/728-3006, summer daily 10 A.M.–5:30 P.M.). Between 1899 and the time of its closure in 1972, the creamery won many awards for its fine-quality butters. Tours ($2) led by costumed guides follow the butter-making process, or relax in the *kaffistofa* (café) with a choice of Icelandic specialties.

The most famous of the Icelandic immigrants was Stephan A. Stephansson, one of the Western world's most prolific poets. He spent the early part of his life in his homeland, most of his poetry was written in Canada. Just north of Markerville is his restored home, the distinctive pink and green **Stephansson House** (403/728-3929,

Markerville is one of Alberta's most attractive towns.

mid-May–Aug. daily 10 A.M.–6 P.M., $2). Interpretive panels beside the parking lot tell the story of Stephansson and his fellow immigrants while a short trail leads through a grove of trees to the house itself.

CALGARY TO RED DEER VIA HIGHWAY 21

To Three Hills

Highway 9 intersects Highway 1 approximately 31 kilometers (19 mi.) east of Calgary and heads north to **Irricana.** Two kilometers (1.2 mi.) northwest of town, **Pioneer Acres** (403/935-4357, May–Sept. daily 9 A.M.–5 P.M., $5) displays a large collection of working farm machinery and holds a festival early in August, with demonstrations of pioneer farming and homemaking activities.

Torrington

Torrington, on Highway 27, 25 kilometers (15.5 mi.) west of Highway 21, has more gophers than residents. This normally wouldn't be unusual for a prairie town, except that Torrington's gophers are all stuffed. The town made world headlines in 1997 with the opening of the **Gopher Hole Museum** (208 1st St., 403/631-3931, summer daily 10 A.M.–5 P.M., $2), which, as the brochure describes, is "a whimsical portrayal of daily life in our tranquil village." Approximately 40 dioramas house stuffed gophers in various poses, including gophers in love, gophers playing sports, trailer court gophers, and even gophers wearing shirts declaring that animal rights activists, who were incensed at the idea of the museum, should "Go stuff themselves." Admission includes a copy of the words to the "Torrington Gopher Call Song," which wafts through the quiet streets of the village whenever the museum is open.

Trochu

On the southeast side of Trochu, **St. Ann Ranch** (403/442-3924) was established in 1905 by a group of aristocratic French settlers and is now a Provincial Historic Site. A French settlement, including a school, a church, and a post office, grew around it. The thriving community suffered a blow during World War II when many townsmen returned to France to defend their country. Descendants of an original settler now operate the ranch, which has been mostly restored. A small museum displays many historic items, and a large tearoom (summer daily 2–5 P.M.) serves, among other delicacies, delicious fruit pies. The main residence operates as St. Ann Ranch Country Inn, with nine guest rooms in all, each decked out in period antiques; the more expensive ones have fireplaces. Rates of $50–70 s, $65–95 d include breakfast.

Dry Island Buffalo Jump

This 1,180-hectare (2,900-acre) park is named for both an isolated mesa in the Red Deer River Valley and the site where natives stampeded bison over a cliff approximately 2,000 years ago. The buffalo jump—a 50-meter (164-ft.) drop—is much higher than other jumps in Alberta and is in an ideal location; the approach to the jump is uphill, masking the presence of a cliff until the final few meters. Below the prairie benchland, clifflike valley walls and banks of sandstone have been carved into strange-looking badlands by wind and water erosion. A great diversity of plant life grows in the valley; more than 400 species of flowering plants have been recorded. The park is a day-use area only; apart from a picnic area and a few trails, it is undeveloped. Access is along a gravel road east from Huxley on Highway 21. From the park entrance, at the top of the buffalo drop, the road descends steeply for 200 vertical meters (660 ft.) into the valley (it can be extremely slippery after rain).

HIGHWAY 22 NORTH

This highway follows the eastern flanks of the foothills from Cochrane, northwest of Calgary, through the small communities of Cremona, Sundre, and Caroline, and the larger town of Rocky Mountain House. The Canadian Rockies dominate the western horizon for much of the route and are especially imposing around Sundre.

Sundre

This town of 2,300, on the banks of the Red Deer River, is the quintessential Albertan town.

Surrounded in rolling foothills that are historically tied to the ranching industry, oil and gas now keep the local economy alive. The **Pioneer Museum and Village** (130 Centre St., 403/638-3233, summer Mon.–Sat. 10 A.M.–4 P.M. and Sun. noon–4 P.M.) displays a large collection of artifacts from early pioneer days, including farm machinery, a blacksmith shop, and an old schoolhouse.

The most appealing of Sundre's four motels is the **Chinook Country Inn** (120 2nd St. SW, 403/638-3300), where the rates of $62 s, $66 d include a light breakfast. **Greenwood Campground** (403/638-2680, mid-May–mid-Sept., unserviced sites $15, hookups $20–25), on the west bank of the Red Deer River within walking distance of downtown, has clean facilities that include showers and a covered cooking shelter complete with a wood stove.

Caroline

Four-time World Men's Figure Skating champion (and four-time professional champion) **Kurt Browning** was born and raised on a ranch just west of Caroline. His portrait adorns local tourist literature, and the town's **Kurt Browning Arena** (48th Ave., Mon.–Fri. 8 A.M.–4 P.M.) houses Kurt's Korner, a display of personal memorabilia.

Caroline Municipal RV Park (east end of town, 403/722-2210, mid-May–mid-Sept., $13–15) has showers and powered sites.

ROCKY MOUNTAIN HOUSE

This town of 6,400, best known simply as "Rocky," straddles the North Saskatchewan River and is surrounded by gently rolling hills in a transition zone between aspen parkland and mountains. Highway 11 (also known as David Thompson Hwy.) passes through town on its way east to Red Deer (82 km/51 mi.) and west to the northern end of Banff National Park (170 km/106 mi.).

Rocky Mountain House National Historic Site

This National Historic Site, seven kilometers (4.3 mi.) west of Rocky Mountain House on Highway

© AVALON TRAVEL PUBLISHING, INC.

11A, commemorates the important role fur trading played in Canada's history at the site of four fur-trading posts built between 1799 and 1875. The forts were used not only for trading but also as bases for exploring the nearby mountains. David Thompson, one of western Canada's greatest explorers, was a regular visitor. By the 1830s, beaver felt was out of fashion in Europe, so traders turned to buffalo robes, and many original forts were abandoned, including those at this site. Today, the protected areas include the sites of the forts, a buffalo paddock, and a stretch of riverbank where the large voyageur canoes would have come ashore to be loaded with furs bound for Europe.

The **visitors center** (403/845-2412, late May–Aug., daily 10 A.M.–5 P.M., adult $2.50, senior $2, child $1.50) is the best place to start; its interpretive displays detail the history of the forts, the fur trade, and exploration of the West. Two trails lead along the north bank of the river. The longer of the two, a 3.2-kilometer (two-mi.) loop, passes the site of the two original forts. Frequent "listening posts" along the trail play a lively recorded commentary on life in the early 1800s. All that remains of the forts are depressions in the ground, but through the commentary and interpretive displays, it is easy to get a good idea of what the forts looked like. To the north of the fort site is an observation deck for viewing a small herd of buffalo that may or may not be visible. The other trail leads one kilometer (0.6 mi.) to two chimneys, remnants of the later forts.

Recreation and Events

The best way to appreciate the history of the area, see some great river scenery, and generally have a good time is to take a float trip with **Voyageur Ventures** (403/845-7878) down the North Saskatchewan River. The voyageur canoes used are replicas of those used by early explorers; they are large and stable, requiring little paddling skill. Half-day trips, which include a stop at the National Historic Site and lunch, are $87; a full day with cooked lunch—prepared along the riverbank while you take a short hike or rest in the sun—is $145. Overnight river trips start at $320.

Another center of water-based activities is **Crimson Lake Provincial Park,** northwest of town.

ALBERTA

Crimson Lake is great for boating and canoeing (rentals available), whereas nearby Twin Lakes, also in the park, is stocked with rainbow trout. The undeveloped northwest side attracts many species of waterfowl, including loons, herons, grebes, sandhill cranes, and a variety of ducks.

Accommodations and Camping

Many motels are spread out along Highway 11 east of town. The least expensive is the **Voyageur Motel** (403/845-3381 or 888/845-5569), which has large, clean rooms from $56 s, $66 d, or pay an extra $8 for a kitchenette.

Riverview Campground (Hwy. 11, 403/845-4422, unserviced sites $15, hookups $18–20), on the North Saskatchewan River, is the only commercial facility in town. The unserviced sites are tucked in among a grove of trees on the riverbank, and above them are serviced sites, with spectacular views along the valley. The campground has a small grocery store, a launderette, showers, and free firewood. Another recommended spot is **Crimson Lake Provincial Park,** northwest of town along an access road off Highway 11, where you'll find two campgrounds; sites along the bank of Crimson Lake are $19–21, whereas those beside Twin Lakes are $16.

Information

Make your first stop in town the **Tourist Information Centre** (54th Ave., 403/845-5450 or 800/565-3793, www.rockychamber.org/vic) beside Highway 11 north of downtown. The center is open late May–August Monday–Saturday 9 A.M.–8 P.M., Sunday 10 A.M.–6 P.M., the rest of the year Monday–Friday 9 A.M.–5 P.M.

NORDEGG AND VICINITY

Westbound Highway 11 climbs slowly from Rocky Mountain House into the dense forests on the eastern slopes of the Canadian Rockies. The only community between Rocky and Banff National Park is Nordegg, 85 kilometers (53 mi.) west of Rocky.

Built in the early 1900s, Nordegg was the first "planned" mining town in Alberta. The

streets were built in a semicircular pattern, centered around the railroad station and shops. Fifty miners' cottages were built, all painted in pastel colors. Gardens were planted, and two churches and a modern hospital were built; miners had never had it better. By the early 1940s, with four briquette presses to convert raw coal, Nordegg had one of the largest such operations in North America. Then trains began converting to diesel fuel and home heating went to natural gas. Brazeau Collieries ceased operations in January 1955. Many miners had spent their entire lives working the mine and had raised families in the remote mining community. By the summer of 1955, the town had been abandoned.

Exploring the Site

The **Nordegg Historical Society,** made up of many former residents of the mining community, has commenced restoration of some of the mine buildings and also operates the **Nordegg Heritage Centre** (403/721-2625, mid-May–Sept. 9 A.M.–5 P.M. Among many interesting displays are newspaper articles telling of the town's ups and downs and extensive photo archives. Also in the building is a gift shop and café. The center is the starting point for member-led tours through Brazeau Collieries Minesite Industrial Museum. The longer of the two options, the Technical Tour, takes in the briquette processing plants and mine entrances. Visitors are free to wander around the townsite themselves, but ask at the heritage center for a self-guided tour brochure.

Abraham Lake

Twenty-three kilometers (14 mi.) from Nordegg, Highway 11 passes a gravel parking area at the trailhead for **Crescent Falls** and **Bighorn Canyon.** Five kilometers (3.1 mi.) farther on, a gravel road leads south to the eastern end of Abraham Lake, one of Alberta's largest reservoirs. An information center (403/721-3952, summer daily 8:30 A.M.–4:30 P.M.) at the dam describes its construction. Back on the highway, the main body of Abraham Lake quickly comes into view, its brilliant turquoise water reflecting the front ranges of the Canadian Rockies. Don't stop for a photo session just yet, though, because the views improve farther west. Across the lake is **Michener Mountain** (2,337 m/7,670 ft.).

Aurum Lodge (45 km/28 mi. west of Nordegg, 40 km/25 mi. east of Banff, 403/721-2117, www.aurumlodge.com, $140–190 s or d) trades on an eco-friendly stance and wonderfully scenic location overlooking Lake Abraham. Owners Alan and Madeleine Ernst used recycled materials wherever possible during construction, natural light streams into all corners, the kitchen uses a wood-fired stove, and much of the waste is recycled. But don't imagine some backwoods cabin without running water—it's a comfortable and modern lodge. Rooms in the main lodge are simply decorated, but bright and immaculately kept. They're equal to the best standard rooms in nearby Banff, but offered at a fraction of the cost. Cozy self-contained cottages offer a bathroom, kitchen with woodstove, and lots of privacy. Spend some time on the sun-drenched deck or curled up in front of the fireplace with a book and you won't even realize there are no televisions. Check the website for meal inclusions and packages.

Kootenay Plains Ecological Reserve

Located at the south end of Abraham Lake, this reserve protects a unique area of dry grasslands in the mountains. As Mary Schäffer noted during her historic journey north to Maligne Lake, to gain full appreciation of the plains you must leave the road and pause in their midst. The climate in this section of the valley is unusually moderate, the warmest in the Rockies. June grass and wheat grass, usually associated with the prairies of southeastern Alberta, thrive here. The valley is a prime wintering area for elk, mule deer, bighorn sheep, and moose. For thousands of years, the Kootenay peoples would cross the mountains from the Columbia River Valley to hunt these mammals and the bison that were then prolific. Because of the dry microclimate and its associated vegetation, mammals are not abundant in summer.

Westward from Kootenay Plains, Highway 11 continues climbing, past a parking area (from which a trail leads to a whirlpool on the North Saskatchewan River) and on into Banff National Park. It ends on the Icefields Parkway at Saskatchewan River Crossing. From here, it's 153 kilometers (95 mi.) north to Jasper and 127 kilometers (79 mi.) south to Banff.

Red Deer

This city of 69,000 (Alberta's fourth-largest) is on a bend of the Red Deer River, halfway between the cities of Calgary and Edmonton, which are 145 kilometers (90 mi.) south and 148 kilometers (92 mi.) north, respectively. From the highway, Red Deer seems to be all industrial estates and suburban sprawl, but an extensive park system runs through the city, and many historic buildings have been restored.

SIGHTS

If you're arriving in Red Deer from either the north or south, stay on Highway 2 until the large red and white **Red Deer Visitor and Convention Bureau** building comes into view (from the north, take the 32nd St. exit and loop back onto

Hwy. 2 northbound). In addition to being a good source of information about the city, it's home to the **Alberta Sports Hall of Fame and Museum** (403/341-8614, summer 9 A.M.–6 P.M., rest of year 10 A.M.–5 P.M., $3), which highlights the feats of sports heroes such as hockey legend Wayne Gretzky and multiple-time World Figure Skating Champion Kurt Browning. From this complex, duck through the Heritage Ranch parking lot to get downtown.

Downtown

The **Red Deer and District Museum** (4525 47A Ave., 403/309-8405, July–Aug. Mon.–Fri. 10 A.M.–5 P.M. and Sat.–Sun. 1–5 P.M., rest of year daily 1–5 P.M.) tells the story of the area from prehistoric times to the present, with emphasis on

A DAY AT THE BEACH

Landlocked Albertans don't have a great deal of choice when it comes to a vacation on the beach, unless they head over the mountains to Invermere, in British Columbia, or jump aboard an airplane. The one exception is **Sylvan Lake,** 22 kilometers (14 mi.) west of Red Deer, which has been a popular summer resort since the beginning of the 20th century. It has more than five kilometers (three mi.) of sandy beaches, clean warm water, a large marina, and plenty of recreation facilities. Kids will love **Wild Rapids Waterslides** (Lakeshore Dr., 403/887-3636) and its 11 water slides, a heated pool, and sailboard and paddleboat rentals. The beachy stretch of lake is lined with surf-clothing shops, water-sport rentals, casual cafés, kid-friendly accommodations, and even a lighthouse.

the growth and development of the last 100 years. If you have youngsters in tow, head for interactive Children's Zone; if you have a love of the tacky and wacky, search out the display of "The World's Most Boring Postcard," a title bestowed on a postcard depicting the museum exterior. The museum is also the starting point for two historical walking tours—ask here for a map. Adjacent to the museum is **Heritage Square,** a collection of historic structures, including the Stevenson-Hall Block, Red Deer's oldest building, and a re-created Norwegian log and sod farmhouse, typical of those lived in by many early settlers in Alberta.

Along the River

On the west side of downtown, **Waskasoo Park** stretches for 11 kilometers (seven mi.) along the Red Deer River. The park has a 75-kilometer (47-mi.) trail system, which is good for walking or biking in summer and cross-country skiing in winter. Drive west along 32nd Street to **Fort Normandeau** (403/346-2010, mid-May–June daily noon–5 P.M., July–Aug. noon–8 P.M.). This replica is built on the site of the original fort, constructed in the spring of 1885 in anticipation of the Riel Rebellion—a Métis uprising led

by Louis Riel. As protection against marauding natives, a hotel by the river crossing was heavily fortified. Its walls were reinforced, lookout towers were erected, and the entire building was palisaded, but it was never attacked.

North of downtown, **Kerry Wood Nature Centre** (6300 45th Ave., 403/346-2010, daily 10 a.m.–5 P.M.) has various exhibits and videos on the natural history of the river valley and provides access to the adjacent 118-hectare (292-acre) **Gaetz Lakes Sanctuary,** home to 128 recorded species of birds and 25 species of mammals.

PRACTICALITIES
Accommodations

Red Deer's location between Alberta's two largest cities makes it a popular location for conventions and conferences, so the city has a lot of hotels. The larger hotels are generally full of conventioneers during the week; weekend rates and web specials usually bring rates down below $100 a night. A cheapie is the **Thunderbird Motel** (Hwy. 2 S, 403/343-8933 or 800/268-7132, $60 s, $65 d) in "Gasoline Alley," the southernmost commercial strip, and as you can guess from the name, it's an older place. The 40 rooms are set around an outdoor pool and barbecue area.

The **Holiday Inn Express** is south of downtown on the northbound side of the road (2803 Gaetz Ave., 403/343-2112, www.hiexpress.com, $119 s or d). The rooms are spacious, modern, and well furnished. Breakfast is included in the rates, as is access to an indoor saltwater pool. Directly across the road is the **Sandman Hotel Red Deer** (2818 Gaetz Ave., 403/343-7400 or 800/726-3626, www.sandmanhotels.com, $100–120 s or d). It features 143 smartly decorated guest rooms, an indoor pool, a fitness center, a lounge, and a restaurant.

Camping

Red Deer has excellent city camping at the **Lions Campground** (4723 Riverside Dr., 403/342-8183, May–Sept.; unserviced sites $18, powered sites $25) on the west side of the river. To get there, follow Gaetz Avenue north through town

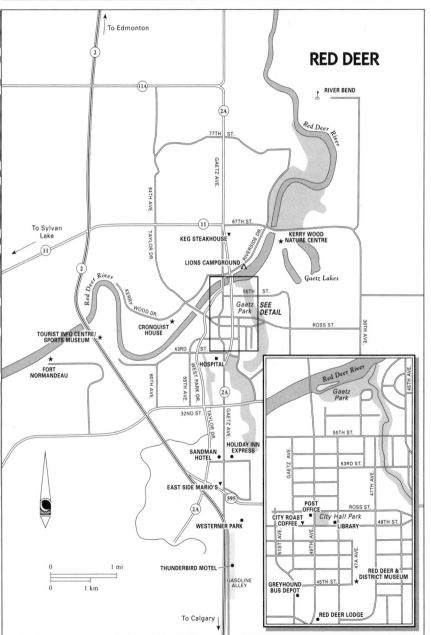

RED DEER

River Bend

Red Deer River

To Edmonton

77TH ST.

GAETZ AVE.

64TH AVE.

TAYLOR DR.

To Sylvan Lake

67TH ST.

KEG STEAKHOUSE

RIVERSIDE DR.

KERRY WOOD NATURE CENTRE

LIONS CAMPGROUND

Gaetz Lakes

Red Deer River

KERRY WOOD DR.

55TH ST.

Gaetz Park

SEE DETAIL

CRONQUIST HOUSE

ROSS ST.

30TH AVE.

TOURIST INFO CENTRE/ SPORTS MUSEUM

43RD ST.

FORT NORMANDEAU

WEST PARK DR.

55TH AVE.

HOSPITAL

60TH AVE.

2A

32ND AVE.

TAYLOR DR.

GAETZ AVE.

SANDMAN HOTEL

HOLIDAY INN EXPRESS

EAST SIDE MARIO'S

595

2A

WESTERNER PARK

THUNDERBIRD MOTEL

GASOLINE ALLEY

To Calgary

0   1 mi

0   1 km

ALBERTA

Detail

Red Deer River

Gaetz Park

45TH AVE.

55TH ST.

GAETZ AVE.

53RD ST.

47TH AVE.

POST OFFICE

CITY ROAST COFFEE

City Hall Park

ROSS ST.

49TH ST.

LIBRARY

51ST AVE.

49TH AVE.

47A AVE.

RED DEER & DISTRICT MUSEUM

GREYHOUND BUS DEPOT

45TH ST.

RED DEER LODGE

and turn right after crossing the Red Deer River. The campground has showers, full hookups, and a laundry room.

Food

Downtown, head to **City Roast Coffee** (4940 Ross St., 403/347-0893, Mon.–Sat. 7:30 A.M.–6 P.M.). It's a big-city-style coffeehouse offering coffees from around the world and light snacks such as soups and sandwiches. Fast-food and family-style restaurants line 50th (Gaetz) Avenue north and south of downtown; Alberta beef dishes at the **Keg Steakhouse** (6365 50th Ave., 403/309-5499) and the Americanized Italian food at **East Side Mario's** (2004 50th Ave., 403/342-2279) are a cut above the rest. Surrounded by tropical greenery, **Botanica Restaurant** (4311 49th Ave., 403/346-8841) takes pride of place within a huge atrium at the Red Deer Lodge. It's open daily for breakfast, lunch, and dinner, but is most popular for the lunchtime buffet and Sunday brunch.

Information

The Red Deer Visitor and Convention Bureau operate the excellent **Tourist Information Centre** (403/346-0180 or 800/215-8946, www.tourismreddeer.net, year-round Mon.–Fri. 9 A.M.–5 P.M., Sat.–Sun. 10 A.M.–5 P.M. and until 6 P.M. in summer) on Highway 2 between the main north and south entrances to the city. It's on the city-side of the highway (if you're arriving from the north, take the 32nd St. exit and loop back onto Hwy. 2 northbound). In addition to providing a load of information, the center has a gift shop, a concession area, restrooms, and is adjacent to a picnic area.

Red Deer Public Library (4818 49th St., 403/346-4576, Mon.–Thurs. 9:30 A.M.–8:30 P.M., Fri.–Sat. 9:30 A.M.–5:30 P.M., Sun. 1:30–5 P.M.) is an excellent facility housed in a single-story, red-brick building behind City Hall. **Chapters** (5250 22nd St., 403/309-2427) is part of a chain of Canadian mega-bookstores.

Aspen Parkland

The aspen parkland lying east of Highway 2, between Red Deer and Edmonton, is a transition zone between the prairies to the south and the boreal forest to the north. Here, groves of aspen and, to a lesser degree, balsam poplar grow around sloughs and pothole-like depressions left by the retreating ice sheet at the end of the last ice age. Although much of the forest has been cleared and cultivated, the region is still home to mammals such as fox, coyote, lynx, white-tailed deer, beaver, and muskrat. The lakes and sloughs attract more than 200 species of birds, including literally millions of ducks that can be seen in almost all bodies of water.

RED DEER TO EDMONTON

It takes little more than an hour to reach the southern outskirts of Edmonton from Red Deer all on divided Highway 2. An alternative is to take Highway 2A, the old highway, which passes through the following towns.

Lacombe

Lacombe, 30 kilometers (19 mi.) north of Red Deer and three kilometers (1.9 mi.) east of Highway 2, was devastated by fire in 1906. The town immediately implemented a bylaw dictating that all new buildings were to be constructed using brick or stone, many of which remain in the business district. One block from the main street (50th Ave.) is **Michener House** (5036 51st St., 403/782-3933, summer Mon.–Fri. noon–4 P.M.), the birthplace of Roland Michener, Canadian governor-general between 1967 and 1974.

Wetaskiwin

This mid-size town (pop. 11,000), halfway between Red Deer and Edmonton on Highway 2A, is named for a Cree word meaning "where peace was made," in reference to nearby hills where a treaty between the Cree and Blackfoot was signed in 1867.

The reason to make the detour is to visit the **Reynolds-Alberta Museum** (780/361-1351, year-round daily 9 A.M.–5 P.M. except Mon. Sept.–May, adult $9, senior $7, child $5), a world-class facility cataloging the history of all types of machinery. Surrounding the main exhibition hall, the complete history of transportation in Alberta is re-created, from horse-drawn carriages to luxurious 1950s automobiles. Over 1,000 vehicles have been fully restored, but some, such as the handmade snowmobile, are in their original condition. At the end of the display, you can peer into a large hall where the restoration takes place. The transportation displays encircle a large area where traditional farm machinery is on show, from the most basic plow to a massive combine harvester. Behind the museum lies an airstrip and a large hangar that houses **Canada's Aviation Hall of Fame.**

Set on two hectares (five acres) of mature gardens, **Country Pleasures** (5712 45th Ave., 780/352-4335, $75–85 s or d) is a delightful bed-and-breakfast that wouldn't look out of place in the English countryside, except it's one block from the bright lights of Wetaskiwin's ubiquitous commercial strip. Common areas include a cozy living room, but on a warm evening it's hard to pass up one of the garden benches for some quiet time. Each of three guest rooms has an en suite bath. Opt for Henry's Den and you'll enjoy a fireplace, claw-foot bathtub, and private patio. Opposite the local golf course, **Wetaskiwin Lions RV Campground** (2.5 km/1.6 mi. east of town along Hwy. 13, 780/352-7258, unserviced sites $15, hookups $20) has free showers, a laundry room, a cooking shelter, a stocked trout pond, and minigolf.

Grandma Lee's Bakery (5103 50th Ave., 780/352-7711, Mon.–Sat. 7:30 A.M.–5 P.M.) is enduringly popular with locals for its small-town atmosphere as much as its food. Recommended are the meat pies and tasty pastries. Continuing east along the main street and over the railway tracks is **MacEachern Tea House** (4719 50th Ave., 780/352-8308, Mon.–Sat. 9 A.M.–5 P.M.). Built by one of the district's early pioneers, this distinctive two-story green and yellow building is open for breakfast, lunch, and afternoon tea. Everything served is made on the premises, including delicious cheesecakes ($4 per slice).

At the junction of Highway 2A and 50th Avenue, the local **Tourist Information Centre** (4910 55th St., 780/352-8003, year-round Mon.–Fri. 9 A.M.–5 P.M., as well as summer weekends 9 A.M.–3 P.M.) is impossible to miss—just look for the colorful water tower across the road.

Pigeon Lake

From Wetaskiwin, head west on Highway 13, beyond Highway 2, to reach Pigeon Lake, a popular recreation area for residents of Edmonton, 105 kilometers (65 mi.) to the northeast. At the southeastern end of the lake is the little hamlet of **Ma-me-o,** where the streets are lined with a colorful array of summer cottages. The beach here is good and is backed by a few shops, including a restaurant.

Pigeon Lake gets very busy in summer. Most visitors are "cottagers," but you can also enjoy the resortlike atmosphere of the area by spending time at **By the Lake Bed and Breakfast** (86 Grandview, 780/586-3598, www.bythelakebnb.com, $70–100 s or d). Two rooms are offered in this modern lakeside home, one in the main house, another in an adjacent building. Both have an inviting atmosphere, en suite baths, and plenty of privacy. In addition to their separate sitting rooms, a patio on the main house opens to gardens and the waterfront. Rates include a gourmet breakfast. The property is signposted off Highway 771 northwest of Westerose.

Also along the western shoreline is **Pigeon Lake Provincial Park.** At the main 300-site campground (unserviced sites $22, powered sites $28), you'll find a beach, showers, cooking shelters, firewood, and the start of an 11-kilometer (6.8-mi.) trail system. **Zeiner Campground** (unserviced sites $22, powered sites $30), a little farther north, has powered sites, cooking shelters, firewood, groceries, canoe rentals, and showers. Both campgrounds are within the provincial park, but are run by a private operator who promotes them as **Pigeon Lake Family Park** (780/586-2644, www.pigeonlakeparks.com).

ALBERTA

EAST OF HIGHWAY 2

It is easy to spend a day—or even longer if you take advantage of the many campgrounds—exploring the parkland region east of Highway 2. Highways 12, 13, and 14 run parallel to each other in a southeasterly direction through this region, with many north–south minor highways providing links. My suggestion is to lay out a map of the area, pick out the attractions below that interest you, and plot a course to Edmonton.

Stettler

Stettler (pop. 5,200) is on Highway 12, 72 kilometers (45 mi.) east of both Red Deer and Lacombe. A highlight of a visit to Stettler is actually *leaving* town—aboard one of Canada's last remaining passenger steam trains. Operated by

THE VIKING RIB STONES

Natives who lived on the plains were nomadic and left few lasting signs of their ever having been there. Buffalo jumps and petroglyphs are the well-documented exceptions. West of Camrose, in an unassuming field, is another. Two rib stones, carved with a design resembling bison ribs, have been dated at 1,000 years old. The stones held special significance for generations of Plains Indians, whose lives revolved around the movement of bison herds. They believed that by conducting certain ceremonial rites and by leaving gifts of beads or tobacco around the stones, their luck in hunting would improve. They then gave thanks by leaving more gifts after a successful hunt.

The site is not well marked. Fourteen kilometers (8.7 mi.) east of Viking on Highway 14 is a historical marker. A little farther east is a gravel road to the south; follow this road two kilometers (1.2 mi.) to Highway 615, turn east (left), then take the first gravel road to the south (right) and follow it for 2.5 kilometers (1.5 mi.) to a low knoll surrounded by fields. A provincial historic cairn marks the site.

Alberta Prairie Railway Excursions (403/742-2811, www.absteamtrain.com, weekends May–Oct., Thurs.–Fri. in July–Aug.; adult $69, child $32), the trains run between an historic railway station at the end of Stettler's main street south to Big Valley. A rollicking good time is had by all, with live music, the occasional train robbery, and a hearty meal served at the turnaround point. Check the website for a schedule. Stettler also offers the **Town and Country Museum** (44th Ave., 403/742-4534, summer only, daily 9 A.M.–4:30 P.M., $3), a surprisingly large complex comprising 22 buildings spread over three hectares (7.5 acres).

The nicest of four accommodations in town is the solid **Super 8 Motel** (5720 44th Ave., at the south end of town, 403/742-3391 or 888/742-8008, $89 s, $99 d), reasonably priced for this chain. **Stettler Lions Campground** is adjacent to the golf course on the west side of town (off Hwy. 12 on 62nd St.). It has showers and hookups for $12–18 per night and is open May–October.

Stettler Tourist Information Centre (403/742-3181, summer Mon.–Fri. 8 A.M.–8 P.M., weekends 9 A.M.–6 P.M., rest of year Mon.–Fri. 8:30 A.M.–5:30 P.M.) is along Highway 12 in front of the Town Centre Mall.

Big Knife Provincial Park

Legend has it that Big Knife Creek was named after a fight between two long-standing enemies—one Cree, the other Blackfoot—that resulted in the death of both men. Recent history is no less colorful. A local farmer named One-eyed Nelson ran a moonshine operation here. His hooch was in demand throughout the prairies; he even exported the popular brew to Montana. Thirty years after he'd left the area, park rangers found the remains of his still in the side of the creek bank.

The small campground ($15) at the park has no services, but the Battle River flows through the park, making for good swimming and canoeing. Sites are situated among towering cottonwood trees. To get to the park from Stettler, head east along Highway 12 approximately 40 kilometers

(25 mi.) to Halkirk, then north on Highway 855 another 20 kilometers (12.5 mi.).

Camrose

Camrose, 84 kilometers (52 mi.) north of Stettler and 40 kilometers (25 mi.) east of Wetaskiwin, is a town of 15,000 that has greatly benefited from the oil-and-gas boom yet retains its agricultural base. As a tribute to early Norwegian settlers, a nine-meter (30-ft.) scaled-down replica of a Viking longship is on display in the **Bill Fowler Centre** (5402 48th Ave., 780/672-4217, summer Mon.–Fri. 8:30 A.M.–7:30 P.M. Sat.–Sun. 9:30 A.M.–5:30 P.M., rest of year Mon.–Fri. 8:30 A.M.–4:30 P.M.). Overlooking Mirror Lake, the center is also home to the local **tourist information center.**

On the first weekend of August, Camrose hosts the **Big Valley Jamboree** (780/672-0224 or 888/404-1234, www.bigvalleyjamboree.com), one of North America's largest gatherings of country-music superstars. Most fans camp out, with one area set aside especially for families. Daily passes are approximately $65, and a three-day weekend pass goes for $170, and camping is $50 for as long as you can handle the heat, the noise, and the booze.

Valleyview Campground (unserviced sites $12, powered $15) has powered sites, showers, a kitchen shelter, and firewood. To get there, follow 53rd Street south from Highway 13 for two kilometers (1.2 mi.) and turn left on 39th Avenue. Within view of the camping area is a massive ski jump and a biathlon range, two sports brought to the area by Norwegian settlers over 100 years ago.

A former residence converted to a teahouse, the **Ruffington** (4803 48th St., 780/672-4500, Mon.–Sat. 10 A.M.–5:30 P.M.) comes with all the decorations but no pretensions. The menu offers a selection of teas (and coffee), plus full-blown lunches such as quiche and a delicious selection of fudges to finish off. It's along Highway 13, just east of the downtown turn-off.

Wainwright

Wainwright, the last town along Highway 14, before Saskatchewan is home to the military's **Western Area Training Camp,** Canada's second-largest military training facility. On its 400 square kilometers (154 sq. mi.) are 22 weapons ranges, two airfields, and a small herd of bison, which can be viewed in **Bud Cotton Buffalo Paddock** beside the base's main gate (turn left at the guarded entrance, then right down the fenceline for best viewing opportunities. The base is two kilometers (1.2 mi.) south of town along 1st Street.

A local restaurant, the **Honey Pot** (825 2nd Ave., 780/842-4094, daily 11 A.M.–10 P.M.) is worthy of a mention. It has been serving hungry locals and travelers alike for more than two decades. In an old building that has served many uses, choose from dishes as varied as T-bone steak and jambalaya, both a reasonable $14.

Miquelon Lake Provincial Park

Originally a bird sanctuary, this 906-hectare (2,240-acre) park lies 30 kilometer (19 mi.) north of Camrose on Highway 833. It is part of the massive 650-square-kilometer (250-sq.-mi.) **Cooking Lake Moraine,** a hummocky region dotted with lakes that extends north to Elk Island National Park. At the end of the last ice age, as the sheet of ice that covered much of the continent receded, it occasionally stalled, as it did in this area. Chunks of ice then broke off and melted, depositing glacial till in mounds. Between the mounds are hollows, known as kettles, which have filled with water. The **Knob and Kettle Trail System** starts behind the baseball diamond and is a series of short interconnecting trails through this intriguing landscape. During summer, rangers conduct guided hikes (Thurs. at 7 P.M. and Sun. at 10 A.M.) and present evening shows in the amphitheater (Fri. and Sat. at 8 P.M.). The campground (unserviced sites $22, powered sites $25) has showers, cooking shelters, and firewood.

Edmonton

Edmonton, Alberta's capital, sits in the center of the province, surrounded by the vast natural resources that have made the city unabashedly wealthy. It's a vibrant cultural center and a gateway to the north, but its reputation as a boomtown may be its defining characteristic. Boomtowns are a phenomenon unique to the west—cities that have risen from the surrounding wilderness, oblivious to hardship, pushed forward by dreams of the incredible wealth to be made overnight by pulling riches from the earth. Edmonton has experienced three major booms, but no big busts, and has grown into one of the world's largest northerly cities. Its population has mushroomed 800 percent in 50 years to 930,000, making it the sixth-largest city in Canada.

The **North Saskatchewan River Valley** winding through the city has been largely preserved as a 27-kilometer (17-mi.) greenbelt of parks—the largest urban park system in Canada. Edmonton's major attractions, though, are indoors—the provincial museum, a cosmopolitan arts district, and the city's biggest attraction, the ultimate shopping experience of **West Edmonton Mall,** the world's largest shopping and amusement complex.

HISTORY

For at least 3,000 years, natives came to the river valley where Edmonton now stands, searching for quartzite to make stone tools. They had no knowledge of, or use for, the vast underground resources that would eventually cause a city to rise from the wilderness.

The First 100 Years

European fur traders, canoeing along the North Saskatchewan River, found the area where Edmonton now stands to be one of the richest fur-bearing areas on the continent. Large populations of beavers and muskrats lived in the surrounding spruce, poplar, and aspen forest. In 1795 a fort was established on the site of the present Legislature Building grounds. It was an ideal location for trading—Cree and Assiniboine could trade beaver, otter, and marten pelts in safety, without encroaching on the territory of fierce Plains Indians, such as the Blackfoot, yet the fort was far enough south to be within range of the Blackfoot, who came north to with buffalo meat and other natural resources. After 100 years, the fur trade ended abruptly. Many of the posts throughout the west were abandoned, but Edmonton continued to be an important stop on the route north. Goods were taken overland from Edmonton to Athabasca Landing, where they were transferred to barges or steamers and taken north on the Athabasca River. Edmonton suffered a setback when the C.P.R. chose a southerly route through Calgary for the TransContinental Railway. A branch built by the Calgary and Edmonton Railway Company arrived in 1891, but it ended on the south side of the North Saskatchewan River, at Strathcona.

Selecting the Capital

The provinces of Alberta and Saskatchewan were both inaugurated on September 1, 1905. Because Regina had been the capital of the Northwest Territories, it was only natural that it continue as the capital of Saskatchewan. The decision about Alberta's capital did not come as easily, however. The Alberta Act made Edmonton the temporary capital, but it had plenty of competition, especially from Calgarians, who believed their city to be the financial and transportation center of the province. Heated debates on the subject took place in the Canadian capital of Ottawa, but Edmonton has remained the capital to this day.

Oil and a Growing City

Fur was Edmonton's first industry and coal was its second (the last of 150 operations closed 1970), but Edmonton's future lay in oil. Since the discovery of "black gold" in 1947 at nearby Leduc, Edmonton has been one of Canada's fastest-growing cities. The building of pipelines and refineries created many jobs, and the city became the center of western Canada's petrochemical industry. As demand continued to rise, hundreds of wildcat wells were drilled around Edmonton. Farmers' fields were filled with derricks, valves, and oil tanks, and by 1956, more than 3,000 producing wells were pumping within 100 kilometers (62 mi.) of the city. A 20-square-kilometer (eight-sq.-mi.) area east of the city was filled with huge oil tanks, refineries, and petrochemical plants. Changes were also taking place within the city as the wealth of the oil boom began to take hold. Restaurants improved and cultural life flourished. The city's businesses were jazzed up, and the expanding business community began moving into the glass-and-steel skyscrapers that form the city skyline today.

Although the original boom is over, oil is still a major part of the city's economy. Planned developments in the surrounding service area total approximately $40 billion this decade, with Edmonton benefiting directly from spin-off infrastructure. A great deal of this development is associated with the **oil sands** of northern Alberta, with a new pipeline and processing facilities being built in the city.

ALBERTA

EDMONTON

To Fort Saskatchewan

To Lloydminster

37

16

To Fort McMurray

To Athabasca
and Slave Lake

37

ALBERTA RAILWAY
MUSEUM ★

15

North Saskatchewan River

MANNING DR.

50TH ST.

66TH ST.

153RD AVE.

82ND ST.

15

111TH AVE.

112TH AVE.

LA BOHEME ●

NORTHLANDS
PARK ■

SKYREACH ■

28

167TH AVE.

137TH AVE.

28

EDMONTON CITY
CENTRE AIRPORT ✈

ALBERTA AVIATION
MUSEUM ★

111TH AVE.

VIA RAIL
STATION ■

2

AVE.

ODYSSIUM ★

156TH ST.

118TH

YELLOWHEAD HWY.

ST. ALBERT TRAIL

170TH ST.

16

16

FATHER LACOMBE CHAPEL ★
ST. VITAL AVE.

ST. ALBERT PLACE ★

2

Big Lake

2157

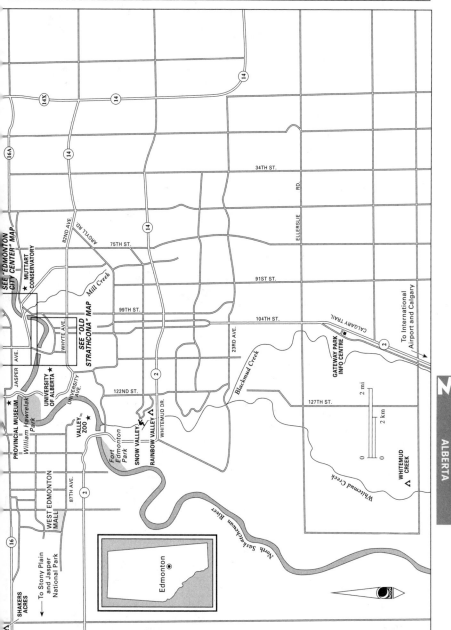

SEE "EDMONTON CITY CENTER" MAP

MUTTART CONSERVATORY

82ND AVE.

ARGYLL RD.

75TH ST.

34TH ST.

ELLERSLIE RD.

91ST ST.

Mill Creek

WHYTE AVE.

SEE "OLD STRATHCONA" MAP

99TH ST.

104TH ST.

CALGARY TRAIL

To International Airport and Calgary

JASPER AVE.

UNIVERSITY OF ALBERTA

23RD AVE.

GATEWAY PARK INFO CENTRE

PROVINCIAL MUSEUM

William Hawrelak Park

UNIVERSITY AVE.

122ND ST.

Blackmud Creek

2 mi

VALLEY ZOO

WHITEMUD DR.

127TH ST.

2 km

SNOW VALLEY

RAINBOW VALLEY

Fort Edmonton Park

WHITEMUD CREEK

0   0

Whitemud Creek

WEST EDMONTON MALL

87TH AVE.

Whitemud Creek

North Saskatchewan River

SHAKERS ACRES

To Stony Plain and Jasper National Park

Edmonton

Edmonton

ALBERTA

Sights

DOWNTOWN AND VICINITY

Looking at Edmonton's dynamic skyline, it's hard to believe that not much more than 100 years ago the main drag was lined with dingy saloons and rowdy dance halls. Since those heady days, the city has seen many ups and downs—its present look is a legacy of the 1970s oil boom. The downtown core is fairly compact; **Jasper Avenue** (101st Ave.) is the main thoroughfare. At the east end of Jasper Avenue is the **Shaw Conference Centre**, a glass-and-steel building that seemingly clings to the wall of the river valley. A few blocks east is the **Arts District**, comprising the provincial government buildings and an array of performing-arts centers.

Throughout all of the development, several historic buildings managed to survive. Many can be seen along **Heritage Trail**, a route taken by early fur traders that linked the old town to Fort Edmonton. Today the trail begins at the Shaw Conference Centre, at the corner of Jasper Avenue and 97th Street, and ends at the legislature grounds. The route is easy to follow—the sidewalk is paved with red bricks and lined with period benches, replica lampposts, and old-fashioned street signs.

The Pedway System

The pedway is unique and necessary this far north. It's a complex system of enclosed walkways linking office buildings, hotels, plazas, the Civic Centre, and public transportation stops. Using the pedways, you can get virtually anywhere downtown, without ever having to step outside into the elements. At first it all seems a bit complicated, but if you're armed with a map, the system soon becomes second nature. Pedways are below, above, or at street level, and the excellent signage makes it easy to find your way. The walkways are spotlessly clean, well lit, and relatively safe, although you wouldn't want to loiter around the Central Light Rail Transit (LRT) Station at night.

Arts District

This complex, in the heart of downtown, oc-cupies six square blocks and is one of the city's showcases. In addition to the main library, a futuristic-looking city hall, Sir Winston Churchill Square, and the magnificent Citadel Theatre, the **Edmonton Art Gallery** (northeast of Sir Winston Churchill Sq. on 99th St., 780/427-6223, Mon.–Wed. and Fri. 10:30 A.M.–5 P.M., Thurs. 10:30 A.M.–8 P.M., and Sat.–Sun. 11 A.M.–5 P.M., adult $5, senior $3, child $2) makes a visit worthwhile. This modern gallery houses an extensive collection of 4,000 modern Canadian paintings as well as historical and contemporary art in all media. Various traveling exhibitions are presented throughout the year.

GETTING ORIENTED IN EDMONTON

Highway 2 from Calgary enters Edmonton from the south and divides just north of Gateway Park Tourist Information Centre. At that point, it becomes known as **Gateway Boulevard** (also known as **103rd St.**). Southbound, it's **Calgary Trail (104th St.)**. From **Whitemud Drive**, a city bypass that delivers you to **West Edmonton Mall**, Gateway Boulevard continues north through **Old Strathcona**, crossing the North Saskatchewan River directly south of downtown.

The **Yellowhead Highway** passes through the city east to west, north of downtown. To get downtown from the east, take 97th Street. From downtown, Jasper Avenue changes to Stony Plain Road as it heads west, eventually joining Highway 16 at the city's western limits.

Avenues run east to west, numbered from 1st Avenue in the south. Streets run north to south, numbered from 1st Street in the east. Even-numbered addresses are on the north sides of the avenues and west sides of the streets. The center of the city is crossed by both 101st Street and 101st Avenue, the latter having retained its original name of **Jasper Avenue.**

ALBERTA

Chinatown

An elaborate gateway designed by a master architect from China welcomes visitors to where Edmonton's small Chinatown *used* to be. The gate spans 23 meters (75 ft.) across 102nd Avenue (also known as Harbin Rd.) at 97th Street. Eight steel columns painted the traditional Chinese color of red support it. Stretched across the center of the arch's roof is a row of ornamental tiles featuring two dragons, the symbol of power in China. The 11,000 tiles used in the gate were each handcrafted and glazed in China. In the last few years, Chinatown has moved up the road a few blocks. The archway now leads into an area of cheap boardinghouses and deserted parking lots, but still forms a colorful break from the pawnshops of 97th Street.

Alberta Legislature Building

Home of the provincial government, this elegant Edwardian building overlooking the North Saskatchewan River Valley is surrounded by 24 hectares (59 acres) of formal gardens and manicured lawns. Its 16-story vaulted dome is one of Edmonton's most recognizable landmarks. The interior features a wide marble staircase that leads from the spacious rotunda in the lobby to the chamber and is surrounded by stained-glass windows and bronze statues. Immediately north of the Legislature Building, beyond the fountains, is the **Legislative Assembly Interpretive Centre** (780/427-7362), which recounts the development of Alberta's political history and serves as the starting point for free tours of the Legislature Building. Between mid-May and October, tours depart on the hour in the morning and every 30 minutes in the afternoon weekdays 8:30 A.M.–5 P.M. and weekends 9 A.M.–5 P.M., the rest of the year hourly weekdays 9 A.M.–5 P.M. and weekends noon–5 P.M.

High Level Bridge

This bridge crosses the North Saskatchewan River at the bottom end of 109th Street. It was built in 1913, linking the new capital to Strathcona. The bridge is 775 meters (2,500 ft.) long and 53 meters (180 ft.) above the river. It has been used as a tramway, a railway, a sidewalk, and a roadway. The rail line was in use until 1951, but in 2000 a local historical society began running a scheduled streetcar over the bridge. It runs from adjacent to the Grandin LRT Station across the bridge

Alberta Legislature Building

ALBERTA

To Edmonton City
Centre Airport

104TH AVE.

MAP TOWN

105TH

104TH

103RD AVE.

DOWNTOWN EDMONTON

109TH

108TH

106TH

ST.

102ND AVE.

ALBERTA CRAFT COUNCIL

ST.

COAST EDMONTON PLAZA HOTEL

ST.

ST.

AUDREY'S

JASPER AVE. (101ST AVE.)

107TH

CAROUSEL PHOTO IMAGING

To West End and
Provincial Museum

112TH

111TH

110TH

100TH AVE.

COMFORT INN & SUITES

ST.

ST.

ALBERTA ENVIRONMENT
INFORMATION CENTRE

ST.

99TH AVE.

ALBERTA

ST.

HIGH LEVEL
STREET CAR
STATION

ALBERTA
LEGISLATIVE
★ BUILDING

98TH AVE.

98TH AVE.

106TH

104TH

VICTORIA GOLF COURSE

TUNNEL

97TH AVE.

GOVERNMENT
CENTRE
COMPLEX

ST.

ST.

96TH AVE.

RIVER VALLEY RD.

To Calgary Trail

HIGH LEVEL
BRIDGE

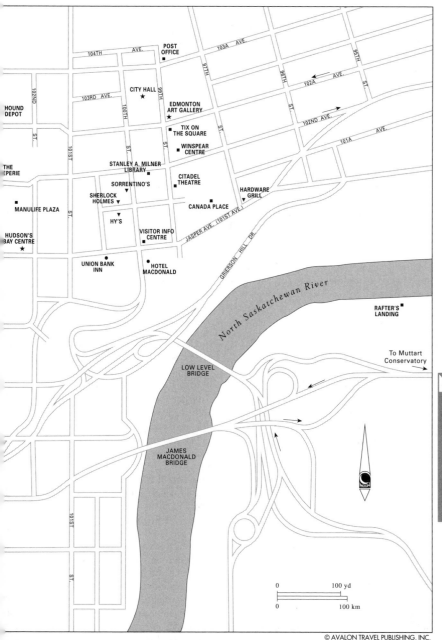

104TH AVE.
POST OFFICE
103A AVE.
96TH ST.
97TH ST.
102ND
ST.
102A AVE.
HOUND DEPOT
103RD AVE.
CITY HALL ★
100TH ST.
96TH ST.
EDMONTON ART GALLERY ★
102ND AVE.
98TH ST.
THE EPERIE
101ST ST.
TIX ON THE SQUARE
97TH ST.
101A AVE.
WINSPEAR CENTRE
STANLEY A. MILNER LIBRARY
SORRENTINO'S
CITADEL THEATRE
HARDWARE GRILL
MANULIFE PLAZA
SHERLOCK HOLMES ▼
ST.
CANADA PLACE
HY'S ▼
HUDSON'S BAY CENTRE ★
VISITOR INFO CENTRE
JASPER AVE. (101ST AVE.)
GRIERSON HILL DR.
UNION BANK INN
HOTEL MACDONALD
North Saskatchewan River
RAFTER'S LANDING
To Muttart Conservatory
LOW LEVEL BRIDGE
JAMES MACDONALD BRIDGE
101ST ST.
MOON

0   100 yd
0   100 km

ALBERTA

© AVALON TRAVEL PUBLISHING, INC.

to as far south as Old Strathcona. The service operates 15 and 45 minutes past the hour Sunday–Friday 11 A.M.–4 P.M., Saturday 9 A.M.–4 P.M. and costs just $3 one-way.

Muttart Conservatory

Across the river from downtown are four large pyramid-shaped greenhouses that make up the Muttart Conservatory (9626 96A St. off 98th Ave., 780/496-8755, Mon.–Fri. 9 A.M.–5:50 P.M., Sat.–Sun. 11 A.M.–5:30 P.M., adult $5.50, senior $4.50, child $3). The greenhouses contain the flora of specific climates. In the arid pyramid are cacti and other hardy plants found in desertlike conditions. The tropical pyramid holds a humid jungle, one of North America's largest orchid collections, and colorful and raucous exotic birds, who live among the palms. The temperate pyramid features plant species from four continents, none of which would grow naturally in Edmonton's harsh environment. The contents of the fourth pyramid change with the season.

John Walter Museum

This historic site located near the Kinsmen Sports Centre consists of three houses—dating from 1875, 1884, and 1900—that were built by John Walter for his family. Walter operated a ferry across the river, as well as a carriage works, a lumber mill, and a coal mine, and at one time even built a steamship. Each house holds exhibits corresponding to the period of its construction and depicts the growth of Edmonton and the importance of the North Saskatchewan River. The buildings (10627 93rd Ave., 780/496-4852) are open only in summer, Sunday 1–4 P.M., with bread-making demonstrations, old-fashioned games, or some other related activity scheduled to correspond with these hours. The grounds are pleasant to walk through at any time. From downtown, take 101st Street south down Bellamy Hill and cross the river at the Walterdale Bridge.

Fort Edmonton Park

An authentic reconstruction of the early trading post from which Edmonton grew is only a small part of this exciting attraction (off Whitemud Dr. near Fox Dr., 780/496-8787, May–June Mon.–Fri. 10 A.M.–4 P.M. and Sat.–Sun. 10 A.M.–6 P.M., July–Aug. daily 10 A.M.–6 P.M., Sept. 10 A.M.–4 P.M., adult $8.25, senior $6.25, child $4.50), Canada's largest historic park. From the entrance, a 1919 steam locomotive takes you through the park to the Hudson's Bay Company Fort, which has been built much as the original fort would have looked in 1846—right down to the methods of carpentry used in its construction. Step outside the fort and you walk forward in time—to 1885 Street, re-creating downtown Edmonton between 1871 and 1891 when the West was opened up to settlers. As you continue down the road, you round a corner and are on 1905 Street, in the time period 1892–1914, when the railway had arrived and Edmonton was proclaimed provincial capital. By this time, you're nearly on 1920 Street. Stop by Bill's Confectionary (noon–4 P.M.) for a soda or sundae, hitch a lift aboard the streetcar, or plan an overnight stay at the Hotel Selkirk (see Accommodations) to round out the roaring 1920s experience.

Valley Zoo

Across the river from Fort Edmonton Park is the city zoo (end of Buena Vista Rd., off 142nd St., 780/496-6911, May–June daily 10 A.M.–6 P.M., July–Aug. 9:30 A.M.–8 P.M., rest of year 9:30 A.M.–4 P.M., adult $6.25, senior $4.75, child $3.75), which holds approximately 350 animals, representing all seven continents. It's designed mainly for kids, with a petting zoo, camel and pony rides, paddleboats, a miniature train, and cut-out storybook characters.

Provincial Museum of Alberta

The Provincial Museum (12845 102nd Ave., 780/453-9100, daily 9 A.M.–5 P.M., Fri. until 9 P.M., adult $10, senior $8, child $5) overlooks the river valley in the historic neighborhood of Glenora, west of downtown. It is one of Canada's largest museums. Exhibits catalog one billion years of natural and human history. The highlight is most definitely the **Wild Alberta Gallery,** where a water setting and the province's four natural regions—mountain, prairie, parkland, and boreal forest—are re-created with incredible accuracy. Lifelike dioramas are only part of the appeal. Much

ALBERTA

of the exhibit encourages visitor input—to solve the mystery of what is Alberta's most dangerous mammal, touch the teeth of a grizzly bear, or soak up the sound of a bull moose calling in the female members of his species.

In front of the museum is **Government House** (780/427-2281, summer tours, Sunday 11 A.M.–4:30 P.M., free), an impressive three-story sandstone structure built in 1913 for Alberta's lieutenant governor, who would entertain guests in the lavish reception rooms or in the surrounding gardens. The building was later used as a hospital, and then restored to its former glory in the 1970s.

Odyssium

Completed in 1984, this multipurpose complex in Coronation Park (11211 142nd St., 780/452-9100, daily 10 A.M.–5 P.M., summer until 9 P.M.) is one of Edmonton's major attractions and a wonderful place to take children. Displays include a look into the future of communications, the chance to solve a crime along Mystery Avenue, a ham radio station hooked up to similar stations around the world, a tribute to RCMP, a laser-light show, an interactive "Eye-lusions" exhibit, Discoveryland for kids, a chance to learn about the environment in Green's House, and Sport II where you can try your hand at sports like wheelchair racing.

A day pass (adults $7, seniors $6, children $5) includes admission to all of the above galleries and theater presentations. Also in the building, an **IMAX theater** presents spectacular video productions—seemingly always of an interesting nature—projected onto a 13- by 19-meter (43-by 62-ft.) screen; adult $10, senior $8, child $7 for the theater only; $16, $13, and $11.25, respectively, for admission to one IMAX feature and the other displays.

OLD STRATHCONA

When the Calgary and Edmonton Railway Company completed a rail line between the province's two largest cities, it decided to end it south of the North Saskatchewan River and establish a townsite there. The town was named Strathcona, and it grew to a population of 7,500 before merging with Edmonton in 1912. Many original brick buildings remain, looking much as they did at the beginning of the 20th century. More modern additions include brick sidewalks and replica lampposts.

Sights

The commercial core of Old Strathcona is centered along Whyte (82nd) Avenue, west of the rail line. Across from the rail line is the **Strathcona Hotel** (corner of 103rd St. and Whyte Ave.), one of the few wood-framed buildings surviving from the pre-1900 period. The two blocks east of the hotel are lined with cafés and restaurants, used bookstores, and many interesting shops. In a converted bus garage one block north is the **Old Strathcona Farmer's Market** (83rd Ave., year-round Sat. 8 A.M.–3 P.M.), with plenty of fresh produce, crafts, and homemade goodies for sale. The **Telephone Historical Centre** (10437 83rd Ave., 780/433-1010, Mon.–Fri. 10 A.M.–4 P.M., Sat. noon–4 P.M., $3) is a surprisingly interesting space that catalogs the history of telecommunications in Edmonton from the introduction of telephones in 1885 to the present. It's housed in Strathcona's original telephone exchange and has many hands-on exhibits, including an early switchboard where you can make your own connections.

Getting There

The best way to get to Old Strathcona from downtown is aboard the **High Level Street Car** (780/437-7721, departs downtown 15 and 45 minutes past the hour summer only Sun.–Fri. 11 A.M.–4 P.M., Sat. 9 A.M.–4 P.M.; $3 one-way), which runs from the west side of the Alberta Legislature Building to the 104th Street and 85th Avenue intersection on Old Strathcona. From the station, wander south to bustling Whyte Avenue.

WEST EDMONTON MALL

Feel like a trip to the beach to do some sunbathing and surfing? Would you like to play a round of golf? How about a submarine trip through a coral reef? Do you like eating at Parisian cafés? Does watching a National Hockey

League team in training seem like a good way to spend the afternoon? Do the kids like dolphin shows? And at the end of the day, would you like to sink into a hot tub, surrounded by a lush tropical forest? All of these activities are possible under one roof at West Edmonton Mall, the largest shopping and indoor amusement complex in the whole world.

Shopping is only one part of the mall's universal appeal. Prices are no less than anywhere else in the city, but the experience of more than 800 stores (including more than 200 womenswear stores, 35 menswear stores, and 55 shoe shops) under one roof is unique.

Attractions

Aside from the shops, many other major attractions fill the mall. **Galaxyland Amusement Park** is the world's largest indoor amusement park, with 25 rides, including "Mindbender"—a fourteen-story, triple-loop roller coaster (the world's largest indoor roller coaster). Off to one side, **Galaxy Kids Playpark** offers the younger generation the same thrills and spills in a colorful, fun-loving atmosphere. Admission is free, but the rides cost money. A Galaxyland day pass, allowing unlimited rides, is adult $29.95, family $74.95, senior or child $21.95.

In the two-hectare (five-acre) **World Waterpark,** you almost feel as though you're at the beach: the temperature is a balmy 30°C (85°F), and a long, sandy beach, tropical palms, colorful cabanas, a beach bar, and waves crashing on the shore all simulate the real thing. The computerized wave pool holds 12.3 million liters (3.2 million gal.) of water and is programmed by computer to eject "sets" of waves at regular intervals. Behind the beach are 22 water slides that rise to a height of 26 meters (85 ft.). Admission to

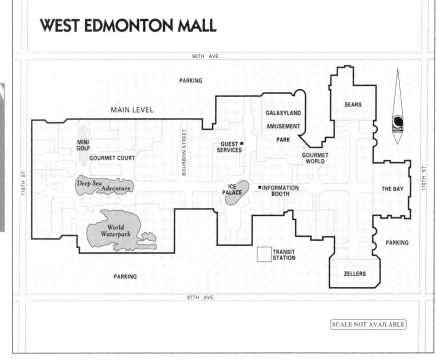

World Waterpark is adult $29.95, family $74.95, senior or child $21.95.

Deep Sea Adventure is a 122-meter (400-ft.) indoor lagoon anchored by a full-size replica of Christopher Columbus's flagship, the *Santa Maria*. You can descend into the depths in one of four self-propelled submarines (adult $12, family $30, senior or child $5) cruising the lake, passing 200 different types of marine life, including real coral. The lake is also the site of scuba-diving courses, canoe rentals, and an underwater aquarium with seals, penguins, and sharks ($6). Beyond the Deep Sea Adventure is the **Playdium** (780/444-7529, 10 A.M.–midnight), opened in 2000 as part of the mall's Phase IV development. This state-of-the-art entertainment center offers more than 150 attractions, from "reality" sports to test your athletic prowess against the professionals to a Speed Zone, which is filled with the latest racing games.

Hours and Other Practicalities

Shopping hours vary seasonally but are generally Monday–Friday 10 A.M.–9 P.M., Saturday 10 A.M.–6 P.M., and Sunday noon–6 P.M. Hours of the various attractions and restaurants vary. Many restaurants stay open later, and the nightclubs stay open to the early hours of the morning.

Mall maps color-code each of four phases to make finding your way around easier (shops and attractions use a Phase number as part of their address). The two official information centers are both on the Main Level near the Ice Palace—a booth on the east side, and Guest Services north toward Entrance 8. For more information, contact West Edmonton Mall (780/444-5200 or 800/661-8890, www.westedmontonmall.com).

The mall is on 170th Street, between 87th and 90th Avenues. Parking is usually not a problem, but finding your car again can be, so remember which of the 58 entrances you parked near (a parking lot along 90th Ave. at 175th St. is designated for RVs). From downtown, take bus no. 100.

WEST EDMONTON MALL TRIVIA

West Edmonton Mall is . . .
- the world's largest shopping and amusement complex, encompassing 483,000 square meters (5.2 million sq. ft.)—that's equivalent to 115 football fields.

West Edmonton Mall has . . .
- over 800 stores
- over 100 eateries
- 58 entrances
- 27 movie screens
- 325,000 light bulbs
- five postal codes
- the world's largest car park (parking for 20,000 vehicles)
- the world's largest indoor amusement park
- the world's largest indoor water park, covering two hectares (five acres) and containing 50 million liters (13.2 million gal.) of water
- the world's largest indoor lake (122 m/400 ft. long)
- the world's only indoor bungee jump

West Edmonton Mall . . .
- cost over a billion dollars to construct
- employs 23,000 people
- uses the same amount of power as a city of 50,000
- attracts 22 million people a year (over 60,000 per day)

ST. ALBERT

The city of St. Albert (pop. 48,000)—northwest of Edmonton along the St. Albert Trail—is one of Alberta's oldest settlements but has today become part of Edmonton's sprawl. Albert Lacombe, a pioneering western Canadian priest, built a mission overlooking the Sturgeon River in 1861, when Fort Edmonton was only a small trading post.

Sights

Father Lacombe Chapel (west of Hwy. 2 on St. Vital Ave., 780/427-3995, mid-May–Aug. daily 10 A.M.–6 P.M., $2), dating from 1861, has been restored to its original appearance. Beside the chapel, a cast-iron statue of Father Lacombe that was made in France overlooks the city. Also

FATHER ALBERT LACOMBE

Dressed in a tattered black robe and brandishing a cross, Father Albert Lacombe, known to natives as "the man with the good heart," dedicated his life to those with native blood. His reputation extended to every corner of the province—he was a spokesman for the Church, an effective influence on government policies, and, most importantly, he had a hand in just about every advance in the often-tense relationship between warring tribes and white men.

Father Lacombe originally came to what is now Alberta in 1852 to serve the Métis and natives who had moved to Fort Edmonton, later founding a mission at what is now St. Albert. He travelled widely, instigating Canada's first industrial school for natives, mediating a dispute between the railway company and angry leaders of the Blackfoot over rights to build a rail line through a reserve, and he wrote the first Cree dictionary. The trust he built up with native leaders was great; during one rebellion of the Blackfoot Confederacy, it is claimed that his influence prevented the slaughter of every white man on the prairies.

on Mission Hill is the **Vital Grandin Centre,** an imposing three-story structure built in 1887 as a hospital.

In stark contrast to the historic buildings overlooking the Sturgeon River is City Hall in **St. Albert Place** on St. Anne Street, a contoured brick building designed by Douglas Cardinal. Inside is the **Musèe Heritage Museum** (780/459-1528, Mon.–Sat. 10 A.M.–5 P.M., Sunday 1–5 P.M.), with displays telling the story of St. Albert's history and the people who made it happen.

St. Albert Information Centre (71 St. Albert Rd., 780/459-1724, Mon.–Fri. 8 A.M.–5 P.M., Sat.–Sun. 10 A.M.–5 P.M.) is in a large, modern building beside Highway 2 on the south side of St. Albert (you can't miss it coming into the city from the south).

Recreation

OUTDOOR ACTIVITIES

River Valley Park System

One of the first things you'll notice about Edmonton is its large amount of parkland. The city has more land set aside for parks, per capita, than any other city in Canada. Most parks interconnect along the banks of the North Saskatchewan River and in adjoining ravines, encompassing 7,400 hectares (18,300 acres) and comprising the largest stretch of urban parkland in North America. Within these parks are picnic areas, swimming pools, historic sites, golf courses, and many kilometers of walking and biking trails. One of the best ways to ensure you make the most of park system is by referring to the brochure *Priceless Fun,* available from Tourist Information Centres and online at the City of Edmonton website (www.edmonton.ca).

Edmonton Queen

The *Edmonton Queen* is a 52-meter (170-ft.) paddlewheeler that cruises along the North Saskatchewan River from Rafter's Landing, near Muttart Conservatory. One-hour cruises (780/424-2628) depart Monday–Saturday at noon and 3 P.M. ($15; lunch extra), evening cruises depart at 7:30 P.M. ($45 including dinner), and the Sunday brunch cruise departs 1 P.M. ($40). To get to Rafter's Landing, take 98th Avenue east along the south side of the river.

Swimming

It's often crowded and it's not cheap, but Edmonton's ultimate swimming, sliding, and sunbathing experience awaits at **World Waterpark** in the West Edmonton Mall (170th St. and 87th Ave., 780/444-5200, adult $29.95, families $74.95, senior or child $21.95).

Edmonton's outdoor swimming season lasts approximately three months beginning at the end of May. Of the five outdoor pools owned by the city, the one in **Queen Elizabeth Park** is in a particularly picturesque location among poplar trees and with a view of the city skyline over the river; access is from 90th Avenue. Another pool, close to the city center, is in **Mill Creek Park,** north of Whyte Avenue (82nd Ave.) on 95A Street. Admission to all outdoor pools is $4. Swimming events of the 1978 Commonwealth Games were held at the **Kinsmen Sports Centre** (9100 Walterdale Hill, 780/496-7300; $4.75), in Kinsmen Park on the south bank of the North Saskatchewan River.

Golf

Canada's oldest municipal course is **Victoria Golf Course** (River Rd., 780/496-4710, $32–37), which is only a little more than 6,000 yards in length but is made challenging by narrow fairways and smallish greens. As a keen golfer, I took time out of my research schedule while last in Edmonton to try a couple of new courses: 7,330-yard **RedTail Landing** (Hwy. 2 by the airport, 780/890-7888, $80), which opened in 2003, and **Jagare Ridge** (14931 9th Ave., 780/432-4030, $72), stretching along both sides of the Whitemud Creek Valley. I can highly recommend both; the well-placed bunkers and multiple water hazards at RedTail prove especially challenging. West of the city, **The Ranch** (52516 Range Rd., Spruce Grove, 780/470-4700, $60) features a water-lined trio of finishing holes (and carts equipped with GPS and electronic scoring). Also in Spruce Grove, **The Links** (off Calahoo Rd., 780/962-4653, $46) is a well-maintained course with rolling fairways, large greens, and around 70 bunkers.

Ballooning

Recreational and competition ballooning is popular in Edmonton throughout the year. One company offering flights is **Windship Aviation** (5615 103rd St., 780/438-0111). Weather permitting, one flight departs at dawn and another in the evening. Launch sites and landing sites change with the wind direction; the grounds of

---

HOCKEY, CANADA'S UNOFFICIAL NATIONAL SPORT

Ask most people—even Canadians—what the national sport of Canada is and they'll say "ice hockey" (simply "hockey" to Canadians), or you'll get a wacky answer like "dog-mushing." Although both answers are wrong (lacrosse is the official national sport), just don't try telling that to the fans of the **Edmonton Oilers** (780/414-4625 or 866/414-4625, www.edmontonoilers.com), or to fans in Calgary and Vancouver, also home to franchises that compete in the National Hockey League for the Stanley Cup.

During the 1980s, when Wayne Gretzky was leading the Oilers, the Cup resided almost permanently in Edmonton, "City of Champions." Since 1988, when Gretzky was sold to the L.A. Kings, the team has met with mixed success. Still, there's no better way to spend a winter's night in Edmonton than by attending a hockey game at the **Skyreach Centre** at Northlands Park, with 20,000 fans who follow every game with a passion. It doesn't really matter if the team is winning or losing; the atmosphere electric. The season runs October–April. Tickets start at $35 and go all the way up to $100–150 for rink-side seats.

Muttart Conservatory are most often used for launching. Flight time is around 60 minutes, and the $200 cost includes transportation back to the launch site, a celebration drink on landing, and a framed picture of your flight, discounted to $130 on weekday mornings.

Skiing and Snowboarding

The closest major alpine resort is Marmot Basin, in Jasper National Park, but Edmonton has a choice of small lift-serviced hills within the city limits. All are great for beginners but won't hold the interest of other skiers or snowboarders for very long. Overlooking downtown from across the river is the **Edmonton Ski Club** (9613 96th Ave., 780/465-0852, Dec.–Mar.), where lift tickets are $15–17. To get there, follow signs to the Muttart Conservatory. Also close to the city center is **Snow Valley** (southwest of downtown, where Whitemud Dr. crosses the river, 780/434-3991), which has a chairlift, a T-bar, and a small terrain park. Tickets are around the same as the ski club, with seniors getting an extra break (ski all day for just $7).

The River Valley Park System provides ample opportunity for cross-country skiing. More than 75 kilometers (47 mi.) of trails are groomed December–early March. The most popular areas are in William Hawrelak Park, up Mill Creek Ravine, and through Capilano Park. For details of trails, pick up the brochure *Cross-country Ski Edmonton* from Tourist Information Centers or download it from the City of Edmonton website (www.edmonton.ca). The **Kinsmen Sports Centre** has cross-country ski rentals; $12 for two hours, or $18 per day, including boots and poles.

ARTS AND ENTERTAINMENT

For details on theater events throughout the city, a listing of art galleries, what's going on where in the music scene, cinema screenings, and a full listing of festivals and events, pick up a free copy of *See Magazine* (www.seemagazine.com) or *Vue Weekly* (www.vueweekly.com). Both are published every Thursday and are available all around town, with all the same information presented on their respective websites. **Tix on the Square**, at street level of Chancery Hall (in the Arts District, across from Sir Winston Churchill Sq., 780/420-1757) sells discounted tickets.

Art Galleries

Scattered throughout the city are commercial art galleries, many of which exhibit and sell Canadian and native art. A group of galleries within six blocks of each other and the corner of Jasper Avenue and 124th Street have formed the **Gallery Walk Association** (www.gallery-walk.com). All are worth visiting, but the **Bearclaw Gallery** (10403 124th St., 780/482-1204) is of special note for those searching out the unique art of the First Nations. Among the shoe shops and souvenir stands in West Edmonton Mall is **Northern Images** (780/444-1995), also with a good collection of native and Nworthern arts

and crafts. Finally, headquarters for the **Alberta Craft Council** (10186 106th St., 780/488-5900) is the Edmonton store.

Theater and Music

Edmonton's 14 theater companies present productions at various locations all year long. For most companies, September–May is the main season. The **Citadel Theatre** (9828 101A Ave., 780/425-1820 or 888/425-1820, www.citadel theatre.com) is Canada's largest theater facility, taking up an entire downtown block and containing five theaters. In addition to a subscription program (Shoctor Theatre), the facility hosts experimental and innovative productions (Rice Theatre); films, lectures, and children's theater (Zeidler Hall); and concerts and recitals across a pond and surrounded by tropical greenery (Tucker Amphitheatre). For slightly more adventurous productions, see what's going on at the **Northern Light Theatre** (11516 103rd St., 780/471-1586, www.northernlightstheatre.com, $10–20). Edmonton's oldest theater is the **Walterdale Playhouse** (10322 83rd Ave., Old Strathcona, 780/439-2845, www.walterdaleplayhouse .com, from $8), which presents historical and humorous material in an October–June season. **Jagged Edge** is a small-time theater company with performances in the Edmonton Centre (10205 101st St., 780/463-4237, Tues.–Fri. 12:10–1 P.M., $8) that are designed especially for the lunchtime crowd.

The **Winspear Centre** (corner of 99th St. and 102nd Ave., www.winspearcentre.com) is home to the **Edmonton Symphony Orchestra** (780/428-1414), and attracts a wide variety of national and international musical acts, ranging from choirs to classical performers.

Bars and Nightclubs

The **Sidetrack Café** (10333 112th St., 780/421-1326, cover $4–8) presents a variety of live entertainment nightly—one night it might be stand-up comedians, the next a blues band, then jazz—and the only thing you can rely on is that it will be busy. Downtown, the **Sherlock Holmes** (10012 101A Ave., 780/426-7784) serves a large selection of British and Irish ales and is the place to head on St. Patrick's Day (March 17). The rest of the year, drinkers are encouraged to join in nightly sing-alongs with the pianist. Sherlock Holmes also has locations in Old Strathcona (10341 82nd Ave., 780/433-9676) and along West Edmonton Mall's Bourbon Street (780/444-1752). Old Strathcona is also home to O'Byrne's Irish Pub (10616 82nd Ave., 780/414-6766), where Celtic bands often play.

Cook County Saloon (8010 Gateway Blvd., 780/432-2665) is consistently voted Canada's Best Country Nightclub by the Canadian Country Music Association. Free two-step lessons are offered on selected weeknights, and on Friday and Saturday nights the action really cranks up, with top Canadian country performers. Beyond West Edmonton Mall is Cowboys (10102 180th St., 780/481-8739), with a Western theme but attracting a young, frat-like crowd with theme nights, popular promotions, white-hatted and scantily clad shooter girls, and a huge dance floor. Another longtime favorite country nightclub is Longriders (11733 8th St., 780/479-7400), where grassroots country bands perform.

Top 40 and dance nightclubs change names, reputations, and locations regularly, but some are reliable fixtures. Even if the names change, the locations don't—Old Strathcona and West Edmonton Mall both offer a range of nightclubbing experiences. In West Edmonton Mall, Red's (780/481-6420) combines a billiards room, restaurant, cigar lounge, dance floor, and a stage that has been graced by some of the biggest names in country music. Also in the famous mall, Rum Jungle (780/486-9494) somehow makes an African safari theme hip, with jungle decor, vine-swinging servers, and a young groovy crowd; Joint (780/486-3013) combines dance and R&B hits with touring acts on the main floor, or you can relax in one of six bars.

SHOPPING

Naturally, any talk of a shopping trip to Edmonton includes West Edmonton Mall (at 87th Ave. and 170th St.), the world's largest shopping and amusement complex. Downtown's major shopping centers are City Centre and ManuLife Place.

FESTIVALS AND EVENTS

Edmonton's Klondike Days

This 10-day event beginning on the third Thursday of each July celebrates Edmonton's links to the Klondike gold rush, when city merchants persuaded approximately 1,600 miners that the best route north was through Edmonton. Events include a massive parade through downtown, an 1890s-style he-man contest at Hawrelak Park, the Sourdough River Race down the river, and a bathtub road race that always gets a laugh. At Northlands Park (7300 116th St.) is Edmonton's Klondike Days Exposition (780/471-7210, www.klondikedays.com), featuring a midway, Klondike Days Casino, free concerts, racing pigs, vaudeville shows, thoroughbred racing, a pavilion featuring a different country each year, and a crafts and country fair. This is the city's biggest annual event, attracting approximately 750,000 visitors, so be prepared for big crowds everywhere.

Other Summer Festivals

During the last week of June, Jazz City International Music Festival (780/433-3333, www.jazzfest.ca) is held at various indoor and outdoor venues. Many foreign stars make special appearances. For 10 days in early July, downtown's Winston Churchill Square come alive during the International Street Performers Festival (780/425-5162, www.edmonton-streetfest.com), with almost 1,000 performances. Fifty outdoor ethnic pavilions at Hawrelak Park are just a small part of Edmonton Heritage Festival (780/488-3378, www.heritage-festival.com), which is held on the August long weekend as a celebration of the city's multicultural roots. During the Edmonton Folk Music Festival (780/429-1999, www.edmontonfolkfest.org), held on the second weekend of August, Gallagher Park comes alive with the sound of blues, jazz, country, Celtic, traditional, and bluegrass music.

North America's largest alternative-theater event is the Fringe Theatre Festival (780/448-9000, www.fringetheatreadventures.ca), held over 10 days in mid-August through Old

ALBERTA

Strathcona with a crowd of half a million watching on. **Symphony Under the Sky** (780/428-1414), held on the weekend closest to August 31, is the last gasp in Edmonton's busy summer festival schedule. Led by the Edmonton Symphony Orchestra, this five-day extravaganza of classical music takes place in William Hawrelak Park.

Fall and Winter

The second week in November, the Skyreach Centre hosts the **Canadian Finals Rodeo** (780/471-7210, www.canadianfinalsrodeo.ca). This $500,000 event is the culmination of the year's work for Canada's top 10 money-earning cowboys and cowgirls in the six traditional rodeo events. The action takes place Wednesday–Saturday at 7 P.M. and 1 P.M. Sunday.

Accommodations and Camping

Nearly all of Edmonton's best hotels are located downtown. Other concentrations of motels can be found along Gateway Boulevard (Hwy. 2 from the south) and scattered along Stony Plain Road in the west. The towns of Leduc and Nisku have several motels close to Edmonton International Airport. Other options include many bed-and-breakfasts, a centrally located hostel, and camping (just five minutes from downtown, or in campgrounds west, east, or south of the city).

DOWNTOWN

$50–100

Between downtown and the Provincial Museum, **Glenora B&B Inn** (12327 102nd Ave., 780/488-6766 or 877/453-6672, www.glenorabnb.com) is a home away from home a short walk from the galleries of 124th Street. The building that houses this bed-and-breakfast was built as a commercial enterprise in 1912 and has been completely renovated with the guest rooms above a guest parlor and street-level restaurant where a full breakfast is served (included in rates). The least expensive rooms share a bathroom ($70 s, $85 d), or pay extra for an en suite (from $80 s, $95 d). For the same price as a mid-priced down hotel ($120 s, $135) upgrade to a spacious deluxe suite, complete with a kitchenette, canopied bed, and clawfoot tub.

Sure, it's a chain hotel, but the **Comfort Inn & Suites** (10425 100th Ave., 780/423-5611 or 888/384-6835, www.comfortinnedmonton.com) is a good choice. The 108 rooms are sensibly furnished for both leisure and business travelers. Parking, local calls, and in-room coffee are complimentary. Rack rates are $99 s or d, but the hotel website offers some great overnight packages.

$100–150

The lobby of the **Coast Edmonton Plaza Hotel** (10155 105th St., 780/423-4811 or 800/663-1144, www.coasthotels.com) has a distinctly alpine feel, yet the rest of the property is nothing but city-style. Handsome rooms come with niceties—such as robes—that make you believe you're paying more than you are. Facilities include an indoor pool, an exercise room, laundry service, a lounge, and a restaurant. Posted rates are $125 s, $135 d, but a quick check of the hotel website uncovered a $129 bed *and* breakfast package for two that included a $50 voucher for West Edmonton Mall—in July!

No, it's not downtown, but it's close. **La Boheme** (6427 112th Ave., 780/474-5693, $95 s, $140 d) is in one of Edmonton's first luxury apartments. Today, La Boheme restaurant downstairs is one of the city's best, and six upstairs rooms have been graciously refurnished and are run as a B&B. The building is certainly charming, right down to its creaky floors. Rates include a continental breakfast.

$150–200

If you're looking for accommodations in this price category, it's very hard to do better than the **Union Bank Inn** (10053 Jasper Ave., 780/423-3600 or 888/423-3601, www.union-bankinn.com) for value, charm, and location.

ALBERTA

The inn is in a restored 1911 bank building in the heart of the city. The new owners have transformed the historic building into a luxurious boutique hotel, featuring a fireplace, down comforters, and bathrobes in each of 34 tastefully decorated rooms spread through two wings. The rates of $150–269 per room also include a cooked breakfast, a wine-and-cheese tray presented to guests each evening, and free parking between 3 P.M. and 9 A.M.

Over $200

The **Fairmont Hotel Macdonald** (10065 100th St., 780/424-5181 or 800/441-1414, www .fairmont.com) has long been regarded as Edmonton's premier luxury accommodation. For many years, it was the social center of the city. It was built in 1915 by the Grand Trunk Railway in the same chateau style used for many of the Canadian Pacific hotels across the country. The 198 guest rooms come in many configurations (many are on the small side). A subtle air of old-world elegance extends throughout the rooms and public areas, such as the upmarket restaurant beautiful lounge overlooking the river valley. Rack rates for a standard Fairmont Room are $219 s or d. Packages offer better deals, or pay more for one of a suite.

Fairmont Hotel Macdonald

© ANDREW HEMPSTEAD

SOUTH OF DOWNTOWN

Gateway Boulevard, an extension of Highway 2 as it enters the city from the south, offers a few cheap roadside motels just beyond Gateway Park, and is then dotted with chain hotels all the way to Old Strathcona. Remember when looking at addresses along this strip that Gateway Boulevard is Highway 2 northbound and Calgary Trail is Highway 2 southbound.

Under $50

Edmonton International Hostel (10647 81st Ave., 780/988-6836 or 877/467-8336, www .hihostels.ca) is sensibly located within walking distance of the hippest Edmonton neighborhood, Old Strathcona. The lounge area is spacious and comfortable, and there's a quiet and private backyard, plenty of space in the kitchen,

and off-street parking. Rates are $22 for members of Hostelling International and $27 for non-members. Check-in is after 3 P.M.

$50–100

Budget-conscious travelers enjoy the best of both worlds at the **Southbend Motel** (5130 Gateway Blvd., 780/434-1418), where guests have access to the recreation facilities at the adjacent Cedar Park Inn while paying just $57 s, $69 d for accommodations.

$100–150

As you drive north along Calgary Trail, it's impossible to miss the 11-story, pastel-colored **Delta Edmonton South** (4404 Gateway Blvd., 780/ 434-6415 or 800/661-1122, www.deltaedmonton .com, $149 s or d), towering over the major intersection with Whitemud Drive. Guests are offered a wide variety of facilities and services, including an indoor pool, restaurant, lounge, airport shuttle, and valet parking.

ALBERTA

Over $150

One of the city's finest accommodations is **The Varscona** (8208 106th St., 780/434-6111 or 888/515-3355, www.varscona.com), situated in the heart of Old Strathcona. The Varscona experience combines the personalized atmosphere of a boutique hotel with all the amenities you'd expect of an upscale chain. The 89 guest rooms are spacious and elegantly furnished in one of three pleasing styles. They all have king-size beds, large bathrooms, and niceties such as bathrobes and gourmet in-room coffee. Midweek rates start at $225 s or d, weekend rates are discounted to below $150. Either way, parking, a light breakfast, a daily newspaper, and an evening wine- and cheese-tasting session is included.

Look no further than the **Hotel Selkirk** (780/496-7227 or 800/717-1277, www.maclab hotels.com) for a unique overnight experience with a historic twist. The original Hotel Selkirk along Jasper Avenue burnt down in 1962, but the historic property has been re-created in minute detail in Fort Edmonton Park, off Whitemud Drive southwest of downtown. The guest rooms have a cozy, Victorian feel but enjoy modern conveniences such as air-conditioning and Internet connections. Rates of $180–200 s, $230–250 d include breakfast and dinner in the downstairs Johnson's Café. Drinks in the Mahogany Room, at a replica of Canada's longest bar, are extra.

WEST EDMONTON

$50–100

If you're on a budget and want to stay out by the mall, consider the **Yellowhead Motor Inn** (five km/3.1 mi. away at 15004 Yellowhead Trail, 780/447-2400 or 800/661-6993, $69 d, $79 d), across from a casino and with an in-house restaurant and lounge.

$100–150

The pick within a cluster of choices along Stony Plain Road, a five-minute drive from the mall, is the **Sandman Hotel West Edmonton** (17635 Stony Plain Rd., 780/483-1385 or 800/726-3626, www.sandmanhotels.com). The rooms are handsomely appointed in sharp tones and comfortable furnishings. The central atrium holds a pool and restaurant—a pleasant respite from the busy road out front. Pay $110 s or d for a standard room or $140 for a very spacious suite.

Over $150

Within West Edmonton Mall is the 355-room **Fantasyland Hotel** (17700 87th Ave., 780/444-3000 or 800/737-3783, www.fantasylandhotel .com), famous for its elaborately themed rooms. The hotel has 118 themed rooms, as well as over 200 regular rooms ($179 s or d) and a few extremely spacious executive suites with jetted tubs ($199 s or d), and three restaurants. No catching a cab back to your hotel after a day of shopping here—just ride the elevator to the room of your wildest fantasy. Each floor has an over-the-top theme, and the choice is yours: Hollywood, Roman, Polynesian, Victorian, African, Arabian, Igloo, Waterpark, Western, Canadian Rail, or Truck—where you can slumber in the bed of a real pickup truck. Each theme is carried out in minute detail. The Polynesian room fantasy, for example, begins as you walk along a hallway lined with murals depicting a tropical beach, floored with grass matting. You'll walk through a grove of palm trees before reaching your room. In the colorful room, an enormous hot tub is nestled in a rocky grotto, and the bed is shaped like a warrior's catamaran, with a sail as the headboard. This escapism comes at a cost, but maybe not as much as you'd expect—$239–309 s or d. (The theme rooms are very popular and are booked far in advance, especially on weekends.)

CAMPGROUNDS

South

The best camping within the city limits is at the **Rainbow Valley Campground** (13204 45th Ave., 780/434-5531 or 888/434-3991, www .rainbow-valley.com, mid-Apr.–early Apr.). The location is excellent and, as far as city camping goes, the setting is pleasant. Facilities include free showers, a laundry room, a barbecue grill, a playground, and a cooking shelter. In summer, all sites are full by noon, so reserve ahead by credit card. Grassed tent sites are $20, powered sites $23. To get there, turn south off Whitemud Drive at 119th Street, then take the first right and follow it into the valley.

West

Continue west from West Edmonton Mall to **Shakers Acres** (21530 103rd Ave., 780/447-3564, www.shakersacresrvpark.com), on the north side of Stony Plain Road. Unserviced sites are

$17 and hookups are $26–60. Farther out, in Spruce Grove, is the **Glowing Embers Travel Centre** (26309 Hwy. 16, 780/962-8100 or 877/785-7275, www.glowingembersrvpark.com, Apr.–Oct., $28). All facilities are modern, and although tents are allowed, they may look out of place among the satellite-toting RVs. Facilities include a recreation hall, a grocery store, an RV wash, a launderette, and service bays with licensed technicians on hand.

Food

From the legendary home-style cooking of Barb and Ernie's (9906 72nd Ave., 780/433-3242) to the historic elegance of Madison's Grill, there's something to suit everyone's taste and budget in Edmonton. Restaurants are concentrated in a few main areas. Downtown in the plazas are food courts that fill with office workers, shoppers, and tourists each lunchtime. This part of the city also has some of Edmonton's finest dining establishments. Old Strathcona offers a smorgasbord of choices, with cuisine from all corners of the world. Gateway Boulevard and Calgary Trail, northbound and southbound, respectively, along Highway 2 south of downtown are lined with family restaurants, buffets, and fast-food outlets.

DOWNTOWN

Cafés and Casual

Zenari's in ManuLife Plaza East (10180 101st St., 780/423-5409) is a trendy lunchtime deli hangout known for its variety of sandwiches and freshly prepared soups, as well as coffees from around the world, ground fresh to order. It's closed on Sunday. One block toward the city center, overlooking Winston Churchill Square, is **Coffee Mania,** in the Chancery Hall building (corner of 102A Ave. and 99th St.). It's part of Tix on the Square, which sells discounted theater tickets, and it has a few outdoor tables in a shaded courtyard.

Surrounded by the city's highest high-rises is **Sherlock Holmes** (10012 101A Ave., 780/426-7784, Mon.–Sat. from 11:30 A.M.), a charming

English-style pub with a shingled roof, whitewashed walls with black trim, and a white picket fence surrounding it. At lunchtime, it's packed with the office crowd. Try traditional British dishes such as Mrs. Hudson's Steak and Kidney Pie ($9), ploughman's ($9.50), liver and onions ($9.50), or fish and chips ($10.50), washed down with a pint of Newcastle ale or Guinness stout. Still hungry? The bread pudding ($5) is a delicious way to end your meal.

Canadian

The **Hardware Grill** (9698 Jasper Ave., 780/423-0969, Mon.–Fri. 11:30 A.M.–2 P.M., Mon.–Sat. from 5 P.M.), one of the city's finest restaurants, is at the street level of an early 1900s hardware store where the white linen and silver table settings contrast starkly with the restored red-brick interior. The menu features dishes using a wide variety of seasonal Canadian produce, including pork, lamb, beef, venison, and salmon, all well prepared and delightfully presented. Lunches such as a grilled Thai chicken salad are less than $15, and dinner entrées run $27–37.

At **Madison's Grill** (10053 Jasper Ave., 780/423-3600), the official-looking architecture of this former bank remains, with contemporary styling balancing columns and ornate ceiling. The kitchen features the best in Canadian ingredients, with the nightly trio of fish choices ($27–33) especially popular. The lunchtime grilled tuna on sourdough bread ($12) keeps the seafood theme up. Good food coupled with impeccable service makes Madison's the perfect place for a splurge.

ALBERTA

Steak, or more precisely, Alberta beef, is the star at **Hy's Steak Loft** (10013 101A Ave., 780/424-4444, Mon.–Fri. from 11:30 A.M., daily from 5 P.M.), one of Canada's most renowned steakhouses. The elegant setting, centered around a Tiffany-style skylight, is slightly dated, but no one seems to mind. The finest cuts of the province's best beef—think classic prime rib ($25–32) and chateaubriand ($33) carved table-side—are complemented by a wine list overloaded with good reds.

European

Among the dozens of Italian restaurants in the city, one of the most popular is **Sorrentino's,** with six city locations including downtown at 10162 100th Street (780/424-7500). The decor at all locations is stylish, with a great old-world Italian charm. The food is simple and satisfying. Begin with gorgonzola (blue cheese) baked in puff pastry then move on to a traditionally rich pasta dish ($14–18), or something lighter such as the veal and wild mushroom ravioli. The menu also features non-Italian choices, such as Australian lamb and Alberta beef.

As you descend the stairs to **The Creperie** below the Boardwalk Market (10220 103rd St., 780/420-6656), a great smell, wafting from somewhere in the depths of this historic building, hits you in the face. It takes a minute for your eyes to adjust to the softly lit dining area, but once you do, its inviting French-provincial atmosphere is apparent. As you've probably guessed, crepes are the specialty. Choose from fillings as varied as the Canadian-influenced Crepe Pacific ($12), filled with shrimp, salmon, and asparagus, or the classic Crepe Suzette ($7) for dessert. It's open weekdays for lunch and daily for dinner.

OLD STRATHCONA AND VICINITY

This historic suburb south of downtown offers Edmonton's largest concentration of cafés and restaurants. There's a great variety of choices, and because it's a popular late-night hangout, many eateries are open to the wee hours. The cavernous **Block 1912** (10361 82nd Ave., 780/

433-6575) offers a great variety of hot drinks, cakes, pastries, and healthy full meals in an inviting atmosphere, which includes several comfortable lounges. Newspapers from around the world are available.

Mexican and Cajun

Julio's Barrio Mexican Restaurant (10450 Whyte Ave., 780/431-0774, daily until midnight) is a huge restaurant decorated with earthy colors and Southwestern-style furniture and has a true south-of-the-border ambience. The menu is appealing but limited. If you just want a light snack, try the warm corn chips with Jack cheese and freshly made Ultimate Salsa ($5.75); for something more substantial, consider the fajitas, presented in a cast-iron pan ($12). This place doesn't get really busy until after 9 P.M.

Da-de-o (10548 Whyte Ave., 780/433-0930, 11:30 A.M.–midnight) is styled on a 1950s diner in New Orleans. The menu features Cajun cuisine, including "po-boys"—Southern-style sandwiches using French bread and fillings such as blackened catfish and tequila salsa ($7 at lunch and all day Mon.–Tues, $10 otherwise)—as well as Southern fried chicken ($13), jambalaya ($13), and inexpensive dishes like barbecue beans and rice ($7.50) that have appeal to the money-watching college crowd. When the hip, evening crowd arrives, service can be blasé at best.

Unheardof

Located a few blocks east of the railway tracks in a renovated shop, is one of Edmonton's most popular restaurants, the Unheardof (9602 82nd Ave., 780/432-0480, Tues.–Sun. from 5:30 P.M.). The main dining room is filled with antiques, and the tables are set with starched white linen and silver cutlery. The menu changes weekly, featuring fresh game such as buffalo tenderloin ($30), homemade chutneys, and relishes during fall, and chicken and beef dishes the rest of the year. Entrées average $24–33 while desserts such as strawberry shortcake at $8 top off your meal. Although it's most obviously an upmarket restaurant, the service is comfortable, and most importantly, the food is absolutely mouthwatering. Reservations are essential.

Information and Services

INFORMATION

If you're driving up to Edmonton from the south along Highway 2, move over to the right lane as you enter the city in preparation for a stop at Edmonton Tourism's **Gateway Park information center** (summer daily 8 A.M.–9 P.M., rest of year Mon.–Fri. 8:30 A.M.–4:30 P.M. and Sat.–Sun. 9 A.M.–5 P.M.). Within this complex, you'll find interpretive displays on the oil industry, stands filled with brochures, and direct-dial phones for Edmonton accommodations. The most central source of tourist information is the main office of **Edmonton Tourism** (downtown at 9990 Jasper Ave. opposite the Fairmont Hotel Macdonald). On the arrivals level of the **Edmonton International Airport** is another information center (year-round daily 7 A.M.–11 P.M.). For pretrip planning, contact **Edmonton Tourism** (780/426-4715 or 800/463-4667, www.edmonton.com).

Bookstores

Audrey's (10702 Jasper Ave., 780/423-3487, Mon.–Fri. 9 A.M.–9 P.M., Sat. 9:30 A.M.–5:30 P.M., Sun. noon–5 P.M.) has the city's largest collection of travel guides, western Canadiana, and general travel writing on two vast floors. **Map Town** (10344 105th St., 780/429-2600, Mon.–Fri. 8 A.M.–5:30 P.M., Sat. 10 A.M.–5 P.M.) stocks topo maps, Alberta wall maps, travel guides, atlases, and a huge selection of specialty guides—for fishing, canoeing, climbing, and the like.

Old Strathcona is an excellent place for browsing through used bookstores. **Wee Book Inn** (10310 82nd Ave., 780/432-7230) is the largest and stocks more recent titles and a large collection of magazines. **Alhambra Books** (upstairs at 10309 82nd Ave., 780/439-4195) specializes in Canadiana and has an extensive collection of Albertan material, including pamphlets and newspapers. **Bjarne's Books** (10533 82nd Ave., 780/439-7123) has older books, including a large selection of hard-to-find western Cana-

diana and Arctic-region material. **Greenwood's** (7925 104th St., 780/439-2005) is an Old Strathcona independent.

Libraries

The Edmonton Public Library System (www.epl.ca) has 13 libraries spread throughout the city. The largest is the **Stanley A. Milner Library** (7 Sir Winston Churchill Sq., 780/496-7000, Mon.–Fri. 9 A.M.–9 P.M., Sat. 9 A.M.–6 P.M., and Sun. 1–5 P.M.). This large, two-story facility, connected to the downtown core by pedways, is a great place to spend a rainy afternoon. It carries newspapers, magazines, and phone books from all corners of the globe, as well as rows and rows of western Canadiana. Throughout the week, author readings take place on the main level.

SERVICES

The main post office is downtown at 9808 103A Avenue. Public Internet access is free at all city libraries, or you can pay approximately $5 for 30 minutes downtown at the **Bohemia Cyber Café** (11012 Jasper Ave., 780/429-3442). In West Edmonton Mall, head to **Bytes Internet Café** (Bourbon St., 780/444-7873).

On the west side of the city is **LaPerle Homestyle Laundry** (9756 182nd St., 780/483-9200), which is handy to the hotels in the area and has large washers and dryers for sleeping bags.

Emergency Services

For medical emergencies, call 911 or one of the following hospitals: **Grey Nuns Community Hospital** (corner of 34th Ave. and 66th St., 780/450-7000), **Northeast Community Health Centre** (14007 50th St., 780/472-5000), **Royal Alexandra Hospital** (10240 Kingsway Ave., 780/477-4111), **University of Alberta Hospital** (8440 112th St., 780/407-8822). For the **Edmonton Police Service,** call 780/945-5330.

ALBERTA

Transportation

GETTING THERE

By Air

Edmonton International Airport (www .edmontonairports.com) is beside Highway 2, 29 kilometers (18 mi.) south of the city center. The airport website has links to airlines serving Edmonton. On the **Arrivals** level are a small information center (year-round, daily 7:30 A.M.–11:30 P.M.), car-rental desks, hotel courtesy phones, a restaurant, and a currency exchange. An Airport Improvement Fee ($15), built into all tickets for departing flights and still collected, helped pay for recent expansion. The **Sky Shuttle** (780/465-8515 or 888/438-2342) departs the airport for downtown hotels every 20 minutes (every 30 minutes on weekends) on three different routes. One-way to downtown is $14, round-trip $22; check in at the counter beside the information center. The cab fare to downtown is set at $44 one-way.

By Rail

The **VIA Rail station** (12360 121st St., 800/561-8630, www.viarail.ca) is northwest of downtown. The ticket office is generally open 8 A.M.–3:30 P.M., later when trains are due. Trains leave Vancouver (1150 Station St.) and Prince Rupert three times weekly for the 23.5-hour trip to Edmonton (via Jasper), continuing on the Canadian route to the eastern provinces. Before paying full price for your ticket, inquire about off-season discounts (up to 40 percent) and the Canrailpass.

By Bus

The **Greyhound** bus depot (10324 103rd St., 780/420-2400 or 800/661-8747, www.greyhound .ca, open Mon.–Sat. 5:30 A.M.–midnight, Sun. 10 A.M.–6 P.M.) is within walking distance of the city center and many hotels. A cab to Edmonton International Hostel from the depot is $18. Within the depot are an A&W Restaurant, a small paper shop, a cash machine, and large lockers ($2). Buses leave daily for all points in Canada, including Cal-

gary (3.5 hours), Jasper (4.5 hours) and Vancouver (15–17 hours).

Red Arrow (780/424-3339, www.redarrow .pwt.ca) buses leave Edmonton 5–7 times daily for Red Deer and Calgary and once daily for Fort McMurray. The downtown office and pickup point is the Holiday Inn Express (10014 104th St.).

GETTING AROUND

Bus

The **Edmonton Transit System** (780/496-1611, www.takeets.com) operates an extensive bus system that links all parts of the city. Not all routes operate on Sunday. For many destinations south of the North Saskatchewan River, you'll need to jump aboard the LRT to the University Transfer Point. Bus fare anywhere within the city is $2 during peak hours (5–9 A.M. and 3–6 P.M.), $1.40 at other times; exact fare only. Transfers are available on boarding and can be used for additional travel in any direction within 90 minutes. For more information and passes, go to the Customer Services Outlet at the Churchill LRT Station (99th St., weekdays 8:30 A.M.–4:30 P.M.).

Light Rail Transit

The LRT has 10 stops running east–west along Jasper Avenue (101st Ave.), northeast as far as Whitemud Park, and south to the University, with an extension to Heritage Mall slated for completion in 2006. The LRT runs underground through the city center, connecting with many pedways. Travel between Grandin and Churchill is free Monday–Friday 9 A.M.–3 P.M. and Saturday 9 A.M.–6 P.M. LRT tickets are the same price as the bus, and tickets, transfers, and day passes are valid for travel on either the LRT or the bus system.

High Level Street Car

A great way to travel between downtown and Old Strathcona is on the High Level Street Car (780/437-7721, $3 one way). Trains and trams originally traveled this historic route over the

High Level Bridge, but today a restored streetcar makes the journey from the west side of the Alberta Legislature Building to Old Strathcona every 30 minutes daily 11 A.M.–4 P.M.

Passengers with Disabilities

Edmonton Transit operates the **Disabled Adult Transit System, or DATS** (780/496-4570), which provides access to various points of the city for passengers with disabilities who are unable to use the regular transit system. The door-to-door service costs the same as Edmonton Transit adult tickets. Priority is given to those heading to work or for medical trips. A Pedway Information Sheet, detailing accessibility, is available from City Hall (780/424-4085).

Taxi

The standard flag charge for cabs is $2.60 plus approximately $1.40 per kilometer, but most companies have flat rates for major destinations within the city. Major companies are **Checker Cabs** (780/484-8888), **Alberta Co-op Taxi Line** (780/425-2525), **Prestige Cabs** (780/462-4444), and **Yellow Cab** (780/462-3456).

Car Rental

Rental agencies and their local numbers are **Avis** (780/448-0066), **Budget** (780/448-2000), **Discount** (780/448-3888), **Enterprise** (780/440-4550), **Hertz** (780/415-5283), **National** (780/422-6097), **Rent-A-Wreck** (780/986-3335), and **Thrifty** (780/890-4555).

TOURS

If you're pressed for time (or even if you're not), a guided tour of Edmonton may be a good idea. As you'd expect from an ex–museum guide, Cameron Malcolm of **Out and About Tours** (780/909-8687) emphasizes the heritage and culture of Edmonton and Old Strathcona on his three-hour city tours ($40), with the option to add a visit to Fort Edmonton Park ($65). **Magic Times** (780/940-7479) takes interested visitors on tours that concentrate on one area, such as Old Strathcona, or historic sites and Fort Edmonton Park. Expect to pay around $40 per person for a four-hour tour. About 50 kilometers (31 mi.) is covered in four hours with Peter Hominiuk of **Peter's Edmonton Tours** (780/469-2641), a personalized service that hits the major historic sites, the university, and the mall, of course. Wayne Millar of **Birds & Backcountry Tours** (780/405-4880) leads visitors through urban parks. Tours depart at dawn or dusk ($65 includes a meal prepared outdoors). Wayne's forte is the areas east of Edmonton including Elk Island National Park and the Cooking Lake Moraine; tours leave on demand.

Northern Alberta

The northern half of Alberta, from Highway 16 north to the 60th parallel, is a sparsely populated land of unspoiled wilderness, home to deer, moose, coyotes, foxes, lynx, black bears, and the elusive Swan Hills grizzly bear. For the most part, it is heavily forested, part of the boreal forest ecoregion that sweeps around the Northern Hemisphere, broken only by the Atlantic and Pacific Oceans. The North Saskatchewan River flows east from the Continental Divide, crossing northern Alberta on its way to Hudson Bay. Alberta's earliest explorers arrived along this river, opening up the Canadian west to the trappers, missionaries, and settlers who followed. The Athabasca and Peace river systems are the region's largest waterways. Carrying water from

hundreds of tributaries, they merge in the far northeastern corner of the province and flow north into the Arctic Ocean.

With few regular "sights," northern Alberta receives fewer tourists than the rest of the province.

Those who do venture north find solitude in a vast, untapped wilderness with abundant wildlife and plenty of recreation—lakes and rivers to fish, historic sites to explore, rivers to float on, and gravel roads to drive just for the sake of it.

Lakeland

Highway 16, east from Edmonton, follows the southern flanks of a region containing hundreds of lakes. History buffs appreciate the legacies of early white settlers that dot the landscape here— restored fur-trading posts, missions, and the Ukrainian Village near Vegreville. Other visitors are attracted by the region's vast areas of un- spoiled wilderness, the opportunities to view large mammals at Elk Island National Park, or just to fish the many waterways.

ELK ISLAND NATIONAL PARK

Heading east from Edmonton on Highway 16, you'll reach Elk Island National Park in well under an hour. This small, fenced, 194-square- kilometer (75-sq.-mi.) park preserves a remnant of the transitional grassland ecoregion—the

aspen parkland—that once covered the entire northern flank of the prairie. It's also one of the best spots in Alberta for wildlife watching; with approximately 3,000 large mammals, the park has one of the highest concentrations of big game in the world. Set aside in 1906 to protect a herd of elk, the fenced park also provides a home for moose, two species of bison, white- tailed and mule deer, coyotes, beavers, muskrats, mink, and porcupines. The many lakes and wet- land areas in the park serve as nesting sites for waterfowl, and approximately 230 species of birds have been observed here.

Park entry for one day is adult $5, senior $4.25 to a maximum of $12.50 per vehicle ($10.50 for seniors); if you've purchased an an- nual pass, you'll be waved straight through the fee station.

THE BISON OF ELK ISLAND

Two species of bison inhabit Elk Island National Park, and to prevent interbreeding, they are separated. All bison on the north side of Highway 16 are **plains bison**, whereas those on the south side are **wood bison.** Wood bison are darker in color, larger (an average bull weighs 840 kg/1,850 lbs.), and have long, straight hair covering the fore- head. Plains bison are smaller, have shorter legs, a larger head, and frizzy hair. In summer they grow distinctive capes of woolly hair that cover their front legs, head, and shoulders.

Before the late 1700s, 60 million plains bison lived on the North American plains. In less than a century, humanity brought these shaggy beasts to the brink of extinction. By 1880, incredibly, only a few hundred plains bison remained. A small herd, the ancestors of today's herd, was corralled at what

was then Elk Island Reserve. A small part of the herd is kept in a large enclosure just north of the Park Information Centre, while the rest roam freely through the north section of the park. Today they number approximately 630 within the park.

The wood bison was thought to be extinct for many years—a victim of hunting, severe winters, and interbreeding with its close relative, the plains bison. In 1957, a herd of 200 was discovered in the remote northwestern corner of Wood Buffalo Na- tional Park. Some were captured and transported to Elk Island National Park, ensuring the survival of the species. Today it's the purest herd in the world and is used as breeding stock for several captive herds throughout North America. To view the herd of 400, look south from Highway 16 or hike the Wood Bison Trail.

NORTHERN ALBERTA

Great Slave Lake

To Yellowknife

Hay River

River

1

1

35

Hwy 35

NORTHWEST TERRITORIES
ALBERTA

BRITISH COLUMBIA
ALBERTA

Bistcho Lake

Zama City

Hay-Zama Lakes

Rainbow Lake

Meander River

High Level

58

35

MACENZIE HWY

Chinchaga River

Caribou Mountains

Buffalo Lake

5

Fort Smith

Wood Buffalo National Park

Lake Claire

Fort Chipewyan

Lake Athabasca

Birch Mountains

River

River

Fort Vermilion

Peace River

La Crete

0   50 mi

0   50 km

ALBERTA

© AVALON TRAVEL PUBLISHING, INC.

Recreation

The 12 trails, ranging in length from 1.4 to 18.5 kilometers (0.9 to 11.5 mi.), cover all areas of the park and provide excellent opportunities to view wildlife. A park information sheet details each one. Make sure to carry water with you, though, because surface water in the park is not suitable for drinking. The paved **Shoreline Trail** (three km/1.9 mi. one-way) follows the shore of Astotin Lake from the golf course parking lot. The **Lakeview Trail** (3.3 km/two mi. round-trip) begins from the northern end of the recreation area and provides good views of the lake. Hike this trail in the evening for a

chance to see beavers. The only trail on the south side of Highway 16 is the **Wood Bison Trail** (18.6 km/11.5 mi. round-trip), which has an interpretive display at the trailhead. In winter, the trails provide excellent cross-country skiing and snowshoeing.

The day use area at **Astotin Lake,** 14 kilometers (8.7 mi.) north of Highway 16, is the center of much activity. There's a pleasant beach and picnic area; canoes, rowboats, and small sailboats can be rented; and the rolling fairways of adjacent **Elk Island Golf Course** (780/998-3161, $32) provide an interesting diversion for golfers.

Practicalities

Sandy Beach Campground ($18 per night plus $4 for firewood permit) on the north side of the Astotin Lake day-use area, is the only overnight facility within the park. It has firepits, picnic tables, flush toilets, and showers. A concession selling fast food and basic camping supplies operates May–October at Astotin Lake, and the golf course (780/998-3161) has a casual restaurant.

The **Park Information Centre** (780/992-5790, May–June weekends only, July–Aug. daily 10 A.M.–6 P.M.) is less than one kilometer (0.6 mi.) north of Highway 16 on the Elk Island Parkway. For online information, click through the links on the Parks Canada website (www.pc.gc.ca).

EAST ALONG THE YELLOWHEAD HIGHWAY

Ukrainian Cultural Heritage Village

This heritage village (50 km/31 mi. east of Edmonton, 780/662-3640, late May–Aug. daily 10 A.M.–6 P.M., Sept. Sat.–Sun. 10 A.M.–6 P.M., Oct.–late May Mon.–Fri. 10 A.M.–4 P.M., adult $8, senior $7, child $4) is a realistic replica of a Ukrainian settlement, common in the rural areas of east-central Alberta at the start of the 20th century. The first, and largest, Ukrainian settlement in Canada was located in this region. Driven from their homeland in Eastern Europe, Ukrainians fled to the Canadian prairies where for many years they dressed and worked in the ways of the Old World. These traditions are kept alive

ELK ISLAND NATIONAL PARK

To Lamont

831

Lakeview Trail

Astotin Lake

SANDY BEACH

ELK ISLAND

Shoreline Trail

Moss Lake

Oster Lake

ELK ISLAND PKWY

Tawayik Lake

★ BISON PADDOCK

Oxbow Lake

Little Tawayik Lake

PARK INFO CENTRE

YELLOWHEAD

HWY

To Edmonton

16

Wood Basin Trail

Flyingshot Lake

To Lloydminster

0   2 mi
0   2 km

The world's largest *pysanka*—a Ukrainian Easter egg—is on the edge of Vegreville.

with costumed guides and a lively program of cultural events.

Vermilion

The reddish-colored iron deposits in a nearby river gave this town of 4,300 at the junction of Highways 16 and 41 its name. Many downtown buildings date from the 1919–1920 period after a fire destroyed the original main street (50th Ave.) in 1918. Made of locally fired brick, many have plaques detailing their history. Pick up a walking tour brochure at the information center (summer daily 10 A.M.–6 P.M.) by the entrance to town. **Vermilion Provincial Park** encompasses 771 hectares (1,900 acres) of aspen parkland and grassland along the banks of the Vermilion River, an ancient glacial meltwater channel. To date, 20 species of mammals and 110 species of birds have been documented here. The park also has 15 kilometers (9.3 mi.) of hiking trails and a campground with showers and a trout pond ($15–19). Access is from the west side of town, north along 62nd Street.

LLOYDMINSTER

North America has several "twin cities" that straddle borders (such as Minneapolis and St. Paul), but Lloydminster is the only one that has a single corporate body in two provinces (or states, depending on the case). Approximately 60 percent of the city's 20,000 residents live on the Alberta side, separated from their Saskatchewan neighbors by the main street.

Sights

The **Barr Colony Heritage Cultural Centre** (in Weaver Park on Hwy. 16, 306/825-5655, daily 10 A.M.–8 P.M., rest of year Wed.–Sun. 1–5 P.M., adult $4, child $3) houses the Richard Larsen Museum featuring a collection of artifacts and antiques used by a group of British immigrants who followed the Reverend George Lloyd to the site of Lloydminster in search of productive land.

Accommodations and Camping

Traill Country Inn (306/825-4176, www.traillcountryinn.com, $69–139 s or d) enjoys a pleasant rural setting 10 kilometers (6.2 mi.) north of town along Highway 17. Even the least expensive room has a private bathroom (but not en suite), while the largest room is an elegant space with its own hot tub. Although it looks decidedly untropical from outside, kids will love the **Tropical Inn** (5621 44th St., 780/825-7000 or 800/219-5244, www.tropicalinns.com, $75–125) for its indoor waterslide and pool complex.

Rolling Green Fairways (780/875-4653, $18–24), two kilometers (1.2 mi.) west of the city on Highway 16, then one kilometer (0.6 mi.) north, is in a pleasant rural setting and adjacent to a golf course. Facilities include showers and a laundry.

Food

The **Tea House** (south side of Hwy. 16, just east of the border post, 306/825-9498, Tues.–Sat. 10 A.M.–6 P.M.) was built in 1942 and is surrounded by well-established gardens. Afternoon tea and light lunches are served April–December. A local favorite are the two restaurants in the **Tropical Inn** (5621 44th St., 780/825-7000 or 800/219-5244).

Information

Tourism Lloydminster (780/871-8333 or 800/825-6180, www.lloydminsterinfo.com) operates a website, but the best source of information once you arrive in town is the provincially operated **Travel Alberta Information Centre** (one km/0.6 mi. east of town, mid-May–mid-June daily 9 A.M.–6 P.M., summer daily 8 A.M.–7 P.M.).

EDMONTON TO COLD LAKE

Highway 28 leaves Edmonton heading north through the suburbs. After a series of 90-degree turns—first one way, then the other, then back again—it comes to **Waskatenau,** where it straightens out to pursue an easterly direction heading toward Cold Lake.

Long Lake Provincial Park

During the last ice age, the low-lying area occupied by this 764-hectare (1,890-acre) park was part of a deep glacial meltwater channel that has now filled with water. Fishing is great for northern pike, perch, and walleye. The campground ($18–20) is right on the lake and has flush toilets, showers, a grocery store, and canoe rentals. To get there from Highway 28, head north from Waskatenau on Highway 831 for 48 kilometers (30 mi.).

STILL WAITING . . .

St. Paul, 210 kilometers (130 mi.) northeast of Edmonton, has spent many thousands of dollars developing an attraction that hasn't had a single official visitor in over 30 years. And the skeptics doubt it ever will.

You guessed it (or maybe you didn't): St. Paul has the world's only **UFO landing pad**—a raised platform forlornly waiting for a visitor from outer space. Beside the pad, the **Tourist Information Centre** (50th Ave. at 53rd St., 780/645-6800, daily 9 A.M.–5 P.M.) has interesting displays including photos of "real" UFOs as well as descriptions of some famous hoaxes. The building is a raised, UFO-shaped circular structure; if approaching from outer space, look for the green flashing light on top.

Smoky Lake and Vicinity

Named for a lake 93 kilometers (58 mi.) west of St. Paul, where natives once rested and smoked pipes during hunts, this small town is home to the **Great White North Pumpkin Fair & Weigh-off** (780/656-3674), an annual competition to find the world's largest pumpkin. Weigh-offs are held the first weekend of October at select locations around the world, but don't waste time scanning the vegetable section at your local grocery store for a winner—you'll need a pumpkin weighing at least 340 kilograms (750 lbs.) to take the day at Smoky Lake (the world record is 513 kg/1,130 lbs.). For those who don't consider size important, there's always a prize for the ugliest pumpkin (officially, only "aesthetically challenged" pumpkins can be entered, appeasing the politically correct) and the pumpkin that's traveled the farthest.

Victoria Settlement (21 km/13 mi. south and east of Smoky Lake, 780/656-2333, mid-May–Aug. daily 10 A.M.–6 P.M., adult $2, child $1.50) was originally the site of an 1864 Hudson's Bay Company post, which was abandoned in 1897. In the early 1900s a group of Ukrainians moved in and the settlement became known as Victoria-Pakan. When the railway bypassed the settlement in 1918, it was abandoned once again. Head to the 1906 Methodist church for a slideshow about the settlement or wander past the clerk's 1864 log cabin to the river and to the site of the McDougall Mission and the graves of the founder's three daughters.

South to Highway 16

East of St. Paul 28 kilometers (17 mi.), Highway 28 jogs north to Cold Lake and Highway 41 heads south 66 kilometers (41 mi.) to Highway 16 at Vermilion. The following attractions are accessed from this route.

On the north bank of the North Saskatchewan River, 13 kilometers (eight mi.) east of Elk Point, **Fort George/Buckingham House** (780/724-2611, mid-May–Aug. daily 10 A.M.–6 P.M., $3) is the site of two fur-trading posts established in the 1790s. Both posts were abandoned in the early 1800s and have long since been destroyed; depressions in the ground, piles of stone, and indistinct pathways are all that remain. Above the site is an interpretive center with audio and visual presentations explaining the rivalry between the Hudson's Bay and Northwest companies and the history of the forts.

Whitney Lakes Provincial Park

This mid-sized park along Highway 646 protects a string of lakes in a transition zone of diverse plant, mammal, and bird species. Beavers are common—look for their ponds on the north side of Laurier Lake. Other resident mammals include porcupines, white-tailed deer, coyotes, and, during berry season, black bears. Birds are abundant, especially waterfowl and shorebirds. A 1.5-kilometer (0.9-mi.) interpretive trail starts at the day-use area at the northeast corner of Ross Lake. Fishing is best for northern pike, perch, and pickerel. Within the park are two campgrounds ($20) totaling more than 200 sites, many with powered hookups.

Bonnyville

Along Highway 28, this town of 5,500 is an agriculture center surrounded by many good fishing and swimming lakes. On the southern edge of town is **Jessie Lake,** where more than 300 species of waterfowl and shorebirds have been recorded. Spring and fall are the best viewing times, although many species are present year-round, nesting in the marshes and aspen parkland surrounding the lake. Numerous viewing platforms, linked by the **Wetlands Nature Trail,** are scattered along Lakeshore Drive and Highway 41.

West of Bonnyville between Highways 28A and 660, **Moose Lake Provincial Park** surrounds a large, shallow body of water with good fishing for northern pike, perch, and walleye. The park's namesake—moose—are long gone, but a choice of forested trails lead along the lake, and to a wetland that is home to many species of birds. The small campground (unserviced sites $17, powered sites $20) has 59 sites on two loops, both of which have access to the beach.

COLD LAKE

At the end of Highway 28, a little less than 300 kilometers (186 mi.) northeast of Edmonton, is

Cold Lake (pop. 13,000), created in 1997 when the administration of three existing towns—Cold Lake, Grand Centre, and Medley—amalgamated. It's Cold Lake itself you'll want to make your final destination.

The town still marked on many maps as "Medley"—now part of Cold Lake South—is **4 Wing Cold Lake,** Canada's largest jet-fighter base. Over 5,000 military personnel and their families live on the base, using an air weapons range that occupies a large tract of wilderness to the north. Although the military has been present for over half a century, it is the **Cold Lake Oil Sands** that hold the key to the region's economic future.

Sights and Recreation

Cold Lake, 22 kilometers (13.6 mi.) wide and 27 kilometers (13.6 mi.) long, is frozen for five months of the year (the tackle shop at the marina has a sheet showing breakup dates for the last 50 years), but when the ice has gone, anglers come to play. Fishing is best for northern pike, lake trout, and walleye, with the center of most activity being a big **marina** (780/639-3535) on the southern shore where small aluminum boats with outboard engines can be rented for $10 per hour or $70 per day. **Hook, Line, and Sinker Fishing Tours** (780/639-3474) offers varying packages in a modern 5.5-meter (18-ft.) fishing boat. Charters are from $15 per person per hour for two people, but it's least expensive for four, when a full day of guided fishing is a reasonable $65 per person. Beside the marina is the **Cold Lake Information Centre** (780/594-7750 or 800/840-6140, www.coldlake.com, May–Aug. daily 9 A.M.–8 P.M., Sept.–Apr. Mon.–Fri. 9 A.M.–5 P.M.).

East of town is 5,855-hectare (14,470-acre) **Cold Lake Provincial Park,** on a low isthmus of land with a diversity of plant species and good fishing. **Hall's Lagoon,** on the northwest side of the isthmus, is a thickly weeded body of water with an observation platform and identification boards set up for bird-watchers.

Accommodations and Camping

On the shore of Cold Lake, a short stroll from town, is the **Harbour House Inn** (615 Lakeshore Dr., 780/639-2337), one of Alberta's finest bed-and-breakfasts. Each of the 11 rooms is tastefully decorated in a unique theme. The Hearts Afire room is decorated in pastel colors and has a lake view, a fireplace, a bath, and a magnificent mahogany canopy bed. Rooms range $60–80 s, $70–100 d; you'll need reservations in summer. Along the same stretch of lakefront is **Bloom N Breakfast Inn** (607 Lakeshore Dr., 780/639-4730 or 877/307-8740, www.bloomnbreakfast.com, $80 s, $85 d), a small bed-and-breakfast offering four guest rooms possessing individual charm—a couple with private balconies, another with a countrified feel, and a third-floor charmer with a bright blue color scheme.

Along 1st Avenue, past Kinosoo Beach, is the **Cold Lake MD Campground** (780/639-4121, mid-May–mid-Sept., $13–17), but a more pleasant option is **Cold Lake Provincial Park,** east of town. The campground (unserviced sites $17, powered sites $19) has coin-operated showers, firewood sales, a beach, summer interpretive programs, and is open year-round.

Food

A pleasant walk along the lakeshore reaches **Harbour House Tea House** (615 Lakeshore Dr., 780/639-2337), associated with the inn of the same name. It opens each afternoon with a changing menu of mouthwatering desserts to accompany tea and coffee.

LAC LA BICHE AND VICINITY

The historic town of Lac La Biche (pop. 2,600) is on the southern flanks of the boreal forest, 225 kilometers (140 mi.) northeast of Edmonton. The town itself has little of interest, but nearby you'll find a restored mission, two interesting provincial parks, and many excellent fishing lakes. The town lies on a divide that separates the Athabasca River system, which drains into the Arctic Ocean, from the Churchill River system, which drains into Hudson Bay. The historic Portage La Biche, across this strip of land, was a vital link in the transcontinental route taken by the early fur traders. Voyageurs would paddle up the Beaver River from the east to Beaver Lake and portage the five kilometers (3.1 mi.) to Lac La Biche, from where passage could be made to the rich fur-trapping regions along the Athabasca River. **Lac La Biche Mission** 11 kilometers (6.8 mi.) northwest of Lac La Biche, was a base for priests who had missions along the Athabasca, Peace, and Mackenzie Rivers and was used as a supply depot for voyageurs still using the northern trade route. Take a guided tour around the original buildings (780/623-3274, summer daily 10 A.M.–6 P.M., adult $5, senior $4.25, child $3.50).

Local Parks

Sir Winston Churchill Provincial Park is on the largest of nine islands in Lac La Biche and is linked to the mainland by a 2.5-kilometer (1.6-mi.) causeway. The island is covered in a lush, old-growth coniferous forest, that, due to its island location, has escaped fires. Along the loop road, short trails lead to sandy beaches (the best on the northeast side of the island), marshes rich with birdlife, and a bird-viewing platform where a mounted telescope lets you watch white pelicans and double-crested cormorants resting on a gravel bar. Camping is $15.

East of Lac La Biche, **Lakeland Provincial Park and Recreation Area** encompasses 60,000 hectares (148,000 acres) of boreal forest that is mostly in its natural state. Deer, moose, beavers, red foxes, lynx, coyotes, a few wolves and black bears, and more than 200 species of birds can be spotted in the area. A colony of great blue herons, Alberta's largest wading bird, lives at **Pinehurst Lake,** 27 kilometers (17 mi.) off Highway 55. Campgrounds are scattered through the park, with rates in the $9–13 range.

Practicalities

La Biche Inn (101st Ave., 780/623-4427 or 888/884-8886, $54 s, $60 d) has a restaurant and a nightclub where the disc jockey sits in a big rig. **Beaver Lake Campground** (780/623-3930, $15–18), three kilometers (1.9 mi.) east and nine kilometers (5.6 mi.) south of town, is a full-service RV park with a large marina, boat rentals, a general store stocked with fishing tackle, and barbecues ($10 per day), perfect for cooking up freshly caught walleye.

On the lakefront is a **Tourist Information Centre** (780/623-4804, May–Aug. Mon.–Thurs. 8:30 A.M.–4 P.M., Fri.–Sat 8:30 A.M.–6 P.M., Sun. 10 A.M.–6 P.M.) and a trail that leads along the shoreline to a statue of explorer extraordinaire David Thompson.

Fort McMurray and Vicinity

It's a long drive up a one-way highway to reach Fort McMurray, 450 kilometers (280 mi.) north of Edmonton, but it's far from a dead-end town. This city of 48,000 is a modern-day boomtown that revolves around the Athabasca Oil Sands, the world's largest deposit of oil. The city is awash with money—and workers spending it. So if you're not a construction worker or oilman, why should you make the long trek north? Actual "sights" are oil sands–related (tours through the mining operations are very popular), but nowhere in the world has so much economic development ever been concentrated in one place, which makes simply "being there" an interesting study in socioeconomics.

SIGHTS AND RECREATION

Oil Sands Discovery Centre

For an insight into the history, geology, and technology of the Athabasca Oil Sands mining process, head to this large interpretive center (corner of Hwy. 63 and Mackenzie Blvd., 780/743-7167, mid-May–Aug. daily 9 A.M.–5 P.M., rest of year Tues.–Sun. 10 A.M.–4 P.M., adult $6, senior $4, child $2.50). Start your visit by watching *Quest for Energy,* a multimedia, big-screen presentation about the industry that has grown around the resource. The center houses an interesting collection of machinery and has interactive displays, hands-on exhibits, and interpretive presentations. Outside is the Industrial Equipment Garden, where an older-style bucket-wheel excavator and other machinery are displayed.

Syncrude/Suncor Plant Tours

Touring the oil sands plants is the best way to experience the operation firsthand. The scope of the developments is overwhelming, while the size of the machinery is almost inconceivable. Syncrude is the larger, more imposing operation of the two,

but it enforces more rules and keeps you farther from the action (tours June Fri.–Sat., July–Aug. Wed.–Sat., and Sept.–Oct. Fri.–Sat. at 9 A.M.). The Suncor tour gives you a better feel for the sheer size of the equipment (tours depart June Sun.–Mon., July–Aug. Sun.–Tues. at 1 P.M.). Tour cost is adult $18, senior $15; reservations are essential and can be made at the Fort McMurray Visitors Bureau (780/791-4336 or 800/565-3947).

To Fort McKay

Fort McKay is a small native settlement on the west bank of the Athabasca River. The town itself has little of interest (and no services), but the drive out to the end of Highway 63 is pleasant and gives you a chance to view the mining operations, albeit at a distance. The **Oil Sands Viewpoint,** 40 kilometers (25 mi.) from Fort McMurray, looks out over tailing ponds and reclaimed land from the Suncor operation. Immediately north is a fenced herd of 300 bison. The road then continues toward Fort McKay along a causeway over **Mildred Lake,** Canada's largest reservoir.

Gregoire Lake Provincial Park

Southeast of the city 34 kilometers (21 mi.) is Gregoire Lake, the only accessible lake in the Fort McMurray area. The 690-hectare (1,700-acre) park on the lake's west shore is a typical boreal forest of mixed woods and black-spruce bogs. Many species of waterfowl nest on the lake, and mammals such as moose and black bears are relatively common. Some short hiking trails wind through the park, and canoes are rented in the day-use area.

Wilderness Tours

Majic Country Wilderness Adventures (780/743-0766, www.wildernesscountry.com) offers tours from Fort McMurray. The most popular outing for money-laden workers with a day off is chasing northern pike down the Clearwater River

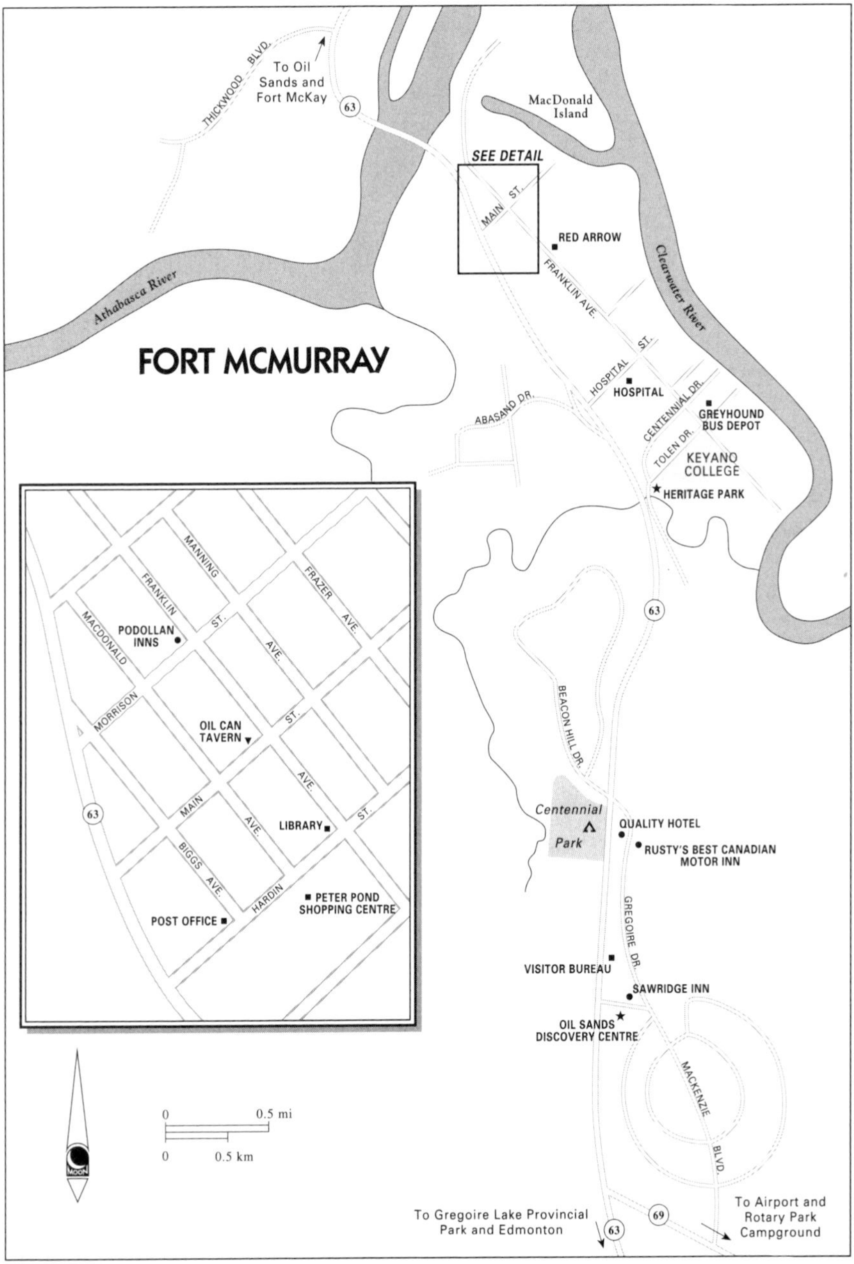

FORT MCMURRAY

To Oil Sands and Fort McKay

MacDonald Island

SEE DETAIL

RED ARROW

Hospital

GREYHOUND BUS DEPOT

KEYANO COLLEGE

Heritage Park

PODOLLAN INNS

OIL CAN TAVERN

LIBRARY

PETER POND SHOPPING CENTRE

POST OFFICE

Centennial Park

QUALITY HOTEL

RUSTY'S BEST CANADIAN MOTOR INN

VISITOR BUREAU

SAWRIDGE INN

OIL SANDS DISCOVERY CENTRE

To Gregoire Lake Provincial Park and Edmonton

To Airport and Rotary Park Campground

© AVALON TRAVEL PUBLISHING, INC.

ALBERTA

in a jet-boat ($500 per day for four people). Other jet-boat tours take in the Suncor site and a chunk of exposed oil sands from river-level, or head out early for the best chance at spotting the abundant bird species drawn to local waterways. Other options include an overnight stay at a remote riverside cabin and horseback riding, or just rent a canoe ($35 per day) and set your own schedule.

Entertainment

As you'd expect, Fort McMurray has dozens of wild, noisy bars and lounges filled with boisterous construction workers with money to burn. Downtown, the **Oil Can Tavern** in the Oil Sands Hotel (10007 Franklin Ave., 780/743-2211) is legendary as a hard-drinking pub with weekend country or rock and roll bands. A more subdued option

would be to relax with a quiet drink on the leather sofas of the **Pillar Pub** at the Podollan Inns (10131 Franklin Ave., 780/790-2000). It's possible to find some big-city culture if you search it out. **Keyano Theatre** (8115 Franklin Ave., 780/791-4990) puts on a season of live performances September–May at the local college.

ACCOMMODATIONS AND CAMPING

If you're planning to stay indoors, it's imperative you book your Fort McMurray accommodations as far in advance as possible. High demand dictates there are really no bargains in Fort McMurray, although the visitor bureau has some accommodation/tour packages that are a good deal—around

---

ATHABASCA OIL SANDS

The numbers that oil types throw around when talking of the Athabasca Oil Sands are impossible to comprehend—315 billion barrels of recoverable oil (more than present in all of Saudi Arabia) from a 1.7 trillion-barrel reserve (only 800 billion barrels of conventional crude oil are known to remain on this entire planet) just means *lots* to most people. The oil is not conventional oil but a heavy oil, commonly called bitumen. The accepted estimate is that only 315 billion barrels of the total field are recoverable using the technology of today. Still, that's a lot of oil and the math is easy—it will take 100 years to extract just 20 percent of the recoverable oil. Within 500 years, someone will probably have figured out a way to get at the other 60 percent of the deposit.

Extracting and processing it to produce a lighter, more useful oil is expensive. The costs for extracting and processing the oil sands bitumen currently run at $12 per barrel, compared to Middle East crude, which can be pumped out of the ground for just $1 a barrel. Still, with improvements in technology, pipelines connected to the insatiable U.S. market, and world supplies of conventional crude slowly being depleted, the oil sands of Fort McMurray are the focus of big oil companies with *big* money—some $85 billion

worth of planned development is underway to complement existing infrastructure.

All told, around $25 billion has been spent on oil sands development since the mid-1990s, with the major players in the industry having collaborated on a development proposal that guarantees a combined regional investment of a further $30 billion over the next 25 years. The current total production rate of one million barrels a day is expected to increase to 1.8 million barrels by 2010.

The Process

The sands are mined in two different ways—deposits close to the surface are strip-mined, while the oil deeper down is extracted in situ (using steam injection). In the case of surface deposits, the size of the machinery used to scrape off the surface layer of muskeg and excavate the oil sands below it is mind-boggling. Extracting oil sands that lie deep below the earth's surface is very costly. A simplified explanation of the process is that the fields are tapped by parallel wells. Steam is injected in one, loosening then liquefying and separating the oil from the sand. A second, lower well, extracts the resulting oil. Once on the surface, it must be chemically altered to produce a lighter, more useful oil.

ALBERTA

$100 per person for two night's accommodation, a tour, and a t-shirt.

$50–100
Rusty's Best Canadian Motor Inn (385 Gregoire Dr., 780/791-4646, www.bestcdn.com, $84 s, $94 d) is one of a bunch of properties four kilometers (2.5 mi.) south of downtown near the visitors center. All rooms have a fridge and some have kitchens, or dine in the hotel restaurant or lounge.

$100–150
Fort McMurray's largest motel, with 190 rooms, is the **Sawridge Inn and Conference Centre** (530 Mackenzie Blvd., 780/791-7900 or 800/661-6567, www.sawridge.com, $119–129 s or d), which underwent a major revamp in 2003. Rooms have all the standard amenities business travelers demand, while a choice of dining facilities are set around an indoor pool complex.

Across the road from Rusty's is the **Quality Hotel** (424 Gregoire Dr., 780/791-7200 or 800/582-3273). You'll do no better for value than the mid-size Standard rooms ($129 s or d), or splurge on a Superior room ($169 s or d) that really is superior. On the bottom floor are a restaurant, lounge, and indoor swimming pool.

Podollan Inns (10131 Franklin Ave., 780/790-2000 or 888/448-2080, www.podallan.com) is the newest of the downtown hotel. Extra-large guest rooms come with modern conveniences such as card-lock entry and high-speed Internet while downstairs is a restaurant, lounge, and heated underground parking. Standard rooms are $139 s or d, or pay $10 extra for a king-size bed.

Campgrounds
Two campgrounds are south of the city limits. The **Rotary Park Campground** (11 km/6.8 mi. south, 780/790-1581, $20) offers showers, cooking facilities, and powered sites and is open year-round. The park is signposted but easy to miss; turn east along Highway 69 and look for the entrance to the left. **Fort McMurray Centennial Park** (9909 Franklin Ave., 780/791-5497, $14)

doesn't have showers or hookups but is along Highway 63, closer to the city. **Rusty's Best Canadian Motor Inn** (385 Gregoire Dr., 780/791-4646, $20) also has a few RV hookups.

OTHER PRACTICALITIES
Food
The **Keg Steakhouse** (Nomad Inn, 10006 MacDonald Ave., 780/791-4770, Mon.–Sat. 11 A.M.–midnight, Sun. 4–11 P.M.) is part of a Canadian chain renowned for fine cuts of Alberta beef served up in a stylish family restaurant atmosphere. You can't go wrong ordering the prime rib with horseradish sauce, boiled vegetables, and a roast potato ($18–25), or go creative and try the teriyaki sirloin ($24). The **Athabasca Grill** at the Quality Hotel (424 Gregoire Dr., 780/791-7200) spreads out breakfast and lunchtime buffets, the latter featuring different cuisines daily.

Information
The **Fort McMurray Visitors Bureau** (780/791-4336 or 800/565-3947, www.fortmcmurray tourism.com) does an excellent job of promoting the city. They operate an information center south of downtown (mid-May–Aug. daily 8:30 A.M.–6 P.M., Sept.–mid-May Mon.–Fri. 8:30 A.M.–4 P.M.), just north of the Oil Sands Discovery Centre. **Fort McMurray Public Library** (9907 Franklin Avenue, 780/743-7800, open daily) has public Internet access.

Transportation
Although the road out of Fort McMurray is excellent and always seems to be busy, many people prefer to fly. The **airport** is nine kilometers (5.6 mi.) south, then six kilometers (3.7 mi.) east of downtown. **Air Canada** (888/247-2262), **Westjet** (800/538-5696), and **Air Mikisew** (780/743-8218) fly daily to Edmonton.

Wood Buffalo Express (780/743-7096, $1.25 per sector) is a local transit service to outlying suburbs and the Oil Sands Discovery Centre. From downtown, a cab costs $10 to the Oil Sands Discovery Centre and $25 to the airport.

North-Central Alberta

From downtown Edmonton, Highway 2 (called the St. Albert Trail in the vicinity of Edmonton) heads north along the **Athabasca Landing Trail,** a historic route used by natives and then traders and explorers that linked the North Saskatchewan and Athabasca river systems.

ATHABASCA

At the end of the Athabasca Landing Trail, 147 kilometers (91 mi.) north of Edmonton, is the town of Athabasca (pop. 2,300), on a hill that slopes gently to the river. Although the Hudson's Bay Company buildings have long since disappeared, many later buildings from the days of the sternwheelers remain, including the 1912 railway station and a 1913 brick schoolhouse. From town, walk through **Muskeg Creek Park** (good berry-picking in late summer) and you'll emerge

at **Athabasca University** (780/675-6111, www .athabascau.ca). This facility has a fulltime staff of 900, a choice of 500 programs at all levels including graduate, a library with 100,000 books, an extensive art collection, and an annual budget exceeding $30 million—but there's not a single student in sight. That's because it's a correspondence university, one of the largest in North America and open to students regardless of their geographical location or previous academic levels.

Practicalities

Several motels are located on Highway 2, south of town. Try the **Athabasca Hillside Motel** (4804 46th Ave., 780/675-5111 or 888/675-8900, athabascahillsidemotel.com, $55 s or d), with good views of the river and kitchenettes in each of the 17 rooms. **River's Edge Campground** (50th Ave., May–mid-Oct.; unserviced sites $10,

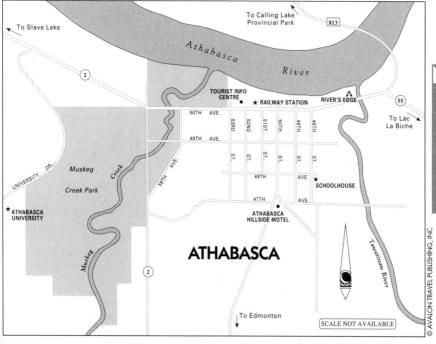

powered sites $15) sits on the edge of town where the Tawatinaw River drains into the much wider Athabasca River.

The **Tourist Information Centre** (beside the railway station on 50th Ave., 780/675-2055, late May–early Sept. daily 11 A.M.–6 P.M.) is in a red CN caboose at the bottom of town.

Calling Lake Provincial Park

Lying along the south shore of one of Alberta's larger lakes, this 741-hectare (1,830-acre) park is on Highway 813, 55 kilometers (34 mi.) north of Athabasca. A boreal forest of aspen surrounds the lake, giving way to a marshy area nearer the shore. Look for deer, moose, and black bears, as well as the occasional white pelican and blue heron. Fishing for northern pike, walleye, perch, and whitefish is the park's main attraction, although swimming and canoeing on the lake are also possible. Camping in the small campground is $15.

SLAVE LAKE AND VICINITY

The town of Slave Lake (pop. 6,500) is on the southeastern shore of **Lesser Slave Lake,** 110 kilometers (68 mi.) west of Athabasca and 250 kilometers (155 mi.) northwest of Edmonton. Once an important staging point for steamboat freight and passengers, the town today is a popular base for anglers and the jumping off point for Highway 88 (**Bicentennial Highway**), which winds its way through uninhabited wilderness to High Level. The first section of this highway passes through **Lesser Slave Lake Provincial Park,** which protects long sandy beaches, unique sand dunes, and wetland and boreal forest habitats supporting diverse wildlife. At the north end of the park, a steep eight-kilometer (five-mi.) road leads to the plateau-like summit of 1,030-meter (3,380-ft.) Marten Mountain, from where views extend across the lake.

Fishing

Lesser Slave Lake (1,150 sq. km/440 sq. mi.) is the largest lake in Alberta accessible by road and has some of the province's best fishing, with northern pike to nine kilograms (19.8 lbs.), walleye to four kilograms (8.8 lbs.), whitefish to 2.5 kilograms (5.5 pounds), and yellow perch to one kilogram (2.2 pounds)—enough to make any self-respecting fisherman quit his job, pack the rod and reel, and head north. The most productive fishing is done from out in the middle of the lake. Ask at the information center for a list of local fishing guides, who rent boats from $20 per hour, $50 half-day, or $100 full day.

Accommodations and Camping

You can stay in town at the **Sawridge Inn and Conference Centre** (200 Main St. S, 780/849-4101 or 800/661-6657, www.sawridge.com, from $75 s or d), but it's worth the drive 30 kilometers (19 mi.) west to **Canyon Creek Hotel** (780/369-3784, $50 s, $60 d). Fronting a sandy beach, the rooms are not particularly attractive, but are comfortable and clean. Meals are available.

Lesser Slave Lake Provincial Park's **Marten River Campground** (at the extreme northern end of the park; unserviced sites $15, powered sites $17) has coin-operated showers, a beach, and a summer interpretive program. Immediately north, outside the park boundary, is **Diamond Willow Resort** (780/849-2292, May–Sept.; unserviced sites $18, powered sites $20), a private campground with coin showers, a grocery store, a pitch-and-putt golf course, and a nature trail.

Information

The **Tourist Information Centre** (off Hwy. 2, west of Main St., 780/849-4611) is open May–August daily 10 A.M.–7 P.M.

West Along Slave Lake

From Slave Lake, Highway 2 westbound follows the southern shore of Lesser Slave Lake to High Prairie. Just west of **Kinuso,** an unpaved road leads north to **Spruce Point Park** (780/775-2117, May–mid-Sept., $17–22), which bustles with families and fisherman throughout summer. From the main camping area, a wide grassed area leads down to a lakefront beach and a marina with boat and canoe rentals and a fish-cleaning shed.

Grouard, near the west end of Lesser Slave Lake, grew up around the St. Bernard Mission. The town was destined to become the center of the north. It had a few thousand people and a rail line on the way, when, because of an unfortunate set of circumstances, everything changed. A sample of water from a nearby lake was sent to the railway headquarters to ensure that it was fit for the steam engines. Along the way it was either dropped, lost, or emptied and replaced by a sample of water from muskeg wetland. The new sample was tested and found to be of poor quality. The proposed route for the railway changed, and the once-thriving town collapsed. **Grouard Native Cultural Arts Museum** (780/751-3915, July–Aug. Tues.–Fri. 10 A.M.–4 P.M., Sat. 10 A.M.–6 P.M., Sept.–June Mon.–Fri. 10 A.M.–4 P.M.) is dedicated to promoting a better understanding of North American native cultures through exhibitions of native arts and crafts as well as the outdoor re-creation of a native village. It's in the Moosehorn Lodge Building on the grounds of the Northern Lakes College, by the lake.

High Prairie

This town of 2,900 near the west end of Lesser Slave Lake has its long history cataloged at the **High Prairie and District Museum** (in the library on 53rd Ave., 780/523-2601, June–Sept. Tues.–Sat. 10 A.M.–5 P.M.), which also has a small exhibit on the missionaries at Grouard.

North of High Prairie on Highway 749, **Winagami Lake Provincial Park** has camping with powered sites ($15–18), and two platforms built for bird-watching. The day-use area has been planted with ornamental shrubs, and a short hiking trail leads along the lakeshore.

McLennan

Known as the "Bird Capital of Canada," this town of 1,000 is on **Kimiwan Lake** at the confluence of three major bird migration paths— the Mississippi, Pacific, and Central. An estimated 27,000 shorebirds and 250,000 waterfowl reside or pass through here; more than 200 different species are sighted annually. An excellent interpretive center (780/324-2004, summer daily 10 A.M.–7 P.M.) overlooking the lake has a display on migration patterns, computers loaded with information on local species, checklists, and binoculars for loan. From the center, a boardwalk leads through a wetland area to a gazebo and a bird blind. Panels along the boardwalk provide pictures and descriptions of commonly sighted species.

HIGHWAY 18 WEST

North of Edmonton 73 kilometers (45 mi.) on Highway 2, Highway 18 heads west through some of Canada's most productive mixed farming land. Major crops include wheat, barley, oats, canola, and hay. Livestock operations include cattle, hogs, poultry, dairy cows, and sheep. At the junction of Highways 2 and 18, a gravel road leads north to **Nilsson Bros. Inc.** (780/348-5893, www.nbinc.com), Canada's largest privately owned cattle exchange. Live auctions are held in summer every Tuesday morning. Buyers come from throughout North America, but anyone is welcome to attend. The auctioneer is lightning fast— Alberta's best beef cattle are sold hundreds at a time by gross weight. The facility is open every day; ask to have a look around. The staff restaurant, open for an hour at lunchtime, serves hearty meat-and-potato meals for a reasonable price. Just don't ask for lamb.

Barrhead and Vicinity

Around 50 kilometers (31 mi.) west of the Highway 2/18 junction is Barrhead, an agriculture and lumber town of 4,200. **Barrhead Centennial Museum** (along Hwy. 33 at 57th Ave., 780/674-5203, mid-May–Aug. Mon.–Sat. 10 A.M.–5 P.M., Sun. 1–5 P.M.), with displays depicting the town's agricultural past, is north of downtown. The town's symbol is the great blue heron; you can see a model of one at the top end of 50th Street, or head 21 kilometers (13 mi.) west of town for the chance to spot a real one at **Thunder Lake Provincial Park.** Three short hiking trails begin from the day-use area, including one along the lakeshore that links to three other trails originating from the campground. The campground is beside the beach and is open year-round. It has pit toilets, coin-operated showers, a concession, firewood sales, cooking shelters, and canoe rentals; unserviced sites are $18, powered sites, found on Loop A, are $21.

HIGHWAY 43 WEST

This major route connects Edmonton with Grande Prairie, a total distance of 460 kilometers (286 mi.). A few towns and parks provide an opportunity to break the journey.

Whitecourt

At the confluence of the Athabasca, McLeod, and Sakwatamau Rivers, 177 kilometers (110 mi.) northwest of Edmonton, this town of 8,000 calls itself the "Forest Centre of Alberta." To learn more about this local industry, make a stop at the **Forest Interpretive Centre** (south side of town, 780/778-2214, year-round Mon.–Fri. 9 A.M.–6 P.M., July–Aug. 9 A.M.–6 P.M.). Displays re-create forest environment and a logging camp, and a series of hands-on, interactive exhibits describe every aspect of the industry. The center also holds the town's information center (780/778-5363) and hands out brochures detailing local forest drives.

Most of Whitecourt's dozen motels are on Highway 43 as it enters town from the southeast. The best of the cheapies is the **Glenview Motel** (780/778-2276, $52 s, $58 d). The **Green Gables Inn** (3527 Caxton St., 780/778-4537 or 888/779-4537, $69–74 s or d), at the top end of the scale, has large and surprisingly nice rooms and a restaurant. The **Lions Club Campground** (unserviced sites $10–13, powered sites $15) at the south end of the service strip, is set in a heavily forested area and has a laundry and showers.

Mountain Pizza & Steak House (780/778-3600) has great pizza from $8.50, or try the restaurant in the **Quality Inn** (5420 47th Ave., 780/778-5477), where the excellent rib-eye steak is $17.

Carson-Pegasus Provincial Park

This 1,178-hectare (2,900-acre) park is on the southern edge of the Swan Hills, 30 kilometers (19 mi.) north of Whitecourt. More than 40 species of mammals have been recorded here, including deer, moose, and black bear. The epicenter of the park is McLeod Lake, where the fishing is excellent for rainbow trout (stocked annually) and the day-use area offers canoe, rowboat, and motorboat rentals ($7, $8, and $14 per hour, respectively) and a sandy beach. A general store (summer, daily 9 A.M.–9 P.M.) sells groceries, fishing tackle, bait, and hot food, and has a laundry room. The campground has flush toilets, showers, cooking shelters, and an interpretive theater. Rates of $22 for tenting or $25 for powered sites include firewood.

Whitecourt to Grande Prairie

Next up along Highway 43 is the service town of **Valleyview,** with the **Horizon Motel** (780/524-3904 or 888/909-3908), which has large rooms in an older wing ($62 s, $72 d) but its newer wing holds nicer ones that are air-conditioned ($79 s, $82 d). Spend the night with Alaska-bound campers at **Sherk's RV Park** (south side of town, 780/524-4949, May–Sept.), a full-service campground where all sites are $19.

Continuing west, **Sturgeon Lake** is known for its excellent northern pike, perch, and walleye fishing and two interesting provincial parks. **Williamson Provincial Park** may be only 17 hectares (42 acres) but has a sandy beach, good swimming, and a campground ($15–17, May–mid-Sept.). Protecting a much larger chunk of forested lakeshore is 3,100-hectare (7,660-acre) **Young's Point Provincial Park.** Here you'll find good bird-watching for forest birds and waterfowl, and productive fishing among the dense aquatic growth close to the shore. Hiking trails begin at the day-use area and lead along the lake and to an active beaver pond. The campground (unserviced sites $15, powered sites $17) has flush toilets, showers, and is near a sandy beach.

West of Edmonton

From the provincial capital, the Yellowhead Highway (Hwy. 16) heads west through a region of aspen parkland and scattered lakes to the Canadian Rockies foothills and the border of Jasper National Park. The region's other main thoroughfare, Highway 40, spurs north off the Yellowhead Highway to Grande Cache and Willmore Wilderness Park. An area of frenzied oil activity during the early 1970s, the region west of Edmonton is the center for a large petroleum industry, as well as for farming, coal mining, forestry, and the production of electricity. The major service centers are Edson and Hinton, both on the Yellowhead Highway.

FROM EDMONTON TOWARD HINTON

Long after leaving Edmonton's city limits, the Yellowhead Highway is lined with motels, industrial parks, and housing estates. The towns of Spruce Grove and Stony Plain flash by, and farming begins to dominate the landscape.

Pembina River Provincial Park and Vicinity

The Pembina River Valley is the first true wilderness area west of Edmonton. The small towns of Entwistle and Evansburg straddle either side of the valley where the park lies. The only structures you'll see in this 167-hectare (413-acre) park are an old single-lane road bridge and the concrete foundations of what once was a railroad trestle. White spruce and aspen blanket the park and provide a habitat for many mammals, including beavers, mule deer, white-tailed deer, and moose. Fishing in the river is particularly good for northern pike and walleye, and those who don't fish might appreciate the deep swimming hole behind a weir, or the hiking trails in the northern part of the park. Open May–October, the campground (unserviced sites $17, powered sites $20) is on the eastern side of the river. It has flush toilets, cooking shelters, showers, an interpretive program, and firewood sales.

Edson

The town of Edson, 199 kilometers (124 mi.) west of Edmonton, relies on natural resource–based industries such as forestry and oil and gas to fuel its economy. The **Galloway Station Museum** is in the RCMP Centennial Park (3rd Ave., 780/723-5696, mid-May–early Sept. daily 10 A.M.–4:30 P.M., $1). It houses artifacts reflecting the importance of transportation and industry to the town's growth. Also on display in the park are a restored 1917 caboose and a 1964 Lockheed jet. Beside the museum is the **Tourist Information Centre** (3rd Ave., 780/723-4918, mid-May–Aug. Mon.–Fri. 8 A.M.–8 P.M., Sat.–Sun. 9 A.M.–8 P.M.).

Most motels are along the main highway through town—locally known as 2nd Avenue (heading east) and 4th Avenue (heading west). **Odyssey Inn** (5601 2nd Ave., 780/723-5505, from $49–59 s, $59–69 d) offers acceptable 1970s-style rooms. The **Sundowner Inn** (5150 2nd Ave., 780/723-5591 or 877/723-5591, $89 s, $99 d) has the basics and a few bonuses too—an indoor pool and a recreation room with a fireplace and pool table.

The **Lions Park Campground** (east end of town, 780/723-3169, May–mid-Sept.; unserviced sites $15, powered sites $18) has treed sites far enough from the highway to be relatively quiet. Facilities include extra hot (and fast) showers and plenty of free firewood, which is just as well because you need a bonfire to cook anything on the oversized fire rings.

HINTON

This town of 10,000, 287 kilometers (178 mi.) west of Edmonton, is just 75 kilometers (47 mi.) from Jasper, but before speeding off to the famous mountain park, take time out to explore Hinton's immediate vicinity—to the south are well-maintained roads leading into the historic Coal Branch; to the north are lakes, streams, canyons, hoodoos, and sand dunes. The town has some interesting sights, and the

ALBERTA

SUNDANCE PROVINCIAL PARK

As an alternative to continuing west along Highway 16 from Edson to Hinton, consider the **Emerson Creek Road,** which links the two towns along an unpaved route north of the main highway. It also provides access to 3,712-hectare (9,170-acre) Sundance Provincial Park, protecting a variety of interesting geological features and the picturesque Emerson Lakes. A 5.7-kilometer (3.5-mi.) trail winds around the lakes to an old trapper's cabin and past some active beaver dams; allow 90 minutes to complete the entire loop. The lakes are stocked with brook trout and Sundance Creek with rainbow and brown trout. A small campground (May–Sept., $9) at the lakes has sites with no services but free firewood.

A good map of local logging roads is required to ensure you stay on the right route. These are available at the information centers in both Edson and Hinton.

motels and restaurants have prices you'll appreciate after spending time in Jasper.

The coal-mining and forestry industries are shown off at Hinton's two main attractions. Don't be put off by the unappealing location of the **Natural Resource Interpretive Park,** behind the Canadian Tire store on the west side of town—much of the park is out of sight in the valley below. Up top is a lookout, a 154-ton dump truck, and panels describing local industry, while a trail leads down to a small arboretum and through an area of wetlands. On the campus of the **Hinton Training Centre** (1176 Switzer Dr., 780/865-8200, Mon.–Fri. 8:30 A.M.–4:30 P.M.), you'll find a small museum dedicated to the history of forestry, including a display on wildfire management. Adjacent is a 1922 ranger cabin.

Accommodations

I recommend giving the regular motels a miss and staying out of town at one of the following accommodations.

Halfway between Hinton and Jasper, **Overlander Mountain Lodge** (780/866-2330 or 877/866-2330, www.overlandermountainlodge.com, $100–275 s or d) has an inviting wilderness setting and energetic hosts with plenty of suggestions to keep you busy through the day. Choose from regular guest rooms in various styles (the Miette Rooms have a particularly appealing decor), cozy cabins, or large, self-contained log chalets. Mountain charm continues through to the dining room, where Canadian specialties anchor a seasonal menu.

The **Black Cat Guest Ranch** (780/865-3084 or 800/859-6840, www.blackcatguestranch.ca) is another mountain retreat. All of the rooms have private baths and mountain views. Horseback riding is available during the day, and in the evening, guests can relax in the large living room or the hot tub. Three meals are included in the rates of $139 s, $176 d. To get to the ranch, take Highway 40 north for six kilometers (3.7 mi.), turn left to Brûlé and continue for 11 kilometers (6.8 mi.), then turn right and follow the signs.

Food

If you've taken my advice and are staying at one of the lodges above, you won't need feeding. If you're just passing through and looking for a quick meal, try **Tokyo Sushi** (Black Bear Inn, 571 Gregg Ave., 780/865-2120), with a modern family-restaurant-style atmosphere and good-value Japanese food. Don't expect anything too adventurous—just tasty, inexpensive favorites like chicken teriyaki ($10) and filling sushi combos (from $12).

Information

The **Tourist Information Centre** (Gregg Ave., 780/865-2777, summer daily 8 A.M.–7 P.M., rest of year weekdays 9 A.M.–4:15 P.M.) is on the south side of the highway, surrounded by gardens in the middle of the commercial strip. It's impossible to miss. Most of the best this region has to offer lies outside of Hinton, and in this regard, the staff does a wonderful job of supplying information on hiking, fishing, and canoeing opportunities that would otherwise be easy to miss.

HIGHWAY 40 TO GRANDE CACHE

Take divided Highway 16 west out of Hinton and, before you know it, Highway 40 spurs north, passing the following sights, reaching Grande Cache after 142 kilometers (88 mi.).

Ogre Canyon

This unique natural feature, between **Brûlé Lake** and the front ranges of the Canadian Rockies, was created by underground streams that dried up, creating sinkholes. Huge chunks of the treed surface above have dropped down, just like an elevator. In most cases, the trees have continued growing, their tops barely reaching the level of the surrounding ground. To get to Ogre Canyon, head north of Highway 16 on Highway 40 and take the first left after crossing the Athabasca River. Continue through Brûlé; the road is rough but passable and ends by Brûlé Lake. The canyon, at the base of the cliffs, is obvious.

William A. Switzer Provincial Park

This 2,688-hectare (6,640-acre) park, 26 kilometers (16 mi.) northwest of Hinton on Highway 40, encompasses a series of shallow lakes. Most of the park is heavily forested with lodgepole pine, spruce, and aspen. The northern section, however, is more wide open, and elk, moose, and deer can often be seen grazing there. The lakes are excellent for canoeing, bird-watching,

and wildlife viewing, but fishing is considered average. Highway 40 divides the park roughly in two, with many access points. From the south, the first road loops around the west side of Jarvis Lake, passing a pleasant picnic area and camping before rejoining Highway 40. At the north end of Jarvis Lake is Kelley's Bathtub day-use area, where a short trail leads to a bird blind. The roads leading into the northern section of the park lead past various hiking trails, three more day-use areas, and three campgrounds.

The main campground is on **Gregg Lake** (unserviced sites $20, powered sites $23). It offers 164 sites, coin-operated showers, cooking shelters, an interpretive theater, and winter camping. For more information on the park, call 780/865-5600.

Roughly in the middle of the park is **Blue Lake Adventure Lodge** (780/865-4741 or 800/582-3305, www.bluelakeadventurelodge.com, from $119 s or d), comprising chalets and cabins in a forested setting and adjacent to Blue Lake. The emphasis is on activities, with nearby hiking trails, a spa and sauna, and a game room as well as canoes, kayaks, mountain bikes, and fishing tackle for rent. Meal and accommodation packages run $90–110 per person per day, discounted October–April. Guests also enjoy discounted rentals, such as canoes for $25 for a full day.

On to Grande Cache

From William A. Switzer Provincial Park, it's 118 kilometers (73 mi.) to Grande Cache. A 32-kilometer (20-mi.) gravel spur to **Rock Lake–Solomon Creek Wildland Provincial Park,** 15 kilometers (9.3 mi.) north of Switzer Park, makes a tempting detour. Ever since a Hudson's Bay Company post was established at Rock Lake, the area has drawn hikers and anglers, attracted by mountain scenery, the chance of viewing abundant big game, excellent fishing for huge lake trout, and the remote location. Hiking trails lead around the lake and three kilometers (1.9 mi.) to the remote northern reaches of Jasper National Park. The large campground ($17) has cooking shelters, firewood, and pit toilets.

From Rock Lake Road, Highway 40 continues to climb steadily, crossing Pinto Creek and Berland River (small campground), then following

Muskeg River for a short while. Continuing north, the road then passes **Pierre Grey Lakes,** a string of five lakes protected as a provincial recreation area. The lakes lie in a beautiful spot, with birdlife prolific and the waters stocked annually with rainbow trout. From the boat launch, a rough trail leads 1.6 kilometers (one mi.) along the lakeshore to the site of a trading post. Camping is $15 per night.

GRANDE CACHE

Grande Cache is a remote town of 3,800, 450 kilometers (280 mi.) west of Edmonton and 182 kilometers (113 mi.) south of Grande Prairie. The surrounding wilderness is totally undeveloped, offering endless opportunities for hiking, canoeing, kayaking, fishing, and horseback riding. It was named by the first European visitors—fur trappers who cached furs near the site of the present town before taking them to major trading posts.

Grande Cache is a planned town. Construction started in 1969 in response to a need for services and housing for miners and their families working at the McIntyre Porcupine Coal Mine. The town was developed 20 kilometers (12.4 mi.) south of the mine to maintain a scenic environment. The mine closed in 2000, but the population level remains stable, with many residents employed at a nearby federal penitentiary.

Grande Cache Tourism and Interpretive Centre

This center (780/827-3300 or 888/827-3790, www.visitgrandecache.com, summer daily 9 A.M.–6 P.M., rest of the Mon.–Fri. 8:30 A.M.–4:30 P.M.) is outstanding, not just considering the size of the town that it represents, but for the wealth of information contained within it. It's easy to spend at least one hour in the two-story complex, where displays include information about the human history of the region, the local industry, taxidermy, tree identification, and Willmore Wilderness Park. Other features include an information desk, a gift shop, and a large deck from where views extend across the Smoky River Valley to the highest peaks of the

Canadian Rockies. Beside it are a 1942 ranger cabin and a few picnic tables.

Willmore Wilderness Park

A northern extension of Jasper National Park, this 460,000-hectare (1.1 million-acre) park lies south and west of Grande Cache, and is divided roughly in half by the Smoky River. The park is accessible only on foot, horseback, or, in winter, on skis. It is totally undeveloped—the trails that do exist are not maintained and are mostly those once used by trappers. The diverse wildlife is one of the park's main attractions; white-tailed and mule deer, mountain goats, bighorn sheep, moose, elk, caribou, and black bears are all common. The park is also home to wolves, cougars, and grizzly bears.

The easiest way to access the park is from **Sulphur Gates Provincial Recreation Area,** six kilometers (3.7 mi.) north of Grande Cache on Highway 40 and then a similar distance along a gravel road to the west. Those not planning a trip into the park can still enjoy the cliffs at **Sulphur Gates,** which rise above the confluence of the Sulphur and Smoky Rivers. The color difference between the glacial-fed Smoky River and spring-fed Sulphur River is apparent as they merge.

Anyone planning an extended trip into the park should be aware that no services are available, most trails are unmarked, and certain areas are heavily used by horse-packers. Led by Dave Manzer, a 20-year veteran of leading trips into Willmore, **Wild Rose Outfitting** (780/693-2296, www.wildroseoutfitting.com) offers pack trips into the park; expect to pay around $205 per person per day, all-inclusive. More information is available by contacting the department of Community Development (780/944-0313, go to www.cd.gov.ab.ca and click the "Preserving Alberta" link).

Other Recreation

Most of the serious hiking and horseback riding takes place in adjacent Willmore Wilderness Park, but a variety of other recreational opportunities around town. For great views of the surrounding area, consider climbing **Grande Mountain.** It's a steep trail, gaining 730 meters (2,400 ft.) of elevation in 3.5 kilometers (2.1

mi.), but from the summit, the view across the Smoky River Valley to the Rocky Mountains is spectacular. The trail follows a power line the entire way to the peak and is easy to follow. To get to the trailhead, head northwest of town one kilometer (0.6 mi.) and turn right at the cemetery gate. Park, walk along the road to the power line, veer right, and start the long slog to the summit. **Grande Cache Lake,** five kilometers (3.1 mi.) south of town, has good swimming, canoeing, and fishing for rainbow trout. **Wild Rose Outfitting** (780/693-2296) and **U Bar Trail Rides** (780/827-3641) have a variety of horseback-riding excursions ranging from one-hour trail rides ($20) to overnight trips into Willmore Wilderness Park. **Grande Cache Golf and Country Club** (780/827-5151, $25) is only nine holes, but you'll want to go around twice, however badly you're playing, because the scenery is distracting to say the least.

In recent years, Grande Cache has placed itself on the calendar of extreme, ultra-marathoners the world over as host of the **Canadian Death Race** series (www.canadiandeathrace.com). Races take place three times annually along the same demanding 125-kilometer (78-mi.) course that summits three peaks; on snowshoes the third weekend of January, on foot the first weekend of August, and on mountain bikes the first weekend of September.

Accommodations and Camping

Room rates in this mountain hideaway are surprisingly inexpensive, but because fewer than 250 rooms are available in the whole town, reservations should be made in advance. On the highway through town, the **Big Horn Motor Inn**

(780/827-3744 or 888/880-2444, www.bighorn inn.com, $50 s, $60 d) is the best value. Each room has a small fridge, some have kitchenettes, and a laundry room and a restaurant are on the premises. Also along the highway are the similarly priced **Alpine Lodge Motel** (780/827-2450) and **Mountain Village Motel** (780/827-2453).

The only camping right in town is at **Marv Moore Campground** (780/827-2404, May–mid-Sept.), which has semiprivate, well-shaded sites and showers, cooking shelters, a laundry, and firewood. Sites in the tenting area are $18, regular powered sites are $20. It's at the north end of town on Shand Avenue beside the golf course.

Food

On a clear day, the view from the **Family Restaurant** (in the Grande Cache Hotel, 780/827-3377) is worth at least the price of a coffee. Soup and sandwich lunch specials are approximately $6, and pizza and pasta dishes start at $8. Across the plaza is **Dragon Place Restaurant** (780/827-3898, daily 11 A.M.–10 P.M.). This is your quintessential small-town Chinese restaurant, with big portions of all the usual westernized Chinese favorites. All entrées except the seafood dishes are under $10. Up on the highway, the **Big Horn Motor Inn** (780/827-3744) has a restaurant that opens daily at 5:30 A.M.

To Grande Prairie

From Grande Cache, a 181-kilometer (112-mi.) gravel road follows the Smoky River out of the foothills and into the wide valley in which Grande Prairie lies. Along the route are service campgrounds and good opportunities for wildlife viewing.

ALBERTA

Grande Prairie

Grande Prairie, a city of 35,000, is in a wide, gently rolling valley surrounded by large areas of natural grasslands. Edmonton is 460 kilometers (286 mi.) to the southeast, while Dawson Creek (British Columbia) and Mile Zero of the Alaska Highway are 135 kilometers (84 mi.) to the northwest. Grasslands are something of an anomaly at such a northern latitude. To the south and west are heavily forested mountains, and to the north and east are boreal forests and wetlands. But the grasslands here, *la grande prairie,* provided the stimulus for growth in the region.

SIGHTS AND RECREATION

Although malls, motels, restaurants, and other services are spread out along Highway 2 west and north of town, the center of the city has managed to retain much of its original charm. The only official "sight" downtown is **Prairie Art Gallery** (10209 99th St., 780/532-8111, Mon.–Fri. 10 A.M.–5 P.M., Sat.–Sun. 1–5 P.M.), whose three galleries display permanent and temporary exhibits of work by artists from throughout Canada. A short walk west of downtown on 100th Avenue is **Bear Creek,** along which most of Grande Prairie's sights lie.

Grande Prairie Museum

Overlooking Bear Creek immediately west of downtown, this excellent museum (780/532-5482, summer daily 10 A.M.–6 P.M., rest of year Sun. 1–5 P.M., $2) is within easy walking distance (30 min.) of Centre 2000 along Bear Creek. If you're driving, access is east along 102nd Avenue from downtown. Indoor displays include the Heritage Discovery Centre, which catalogs the area's early development through interactive exhibit, a natural history display, and dinosaur bones from a nearby dig. Historic buildings outside include a church, a schoolhouse, a blacksmith shop, and a fire station.

Muskoseepi Park

Muskoseepi (Bear Creek, in the Cree language) is a 405-hectare (1,000-acre) park that preserves a wide swathe of land through the heart of the city. At the north end of the park is **Bear Creek Reservoir,** the focal point of the park. Here you'll find an interpretive pavilion, a heated outdoor pool, tennis courts, minigolf, and canoe rentals ($8 per hour). At the magnificent open-plan **Centre 2000,** Grande Prairie's main information center (off the Hwy. 2 bypass at 11330 106th St., 780/539-0211), a stairway leads up to the **Northern Lights Lookout.** From Centre 2000, 40 kilometers (25 mi.) of hiking and biking trails follow both sides of Bear Creek to the city's outer edge.

Saskatoon Island Provincial Park

For thousands of years, natives have come to this area, 20 kilometers (12 mi.) west of the city, to collect saskatoon berries. The "Island" part of the name dates to the 1920s, when much of what is now protected was an island; today the park is an isthmus between Little and Saskatoon Lakes. Sweet, purple saskatoons are still abundant and cover nearly one-third of the 102-hectare (250-acre) park. **Little Lake,** with its abundant aquatic vegetation, provides an ideal habitat for trumpeter swans, North America's largest waterfowl. This park is one of the few areas in Canada where the majestic bird can be viewed during the spring nesting season.

Events

Evergreen Park, south of downtown, hosts many of the city's larger events, including a farmers market each Saturday during summer, horse racing, demolition derbies, and fall harvest festivals. The weekend closest to May 31 is **Stompede** (780/532-4646), a gathering of North America's best cowboys and chuck wagon drivers. On the Canada Day long weekend, **Bud Country Music Festival** hits the city. This large gathering of country music stars from Canada and the United States attracts thousands of fans. The regional fair, with a livestock show, chuck wagon races, and a midway, is the last weekend of July. For further information on these events, call the park

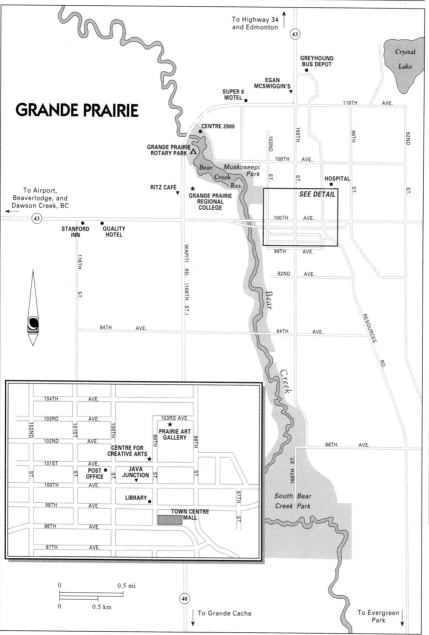

GRANDE PRAIRIE

To Highway 34 and Edmonton

Crystal Lake

GREYHOUND BUS DEPOT

EGAN MCSWIGGIN'S

SUPER 8 MOTEL

CENTRE 2000

GRANDE PRAIRIE ROTARY PARK

Muskoseepi Park

Bear Creek Res.

RITZ CAFÉ

GRANDE PRAIRIE REGIONAL COLLEGE

SEE DETAIL

HOSPITAL

To Airport, Beaverlodge, and Dawson Creek, BC

STANFORD INN

QUALITY HOTEL

WAPITI RD. (108TH ST.)

Bear

Creek

South Bear Creek Park

RESOURCES RD.

104TH AVE.
103RD AVE.
102ND AVE.
101ST AVE.
100TH AVE.
99TH AVE.
98TH AVE.
97TH AVE.

103RD AVE.
PRAIRIE ART GALLERY

CENTRE FOR CREATIVE ARTS

JAVA JUNCTION

POST OFFICE

LIBRARY

TOWN CENTRE MALL

116TH AVE.
108TH AVE.
100TH AVE.
96TH AVE.
92ND AVE.
84TH AVE.
68TH AVE.

0   0.5 mi
0   0.5 km

To Grande Cache

To Evergreen Park

ALBERTA

© AVALON TRAVEL PUBLISHING, INC.

administration (780/532-3279). Muskoseepi Park hosts **National Aboriginal Day** on the fourth weekend of June.

Grande Prairie's climate is perfect for **hot-air ballooning,** and every couple of years the city plays host to a national or international competition.

PRACTICALITIES
Accommodations
All motels are located west and north of downtown along Highway 2. **Stanford Inn** (11401 100th Ave., 780/539-5678 or 800/661-8160, www.stanfordinn.net, $80 s, $85 d) is a large 206-room complex, with newly renovated rooms, a restaurant, and a bar. The **Quality Hotel** (11201 100th Ave., 780/539-6000 or 800/661-7954, www.qualityhotelgrandeprairie.com, $109–139 s or d) stands out not only for its sleek exterior, but inside for modern, well-designed rooms with all the amenities. A fitness center, business center, restaurant, and lounge are on site. Rates include local calls, a light breakfast, and an airport shuttle. The **Super 8 Motel** (10050 116th Ave., 780/532-8288 or 800/800-8000, www.super8.com) is well priced at $89 s, $99 d. Don't expect any surprises here—just the usual high standard of reliable rooms, an indoor pool and water slide, a laundry facility, and a free Continental breakfast.

Camping
Grande Prairie Rotary Park (along the Hwy. 2 bypass, 780/532-1137, May–Sept.) overlooks Bear Creek and is just across from Centre 2000. It has showers and a laundry room but few trees; tent sites down by the water are $15, RVs and trailers pay $23–25 (no reservations taken). **Saskatoon Island Provincial Park** (unserviced sites are $17, powered sites $20), 20 kilometers (12.5 mi.) west of Grande Prairie on Highway 2, then three kilometers (1.9 mi.) north, has showers, groceries, a food concession, and minigolf, and is beside a beach.

Food
The dining scene in Grande Prairie is unremarkable at best. Downtown is **Java Junction** (9926 100th Ave., 780/539-5070, Mon.–Fri. 7:45 A.M.–5:30 P.M., Sat. 9 A.M.–4 P.M.), a small coffee shop with friendly staff; coffee and a muffin is $3, and soup, sandwich, and coffee is $6. The **Ritz Café** (10810 107th Ave., 780/538-3900) doesn't look like much from the outside, but the food (especially breakfast) is as good as you're likely to come across in Grande Prairie and the prices are cheap. Across the road, the Grande Prairie Regional College has a cafeteria that bustles with students (and locals looking for a cheap meal) throughout the school year.

Egan McSwiggin's (upstairs at 11920 100th St., 780/402-7090) has a refined Irish-pub atmosphere with a cross-section of British fare on a long menu.

Information
Overlooking Bear Creek Reservoir, **Centre 2000** (off the Hwy. 2 bypass at 11330 106th St., 780/539-0211) houses the local tourist information center. It's open May–September daily 8:30 A.M.–9 P.M., the rest of the year daily 8:30 A.M.–4:30 P.M. **Grande Prairie Public Library** (9910 99th Ave., 780/532-3580, open Mon.–Thurs. 10 A.M.–9 P.M., Fri.–Sat. 10 A.M.–6 P.M., and Sun. 2–5 P.M.) is an excellent facility.

The Northwest Corner

From its source in the interior of British Columbia, the Peace River has carved a majestic swath across the northwestern corner of Alberta's boreal forest. Explorers, trappers, settlers, and missionaries traveled upstream from Fort Chipewyan on Lake Athabasca and established trading posts along the fertile valley and surrounding plains. The posts at Fort Vermilion and Dunvegan have slipped into oblivion and are now designated as historical sites, but the town of Peace River has grown from a small post into an agriculture and distribution center that serves the entire Peace River region. The river—so named because on its banks peace was made between warring Cree and Beaver Indians—and the surrounding land are often referred to as Peace Country. This moniker is a throwback to the 1930s, when the government refused to build a rail link and many local residents favored seceding from Alberta and creating their own country.

Sexsmith

Make your first stop out of Grande Prairie this pretty little town where main street businesses have spruced themselves up with early-

Sexsmith Blacksmith Shop

1900s–style facades. One block off the main street is the **Sexsmith Blacksmith Shop** (780/568-3668, June–early Sept. Mon.–Fri. 9:30 A.M.–4:30 P.M., Sat.–Sun. 10 A.M.–4 P.M.), a working museum restored to its original 1916 condition. Inside the log structure are more than 10,000 artifacts, including caches of moonshine, which were hidden in the log walls to prevent detection by the NWMP.

From Sexsmith, Highway 2 climbs slowly through a mixed-wood forest connecting the Saddle Hills, to the west, and the Birch Hills, to the northeast. After crossing a low, indistinguishable summit, the road begins descending into the Peace River Valley.

PEACE RIVER VALLEY

The Peace River Valley extends 230 kilometers (143 mi.) from the Alberta–British Columbia border to the town of Peace River. From Highway 49, on the south side of the river, and Highways 64 and 2 on the north side, roads lead down to the river and nine recreation and camping areas. The best way to start a visit to the region is to stop at **Rycroft,** at the junction of Highways 2 and 49. **Courtesy Corner** (780/765-3730, June–Aug. daily 9 A.M.–8 P.M.), an enormous red and white tepee situated right at the highway junction, houses an information center and sells local arts and crafts.

West of Rycroft, **Moonshine Lake Provincial Park and Vicinity** is best known for its rainbow trout fishing, but is also home to more than 100 species of birds. Campsites ($17–20) are scattered among stands of aspen, poplar, and white spruce. Facilities include showers, flush toilets, cooking shelters, a concession, and powered hookups.

Historic Dunvegan

As Highway 2 descends into the Peace River Valley from the south, it crosses Alberta's longest suspension bridge at Dunvegan—a point that was the site of many trading posts and a mission. On the north side of the river is the **Visitor Reception Centre** (780/835-7150, May–Sept.

ALBERTA

daily 10 A.M.–6 P.M.), featuring displays that tell the story of Dunvegan and its role in the early history of northern Alberta. On the riverbank are the restored church and rectory of the St. Charles Roman Catholic Mission, circa 1885. Adjacent to these historic sites is **Dunvegan Provincial Park,** a 67-site campground (open Apr.–Oct.; unserviced sites $17, powered sites $20). Downstream from the fort is **Dunvegan Tea Room** (780/835-4585), in an old greenhouse, which naturally means it's a well-lit place and surrounded by plenty of greenery.

Peace River

Many historic buildings line the main street (100th St.) of this bustling northern town. By the river is the **Peace River Centennial Museum** (10302 99th St., 780/624-4261, daily 9 A.M.–5 P.M., $3), which has displays on native clothing, the fur trade, early explorers, and the development of the town, and an extensive photo collection and archives. For excellent river views, take 101st Street south to 107th Avenue, which links up with Judah Hill Road. This road passes **Sagitawa Lookout,** from which you can see the town, the valley, and the confluence of the Peace and Smoky Rivers.

The least expensive rooms in town are in an older wing of the **Best Canadian Motor Inn** (9810 98th St., 780/624-2586 or 888/700-2264). Pay $55 s, $65 d, or upgrade to newer rooms across the road for $85 s, $95 d; kitchenettes are an extra $10. **Lions Club Park** (on west side of river, 780/624-2120, May–Oct.; unserviced sites $14, hookups $16–20) has well-shaded campsites, showers, a laundry room, and groceries.

The **Mighty Peace Tourist Association** is based out of an old railway station at the top end of 100th Street (780/338-2364 or 800/215-4535, www.mightypeace.com, June–Sept. daily 10 A.M.–6 P.M.).

MACKENZIE HIGHWAY

Named for 18th-century explorer Alexander Mackenzie, this route (Hwy. 35), extends from Grimshaw, 24 kilometers (15 mi.) west of Peace River, for 473 kilometers (294 mi.) north to the Northwest Territories. It passes through a vast, empty land dominated by the Peace River and a seemingly endless forest of spruce, poplar, and jack pine. The main population centers are Manning and High Level.

Grimshaw

Best known as Mile Zero of the Mackenzie Highway, this town of 2,500 has grown around the railway as a farming center. For many years after the railway arrived, it was a jumping-off point for farmers, trappers, and homesteaders in Peace Valley Country. Make a point of stopping at the local **information center** (June–early Sept. 9 A.M.–5 P.M.) in a blue rail car at the main intersection. It's stocked with brochures for onward travel and staffed by friendly locals who seem genuinely interested in your travels. If it's open, they'll recommend a visit to the **Antique Truck Museum** (780/332-2969), right across the road. And so do I—it holds a large collection of lovingly restored vehicles and machinery collected from throughout the north.

Camp at nearby Queen Elizabeth Provincial Park or continue 11 kilometers (6.8 mi.) north to **The Creek Golf Course** (780/332-4949,

The Grimshaw information center, housed in a converted rail car, is a worthwhile stop before heading north along the Mackenzie Highway.

May–Sept.), where camping with hookups and showers is $16 and a round of golf is $15.

Manning

As the highway descends into the picturesque Notikewin Valley, it enters Manning, a service center for the region's agricultural and petroleum industries. At the south end of town, one kilometer (0.6 mi.) east on Highway 691, is the excellent **Battle River Pioneer Museum** (780/836-2374, May–Sept. daily 1 A.M.–6 P.M., July–Aug. from 10 A.M.), which has a large collection of antique wrenches, taxidermy (including a rare albino moose), carriages and buggies, a birch necklace carved out of a single piece of wood, and a collection of prehistoric arrowheads (ask to see the one embedded in a whalebone).

Manning Motor Inn (780/836-2801, $74 s, $86 d) is at the south end of town and has a restaurant. **Manning Municipal Campground** (May–Sept., $15) is immediately west of the Tourist Information Centre in a shaded spot beside the Notikewin River. The campground is small (nine sites), but has powered sites. It is also possible to camp at the golf course north of town, which offers powered sites ($15 per night) and a restaurant.

A Short Detour

North of Paddle Prairie, an unpaved road (Hwy. 697) leads east to the Peace River and Tomkin's Landing and one of only eight ferry crossings in the province (operates in summer, daily 24 hours). It then continues to La Crete and Fort Vermilion, crosses the Peace River, and intersects Highway 58, which heads west, rejoining the Mackenzie Highway at High Level.

La Crete (pop. 900) is an agricultural center on the northern fringe of the continent's arable land. Most residents are Mennonites, from a Protestant sect originating in Holland. Members settled in remote regions throughout the world and established self-sufficient agricultural lifestyles, in hopes of being left to practice their faith in peace. On the streets and in the local restaurants, you'll hear their language, *Plattdeutsch* (Low German).

Fort Vermilion

This town of 750, on the south bank of the Peace River, 40 kilometers (25 mi.) north of La Crete and 77 kilometers (48 mi.) east of High Level grew around a trading post established by the North West Company in 1788. Many old buildings and cabins, in varying states of disrepair, still stand. Pick up a *Fort Vermilion Heritage Guide* from the **Fort Vermilion Heritage Centre** (780/927-3216, July–Aug. Mon.–Thurs. 9 A.M.–9 P.M., Fri.–Sat. 9 A.M.–5 P.M., Sun. 1–9 P.M.) to help identify the many historical sites in town.

Across from the river, the **Sheridan Lawrence Inn** (780/927-4400, $68 s, $76 d) is the only place to stay in town. It has 16 rooms and a small restaurant (open from 7 A.M.) with a Canadian and Chinese menu. Breakfast is reasonable at $7.

High Level and Vicinity

Named for its location on a divide between the Peace and Hay River watersheds, High Level (pop. 3,100), 279 kilometers (173 mi.) north of Grimshaw, is the last town before the Alberta–Northwest Territories border. It's a major service center for a region rich in natural resources. The only worthwhile sight in town is **Mackenzie Crossroads Museum** (at south entrance to town, 780/926-2420, June–Aug. Mon.–Fri. 9 A.M.–9 P.M., Sat.–Sun. 10 A.M.–8 P.M., rest of year Mon.–Sat. 9 A.M.–4:30 P.M., $2). Located in the tourist information center building, the museum is themed on a northern trading post, with interesting displays telling the human history of northern Alberta. A three-dimensional map of northwestern Alberta gives a great perspective of this inaccessible part of the province.

Motel prices in High Level are just a warm-up for those over the border in the Northwest Territories, so don't be surprised at $60 rooms for which you'd prefer to pay $40. Pick of the bunch, the **Best Canadian Motor Inn** (780/926-2272, $68 s, $83 d), undergoes regular revamps and its midsize rooms are air-conditioned. A free municipal campground is immediately east of town on Highway 35 (but it's pretty gross), and a primitive campground lies farther north at **Hutch Lake Recreation Area** (mid-May–September, $11).

Northwest Territories

A s the world's last great wilderness frontiers slowly disappear, Canada's vast northlands—including the 3.4 million square kilometers (1.3 million sq. mi.) of the Northwest Territories—remain relatively untouched, unspoiled, and uninhabited, with a population of just 64,000. Once this land was home only to small populations of indigenous Dene and Inuit people who had adapted to the harsh environment. But explorers, whalers, missionaries, and governments eventually found their way here, bringing rapid changes to native lifestyles. Within the region's borders are two of the world's 10 largest lakes, one of the world's longest rivers, a waterfall twice the height of Niagara, one UNESCO World Heritage Site, three national parks, and an amazing abundance of wildlife.

Today, travelers, adventurers, writers, artists, and scientists come in search of the territories' unlimited opportunities for naturalist and wilderness pursuits. Hiking the **Canol Road**, canoeing the **South Nahanni River**, fishing for trophy-size lake trout in **Great Bear Lake**, and watching beluga whales frolic in the **Beaufort Sea** are just the highlights.

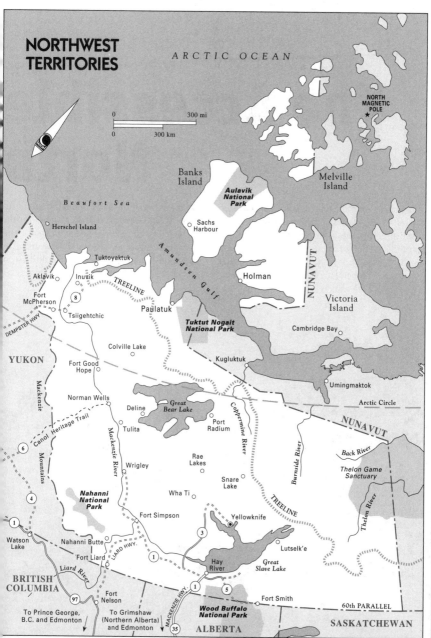

NORTHWEST TERRITORIES

ARCTIC OCEAN

Beaufort Sea

NORTH MAGNETIC POLE ★

0 — 300 mi
0 — 300 km

Banks Island

Aulavik National Park

Melville Island

Herschel Island

Sachs Harbour

Amundsen Gulf

Holman

NUNAVUT

Victoria Island

Tuktoyaktuk

Aklavik
Inuvik

TREELINE

Fort McPherson

8

Tsiigehtchic

Paulatuk

Tuktut Nogait National Park

Cambridge Bay

YUKON

Colville Lake

Fort Good Hope

Kugluktuk

DEMPSTER HWY.

Norman Wells

Deline

Great Bear Lake

Port Radium

Coppermine River

Umingmaktok

Arctic Circle

NUNAVUT

Mackenzie

Canol Heritage Trail

Tulita

Back River

Burnside River

Mackenzie River

6

Mountains

Wrigley

Rae Lakes

Snare Lake

Thelon Game Sanctuary

Wha Ti

TREELINE

Thelon River

4

Nahanni National Park

Fort Simpson

Yellowknife

1

Watson Lake

Nahanni Butte

3

Lutselk'e

LIARD HWY.

Fort Liard

1

Hay River

Great Slave Lake

Liard River

BRITISH COLUMBIA

97

Fort Nelson

1

MACKENZIE HWY.

5

Fort Smith

60th PARALLEL

To Prince George, B.C. and Edmonton

To Grimshaw (Northern Alberta) and Edmonton

35

Wood Buffalo National Park

ALBERTA

SASKATCHEWAN

© AVALON TRAVEL PUBLISHING, INC.

N.W. TERRITORIES

The Accessible North

Whether it's your first time or your 40th, crossing the 60th parallel marks the beginning of a new adventure. And the adventure starts in the most accessible section of the territories, immediately north of Alberta. It's a vast expanse of stunted boreal forest broken only by two of North America's largest rivers, the **Slave** and **Mackenzie.** To the north lies **Great Slave Lake,** named for the Slavey Dene who have trapped and fished along its southern shores for thousands of years. This vast inland freshwater sea is the world's 10th-largest lake. The region's main communities are

Hay River, on the south shore of Great Slave Lake; and Fort Smith, the gateway to Wood Buffalo National Park, the second-largest national park in the world. Paved and improved gravel roads link the two towns and continue around the west and north sides of Great Slave Lake to the territorial capital, Yellowknife.

60TH PARALLEL TO HAY RIVER

The wood-and-stone structure marking the 60th parallel is a welcome sight after the long drive north through northern Alberta up the Mackenzie Highway. North of the border, the highway number changes from 35 to 1, and the road follows the Hay River 118 kilometers (73 mi.) to Great Slave Lake. This stretch is known as the **Waterfalls Route,** for the impressive falls along the way.

Just beyond the border is the **60th Parallel Visitors Centre** (867/920-1021, May–mid-Sept. daily 9 A.M.–9 P.M.), well worth a stop just to have a chat with the friendly hosts. The center offers maps and brochures, camping permits, fishing licenses, and displays of local arts and crafts. And the coffeepot is always on, accompanied by freshly made scones, if you're lucky. Behind the center is the **60th Parallel Campground** ($12), a small facility overlooking the Hay River.

Twin Falls Gorge Territorial Park

North of the border, the Hay River has carved a deep gorge into the limestone bedrock. Punctuating the river's flow are two dramatic waterfalls that formed a major barrier for early river travelers, forcing a portage along the west bank. Encompassing both falls, and the equally impressive is Twin Falls Gorge Territorial Park. From the first day-use area, a short trail leads to a viewing platform overlooking **Alexandra Falls,** where the peat-colored Hay River tumbles 34 meters (112 ft.). **Louise Falls,** three kilometers (1.9 mi.) downstream, is not as high, but its intriguing steps make it just as interesting. **Louise Falls Campground** ($12) has water, pit toilets, and bug-proof cooking shelters.

Hay River

This town of 3,600 lies 118 kilometers (73 mi.) north of the border, 1,070 kilometers (665 mi.) north of Edmonton, and 500 kilometers (310 mi.) from the territorial capital of Yellowknife. Hay River is a vital transportation link for waterborne freight bound for communities along the Mackenzie River and throughout the western and central Arctic.

Within the town limits, several distinct communities surround the delta, which was formed where the Hay River flows into Great Slave Lake. Most modern development, including motels, restaurants, and government offices, is located in **New Town,** on the west bank of the Hay River. A bridge links New Town to **Vale Island,** where the airport, campground, and excellent beaches are located. Also on the island are the communities of **Old Town,** which was partially destroyed by flooding in 1963, and **West Channel Village,** which grew around the commercial fishing industry. Across the mouth of Hay River is the **Hay River Dene Reserve,** the only Indian reserve in the Northwest Territories.

SIGHTS AND RECREATION
New Town Sights

To get oriented, head to the manager's office (2nd floor) at the 17-story **Mackenzie Place Apartment Building.** Ask for a key and ride the claustrophobia-inducing elevator to the roof, where panoramic views of the Great Slave Lake, Hay River, and the boreal forest extend to the horizon. The **Diamond Jenness High School** (Riverview Dr.) was named for a famed Northern anthropologist and is undoubtedly the town's most unusual structure. It was designed by Douglas Cardinal, an Albertan architect whose distinctive work is found throughout that province. Its curved walls alone would have made it a Northern landmark, but the choice of color for the entire exterior was left to the students—and they chose purple! (It's known to the kids as the "Purple People Eater.") Behind the school, the **Kiwanis Nature Trail** leads along the west bank of the Hay River (look for fossils) to various signposted points of interest, then across Highway 2 and along the West Channel to Great Slave Lake.

Vale Island

The boarded-up shop fronts, dusty streets, and empty houses of Vale Island belie the activity that still takes place along the waterfront. The large **Canadian Coast Guard Base** is responsible for all search-and-rescue operations in the western Arctic. And the facilities of the **Northern Transportation Company Ltd.** (NTCL), a large shipping concern, include shipyards, a dry dock, freight-storage areas, and a syncrolift—a hydraulic device that removes vessels from the water for easy maintenance (it's one of only four in Canada; it can be seen to the right along 106th Ave.).

From Old Town, Mackenzie Drive—the island's main thoroughfare—continues past a popular swimming beach and a radio observatory before it dead-ends in **West Channel Village,** a once-prosperous fishing community.

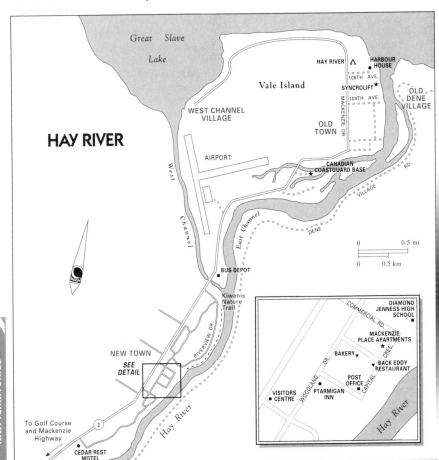

Swimming and Fishing

The beaches of Vale Island are very popular during summer, even if the water may be a little cold for most. The best beach is at the end of 106th Avenue; those farther around the island are quieter. Anglers will find plentiful northern pike and pickerel in the Hay River.

Golf

Hay River Golf Club (13 km/eight mi. south of town, 867/874-6290) is the finest course in the territories. It has nine holes with grassed fairways, artificial greens, a driving range, and a superbly crafted log clubhouse (well worth a look, even for nongolfers). A round of golf (18 holes) is $26, or play all day for $34. The course also has a driving range, and club rentals are available. On the Labour Day weekend (early Sept.), the course hosts the 54-hole **NWT Open,** which everyone is welcome to enter.

ACCOMMODATIONS AND CAMPING

$50–100

Harbour House Bed and Breakfast (106th St., 867/874-2233) is an excellent choice for accommodations in Hay River. Located across from Vale Island's best beach, the setting is wonderful and the mood casual. Rates of $60, $70 d include breakfast. Located a couple of kilometers (1.2 mi.) from downtown is the **Cedar Rest Motel** (867/874-3732, $75 s, $85 d), a place that looks half finished, with a massive gravel parking lot out front.

$100–150

The best rooms in town are at the **Ptarmigan Inn** (867/874-6591 or 800/661-0842, $125 s, $135 d), in the center of town. There's an adjacent restaurant and lounge.

Campground

Hay River Campground (Vale Island, mid-May to mid-Sept., $12–15) is a short walk from the beach and seven kilometers (4.3 mi.) from downtown. The sites are private, a few have power, and all have picnic tables and fire rings.

OTHER PRACTICALITIES

Food

Beside Northern, **Hay River Bakery** (867/874-2322) has a wide variety of cakes and pastries and is a good place for an inexpensive lunch. Worth the effort to find is **Back Eddy Restaurant** (867/874-6680, Mon.–Fri. 11 A.M.–2 P.M., 5–9 P.M., Sat. 11 A.M.–10 P.M.), above Rings Drug Store on Capital Crescent. Meals are served in the lounge or, for families, in a separate dining area. The menu features pickerel and whitefish fresh from the lake. Expect to pay $7–12 for lunch and a few dollars more for dinner.

Information

The **Visitors Centre** (867/874-3180, mid-May–mid-Sept. daily 9 A.M.–9 P.M.) is at the south entrance to town. It has bundles of brochures and books, and, almost as importantly, the coffeepot is always on. The **NWT Centennial Library,** opposite Northern (Woodland Dr., 867/874-6486, Mon.–Thurs. 10 A.M.–5 P.M., Fri.–Sat. 7–9 P.M.), is headquarters for the Northwest Territories library system. Books are transported by road, air, and sea to other libraries, including those in the most remote communities.

Transportation

Hay River Airport is on Vale Island, a $10 cab ride from town. During freeze-up and breakup of the Mackenzie River, road traffic through to Yellowknife is blocked, and Hay River Airport becomes the center of frenzied activity; freight and passengers arriving by road from the south transfer to planes for the short hop over Great Slave Lake. **Northwestern** (867/669-7606) flies daily between Hay River and Yellowknife, while local flightseeing is handled by **Landa Aviation** (867/874-3500).

The bus depot is at the south end of Vale Island. **Greyhound** departs daily for Edmonton (16 hours). Connecting with the Greyhound services is **Frontier Coachlines** (867/874-6966), using the same depot.

To Fort Smith

The 270-kilometer (168 mi.) road linking Hay River to Fort Smith (Hwy. 5) is paved for the first 60 kilometers (37 mi.) then turns to improved gravel. No services are available along this route. The road bisects a typical boreal forest of stunted spruce and aspen. A gravel road to the north, 49 kilometers (30 mi.) from Highway 2, leads two kilometers (1.2 mi.) to **Polar Lake.** The lake is stocked with rainbow trout and has good bird-watching around the shoreline. Camping is $5, picnicking $3.

Another 11 kilometers (6.8 mi.) beyond the Polar Lake turn-off, the highway divides: The right fork continues to Fort Smith, the left to Fort Resolution.

Fort Resolution

This historic community of 500 is in a forested area on the shore of Great Slave Lake around 170 kilometers (106 mi.) east of Hay River. The original fort, built by the North West Company in 1786, was to the east, on the Slave River Delta. When the post was moved, a Chipewyan Dene settlement grew around it, and in 1852 Roman Catholic missionaries arrived, building a school and a hospital. A road connecting the town to Pine Point was completed in the 1960s, and today the mainly Chipewyan and Métis population relies on trapping and a sawmill operation as its economic base.

Continuing to Fort Smith on Highway 5

From the Fort Smith/Fort Resolution junction, 60 kilometers (33 mi.) east of Hay River, it's another 210 kilometers (130 mi.) southeast to Fort Smith. After an hour of smooth sailing, the road enters **Wood Buffalo National Park,** the largest national park in North America. Five kilometers (3.1 mi.) beyond the park entrance sign is the **Angus Fire Tower.** Behind the tower is one of many sinkholes found in the northern reaches of the park. This example of karst topography occurs when underground caves collapse, creating a craterlike depression. This one is 26 meters (85 ft.) deep and 40 meters (130 ft.) across. The next worthwhile stop is at **Nyarling River,** 14 kilometers (8.7 mi.) farther east. The dried-up riverbed is actually the path of an underground river, hence the name *Nyarling* (underground, in the Slavey language).

As the highway continues east, it enters an area where the Precambrian Shield is exposed, making for a rocky landscape where stunted trees cling to shallow depressions that have filled with soil. To the north, an access road leads to several small waterfalls in **Little Buffalo Falls Territorial Park** and a campground ($12) with pit toilets, a kitchen shelter, and firewood.

FORT SMITH

Until 1967, this town of 2,500 was the territorial capital. It still functions as an administrative center for various governmental offices and is the educational center for the Northwest Territories. The town was established because of formidable rapids on the Slave River, a vital link for all trav-

PINE POINT: A MODERN GHOST TOWN

In 1951 the mining giant Cominco began extracting lead and zinc from an open-pit mine east of Hay River at a site known as Pine Point. With production on the increase, a town was built, at one time boasting more than 2,000 residents. Low lead and zinc prices, coupled with rising operational costs, forced Cominco to close the mine in 1988. One of the lease conditions was that Cominco was to restore the land to its original condition when it left. As a result, the whole town—a school, a hospital, a supermarket, and hundreds of houses—had to be moved. After standing empty for a few years, the buildings were moved to various locations throughout the north. Today all that remains are tailing piles from the mine, paved streets, sidewalks, and a golf course with a rough that makes the U.S. Open look tame.

elers heading north. In 1872, the Hudson's Bay Company opened a post, later known as Fort Fitzgerald, at the southern end of the rapids. Two years later, the company established a fort near the northern end of the portage route, at Fort Smith.

Sights

Most people who venture to Fort Smith do so to visit Wood Buffalo National Park (see the Northern Alberta chapter).

In the 1920s, when Fort Smith was capital of the Northwest Territories, administrative duties fell to the local bishop, whose house and gardens are now part of **Fort Smith Mission Historic Park** (corner of Mercredi Ave. and Breynat St.). Declared a Territorial Historic Park in 1991, it's an ongoing restoration project; at this stage, interpretive signs explain the various buildings, and gardens are planted for each summer. The fort-shaped **Northern Life Museum** (110 King St., 867/872-2859, summer daily 1–5 P.M.) houses a large collection of artifacts from the days of the fur trade, as well as dog-mushing equipment, Inuit carvings, the first printing press in the north, and displays on bison. Along the riverfront on Marine Drive, is the **Slave River Lookout.** Use the spotting scope here to search out white pelicans nesting on rocks scattered through the river.

Recreation and Tours

Pelican Rapids Golf and Country Club (867/872-4653) through town to the southeast, has been carved out of the forest by the town's surprisingly large golfing population. It has grassed fairways and oil-soaked greens. The year's biggest tournament is the 54-hole Merchants Classic Golf Tournament, held during the August long weekend. Everyone is welcome to enter, and a great time is had by all. Regular greens fee is $18 per day. The clubhouse has rentals, but for all your other golfing needs, you should head to **Northwind Sports** (182 McDougal Rd., 867/872-5660). This shop also stocks fishing tackle and camping gear.

Accommodations and Camping

Thebacha Tourist Home (53 Portage Ave., 867/872-2060, $75 s, $90 d) offers four guest rooms, breakfast, and the use of a kitchen in a centrally located residence. For motel accommodations, consider **Pelican Rapids Inn** (152 McDougal Rd., 867/872-2789, $120 s or d), with basic but spacious rooms.

The only campground close to town is the **Queen Elizabeth Campground,** four kilometers (2.5 mi.) west toward the airport; turn north on Teepee Trail Road. Sites cost $12 per night and are spread out and private, with pit toilets and cooking shelters. Showers and flush toilets are available in the warden's compound.

Information

Fort Smith Visitor Information Centre (King St., 867/872-2515) is open mid-May–mid-September 10 A.M.–10 P.M.

WOOD BUFFALO NATIONAL PARK

From Fort Smith, Highway 5 continues through town and loops back south and into Alberta (just beyond town limits). The border is also the northern boundary of Wood Buffalo National Park, the second-largest national park in the world (the largest is in Greenland). Throughout this 45,000-square-kilometers (17,400-sq.-mi.) chunk of boreal forest, boreal plains, shallow lakes, and bogs flow two major rivers—the Peace and Athabasca. These drain into **Lake Claire,** forming one of the world's largest freshwater deltas. The Peace-Athabasca Delta is a mass of confusing channels, shallow lakes, and sedge meadows, surrounded by a wetland that is a prime wintering range for bison, rich in waterfowl, and home to beavers, muskrats, moose, lynx, wolves, and black bears. From the delta, the Slave River, which forms the park's eastern boundary, flows north into Great Slave Lake.

Probably best known for being the last natural nesting habitat of the rare whooping crane, the park is also home to the world's largest free-roaming herd of bison. It has extensive salt plains and North America's finest example of gypsum karst topography—a phenomenon created by underground water activity. For all of these reasons, and as an intact example of the boreal forest that once circled the entire Northern Hemisphere, the park was declared a UNESCO World Heritage Site in December 1983.

Sights

The expansive **Salt Plains** in the northeast of the park are one of Wood Buffalo's dominant natural features. Underground water flows through deposits of salt left behind by an ancient saltwater ocean, emerging in the form of salt springs. Large white mounds form at their source, and where the water has evaporated the ground is covered in a fine layer of salt. The best place to view this phenomenon is from the **Salt Plains Overlook,** 35 kilometers (22 mi.) west of Fort Smith, then 11 kilometers (6.8 mi.) south on Parson's Lake Road. The panoramic view of the plains is spectacular from this spot, but it's worth taking the one-kilometer (0.6-mi.) trail to the bottom of the hill.

In the same vicinity, a bedrock of **gypsum karst** underlies much of the park. Gypsum is a soft, white rock that slowly dissolves in water. Underground water here has created large cavities beneath this fragile mantle. This type of terrain is known as karst, and this area is the best example of karst terrain in North America. As the bedrock continues to dissolve, the underground caves enlarge, eventually collapsing under their own weight, forming large depressions known as **sinkholes.** The thousands of sinkholes here vary in size from a three meters (10 ft.) to 100 meters (330 ft.) across. The most accessible large sinkhole is behind the Angus Fire Tower, 150 kilometers (93 mi.) west of Fort Smith.

The **Peace-Athabasca Delta** is in a remote part of this remote park and is rarely visited. Getting to the delta requires some planning because no roads access the area. The most popular visitor destination on the delta is **Sweetgrass Station,** located 12 kilometers (7.5 mi.) south of the Peace River. The site is on the edge of a vast meadow that extends around the north and west shore of Lake Claire, providing a summer range for most of the park's bison. A cabin with bunks and a woodstove is available for visitors to the area at no charge, although reservations at the park information center are required. The cabin is an excellent base for exploring the meadows around Lake Claire and viewing the abundant

WHOOPING CRANES

Through a successful captive-breeding program, the whooping crane, *Grus americana,* has become a symbol of human efforts to protect endangered species in North America. Whoopers, as they are commonly called, have never been prolific. They stand 1.3 meters (four ft.), have a wingspan of 2.4 meters (eight ft.), and are pure white with long black legs. (They are often confused with the slightly smaller, reddish-brown sandhill crane, which is common in the park.) Their naturally low reproduction rate, coupled with severe degradation of their habitat, caused their numbers to dip as low as 21 in 1954—a single flock nested in Wood Buffalo National Park. Today, the population of the highly publicized and heavily studied flock has increased to more than 170, more than half the number that remain worldwide (most of the others are in captivity). The birds nest in a remote area of marshes and bogs in the northern reaches of Wood Buffalo far from human contact, migrating south to the Texas coast each fall.

wildlife. From Fort Smith, **Northwestern Air** (867/872-2216), charges $380 each way to fly two people and their gear to Sweetgrass Station.

Park Practicalities

The **Park Information Centre** (126 McDougal Rd., Fort Smith, 867/872-7900, Mon.–Fri. 8:30 A.M.–5 P.M. plus summer weekends 10 A.M.–5 P.M.) offers trail information, a short slideshow, and an exhibit room. Another small park office (780/697-3662, Mon.–Fri. 8:30 A.M.–5 P.M.) is in Fort Chipewyan. It has an interesting exhibit on the Peace River.

Within the park itself, the only developed facilities are at **Pine Lake,** 60 kilometers (37 mi.) south of Fort Smith. The lake has a campground ($12) with pit toilets, covered cooking shelters, and firewood. On a spit of land jutting into the lake beyond the campground is a picnic area with bug-proof shelters. The park staff presents a summer interpretive program at various locations; check the schedule at the park information center or on the campground notice board.

N.W. TERRITORIES

Hay River to Yellowknife

Yellowknife, on the north shore of the Great Slave Lake, is a long 480-kilometer (300-mi.) haul from Hay River, through a monotonous boreal forest of spruce, poplar, and jack pine. Twice a year, for 3–6 weeks in spring and again in late fall (at breakup and freeze-up, respectively, of the Mackenzie River), the road to Yellowknife is not passable (call 800/661-0751 for closure dates).

Lady Evelyn Falls

From Enterprise, south of Hay River, Highway 1 heads northwest, coming to Lady Evelyn Falls after 53 kilometers (33 mi.). These falls, where the wide **Kakisa River** cascades off a 15-meter (50-ft.) escarpment, are easily accessible from the highway, seven kilometers (4.3 mi.) down a gravel road. A short trail leads from the day-use area down to a platform overlooking the falls. The falls are part of a territorial park that has a campground ($12) with pit toilets, bug-proof cooking shelters, and firewood.

Fort Providence

The highway forks 85 kilometers (53 mi.) from Enterprise: To the left, Highway 1 continues west to Fort Simpson, and to the right, Highway 3 heads north toward Yellowknife. Highway 3 crosses the Mackenzie River, via a ferry (operating 6 A.M.–midnight), 24 kilometers (15 mi.) from the junction. Across the river and just up the highway, a spur road leads eight kilometers (five mi.) to the Slavey Dene community of Fort Providence (pop. 650), perched high above the river on its steep northern bank. On the riverfront is a **visitors center,** and farther along, historical markers honor the roles played by Alexander Mackenzie and the Church in the region's history.

Rae-Edzo

Rae-Edzo, 214 kilometers (133 mi.) north of Fort Providence, is the largest Dene community in the Northwest Territories, with a population of 1,500 Dogrib Dene. They settled around a Hudson's Bay Company post as early

Lady Evelyn Falls

as 1852. In the 1960s, the government began developing a new townsite, Edzo, closer to the highway. The school at Rae was closed, and a new one opened at Edzo. Today, most of the people continue living at Rae, where the water access is better for fishing and hunting, whereas the government buildings are up on the highway at Edzo. The 10-kilometer (6.2-mi.) side trip to Rae is worth taking. The resilient community is perched on a rocky outcrop jutting into **Marian Lake.** The main road through town leads to a small island, where the rocky beaches are littered with boats, fishing nets, and dogs tied up waiting for snow. Apart from the snowmobiles, the village looks much as it did 100 years ago.

Yellowknife and Vicinity

Built on dreams, perseverance, and the ingenuity of a small group of pioneers who came in search of gold, the territorial capital of Yellowknife has grown into a modern urban center of 18,000. Its frontier-town flavor and independent spirit distinguish it from all other Canadian cities. It's the northernmost city in Canada, the *only* city in the Northwest Territories, and the only predominantly nonnative community in the territories. Located on the North Arm of the Great Slave Lake, the city clings precariously to the ancient, glacial-scarred rock of the Canadian Shield. Edmonton is 1,530 kilometers (950 mi.) south by road, 965 kilometers (600 mi.) by air. The Arctic Circle is 440 kilometers (273 mi.) north.

At first, Yellowknife looks little different from other small Canadian cities, but unique contrasts soon become apparent. Some residents write computer programs for a living, whereas others prepare caribou hides; architect-designed houses are scattered among squatters' log cabins; and the roads are seemingly always under repair, a legacy of permafrost. To the Dene, Yellowknife is known as *Som bak'e* (Place of Money).

History
Samuel Hearne dubbed the local Dene natives the Yellowknife for the copper knives they used. Miners on their way to the Klondike were the first to discover gold in the area, but they didn't rush in to stake claims because of the area's remote location and the difficulty of extracting the mineral from the hard bedrock. But as airplanes began opening up the north, the area became more attractive to goldseekers. Hundreds of claims were staked between 1934 and 1936, and a

boomtown sprang up along the shore of Yellowknife Bay. After the war, growth continued, and soon the original townsite around the bay was at full capacity. A new town, just up the hill, was surveyed, and by 1947 the city center of today began taking shape. In 1967, a road was completed to the outside, and the city came to rely less on air travel. The city was named territorial capital the same year.

SIGHTS
Prince of Wales Northern Heritage Centre
The entire history of the territories is cataloged at this modern facility (867/873-7551, July–Aug. daily 10:30 A.M.–5:30 P.M., rest of year Mon.–Fri. 10:30 A.M.–5 P.M. and Sat.–Sun. noon–5 P.M.) on the shore of Frame Lake. The South Gallery displays a collection of Dene, Métis, and Inuit artifacts. The North Gallery catalogs the arrival of European explorers, miners, and missionaries and their impact on the environment. The Aviation Gallery presents a realistic display of a bush pilot and his plane and a wall of fame for the pilots who helped open up the north. Also here is a live hookup to the traffic controllers at Yellowknife Airport. A library stocks 6,000 historical and fiction books on the north.

Legislative Assembly of the Northwest Territories
This building on the shore of Frame Lake is the heart of territorial politics. Opened in 1993, it was designed to blend in with the surrounding landscape and made use of Northern materials.

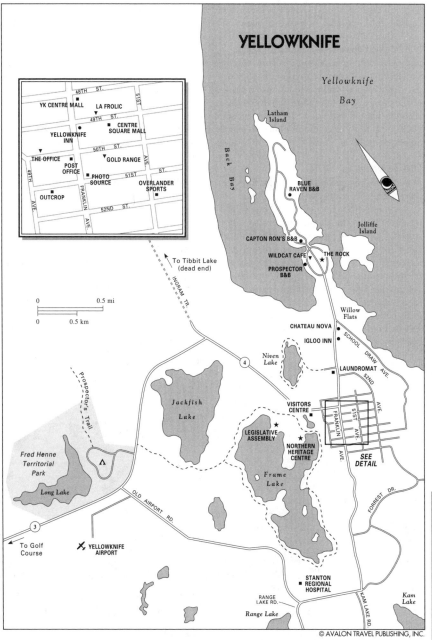

YELLOWKNIFE

Yellowknife Bay

Latham Island

Back Bay

Jolliffe Island

BLUE RAVEN B&B

CAPTON RON'S B&B

WILDCAT CAFE ★ THE ROCK

PROSPECTOR B&B

To Tibbit Lake (dead end)

INGRAM TR.

Willow Flats

CHATEAU NOVA

IGLOO INN

SCHOOL DRAW AVE.

LAUNDROMAT

52ND

Niven Lake

4

Jackfish Lake

VISITORS CENTRE

LEGISLATIVE ASSEMBLY ★

★ NORTHERN HERITAGE CENTRE

FRANKLIN AVE.

51ST AVE.

SEE DETAIL

Frame Lake

Prospector's Trail

Fred Henne Territorial Park

Long Lake

OLD AIRPORT RD.

FORREST DR.

3

To Golf Course

✈ YELLOWKNIFE AIRPORT

STANTON REGIONAL HOSPITAL

RANGE LAKE RD.

Range Lake

KAM LAKE RD.

Kam Lake

0   0.5 mi
0   0.5 km

Detail inset:

48TH ST.

YK CENTRE MALL   LA FROLIC   51ST

49TH ST.

YELLOWKNIFE INN   CENTRE SQUARE MALL

THE OFFICE   50TH ST.

POST OFFICE   GOLD RANGE AVE.

PHOTO SOURCE   51ST ST.

49TH AVE.   OUTCROP   OVERLANDER SPORTS

FRANKLIN AVE.   52ND ST.

N.W. TERRITORIES

© AVALON TRAVEL PUBLISHING, INC.

Through the front doors of a massive glass-walled facade is the Great Hall, topped by skylights and lined with the artwork of Angus Cockney. The building's centerpiece is the circular Chamber, in which the members of the legislative assembly sit facing the Speaker. Behind the Speaker stretches a massive zinc-plated mural of a Northern landscape. One-hour tours (867/669-2300) are offered in July and August Monday–Friday at 10:30 A.M., 1:30 P.M., and 3:30 P.M. as well as Sunday at 1:30 P.M.

Old Town

From the city center, Franklin Avenue (50th Ave.) descends a long, dusty hill to Yellowknife's Old Town. In the 1930s, the first log and frame buildings were erected at this site. Along the narrow streets, Quonset huts, original settlers' homes, converted buses, old boats, and tin shanties look incongruous in a Canadian capital city. Some of the most unusual housing is in **Willow Flats,** east of Franklin Avenue. **Ragged Ass Road,** named for a mine claim, has the most unusual houses, many posting signs telling the story of the building. Farther north along Franklin Avenue is an area known simply as **The Rock,** for the huge chunk of

Canadian Shield that towers above the surrounding landscape. At the top of The Rock is the **Pilot's Monument,** dedicated to the bush pilots who opened up the north. At the corner of Pilots Lane and Wiley Road is **Weaver & Devore,** an old-time general store selling just about everything. Many of their larger orders have to be flown in to buyers scattered throughout the north. East of The Rock, in Yellowknife Bay, is **Jolliffe Island,** once a fuel depot but now a residential area. The homes are reached by boat or canoe in summer and by road in winter. At the north end of The Rock, a causeway, built in 1948, connects **Latham Island** to the mainland. At the south end of the island are floatplane bases, where the constant buzz of small planes taking off and landing symbolizes the north.

Ingraham Trail

Apart from Highway 3 from the south, the Ingraham Trail (Hwy. 4 East) is the only route out of the city. It then crosses the Yellowknife River and passes **Prosperous, Pontoon,** and **Prelude Lakes,** each with day-use areas and great for fishing, boating, and swimming. Continuing east, the road parallels the **Cameron River,** 48 kilo-

The eclectic housing along Ragged Ass Road is a reminder of the city's earliest days.

meters from Yellowknife. Trails lead down to the riverbank, and waterfalls dot the route. The road ends at **Tibbit Lake,** 71 kilometers (44 mi.) from Yellowknife.

RECREATION
Fred Henne Territorial Park
Forest-encircled **Long Lake,** opposite Yellowknife Airport, is used by visitors mainly for the excellent camping facilities, but it's also a good example of the wilderness surrounding the city. The four-kilometer (2.5-mi.) round-trip **Prospector's Trail,** which begins from the campground, is a good way to experience the unique landscape. You can hike to the park from the city center along the trails around **Frame Lake.**

Fishing and Canoeing
The brochures of many fishing-charter operators fill the Northern Frontier Regional Visitors Centre, but **Bluefish Services** (867/873-4818) offers the widest range of fishing opportunities, including fishing for arctic grayling from local river banks, chasing northern pike out on North Arm, and trawling the deepest parts of Great Slave Lake for massive lake trout. Rates are from $65 per person for four hours and $105–160 for a full day. **Enodah Wilderness Travel** (867/873-4334, www.enodah.com) has a lodge on Trout Rock, a small island 30 kilometers (19 mi.) west of Yellowknife that was once the site of a Dogrib community; three-day fishing trips start at $675 per person.

    Overlander Sports (5103 51st Ave., 867/873-2474) rents canoes for $20 for four hours, the perfect length of time to explore nearby Jolliffe Island and its surrounding waters. For those interested in longer trips, canoes are $30 per day.

Golf
The **Yellowknife Golf Course** (west of town along Hwy. 3, 867/873-4326, May–Sept.) features "greens" of artificial grass and rock and gravel fairways. Each shot must be hit from a small mat that players carry around the course; greens fee is $25. Aside from the unique playing conditions, facilities are similar to those at any regular golf course: a pro shop with rentals, a driving range, a restaurant, and a beer cart, of course. Also look for some great photos of the course's early days in the clubhouse.

ENTERTAINMENT
Entertainment at the **Gold Range Hotel** (5010 50th St., 867/873-4441), best known as the "Strange Range," is like no other in the country. Don't be put off by the unusual characters, hundreds of empty beer glasses, and bouncers with legs like tree trunks; it isn't as rowdy as it seems. If you like to mix with the locals, this is the place to do it, and you may help them claim the title for highest beer sales per capita in Canada; so far they run only second.

Festivals and Events
The week closest to Summer Solstice (June 21) is the **Solstice Festival,** featuring street entertainment and a midnight-sun golf tournament (this event is popular with visitors, so make reservations in advance, 867/873-2386). The **Under the Midnight Sun Festival** (867/873-4950) comprises performing arts at various locales around the city. **Folk on the Rocks,** held during the third weekend of July, takes place on the shore of Long Lake and attracts Northern and Southern performers of folk, reggae, and Inuit music.

ACCOMMODATIONS AND CAMPING
$50–100
The only accommodations with rooms for less than $100 are bed-and-breakfasts. Ask at the Visitors Centre for a current list of B&Bs, or contact the following. **Captain Ron's** (8 Lessard Dr., 867/873-3746, $85 s, $95 d), overlooking the floatplane base, has four rooms, a sundeck, a library, and a guest lounge. In the same vicinity, **Blue Raven B&B** (37B Otto Dr., 867/873-6328, $70 s, $80 d), on top of a hill on Latham Island, overlooks Great Slave Lake.

$100–150
Yellowknife's least expensive motel is the **Igloo**

Inn (4115 Franklin Ave., 867/873-8511, $98 s, $108 d), halfway between downtown and Old Town. It could do with a revamp, but rooms are in reasonable shape.

Chateau Nova (4401 50th Ave., 867/873-9700 or 877/839-1236, www.chateaunova.com) is the rather grand name of a newish hotel a few blocks from downtown on the way to Old Town. Rooms are modern and come with niceties such as bathrobes and a writing desk. Other amenities include a small fitness room with a big hot tub, a business center with Internet access, spa services, a restaurant, and a lounge. Rates start at $146 s or d for a standard room.

$150–200

The Yellowknife Inn (5010 49th St., 867/873-2601 or 800/661-0580, www.yellowknifeinn .com) is right in the center of the city. A Double Room here means a double bed, so request a Queen Room, as rates are the same ($160 s or d). Better still, pay an extra $30 for a Deluxe Suite with more room and upgraded everything.

Campgrounds

The city's only campground is at Fred Henne Territorial Park (867/920-2472, $12–15), across from the airport and a one-hour walk from downtown. Facilities include bug-proof cooking shelters, woodstoves, showers, and some powered sites. Along the Ingraham Trail, at Reid Lake, and at Prelude Lake are primitive campgrounds. All three sites are open late May–September.

FOOD

The Red Apple (in the Discovery Inn, 867/873-2324) opens at 6 A.M. and is a popular spot for breakfast. It also serves a variety of dishes starting at $8 the rest of the day. L'atitudes (in Centre Square Mall below the Yellowknife Inn, 867/920-7880) is a stylish, dimly lit restaurant open daily for breakfast and lunch and Thursday–Friday until 9 P.M. Cooked breakfasts are $7, and the rest of the day main meals start at $12.

Northern Specialties

Head down the hill from the city center to enjoy Northern cuisine and typically hospitable Northern atmosphere at any of the following restaurants. The Wildcat Café (3904 Wiley Rd., 867/873-8850, June–Aug. Mon.–Sat. 7:30 A.M.–9 P.M., Sun. 10 A.M.–9 P.M.) has been famous since it was opened by Willy Wiley and Smoky Stout in 1937, becoming the first place in Yellowknife to sell ice cream. The café closed its doors in 1959 but reopened with some remodeling in 1977. The distinctive Northern feel hasn't been lost—log walls, wooden tables, a sloping floor, and a congenial atmosphere are part of the charm. It only has a few tables and is perpetually full, so chances are you'll end up sharing a table. The blackboard menu changes daily but features dishes such as lake trout, whitefish, and musk ox from $18.

Le Frolic (5019 49th St., 867/669-9852) is the downstairs half of a French restaurant combo (L'Heritage, upstairs, is more formal and expensive) that presents game like arctic char, musk ox, and caribou with French flair. With the bison burger at $13, you don't need to spend a fortune, but the wild-game fondue ($33 per person) is hard to pass up. Small and dimly lit, The Office (4915 50th St., 867/873-3750) serves delicious arctic char and other seasonal game from $20. Finally, head to Northern Fancy Meats (314 Woolgar Ave., 867/873-8767, Mon.–Sat. 9 A.M.–6 P.M.) for Northern game meat and in-house sausages and jerky.

INFORMATION AND SERVICES

The Northern Frontier Regional Visitors Centre (4807 49th St., 867/873-4262 or 877/881-4261, www.northernfrontier.com) overlooks Frame Lake. It's stocked with brochures on everything you'll need to know about Yellowknife, historic photographs, and interesting displays. It's open in June–August daily 8:30 A.M.–6 P.M., the rest of the year Monday–Friday 8:30 A.M.–5:30 P.M. and Saturday–Sunday noon–4 P.M.

Books and Bookstores

On the second floor of Centre Square Mall is Yellowknife Public Library (5022 49th St., 867/920-5642, Mon.–Thurs. 10 A.M.–9 P.M., Fri.–Sat. 10 A.M.–6 P.M.). Although small, it has newspapers from throughout Canada, lots of literature on the north, and public Internet access. **Yellowknife Book Cellar** (Panda II Mall, 867/920-2220) has a wide selection of Northern and Canadian literature. The north's biggest publisher, **Outcrop** (4920 52nd St., 867/920-4343 or 800/661-0861), has back issues of *Up Here* for sale and catalogs of all books they publish.

Services
The post office is at 4902 50th Street. Wash clothes at the **Arctic Laundromat** (4310 Franklin Ave., daily 8:30 A.M.–11 P.M.). **Henry's Camera and Photo Lab** (Centre Square Mall, 867/873-2389) develops film in one hour and has a limited range of camera supplies. On the main drag, **Yellowknife Foto Source** (5005 Franklin Ave., 867/873-2196) has the same services.

Stanton Regional Hospital (867/920-4111) is on Old Airport Road at Range Lake Road. For the **RCMP,** call 867/669-5100.

TRANSPORTATION
Getting There
Yellowknife Airport, five kilometers (3.1 mi.) west of the city along Highway 3, is the hub of air travel in the Northwest Territories. It's open daily 24 hours, has an inexpensive café (5:30 A.M.–10 P.M.), a bar, lockers, and rental cars. **First Air** (867/669-8500 or 800/267-1247) uses Yellowknife as its western hub, with flights arriving and departing daily from Edmonton, Inuvik, and many Nunavut communities.

Frontier Coachlines (113 Kamlake Rd., 867/873-4892) offers bus service five times weekly from Hay River to Yellowknife, with connections from there to Greyhound's other Canadian services.

Getting Around
Arctic Frontier Carriers (867/873-4437) operates the **Public Transit System** along two routes, including out to the campground and airport, Monday–Friday and with a limited Saturday service. Cab companies are **City Cab** (867/873-4444) and **Sunshine Taxi** (867/873-4414). Rental-car agencies include **Budget** (867/920-9209), **Hertz** (867/766-3838), and **National** (867/873-3424). Rates start at $60 per day and $340 per week for a small car, plus $.20 per kilometer.

City Tours
Raven Tours (867/873-4776, www.raventours .yk.com) runs a 2.5-hour City Sightseeing Tour that takes in all the sights of New Town, Old Town, Latham Island, and a sled-dog kennel for $28 per person. The company also offers guided hikes to Cameron River Falls ($42 per person), and a two-hour lake cruise ($28 per person). In winter, the company specializes in aurora tours.

Mackenzie River and Western Arctic

Between the treeless barren lands of central NWT and the jagged peaks of the Mackenzie Mountains flows one of the world's mightiest rivers—the Mackenzie, which drains one-fifth of Canada before emptying into the Arctic Ocean. It is a wild and mostly uninhabited region, with jagged peaks, thundering rivers, a waterfall twice the height of Niagara, and pristine lakes so full of fish that you'll need to bait your hook behind a tree. From Hay River, the Mackenzie Highway provides access to the southern part of the region and Fort Simpson, the jumping-off point for Nahanni National Park, a UNESCO World Heritage Site. Communities along the

Mackenzie River are mostly made up of Dene, who have lived along the *Deh Cho* (Big River) for thousands of years. In the far north, Inuvik is a modern, planned town linked to the outside world by the Dempster Highway from Dawson City. This chapter covers all these towns, as well as other worthwhile destinations and activities in the region—fishing on Great Bear Lake, swimming in the Arctic Ocean at Tuktoyaktuk, and more.

Deh Cho (Mackenzie River) Region

HAY RIVER TO FORT SIMPSON

From the Yellowknife junction, the Mackenzie Highway continues west through a typical northern boreal forest, reaching the largest town in the region, Fort Simpson, after 268 kilometers (166 mi.). The road is unpaved but well maintained.

Sambaa Deh Falls Territorial Park

Approximately 136 kilometers (84 mi.) from the turn-off at Highway 3, the Mackenzie Highway reaches Saamba Deh Falls on the Trout River. The falls are directly downstream from the road bridge and are easily accessible from the day-use area, on the other side of the road. Here, the river is forced through a narrow gorge, exploding into the deep pond below. A one-kilometer (0.6-mi.) trail upstream leads to a fossil-filled limestone outcrop. The park has camping (showers, bug-proof cooking shelters, and well-maintained sites for $12 per night) and a **Visitors Centre** (mid-May–mid-Sept. daily 8 A.M.–8 P.M.) with a fossil display and TV room where nature videos are shown.

FORT SIMPSON

Best known as the jumping-off point for Nahanni National Park, the town of Fort Simpson (pop. 1,000) is at the confluence of two major rivers—the Liard and Mackenzie—with ferry crossing (late May–late Oct. daily 8 A.M.–11:45 P.M., free) required to reach town from the Mackenzie Highway. Throughout summer, the town is a hive of activity, a constant buzz of floatplanes taking off to remote fly-in fishing lakes and hunt camps, groups of Gore-Tex–clad adventurers from around the world checking their equipment before heading off for the adventure of a lifetime down the South Nahanni River, and the occasional canoe-load of paddlers stopping in on their way to the Arctic Ocean.

Sights and Recreation

The main street through Fort Simpson is typical of Northern towns, with all the usual services, a couple of motels, and lots of modular buildings. The most interesting sights are one block east on Mackenzie Drive, running alongside the Mackenzie River. This was the main street before the

ALBERT FAILLE

Each breakup from 1916 to 1961, Albert Faille left Fort Simpson by scow in a feverish, determined quest for the elusive Nahanni gold. Some said it was sheer lunacy, others a waste of time. But his relentless obsession and exploits against insurmountable odds created the Faille legend, which has become synonymous with the Nahanni.

Of Swiss descent, Faille was born in Minnesota. He was one of the earliest men to tackle the river alone, and at the time, the first to winter there in seven years. He built a cabin at the mouth of the Flat River, but it was at Murder Creek, upstream from the cabin, that Faille believed his fortune in gold lay. At times he'd be given up for dead, and rumors and tales would begin to unfold—but then he would turn up at Fort Simpson for supplies. He spent most winters in a small cabin that still stands today, overlooking the Mackenzie River in Fort Simpson. He died there in 1974. His scows still lie out front, ready for breakup and another attempt for the elusive key to finding gold. His final trip is documented by a 1961 National Film Board production that can be seen in the Fort Simpson and Blackstone visitors centers.

N.W. TERRITORIES

highway was completed and businesses moved closer to it. At the south end, a beached sternwheeler on the riverbank soon comes into view. Built in 1920, this boat was one of many that plied the Mackenzie River. Also here is a small monument noting the importance of the river in the town's history. Across the road is the site of the Hudson's Bay Company post (the only original building remaining is the company's outhouse). Continuing farther along the river, you pass plaques noting the historic importance of various structures, including the cabin of Nahanni legend **Albert Faille,** who wintered here between his goldseeking trips. Peering through the windows and marveling at the wooden scows laying in the yard gives you some insight into the life of this amazing man, particularly if you've watched the National Film Board documentary about him shown at the Visitors Centre.

Many local lakes have great fishing for northern pike, pickerel, lake trout, and arctic grayling, but are only accessible by air. **Simpson Air** (867/695-2505) flies to Little Doctor Lake, where they operate a lodge, as well as **McGill Lake** and **Mustard Lake.** Down by the entrance to town on Antoine Drive is the local golf course, which has nine holes with oil-soaked greens. There are no club rentals, but the local golfing population is proud of it.

Accommodations and Food

Along the road into town is **Bannockland Inn** (867/695-3337, $130–16 s or d). It's the home of long-time Northerners Susan and Glen Sibbeston, who have opened five rooms in their modern riverfront home to visitors. Each spacious room has an en suite, and rates include a cooked breakfast and airport transfers. Rooms in both of Fort Simpson's hotels are little more than basic and both charge from $110 s, $120 d. They are the **Maroda Motel** (867/695-2602), where some rooms have kitchenettes, and the **Nahanni Inn** (867/695-2201), which has a coffee shop (open daily at 8 A.M.) and dining room.

On the road to the Papal Grounds is **Fort Simpson Campground** (mid-May–mid-Sept., $10), where sites (four with power hookups) provide ample privacy and a large supply of firewood is available.

Information and Services

At the south entrance to town is the excellent **Fort Simpson Visitor Centre** (867/695-3182, May 15–Sept. 15 daily 8 A.M.–8 P.M.), which contains a re-creation of the original Hudson's Bay Company post and some interesting historical displays. Don't miss the 1961 National Film Board documentary on Nahanni legend Albert Faille, which is shown, along with others, in the theater. Diagonally opposite the Visitors Centre is the **Tourist Service Centre,** with coin showers, a car wash, and a launderette. The library (Antoine Dr.) has public Internet access.

LIARD HIGHWAY

From the Mackenzie Highway, southeast of Fort Simpson, to Fort Nelson (British Columbia) is 394 kilometers (245 mi.) of relatively straight road through a boreal forest of spruce, aspen, and poplar. Wildlife along this route is abundant; chances are you'll see moose and black bears, especially at dawn and dusk. The only services are at Fort Liard.

Blackstone Territorial Park

A little over 100 kilometers (62 mi.) from the Mackenzie Highway, where the Blackstone River drains into the Liard River, a small territorial park has been established at a site known as **Blackstone Landing.** Inside the park visitors center (mid-May–mid-Sept. daily 8 A.M.–8 P.M.) are some interesting displays on the area's history and a good selection of locally made documentaries to watch. The center is the starting point for a short trail that leads to a trapper's cabin. The park's campground ($14) has flush toilets, showers, and two bug-proof, woodstove-equipped cooking shelters. Black bears are common, so keep your food securely stored.

FORT LIARD

Best known as the "Tropics of the North" for its warm microclimate (many locals maintain vegetable gardens), this town of 400 is set among a lush forest of poplar and birch on the banks of the Liard River. The area has been settled since 1807, when the North West Company established where the Petitot River drains into the Liard. Until the 1960s, most of the Dene inhabitants spent winter away from Fort Liard, and modern development didn't begin until the highway opened to Fort Nelson. Traditional lifestyles are still important to residents, nearly all of whom spend time trapping, hunting, fishing, and making clothing and crafts.

Birchbark Baskets

The women of Fort Liard are famous for these baskets, made for storing food, collecting berries, carrying supplies, or even boiling water. Birch is abundant in the area and has a remarkably pliable nature, ideal for bending and sewing. The bark contains a natural wax, making it not only rot-resistant but also waterproof. Baskets are still made in the long, tedious process handed down from generation to generation. They are sewn together with specially prepared roots and decorated with porcupine quills. Available from the small gift store on Fort Liard's main street (or in Fort Simpson and Hay River), they make a wonderfully authentic Northern souvenir.

Practicalities

The small but well-maintained **Hay Lake Campground** has pit toilets, firewood, and drinking water. It's along the Fort Liard access road. Accommodations above the **Liard Valley General Store** (867/770-4441) sleep 24 in 12 basic rooms, for $90 single, $100 double, or with kitchenette $120 and $130, respectively. Back out on the highway is the only gas station (7 A.M.–11 P.M.) between Fort Simpson and Fort Nelson.

NAHANNI NATIONAL PARK

One of the most beautiful, wildest, and purest stretches of white water in the world is the **South Nahanni River.** Protecting a 300-kilometer (186-mi.) stretch of this remote river is 4,766-square-kilometer (1,234-sq.-mi.) Nahanni National Park. This roadless park is a vast wilderness inhabited only by bears, mountain goats, Dall's sheep, caribou, moose, and wolves.

Accessible only by air, the best way to really experience the park is on a raft or canoe trip down the South Nahanni River. Many visitors just fly in for the day. However you decide to visit the park, the adventure will remain with you for the rest of your life. But with names on the map like Headless Creek, Deadmen Valley, Hell's Gate, Funeral Range, Devils Kitchen, Broken Skull River, and Death Canyon, you'd better tell someone where you're going before heading out.

History

Slavey Dene, who lived on the lowlands along the Mackenzie and Liard Rivers, feared a mysterious group of natives living high in the Mackenzie Mountains, calling them the *Nahanni* (People Who Live Far Away). The first white men to travel up the South Nahanni River were fur trappers and missionaries, followed by men lured by tales of gold. In 1905, Willie and Frank McLeod began prospecting tributaries of the Flat River in search of an elusive mother lode. Three years later, their headless bodies were discovered at the mouth of what is now known as Headless Creek; for many years thereafter, the entire valley was called Deadmen Valley. Very quickly, stories of gold mines, murder, lush tropical valleys, and a tribe of Indians dominated by a white woman became rampant. These stories did nothing but lure other prospecting adventurers to the valley—Jorgenson, Shebbach, Field, Faille, Sibbeston, Kraus, and Patterson. Many died mysteriously: Jorgenson's skeleton was found outside his cabin, his precious rifle gone; Shebbach died of starvation at the mouth of Caribou Creek; the body of Phil Powers was discovered in his burned-out cabin; Angus Hall just plain disappeared.

The Land

The headwaters of the **South Nahanni River** are high in **Mackenzie Mountains,** which form the remote border between the Northwest Territories and the Yukon. Flowing in a roughly southeasterly direction for 540 kilometers (336 mi.) it drains into the Liard River, a major tributary of the Mackenzie River. The South Nahanni, cut deeply into the mountains, is known as an "antecedent"; that is, it preceded the mountains. It once meandered through a wide-open plain. As uplift in the earth's surface occurred, the river cut down through the rising rock strata and created the deep, meandering canyons present today.

The starting point for many river trips and the destination of most day trippers is **Virginia Falls,** at 92 meters (300 ft.) they are twice as high as Niagara Falls. Over many thousands of years, erosion has forced the falls upstream, creating a canyon system with walls over one kilometer (0.6 mi.) high immediately downstream of the falls.

Running the South Nahanni with an Outfitter

For most people, whether experienced canoeists or never-evers, the advantages of a trip down the South Nahanni River with a licensed outfitter far outweigh the disadvantages.

The two outfitters I recommend are **Nahanni River Adventures** (867/668-3180 or 800/297-6927, www.nahanni.com) and **Nahanni Wilderness Adventures** (403/678-3374 or 888/897-5223, www.nahanniwild.com). Each offers trips of varying lengths—8–12 days from Virginia Falls, two weeks from Rabbitkettle Lake, or up to three weeks from Moose Ponds. Craft used are rafts, two-person canoes, or longer voyageur-type canoes. Trips start at $3,500 for an eight-day float. The best way to get a feeling which trip suits your needs and interests is by talking to the outfitters (they all love "their" river, so getting them to talk is no problem). Guided trips operate mid-June–early September, and many dates fill up fast. The staging area for both outfitters is the north end of the old airstrip in downtown Fort Simpson.

Your Own White-Water Expedition

Experienced white-water enthusiasts planning their own trip down the Nahanni have four main components to organize: permits and fees, transportation into the park, transportation down the river, and supplies. The best place to start planning your trip is the Parks Canada website (www.pc.gc.ca/nahanni), where you can download reservation forms and pay the park use fee ($100 per person). Only 12 nonguided visitors

are allowed to start down the river each day, so reservations are an absolute necessity. Most expeditions begin with a floatplane trip to Virginia Falls and end outside of the park, where the Liard River flows alongside the Liard Highway. The charter cost from Fort Simpson to Virginia Falls for two people, one canoe, and 500 pounds of gear, is around $1,100. This is just an example—if there are four of you, you would travel in a bigger plane (a Beaver) and the cost would run around $1,500. For detailed quotes contact **Simpson Air** (867/695-2505), **South Nahanni Airways** (867/695-2007), or **Wolverine Air** (867/695-2263). These are same companies used by commercial operators, so they're flying into the park all the time. A few years ago, I picked up a guy who'd just come down the river and was hitchhiking back to Watson Lake from Blackstone Landing. He'd started at Moose Ponds, which is closer to Watson Lake (Yukon) than any Northwest Territories community, therefore chartering a plane from Watson Lake cost less, but it seemed an inconvenient way to save a couple hundred bucks. If you need a canoe or other equipment, contact the floatplane companies or the commercial outfitters.

Flightseeing

Calling a flightseeing trip into Nahanni "awe-inspiring" doesn't do it justice—it is simply one of the most memorable flights I have ever taken. Getting into the park for just the day is problematic but well worth the effort and cost. Typically, charter operators use a floatplane to fly from Fort Simpson to Virginia Falls, with up to two hours spent at the falls, enough time to walk the 1.3-kilometer (0.8-mi.) portage to the base of the falls. If you have three or more people in your group, there are no problems; just call each operator for the best quote (or get the staff at Fort Simpson Visitor Centre to do it for you). Groups of less than three have the choice of chartering an entire plane (from approximately $900) or waiting around for other interested parties to turn up. Each of the air charter companies can tailor flights to suit your needs. By waiting around until the plane is full, or by booking in advance, you have a better chance of keeping the cost down. Fort Simpson operators are the following: **Simpson Air** (867/695-2505), **South Nahanni Airways** (867/695-2007), and **Wolverine Air** (867/695-2263).

Information

The outfitters on the river are experts in their own right and can answer many of your questions long before you arrive. For specific information on the park, check the website (www.pc.gc.ca/nahanni) or contact **Park Headquarters** in Fort Simpson (867/695-3151). The **Fort Simpson Visitor Centre** (867/695-3182, May 15–Sept. 15 daily 8 A.M.–8 P.M.) has park displays as well as relevant videos and books for visitor use.

TOWNS ALONG THE MACKENZIE RIVER

In 1789, Alexander Mackenzie became the first European to travel the river that now bears his name. After his reports of rich fur resources reached the outside, the North West Company established fur-trading posts along the river. The Dene, who were originally nomadic, settled at the trading posts, forming small communities that still exist today. The only road into the region begins at Fort Simpson and extends north to Wrigley.

Wrigley

The road between Fort Simpson and Wrigley traverses thick boreal forest, breaking only for a short ferry trip at **Ndulee** (daily 9–11 A.M. and 2–8 P.M.), 84 kilometers (52 mi.) out of Fort Simpson.

Most of the community's 160 residents are Slavey Dene who live a semitraditional lifestyle. Across the Yukon River from the village is **Roche qui-Trempe-à-L'eau** (The Rock that Plunges into the Water), an isolated hill that has been eroded away by the river on one side, creating a sheer cliff that drops 400 meters (1,300 ft.) into the water below.

The **Petanea Hotel** (867/581-3121, www.wrigleyhotel.com) is in a modular building that holds five guest rooms. Rates are $190 pp per day with three meals. The hotel also has a small coffee shop and a dining room that opens in the evening. Enquire here about boat rentals and tours.

Norman Wells

Oil is the lifeblood of Norman Wells (pop. 800), which lies along the Mackenzie River halfway between Fort Simpson and Inuvik. Unlike other settlements along the Mackenzie River, Norman Wells did not originate as a trading post but owes its existence to oil. Imperial Oil produces 10 million barrels annually from field tapped by over 150 wells (the company's largest source of conventional crude oil), shipping to market by pipeline. The infrastructure is unique in that it comprises manmade islands in the middle of the Mackenzie River, directly offshore from town, allowing oil extraction to continue throughout breakup and freeze-up of the river. The **Norman Wells Historical Centre** (867/587-2415, summer daily 10 A.M.–10 P.M.) tells the story of the Canol Project through historical displays, photographs, artifacts recovered from along the road, and an excellent propaganda movie that was commissioned to help finance the project. Next door is an interesting church. Actually, the church

Floatplanes are the only way to access much of the Mackenzie region.

is fairly normal, but the congregation is unusual. Roman Catholics meet on one side, Protestants on the other.

The center of town, a 20-minute walk from the airport, is a semicircle of semipermanent buildings around a dusty parking lot. Here you'll find the **Yamouri Inn** (867/587-2744, $120 s, $130 d), which has rooms, a dimly lit cocktail lounge, a coffee shop, and a restaurant. Closer to the airport is the **Mackenzie Valley Hotel** (867/587-2511, www.mackenzievalleyhotel.com, $130 s, $160 d). The 34 rooms are cheerfully painted and each comes with a TV and phone.

Norman Wells has an impressive three-story airport complete with an observation deck and revolving baggage claim—not bad for a town of 800 people. It is a one-kilometer (0.6-mi.) walk into town. **North-Wright Airways** (867/587-2333, www.north-wrightairways.com) has daily flights from Yellowknife to Norman Wells, as well as from Norman Wells to all Mackenzie River communities.

Canol Heritage Trail

The large U.S. military force present in Alaska during World War II needed oil to fuel aircraft and ships, which were in place for expected Japanese attacks. The strategically located Norman Wells oil fields were chosen as a source of crude oil, with little regard for the engineering feat needed to build a pipeline over the Mackenzie Mountains. To this day, it remains one of the largest projects ever undertaken in northern Canada. More than $300 million was spent between 1942 and 1945, employing 30,000 people who laid 2,650 kilometers (1,650 mi.) of four- and six-inch pipeline and built a road over some of North America's most isolated and impenetrable mountain ranges. It was abandoned less than a year after completion. Today, the roadbed remains—strewn with structures, trucks, and equipment used in the project's construction—and is considered by many to be one of the world's great wilderness hikes. It follows the original route for 372 kilometers (231 mi.), from the Mackenzie River across from Norman Wells to the Yukon border. Following the road causes little problem, but the logistics of getting to the beginning of the trail, arranging food drops, crossing

rivers (most bridges have been washed out), and returning to Norman Wells require much planning. **Mountain River Outfitters** (867/587-2285, www.mountainriver.nt.ca) can provide transportation and logistical support.

Tulita

This small Slavey Dene community (pop. 300) is south of Norman Wells, where the Great Bear River drains into the Mackenzie River. This strategic location has made it a transportation hub since the days of Sir John Franklin. An Anglican church, built of squared logs and dating to the 1860s, sits on the riverbank, beside the Hudson's Bay Company post. Many houses have colorful tepees in their yards, which are used for drying and smoking fish, standing in stark contrast to a modern school building.

The **Two Rivers Hotel** (867/588-3320, $149 s, $199 d) has four rooms with single and double beds, all with a shared bathroom and kitchen. Meals can also be arranged in the dining room. If you're interested in a boat trip chasing arctic grayling in the Great Bear River or to the **Smoking Hills,** where an exposed seam of coal burns permanently, make enquires at the hotel.

Great Bear Lake

East of the Mackenzie River, Great Bear Lake is one of the world's best freshwater fishing lakes, and it has the records to prove it. This lake holds world records for *all* line classes of lake trout; the overall world record, caught in 1993, weighed in at a whopping 32.2 kilograms (71 lbs.) and measured more than one meter (three ft.). The lake also holds world records for most classes of arctic grayling, including the overall record.

Around the lake are small fishing lodges offering all-inclusive packages, including three operated by **Plummer's Arctic Lodges** (204/774-5775 or 800/665-0240, www.plummerslodges.com). Accommodations, all meals, guides, professionally equipped boats, and round-trip air charters from Winnipeg or Edmonton are included in the package; US$4,200 for seven days.

Formerly known as Fort Franklin, **Déline** (Flowing Water) is the only community on the lake. In 1825, Sir John Franklin wintered at the trading post here before setting off on one of his many expeditions in search of the Northwest Passage. Today, the Slavey Dene of Déline live a traditional lifestyle, trapping, fishing, and making crafts, including moccasins for which they are well known. The tepee-shaped church is worth visiting, and the hike along the shore of Great Bear Lake offers rewarding vistas and passes several historic sites. Right in town, **Grey Goose Lodge** (867/589-3117, www.greygooselodge.ca, $145 pp including breakfast) is a modern accommodation with 12 guest rooms, canoe and motorboat rentals, and fishing charters.

Fort Good Hope

Overlooking the Mackenzie River and flanked by boreal forest, this Slavey Dene community of 550 is on the east bank of the Mackenzie River, 190 kilometers (118 mi.) downstream of Norman Wells and just south of the Arctic Circle. A trading post was established here in 1805 by the North West Company, but the oldest building in town is the 1860 **Our Lady of Good Hope Church,** which has been declared a National Historic Site. The church's interior, decorated in ornate panels and friezes painted by an early missionary, Father Emile Petitot, depicts aspects of his travels and life in the north.

One of the highlights of a trip to Fort Good Hope is visiting **The Ramparts,** where 200-meter-high (660-ft.) cliffs force the Mackenzie River through a 500-meter-wide (1,640-ft.) canyon. Although the cliffs continue for many kilometers, the most spectacular section is upstream of town and can be reached on foot or by boat. Arrange boat rentals and tours through the **Ramparts Hotel** (867/598-2500, $120 pp). Overlooking the river, this hotel has a restaurant with a simple menu (entrées $15–25).

Colville Lake

This community of 50 North Slavey Dene, just north of the Arctic Circle on the southeast shore of Colville Lake, was established in 1962 when a Roman Catholic mission was built. It is the territories' only community built entirely from logs. The largest building is the church, which supports a bell weighing 454 kilograms (1,000 lbs.). The mission was built by Father Bern Will Brown, who has now left the church and is one of the north's most respected artists. His paintings, which depict the lifestyle of Northerners, are in demand across North America. Brown is also the host at **Colville Lake Lodge** (867/709-2500), which combines excellent fishing for lake trout, arctic grayling, northern pike, whitefish, and inconnu, with a small museum highlighting life in the north. The lodge also has an art gallery, boat and canoe rentals, and common kitchen facilities.

Western Arctic

The northwestern corner of the Northwest Territories, where the Mackenzie River drains into the Arctic Ocean, is linked to the outside world by the Dempster Highway, the continent's northernmost public road. The region, which is entirely above the Arctic Circle, encompasses the Mackenzie River valley and the vast barrens flanking the Arctic Ocean.

The **Mackenzie Delta,** 90 kilometers (56 mi.) long and 60 kilometers (37 mi.) wide, is one of the world's greatest waterfowl nesting grounds. Hundreds of thousands of birds migrate to the delta each spring; among them are swans, cranes, hawks, bald eagles, and peregrine falcons. In the vicinity of the delta live red foxes, lynx, wolves, black bears, and moose. Many woodland and barrenground caribou migrate through the region in early spring and fall; the Porcupine herd, named for the Porcupine River, migrates as far as Alaska. Beluga whales spend summer in the shallow waters around the delta and can be viewed from the air or in a boat.

INUVIK

You must see Inuvik (pop. 3,200) with your own eyes to believe it, and then you may still doubt what you see: brightly painted houses on stilts, a

N.W. TERRITORIES

INUVIK

0   250 yds
0   250 m

INDUSTRIAL RD.

NAVY RD.

MARINE BYPASS RD.

WOLVERINE RD.

KUGMALLIT

BONNET

RD.

PLUME RD.

INGAMO HALL ★

MACKENZIE RD.

FRANKLIN RD.

KINGMINGYA

RELIANCE ST.

INUIT RD.

BREYNAT ST.

Twin

HAPPY VALLEY △

ROBERTSON'S B&B ●

RD.

LOUCHEAUX RD.

Lakes

POLAR B&B/ TO GO'S ●

LIBRARY ■

▼ TRAPPER PUB

NORTHERN IMAGES ■

● NORTHERN ▼

ESKIMO INN ●

IGLOO CHURCH ★

ARCTIC NATURE TOURS ■

MACKENZIE HOTEL ●

WATER ST.

DISTRIBUTOR ST.

AURORA RESEARCH INSTITUTE ★

POST OFFICE ■

MACKENZIE RD.

WESTERN ARCTIC VISITOR CENTRE ■

FINTO LODGE ●

■ DOCK

Duck Lake

BOOT LAKE RD.

HOSPITAL ■

To Chuk Park, Airport, and Dempster Highway

Mackenzie River (East Channel)

DUCK LAKE ST.

Boot Lake

N.W. TERRITORIES

monstrous church shaped like an igloo, metal tunnels snaking through town, and a main street where businesses have names such as Eskimo Inn, 60 Below Construction, and Polar TV. *Inuvik* (Place of Man, in Invialuktun) is obviously a planned community, transformed from some architect's drafting board into full-blown reality high above the Arctic Circle. All aspects have been scientifically planned, right down to the foundations—all structures sit on piles of rock, ensuring stability in the permafrost and preventing heat from turning the ground into sludge.

Inuvik marks the end of the Dempster Highway, as far north as you can drive on a public road in North America, which is reason enough for many visitors to make the trek to town. If you come up from Calgary, you will have driven 3,560 kilometers (2,210 mi.), from Seattle 4,030 kilometers (2,500 mi.), from Los Angeles 6,100 kilometers (3,790 mi.), or from New York 7,600 kilometers (4,720 mi.).

Sights

It's easy to spend a whole day walking around town, checking out the unique considerations involved in living above the Arctic Circle. *Utilidors,* for example, snake around town, linking businesses and houses and passing right through the middle of the schoolyard. These conduits contain water, heat, and sewerage pipelines and are raised above the ground to prevent problems associated with permafrost. Inuvik's most famous landmark is **Our Lady of Victory Church,** commonly known as the **igloo church** for its distinctive shape. The church, on Mackenzie Road, is not always open; ask at the rectory for permission to enter. The interior is decorated with a series of paintings by Inuvialuit artist Mona Thrasher, depicting various religious scenes. A few blocks to the east is the **Aurora Research Institute** (867/777-3298, Mon.–Fri. 9 A.M.–5 P.M.), one of three support facilities for scientific projects throughout the Arctic. West along Mackenzie Road is **Ingamo Hall,** a three-story structure built with more than 1,000 logs. The best views of the delta are, naturally, from the air, but the next best thing is to climb the 20-meter (66-ft.) observation tower in **Chuk Park,** six kilometers (3.7 mi.) south of downtown.

Tours

It seems that everyone who visits Inuvik takes at least one tour, whether it's around town, on the delta, or to an outlying community. **Arctic Nature Tours** (beside the igloo church on Mackenzie Rd., 867/777-3300, www.arcticnaturetours.com) offers an extensive variety of tours June–early September; those that require flying include transportation from town out to the airport. The town tour ($30 pp) lasts approximately two hours, taking in all the sights. Another popular excursion is to the camp of an Inuvialuit elder ($85 pp), where tea and bannock is served. In addition to Tuk Tours, the company has trips to remote **Herschel Island** located in the Beaufort Sea. The island was a major whaling station during the early 1900s, but today only ruins remain. This trip is especially good for bird-watchers because more than 70 avian species have been recorded on the island. The flight to the island passes **Ivvavik National Park** in the northern Yukon, providing opportunities to see musk oxen, caribou, and grizzly bears. A two-hour stay on the island costs $325 per person, including the 90-minute (each way) flight. Overnight stays begin at $650 per person.

Nightlife

Inuvik's most famous nightspot is **The Zoo,** in the Mackenzie Hotel, where a colorful mixture of oil field workers, German backpackers, drunken Aussies, fur-coated southerners, pin-striped businessmen, and locals who've been kicked out of every other place in town converge to listen to some band that lost its way down in Whitehorse and wound up in Inuvik. Also in the Mackenzie Hotel is the more mellow **Brass Rail Lounge,** where the bar is covered in roofing materials—a legacy of the original owner's profession before becoming involved in the hotel business. Down the hill is the **Mad Trapper Pub,** where local musicians jam on Saturday afternoons at 4 P.M., hoping one day to play at the Zoo.

Festivals and Events

Summer Solstice in June is celebrated by **Midnight Madness,** although because the sun doesn't set for a month, the actual date of the festival is of little importance. Celebrations on the weekend closest to the solstice (June 21) include traditional music and dancing and a feast of lobster imported from the east coast for the occasion. The **Great Northern Arts Festival** (867/777-3536, www.gnaf.ca), held during the third week of July, features demonstrations, musical performances such as Inuit drumming, displays, and sales of Northern art.

Accommodations and Camping

A few locals run bed-and-breakfasts, which are relatively inexpensive and a friendly alternative to the impersonal hotels. Accommodations at the centrally located **Polar B&B** (75 Mackenzie Rd., 867/777-2554, $105 s, $115 d) are comfortable, with a shared bathroom, kitchen, laundry, and lounge with television. Rates include a self-serve breakfast. One block farther down the hill is **Robertson's B&B** (41 Mackenzie Rd., 867/777-3111, June–Sept., $80 s, $90 d). This place has a large deck with great view of the delta. The two guest rooms share a single bathroom, but the price is right.

Inuvik's three motels are owned by the Mackenzie Delta Hotel Group (www.inuvikhotels.com), a native co-operative. Each has a coffee shop, a restaurant, and basic rooms with private baths. They are **Mackenzie Hotel** (185 Mackenzie Rd., 867/777-2861, $149 s, $164 d); **Eskimo Inn** (133 Mackenzie Rd., 867/777-2801, $149 s, $179 d), with some rooms designated as nonsmoking; and, on the way to the airport, the **Finto Lodge** (288 Mackenzie Rd., 867/777-2647, $159 s, $174 d), with delta views and some rooms with a fridge and microwave for a few dollars extra.

Happy Valley Campground (unpowered sites $12, powered $15) is on a bluff overlooking the delta, yet one block from the main street. It has 20 private, unserviced sites and a gravel parking area for RVs and trailers that need power. Facilities include flush toilets, showers, and firewood. Outside of town toward the airport is the **Chuk Park** ($10)—it's quiet but has limited facilities.

Food

The thing to do this far north is to sample local fare such as musk ox, caribou, and arctic char. The least expensive way to do this is at **To Go's** (71 Mackenzie Rd., 867/777-3030), which has a few tables and a take-out menu. Caribou burgers and musk ox burgers ($6.50) are the same price as regular hamburgers but cheaper than mushroom burgers. Pizza starts at $12; extras such as musk ox are $2, and the Northern Pizza—with the works—is $19. The coffee shop in the **Mackenzie Hotel** (185 Mackenzie Rd., 867/777-2861, daily from 7 A.M.) is the most popular breakfast hangout, but it can get smoky. The **Green Briar Dining Room** (Tues.–Sat. 6–10 P.M.), also in the Mackenzie Hotel, serves a good selection of Northern cuisine (starting at $14.95 for a caribou burger). The **Peppermill Restaurant** (Finto Lodge, 288 Mackenzie Rd., 867/777-2647) offers much of the same; try caribou steaks smothered in blueberry sauce (made from locally picked blueberries) for $22.50. The town's only supermarket (120 Mackenzie Rd., daily 10 A.M.–midnight) has a decent selection with prices not as high as you might expect.

Information and Services

The **Western Arctic Visitor Centre** (867/777-4727, www.town.inuvik.nt.ca, summer daily 9 A.M.–8 P.M.) is at the entrance to town, a 10-minute walk from downtown. This modern facility features displays on the people of the north, details on each of the western Arctic communities, and all the usual tour information. Out back, a trail leads through a re-creation of an Inuvialuit whaling camp and a Gwich'in fishing camp. **Inuvik Centennial Library** (Mackenzie Rd., 867/777-2749, Mon.–Thurs. 10 A.M.–9 P.M., Fri. 10 A.M.–6 P.M., Sat.–Sun. 1–5 P.M.) has a fairly extensive collection of Northern books and literature.

The post office is at 817 Mackenzie Road. **Northern Images** (upstairs at 115 Mackenzie Rd., 867/777-2786) has a fantastic collection of paintings and sculptures from throughout the territories. The hospital (867/777-2955) is on the east end of town.

Transportation

Mike Zubko Airport, 12 kilometers (7.5 mi.) south of town, is the hub of air transport in the western Arctic. A cab between the airport and downtown is $32 for one or two passengers. First Air (867/777-2341), a code-share carrier for Air Canada, flies into Inuvik daily from Yellowknife. Sit on the left side of the plane for views of the Mackenzie Mountains.

For a cab, call **United Taxi** (867/777-5050). The cabs don't have meters because fares are set: $6 anywhere around town, $32 to the airport, and $320 to Tuktoyaktuk on the winter road.

AKLAVIK

Theoretically, this community in the middle of the Mackenzie Delta was abandoned more than 35 years ago when the government built Inuvik, but don't tell that to the 700 Dene and Inuvialuit who call Aklavik, 58 kilometers (36 mi.) to the west, home. Wooden sidewalks, a legacy of Aklavik's one-time importance, link the original Hudson's Bay Company post and a mission church (now a small museum) to newer structures, built before the big move east was announced. Many large houses still stand, testimony to the fortunes made by prosperous traders in days gone by. Trails lead in all directions from town, inviting the curious to explore this small delta island.

Tours

Most people arrive in Aklavik as part of a tour from Inuvik with **Arctic Nature Tours** (867/777-3300). On clear days, the 20-minute flight is awe-inspiring. The company offers flights to Aklavik with a one-hour town tour ($160), but a better way to experience the delta is by boat. To boat one-way then fly the other is $185. For independent travelers, this company will arrange flights and advise on accommodation in the town's only hotel.

TUKTOYAKTUK

Most travelers, not satisfied with driving to the end of the road, hop aboard a small plane in Inuvik for the flight along the Mackenzie Delta to Tuktoyaktuk, a small community perched precariously on an exposed gravel strip on the Beaufort Sea. Although it would be a harsh and unforgiving place to live, a visit to "Tuk," as it is sensibly known, is a delightful eye-opener. The community is spread out around **Tuktoyaktuk Harbour** and has spilled over to the gravel beach, where meter-high (three-ft.) waves whipped up by cold Arctic winds roll in

beached boat, Tuktoyaktuk

off the Beaufort Sea and thunder up against the shore. The most dominant natural features of the landscape are **pingos,** massive mounds of ice forced upward by the action of permafrost. The mounds look like mini-volcanoes protruding from the otherwise flat environs. The ice is camouflaged by a natural covering of tundra growth, making the pingos all the more mysterious. Approximately 1,400 pingos dot the coastal plain around Tuk, one of the world's densest concentrations of these geological wonders peculiar to the north.

Around Town

Most visitors see Tuk from the inside of a transporter van driven by accommodating locals who never tire of the same hackneyed questions about living at the end of the earth. The bus stops at *Our Lady of Lourdes,* once part of a fleet of vessels that plied the Arctic delivering supplies to isolated communities. Here also are two mission churches built in the late 1930s. A stop is also made at the Arctic Ocean, where you are encouraged to dip your toes in the water or go for a swim if you really want to impress the folks back home. (Tuk is actually on the Beaufort Sea, an arm of the Arctic Ocean, but who's telling?) For a few extra bucks, you are given some time to explore on your own, including walking along the beach, climbing a nearby pingo, and checking out the well-equipped ocean port.

Practicalities

Tuk is the most popular flightseeing destination from Inuvik, and a variety of trips are offered from Inuvik. Trips start at $195, which includes the return flight (worth the price alone) and a tour of the town. The flight into Tuk is breathtaking—the pilots fly at low altitudes for the best possible views. For those who wish to spend longer in Tuk (there are enough things to do to hold your interest for at least one day), extended tours visit community's unique cool room and include lunch with an Inuvialuit family, for $290 per person. For tour details, contact **Arctic Tour Co.** (867/977-2230) or **Arctic Nature Tours** (867/777-3300).

PAULATUK

Meaning "Place of the Coal" in the local language, Paulatuk, 400 kilometers (250 mi.) east of Inuvik, is a small community 190 Inuvialuit, most of whom live a traditional lifestyle of hunting, trapping, and fishing. A Roman Catholic mission and trading post, established in 1935, attracted Inuvialuit families from camps along the Arctic coast. Their descendants continue living off the abundant natural resources. To the northeast are the **Smoking Hills,** seams of coal, rich with sulfide, that were ignited centuries ago and still burn today, filling the immediate area with distinctively shaped clouds of smoke. Sprawling across Parry Peninsula, to the west of Paulatuk and partly within Nunavut, is **Tuktut Nogait National Park,** the major staging area for the 125,000-strong **Bluenose caribou herd,** which migrates across the north.

Practicalities

The only accommodation in town is the **Paulatuk Hotel** (867/580-3027, $145 pp), with eight rooms that share bathrooms and a small restaurant. The only scheduled flights to Paulatuk are with **Aklak Air** (867/777-3777, www.inuvialuit .com/aklak) from Inuvik.

BANKS ISLAND

Banks Island is one of the best places in the world for viewing musk oxen. Approximately 60,000 (half the world's population and the largest concentration of these shaggy beasts call the island's **Aulavik National Park** home. Separated from the mainland by **Amundsen Gulf,** Banks is the most westerly island in the Canadian Arctic archipelago. Throughout the barren, low, rolling hills that characterize this island flow some major rivers, including the **Thomsen,** the northernmost navigable river in Canada.

Sachs Harbour (Ikaahuk)

The only permanent settlement on Banks Island is Sachs Harbour (pop. 150), at the foot of a low bluff along the southwest coast, 520 kilometers (323 mi.) northeast of Inuvik. The least expensive way to visit Sachs Harbour is on a tour organized by **Arctic Nature Tours** (867/777-3300). Airfare from Inuvik and a town tour is $500 per person, but this tour leaves only if at least four people are interested. Another tour includes airfare, two nights' accommodations, meals, and tours by boat and all-terrain vehicle to see local wildlife populations, including musk oxen, for approximately $1,200 per person. The town has no restaurants, only a small co-op grocery store (closed Sun.). **Aklak Air** (867/777-3777) has a twice-weekly scheduled flight to Sachs Harbour from Inuvik. This flight is used by Arctic Nature Tours, so inquire about cheaper fares.

HOLMAN (ULUQSAQTUUQ)

Most of **Victoria Island,** separated by the Prince of Wales Strait from Banks Island, falls within Nunavut. The exception is the island's western corner, including Diamond Jenness Peninsula, where the community of Holman (pop. 360) lies. Holman is on a gravel beach at the end of horseshoe-shaped Queens Bay and is surrounded by steep bluffs that rise as high as 200 meters (660 ft.). The village was founded around a Hudson's Bay Company post in 1939. Inuit that moved to the post were taught printmaking by a missionary, Reverend Henri Tardi, and to this day printmaking is a major source of income for the community. Holman also has a golf course, the northernmost in the world. Playing a round of golf here is really something to tell the folks back at the country club about; for the record, the course is at a latitude of 70°44' North. In mid-July, the course hosts the **Billy Joss Open** (867/396-3080) attracting entrants from as far away as the United States.

Practicalities

Holman's only hotel is the **Arctic Char Inn** (867/396-3501). Rates are $180 per person, including meals. Scheduled flights into Holman are three times weekly from Yellowknife with **First Air** (867/396-3063).

Yukon Territory

The Yukon sits like a great upside-down wedge—bordered by Alaska, British Columbia, Northwest Territories, and the Arctic Ocean—at the north corner of western Canada. Wilderness and history enriched by the Klondike gold rush combine to create a unique destination, very different from the rest of the country, but easily accessible by plane or by the Alaska Highway.

The territory's 483,450 square kilometers (208,000 sq. mi.) cover under 5 percent of Canada's total land area yet the Yukon is 25 percent larger than California. The massive **St. Elias Mountains** pass through the territory's southwest corner, while the rest of the Yukon is a huge expanse of rolling hills, long narrow lakes, and boreal forests that give way to rolling tundra north of the Arctic Circle. Through the heart of it all flows the **Yukon River**.

Wildlife is present in amazing numbers: 300,000 caribou, 50,000 moose, 22,000 Dall and Stone sheep, 10,000 black bears, 7,000 grizzlies, 4,500 wolves, and 2,000 mountain goats. The human population is just 31,000, almost 75 percent of them living in the capital, **Whitehorse**. The next biggest town is **Dawson City**, site of the world's most frenzied and famous gold rush and now one of the region's premier tourist destinations.

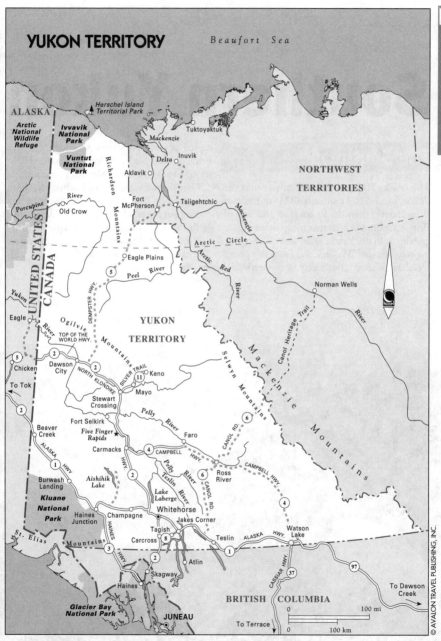

YUKON TERRITORY

Beaufort Sea

ALASKA

Arctic National Wildlife Refuge

Herschel Island Territorial Park

Ivvavik National Park

Vuntut National Park

Tuktoyaktuk

Mackenzie

Delta

Inuvik

Aklavik

NORTHWEST TERRITORIES

Richardson Mountains

Porcupine

River

Old Crow

Fort McPherson

Tsiigehtchic

Arctic Circle

UNITED STATES

CANADA

Yukon

Eagle

River

Eagle Plains

Peel River

Arctic Red River

Mackenzie River

Norman Wells

Ogilvie Mountains

YUKON TERRITORY

DEMPSTER HWY.

5

TOP OF THE WORLD HWY.

Selwyn Mountains

Canol Heritage Trail

Mackenzie Mountains

5

Chicken

To Tok

2

Dawson City

NORTH KLONDIKE

SILVER TRAIL

11

Keno

Mayo

2

Stewart Crossing

Beaver Creek

ALASKA HWY.

1

Fort Selkirk

Five Finger Rapids

Carmacks

Pelly River

4

CAMPBELL HWY.

Faro

CANOL RD.

6

Burwash Landing

Aishihik Lake

2

HAINES

Pelly River

Teslin River

6

Ross River

CANOL RD.

CAMPBELL HWY.

Kluane National Park

Haines Junction

Champagne

Lake Laberge

Whitehorse

Jakes Corner

4

Watson Lake

St. Elias Mountains

Tagish

3

HAINES HWY.

Carcross

8

2

Atlin

Teslin

1

ALASKA HWY.

CASSIAR HWY.

37

97

Haines

Skagway

BRITISH COLUMBIA

To Dawson Creek

Glacier Bay National Park

JUNEAU

To Terrace

0   100 mi

0   100 km

© AVALON TRAVEL PUBLISHING, INC.

Southern Yukon

The Southeast

The Alaska Highway (Alcan) crosses into the Yukon some 520 kilometers (323 mi.) east of Whitehorse, then ducks back in and out of British Columbia a couple more times before crossing into the Yukon again and reaching the highway town of Watson Lake. From this point, travelers either continue east to the territorial capital or complete the loop through northern British Columbia by taking the Cassiar Highway (Hwy. 37) south to Meziadin Junction.

Over the years, the Alaska Highway has been shortened by straightening some sections and cutting out big bends completely. Mileage posts in British Columbia have been replaced to reflect these new distances, but those on the Yukon side haven't—so you'll see a 40-kilometer (25-mi.) discrepancy at the border.

WATSON LAKE

This is the first town in Yukon Territory for all drivers heading north from British Columbia. Even though it's not pretty, it's a welcome sight after the several hundred kilometers on the Cassiar Highway or the all-day ride from Fort Nelson on the Alaska Highway.

Originally inhabited by Kaska Indians, Watson Lake (the town) was created to serve one of a string of airfields constructed across the northern Canada in 1940, and its existence was ensured when the Alcan was routed through to service the airfield. Today Watson Lake functions as the hub of a large area of southern Yukon, southwestern Northwest Territories, and northern British Columbia. With a population of 1,600, it's the third-largest town in the territory.

Sights

Stop first at the **Watson Lake Visitor Reception Centre** (corner of Alaska Hwy. and Robert Campbell Hwy., 867/536-7469, mid-May–mid-Sept. daily 8 A.M.–8 P.M.). Here you'll get a graphic lesson, through photos, displays, dioramas, and a three-projector audiovisual presentation, on the monumental engineering feat that is the Alcan.

Beside the visitors center is the famous **Signpost Forest,** originated in 1942 by a G.I. working on the highway who, when given the task of repainting the road's directional sign, added the direction and mileage to his hometown of Danville, Illinois. Since then, more than 40,000 other signs have been added to the collection with town signs, license plates, posters, pie tins, gold-panning pans, mufflers, driftwood, even flywheels stating where the contributor is from and who he/she is. You can put up your addition personally or take it inside the visitors center and have them put it up for you. The chamber of commerce maintains the site and installs new posts as they're needed.

The nearby **Northern Lights Centre** (867/536-7827) has a planetarium-type theater which takes you on an exploration of the northern lights several times daily in the summer.

Take Eighth Street north a few blocks up from the Alaska Highway to **Wye Lake,** where a trail encircle the lake, complete with a boardwalk platform from which to view migrating shorebirds and resident grebes. If you're traveling with kids, make a stop five kilometers (3.7 mi.) south of town at **Lucky Lake** (June–Aug.), a day-use recreation area complete with a water slide that will land them into the surprisingly warm lake.

Accommodations and Camping

Coming into Watson Lake from the road, you'll be tired and hungry, guaranteed. Half a dozen motels, several campgrounds, and a handful of restaurants are there to serve. **Cedar Lodge Motel** (867/536-7406, www.cedarlodge.yk.net) has standard motel rooms with phones and cable TV for $75 s or d, or pay $85 for a kitchenette. The hands-on owners have also developed suites in a building they moved from an abandoned mining town (from $95 s or d). Also in town is the more modern **Big Horn Hotel** (867/536-2020) with attractively appointed rooms, including kitchen suites, starting at $115 s or d.

Nugget City (867/536-2307, www.nuggetcity.com, May–Oct.) is a large tourist complex 20 kilometers (12 mi.) west of Watson Lake (just past the Cassiar turn-off). The wooden cabins here are spotlessly clean and come with a deck and satellite TV. Even taking into consideration the nondescript interiors, at $94 s or d they are good value. Fancier suites with jetted tubs range $148–188 per night. Part of the operation is a campground (called Baby Nugget RV Park), with facilities (bathroom, laundry, and so on) as good as any along the highway. Serviced sites come with power, water, and satellite TV hookups for $26–35. The on-site restaurant has a good selection of Northern foods and a nice deck.

Other camping options are **Downtown RV Park** (right in the middle of town, 867/536-2646, $15–22) with full hookups and showers, and **Watson Lake Public Campground,** which is three kilometers (1.9 mi.) off the highway at Km 1,025 and has no services for $8 per night.

Food

Both the **Belvedere** (867/536-7712) and **Watson Lake Hotels** (867/536-7781) have coffee shops and dining rooms open from 6 A.M. Both also have bars, the latter decorated with Northern memorabilia.

The **Wolf it Down Restaurant** (20 km/12 mi. west of town, 867/536-2307, May–Oct. 6:30 A.M.–9:30 P.M.) is a touristy place with decent food and an in-house bakery.

WATSON LAKE TO WHITEHORSE

It's 454 kilometers (282 mi.) from Watson Lake to Whitehorse. A pullout at Km 1,163 marks the **Continental Divide** between rivers that drain (via the Mackenzie system) into the Arctic Ocean and those that empty (via the Yukon) into the Pacific.

Dawson Peaks Resort & RV Park (Km 1,282, 867/390-2244, mid-May–mid-Sept.) stands out above other lodges between Watson Lake and Teslin for both location and services. Right on Teslin Lake, it features treed tent sites ($10), RV sites ($18), dorm beds ($15), motel rooms ($59 s or d), and lakeside cabins ($79 s or d). The restaurant not only has good food (entrées $12–19, delicious rhubarb pie $3.50 per slice), it has table settings on a wonderful deck overlooking the lake. Owners David Hett and Carolyn Allen will make you feel welcome, tempting you to make your stop more than a simple overnight stay with canoe and motorboat rentals ($24 and $40, respectively, for a half-day); guiding fishing for trout, pike, and inconnu ($55 per hour); and land and river tours ($55 per hour).

Teslin

Just over halfway between Watson Lake and Whitehorse, Teslin (Km 1,293) is reached after crossing the impressive Nisutlin Bay Bridge (longest on the Alaska Hwy.). Its mostly Tlingit population live a traditional lifestyle: hunting, fishing, trapping, carving, and sewing. The **George Johnston Museum** (867/390-2550, summer daily 9 A.M.–7 P.M., $2.50) has displays native culture, Yukon frontier artifacts, and one-of-a-kind photographs taken 1910–1940 by Johnston, a Tlingit hunter and trapper.

Teslin has the aforementioned **Dawson Peaks Resort & RV Park** as well as the in-town **Yukon Motel** (867/390-2443, www.yukonmotel.com), with biggish rooms for $75 s, $79 d, RV parking ($22 per night), boat rentals, gas, a restaurant, and a room filled with wildlife dioramas. Another camping option is **Teslin Lake Campground** ($8), through town at Km 1,307.

Teslin to Whitehorse

It's 183 kilometers (114 mi.) between Teslin and Whitehorse with the Alaska Highway closely paralleling Teslin Lake for the first 40 kilometers (25 mi.) or so. At the lake's northern outlet is **Johnson's Crossing** (Km 1,346, 867/390-2607, May–mid-Oct.) has the usual Alaska Highway set-up—campground (some sites with electricity), gas, groceries, a restaurant (famous cinnamon buns), and showers.

At Km 1,413, halfway between Jake's Corner and Whitehorse, is **Inn on the Lake** (867/660-5253, www.exceptionalplaces.com, June–Sept. and Dec.–Mar.), the most upscale lodging along the entire Alaska Highway. The main lodge is a peeled-log building with a living room, library, solarium, and spiffy dining room with a vaulted ceiling. Each guest room is decorated with stylish furnishings and has a comfortable bed, quality linens, and a well-appointed bathroom. The Classic Suites ($169 s or d) and Vacation Cottage ($199 s or d) have a luxurious yet woodsy feel.

ATLIN

The small community of Atlin lies 100 kilometers (62 mi.) south Jake's Corner, back over the border in British Columbia. It is British Columbia's northernmost and westernmost settlement. Although isolated from the rest of British Columbia, it is one of that province's most picturesque communities. The glaciated peaks of the Coast Mountains form a stunning backdrop for the town, which is on a gently sloping hill overlooking beautiful 140-kilometer-long (85-mi.) **Atlin Lake.**

Atlin was a boomtown with more than 8,000 people during the 1898 Klondike gold rush, when gold was discovered in nearby Pine Creek. Today they're still finding some color hereabouts, but the town's population has dwindled to about 450.

The highlight of Atlin is the surrounding scenery. Wandering along the lakeshore you'll have outrageous views of sparkling peaks, glaciers, waterfalls, and mountain streams. Tied up on the lake in front of town is the **SS Tarahne,** a 1916 steamer that has been restored. If you want to get out on the lake yourself, contact **Norseman Adventures** (250/651-7535), which rents small motorboats ($20 per hour) and modern houseboats ($625–1,000 for four days) as well as offering guided fishing and wildlife watching trips ($60 per hour).

Sights

Atlin Historical Museum (3rd St. and Trainor St., 250/651-7522, June–early Sept. daily 9 A.M.–5:50 P.M., $3), housed in a 1902 schoolhouse, lets you relive the excitement of the gold rush. Scattered through town are many historic buildings and artifacts pretty much untouched from the gold-rush era.

South of Atlin along Warm Springs Road are various lakes, camping areas, and, at the end of the road, **warm springs.** The springs bubble out of the ground at a pleasant 29°C (84°F) into shallow pools surrounded by flower-filled meadows.

Practicalities

Holding a prime downtown, lakefront location is the **Atlin Inn** (1st St., 250/651-7546 or 800/682-8546) which comprises 18 motel rooms ($115 s or d) and a string of similarly priced kitchen-equipped cottages. It also has a restaurant open daily at 7 A.M. and a lounge with a great patio.

RVers can park their rigs on the lakeshore at the **Norseman Adventures** (250/651-7535) marina for $16 per night, including power and water hookups. For more primitive camping, the first of four spots through Atlin to the south is **Pine Creek Campground** ($7), with pit toilets and firewood (no drinking water).

CARCROSS AND VICINITY

Rather drive straight through to Whitehorse, many travelers hang a left a Jake's Corner to Carcross (a contraction of "caribou crossing"), on Highway 2 between Skagway (Alaska) and Whitehorse. This picturesque village of 400 sits at the north end of Lake Bennett, which forms the headwaters of the Yukon River. It was an important stopping point for miners during the Klondike gold rush and today is chock-a-block with buildings from this era.

Sights

Carcross lost its most prized possession, the *Tutshi* sternwheeler, to fire in 1990, but there still remains a lot to see. Start by visiting the **Yukon Visitor Reception Centre** (867/821-4431, mid-May–late Sept. daily 8 A.M.–8 P.M.), housed in a railway station that served passengers along the White Pass & Yukon Route (WP&YR). It contains not only brochures from all over the Yukon, but also fine historical exhibits. WP&YR trains crossed the original "swing bridge" in town, built to allow the riverboats to pass; walk across the bridge for a look back. A footbridge is just north of this. In business since 1909, **Mathew Watson General Store** (867/821-3501) is the oldest store in the Yukon, and the flamingo-pink exterior makes it easy to find. Inside are old fixtures (including classic cash registers), along with trinkets, gifts, and an ice cream shop. In the old Carcross **cemetery,** two kilometers (1.2 mi.) away, rest such stampede-starting notables as Skookum Jim, Tagish Charlie, and Kate Carmack.

Accommodations and Food

Two of the best local lodgings are on Spirit Lake, a 10-minute drive north of Carcross toward Whitehorse. **Spirit Haven B&B** (867/821-4722) has three bedrooms with shared bath for $70 s, $95 including a delicious full breakfast. At **Spirit Lake Wilderness Resort** (867/821-4337, www.spiritlakeyukon.com) the lakeside cabins ($59 s or d) are my pick for the views and rustic charm, although they don't electricity or running water (share shower facilities). Other choices are cottages ($59 s, $69 d) and motel rooms ($89 s, $99 d) that lack the atmosphere but are more comfortable. Tent sites are $14 and hookups $17–20. Activities include canoeing and horseback riding and there's an on-site restaurant.

Wheaton River Wilderness B&B (867/333-1364, www.wheatonriver.net) is truly in the wilderness, 22 kilometers (13.7 mi.) along Annie Lake Road, which branches off Highway 2 north of Spirit Lake. The lodge is solar-powered and a wood stove is used for cooking. Accommodation is in the main building or a riverfront cabin,

with both options laid out with wooden furniture carved by the owners. Rates are $90 s or d, which includes a cooked breakfast. Dinner is available for an additional $15, or cook up a feast yourself on the wood stove or barbecue.

Whitehorse

Whitehorse is a friendly oasis in the heart of an unforgiving land. With 20,000 residents, Whitehorse is the largest city in northern Canada. It squats on the western bank of the Yukon, hemmed in by high bluffs that create something

of a wind tunnel along the river. To the east, the bare rounded hulk of Grey Mountain (1,494 m/4,900 ft.) fills the horizon. Whitehorse has its share of gold-rush history and nostalgia, but is not dominated by it; as the capital of Yukon

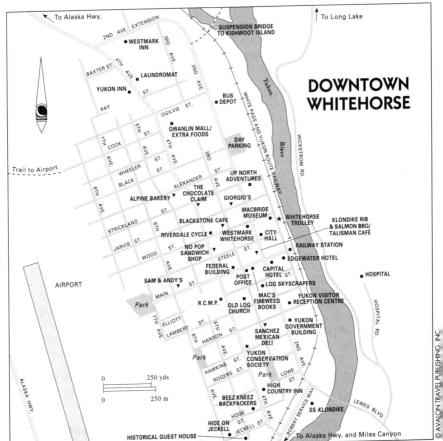

DOWNTOWN WHITEHORSE

© AVALON TRAVEL PUBLISHING, INC.

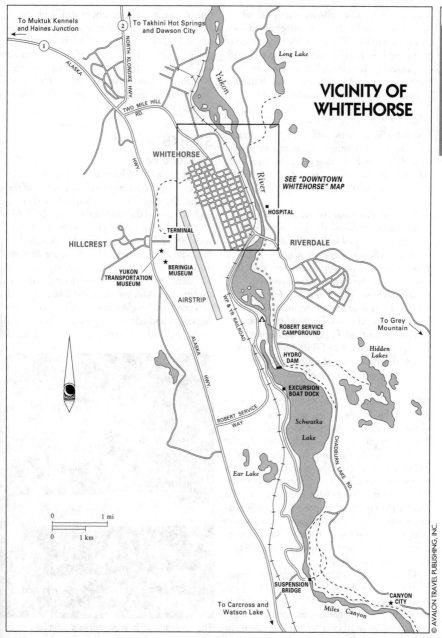

VICINITY OF WHITEHORSE

SEE "DOWNTOWN WHITEHORSE" MAP

To Muktuk Kennels and Haines Junction

To Takhini Hot Springs and Dawson City

Long Lake

WHITEHORSE

NORTH KLONDIKE HWY.

ALASKA

TWO MILE HILL RD.

HWY.

Yukon River

HOSPITAL

TERMINAL

HILLCREST

RIVERDALE

YUKON TRANSPORTATION MUSEUM

BERINGIA MUSEUM

AIRSTRIP

WP & YR RAILROAD

ALASKA HWY

To Grey Mountain

ROBERT SERVICE CAMPGROUND

HYDRO DAM

Hidden Lakes

EXCURSION BOAT DOCK

ROBERT SERVICE WAY

Schwatka Lake

CHADBURN LAKE RD.

Ear Lake

MOON

0   1 mi

0   1 km

SUSPENSION BRIDGE

CANYON CITY

To Carcross and Watson Lake

Miles Canyon

YUKON TERRITORY

© AVALON TRAVEL PUBLISHING, INC.

Territory for the past half-century, this small city has a brash, modern frontier energy all its own. It's easy to slip into Whitehorse's strong stream of hustle and bustle, which seems to keep pace with the powerful Yukon itself. Yet the town also has a warm, homespun vitality to it, like huddling around the fire on a cold northern night.

History

The name Whitehorse was given to the treacherous rapids encountered by stampeders, who likened them to the flowing manes of Appaloosas. An entry in an early edition of the *Klondike Nugget* described the scene:

> *Many men who ran these dangerous waters had never handled a boat in their lives until they stopped at Lake Bennett to figure out which end of their oar went into the water. . . . The boats filed into that tremendous first section of the canyon, dodged the whirlpool in the middle, rushed down the second section of the canyon, tossed around for a while in the seething water of the rapids, made that stupendous turn into White Horse, as with rapidly accelerating speed they plunged into the final chaos of angry water. . . .*

A few men drowned; many managed to hang onto their lives but lost their boats and grubstakes. Regulations were put in place that allowed only expert handlers to pilot the rapids. Undoubtedly, this saved countless lives and supplies in the more than 7,000 boats that passed through in the first, crazy rush to the Klondike. Soon after, an eight-kilometer (five-mi.) horse-drawn tramway was built around the rapids to the present site of Whitehorse, where goods were reloaded into boats to complete the journey to Dawson City. A tent city sprang up at the tramway's lower end, and Whitehorse was born.

The town's role as a transportation hub began in 1900, when the WP&YR reached Whitehorse, finally connecting Skagway (Alaska) to the Yukon. At Whitehorse, passengers and freight transferred to riverboats for the trip down the Yukon River to Dawson City. In 1942–1943

this role grew substantially, as did Whitehorse along with it, during the construction of the Alaska Highway. In 1953, Whitehorse eclipsed declining Dawson in population and importance and became the territorial seat of government. Whitehorse today thrives on highway traffic, territorial administrative duties, and its function as a supply center for Yukon mines.

SIGHTS

SS Klondike

Start your visit to Whitehorse with a tour of the largest sternwheeler ever to ply the waters of the Yukon, the *Klondike*, which is dry-docked along 2nd Avenue and the south end of town (867/667-3910, mid-May–mid-Sept. daily 9 A.M.–6 P.M., adult $5, senior $4.50, child $3). Launched in 1929 and rebuilt after it sank in 1936, the *Klondike* made 15 round-trips a season, requiring one and a half days and 40 cords of wood for the downstream trip to Dawson, four and a half days and 120 cords back to Whitehorse. The *Klondike* is beautifully and authentically restored, right down to the 1937 *Life* magazines and the food stains

The SS *Klondike* is Whitehorse's premier attraction.

COURTESY OF YUKON GOVERNMENT

on the waiters' white coats. Bridges erected along the road to Dawson in the mid-1950s blocked the steamer's passage and she has sat in the same spot since her last run in 1955. The best way to learn about the vessel and her colorful history is by joining a tour (included with admission) that runs every 30 minutes, proceeding from the boiler, freight, and engine deck, up to the dining room and first-class cabins, and finally up to the bridge.

MacBride Museum

North of the visitors center and across the road from the river is the excellent MacBride Museum (1124 1st Ave. at Wood St., 867/667-2709, mid-May–Sept. Mon.–Fri. 10 A.M.–9 P.M., Sat.–Sun. 10 A.M.–7 P.M., rest of year Thurs.–Sat. noon–5 P.M., adult $5, senior $4, child $3.50). The main building is a sod-roofed log cabin filled with historical items, including stuffed Yukon wildlife and hundreds of gold-rush photographs. Surrounding it are other buildings and equipment: the old government telegraph office, engine no. 51 from the WP&YR, Sam McGee's cabin, and even a one-ton copper nugget.

Directly across from the museum is the **Waterfront Trolley** that runs along the waterfront daily in the summer and costs $1.

Yukon Beringia Interpretive Centre

This dramatic multimedia center (Alaska Hwy., 867/667-8855 May–Sept., daily 9 A.M.–6 P.M., rest of the year Sunday 1–5 P.M., adult $6, senior $5, child $4) out by the airport contains life-size exhibits of animals from the last ice age, including a spectacular 12,000-year-old, four-meter-tall (12-ft.) woolly mammoth skeleton. Visitors will learn about the animals that once roamed the north through exhibits, computer kiosks, dioramas, and a fascinating 30-minute film. A reconstruction of a 24,000-year-old archaeological site is also here, plus a gift shop and café.

Yukon Transportation Museum

Located next to the Beringia Interpretive Centre, this is one of the finest museums in the north (30 Electra Cres., 867/668-4792, summer daily 10 A.M.–6 P.M., adult $4.50, senior and child $3.50). You could easily spend a few hours examining the many excellent displays and watching the long historical videos. Here's just a sample: Look up to view *Queen of the Yukon,* the first commercial aircraft in the territory, hanging from the ceiling; take the Golden Stairs up to the second floor, where murals and artifacts re-create the gold rush from Skagway to Dawson; sit in Lake Annie, a WP&YR railcar, and watch the 30-minute video while the model train circles the track; and check out the Alcan room with a fascinating video on the highway's construction. Out front is a DC-3 that acts as the world's largest weathervane.

Schwatka Lake and Miles Canyon

Cross the bridge beside the *Klondike* and take Lewis Boulevard south or walk along the trail riverside trail south 4.5 kilometers (2.8 mi.) toward the **Whitehorse Dam** that created Schwatka Lake, tamed the once-feared White Horse Rapids, and now provides electricity for the city. The world's longest wooden **fishway** (366 m/1,200 ft.) allows fish to get around the dam and up to their spawning grounds upriver. Three underwater windows inside the fishway building (867/633-5965, June–early Sept. 8:30 A.M.–8:30 P.M.) give you a good look at the chinook (king) salmon (late July–early Sept. is best).

From the dam, continue south on Chadburn Lake Road to the head of the lake where the Yukon River flows through spectacular Miles Canyon. A path along the canyon leads to the distinctive **Lowe Suspension Bridge** (1923), first bridge across the Yukon—the views are superb.

Continue two kilometers (1.2 mi.) beyond the bridge, staying on the east side, to reach the site of **Canyon City,** which slipped into oblivion after the opening of the railway in 1900 put an end to river travel above Whitehorse.

As an alternative to accessing these sights by road, consider walking. It's 10-kilometers (6.2-mi.) round-trip from downtown, with the option of crossing the suspension bridge and returning along the west bank of the river, or jumping aboard a city transit bus (hourly along South Access Rd.) to get back to town. Another way to see the lake and surrounding sights is aboard the **MV *Schwatka*** (867/668-4716, $24), a tour boat that departs June–August daily at 2 P.M. (plus

6:30 P.M. in July) for two-hour cruises. The departure point is one kilometer (0.6 mi.) south of downtown on the *west* side of the dam.

Takhini Hot Springs

These odorless (no sulfur) hot springs (867/633-2706, mid-May–mid-June daily noon–10 P.M., mid-June–mid-Sept. daily 8 A.M.–10 P.M.) bubble out of the ground at 36°C (96°F) north of Whitehorse. They have been developed and are as popular with locals as they are with visitors. All-day access is adult $7, senior $5.50, child $5.25. (If you don't want to pay, follow the overflow "creek" to where some locals have dug out a public pool.) The attached café has some of the best chicken soup north of Vancouver. The adjacent campground costs $14.50 for tents and $17–22 for RVs and trailers (this is a good place to spend the night, take an early dip, then hit the road to Dawson). Get to Takhini by driving 18 kilometers (11.2 mi.) north from Whitehorse toward Dawson City, then take the 10-kilometer (6.2-mi.) side road to the west (it's well signposted).

RECREATION AND SHOPPING
Historical and Nature Walks

Whitehorse is small enough that you can cover downtown by foot. A pleasant paved **walkway** follows the Yukon River from the SS *Klondike* to the north end of town.

To learn more about local history, take a volunteer-led 45-minute historical walking tour (Mon.–Sat. at 9 A.M., 11 A.M., 1 P.M., and 4 P.M.) of downtown Whitehorse buildings offered by the **Yukon Historical & Museums Association.** It leaves from Donnenworth House (3126 3rd Ave., 867/667-4704). If the tour times don't fit into your plans, stop by the Donnenworth House, pick up the walking tour book, and take a self-guided tour.

The **Yukon Conservation Society** (302 Hawkins St., 867/668-5678, Mon.–Fri. 10 A.M.–4 P.M.) leads a variety of hikes, from two to six hours, several times a day in July and early August. One of the most interesting is a two-hour trip to Miles Canyon, or if the family is with you, the kids may enjoy joining the as-

sociation's Ed-Ventures program for a morning. The hikes are free; bring bug spray, wear sturdy boots, and have a lunch for the longer excursions. You can also buy self-guiding trail booklets at its office and set out on your own.

Other Recreation Opportunities

Whitehorse is home to the Yukon Campus of the **National Outdoor Leadership School** (867/668-3578; www.nols.edu). From this base, NOLS leads a range of courses that involve backpacking, canoeing (its specialty), and leadership courses in remote parts of the Yukon.

Whitehorse is relatively flat, making biking easy and fun. Rent mountain bikes from **Up North Adventures** (103 Strickland St., 867/667-7035) or **Fireweed Hikes and Bikes** (102 Wood St., 867/668-7313) or take a guided ride with the latter company. If you're interested in joining up with some locals, drop by **Riverdale Cycle** (310 Wood St., 867/668-7505) and ask about evening group rides after the shop closes at 6 P.M.

FLOATING THE YUKON

Every year hardy souls re-create the route taken by stampeders heading to Dawson and float the Yukon River from Whitehorse. The most authentic way to travel is by canoe, which takes 12–15 days. This is easily arranged; several outfits in Whitehorse supply everything required at a reasonable price.

Kanoe People (1st Ave. and Strickland St., 867/668-4899, www.kanoepeople.com) has been around the longest (since 1974), and rents canoes for $25 per day or $150 per week. They specialize in one-way rentals to Carmacks or Dawson and guided tours, such as an eight-day river trip with meals and accommodations for $1,600. **Up North Adventures** (103 Strickland St., 867/667-7035, www.upnorth.yk.ca) also offers canoes rentals (as well as bike and kayak rentals) with a local drop-off and pick-up service perfect for a single day on the river. For example, pay $55 pp for a full-day rental and return transportation from Lake Laberge.

Frank Turner, a Yukon Quest winner, offers summertime **dog mushing** demonstrations and tours at **Muktuk Kennels** (west of Whitehorse toward Haines Jct., 867/393-1799, www.muktuk .com). In summer, tours of the kennels take place 7 A.M.–1 P.M. ($25), in fall (Aug.–Nov.) you can join a training run aboard an ATV ($50), and then in winter the action really cranks up with options that run from a full-day mushing trip ($175 pp) to joining Frank and his crew on the road as they compete in the Yukon Quest.

Shopping

Whitehorse is a great place to shop, particularly if you've just arrived from Skagway and are accustomed to paying in greenbacks. The favorable exchange rate doesn't hurt, and the selection is great.

A number of fine galleries are scattered around town. The Northern Fibres Guild produces a free booklet that describes local artists with illustrations of their work; it's available at the Visitors Reception Centre. Well worth a visit are the **North End Gallery** (118 1st Ave., 867/393-3590) and the **Midnight Sun Gallery** (250 Main St., 867/668-4350), the latter featuring the brightly colored, Northern-themed paintings of Ted Harrison.

Folknits (2151 2nd Ave., 867/668-7771) sells spinning fiber and finished knitwear made from *quviuq,* the fine underhair of the musk ox. Look for the log cabin with two moose on the roof.

ENTERTAINMENT AND EVENTS

Frantic Follies is one of many vaudeville revues along the route north that is styled on the stage shows that entertained stampeders back in the days of the Klondike gold rush. The Follies are performed nightly at the Westmark Whitehorse (2nd Ave. and Wood St., 867/668-2042, June–early Sept. nightly 7 P.M. and 9:15 P.M.; adult $20, child $10).

Whitehorse has no lack of rowdy bars and none are as popular as **"The Cap"** (in the Capital Hotel, 103 Main St., 867/667-2565)—music central for Whitehorse, with rock bands seven nights a week.

Yukon Brewing Company (102 Copper Rd., 867/668-4183) is the only brewery in the territory. Free tours (with samples) are offered daily at 11 A.M. and 4 P.M. and a gift shop is open daily 11 A.M.–6 P.M.

One of the Yukon's biggest events is the **Yukon Quest** (867/668-4711, www. yukonquest.com) a 1,600-kilometer (1,000-mi.) dog-mushing race between Whitehorse and Fairbanks held each February. As the race is winding down, Whitehorse spins into action with the **Frostbite Music Festival** (867/668-4921), featuring an eclectic mix of concerts, dances, and workshops.

The summer solstice (June 21) is celebrated with a **Midnight Sun Golf Tournament** at Mountainview Golf Course (867/633-6020). **Canada Day** (July 1) features a parade, followed in mid-July by the **Whitehorse Rodeo** with bronc and bull rides, calf roping, steer wrestling, team roping, and barrel racing. Say goodbye to summer on the last full weekend in August at the **Klondyke Harvest Fair,** where you'll see crafts, livestock, fruits, veggies, and more.

ACCOMMODATIONS AND CAMPING

Whitehorse has a surprising number of motels and hotels for its size: 23, accounting for over 900 rooms. The competition, of course, works to the traveler's advantage, and some of the digs are actually affordable.

Under $50

Beez Kneez Bakpakers (408 Hoge St., 867/456-2333, www.bzkneez.com) has beds for $20 in dorm rooms and private rooms (two single beds). Other facilities include a living room, a communal kitchen, laundry facilities, free use of bikes, and Internet access. **Hide on Jeckell** (410 Jeckell St., 867/633-4933, www.hide-on-jeckell.com) is a similar set-up, with all the same services on offer.

$50–100

Historical Guest House (5128 5th Ave., 867/668-3907, www.yukongold.com, $75 s, $85 d) is a comfortable downtown home that was built in 1908 and has been extensively restored, exposing much of the original hand-hewn log work. Each of the two upstairs guest rooms has its own bathroom while downstairs is a kitchen and living area and out back is a garden and barbecue. Rates include a light, self-serve breakfast. The owners live next door.

Barton's B&B (19 Boxwood Cres., 867/668-7075, www.bartonsbb.com, $89–98 s, $98–110 d) is ideally situated across the river from downtown and overlooking a small lake. My favorite of the three guestrooms is the Fireweed Room, which has a private entrance and enjoys an easterly exposure that catches the morning sun. Guests have use of a kitchen, barbecue, and laundry, and rates include breakfast.

If you're planning on traveling as far north as Whitehorse, you're more adventurous than most travelers, so why not do something really unique and stay on a ranch with 100 mushing dogs? You can at **Muktuk Cabins** (west of Whitehorse toward Haines Jct., 867/393-1799, www.muktuk.com), on the property of mushing legend Frank Turner. The smallest wood cabins are $65 s or d and larger ones, with woodstoves, are $85. Meals are provided at an extra charge ($41 per day for three hot meals). The property is right on the Takhini River and in addition to touring the facility, there are canoe rentals, hiking, and trail riding.

$100–150

My choice in this price range for downtown hotel accommodation is the **High Country Inn** (4051 4th Ave., 867/667-4471 or 800/554-4471, www.highcountryinn.ca), a large and well-appointed hostelry with a variety of accommodations, starting at $119 s or $139 d for standard rooms, and going all the way up to $229 for a Jacuzzi suite. The hotel has a fitness room, a business center with Internet access, and its own airport shuttle. Downstairs is a Western-style saloon where you can pan for gold, dine on Northern dishes, or enjoy a cold one on the patio.

Hawkins House (303 Hawkins St., 867/668-7638, www.hawkinshouse.yk.ca, $129 s, $149 d, breakfast an extra $7 pp) is Whitehorse's most luxurious bed-and-breakfast. The property features hardwood floors and high ceilings throughout. Each of the guest rooms is themed differently, but all feature a bright, Victorian color scheme

and come with a well-appointed en suite bathroom that has a jetted tub with bathrobes at the ready. As you may expect, breakfast is memorable. Dishes incorporate many local delicacies—moose sausage, smoked salmon, rose-hip jelly, and more—prepared by the hosts.

Campgrounds

The prime choice for tenters (no RVs allowed) is **Robert Service Campground,** a two-kilometer (1.2-mi.) drive or 20-minute walk south of town along the river (South Access Rd., 867/668-3721, May–Sept., $14). It has a small store and showers. Government-run **Wolf Creek Campground** ($8) 11 kilometers (6.8 mi.) south of Whitehorse along the Alaska Highway, has campsites for both tents and RVs (but no hookups), a nature trail, water, outhouses, and cooking shelters.

Near the south entrance to town, **Hi Country RV Park** (867/667-7445 or 877/458-3806, www.hicountryrv.ca) is one of a half-dozen private campgrounds spread along the Alaska Highway within a five-minute drive of downtown. It has 130 sites spread among the trees, modern shower facilities, a laundry, RV wash, dump station, and convenience store. Farther south, **Pioneer RV Park** (867/668-5944, www.pioneer-rv-park.com) has a similar setting as well as an on-site mechanic, discounted fuel for guests, and high-speed Internet access linked to every site. Both parks charge a reasonable $17–24 per night.

FOOD

Coffeehouses and Bakeries

Even though Whitehorse isn't a latte type of town, the coffee at **Midnight Sun Coffee Roaster** (4168 4th Ave., 867/633-4563) is as good as you'll find anywhere. Roasted in-house, it comes with locally inspired monikers like Sam McGee's Black. Grab a cup, along with a blueberry muffin, and with the smell of roasting beans filling the air, sit down with the *Whitehorse Daily Star* to catch up on the world. Also well worth a visit is **The Chocolate Claim** (305 Strickland St., 867/667-2202), an arty space with handmade chocolates, freshly baked sunflower bread, sandwiches, savory soups, and cappuccino.

In a two-story log building just off 4th Avenue on the north side of downtown, **Alpine Bakery** (411 Alexander St., 867/668-6871, Mon.–Sat. 8 A.M.–6 P.M.) bakes wholesome European-style breads with organic ingredients, but they aren't cheap. Also here is a café and deli.

Cheap and Cheerful

No Pop Sandwich Shop (312 Steele St., 867/668-3227, Mon.–Sat. 9 A.M.–8:30 P.M., Sun. 10 A.M.–3 P.M.) looks like a dive outside, but inside you'll find a homey setting with reasonable prices and good food. Breakfast includes eggs Benedict, crepes, and omelets; it also offers a popular Sunday brunch. The lunch menu has a variety of wholesome yet inexpensive sandwiches and there are always a couple of specials around $10 for dinner. It's licensed to sell liquor but, as the name suggests, there's no pop.

The **Loose Moose Café** (Yukon Inn, 4220 4th Ave., 867/668-2527, Mon.–Sat. 7 A.M.–9 P.M., Sun. 8 A.M.–9 P.M.) is at the north end of downtown. It does some good omelets and eggs Benedict for under $10. The rest of the day, there are no surprises (burgers, pizza, steaks) on a menu where most dishes are under $18.

Dinner Delicacies

Right downtown, dining at the **Yukon Mining Company** (High Country Inn, 4051 4th Ave., 867/667-4471, 7 A.M.–9:30 P.M.) combines Northern favorites with a clean, comfortable Western atmosphere and reasonable prices. The best choices focus on classic dishes with a Northern twist such as a caribou burger ($13) and reindeer sausage penne ($17). Most steak and seafood mains are under $20. It also has a heated deck and a trough in which to try your hand at gold-panning between courses.

Housed in Whitehorse's oldest commercial building, the **Klondike Rib & Salmon BBQ** (2116 2nd Ave., 867/667-7554) has a family-friendly atmosphere of long tables covered with checked tablecloths and a finger-lickin' menu. The house specialty is barbecued ribs ($17), but you'll also find steaks, Caesar salad, smoked salmon, halibut fish & chips, miner's soup with caribou sausage, and bumbleberry pie. It's busy, noisy, fun, and tasty. Next door, the **Talisman Café** (2112 2nd Ave., 867/667-2736, Mon.–Wed. 9 A.M.–7 P.M., Thurs.–Sat. 9 A.M.–9 P.M., Sun. 10 A.M.–3 P.M.) is very different. The atmosphere is heady and the food runs the entire spectrum—from bannock and jam ($3) at breakfast to couscous salad ($7) and a Mediterranean platter ($18) in the evening.

Sanchez Mexican Deli (211 Hanson St., 867/668-5858, Mon.–Sat. 11:30 A.M.–3:30 P.M. and 4:30–9:30 P.M.) is a casual, quiet place with familiar Mexican favorites. Sides of salsa and guacamole are made in-house and are delicious. Everything is under $15. Also on the international front is **Giorgio's** (202 Motor Inn, 206 Jarvis St., 867/668-4050, daily 4:30–11 P.M.), an upscale restaurant with classic Italian cuisine.

INFORMATION

The **Yukon Visitor Reception Centre** (Hanson St. and 2nd Ave., 867/667-3084, May–Sept. daily 8 A.M.–8 P.M., rest of year Mon.–Fri. 9 A.M.–4:30 P.M.) promotes both Whitehorse and the Yukon. The **City of Whitehorse** website (www.city.whitehorse.yk.ca) is a handy pre-trip reference.

Books and Bookstores

The excellent **Whitehorse Public Library** (2nd Ave., 867/667-5228, Mon.–Fri. 10 A.M.–9 P.M., Sat. 10 A.M.–9 P.M., Sun. 1–9 P.M.) is directly across from the visitors center. It has a good selection of Northern literature, newspapers from around the world, and public Internet access.

Mac's Fireweed Books (203 Main St., 867/668-6104, www.yukonbooks.com) is the biggest and most complete bookstore in the Yukon, with a large selection of local- and general-interest books, children's books, and magazines. It's open daily until midnight in the summer. If you can't find what you're looking for using the in-store searchable database at **Well-Read Books** (4194 4th Ave., 867/393-2987, www.wellreadbooks .yk.net), the knowledgeable staff will lead you in the right direction when it comes to looking through their used book collection.

TRANSPORTATION

By Air

The airport is right above town on the bluff. You can't miss the "world's largest weathervane"—the restored DC-3 (mounted on a moveable pedestal) that points its nose into the wind. Get to the airport by going north along 4th Avenue to the Alaska Highway and take a left, or go south out 2nd Avenue and turn right. Most hotels provide a shuttle, or you can catch a cab for around $12 to downtown.

For a city of its size, Whitehorse has an astounding number of regional and even international flights. **Air Canada** (888/247-2262) has service to and from Vancouver several times a day. **Air North** (867/668-2228) has expanded greatly in recent years and now has flights to Whitehorse from Edmonton, Calgary, Vancouver, and Juneau, as well as onward flights to Dawson City, Inuvik, and Fairbanks. **First Air** (867/695-2020) has scheduled service between Whitehorse and Yellowknife (NWT) three times a week.

By Bus

The **Whitehorse Bus Depot** (2nd Ave. behind Qwanlin Mall, 867/668-2223) is the northern terminus for **Greyhound.** In summer, one bus a day (departs 1 P.M.) heads south along the Alaska Highway.

The only bus service that continues west from Whitehorse to Alaska is **Alaska Direct Bus Line** (867/668-4833 or 800/770-6652), to Anchorage (US$175) and Fairbanks (US$150). **Alaska Overland** (867/667-7896) runs a summer-only daily scheduled service between Whitehorse and Skagway for $42 each way.

Dawson City Courier and Taxi (867/993-6688, www.dawsonbus.ca) runs vans between Whitehorse and Dawson City daily in the summer; $94 each way or $168 round-trip.

Getting Around

Whitehorse Transit (867/668-7433, Mon.–Sat. 6 A.M.–7 P.M., Fri. to 10 P.M.; $1.50) operates a citywide public bus service. Pick up a schedule at the visitor centre or from the drivers. Day passes are available from drivers for $4, as are transfers. All routes begin and end beside Canadian Tire, opposite Qwanlin Mall. Bus stops are clearly marked with blue-and-white signs.

Local taxi companies are **5th Avenue Taxi** (867/667-4111), **Whitehorse Taxi** (867/393-6543), and **Yellow Cab** (867/668-4811).

All major car-rental companies are represented at the airport. If you're planning on renting a vehicle in Whitehorse, check mileage allowances. Not all companies include unlimited travel. For example, **Budget** charges $60 a day and $330 a week for an economy vehicle, with a maximum of 150 free kilometers (93 mi.) per day. **Norcan** (867/668-2137, www.norcan.yk.ca) is a local company with competitive rates.

Whitehorse is a popular starting point for European travelers who want to explore the Yukon and Alaska in a campervan, so you'll find plenty of choices. Plan on spending around $900 per week for a truck and camper, or $1,400 per week for a 24-foot motor home, both with 100 kilometers (62 mi.) free per day. Local rental companies include **Big Bear Adventure Tours** (867/633-5642 or 888/663-5657, www.helloyukon.com), **CanaDream Campers** (867/668-3610, www.canadream.com), **Klondike Recreational Rentals** (867/668-2200, www.klondike-rv.com), and **Motorhome Vacation Rentals** (867/668-3900 or 888/999-9450, www.motorhomevacation.com).

Whitehorse to Beaver Creek

Before leaving Whitehorse, you need to decide whether to take the Alaska Highway straight through to Alaska or continue north to Dawson City then continue along the Top of the World Highway which loops back down to the Alaska Highway at Tok. The latter option adds less than 200 kilometers (120 mi.) to the distance between Whitehorse and Tok and Dawson City, a must-stop on any Northern itinerary. The entire loop, taking in Dawson and Tok, is 1,480 kilometers (920 mi.).

This section covers the direct route to Alaska, along the Alaska Highway to Beaver Creek. The total distance is 460 kilometers (187 mi.). Haines Junction is the only town of any consequence en route, beyond which the highway parallels Kluane National Park.

Whitehorse to Haines Junction

It's an easy 160-kilometers (100-mi.) drive to Haines Junction from the capital. The scenery doesn't really hot up until the highway closes in on Haines Junction, when the Kluane Icefield Ranges and the foothills of the St. Elias Moun-

tains start to dominate the view; when it's clear, Mount Hubbard (4,577 m/15,000 ft.) loom high and white straight ahead.

A worthwhile stop is Km 1,604, 21 kilometers (13 mi.) east of Haines Junction. Here a log bridge dating to the early 1900s has been rebuilt. Walk out onto it to compare the log action with the steel-supported highway bridge.

Government campgrounds between Whitehorse and Haines Junction are located at Km 1,543; Km 1,602; and Km 1,628.

HAINES JUNCTION

Established in 1942 as a base camp for Alaska Highway construction, this town of 850 is the largest between Whitehorse and Tok and is the gateway to Kluane National Park, the most accessible of the Yukon's three national parks. It's also the first town north of Haines (Alaska), so sees a lot of traffic from the ferry passing through.

Sights

At the village square near the intersection of the

driving the Alaska Highway

COURTESY OF YUKON GOVERNMENT

Alaska and Haines Highways, a grotesque sculpture of mountains, mammals, and humans has been placed. Ironically, it's part of a Yukon beautification program. It looks more like a misshapen cupcake with really ugly icing. Here you can also read the signboards describing the history and attractions of the Haines Junction area and sign your name in the gigantic guest book. Just up the road toward Whitehorse is **Our Lady of the Wake Church,** built in 1954 by a Catholic priest who converted an old Quonset hut by adding a wooden front, a shrine on top, and a steeple with bell in back.

Accommodations

Haines has a bunch of motels to choose from (listed in the territorial tourism guide), along with the following three choices.

Paddle Wheel Adventures (867/634-2683, www.paddlewheeladventures.com) rents Quonset-style huts, each with a cooking facilities and a private bathroom, for a reasonable $50 per night. Primarily outfitters, they also rent canoes and bikes and lead guided raft and fishing tours.

The Cabin B&B (27 km/16.8 mi. south of Haines Jct. on Hwy. 3, 867/634-2626, $74 s, $80 d) comprises five rustic cabins, each with a kitchenette and deck with views extending over Kluane National Park.

The nonsmoking **Raven Hotel** (867/634-2500, May–Sept., $110 s, $125 d including breakfast) offers the 12 nicest motel rooms in town, a fine-dining restaurant, and an art gallery/gift shop. You can't miss it; the Raven looks like a modular mansion, right in the middle of town.

Camping

Right downtown, **Kluane RV Kampground** (867/634-2709 or 866/634-6789) separates tenters from RVers, but offers lots of services for both. For in-town camping, the tent sites ($12) are pleasant, with lots of trees, and barbeques and firewood supplied. The sites with hookups ($15–20) come with cable TV and Internet access. Other amenities include a shower block, laundry, car and RV wash, grocery store, and gas. Nearest public camping is at **Pine Lake** ($8), seven kilometers (4.3 mi.) east of town on

the Alaska Highway with drinking water, firewood, picnic tables, playground, and decent fishing in the lake.

Food

Village Bakery & Deli (867/634-2867) is a popular hangout, with delicious muffins, strudels, doughnuts, and cheese sticks, as well as breads, croissant sandwiches, soups, quiche, sourdough pizzas, lasagna, meat pies, and whatever else the good cooks feel like creating.

Several of the hotels also serve meals, including—most notably—the **Raven Hotel** (867/634-2500, May–Sept. daily 5:30–10 P.M.). The menu here changes daily, but the choices are always varied and thoughtful. Considering the remote location, the owners do a great job of sourcing fresh produce to go with lots of local game and seafood. Entrées are in the $15–22 range. Views to the snowcapped peaks of Kluane National Park are a bonus. Reservations recommended.

The motto at **Madley's General Store** (103 Haines Rd., 867/634-2200) is We've Got It All, and it's not too far from the truth. Here you can pick up groceries, fruit and meat, deli sandwiches, camping supplies, and more; the bank, an ATM, and a post office are also inside.

KLUANE NATIONAL PARK

The lofty ice-capped mountains of southwest Yukon, overflowing with glaciers and flanked by lower ranges rich in wildlife, have been set aside as 21,980-square-kilometer (8,490-sq.-mi.) Kluane (Kloo-AH-nee) National Park. Although the Alaska and Haines Highways, which run along the fringe of the park, make it accessible, Kluane is a wilderness hardly touched by human hands; once you leave the highways you'll see few other people. No roads run into the park itself, so to experience the true magnificence of this wilderness you must embark on an overnight hike or take a flightseeing trip.

The Land

The St. Elias Range, running from Alaska through the Yukon to British Columbia, is the highest mountain range in North America and the second-highest coastal range in the world (only the Andes are higher). **Mount Logan,** at 6,050 meters (19,850 ft.), is the highest peak in Canada. The ranges you see from the Alaska Highway are impressive enough, but only through gaps can you glimpse the fantastic Icefield Ranges lying directly behind. These peaks are surrounded by a gigantic icefield plateau 2,500–3,000 meters (8,200–9,800 ft.) high, the largest nonpolar icefield in the world, occupying a little over half the park. Radiating out from the icefield like spokes on a wheel are valley glaciers up to 60 kilometers (37 mi.) long, some very active. Such is the importance of this area that—together with Wrangell–Saint Elias and Glacier Bay National Parks in Alaska, and Tatshenshini-Alsek Provincial Park in British Columbia—Kluane has been declared a World Heritage Site by UNESCO.

Although more than half of Kluane is ice, rock, and snow, the remainder includes habitat that holds large populations of wildlife. Some 4,000 Dall sheep—one of the world's largest populations—reside on the high open hillsides northwest of Kaskawulsh Glacier and elsewhere in the park. Many can be seen from the highway in the vicinity of Sheep Mountain. Kluane also has significant numbers of moose, caribou, mountain goats, and grizzly bears.

Flightseeing
Flightseeing over the park is available from the Haines Junction Airport. The one-hour flight affords a spectacular view of Mount Logan plus several glaciers and is highly recommended if you happen to be there on a clear day. Contact **Sifton Air** (867/634-2916). Prices with **Trans North Helicopters** (867/634-2242) start at $150 pp for a 30-minute glacier tour. Trans North is based beyond Haines Junction around Km 1,698.

Visitors Centers
In Haines Junction, the **Haines Junction Visitor Reception Centre** (867/634-2293, www.pc.gc.ca, mid-May–mid-Sept. daily 9 A.M.–9 P.M.) has a relief map of the park and an excellent 20-minute sight-and-sound slide show presented every half hour. Situated in the Slim's River Valley, 72 kilometers (45 mi.) north of Haines Junction,

Sheep Mountain Visitor Information Centre (867/734-7250, mid-May–mid-Sept. daily 9 A.M.–5 P.M.) has a spotting scope to look for wild sheep on nearby Sheep Mountain (late Aug.–mid June is the best time of year for sheep-spotting).

HAINES JUNCTION TO BEAVER CREEK
For most of the 300 kilometers (186 mi.) to Beaver Creek, the Alaska Highway parallels Kluane National Park or Kluane Wildlife Sanctuary—a comparatively well-populated, civilized, and stunningly scenic stretch of the road. Along the way are three provincial campgrounds (Km 1,725, Km 1,853, and Km 1,913), three little settlements, and a dozen lodges.

At **Soldier's Summit,** Km 1,707, a sign commemorates the official opening of the Alcan on November 20, 1942, a mere eight months after construction began; an interpretive trail from the parking area leads up to the site of the dedication ceremony.

Destruction Bay
This tiny town at Km 1,743 was named when the original road-construction camp was destroyed by a windstorm in 1942. Destruction Bay has a gas station, the 32-room **Talbot Arm Motel** (867/841-4461), a cafeteria and dining room, an RV park, showers, general store, and gift shop.

Burwash Landing
On Kluane Lake, 127 kilometers (79 mi.) northwest of Haines Junction, is Burwash Landing, population 90. The fine **Kluane Museum of Natural History** (867/841-5561, summer daily 9 A.M.–8 P.M., adult $3.75, child $3.25) includes a wildlife exhibit, native artifacts, a large model of the area, a theater where a wildlife video is shown, and some interesting fossils. Also take a gander at **Our Lady of the Rosary Church,** a log structure built in 1944.

Burwash Landing Resort (867/841-4441) has hotel rooms, a restaurant, lounge, RV park, and boat rentals. The cafeteria is huge, there's a fine dining room, and the bar gets raucous most nights—check out the back wall papered with money. You can boat and fish in the lake from here; guides are available.

BEAVER CREEK

The last place with facilities in the Yukon, Beaver Creek is a tiny town (pop. 110) with a big travel-based economy. Canadian Customs is here, as is an Alaska Highway road crew.

Accommodations and Food

Through town, the **1202 Motor Inn** (867/862-7600, 800/764-7601 in Alaska or 800/661-0540 in western Canada, www.1202motorinn.com) has motel rooms in an older wing ($65 s or d), more modern units ($95 s or d), large kitchen-equipped suites ($175 s or d), and parking for RVs ($16). The complex also has a rustic log dining room, a lounge, public Internet access, and gas (which will be cheaper on the U.S. side of the border). The biggest place in town is the **Westmark Inn Beaver Creek** (867/862-7501 or 800/544-0970, www.westmarkhotels.com, mid-May–mid-Sept., $95 s, $105 d), with tiny nondescript rooms aimed at the escorted-tour crowd.

The Westmark hosts performances of **Beaver Creek Rendezvous,** a lighthearted musical theatre nightly in the summer. It costs $40 for dinner and the show or $15 for the show alone.

Information

The **Beaver Creek Visitor Reception Centre** (867/862-7321, mid-May–mid-Sept. daily 9 A.M.–9 P.M.) is operated by the Yukon government as an information resource for travelers entering the territory from Alaska.

Onward to Alaska

The Canada–U.S. border is 32 kilometers (20 mi.) west of Beaver Creek and the **U.S. Customs post** is a further one kilometer (0.6 mi.) west. Heading into Alaska, be sure to turn your watches back one hour to Alaska Standard Time. Traveling in the opposite direction, **Canadian Customs** is well inside Canada, just three kilometers (1.9 mi.) northwest of Beaver Creek. Both posts are open 24 hours a day, year-round.

If you're reading this before leaving home, begin planning your Alaska travels by contacting the **Alaska Division of Tourism** (907/465-2017; www.travelalaska.com) and requesting an information package. The best guidebook out there is Don Pitcher's *Moon Handbooks Alaska* (Avalon Travel Publishing). In Whitehorse, you'll find copies at Mac's Fireweed Books.

Klondike Loop

The **Klondike Highway** runs 536 kilometers (333 mi.) from Whitehorse to Dawson City. Travel 105 kilometers (65 mi.) from Dawson along the Top of the World Highway to the border with Alaska, followed by another 175 kilometers (109 mi.) on the Taylor Highway back to the Alaska Highway outside of Tok to complete the Klondike Loop.

As you drive this route you can soak up the raw history of Dawson City, the scene of world's greatest gold rush. The trip north from Whitehorse along the Yukon River follows the same route taken by thousands of stampeders in the late 1890s, except instead of riverboats it's RVs and rental cars filled with modern-day travelers in search of adventure. Many of Dawson's historic buildings have been given cheerful coats of paint, others have very effectively been left to the ravages of Mother Nature. Walking tours are the best way to take in the history, but you can also listen to Robert Service recitals at the cabin this famous poet once called home, try your hand at panning for gold, or gamble the night away at an old-time casino.

WHITEHORSE TO DAWSON CITY

Lake Laberge, 62 kilometers (38.5 mi.) from Whitehorse, is famous primarily as the site of the burning of the corpse in Robert Service's immortal "Cremation of Sam McGee." The excellent trout fishing here has also been well known since stampeder days, when the fish were barged to Dawson by the ton. Lakeside camping is $10, or continue 22 kilometers (14 mi.) north to **Fox Lake Campground,** with summertime swimming.

Carmacks

A little more than 180 kilometers (120 mi.) from Whitehorse, the river town of Carmacks (pop. 550) is named for George Washington Carmack, credited with the Bonanza Creek strike that triggered the famous Klondike gold rush.

Get the lay of town by driving down Three Gold Road (at the Carmacks Hotel) to the Yukon River. A two-kilometer (1.2 mi.) **boardwalk** runs along the river from here to a park, complete with a gazebo. There are benches, viewing platforms, and interpretive signs along the way. If you're interested in getting out on the river, contact **Experience Yukon** (867/863-6021) to reserve a spot on their 9:30 A.M. tour boat or to rent a canoe. The **Tage Cho Hudan Interpretive Centre** (867/863-5830) exhibits archaeological displays and a diorama of a mammoth snare, plus interpretive trails and a gift shop. Find it at the second driveway north of the bridge.

Hotel Carmacks (867/863-5221) rents modern rooms and cabins. A large lounge is attached, sporting a couple of pool tables and an interesting brass railing along the bar, perfect for bellying up to. Part of its restaurant occupies the old Carmacks roadhouse, built in 1903 and the only remaining roadhouse of the 16 that once operated between Whitehorse and Dawson. Camp at the village-run **Tantalus Campground** (867/863-6271) on the banks of the river. The **Carmacks Visitor Reception Centre** (867/863-6330) is next to the campground and open seasonally.

Five Finger Rapids

North of Carmacks 25 kilometers (15.5 mi.) is a pullout overlooking Five Finger Rapids, where four rock towers here choke the river, dividing it into five channels through which the current rips; only the eastern. At **Five Finger Rapids Recreation Site** a wooden platform overlooks the river, and stairs lead down to the river. Allow an hour or so for the round-trip to the river—a nice little walk to break up the drive.

Pelly Crossing

In another 108 kilometers (67 mi.) you come to Pelly Crossing, roughly halfway between Whitehorse and Dawson. Downtown, interpretive panels describe the town and its native population, who moved upstream from remote Fort Selkirk after the Klondike Highway was completed in the 1950s.

Silver Trail

The first settlement north of Pelly River is **Stewart Crossing,** the site of an 1883 trading post and the last gas stop before Dawson City, a further 181 kilometers (112 mi.) north.

At this point, the Silver Trail (Hwy. 11) branches northeast through a heavily mined area or silver deposits. Two small towns and loads of history make a detour worthwhile.

Mayo (pop. 500), above a wide bend of the Stewart River, was once a bustling silver-mining center, with the ore transported out of the wilderness by sternwheeler, eventually reaching smelters in San Francisco. Stop by the **Binet House Interpretive Centre** (867/996-2926) for a rundown of the Mayo District, including historical photos; displays on the geology, minerals, flora, and fauna of the area; and silver samples. The **Bedrock Motel** (north side of town, 867/996-2290, $80 s or d) has clean, comfortable rooms as well as RV parking.

From Mayo, it's another 59 kilometers (36.6 mi.) on hard-packed gravel to **Keno City,** passing **Elsa,** the site of a silver mine that closed as recently as 1989, along the way. Once a booming silver town, Keno's population has dwindled to just 25. Its long and colorful history is cataloged at the **Keno City Mining Museum** (867/995-2792, June–Aug. 10 A.M.–6 P.M.), fittingly housed in a 1920s saloon.

On the south side of town, **Keno City Cabins** (867/995-2829, $69–95 d)—there's only two of them—are modern and well-equipped, with cooking done on a woodstove. Or stay downtown at the classic **Keno City Hotel** (867/995-2312, May–Aug., from $55 s or d).

Dawson City

Of all the towns in Canada, Dawson City (not to be confused with Dawson Creek, British Columbia) has the widest fame and the wildest past. Although the Klondike gold rush was short lived, tourists have rediscovered Dawson's charms in a big way. It's a long way north, some 536 kilometers (333 mi.) from Whitehorse, but 60,000 visitors make the trek annually to this delightful salmagundi of colorful historic facades and abandoned buildings, tiny old cabins and huge new ones, rusted old sternwheelers and touristy casinos.

HISTORY

The Klondike gold fields cover an area of 2,000 square kilometers (770 sq. mi.) southeast of Dawson. It was in 1896 that a Nova Scotian prospector, Robert Henderson, discovered the first gold—about 20 cents' worth per pan—in a creek he went ahead and named Gold-Bottom Creek. He spent the rest of the summer working the creek, while passing news of his find to fellow prospectors who were in the area. One such man was George "Siwash" Washington Carmack, who with partners Tagish Charlie and Skookum Jim struck gold in extraordinary quantities—$3–4 a pan—on nearby Rabbit Creek (soon to be renamed Bonanza). They staked three claims before word began to spread. By fall most of the richest ground had been claimed.

Gold Fever

News of the strike reached the outside world a year later, when a score of prospectors, so loaded down with gold that they couldn't handle it themselves, disembarked in San Francisco and Seattle. The spectacle triggered mass insanity across the continent, immediately launching a rush the likes of which the world had rarely seen before and has not seen since. Clerks, salesmen, streetcar conductors, doctors, preachers, generals (even the mayor of Seattle) simply dropped what they were doing and started off "for the Klondike." City dwellers, factory workers, and men who had never climbed a mountain, handled a boat, or even worn a backpack were outfitted in San Francisco, Seattle, Vancouver, and Edmonton, and set out on an incredible journey through an uncharted wilderness with Dawson—a thousand miles from anywhere—as the imagined grand prize.

Out of an estimated 100,000 "stampeders" that started out, 35,000 made it to Dawson.

Meanwhile, the first few hundred lucky stampeders to actually reach Dawson before the rivers froze that winter (1897) found the town in such a panic over food that people were actually fleeing for their lives. At the same time tens of thousands of stampeders were heading toward Dawson along a variety of routes, including over the **Chilkoot Pass** and down the Yukon River. Most hopefuls were caught unprepared in the bitter grip of the seven-month Arctic winter, and many froze to death or died of scurvy, starvation, exhaustion, heartbreak, suicide, or murder. And when the breakup in 1898 finally allowed the remaining hordes to pour into Dawson the next spring, every worthwhile claim had already been staked.

Heyday and Paydirt

That next year, from summer 1898 to summer 1899, was a unique moment in history. As people and supplies started deluging Dawson, all the hundreds of thousands in gold, worthless previously for lack of anything to buy, were spent with a feverish abandon. The richest stampeders established the saloons, dance halls, gambling houses, trading companies, even steamship lines and banks—much easier ways to get the gold than mining it. The casinos and hotels were as opulent as any in Paris. The dance-hall girls charged $5 in gold per minute for dancing (extra for slow dances), the bartenders put stickum on

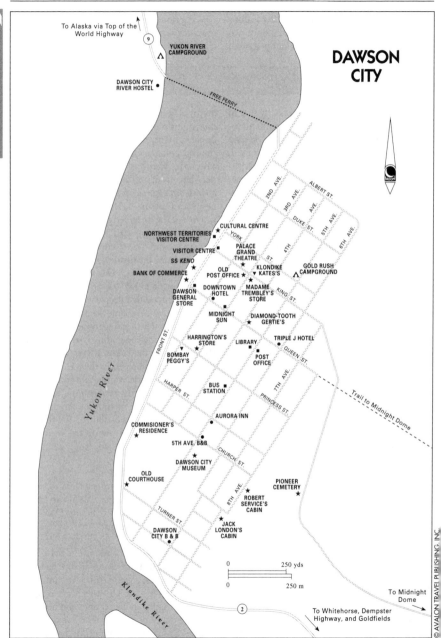

YUKON TERRITORY

DAWSON CITY

To Alaska via Top of the World Highway

9

YUKON RIVER CAMPGROUND

DAWSON CITY RIVER HOSTEL

FREE FERRY

Yukon River

2ND AVE.
3RD AVE.
AVE.
5TH AVE.
6TH AVE.
ALBERT ST.
DUKE ST.

NORTHWEST TERRITORIES VISITOR CENTRE
CULTURAL CENTRE
YORK
PALACE GRAND THEATRE
VISITOR CENTRE
SS KENO
BANK OF COMMERCE
OLD POST OFFICE
KLONDIKE KATE'S'S
GOLD RUSH CAMPGROUND
4TH ST.
DAWSON GENERAL STORE
DOWNTOWN HOTEL
MADAME TREMBLEY'S STORE
KING ST.
MIDNIGHT SUN
DIAMOND-TOOTH GERTIE'S
FRONT ST.
HARRINGTON'S STORE
LIBRARY
TRIPLE J HOTEL
QUEEN ST.
BOMBAY PEGGY'S
POST OFFICE
HARPER ST.
BUS STATION
7TH AVE.
PRINCESS ST.
Trail to Midnight Dome
AURORA INN
COMMISSIONER'S RESIDENCE
5TH AVE. B&B
CHURCH ST.
DAWSON CITY MUSEUM
OLD COURTHOUSE
PIONEER CEMETERY
8TH AVE.
ROBERT SERVICE'S CABIN
TURNER ST.
JACK LONDON'S CABIN
DAWSON CITY B & B

Klondike River

0   250 yds
0   250 m

2

To Midnight Dome

To Whitehorse, Dempster Highway, and Goldfields

© AVALON TRAVEL PUBLISHING, INC.

their fingers to poke a little dust during transactions, and the janitors who panned the sawdust on the barroom floors were known to wash out $50 nightly. Dawson burned with an intensity born of pure lust, the highlight of the lives of every single person who braved the trails and experienced it.

In 1899, most of Dawson burned to the ground, and at the same time, word filtered in that gold had been discovered on the beaches of Nome, and just as the Klondike strike had emptied surrounding boomtowns, Nome emptied Dawson. By the summer of 1899, as the last bedraggled and tattered stampeders limped into Dawson two years after setting out, the 12-month golden age of Dawson was done. The city's heyday was as brief as its reputation was beefy, and Dawson quickly declined into another small town on the banks of the Yukon.

SIGHTS

Dawson's plentiful free or inexpensive attractions can keep you happily busy for several days. The compact downtown area mixes dirt streets and crumbling wooden storefronts with faux goldrush-era buildings and bustling tourist businesses. The actual goldfields are out of town, while it will take a trip up Midnight Dome to see the town and Yukon River laid out in their glory.

Start your exploration of Dawson at the **Visitor Reception Centre** (867/993-5566; mid-May–mid-Sept., daily 8 A.M.–8 P.M.), right in the thick of things at Front and King Streets. Outstanding one-hour, historically loaded **walking tours** of the town core leave from the visitors center several times a day; a schedule is posted at the center.

While you're exploring town, keep your eyes open for **Red Serge,** an RCMP in the famous red dress uniform on horseback. He generally patrols town Monday–Saturday 10:30 A.M.–4:30 P.M., and will be happy to pose for a photo.

Dawson City Museum

If possible, before you do anything else in town, try to visit this excellent and extensive museum (5th Ave. and Church St., 867/993-5291, mid-

May–early Sept. daily 10 A.M.–6 P.M., adult $5, senior $4.50, child $3).

The south and north galleries present an enormous amount of history, from fossils and flora and fauna through northern Athabascan lifestyles up to the gold rush and the subsequent developments. The museum has a wealth of material to draw from and it's all nicely presented. The mining-history displays alone, from hand mining to dredges, are worth the price of admission; also check out the display on law and order during

Dawson City Museum

the gold rush. The "visible storage area" houses about one-fifth of the museum's collection of 30,000 artifacts.

SS Keno

The restored riverboat **SS Keno,** built in 1922 in Whitehorse, is beached on Front Street. It was used to transport ore from the mining area around Mayo down to the confluence of the Yukon, where larger riverboats picked transported it upriver to Whitehorse and the railhead. The *Keno* sailed under its own steam to its resting place here in 1960 but wasn't restored until 40 years later. Tour cost is adult $5, senior $4.50, child $2.50.

Historic Buildings

Parks Canada and the Klondike Visitors Association (KVA) have been doing an outstanding job bringing the color of life back to town. Many ramshackle buildings have been spruced up with brightly painted facades and informative window displays, and most of the commercial hotels, gift shops, restaurants, beauty parlors, bed-and-breakfasts, and other businesses have followed suit. Thankfully, much of the semi–ghost town flavor remains. The most historically important buildings are protected as **Dawson Historical Complex National Historic Site** and the most picturesque ruins of permafrost, gravity, and neglect have purposely been left alone.

The exterior of the **Bank of Commerce,** next to the *Keno,* hasn't changed much since Robert Service worked here in 1908, though the building was in dire need of work when I last saw it. On King Street, up a block from the visitors center, is the **Palace Grand Theatre,** built in 1899 by "Arizona Charlie" Meadows, the most famous bartender/gunslinger on the Trail of '98. At the time, the Grand was one of the most luxuriously appointed theaters in the west, hosting everything from Wild West shows to opera. Take a tour daily at 2 P.M. (adult $5, senior, $4.50, child $3). In the vicinity of the theater are many buildings with historic window displays. Walk three blocks south down 3rd Avenue (at Harper St.) to take a snap of the terribly slanted, oft-photographed **Strait's Auction House.**

The beautifully restored **Commissioner's Residence** on Front Street near Church Street was the official residence of the Commissioner of the Yukon from 1900 to 1916. Tours (adult $5, senior $4.25, child $2.50) of the mansion and gardens are given daily by costumed interpreters or come for afternoon tea (adult $15, senior $13, child $7.50).

Robert Service Cabin

Stroll three blocks uphill from the museum to 8th Avenue (at Hanson St.) to see the log cabin that Robert Service called home 1909–1912. Service, who never took shovel nor pan to earth nor water, wound up as a troubadour–bank teller in Dawson and made his fame and fortune unexpectedly while living here, penning such classic prose poems as "The Cremation of Sam McGee" and "The Shooting of Dan McGrew." No one has lived in this cabin since Service left Dawson a celebrity in 1912, and people have been making pilgrimages to it ever since. The cabin is open daily 9 A.M.–5 P.M. in the summer, and Charlie Davis does recitations of Service's best-known poems at 3 P.M. for adult $5, senior $4.25, child $2.50.

Midnight Dome

This 885-meter (2,900-ft.) hill provides a 360-degree view of the area. The Yukon River stretches out in both directions and Dawson is right below you, to the west the Top of the World Highway winds away to Alaska, and to the south you look directly up Bonanza Creek, past the wavy tailings and hillsides pitted by hydraulic monitors that still bring pay dirt down for sluicing. The sign on top identifies all the topographic features. If you're driving, take King Street through downtown from Front Street and follow the signs; it's seven kilometers (4.3 mi.) to the top. A steep hiking trail begins at the end of Queen Street (ask at the visitors center for a trail map).

The Gold Fields

For a close-up look at where the Klondike gold frenzy took place, head two kilometers (1.2 mi.) back out of town and take Bonanza Creek Road south.

The highlight of the drive is a visit to **Dredge No. 4,** the largest wooden-hulled gold dredge in North America. Built in 1912, this massive machine scooped pay dirt from the creek beds right up until 1966. Tours are offered May–August and cost adult $5, senior $4.50, child $2.50 (or are included in the Parks and Partner's Pass).

The Klondike Visitors Association owns **Claim 6** on the famous Bonanza Creek. You can pan for gold free of charge mid-May–mid-September. Buy a pan from any one of many shops in Dawson or rent one from the RV park at the Bonanza Creek Road turn-off. Downstream a ways, **Claim 33** (867/993-5303) is a commercial panning operation where you pay to pan for guaranteed "color." Hope I don't give away any secrets, but it's spiked. Still, it's good fun and a way to practice your technique.

A monument at **Discovery Claim,** 16 kilometers (10 mi.) south from the main highway, marks the spot where George Carmack made the strike in 1896 that set the rush into motion.

The road continues beyond the monument to the confluence of Bonanza and Eldorado Creeks, site of the gold-rush town of Grand Forks, and then splits. The left fork is part of a 100-kilometer (62-mi.) loop through some seriously isolated country before rejoining the Klondike Highway near the airport.

ENTERTAINMENT AND SHOPPING

Diamond Tooth Gerties Gambling Hall

Canada's first legal casino, Diamond Tooth Gerties (4th and Queen, 867/993-5575, mid-May–mid-Sept., Mon.–Fri. 7 P.M.–2 A.M., Sat.–Sun. 2 P.M.–2 A.M.) was named for a Dawson dance hall queen with a diamond between her two front teeth. Though casinos were as common as sluice boxes and saloons at the height of the Dawson madness, gambling in the Yukon (and throughout Canada) wasn't formally legalized until 1971, the year this place opened. Games include slot machines, blackjack, poker, sic bo, and roulette, with odds that decidedly favor the house. Drinks are not free, even if you're dropping major-

ONLY IN THE NORTH . . .

Dawson's most infamous nightcap can be "enjoyed" at the **Downtown Hotel** (Queen St. and 2nd Ave., 867/993-5346). It all began in 1973 when "Captain" Dick Stevenson was searching though an abandoned cabin and he came across a pickle jar that held a toe that had been severed by an ax. Inspiration (if it could be called that) struck, and the toe landed in a drink. The original toe is long gone—it was swallowed by an overzealous patron—but at last check, the bar in the Downtown Hotel had eight toes to choose from, all looking ghastly at best. They're preserved in salt, and came from donations by folks who lost them in accidents or because of frostbite. It's pretty gross, but amazingly popular—2,000 or so folks become members of the Sourtoe Cocktail Club annually. Sourtoe cocktails are $5 (you can put the toe in any drink). The bartenders make sure the toe touches your lip to receive an official certificate showing your prowess in stupid bar tricks.

league cash. This sure isn't Vegas! The 30-minute floorshow of Geritol oldies and cancan kicks is presented nightly at 8:30 P.M., 10:30 P.M., and midnight. Cover charge is $6.

Gerties is run by the KVA as a money-maker to restore and promote Dawson City. Take a look around town and you'll see how much money they make at Gerties (or how much the tourists lose)—around $1 million annually. I'm not saying that you won't come out in front, but just approach this joint with the attitude that you're making a donation. And why not? It's a very good cause.

Palace Grand Theatre

Arizona Charlie Meadows was a young impresario and theater builder who arrived in Dawson in 1898. Within a year he erected the Palace Grand Theatre (King St. between 2nd Ave. and 3rd Ave., 867/993-6217) from wood salvaged off sternwheelers. The original horseshoe balcony, private box seats, and lavish interior have been lovingly restored. Today, the theater hosts *Gaslight Follies,* one of the best of the many vaudeville revues in the

Yukon. Hour-long shows are presented every night mid-May–early September at 8:30 P.M.; $15 adults ($17 for a balcony seat), $7.50 children.

Galleries and Gifts

The **Klondike Institute of Art and Culture** (2nd Ave. and Princess St., 867/993-5005) hosts exhibits of art by Yukoners and organizes the mid-August **Yukon Riverside Arts Festival** in a park beside the Yukon. **Art's Gallery** (3rd Ave. and King St., 867/993-6967) sells excellent hand-blown art glass, scrimshaw, pottery, batiks, and baskets woven from birch, cedar, or spruce root.

The most interesting of touristy Dawson's many gift shops is the **Gold Claim** (3rd Ave. and Princess St., 867/993-6387) operated by Stuart Schmidt, whose grandfather was one of the original Klondikers. Schmidt uses gold he's mined himself to make hand-forged jewelry. **Forty Mile Gold Workshop** (3rd Ave. and York St., 867/993-5690) is in the business of selling and buying claims, but also sells raw gold out of its offices.

ACCOMMODATIONS AND CAMPING

Check the **Klondike Visitors Association** website (www.dawsoncity.ca) for a complete list of local lodgings. If you arrive in Dawson without reservations, be sure to check out the lodging notebook in the Visitor Reception Centre; often hotels, motels, and bed-and-breakfasts will advertise special rates for the night here.

Under $50

Dawson City River Hostel (867/993-6823, www.yukonhostels.com, mid-May–mid-Sept.) is Canada's northernmost hostel. Located on the west side of the Yukon, it's a quick ferry ride from Dawson. A back-to-the-land spirit infuses this friendly place where dorm-style lodging in cabins is $15 for members of Hostelling International (nonmembers $19), private rooms are $39 s or d, and tent spaces cost $12. The hostel doesn't have electricity (and therefore it's cash only), but does have a cooking area with woodstove, canoe and mountain bike rentals, a communal cabin, plus the funkiest bathhouse going.

The cheapest place right downtown is the shockingly pink **Westminster Hotel** (975 3rd Ave., 867/993-5463, www.westminsterhotel.ca), where basic rooms with shared bath start at $40 s or d. The Westminster is definitely not for everyone and it helps to be a heavy sleeper as the downstairs bar gets noisy Friday–Saturday when the countrwy house band gets going.

$50–100

In addition to having great breakfasts, **Klondike Kate's** (3rd and King, 867/993-6527, www.klondikekates.ca, June–Sept.) has 16 spacious wood cabins, each with a bathroom, cable TV, and a phone. Rates are a reasonable $95–125 s or d.

Next to the museum, **5th Avenue B&B** (867/993-5941 or 866/631-5237, www.5thave bandb.com, $85–105 s, $95–115 d) may have an uninspiring name but the aquamarine exterior is impossible to miss. It features seven comfortable guest rooms with shared or private baths and a large sitting area. Rates include a hearty all-you-can-eat breakfast.

If you really want to immerse yourself in the gold-mining culture of Dawson, consider staying at a camp set up by **Eureka Gold Panning Adventures** (867/633-6519, www.eurekagold panning.com) beyond Bonanza Creek Road along Hunker Creek. Morris and Sandy George supply wall tents, cooking facilities, wood-burning heaters, and solar showers. You supply sleeping bags and food. Rates are well under $100 d per night, but most visitors stay as part of a package, such as $120 s, $195 d for one night accommodation and two full days of gold-panning. Transportation from Dawson if required is $45 for one person, $60 for two.

$100–150

Across from Diamond Tooth Gertie's is the **Triple J Hotel** (5th and Queen, 867/993-5323 or 800/764-3555, www.triplejhotel.com, mid-May–mid-Sept.) a gold-rush-era-looking hotel that, beyond the facade, is a modern complex of motel rooms ($99 s, $119 d), hotel rooms ($109 s, $119 d), and cabins ($119 s, $129 d).

The **Aurora Inn** (5th Ave., 867/993-6860, www.aurorainn.ca, $119 s, $129 d) is a modern wooden lodging with a distinctive yellow facade. The rooms are bright and spacious, with simple furnishings and practical bathrooms. Add $10 pp for a continental breakfast.

On the outskirts of town and less than a block from the Klondike River, **Dawson City B&B** (451 Craig St., 867/993-5649, www.dawsonbb .com) is a neat two-story home with a pleasing blue and white exterior. Rates of $100–130 s or d include breakfast, bikes, fishing poles, and airport transfers.

Fun and funky on the outside, the rooms at the **Downtown Hotel** (Queen at 2nd, 867/993-5346 or 867/993-5346, www.downtownhotel.ca, $116 s, $126 d) are somewhat clinical. Still, it's close to everything and the on-site bar has a rocking nighttime atmosphere.

Over $150

Bombay Peggy's Inn & Lounge (2nd at Princess, 867/993-6969, www.bombaypeggys.com) is named for the former madam of a brothel that once operated in the building. Not only has it been totally renovated, it was moved from its original location. Most rooms are suites (from $169 s, $179 d), decorated in bold Victorian colors, with hardwood floors, and lavish bathrooms with antique tubs. Also available is one room that shares a bathroom ($85 s, $95 d). You don't have to abandon modern comforts for the sake of atmosphere—there's also high-speed Internet. Rates include a light breakfast. About the only reminders of the building's past are a racy cocktail list in the downstairs lounge and the phone number. It's also one of the few lodgings open year-round.

Campgrounds

The **Yukon River Campground** (across the river from town, mid-May–mid-Sept., $10) is convenient but lacks facilities (drinking water, pit toilets, and firewood only). The free ferry from town runs 24 hours daily. Walk downstream from the campground to reach three rusting riverboats that are slowly disintegrating where they were beached many years ago.

RVers can circle their rigs right downtown at the **Goldrush Campground** (5th and York, 867/993-5247, www.goldrushcampground.com, mid-May–mid-Sept., unserviced sites $16, hookups $23–30). Facilities include coin showers and a launderette. South of town, **Bonanza Gold RV Park** (867/993-6789, www.bonanza gold.ca) and **GuggieVille RV Park** (867/993-5008) both have modern facilities, but tents are not permitted at the former.

FOOD

Dawson is great for eating out; check the menu book at the Visitor Reception Centre to see which places look inviting.

River West Cappuccino Bistro (Front St., 867/993-6339, daily from 7:30 A.M.) has good coffee plus a deli with the best sandwiches in town and a delightful selection of baked goods. **Rio Grill** is a simple fast-food place across from the SS *Keno* that serves steak sandwiches ($9), burgers, and other delights. Very good, and it's open 24 hours a day in the summer; closed the rest of the year.

The breakfast special at **Klondike Kate's** (3rd Ave. and King St., 867/993-6527, 6:30 A.M.–11 P.M.) isn't as legendary as the restaurant's namesake was during the gold rush, but it's still mightily popular. Bacon and eggs with real live homefries will set you back $5. Pancakes and omelets are similarly priced. At lunch, salads and gourmet sandwiches are all under $10 while at dinner, plan on starting with a platter of Mediterranean delicacies ($12 for two), and go on to grilled salmon or arctic char for $17. This place has Dawson's nicest patio.

Groceries

Dawson City General Store (540 Front St., 867/993-5813, 8 A.M.–9 P.M.) has a bakery and groceries, while your best bet for fresh meat and deli items is the **Bonanza Market** (2nd and Princess, 867/993-6567, Mon.–Sat. 9 A.M.–7 P.M.).

INFORMATION

The centrally located **Visitor Reception Centre** (Front St. and King St., 867/993-5566, www.tourdawsoncity.com, mid-May–mid-Sept., daily 8 A.M.–8 P.M.) is extremely well organized and prepared for the most common questions from the hordes of hopefuls that are, after all, Dawson's legacy. It stocks books of menus, hotel rates, and gift shops; schedules of tours; hours of attractions; and much, much more. In advance of your trip, you can order an order an information package from the **Klondike Visitors Association** (867/993-5575 or 877/465-3006, www.dawsoncity.ca).

Books and Maps

The library is at 5th and Queen in the same building as the public school (remove your shoes before entering). **Maximillian's Gold Rush Emporium** (Front St., 867/993-5486) has a great selection of northern literature. One of the most unique souvenirs you can get in Dawson is an authentic **placer map** showing all the gold fields and claims. They are available along with topo maps at the **mining recorder's office** (5th Ave. between Queen St. and Princess St.).

TRANSPORTATION

Dawson is accessible from the south via the year-round **North Klondike Highway** (536 km/333 mi. from Whitehorse), with westward connections to Alaska over the seasonal **Top of the World Highway** (280 km/174 mi. to Tok, Alaska).

Getting There

Dawson's airport is 17 kilometers (10.6 mi.) east of town. **Air North** (867/668-2228) links Dawson with Fairbanks and Whitehorse as well as Inuvik to the north. Taxis and a shuttle bus meet all flights.

Dawson City Courier and Taxi (867/993-6688) runs a minibus between Whitehorse and Dawson City daily in the summer; $94 one way, $168 round-trip. **Alaska Trails** (888/600-6001, www.alaskashuttle.com) has a thrice-weekly bus service connecting Dawson City with Fairbanks (US$135).

Tours

One local tour company has been doing city, Midnight Dome, Arctic Circle, and gold fields van tours for many years, and gets high recommendations from travelers: **Gold City Tours** (Front St. across from the riverboat SS *Keno*, 867/993-5175, www.goldcitytours.info). The most interesting option is the 3.5-hour City and Goldfields Tour ($42) that departs daily at 1 P.M., or take a one-hour city tour or gold-panning trip. As an alternative to the fast-paced *Yukon Queen* tours described following, several local folks guide river trips at a more leisurely pace. Get details at the Visitor Reception Centre or at **Dawson Trading Post** (5th Ave. and Harper St., 867/993-5316, www.dawsontradingpost.ca).

CONTINUING WEST TO ALASKA

If you arrived in Dawson City by road from Whitehorse, you have the option of returning the way you came or continuing to Alaska along the Top of the World Highway. If you arrived in town by public transportation, your options are a little more varied—fly or bus it out in either direction or catch the *Yukon Queen* to Eagle.

Top of the World Highway

Heading west toward Alaska, the Top of the World Highway crosses the Yukon River at the edge of Dawson. A free **ferry,** with room for up to eight regular-sized vehicles, crosses the Yukon River mid-May–mid-September, 24 hours a day (except 5–7 A.M. Wed.). It's a fun ride even if you're not heading up the Top of the World Highway. The ferry can get seriously backed up in the summer, with lengthy two- or three-hour waits at times (local vehicles go first).

From the west bank of the Yukon, the highway climbs out of Dawson into the alpine tundra of the lower White Mountains, with vast vistas in which you can see the road running along the ridge tops in the distance. Civilization along the highway, however, is nonexistent until you reach **Poker Creek, Alaska** at Km 106 (Mile 66). With a population of two, this is the northernmost border station in the United States. It's open for as long as the Dawson car ferry operates (usually mid-May–mid-Sept.), daily 9 A.M.–9 P.M. **After crossing into Alaska, you must also turn your**

DEMPSTER HIGHWAY

Dawson is the jumping off point for the 741-kilometer (460-mi.) Dempster Highway that leads across the **Arctic Circle** to **Inuvik** in the Northwest Territories. Unpaved all the way, it traverses endless tundra and snowcapped mountain ranges; it crosses the migration path of the Porcupine caribou herd; and, in winter, you can drive clear through to the **Arctic Ocean** on the frozen Mackenzie River. But it's also one of the most remote public roads in North America, one for which you must be prepared with a full gas tank and spare tires. You also need to turn around at the end and return to Dawson along the same route.

Driving the Dempster

Request information packages from either of the territorial tourism bureaus before leaving home, then make a stop at the **Northwest Territories Visitor Centre** (Front St., 867/993-6167, mid-June–late Sept. daily 9 A.M.–8 P.M.) once you arrive in Dawson. The ferry crossing of the Peel River operates mid-June–October. For a schedule and general highway conditions call 800/661-0750 or go online to www.gov.nt.ca/transportation.

Numerous campgrounds and three lodges dot the route. A good spot to spend the night before hitting the highway is **Klondike River Lodge** (867/993-6892), east of Dawson at the start of the highway. Tent sites are $6, hookups $22, and motel rooms $105 s or d. They also have gas pumps. The **Arctic Circle** is reached at Km 403 (Mile 250) and the Yukon/Northwest Territories border at Km 471 (Mile 293). **Fort McPherson,** 550 kilometers (342 mi.) from Dawson, is a Gwich'in Dene village of 800 with a visitors center and other highway services.

The town at the end of the road, Inuvik, is covered in the Mackenzie River and the Western Arctic chapter of this book.

watch *back* one hour to Alaska Time (which means if you're traveling to Dawson from Alaska, the border station is open 8 A.M.–8 P.M.).

One important note: The Dawson ferry can get heavily backed up in mid-summer, with delays of up to three hours at the busiest times (7 A.M.–11 A.M. and 4–7 P.M.). Don't head off too late in the day if you intend to make the border crossing before it closes.

Yukon Queen II

The *Yukon Queen II* is a modern riverboat that blasts between Dawson City and the fascinating and historic town of Eagle, Alaska, every day in the summer. The 120-passenger boat travels at 65 kph (40 mph). Most passengers are part of a Holland America tour through Alaska and the Yukon, with a bus picking them up in Eagle for the next leg of their trip (or vice versa). The boat leaves Dawson at 9 A.M., arrives in Eagle at noon, and then departs again at 2:30 P.M., with an 8 P.M. arrival in Dawson. The cost is US$126 each way or US$209 round-trip, including the same bland meal in each direction. Buy tickets at the **Yukon River Cruises** office (Front St., Dawson City, 867/993-5599).

Resources

Suggested Reading

NATURAL HISTORY

The Atlas of Breeding Birds of Alberta. Edmonton: Federation of Alberta Naturalists, 1992. Comprehensive study of all birds that breed in Alberta with easy-to-read distribution maps, details on nesting and other behavioral patterns, and color plates.

Baldwin, John. *Mountain Madness: Exploring British Columbia's Ultimate Wilderness.* Vancouver: Harbour Publishing, 1999. Filled with stunning photography, this coffee table book is a worthwhile purchase for climbers or anyone interested in the natural landscapes of the Coast Mountains.

Cannings, Richard. *British Columbia: A Natural History.* Vancouver, Douglas & McIntyre, 1996. The natural history of the province divided into 10 chapters, from the earliest origins of the land to problems faced in the new millennium. It includes lots of color photos, diagrams, and maps.

Folkens, Peter. *Marine Mammals of British Columbia and the Pacific Northwest.* Vancouver: Harbour Publishing, 2001. In a waterproof, fold-away format, this booklet provides vital identification tips and habitat maps for 50 marine mammals, including all species of whales present in local waters.

Foster, John E., Dick Harrison, and I.S. MacLaren, eds. *Buffalo.* Edmonton: University of Alberta Press, 1992. A series of essays by noted historians and experts in the field of the American bison, addressing their disappearance from the prairies, buffalo jumps. One essay deals with Wood Buffalo National Park.

Gadd, Ben. *Handbook of the Canadian Rockies.* Jasper: Corax Press, 1999. The latest edition of this classic guide is in color, and although bulky for backpackers it's a must-read for anyone interested in the natural history of the Canadian Rockies.

Gill, Ian. *Haida Gwaii: Journeys through the Queen Charlotte Islands.* Vancouver: Raincoast Books, 1997. A personal and touching view of the Queen Charlottes complemented by the stunning color photography of David Nunuk.

Gross, Renie. *Dinosaur Country.* Wardlow: Badlands Books, 1998. Combines descriptions of the various dinosaurs that once roamed Alberta with stories of their discovery and an in-depth look at dinosaur-hunting today.

Haig Brown, Roderick. *Return to the River.* Vancouver: Douglas & McIntyre, 1997. Although fictional, this story of the life of one salmon and its struggle through life is based on fact, and is a classic read for both anglers and naturalists. It was originally published in 1946 but has recently been reprinted and is available at most bookstores.

Herrero, Stephen. *Bear Attacks: Their Causes and Avoidances.* New York: Nick Lyons Books, 1995. Through a series of gruesome stories, this book catalogs the stormy relationship between people and bruins, provides hints on avoiding attacks, and tells what to do in case you're attacked.

Hudson, Rick. *Gold, Gemstones, and Mineral Sites of British Columbia.* Victoria: Orca Books, 1999. This still-evolving series currently has two volumes in print. Volume 1 details sites on Vancouver Island. Volume 2 covers sites around Vancouver and within a day's drive of the city. The history of each location, along with a map, what the site holds today, and interesting related facts make this a must-read for keen rockhounds.

Jones, Karen. *Wolf Mountains.* Calgary: University of Calgary Press, 2002. Explores the history of wolves in the Canadian Rockies, with emphasis on the often controversial relationship between man and wolf.

Osborne, Graham (photographer). *British Columbia: A Wild and Fragile Beauty.* Vancouver: Douglas & McIntyre, 1993. In my opinion this coffee-table book depicts the natural beauty of British Columbia better than any other edition currently in print. A short section of moving text accompanies each photograph.

Patterson, W. S. *The Physics of Glaciers.* Toronto: Pergamon Press, 1969. A highly technical look at all aspects of glaciation, why glaciers form, how they flow, and their effect on the environment.

Rezendes, Paul. *Tracking and the Art of Seeing.* Charlotte, Virginia: Camden House Publishing, 1992. This is one of the best of many books dedicated to tracking the North American mammals. It begins with a short essay on the relationship of humans with nature.

Sharp, Robert P. *Living Ice: Understanding Glaciers and Glaciation.* Cambridge, England: Cambridge University Press, 1988. A detailed but highly readable book on the formation, types, and results of glaciers.

Vacher, André. *Summer of the Grizzly.* Saskatoon: Western Producer Prairie Books, 1985. True story of a grizzly bear that went on a terrifying rampage near the town of Banff.

Whitaker, John. *National Audubon Society Field Guide to North American Mammals.* New York: Random House, 1997. One of a series of field guides produced by the National Audubon Society, this one details mammals through color plates and detailed descriptions of characteristics, habitat, and range.

Wilkinson, Kathleen. *Wildflowers of Alberta.* Edmonton: University of Alberta Press, 1999. Color plates of all flowers found in the mountain national parks and beyond. Color plates and line drawings are indispensable for identification.

HUMAN HISTORY

Allen, D. *Totem Poles of the Northwest.* Surrey, British Columbia: Hancock House Publishers Ltd., 1977. Describes the importance of totem poles to native culture and totem pole sites and their history.

Bone, Robert. *The Geography of the Canadian North.* Toronto: Oxford University Press, 1992. An in-depth look at the role Canada's north has played and will play in the management of world resources, and the impact of self-government on the region.

Burton, Pierre. *Klondike: The Last Great Gold Rush, 1896-1899.* The Klondike gold rush is brought to life by Canada's preeminent historian/writer in this book that has been reprinted many times, most recently by Doubleday in 2001.

Coull, Cheryl. *A Traveller's Guide to Aboriginal B.C.* Vancouver: Whitecap Books, 1996. Although this book covers native sites throughout British Columbia, the Lower Mainland (Vancouver) chapter is very comprehensive. Also included are details of annual festivals and events and hiking opportunities with a cultural slant.

Duff, Wilson. *The Indian History of British Columbia: The Impact of the White Man.* Victoria: University of British Columbia Press, 1997. In this book Duff deals with the issues faced by natives in the last 150 years but also gives a good overview of their general history.

Engler, Bruno. *Bruno Engler Photography.* Rocky Mountain Books, 2002. Swiss-born Engler spent 60 years exploring and photographing the Canadian Rockies. This impressive hardcover book showcases over 150 of his most timeless images.

Jenness, Diamond. *The Indians of Canada.* Toronto: University of Toronto Press, 1977. Originally published in 1932, this is the classic study of natives in Canada, although Jenness's conclusion, that they were facing certain extinction by "the end of this century" is obviously outdated.

Johnson, Pauline. *Legends of Vancouver.* Vancouver: Douglas & McIntyre, 1998. First published in 1911, this book contains the writings of Pauline Johnson, a well-known writer and poet in the early part of the 1900s. She spent much of her time with native peoples, and this is her version of myths related to her by Joe Capilano, chief of the Squamish.

Lavallee, Omer. *Van Horne's Road.* Montreal: Railfare Enterprises, 1974. William Van Horne was instrumental in the construction of Canada's first transcontinental railway. This is the story of his dream, and the boomtowns that sprung up along the route. Lavallee devotes an entire chapter to telling the story of the railway's push over the Canadian Rockies.

McMillan, Alan D. *Native Peoples and Cultures of Canada.* Vancouver: Douglas & McIntyre, 1995. A comprehensive look at the archaeology, anthropology, and ethnography of the native peoples of Canada. The last chapters delve into the problems facing these people today.

Murphy-Lamb, Lisa. *Dinosaur Hunters.* Canmore: Altitude Publishing, 2003. A small, inexpensive book comprising short stories of dinosaur hunting in Alberta, from the first recorded dinosaur find by George Dawson

to the province's own Dr. Phil Currie, one of the world's preeminent paleontologists.

Patterson, Bruce. *The Wild West.* Canmore: Altitude Publishing, 1993. From the Calgary Exhibition and Stampede to the working ranches of Alberta's foothills, this book covers all aspects of life in the west.

Reksten, Terry. *Rattenbury.* Victoria: Sono Nis Press, 1998. The biography of Francis Rattenbury, British Columbia's preeminent architect at the beginning of the 20th century. The histories of his most famous Victoria and Vancouver buildings are given, and the final chapter looks at his infamous murder at the hands of his wife's young lover.

Schäffer, Mary T. S. *A Hunter of Peace.* Banff: Whyte Museum of the Canadian Rockies, 1980. This book was first published in 1911 by G. P. Putnam & Sons, New York, under the name *Old Indian Trails of the Canadian Rockies.* Tales recount the exploration of the Rockies during the turn of the century. Many of the author's photographs appear throughout.

Scott, Chic. *Pushing the Limits.* Calgary: Rocky Mountain Books, 2000. A chronological history of mountaineering in Canada, with special emphasis on many largely unknown climbers and their feats, as well as the story of Swiss guides in Canada and a short section on ice climbing.

Turner, Dick. *Nahanni.* Surrey, British Columbia: Hancock House, 1975. One of the north's most celebrated authors recounts stories of early life in the north and particularly on the South Nahanni River.

Woodman, David C. *Unravelling the Franklin Mystery.* Montreal: McGill-Queen's University Press, 1991. Many volumes have been written on the ill-fated Franklin Expedition. This one, using Inuit recollections, is among the best.

RECREATION

Christie, Jack. *Inside Out British Columbia.* Vancouver: Raincoast Books, 1998. Although the organization of this book is sometimes difficult to follow, it is the most comprehensive guide available to all recreational opportunities the province has to offer, especially the provincial parks. Jack Christie is a prolific author who also writes *Day Trips from Vancouver* and *One-day Getaways from Vancouver* (both published by Douglas & McIntyre, Vancouver).

Corbett, Bill. *Day Trips from Calgary.* Vancouver: Whitecap Books, 2002. Multiple books have been written about recreation in the Canadian Rockies, which this book covers along with dozens of ideas for day-tripping away from the mountains.

Eastcott, Doug. *Backcountry Biking in the Canadian Rockies.* Calgary: Rocky Mountain Books, 1999. Details over 220 bicycling routes using simple maps, road logs, and black and white photography.

Johnson, Leslie. *Basic Mountain Safety from A to Z.* Canmore: Altitude Books, 2000. Everything you need to know about safety in the mountains, including a large section on camping.

Kane, Alan. *Scrambles in the Canadian Rockies.* Calgary: Rocky Mountain Books, 1999. Routes detailed in this guide lead to summits, without the use of ropes or mountaineering equipment.

Mitchell, Barry. *Alberta's Trout Highway.* Red Deer: Nomad Creek Books, 2001. "Alberta's Trout Highway" is the Forestry Trunk Road (Hwy. 40), which runs the length of Alberta's foothills. Entertaining and useful descriptions of Mitchell's favorite fishing holes are accompanied by maps and plenty of background information.

Patton, Brian, and Bart Robinson. *The Canadian Rockies Trail Guide.* Banff: Summerthought,

2000. This regularly updated guide, first published in 1971, covers 230 hiking trails and 3,400 kilometers (2,100 mi.) in the mountain national parks as well as in surrounding provincial parks. A full page is devoted to each trail, making it the most comprehensive hiking book available.

Pratt-Johnson, Betty. *101 Dives from the Mainland of Washington and British Columbia.* Surrey, British Columbia: Heritage House Publishing, 1999. This book and its companion volume, *99 Dives from the San Juan Islands in Washington to the Gulf Islands,* are the best sources of detailed information on diving in British Columbia.

Woodsworth, Glenn. *Hot Springs of Western Canada.* West Vancouver: Gordon Soules Book Publishers, 1997. Details every known hot springs in western Canada, including both commercial and undeveloped sites. A short history, directions, and practicalities are given for each one.

OTHER GUIDEBOOKS AND MAPS

Gem Trek Publishing. Cochrane, Alberta. This company produces tear-proof and waterproof maps for all regions of the Canadian Rockies. Relief shading clearly and concisely shows elevation, and all hiking trails have been plotted using GPS. On the back of each map are descriptions of attractions and hikes, along with general practical and educational information. www.gemtrek.com.

MapArt. Driving maps for all of Canada, including provinces and cities. Maps are published as old-fashioned fold-out versions, as well as laminated and in atlas form. www.mapart.com.

The Milepost. Bellevue, Washington: Vernon Publications. This annual publication is a must-have for those traveling through western

Canada and Alaska. The maps and logged highway descriptions are incredibly detailed. Most northern bookstores stock *The Milepost,* or order by calling 800/726-4707 or visiting the website www.milepost.com.

Pantel, Gerda. *The Canadian Bed and Breakfast Guide.* Toronto: Penguin Books Canada, 2002. Lists all bed-and-breakfasts that pay a fee, so the reviews aren't very objective. Also lists prices.

MAGAZINES

Beautiful British Columbia. Victoria. This quarterly magazine depicts the beauty of the province through stunning color photography and informative prose. It's available by subscription (250/384-5456 or 800/663-7611, www.beautifulbc.ca).

The Canadian Alpine Journal. Canmore, Alberta. Annual magazine of the Alpine Club of Canada with articles from its members and climbers from around the world. www.alpineclubofcanada.ca.

Canadian Geographic. Ottawa: Royal Canadian Geographical Society. Bimonthly publication pertaining to Canada's natural and human histories and resources. www.canadiangeographic.ca.

Explore. Calgary. Bimonthly publication of adventure travel throughout Canada. www.explore-mag.com.

Nature Canada. Ottawa, Ontario. Quarterly magazine of the Canadian Nature Federation. www.cnf.ca.

Up Here. Yellowknife. Magazine of life in Canada's north published by Outcrop Ltd. Eight issues annually. www.uphere.ca.

Western Living. Vancouver, British Columbia. Lifestyle magazine for western Canada. Includes travel, history, homes, and cooking. www.westernliving.ca.

FREE CATALOGS

Accommodations. Tourism British Columbia. Updated annually, this free booklet is available at information centers throughout British Columbia or by calling 250/387-1642 or 800/435-5622, or online at www.hellobc.com.

Alberta Accommodation Guide. Alberta Hotel & Lodging Association. Lists all hotel, motel, and other lodging in the province. Available through Travel Alberta (780/427-4321 or 800/252-3782, www.travelalberta.com) or from local information centers. The online version is at www.explorealberta.com.

Alberta Campground Guide. Alberta Hotel & Lodging Association. Lists all campgrounds in the province. Available through Travel Alberta (780/427-4321 or 800/252-3782, www.travel alberta.com) or from local information centers. The online version is at www.explorealberta.com.

Tour Book: Western Canada and Alaska. Booklet available to members of the Canadian or American Automobile Association.

Western Canadian Bed and Breakfast Innkeepers Association. Contact this association for a copy of its annual accommodations guide (604/255-9199, www.wcbbia.com). It contains descriptions and prices of more than 120 properties.

Internet Resources

ACCOMMODATIONS

Accent Inns: www.accentinns.com
Banff Central Reservations:
www.banffreservations.com
Bed & Breakfast Association of Calgary:
www.bbcalgary.com
Bed & Breakfast Association of the Yukon:
www.yukonbandb.com
Bed and Breakfast Online: www.bbcanada.com
Best Western: www.bestwestern.com
Charming Inns of Alberta:
www.charminginnsofalberta.com
Days Inn: www.daysinn.com
Delta Hotels and Resorts:
www.deltahotels.com
Fairmont Hotels and Resorts:
www.fairmont.com
Holiday Inns: www.holiday-inn.com
Hostelling International–Canada:
www.hihostels.ca
Howard Johnson: www.hojo.com
International Youth Hostel Federation:
www.iyhf.com
Jasper Home Accommodation Association:
www.stayinjasper.com
Radisson: www.radisson.com
Sandman Hotels: www.sandmanhotels.com
Super 8: www.super8.com
Western Canada Bed and Breakfast
Innkeepers Association: www.wcbbia.com

AIRLINES

Air Canada: www.aircanada.ca
Air Canada Jazz: www.flyjazz.com
Air New Zealand: www.nzair.com
Air North: www.flyairnorth.com
Air Pacific: www.airpacific.com
Alaska Airlines: www.alaksaair.com
All Nippon Airways: www.ana.co.jp
American Airlines: www.aa.com
British Airlines: www.britishairlines.com

Continental Airlines: www.continental.com
First Air: www.firstair.ca
Harbour Air: www.harbour-air.com
Hawk Air: www.hawkair.net
Japan Airlines: www.jal.co.jp
KLM: www.klm.nl
Lufthansa: www.lufthansa.de
Northwest Airlines: www.nwa.com
North-Wright Airways:
www.north-wrightairways.com
Pacific Coastal: www.pacific-coastal.com
Qantas: www.qantas.com.au
Singapore Airlines: www.singaporeair.com
Tango: www.flytango.com
United Airlines: www.ual.com
WestJet: www.westjet.com

CAR AND RV RENTAL

Avis: www.avis.com
Budget: www.budget.com
C.C. Canada Camper:
www.canada-camper.com
Cruise America: www.cruiseamerica.com
Cruise Canada: www.cruisecanada.com
Discount: www.discountcar.com
Dollar: www.dollar.com
Enterprise: www.enterprise.com
Go West: www.go-west.com
Hertz: www.hertz.com
National: www.nationalcar.com
Rent-A-Wreck: www.rentawreck.ca
Thrifty: www.thrifty.com

OTHER TRANSPORTATION AND TOURS

Alaska Marine Highway: www.alaska.gov/ferry
Banff Airporter: www.banffairporter.com
BC Ferries: www.bcferries.com
Brewster: www.brewster.ca
Canadian Mountain Holidays:
www.cmhhike.com

Clipper Navigation: www.victoriaclipper.com
Good Earth Travel Adventures:
  www.goodearthtravel.com
Gray Line Canada: www.grayline.ca
Greyhound: www.greyhound.ca
MV *Coho:* www.cohoferry.com
Pacific Coach Lines: www.pacificcoach.com
Perimeter: www.perimeterbus.com
Red Arrow: www.redarrow.pwt.ca
Rocky Mountaineer Railtours:
  www.rockymountaineer.com
Rocky Mountain Sky Shuttle:
  www.rockymountainskyshuttle.com
VIA Rail: www.viarail.ca
Washington State Ferries:
  www.wsdot.wa.gov/ferries

TOURISM OFFICES

Banff/Lake Louise Tourism Bureau:
  www.banfflakelouise.com
Canadian Tourism Commission:
  www.canadatourism.com
**Chinook Country Tourist Association
  (Southern Alberta):**
  www.chinookcountry.com
City of Whitehorse:
  www.city.whitehorse.yk.ca
City of Yellowknife:
  www.city.yellowknife.nt.ca
Drumheller Tourism:
  www.canadianbadlands.com
Edmonton Tourism: www.edmonton.com
Fort McMurray Visitors Bureau:
  www.fortmcmurraytourism.com
Jasper Tourism and Commerce:
  www.jaspercanadianrockies.com
Kelowna Chamber of Commerce:
  www.kelownachamber.org
Klondike Visitors Association:
  www.dawsoncity.ca
Nelson Chamber of Commerce:
  www.discovernelson.com

Northwest Territories Tourism:
  www.explorenwt.com
Powell River Visitors Bureau:
  www.discoverpowellriver.com
Tofino Visitor Info Centre:
  www.tofinobc.org
Tourism Calgary: www.tourismcalgary.com
Tourism Canmore:
  www.tourismcanmore.com
Tourism Nanaimo:
  www.tourismnanaimo.bc.ca
Tourism Red Deer: www.tourismreddeer.net
Tourism Richmond:
  www.tourismrichmond.com
Tourism Vancouver:
  www.tourismvancouver.com
Tourism Vancouver Island:
  www.islands.bc.ca
Tourism Victoria: www.tourismvictoria.com
Tourism Whistler: www.mywhistler.com
Tour Yukon: www.touryukon.com
Travel Alberta: www.travelalberta.com
Venture Kamloops:
  www.adventurekamloops.com
Vernon Tourism: www.vernontourism.com

GOVERNMENT

**Canada Customs and Revenue (Visitor
  Rebate Program):** www.ccra-adrc.gc.ca
Citizenship and Immigration Canada:
  www.cic.gc.ca
Government of Alberta: www.gov.ab.ca
Government of British Columbia:
  www.gov.bc.ca
Government of Canada: www.gc.ca
Government of the Northwest Territories:
  www.gov.nt.ca
Government of Yukon: www.gov.yk.ca
Parks Canada: www.pc.gc.ca

Index

Index

Index

Cycling

Fish/Fishing

Hiking

Index

M

Index

Rodeos

Index

U.S. ~ Metric Conversion

1 inch	=	2.54 centimeters (cm)
1 foot	=	.304 meters (m)
1 yard	=	0.914 meters
1 mile	=	1.6093 kilometers (km)
1 km	=	.6214 miles
1 fathom	=	1.8288 m
1 chain	=	20.1168 m
1 furlong	=	201.168 m
1 acre	=	.4047 hectares
1 sq km	=	100 hectares
1 sq mile	=	2.59 square km
1 ounce	=	28.35 grams
1 pound	=	.4536 kilograms
1 short ton	=	.90718 metric ton
1 short ton	=	2000 pounds
1 long ton	=	1.016 metric tons
1 long ton	=	2240 pounds
1 metric ton	=	1000 kilograms
1 quart	=	.94635 liters
1 US gallon	=	3.7854 liters
1 Imperial gallon	=	4.5459 liters
1 nautical mile	=	1.852 km

To compute Celsius temperatures, subtract 32 from Fahrenheit and divide by 1.8. To go the other way, multiply Celsius by 1.8 and add 32.

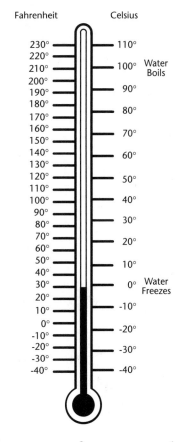

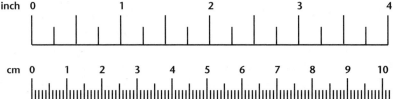

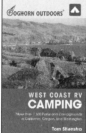
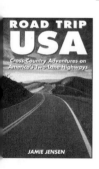

Keeping Current

Although we strive to produce the most up-to-date guidebook humanly possible, change is unavoidable. Between the time this book goes to print and the moment you read it, a handful of the businesses noted in these pages will undoubtedly change prices, move, or even close their doors forever. Other worthy attractions will open for the first time. If you have a favorite gem you'd like to see included in the next edition, or see anything that needs updating, clarification, or correction, please drop us a line. Send your comments via email to atpfeedback@avalonpub.com, or use the address below.

Moon Handbooks Western Canada
Avalon Travel Publishing
1400 65th Street, Suite 250
Emeryville, CA 94608, USA
www.moon.com

Editor: Amy Scott
Series Manager: Kevin McLain
Acquisitions Editor: Rebecca K. Browning
Copy Editor: Kate McKinley
Production Coordinators: Jacob Goolkasian, Emily Douglas
Graphics Coordinator: Justin Marler
Cover Designer: Kari Gim
Interior Designers: Amber Pirker, Alvaro Villanueva, Kelly Pendragon
Map Editor: Olivia Solís
Cartographers: Suzanne Service, Kat Kalamaras, Mike Morgenfeld
Indexer: Deana Shields

ISBN: 1-56691-665-8
ISSN: 1548-2170

Printing History
1st Edition—June 2004
5 4 3 2 1

Text © 2004 by Andrew Hempstead.
Maps © 2004 by Avalon Travel Publishing, Inc.
All rights reserved.

Avalon Travel Publishing is a division of Avalon Publishing Group, Inc.

Some photos and illustrations are used by permission and are the property of the original copyright owners.

Front cover photo: © timfitzharris.com
Table of contents photos: © Andrew Hempstead

Printed in USA by Worzalla